Finnish Yearbook of International Law

Finnish Yearbook of International Law

Volume 23, 2012–2013

Ius Gentium Association

• HART •
PUBLISHING

OXFORD AND PORTLAND, OREGON
2016

Published in the United Kingdom by Hart Publishing Ltd
16C Worcester Place, Oxford, OX1 2JW
Telephone: +44 (0)1865 517530
Fax: +44 (0)1865 510710
E-mail: mail@hartpub.co.uk
Website: http://www.hartpub.co.uk

Published in North America (US and Canada) by
Hart Publishing
c/o International Specialized Book Services
920 NE 58th Avenue, Suite 300
Portland, OR 97213-3786
USA
Tel: +1 503 287 3093 or toll-free: (1) 800 944 6190
Fax: +1 503 280 8832
E-mail: orders@isbs.com
Website: http://www.isbs.com

Hart Publishing is an imprint of Bloomsbury Publishing plc.

The editors welcome unsolicited contributions related to international law. General information for authors and a detailed guide to the Yearbook's house style can be found at www.fybil.org.
Communications to the editors should be addressed to:

Finnish Yearbook of International Law
Erik Castrén Institute of International Law and Human Rights
P.O. Box 4 (Yliopistonkatu 3)
FI-00014 University of Helsinki, Finland
E-mail: fybil@fybil.org

The Ius Gentium Association gratefully acknowledges the support of the Legal Department of the Finnish Ministry for Foreign Affairs to the publication of the Yearbook.

British Library Cataloguing in Publication Data
Data Available

ISBN: 978-1-84946-566-3
ISSN: 0786-6453

Typeset by Compuscript Ltd, Shannon
Printed and bound in Great Britain by
TJ International Ltd, Padstow, Cornwall

Finnish Yearbook of International Law

Contents

Special Section: Rule of Law

Articles

Book Reviews

Edited by Rain Liivoja

New Finnish Doctoral Dissertations in International Law

Finnish State Practice

Special Section:

Rule of Law

The Rule of Law as Morality Play

Stephen Humphreys*

ABSTRACT: Since the Cold War ended, the world's principal financial and development institutions have focused extensive attention on 'rule of law assistance' or 'promotion' in poor and developing countries. This body of work generally treats law in some isolation from broader social and political questions, presented as a technical exercise, recalibrating law in pursuit of undisputed universal goals, such as eradicating poverty or fulfilling human rights. In this article, I undertake a close reading of the literature of two major rule of law funders in the field of market-building—as distinct from, albeit related to, the state-building work also undertaken under this rubric at the UN and elsewhere. My aim is to show how this body of work promotes a thoroughgoing vision of a particular social and political order. Noting that the techniques of rule-of-law promotion align poorly with fundamental principles generally attributed to the rule of law, and that there is little or no evidence that this vision does—or even can—achieve its stated aims, I redescribe rule of law promotion as a kind of rhetorical intervention, a morality play concerned with the universalisation and naturalisation of certain ideas about society, polity and economy. In this essentially pedagogical role, rule of law promotion can claim some modest success.

KEYWORDS: rule of law, World Bank, USAID, Habermas, Hayek, Weber, corruption, privatisation, civil society

1. A Theatre of the Rule of Law

Over two decades of 'promoting the rule of law' an immense literature has been generated by the public and private 'donor' agencies who commission, guide, implement and explain this expansive field of activity. Often presented as mere 'technical assistance', a close examination of this literature reveals a quite complete vision of what society is and how it should work, including detailed prescription on the activities appropriate to the state, the role of civil society, the correct approach to the economy, and the optimal construction of legal and judicial institutions. In each 'beneficiary' country, the

* Associate Professor of International Law, London School of Economics. This article summarises arguments made at greater length in my book, *Theatre of the Rule of Law* (Cambridge University Press, 2010, paperback 2012).

literature proposes essentially the same stylised drama, peopled by familiar actors performing from a limited and, by now, well-known repertory. This article examines the themes and *dramatis personae* that habitually reappear on the rule of law stage, with the aim of describing what might be termed the 'latent theory' of rule of law promotion.

I will argue that rule of law assistance not only presupposes a certain vision of society, it proactively sets about making it flesh. It does so by funding, 'nurturing' and training whole sections of society—judiciaries, police, soldiers and civil servants, of course, but also nongovernmental organisations, the media, 'civil society' itself. The goal of 'rule of law programs' is not simply to construct or reform 'institutions', it is actively to reform the way people in general in host countries behave, public and private persons alike. The aim is, apparently, to normalise and universalise very specific ideas about state, society and their inter-relation.

Ambitious though the program literature—to which I will turn for detailed accounts of the field—is, it rarely expresses the full implications of its own presuppositions. These larger claims, hopes and intentions are rarely openly acknowledged or proclaimed, indeed, they are perhaps not always fully appreciated. And yet, as I will show, they are pervasive. They are indicated by, and necessary to, a consistent narrative which is thoroughly embedded in the body of programs wherever performed. They are *staged* rather than stated. Furthermore, the extraordinary scale of ambition behind this work is, unsurprisingly, not generally met in practice—indeed it is difficult to see how it could be. Yet, perhaps because the larger premise is so rarely articulated, the literature evinces recurrent surprise and disappointment at the failure to achieve its stated aims, as though these more modest objectives could somehow be uncoupled from the wider transformation rule of law programs mutely expect.

I will suggest that it is most appropriate to characterise the world of rule of law promotion as a kind of theatre or performance—as the staging of a certain story or morality tale about the good life: about state and society, about law and economy, about the appropriate way to set priorities, about the appropriate priorities to set. As pedagogical. Rule of law promotion is theatrical in its mode of persuasion: it does not attempt to *demonstrate* the rightness of its propositions through empirical evidence (there is little), nor through the discipline of reasoned competitive discourse in the public sphere (it is not itself open for debate), nor through the clarity of historical analogy (no analogy seems appropriate). Rather, the field bases its appeal on the force of repeated narrative itself, and on the consistent reproduction of a cast of strangely inscrutable terms that follow a similar choreography regardless of context. These comprise, on one hand, a set of immutable themes (governance, corruption, privatisation, transparency, accountability, impunity, judicial independence) and, on the other, a group of recurrent morally-tagged actors (civil society, the judiciary, 'the poor', 'the elite', the media, public officials, 'reform-minded constituencies').

The plotlines too are simple, bold, familiar and repeated. Governments tend to tyranny. Independent courts protect the rights of ordinary people. Corruption obstructs 'governance' and constitutes a tax on the poor. Privatised services are more efficient than public. An 'enabling environment' for investment is a prerequisite of 'development'. 'Integration' in the global economy is good for everyone, local and global alike. 'The poor' are essentially entrepreneurial, waiting for the right environment to step forward and contribute to (and benefit from) wealth generation. The 'right environment' is a matter of incentives.

The background motif that consistently figures, implicitly or explicitly, in this drama is modernisation. This provides an immediate, intuitive, distinctive and enduring base-note: we are concerned with two sets of countries bound together by a particularly contemporary form of transaction—aid donors and recipients. Their relationship is premised on the reproduction in the latter of certain structural conditions that already exist in the former. The action takes place in the host country, dramatising the complementary, if contrasting, obligations of public and private actors, each of whom must learn and internalise irreducible difference: the former must be bound in order that the latter might be free. The plot thematises austerity: public officers are subjected to rituals of hygiene (anti-corruption), self-discipline (governance) and abnegation (privatisation).[1] The accompanying narrative, however, prioritises freedom: public restraint, it turns out, is the price and condition of private freedom.

In practice, much of the action centres on mediating figures—the judiciary, 'civil society' and the media—characters expected, in different ways, to reinforce and refine the public-private divide. A 'reform constituency' in the host country is a key stock character without whom the action cannot progress. Complex character development is expected of another central figure: 'the poor', the nominal beneficiaries, passive, awaiting the right incentives to awaken. The drama's projected ending looks forward to the recipient state's 'integration' in a global community.

1. In this the rule of law narrative retraces Weber's account of bureaucracy. See Max Weber, *Economy and Society* (first published 1922) (2 vols, University of California Press, 1978) at 956–58. There are echoes of a more ancient secular theology in the subjection of government to poverty (privatisation), chastity (anti-corruption) and obedience (governance).

These themes and actors are so basic to the rule of law narrative that their appearance here may seem banal to those familiar with the field. Still, by revisiting them in a spirit of naiveté, my aim in this article is to allow them to serve as windows onto the heart of contemporary rule of law promotion. Throughout I will rely on a broad body of materials gathered from donors, in particular the two earliest and most vigorous actors in this domain, the World Bank and the US Agency for International Development (USAID). Following their own proclivities in their project and strategic literature, I will treat the 'rule of law' theme in combination with the closely related themes of 'governance', corruption and privatisation.

Although I am not attempting in what follows to fix a definition of 'rule of law'—a complicated task for a term which owes its prominence largely to its plasticity—it is nevertheless striking that the modes of practice of rule of law assistance deviate sharply from the procedural rigour and conservative caution with which the term is generally associated.[2] However, my interest here is rather to investigate certain concrete activities undertaken by a particular group of actors mobilising the *rhetoric* of 'rule of law' in ways that are often familiar, sometimes innovative. The point is to identify how that rhetoric aligns with a practice (hence 'latent theory'), to show what can be justified 'in the name of' the rule of law, and to reconstruct the sort of world imagined by those who support this kind of activity. While I liken rule of law promotion to 'theatre' in the sense of *staging* (a morality tale, spectacle or drama), I also have in mind the sense of a 'theatre of war'—something projected from one place into another, a notionally bounded space of activity 'over there', in which undertakings follow an existing playbook or strategy, even if the ultimate outcome remains unknown.

2. The Guiding Motif: Modernisation

Although rule of law project documents regularly introduce modernisation as a motivating premise, the term is not defined in the literature: rather its rhetorical function is to provide an intuitive rationale for systemic interventions.[3]

2. I provide fuller discussion of this point in the prologue and first three chapters of Stephen Humphreys, *Theatre of the Rule of Law: Transnational Legal Intervention in Theory and Practice* (Cambridge University Press, 2010).
3. As of January 2014, the project database on the World Bank website lists 879 'rule of law'-themed projects, and 7,131 projects dealing with 'public administration, law and justice'. 'Modernisation' is tagged as a key word for over 1,000 projects, 50 of which involve 'legal institutions for a market economy', 19 on 'judicial and other dispute resolution institutions', and 34 'law reform' projects, among others. The list includes 'Judicial

That rationale hinges on three notions of modernisation: political, historical and technological.

Politically, the notion of modernisation counterposes 'state of the art' laws and institutions with those that are or have become 'outdated' along with the regimes or ideologies that spawned them. A project in Russia, for example, claims to address something 'universally recognised as among the most pressing problems in transition countries: the incomplete, out of date, and contradictory legal framework'.[4] Kazakhstan, according to one USAID project document, has had 'no experience with … the modern rule of law'.[5] A key constraint to Zambia's 'long term development program', on the Bank's assessment, is the country's 'outdated policies and legal framework'.[6] The implication is that much of the apparatus of the state in target countries was made for a different—colonial or communist—reality and is not suited to the post-present. With the recession of a colonial/communist apparatus, state laws and institutions need to be 'overhauled' to suit a new configuration. So reflexive is this approach that it is even applied in many Latin American countries where, despite the remoteness of the colonial era,[7] USAID observes that decades of dictatorial and authoritarian leadership allowed the inherited colonial judicial system to fall into disrepair.[8] More broadly, the legal framework

Modernisation' projects in countries such as Azerbaijan, Georgia, Mexico and El Salvador and 'Public Sector Modernisation' projects in Kosovo, Jamaica, Argentina, Armenia, Honduras and elsewhere.

4. World Bank, *Implementation Completion Report on a Loan in the Amount of US$58 Million to the Russian Federation for a Legal Reform Project* (2006) at 4.
5. Chemonics International, *Strengthening the Rule of Law in Kazakhstan: Kazakhstan Judicial Assistance Project Phase I, Final Report* (USAID, 2007) at 3.
6. International Development Association, *Country Assistance Strategy for the Republic of Zambia* (World Bank, 2008) at 46. See also World Bank, *Implementation Completion Report (TF-26063 TF-23757) on a Credit in the Amount of US$2.49 Million to the West Bank and Gaza for a Legal Development Project, Report No: 29066* (June 9, 2004) at 2; World Bank, *Project Appraisal Document on a Proposed Credit in the Amount of SDR 6.80 Million (US$10.15 Million Equivalent) to the Republic of Armenia for a Public Sector Modernization Project*, Report No: 27563-AM (April 8, 2004) at 53.
7. See Malcom Rowat, Waleed H. Malik and Maria Dakolias (eds), 'Judicial Reform in Latin America and the Caribbean: Proceedings of a World Bank Conference', World Bank Technical Paper Number 280 (World Bank, 1995), especially contributions to Part VIII. Assessments on these lines were already common during the 'law and development' wave of the 1960s/1970s; see, for example, Keith S. Rosenn, 'The Jeito: Brazil's Institutional Bypass of the Formal Legal System and its Developmental Implications', 19 *American Journal of Comparative Law* (1971) 514–49.
8. 'In the LAC [*sic*: Latin American and Caribbean] region … the civil code system had generally failed to modernize; codes had largely become antiquated and anachronistic; and abuses stemming from the opacity of the inquisitorial system had been allowed to develop.'

of any 'transition' economy is likely to contain outmoded elements and need updating in the post-1989 era, whether 'transiting' from dictatorship, communism or colonialism.

By foregrounding modernisation, donors effectively distance themselves from their colonial or communist forerunners, and invite partner governments to do likewise. Specificity of historical circumstance is easily elided in the common failure of different countries to achieve rule of law.[9] In practice, the implications differ somewhat for postcolonial and post-communist countries. In the former, the fact that laws and courts are 'outdated' is associated with a lack of investment and/or under-utilisation of the formal machinery of justice.[10] A common implication, as the World Bank concluded in a pivotal 1989 report on sub-Saharan Africa—a report that is sometimes credited with sparking the turn to the 'rule of law'[11]—is that post-independence governments are to blame where once-functional laws and institutions have fallen into desuetude or disrepair, or have become dysfunctional due to incoherent

---

Management Systems International (MSI), *Achievements in Building and Maintaining the Rule of Law: MSI's Studies in LAC, E&E, AFR, and ANE*, USAID Occasional Papers Series (USAID, 2002) at 4 (also at 3, 58, 66, 77). See too Thomas Carothers, *In the Name of Democracy: US Policy towards Latin America in the Reagan Years* (University of California Press, 1991); Yves Dezalay and Bryant Garth, *Dealing in Virtue: International Commercial Arbitration and the Construction of a Transnational Legal Order* (University of Chicago Press, 1996); on El Salvador, Robert Orr, 'Paradigm Lost? United States Approaches to Democracy Promotion in Developing Countries', PhD thesis, Princeton University (1996).

9. See, for example, MSI, *USAID in LAC, E&E, AFR, and ANE, supra* note 8, at 25, noting that, despite, their differences, Bangladesh, Egypt, the Philippines, Mongolia and Nepal 'share the common experience of dominance by authoritarian, repressive regimes [who] systematically weakened the courts and marginalised the rule of law'.
10. In Guinea Bissau, 'the legal system is antiquated and constraining, as most of the legislation in force today dates back to the early colonial period.' World Bank, *Project Appraisal Document on a Proposed Credit in the Amount of SDR 21.0 Million (US$26.0 Million Equivalent) to the Republic of Guinea-Bissau for a Private sector Rehabilitation and Development Project* (28 February 2002) at 8. See also World Bank, *Project Appraisal Document on a Proposed Credit in the Amount of SDR 12 Million (US$15 Million Equivalent) to the Republic of the Gambia for a Capacity Building for Economic Management Project*, Report No. 22516 GM (6 July 2001) at 3.
11. See World Bank, *Sub-Saharan Africa: From Crisis to Sustainable Growth. A Long-Term Perspective Study* (World Bank, 1989) and for discussion of its influence, Ibrahim Shihata, 'The World Bank and "Governance" Issues in Its Borrowing Members', in Ibrahim Shihata, *The World Bank in a Changing World: Selected Essays* (Martinus Nijhoff: Leiden, 1991) at 53–96. A full account of the World Bank's turn to the rule of law is provided in Humphreys, *Theatre of the Rule of Law, supra* note 2, at ch. 4.

policies and legislation or corruption in the intervening years.[12] Post-colonial countries drifted into a 'suffocating' developmentalism: an overweening state itself breeds corruption and stifles creativity. For post-communist countries, on the other hand, the laws and institutions were never really acceptable even when first instituted. There, overhaul was always needed, but is only now possible.

Everywhere, though, the implication is that while *the world*, or *society*, has moved inexorably forward—has progressed, politically—this particular *state* has failed to keep up. It is the state's job now to meet the more sophisticated needs of a contemporary national/global/cosmopolitan society. Even while it assails the government, in short, such a language is designed to appeal to 'modernisers' within government, a 'reform constituency' framed as representing the 'progressive' sectors of 'public opinion': to pull the country forward out of the 'backwardness' of the past.[13]

Modernisation is, second, a cultural concern in that 'modern' states are distinct from *traditional*, rural, or customary ones. To give but one example: in Yemen, one World Bank report found that despite 'substantial military and technical assistance ... its governance remained traditional in character, and the size of its public sector was small ... Many of the institutions of modern governance were absent'.[14] Modern in this sense refers not to the modernism of a particular moment in time, but the modernism of a particular regional tradition or culture. Mapping roughly onto the UN usage of 'developed country', this is the 'modern' of Max Weber's *modern state*, by which is meant the ideal type of a particular European tradition; a state, no matter its geographical location, that shares certain basic structures and premises with this tradition.[15] The Weberian state is famously one in which the sovereign commands unrivalled dominance throughout its territory; but it is also, in

12. Thus in Ghana, 'The intractable land problems and disputes ... cannot be resolved without the streamlining and harmonisation of the prevailing contradictory policies and legislation and reforming the non-collaborating and inefficient public sector land agencies.' World Bank, *Project Appraisal Document on a Proposed Credit in the Amount of SDR 15.1 Million to the Republic of Ghana for a Land Administration Project* (2003) at 15.
13. 'Backwardness' can apply as easily to communist or socialist post-independent structures as to precolonial polities. See, for a rich example, the World Bank, *World Development Report 1991: The Challenge of Development* (World Bank, 1990) ('A consensus is forming in favour of a "market-friendly" approach to development') at 1, 19 and 33.
14. World Bank, *World Bank Independent Evaluation Group, Project Performance Assessment Report, Republic of Yemen, Institutional Development for Public Administration Project, Legal and Judicial Development Project, Public Sector Management Adjustment Credit, Country Evaluation and Regional Relations* (October 16, 2008) at para. 1.1.
15. Weber, *Economy and Society*, *supra* note 1, at 880–892.

its Habermasian reworking, a state that has surpassed the parochialism of the community, and replaced it with a pluralist 'tolerance' among strangers who need not share the same backgrounds and belief systems.[16] The 'traditional', by contrast, retains just these elements—communal, shared (ethnic or religious) belief systems, parochialism, and a continued jostling over authority. Since such a system cannot perform statehood, it survives under the wing of a protecting state or remains residually dominant where the supposedly authentic state is absent, weak, or illegitimate. A predominance of 'traditional' justice sectors outside the 'formal' structures of the state is, then, prima facie evidence of weak rule of law. Afghanistan's 'traditional' justice mechanisms have, for example, attracted intense donor interest since efforts commenced, after the 2001 invasion, to establish the rule of law there.

> The 'informal justice sector' or 'customary law sector' covers a wide variety of clusters of norms and practices, often uncodified and orally transmitted, usually combined together in varying mixes. This includes customary law ... local understanding of Islamic legal traditions ... and even some modern laws ... The only thing these methods have in common is that they reflect a level of fairness and justice broadly accepted by the majority of the population and they are all outside the scope of the formal state justice system. Whereas the authoritative purveyors of this decision making and dispute resolution system may enjoy some degree of state endorsement ... the sources of their authority are invariably based in their communities and in local power structures.[17]

In this context, reference to the 'modern' activates and accentuates the difference between donor and recipient countries primarily in terms of the relative capacity of the state. Of particular importance in post-conflict settings—but of insidious significance wherever the capacity of the state is at issue—it sets up a quasi-paternal relation, in which the donor is the bearer of a knowledge

16. Jürgen Habermas, *Between Facts and Norms: Contributions to a Discourse Theory of Law and Democracy* (Polity Press: Cambridge, UK, 1998) at 448; Michael Oakeshott, *On History and other Essays* (Liberty Fund: Indianapolis, IN, 1999); for a World Bank view, Shihata, 'The World Bank and "Governance" Issues', *supra* note 11, at 85.
17. Checchi and Company Consulting, Inc., *Afghanistan Rule of Law Project: Field Study of Informal and Customary Justice in Afghanistan and Recommendations on Improving Access to Justice and Relations between Formal Courts and Informal Bodies* (USAID, 2005) at 3–4. See also United Nations Development Program, *Afghanistan Human Development Report, Bridging Modernity and Tradition: Rule of Law and the Search for Justice* (UNDP, 2005); United States Institute for Peace, 'Establishing the Rule of Law in Afghanistan', USIP Special Report 117 (United States Institute for Peace, 2003); Thomas Barfield, 'Afghan Customary Law and Its Relationship to Formal Judicial Institutions' (United States Institute for Peace, 2003); Thomas Barfield, Neamat Nojumi and Alexander Thier, *The Clash of Two Goods: State and Non-State Dispute Resolution in Afghanistan* (United States Institute of Peace, 2007).

and expertise that the recipient cannot be expected to match. Both colonial and communist states were 'modernising' in this sense; both characterised the 'traditional' as 'backward', 'primitive' or 'childlike' and sought to develop it.[18] In the colonial context this involved a paternalist modernisation, nurturing and shaping rather than merely rejecting or overruling the 'traditional'.[19] Legal intervention during the colonial era had, among its objectives, the cultivation of 'native courts' to capitalise upon and reshape 'customary' law to fit modern ends.[20] Contemporary rule of law reform too retains gentler overtones in the traditional context than in the post-communist setting, speaking of 'formalising' or 'clarifying' land tenure systems, not replacing them outright,[21] and of 'integrating' traditional or customary legal systems into the 'formal' system to ensure they are in line with constitutional or 'international human rights' norms.[22] As with colonial 'repugnancy' clauses, it is the subordination of 'traditional authorities' to the state's overarching authority—not their elimination—that is desired.[23] In this sense of 'modernisation', then, contemporary rule of law reform is recognisably descended from its colonial forebear.

Finally, 'modernisation' is about technology. Modern here refers back to its Enlightenment signification, the reliance on science to dispel myth and superstition and to engender progress. Technology has always constituted evidence of that progress: in any given environment, access to and application

18. See, for example, Beatrice Wede, 'Legal Systems and Economic Performance: The Empirical Evidence', in Rowat, Malik and Dakolias (eds), 'Judicial Reform in Latin America', *supra* note 7, 21–27 at 21; Leila Chirayath, Caroline Sage and Michael Woolcock, 'Customary Law and Policy Reform: Engaging with the Plurality of Justice Systems', prepared as a background paper for the World Bank, *World Development Report 2006: Equity and Development* (World Bank, undated 2005) at 4.
19. Humphreys, *Theatre of the Rule of Law, supra* note 2, at 109–22; Stephen Humphreys, 'Laboratories of Statehood: Legal Intervention in Colonial Africa and Today', 75(4) *Modern Law Review* (2012) 475–510.
20. See, for example, Frederick Lugard, *The Dual Mandate in British Tropical Africa* (William Blackwood & Sons: Edinburgh, London, 1926) at 547–549.
21. For example, World Bank, *Project Appraisal Document on a Proposed Credit in the Amount of SDR 15.1 Million to the Republic of Ghana for a Land Administration Project* (World Bank, 2003).
22. For example, World Bank Legal Vice Presidency, *The World Bank, Initiatives in Legal and Judicial Reform* (World Bank, 2004) at 13.
23. Chirayath, Sage and Woolcock, 'Customary Law and Policy Reform', *supra* note 18; World Bank, *World Development Report* 1996: *From Plan to Market* (World Bank, 1995). On 'repugnancy' clauses, with which colonial authorities circumscribed the application of 'native customary law' in colonial contexts, see Humphreys, *Theatre of the Rule of Law, supra* note 2, at 117–118. The broader discussion in Mahmood Mamdani, *Citizen and Subject* (Princeton University Press, 1996) is invaluable.

processes—Kant's public use of private reason (Giddens describes this as the 'quintessential modern trait').[33]

Clearly, 'modernisation' in rule of law programming describes a very different process, substituting the epiphenomena of modernity—a smorgasbord of laws and technologies, and an insistent pressure on the 'traditional'—for the social processes that, in earlier accounts, *produce* these phenomena. No theoretical account is offered in the rule of law literature as to why such reverse engineering might be expected to work. Of course there are well-known historical precedents for what we might call 'forced modernisation' under both colonial and communist rule. It is a technique contemporary rule of law promotion appears to have partially borrowed, despite its meticulous self-distancing from these earlier experiments.

3. Lead Roles: Public and Private

Rule of law literature does not offer a theoretical account of the public-private distinction, yet both terms recur with the regularity of a muezzin: we hear much about public accountability and private development, public policy and private incentives; the public and private *sectors* are each supported in different ways. The distinction is treated as natural—it is assumed rather than explained—and the private is consistently privileged over the public, often implicitly: a primary role of the public is to facilitate the freedom of the private. The law, in rule of law literature, sharpens the distinction even if it rarely articulates it: public and private sectors are each addressed in their own registers and relations between the two are subject to a specific form of regulation.

For context, it might be helpful to provide some background to this critical conceptual divide. Perhaps the most thorough, and certainly the most influential, account of the emergence of the public-private distinction is Jürgen Habermas's description of the rise of what he called the 'public sphere' in Europe during the eighteenth and nineteenth centuries. Habermas characterised the public sphere 'as the sphere of private people come together as a public' to exercise control over the state 'in the public interest'.[34] Habermas showed how the principal constitutional guarantees that arose across 19th century Europe were premised on preserving the integrity of the 'public

33. Anthony Giddens, *Modernity and Self-Identity* (Polity Press: Cambridge, UK, 1991); Immanuel Kant, 'An Answer to the Question: What is Enlightenment?', in Kant, *Perpetual Peace and Other Essays* (first published 1784) (Hackett Publishing Company: Indianapolis, IN, 1983) 41–48 at 42.

34. Habermas, *Structural Transformation, supra* note 32, at 27.

sphere' and its autonomy from the 'public realm' of government. The passage is worth quoting in some detail:

> A set of basic rights concerned the sphere of the public engaged in a rational-critical debate (freedom of opinion and speech, freedom of press, freedom of assembly and association, etc.) and the political function of private people in this public sphere (right of petition, equality of vote, etc.). A second set of basic rights concerned the individual's status as a free human being, grounded in the intimate sphere of the patriarchal conjugal family (personal freedom, inviolability of the home, etc.). The third set of basic rights concerned the transactions of the private owners of property in the sphere of civil society (equality before the law, protection of private property, etc.). The basic rights guaranteed: the spheres of the public realm and of the private (with the intimate sphere at its core); the institutions and instruments of the public sphere, on the one hand (press, parties) and the foundation of private autonomy (family and property), on the other; finally, the functions of the private people, both their political ones as citizens and their economic ones as owners of commodities.[35]

This idea or ideal of the public sphere flourished under a particular set of historical circumstances. One necessary condition was the cultural and social development of technologies, notably communication technologies (printing presses, newspapers), supportive of concrete and differentiable public and private activities. On Habermas's account, a consolidating notion of 'privacy' applying to individuals 'in their own homes'—accessing information, 'culture' and 'news' in private—soon extended to the economic independence of the bourgeoisie (from community or family) and this in turn provided individuals with a basis for stepping forward into a notional public sphere. There, as members of civil society—in debating halls and coffee salons, at public events and in the pages of newspapers and journals—private individuals debated among themselves with a view to determining the public interest—eventually transmitted (as 'public opinion') to a state that was increasingly constrained (through constitutional safeguards) to deliver it.[36] The public/private divide, in this idealised form, is thus perhaps better conceived as a *tripartite* distinction between (i) private persons as such (the private or family sphere), (ii) a public sphere, comprised of private persons and economic actors ('civil society'), and (iii) a public sector, the state.[37]

35. *Ibid*, at 83.
36. Humphreys, *Theatre of the Rule of Law*, *supra* note 2, at 45–55.
37. This tripartite distinction picks up the Hegelian description of the polity composed of family, civil society and state. See Humphreys, *Theatre of the Rule of Law*, *supra* note 2, at 49–50.

Contemporary rule of law programs do not advert to this theoretical underpinning; nor do they problematise the world wherein they act. Nevertheless, Habermas's presumptions run through the project literature in the manner of an *a priori* premise. The work tends to assume the desirability of this set of structural conditions in countries of implementation and aims to ignite, develop or reinforce them. Rule of law and associated language—governance, corruption, privatisation, civil society, judicial independence—provide a conceptual armoury and interdependent framework for nurturing the public-private distinction. They do so in part by emphasising the non-identity of public and private (as a matter of principle) and insisting upon the desirability of achieving their complete separation (as a matter of practice). And they proceed by assuming that the relevant constituencies already exist in target countries, but have become submerged or displaced; they must be helped to re-emerge and equipped to take their proper place in a recognisably 'modern' theatre of public life. There is an apparent paradox here: much as these actors are 'activated' from without, the process is conceived of as *self*-actualising as though the various roles already exist in latent form within the polity, simply awaiting ignition.[38] So whereas the *public*—that is, the new, surviving, or residual state—is to be shaped, disciplined and pruned, the private is to be coaxed, seduced and incentivised. The assumption that appropriate incentives will simply call forth private and civil society sectors appears much less presumptuous when it is remembered that these actors do, in fact, already exist *trans*-nationally—ready to mobilise, in the form of multinational companies, international investors and a global civil society.

As a next step, I will examine these themes through the deployment of certain keywords in the project and strategy-level documentation of the World Bank, USAID and the UN: governance, corruption, and privatisation—and the activating medium of a 'reform constituency'.

3.1. The Reform Constituency

An arresting theme that recurs throughout rule of law project documentation is the conviction that in order to 'push through' reform, donors will need to work with a small 'reform-minded' minority in government,

38. A similar paradox is captured in Nikolas Rose's description of a cognate phenomenon, 'government through community'. According to Rose, in this model of government, the community 'is to be achieved, yet the achievement is nothing more than the birth-to-presence of a form of being which pre-exists.' Cited in Tania Murray Li, 'Neo-Liberal Strategies of Government through Community: The Social Development Program of the World Bank in Indonesia', NYU Institute for International Law and Justice Working Paper 2006/2 (2006) at 4.

sometimes in disregard of the formal legislative process. 'Without reform-minded and active leadership in the Government of Egypt', one project report notes, 'USAID … efforts would have been futile. This point cannot be overemphasised'.[39] The importance of working through a 'reform constituency' was flagged early on in rule of law work: the first of four 'essential needs', according to a 1994 evaluation of USAID's rule of law work, is 'host country political leadership in support of ROL [*sic*] reforms'.[40] If this support is lacking, 'donors will need to support constituency and coalition building strategies to strengthen political and public pressure for reform.' One project document puts it thus: 'Skills training not only develops skills but also develops a cadre of change agents'.[41] In practice, donors frequently rely on close links with key figures in government to accelerate reform processes and avoid lengthy public or parliamentary debate. USAID, for example, explains the advantages of grantmaking over loans in these terms:

> Even highly concessional loans typically require ratification by the legislature, whereas grants can be implemented by the executive branch. The process of legislative approval can stretch the gap between initial project agreement and the start of implementation into months or years. In the meantime conditions may change—a dedicated minister is replaced by one less committed to reform, or the conditions necessary for the passage of a key law or regulation are no longer in place. USAID's grant funding helps avoid this problem.[42]

The World Bank observes that, in practice, successful reforms often avoid the 'process of legislative approval' altogether:

> Macroeconomic reforms are often carried out in times of crisis by a stroke of the pen—achieved by administrative decree and a few key actors. The benefits are usually immediate, visible, and spread across the population, with losers or potential losers often too dispersed or too small in number to be of political importance.[43]

Project documents are replete with references to key legislative hooks introduced by decree, which often turn out to be instrumental in allowing relevant projects to take place at all.[44] Indeed, these begin with the shaping of

39. Nathan Associates Inc., *Assistance for Trade Reform, Final Report* (USAID, 2006) at vi.
40. Blair and Hansen, *USAID Scales of Justice*, *supra* note 25, at 3.
41. Yeager, *Final Report: USAID Croatia Commercial Law Reform*, *supra* note 27, at 6.
42. USAID, *Economic Growth Strategy: Securing the Future* (prepublication edition, 2008) at 12.
43. Sunita Kikeri, Thomas Kenyon and Vincent Palmadem, 'Reforming the Investment Climate: Lessons for Practitioners', World Bank Policy Research Working Paper 3986 (World Bank, 2006) at 2.
44. See, for example, World Bank, *Azerbaijan Judicial Modernization Project*, *supra* note 24, at 1; World Bank, *Project Appraisal Document on a Proposed Loan in the Amount of US$17.1*

constitutions, an area where USAID was extremely active in the early 1990s in former communist countries.[45] Delivery of the appropriate legislative environment is typically a core project output; the process through which it is achieved remains secondary. Donors not only 'assist' in drafting legislation, they frequently pre-draft it, sometimes without even visiting the country in question.[46] Indeed, even where the work remains local, donor influence is often very hands-on. Here, for example, is the description provided by a USAID consultant on inserting WTO-friendly language into Tajikistan's Civil Procedure Code:

> Specifically, the project carefully and successfully guided the development of the draft [Code] so that [it] now contains preliminary relief provisions as required for WTO accession ... We argued most loudly for these provisions ... and were not successful until the eleventh hour, when [project staff] met the Minister of Justice and urged [their] inclusion. The project helped draft the necessary language, translated it into Tajik, and worked with the Minister and his colleagues on the reasons for which the provisions were important for Tajikistan's future.[47]

An implicit assumption in much of the literature, as the above citations indicate, is that the beneficiaries of reform are not necessarily apprised of their own best interests—which in turn increases the value of the reform constituency. If they lose ground, projects can suffer or be abandoned.[48] There is thus a constant concern in rule of law reform circles with 'political will', its presence or absence, its inducement and encouragement:

> How can the political will to bring about basic, systemic reform be generated? Such political will is generated from three directions: from below, from within, and from outside. Organised pressure from below, in civil society, plays an essential

million to the Republic of Indonesia for a Private Provision of Infrastructure Technical Assistance Loan, Report No: 25820 (25 April 2003) at 8.

45. MSI, *USAID in LAC, E&E, AFR, and ANE, supra* note 8, at 12 recounts USAID aid in drafting the constitutions of Albania, Armenia, Bulgaria, Georgia, Russia, and Ukraine.
46. For example, Booz Allen Hamilton, *Final Report for Cape Verde WTO Accession Project under The Doha Project for WTO Accession and Participation* (USAID, 2005).
47. ARD Inc. and Checchi & Co. Consulting, *Assistance in Establishing the Legal and Institutional Framework Necessary to Support a Market-Based Economy (LIME 2) Kyrgyzstan and Tajikistan. Final Report* (USAID, 2006) at 45.
48. Thus the World Bank withdrew support for a follow-up to its 'legal and judicial development project' in Yemen after '[t]he implementation of the Judicial Development Component, in particular, was compromised in mid-2001 by the replacement of a reform-minded minister with a significantly more conservative minister' which 'sent a message that modernization of the judiciary was not a priority', World Bank, *Implementation Completion Report on a Credit in the Amount of SDR1.8 Million Equivalent to the Republic of Yemen for a Legal and Judicial Development Project* (2003) at 6.

> role in persuading ruling elites of the need for institutional reforms to improve governance. There may also be some reform-minded elements within the government and the ruling party or coalition who, whether for pragmatic or normative reasons, have come to see the need for reform but are reluctant to act in isolation. Finally, external actors in the international community often tip the balance through persuasive engagement with the rulers and the society and by extending tangible rewards for better governance and penalties for recalcitrance.[49]

The reform constituency is not, however, to be confused with 'the elite'. The latter term, which likewise appears regularly throughout rule of law literature, carries the consistently negative connotation of status quo power-brokers with the most to lose from reform.[50] Corrupt and collusive, the elite—defined as 'any economic, political, ethnic, social or other group trying to promote their interests at the expense of the interests of non-elite members'[51]—are often assumed to have 'captured' the state.[52] Reformers are thus pitted against the elites, aided by the internal divisions within, and popular suspicion regarding, the incumbents:

> The champions of reform are many but varied, and they tend to lack the resources commanded by those who benefit from the status quo. However [two] elements ... bode well for reform. The first is that those elites with vested interests in the informal networks of patronage are increasingly divided ... Secondly, the increasing demands placed upon the political elite by the population means that the frailties of the existing political system have become raw and exposed, and threaten to cast the political order into conflict and turmoil.[53]

49. USAID, *Foreign Aid in the National Interest: Promoting Freedom, Security and Opportunity* (USAID, 2002) at 48.
50. An early USAID paper put it thus: 'In developing countries, elite segments of society (which often include the civil service) may use the state as an instrument to pursue their own narrow interests, setting aside the legitimate needs and aspirations of the majority'. USAID, *Policy, Democracy and Governance* (1991) at 9.
51. Klaus Decker, Caroline Sage and Milena Stefanova, *Law or Justice: Building Equitable Legal Institutions*, prepared as a background paper for World Bank, *World Development Report 2006: Equity and Development* (World Bank, 2005) at 4.
52. 'Elite capture' is a term of art in Bank literature, extending to the judiciary ('Corruption and elite capture within judicial systems are among the obstacles to development to overcome through legal and judicial reform'): Robert Danino, 'Reforming Legal and Judicial Systems', in Ruth Kagia (ed.), *Balancing the Development Agenda: The Transformation of the World Bank Under James D. Wolfensohn, 1995–2005* (World Bank, 2005) 62–67 at 66. See also Joel Hellman, G Jones and Daniel Kaufmann, 'Seize the State, Seize the Day: State Capture and Influence in Transition Economies', 31 *Journal of Comparative Economics* (2003) 751–773.
53. ARD Inc., *Democracy and Governance Assessment of Nigeria* (USAID, December 2006) at v. See also Management Systems International (MSI), *Corruption Assessment Senegal,*

On this account, the true protagonists in the rule of law narrative are the 'population' against the 'elite', with the 'reformers' valiantly standing up on behalf of the general interest. Since the elite can manipulate the resources at their disposal, including the media, to capture popular acquiescence, reformers must also often struggle against popular reticence or misunderstanding. Reform is thus frequently presented as a heroic endeavour, pursued in the face of populist opposition, by a handful of far-sighted and selfless reform-minded politicians or bureaucrats, idealistic civil society agitators, the 'business community', often mobilised in chambers of commerce (who play frequent cameos in rule of law project scripts) and other 'stakeholders'.[54] Moreover, less obviously, perhaps, 'stakeholders' may also include non-nationals. Thus a World Bank project in Georgia cites among its target audiences 'international investors' and adds 'the international business community should be aware of the efforts undertaken in Georgia to set in place a competent and fair judiciary and ensure the rule of law'.[55]

3.2. Governance

> Governments determine how well, or how poorly, markets function. This simple truth explains the current concern with 'governance' as the world shifts toward an overwhelming endorsement of markets as the base of economic activity.[56]

'Governance' has come, over time, to define the boundaries and scope of the public sector in rule of law literature. The International Development Association (IDA)—the World Bank's grant arm for the poorest countries—defines it as 'the way the state acquires and exercises the authority to provide and manage public goods and services—including both public capacities

---

Contracted under USAID Contract No. DFD-I-00-03-00144-00, Task Order 1 (USAID, 31 August 2007); Paul J. Bonicelli [USAID Assistant Administrator for Latin America and the Caribbean], 'Assessing the State of Democracy in the Hemisphere' (Council of the Americas, 8 November 2007).

54. See, for example, International Development Association, *Country Assistance Strategy for the Republic of Zambia* (World Bank, 2008) at 2.
55. World Bank, *Project Appraisal Document on a Proposed Credit in the Amount of SDR 9.9 Million to Georgia for a Judicial Reform Project* (1999) at 25.
56. Deborah Brautigam, 'Governance and Economy: A Review', Policy Research Working Papers 815 (World Bank, 1991) at 1. See also Brian Van Arkadie, 'The Role of Institutions in Development', in World Bank, *Proceedings of the World Bank Annual Conference on Development Economics* 1989 (World Bank, 1990) 153–193; World Bank, *Governance and Development* (World Bank, 1992); James Anderson and Cheryl Gray, *Transforming Judicial Systems in Europe and Central Asia* (World Bank, 2007).

and public accountabilities', further broken down to encompass protections of property, budget management, efficient resource mobilisation and public administration, transparency and accountability, notably in procurement processes.[57]

At root, these principles of a functional bureaucracy—similar to those identified by Weber—supply a disciplinary category, the boundaries that circumscribe the activities of public officials. They outline the 'economic governance' functions of the state.[58] In rule of law interventions, the 'international community' acts as 'mentor' to a generation of responsible public officials, demonstrating the correct activation and deployment of the coercive machinery of the state. However, once control of that coercive machinery is in the hands of local officials, they have an incentive to 'free-ride' by using their coercive levers to steal from the public wealth. 'Governance' thus describes the parameters of *legitimate* state coercive activity. Its disciplinary character is reinforced by donors (including the IDA) who measure it as a basis for dispensing funds.[59] To assess 'governance' is to determine whether the public sector has deviated from its core function (creating an 'enabling environment' for investment), and to take punitive steps if so.

3.3. Corruption

Corruption is the flipside of governance: its absence or infringement. Usually defined as 'the abuse of public office for private gain', the term focuses on the boundary between public and private and provides criteria for policing that boundary.[60] The 'private gain' in question may refer to the private interest of *others* in transaction with the public official, but more precisely refers to the public official's *own* private interest, which is strictly illegitimate.

57. International Development Association, *IDA's Performance-Based Allocation System: A Review of the Governance Factor, International Development Association Resource Mobilization* (World Bank, 2006) at 1 and 6. Nine definitions of 'governance' are supplied in Navin Girishankar et al., 'Governance', in World Bank, *Poverty Reduction Strategy Sourcebook* (World Bank, 2002).

58. See Humphreys, *Theatre of the Rule of Law, supra* note 2, at ch. 5.

59. IDA, *A Review of the Governance Factor, supra* note 57. See also the Millennium Challenge Account: Millennium Challenge Corporation, *Fiscal Year 2007 Guidance for Compact-Eligible Countries* (MCC, 2006); Millennium Challenge Corporation, *Guide to the MCC Indicators and the Selection Process Fiscal Year 2008* (MCC, 2007).

60. For example, World Bank, *Implementation Plan for Strengthening World Bank Group Engagement on Governance and Anticorruption* (World Bank, 2007) at para. 3; USAID, *A Handbook on Fighting Corruption* (USAID, 1999).

Wherever the boundary between public and private (even, or especially, as that boundary exists within a specific person—that is, within any given 'office') is transgressed, ignored or misperceived, the result is 'corruption':

> [U]naccountable and nontransparent public governance can lead to a blurring of the lines between the public and private sectors and to … excessive government interference, corrupt capital market or utility regulation, or government 'capture' by private interests, as in 'crony capitalism'.[61]

Corruption is thus effectively twinned with 'governance' as its other—the confusion of public and private realms is to be criminalised.[62] The problematisation of corruption is an occasion for intensive scrutiny of the appropriate boundaries between public and private—as witness the United Nations Convention Against Corruption, with its meticulous and sometimes tortuous refinement of the relevant actors in each listed instance of possible corruption.[63] Steps to address corruption further explicate and reinforce these roles, by creating private pressures and public obligations. Thus there has been, on one hand, a significant (and largely privately funded) push to create an 'anti-corruption movement' by replicating human rights techniques of civil society monitoring and 'naming and shaming'. On the other, the repeat *source* of information on corruption is the private sector. By soliciting the perceptions—rather than monitoring the behaviour—of private actors, corruption indicators such as Transparency International's well known Corruption Perceptions Index effectively assume the latter as members of the 'movement'.

So while privately-funded anti-corruption work responsibilises the public *sphere*—mobilised to police the boundaries—Bank work places the burden of correction on the public (rather than private) *sector*. At project level, anti-corruption work involves the inculcation of criteria for recognising and activating the boundary between public and private—codes of ethics; reporting and other transparency procedures; public information campaigns—intended to encourage (or initiate) exposure to public scrutiny. In principle, then, the achievement of governance necessarily involves the elimination of corruption, so the latter goal appears to add merely rhetorical (and moral) weight to the former.

---

61. World Bank 'Reforming Public Institutions and Strengthening Governance: A World Bank Strategy', Public Sector Group, Poverty Reduction and Economic Management (PREM) Network (World Bank, 2000) at 14.
62. See in this context, Arts. 15–42, UN Convention against Corruption, 31 October 2003, in force 14 December 2005, 2349 UNTS 41 (UNCAC).
63. See, for example, *ibid*, Article 2(a).

3.4. Privatisation

The tremendous enthusiasm for the self-abnegation of the state—the obligatory ritual of renouncement that constitutes privatisation—at the Bank, within USAID, and elsewhere, was (and is) driven in part by the clarity it introduces between the private and public sectors, attentive to their differing roles (entrepreneurship, on one hand, governance, on the other).[64] On one hand, the massive transfer of assets from nominally public to private hands, with the number of annual privatisations growing apace since 1989, clearly signals the central importance of their mutual differentiation and relative privileging.[65] On the other, a perhaps more crucial effect is the *clarification* of control over assets—with the assumption that ownership is in fact more sharply defined as well as more efficiently allocated in private than in public hands. For example, a World Bank project in Romania was 'geared to strengthening financial discipline in the state enterprise sector, liquidating nonviable loss-making enterprises, privatising most remaining state enterprises and cutting overall losses and subsidies in the state enterprise sector by 22 percent'.[66] According to a fiercely defended discourse, privatisation of state-run enterprises permits the costs of inefficiencies and the rewards of efficiencies to be properly allocated to, and so felt by, the responsible individuals, rather than being absorbed into an amorphous and unaccountable leviathan.[67]

There is thus a clear ideational linkage between 'governance', 'corruption' and 'privatisation'. Privatisation is championed for reducing the scope for corruption (an informal tax on the private sector), not only by altering

64. The World Bank's privatisation database records over 1,800 privatisations valued at over US$ 1 million each between 2000 and 2008 (the database end date), <go.worldbank.org/W1ET8RG1Q0> (visited 10 March 2015).
65. The value of privatisations peaked in 2007 at US$133 billion, 'a record in nominal terms'. Sunita Kikeri and Verena Phipps, 'Privatization Trends: A Record Year in 2006', *Public Policy for the Private Sector*, Note No. 317 (World Bank, 2008) at 1 and Sunita Kikeri and Verena Phipps, 'Privatization Trends: A Record Year for Initial Public Offerings in 2007', *Public Policy for the Private Sector*, Note No. 321 (World Bank, 2008) at 1.
66. World Bank, *Implementation Completion Report on a Loan in the Amount of US$25 Million to Romania for a Private Sector Institution Building Project* (2005) at 5: 'These objectives were all met and this component can be rated as satisfactory'.
67. See generally: Friedrich Hayek, *The Road to Serfdom* (first published 1944) (University of Chicago Press, 1994); Ronald Coase, 'The Problem of Social Cost', 3(1) *Journal of Law and Economics* (1960) 1–44; Anne Krueger, 'Aid in the Development Process', 1(57) *Research Observer* (January 1986) 57–78.

incentive structures, but also by merely recategorising revenues.[68] Thus 'corrupt' payments to a public official for a public service reappear as profit to a service provider once the service is privatised: but in the process, income from the service is formalised and rationalised, the 'profit' moved from a public gatekeeper to a private owner—who, much as they might reinvest it 'more efficiently', might also simply expatriate it.

The extensive theoretical baggage that aligns privatisation, governance and anti-corruption with economic growth all moves in and around the edges of the ordinary rule of law penumbra as it has come down to us in association with the discipline of economics. As a limitation of public interference with private rights (or assets), a strong associative presumption links privatisation and the rule of law in Bank and other literature. On any account, as we have seen, the rule of law assumes a clear distinction between public and private and reinforces the boundary between them; accounts differ, however, on where precisely the boundary should be drawn. But a strong association with privatisation, such as that adopted by the Bank, USAID and others, will tend to redirect rule of law language toward the most parsimonious delineation. And this assumption is easily compatible with most accounts of the rule of law in the Hayekian and the new post-1989 tradition, even if it has little traction with its classical normative scope.[69]

3.5. A Public Sphere of Private … Investors?

It should already be clear that this account of the public sphere differs from Habermas's in some crucial respects. Whereas both privilege private over public, the contemporary account does so in a manner that is at the same time narrower and broader than the Habermasian ideal. It is narrower in that it consistently privileges a mere slice of private activity—commercial entrepreneurship—above all others: the private sector, and even more, the private investor, are fetishised to the point that they occupy almost the entire space of 'the private' in rule of law literature. 'Civil society', the principal agent of the political theory of an earlier era, appears in this account not only secondary in importance to, but ultimately parasitic upon, the private sector. Characterised in the diminished guise of advocacy-oriented

68. The point was made early on: 'Privatization, or the reduction of government controls and regulations and the sale of public enterprises to the private sector, has potential to increase transparency and reduce corruption abuses.' Deborah Brautigam, 'Governance and Economy', *supra* note 56, at 24.

69. Hayek, *Road to Serfdom*, *supra* note 67, and Friedrich Hayek, *The Constitution of Liberty* (first published 1960) (Routledge: London, 2006).

NGOs—rather than as the cumulative product of rational exchange in the public domain—civil society is (as we shall see in more detail below) expected to turn to private funding for sponsorship, and to launch 'public awareness' campaigns to jostle and compete in the media with commercial advertising.[70]

The scope of the private in rule of law activity is also *broader* than usually conceived, however, in that it abandons the implicit rootedness of the private realm within the bounds of the nation-state. Private investors, and the private sector, are transnational from the outset, with no necessary relation to a given 'public sector', except as incidental (and fundamentally interchangeable) locus of protection/regulation. The same is true of civil society and the media, both of which are conceived of as *essentially* transnational, even if nationally-inflected in a given context. Much as specific projects focus on national actors, the beneficiaries are also always transnational. The public sphere and public sector no longer map onto one another in the associative form assumed in the Habermasian model: an implicit symmetry between public and private, or state and society, that underpins relevant models from Kant through Weber is discarded in contemporary rule of law discourse. The 'society' that is to 'control' the state turns out itself to be trans-statal.

And yet, both 'public' and 'private' are imagined throughout this literature in a highly attenuated and idealised manner. On one hand, the selfless civil servant or functionary, efficient and productive, and differing from the Weberian bureaucrat only in his special regard for the market economy. On the other, the private individual in one of two guises: as latent entrepreneur ready to 'unleash market forces' or as active member of 'civil society'.

4. Supporting Roles

If 'governance' describes the proper limited role of a public sector clearly separated from the private realm and 'corruption' describes a condition whereby these spheres or the boundaries between them become blurred or confused, the rule of law is introduced as a means to hold public and private apart. This role of the rule of law is so deeply embedded in the literature's self-representation—so self-evident—that it is easily overlooked. The rule of law comprises basic civil controls over the public realm, thus *presupposing* two distinct realms; the corollary, evidenced in contemporary reform, is that the rule of law and the public/private distinction are mutually constitutive.

70. See Preeti Shroff-Mehta, *Romania Civil Society Strengthening Program, Final Report* (USAID & World Learning, 31 March 2008). See also Part Two of Habermas, *Structural Transformation, supra* note 32.

In states where the rule of law is said to be weak or absent, it is, in effect, the distinction between public and private itself that is weak, blurred, collapsed, or underdeveloped. To 'strengthen the rule of law' in such circumstances means to provide clarity and definition between distinct public and private realms, to supply mechanisms for negotiation between them, and to reinforce each in its own role. Rule of law culture relies on (at least) three such mechanisms: the disinterested figure of the judge, the interested figure of the private citizen (civil society), and the passive beneficiary ('the poor').

4.1. The Judiciary: Autonomy and Prestige

In the ideal rule of law configuration, the judiciary is the key guarantor of the divide between public and private, but only insofar as it is independent of both.[71] Its multifold remit is well captured in an $11 million Armenian 'Judicial Modernisation' project:

> Both domestic and foreign investors were expected to benefit from an efficient, independent and impartial judiciary thus promoting private sector development and economic growth in Armenia. Judges and court personnel were expected to benefit in terms of enhanced professional training, administrative independence and security, improved working conditions and better access to legal information. The general public and legal professionals would benefit from improved access to the courts and legal information, and impartial and professional functioning of the judiciary.[72]

I will return to the second and third beneficiaries cited here in a moment (the 'general public' and 'legal professionals'). As to the first, however, the notion that 'foreign and domestic investors' are viewed as personifying, or at least representing, the general interest will come as a surprise to many. Yet that implicit claim is a staple of contemporary project literature.[73] What appears to have happened is that the literature has identified the public interest with

71. Edgardo Buscaglia and Maria Dakolias, 'An Analysis of the Causes of Corruption in the Judiciary', The World Bank, Legal and Judicial Reform Unit (World Bank, 1999).
72. World Bank, *Armenia Judicial Reform Project, supra* note 28, at 3. The project included the objective of a constitutional amendment to improve judicial independence, which, according to the project report, 'was a challenging task for the authorities. After the first unsuccessful attempt in 2003, the government was able to secure a successful outcome in November 2005.' World Bank, *Armenia Judicial Reform Project, supra* note 28, at 8. See too USAID, *A Global Guide to Judicial Independence* (USAID, 2001).
73. For example, the World Bank claims for one project that it 'would benefit the entire population of Georgia, and in particular, the business community and foreign investors through the establishment of an independent and competent judicial system, leading to the enforcement of more secure property rights and contractual obligations and an

'investors' and the rule of law itself—the guardianship of the law—with the courts. I will take these two themes in order.

First, as to the location of the public interest, the implicit claim is that an independent and impartial judge disentangles the 'public interest' from the 'public sector' and (re)associates it with the private realm.[74] In this context, project documents on former socialist countries speak disparagingly of 'telephone justice', or judicial responsiveness to communications from their 'political masters'.[75] A properly independent judiciary will instead ratify public recognition of the legitimacy and authority of *private* interests as the proper content of the public sphere. In project literature, the identification of the public interest with private interests is justified largely on economic grounds—but it fits well with a wholesale vocabulary of individual freedoms and human rights that usually accompanies rule of law reform. By the same token, no particular private actor is to be privileged. Where a fuzzy or bloated public realm had previously provided special protection to government and select private interests—think 'crony capitalism'—a rule of law culture instead treats all equally.

There are two further implicit claims here. One is that in Armenia (and other rule of law recipient countries), foreign investors were previously discriminated against, by means of subsidies, tariffs, taxes, regulations and other forms of economic nationalism. By lifting that discrimination, equality under law is returned, and development furthered.[76] This claim further supports, and is supported by, the consistent rule of law preference for trade liberalisation and push for the internalisation of WTO principles into national law

---

environment conducive to the establishment of the rule of law'. World Bank, *Implementation Completion and Results Report on a Credit in the Amount of SDR 9.87 Million to Georgia for Judicial Reform Project* (2007) at 3.

74. World Bank, 'The Law and Economics of Judicial Systems', Preliminary Notes No. 26 (World Bank, 1999); Buscaglia and Dakolias, 'Corruption in the Judiciary', *supra* note 71.
75. Examples: Chemonics International, *Strengthening the Rule of Law in Kazakhstan, supra* note 5, at 3; World Bank, *Project Appraisal Document on a Proposed Loan in the Amount of US$50 Million to the Russian Federation for a Judicial Reform Support Project* (January 19, 2007) at 2; World Bank, *Project Appraisal Document on a Proposed Loan in the Amount of Euro 110.0 Million (US$130.0 Million Equivalent) to Romania for a Judicial Reform Project* (22 November 2005) at 27; MSI, *USAID in LAC, E&E, AFR, and ANE, supra* note 8, at 119.
76. For example, Chirayath, Sage and Woolcock, 'Customary Law and Policy Reform', *supra* note 18, at 95; *National Security Strategy of the United States of America 2006* (White House, 2006) at 27: 'While most of the world affirms in principle the appeal of economic liberty, in practice too many nations hold fast to the false comforts of subsidies and trade barriers. Such distortions of the market stifle growth in developed countries, and slow the escape from poverty in developing countries. Against these short-sighted impulses, the United States promotes the enduring vision of a global economy that welcomes

(about which more below). The second claim is that investors are in some way *particularly* representative of the public interest. This claim is indissociable from a familiar economic view, with roots traceable to Adam Smith, later expressed most clearly, perhaps, in Friedrich Hayek and Harnando de Soto—that by reallocating resources to where they will be most efficient, investors perform the ultimate public good.[77] In rule of law literature, this notion gains the force of proven fact; and so it appears self-evident that a truly independent judiciary will understand the importance of investment generally, and respect the autonomy of foreign investors in particular, in a national economy, all else being equal.

Second, as to the role of the courts, the assumption appears to be that if law is to rule, its priests and guardians must be tended. An important background theme in rule of law projects has been to increase the *prestige* of the judiciary.[78] Judicial independence derives from many sources, mostly structural.[79] Among these, the literature agrees that good remuneration and working conditions are essential.[80] Prestige further depends upon the inculcation among legal actors of professional pride in their unique guardianship of the rule of law. Project literature is full of examples of demoralised, underpaid and unprofessional judicial actors. In Georgia, one project notes: 'Judges received poor remuneration, and held little if any prestige. For these reasons, the judiciary was staffed with individuals who were often unwilling or incapable of providing independent, professional judicial decisions'.[81] Courthouse rehabilitation,

all participants and encourages the voluntary exchange of goods and services based on mutual benefit, not favouritism.'

77. See Humphreys, *Theatre of the Rule of Law*, *supra* note 2, at ch. 1.
78. MSI reports on USAID's support for judicial associations in Eastern Europe that 'the need for such professional associations has been particularly important in post-communist societies because their judiciaries have typically been accorded less power, prestige, and resources than their western counterparts. USAID has made a very important contribution in helping develop judicial associations throughout the region.' MSI, *USAID in LAC, E&E, AFR, and ANE*, *supra* note 8, at 16.
79. For an overview of the ingredients of judicial independence, see USAID, *Guidance for Promoting Judicial Independence and Impartiality* (USAID, 2002) at 12–41. Among the priority areas identified are: selection processes, security of tenure, length of tenure, and structure of the judiciary (including budgets). For increasing 'judicial capacity', recommendations include training programs, access to legal materials, codes of ethics, increasing the status of judges, and creating judicial associations.
80. *Ibid*, at 31: 'The question is: How to increase the self-respect of judges? … In terms of affecting the attitude of the judges themselves, salaries and benefits are key factors.'
81. World Bank, *Georgia Judicial Reform Project*, *supra* note 55, at 3. See also World Bank, *Russia Judicial Reform Support Project*, *supra* note 75, at 10; World Bank Legal Vice Presidency, *The World Bank, Ethiopia: Legal and Judicial Sector Assessment* (World Bank, 2004) at 20.

new computers, better wages, professional training: according to project documents, all of these elements help build the prestige of the judiciary. The World Bank thus describes two lessons derived from its 'depth of experience in the reform and development of legal and judicial institutions, particularly in transition countries':

> The first is that judicial independence relies as much on the constitutional empowerment of the judiciary to self-governance as it does on the capacity of the judiciary to manage and administer its own resources—human, financial, informational, technical and physical. The latter [is] sometimes called operational independence ... The second lesson is that the effectiveness of a judiciary lies in its ability to deliver efficient services to the public as much as in its role as a check and balance on the executive. As such, developing effective service delivery mechanisms through IT systems, courthouse modernization, training, and public education are essential corollaries to strengthening independence.[82]

Funding judicial associations and supporting conferences on 'the role of judges in society' or 'the importance of the rule of law' address these shortcomings, nurture professional pride, and sensitise the courts to their public role.[83] If legal professionals and judges are themselves persuaded of the importance of their calling, the logic goes, they will better serve as impartial arbitrators. In a virtuous cycle, this will lead to greater 'societal respect', which will in turn boost their capacity to apply the law independently.[84] If the judge is gently prodded in the appropriate direction, other good things follow.[85]

---

82. World Bank, *World Bank Report No: 38361-AM, Project Appraisal Document on a Proposed Credit in the Amount of SDR 15.2 million (US$22.5 Million Equivalent) for a Second Judicial Reform Project, Republic of Armenia* (9 February 2007) at 2.
83. See for example, USAID, *The Vermont-Karelia Rule of Law Project, Final Report,* January 1, 1997–December 31, 1997 (USAID, 1998); American Bar Association, *Program of the 2nd Annual IBA Bar Leader's Conference, 16–17 May 2007, Zagreb, Croatia* (American Bar Association, 2007): 'How Can Bar Associations Promote the Rule of Law ... Promoting the rule of law [involves] "public education". More often than not, it is a country's government itself which is most in need of education. However, educated support for the rule of law among the population at large is essential if the rule of law is to become embedded in a society.'
84. For example, USAID, *Promoting Judicial Independence, supra* note 79, at 36, under the header 'Promoting Societal Respect for the Role of an Impartial Judiciary' and referring to 'the most important factor affecting judicial independence: the expectations of society. If a society expects and demands an honest judiciary, it will probably get one. If expectations are low, the likelihood that the judiciary will operate fairly is equally low.'
85. So, for example, MSI, *USAID in LAC, E&E, AFR, and ANE, supra* note 8, at 58: '[In the Dominican Republic] USAID facilitated a dialogue that led to placing the role of the judiciary in the proper perspective. For the first time, objectives for fair and efficient court performance were established. These included a Supreme Court mission statement, which informs judges and court administrators what is expected of them by the public. Court

In the ideal horizon, judicial integrity would be entirely governed by internal disciplinary mechanisms, such that neither public imperatives nor private incentives can claim the allegiance of the judge. Allegiance is instead transferred to a body of norms characterised as 'the rule of law', the source of which is removed from ordinary politics and returned, in theory, to the discipline of legal practice itself, now universalised. Just as judicial independence affirms the independence of the law itself, so a prestigious judiciary brings dignity to the law. In rule of law culture, then, a primary role of the courts and the figure of the judge is iconic—to *symbolise* the gravity, stolidity, prestige of law; its capacity to rule and its fittedness to do so. The judge evokes and advertises the autonomy of law—a role she can play even if that autonomy itself is in fact ultimately untraceable or illusory, and even if her own role in doing so derives primarily from a series of funded initiatives hailing from a handful of institutions mostly based in Washington, D.C.

4.2. Civil Society

The public sphere as such generally appears in project literature in the guise of 'civil society'. In project documentation, civil society today is freighted with an attenuated reconstruction of its role in the classical public sphere. Where, for Habermas, civil society signified the collective and active body of private individuals acting in the public interest,[86] in today's rule of law world it is synonymous with CSOs (civil society organisations) or NGOs ('non-profit' as well as non-governmental)—specific niche mediators between public and private realms. NGOs have three main roles in rule of law projects. They are, first, representatives of the general public; a relevant audience or constituency for project outputs, who are counted on to activate the project's wider goals.[87]

---

staff and judges were made aware that court performance and judges' and administrators' actions should facilitate access to justice, expeditious procedures, impartiality and integrity, political independence, accountability, and public confidence in the judicial system.'

86. Habermas, *Structural Transformation*, *supra* note 32, at 73–79.
87. Here is an example from a World Bank 'judicial reform support project' in the Philippines. '*Improvements in information provided to the public and greater collaboration with civil society*. The public has little understanding of how the courts operate and what their rights are under the law. This has profound implications for access to justice, especially by the poor. It also contributes to a situation where the courts are extremely vulnerable to graft and corruption and political pressures. There is a need to improve public information and collaboration with civil society, organised groups, the legal profession and media, in order to improve access, improve the utilisation of judicial services, and enhance accountability of judicial personnel.' (World Bank, *Project Appraisal Document on a Proposed Loan in the Amount of US$21.9 Million to the Republic of the Philippines for a Judicial Reform Support Project* (2003) at 6).

Second, CSOs are themselves a vehicle for project activities—project funding is channelled through them to 'monitor' the public sector and 'hold it accountable'. Third, as a constituent part of a modern polity, rule of law projects aim themselves to build and nurture civil society.[88] In the rule of law vision, civil society actors effectively constitute the public sphere; as private citizens, they monitor and pressure the public sector to act in the public interest. They are not themselves subject to the discipline of 'governance'; rather they police its boundaries. A sharpened public/private distinction does not therefore need to result in mutual isolation of these two spheres; rather it provides a platform for interchange between them, which in turn provides the basis for 'public policy in the private interest' (the title of a Bank publication). Once properly distinct, contact between public and private spheres is encouraged through 'civil society consultation' and 'public-private dialogue'.[89]

The consciously constructed nature of 'civil society' in this vision is well outlined in the following activities of a USAID 'civil society strengthening' project undertaken in Romania. It is worth quoting at length:

> Organizational and financial sustainability grants [were] provided [to] watchdog and public policy NGOs with specific opportunities to develop products and systems that made them potentially more attractive to donors and to their members, supporters and constituents while providing opportunities to develop local funding bases ... NGOs established and put into operation realistic business plans ... and introduced new mechanisms for revenue generation; staff training and appropriate systems of remuneration were introduced so as to retain staff ... and finally, they tapped increasing volunteerism and expanded their volunteer base to enjoy the benefits of this human resource ... Financial sustainability was enhanced by the NGOs' better documentation of the impact that their advocacy activities

88. For example, the 'Romania Civil Society Strengthening Program' was implemented between September 2005 and December 2007, involving a USAID grant of US$4.8 million, of which US$2.4 million was allocated as grant support for Romanian NGOs that agreed to partner with USAID's contractor, World Learning for International Development (WLID). Preeti Shroff-Mehta, *Romania Civil Society Strengthening Program*, *supra* note 70.

89. Many projects include mechanisms for public-private and civil society dialogue. On public-private dialogue, see USAID, *Final Report, Assessment of the Bulgarian Enterprise, Growth and Investment Project (EGIP) (Formerly the Policy Reform and Advocacy Strengthening Project), Funded by USAID/Bulgaria, Conducted by Stephen C. Silcox, Kristin Lobron, Neal Nathanson* (22 February 2005) and World Bank, *Project Appraisal Document on a Proposed Grant in the Amount of SDR 10 Million (US$15 Million Equivalent) to the Republic of Malawi for a Business Environment Strengthening Technical Assistance Project (BESTAP), Report No: 39633-MW* (27 April 2007). On civil society consultation, Preeti Shroff-Mehta, *Romania Civil Society Strengthening Program*, *supra* note 70 and World Bank, *Philippines Judicial Reform Support Project*, *supra* note 87.

> had for marketing purposes and for increasing the credibility of the watchdog and public policy NGO sub-sector; citizen and organizational membership schemes were developed to assist in creating identifiable constituencies as well as to enhance local fundraising strategies ...[90]

Indeed civil society, in this construction, faces both ways—not only do CSOs monitor and pressure the government (the public *sector*), they also monitor and pressure the public *sphere*, albeit in the vein of agitation rather than accusation. As CSOs agitate for reform and to mobilise the public, they must rely upon a functional media. 'Public information' and 'public awareness' are of immense significance to rule of law projects.[91]

Another favourite area of 'awareness raising' concerns rights—the injunction to 'know your rights' repeatedly arises as a vehicle of public mobilisation, and a concretisation of the public/private separation, with 'human' or 'civil' rights both held against the state and enforced through it. In one fascinating case in Armenia, a TV program funded by the World Bank as part of a justice sector reform project, *My Right*, became the most popular show on Armenian television:

> *Public Awareness and Education*. The image of the judiciary, as an open, fair and accessible institution, was improved as a result of several project activities. The main output of the Public Awareness component was the "My Right" television show, which was developed and broadcasted on Armenian Public Television starting September 2004. By 2006 the show had been rated number one by the Public Television of Armenia for two consecutive years making it a real success. The show also has an official website that provides useful legal information and opportunities for the public to ask questions. In response to the large number of citizens requests for legal information, the MOJ organised a number of free consulting sessions where the "My Right" TV judge and Ministry legal experts provided advice. Some activities of this component, such as journalism training and publication of brochures were dropped due to the Government's view that they were relatively ineffective and the availability of other donor resources for such activities.[92]

This example succinctly illustrates the dislocation between the classical public/private distinction (as it appears in the writings of Habermas and others), and the contemporary distinction promoted through rule of law projects. The show popularises a primary theme of the public sphere according to the rule of law—enforceable rights held against the state—and no doubt increases and mobilises faith in the capacity of that public sphere to self-mobilise. And yet, while it appears to instantiate a Habermas-like collective of private

90. Preeti Shroff-Mehta, *Romania Civil Society Strengthening Program*, *supra* note 70, at 2–3.
91. USAID, *The Role of Media in Democracy: A Strategic Approach* (USAID, 1999).
92. World Bank, *Armenia Judicial Reform Project*, *supra* note 28, at 17.

interests, it is in fact wholly a creature of the public sector itself; the product of an agreement between the World Bank and the government, implemented with public funding and projected into the public sphere to help in the latter's self-consolidation or emergence, in a process that not only relies upon government support for its success but defers to government suggestion in its execution. The secret paradox disclosed by this remarkably controlled projection of the rule of law—its managed consolidation of a public/private distinction so attenuated as to have effectively vanished—is the inescapability of the public in the construction of the private; precisely the reverse of the ideal type process described by Habermas.[93] We might call the production of these pseudo-adversarial public and private figures, a pedagogy of the rule of law.[94]

4.3. 'The Poor': Investors in Waiting

Ostensibly, the principal 'stakeholder' of rule of law reform is 'the poor'. This amorphous group-noun recurs with extraordinary frequency in the documentation of the Bank in particular—whose oft-cited mission is to 'eradicate poverty'. The vocabulary of poverty does enormous work for the Bank. First, in aid-recipient countries, 'the poor' generally comprise the majority of the population—they are therefore the relevant 'public' who are to benefit from reform; moreover, their prioritisation feels substantively democratic. However, second, 'the poor' are not really represented as a 'public' at all, in that they do not possess the attributes of a public sphere—indeed, insofar as 'poverty' aims to indicate that the conditions of autonomy (security of health, food and education, political participation, and so on) are weak or lacking, the aggregate 'poor' of the Third World are defined in opposition to the notion of a 'public sphere'.[95] By corollary, 'the poor' as such do not comprise 'civil

93. Habermas does not claim this to be an actual historical process: the notion that the public sphere takes command of the state is rather an ideal, or ideological, explanation of the relationship between state and society. See Jürgen Habermas, 'Further Reflections on the Public Sphere', in Craig Calhoun (ed.), *Habermas and the Public Sphere* (MIT Press: Cambridge, 1992) at 422; Habermas, *Structural Transformation, supra* note 32, at xvvii, 83 and 88; Humphreys, *Theatre of the Rule of Law, supra* note 2, at 44 and 50–52.

94. A Philippines project provides a literal example: to develop 'community outreach programs … for children in primary schools to inculcate an understanding of the rule of law and the role of judges, in partnership with the department of education'. World Bank, *Philippines Judicial Reform Support Project, supra* note 87, at 36.

95. This is not, of course, to claim that the condition of poverty is a bar to being a 'private person'. It is merely to recall the obvious point that the condition of 'privacy' is not a simple natural attribute, but a historical and conceptual one. The point is that where the term 'poor' is used in the abstract as a categorical term, it denies or assumes the absence of the attributes of private personhood *per se.*

society'. Although 'grassroots' and 'social' movements may be of immense political significance, the poor *per se*, defined merely by the absence of wealth, form neither an 'interest' in themselves nor a forum wherein a shared (public) interest might be identified and promoted. Nevertheless, third, the poor appear to donors as a natural 'constituency for reform', since the quality that defines them—the absence of wealth—itself constitutes the undesirability of the status quo; the poor are the *raison d'être* of reform and development. Fourth, as such—a constituency for reform that does not in itself constitute a public—the poor need protection or representation. As their home elites, in rule-of-law deficient countries, do not protect or represent them adequately, the role is left to others. The Bank supplies this representation; Bank documents on every topic reflexively note the benefits for 'the poor' of recommended measures. Here are some examples:

— *Crime*: Increasing the rule of law, by reducing crime, benefits the poor as 'the poor suffer more from crime, the impact of crime on their livelihood is greater, and they are less able to access the justice systems'.[96]
— *Trade*: Reducing trade protection 'generally promotes exports and raises the incomes of the poor by supporting labor-intensive activities'.[97]
— *Finance*: 'Improving access to financial services such as savings, credit, insurance, and remittances is vital to enabling the poor to take advantage of economic opportunities and guard against uncertainty'.[98]
— *Governance*: The World Bank focus on governance and corruption 'is based on its mandate to reduce poverty [since] a capable and accountable state creates opportunities for the poor'.[99]
— *Corruption*: 'Corrupt bureaucracies and biased enforcement of contract and property rights inhibits the poor from making investments in physical and human capital that could raise their incomes';[100] 'Corruption is an especially regressive tax, with the poor hit hardest by even small demands for bribes or fees when they want public services.[101]

96. Kirsti Samuels, 'Rule of Law Reform in Post-Conflict Countries Operational Initiatives and Lessons Learnt', World Bank Conflict Prevention and Reconstruction Paper No. 37 (World Bank, 2006) at 3.
97. World Bank, *World Development Report 1991*, *supra* note 13, at 10.
98. World Bank, *The World Bank Annual Report 2006* (World Bank, 2006) at 21.
99. Ksenia Yudaevam (ed.), *Beyond Transition* (World Bank, 2007) at 2.
100. World Bank, *2004 Annual Review of Development Effectiveness: The World Bank's Contributions to Poverty Reduction* (World Bank, 2005) at 40.
101. World Bank, *World Development Report 2002: Building Institutions for Markets* (World Bank, 2001) at 5. This common refrain, supported by scant evidence, is counter-intuitive. Since bribes, unlike for example, VAT, are often modulated to match individual capacity

A recurrent motif that runs through many of the above quotes and through a preponderant section of the Bank's voluminous writing on poverty associates its relief with 'opportunities' in a liberated economy, and pairs 'the poor' with 'small and medium enterprises'.[102] The recurrent interest in micro-business and micro-financing evinces a similar conviction that an enabling environment for private sector development suits 'the poor' just as well as the foreign investor precisely because the poor are themselves, essentially, investors-in-waiting. The poor are the ordinary folk of rule of law literature, a collection of *tabulae rasae* upon which is quickly drawn the outline of *homo economicus*. And, since the 'poor' are neither a public nor a lobby group, who is to object?

One source of objection turned out to be the Bank itself, in a rare display of dissenting research.[103] A large Bank survey into the conditions for 'the poor' in 23 countries reported that most of the tens of thousands interviewed, far from uncovering new opportunities and investments, were instead struggling in deteriorating circumstances, and attributed their new hardships to the measures the Bank had claimed should help.[104] In general, the report found that 'households are crumbling under the stresses of poverty' and the 'social fabric, poor people's only "insurance", is unraveling'.[105] Despite its 1,000-page length, the study does not investigate the underlying causes of the malaise it describes—the authors explain that the report 'was not designed to disentangle and evaluate the effects of specific economic policies or trends on the lives of poor people', but merely to 'present the analyses of those who are currently poor, who recount the negative impact that certain economic policies and market changes have had on them and on their households and communities'.[106] The result is a litany of accounts of misfortune and misery, striking in their near uniformity across the world's different regions, recounting the hardship experienced by 'the poor' everywhere as public services recede

to pay, it seems more likely that corruption would constitute a progressive tax. See also USAID, *A Handbook on Fighting Corruption* (USAID, 1999).

102. Thus, for example, Yudaevam (ed.), *Beyond Transition*, *supra* note 99, at 2: 'the abolishment of such barriers [to banking] and financial development disproportionately benefit the poor and small businesses.'
103. There are, of course, other available descriptions of the effects of what has come to be known as 'neoliberalism', but it seems most appropriate in the present context to use the Bank's own account.
104. Deepa Narayan and Patti Petesch (eds), *Voices of the Poor: From Many Lands* (World Bank, 2002). For the response within the Bank to these findings, see *ibid*, at 8.
105. Deepa Narayan, *Can Anyone Hear Us? Voices From 47 Countries, Voices of the Poor Volume 1* (World Bank, 1999) at 6–7. See also Deepa Narayan, Robert Chambers, Meera K. Shah and Patti Petesch, *Voices of the Poor: Crying Out for Change* (Oxford University Press, 2000). Together these three volumes comprise the full study.
106. Narayan and Pretesch, *From Many Lands*, *supra* note 104, at 471.

and/or are privatised, labour protections vanish, living standards drop, and medical services deteriorate.[107] A number of examples are worth recounting:

> Poor people from several countries expressed deep concern over the economic upheavals and policy changes that are buffeting their lives … Depending on the country, poor people mentioned privatization, factory closures, the opening of domestic markets, currency devaluation, inflation, reductions in social services, and other related changes as having depleted their assets and increased their insecurity.
>
> Cynicism and anger over this abandonment [of public services] are evident everywhere but are especially prominent in countries of the former Soviet Union, where people once experienced effective delivery of basic services and now face both high state capture and widespread corruption.
>
> In the wake of the transition to market economies in the four countries visited in Eastern Europe and Central Asia, people reported steep drops in living standards. Especially hard hit were the "one-company towns" and villages that once revolved around large state farms.
>
> In all countries visited in this region, poor people connected extensive unemployment and underemployment to the dismantling of the state before functioning markets were in place.
>
> In all four countries of Latin America and the Caribbean, people described the economic and social devastation of their communities in the wake of macroeconomic crises and policy reforms.
>
> Poor men and women in the four European and Central Asian countries described the wrenching effects created by the elimination of free medical services. Participants related frightening experiences of going without needed medical services and medications and of receiving surgery without anesthesia.

Despite these observations, *Voices of the Poor* concludes that the key 'challenges' for the Bank concern the relative weakness of national-level institutions. Institutional state failures, the report says, create and exacerbate problems for the poor: corruption; clientelism and patronage; lawlessness, crime, and conflict; discriminatory behaviour.[108] In response, the report urges tweaks on existing orthodoxy: 'pro-poor' economic policies; 'investing in poor peoples' assets'; supporting partnerships with poor people; addressing 'gender inequities'; and protecting poor peoples' rights.[109]

---

107. *Ibid*, at 471–6.
108. Narayan and Petesch (eds), *From Many Lands*, *supra* note 104, at 477–80.
109. *Ibid*, at 487–93.

It would appear, then, that faced with the spectre of 'social chaos' the choice has been to soldier on. In response to the apparent dissonance, at the Bank and elsewhere, between the rhetoric of 'pro-poor growth' and the observed experience, in much of the world, of the reverse, a new term was added to the rule of law lexicon: 'legal empowerment'. In its initial formulation, this term signified a shift in process and focus, rather than in the content, of rule of law work. Still frankly instrumental, law reform would abandon some of the formal pretensions of a 'rule of law orthodoxy' while nevertheless remaining broadly within the field's mainstream themes.[110] Legal empowerment meant using the law to alleviate poverty; although it would be 'rights-based' and concerned with enforcing existing protections already 'on the books', the initial focus on 'paralegals' (that is, legal help from trained non-lawyers) and using law to address poverty indicated an apparently substantivist orientation.[111]

When a 'Commission on Legal Empowerment of the Poor' was created in 2005, however, the focus soon shifted towards more, rather than less, formalism. The Commission's 2008 report opens with the astonishing claim that 'four billion people around the world are robbed of the chance to better their lives and climb out of poverty, because they are excluded from the rule of law'.[112] The central premise of the report is that poverty is in part due to and exacerbated by exclusion from the (formal) legal system *per se*—and that inclusion in some form is thus, in itself, a step to curing poverty. The Commission's response is to call for the formalisation of labour, property, and 'business' rights, and to ensure greater 'access to justice' and court processes.[113] The assumption implicit in many Bank materials that 'the poor' are in fact embryonic entrepreneurs awaiting only a formally secure system to incentivise them to creativity is embraced by the Commission:

> For all these people, protection of their assets is fundamental. But protection of what they have is not enough, for they are poor and their possessions meagre.

110. Frank Upham, 'Mythmaking in the Rule of Law Orthodoxy', in Thomas Carothers (ed.) *Promoting the Rule of Law Abroad: In Search of Knowledge* (Carnegie Endowment for International Peace: Washington, D.C., 2006) at 75–104.
111. Stephen Golub, 'The Legal Empowerment Alternative', in *ibid*, 161–190 at 161–65.
112. Commission on Legal Empowerment of the Poor, *Making the Law Work for Everyone* (UNDP, 2008), vol. I at 1. 'At best', the report adds, 'they live with very modest, unprotected assets that cannot be leveraged in the market due to cumulative mechanisms of exclusion.' *Ibid*, at 19.
113. With regard to property rights, see Commission on Legal Empowerment of the Poor, *Making the Law Work for Everyone* (UNDP, 2008), vol. II at 75. For relevant background, Hernando De Soto, *The Mystery of Capital: Why Capitalism Triumphs in the West and Fails Everywhere Else* (Basic Books: New York, 2000). According to the report: '"Business rights" need not yet be regarded as a new term in law, but rather as derived

> They deserve a chance to make their business operations, no matter how small or even micro they are, more productive, and they are entitled to decent working conditions. Reforms of the institutions they relate to are essential for their empowerment. Only through such systemic change will the poorest be able to take advantage of new opportunities and be attracted to joining the formal economy.[114]

It is not clear here or elsewhere whether the authors are aware that formalising the 'property rights' of the poor may open the way to dispossession as much as to investment;[115] that 'business rights' can be mobilised by well-resourced actors against poorer ones; or that 'labour rights', if reduced to 'job opportunities' with 'social protection' languishing as a mere aspiration, need not provide more security for workers than the informal market (which can also be, for example, kin or clan based). By assimilating 'the poor' to proto-investors, the Commission's authors appear to miss the possibility that, absent strong and specific protections of a kind they do not suggest, poor people stand to lose at least as much as they gain from a formal legal system, or that gains might need to be weighed against losses—or, most pertinently, that a functional legal framework may actually facilitate loss.

Such impoverished analysis is facilitated by the report's frankly ideological embrace of the entire edifice of rule of law economics, now washed in a newly utopian abstraction:

> The law is the platform on which rests the vital institutions of society. No modern market economy can function without law, and to be legitimate, power itself must submit to the law. A thriving and inclusive market can provide the fiscal space that allows national governments to better fulfil their own responsibilities. The relationship between society, the state and the market is symbiotic. For example, the market not only reflects basic freedoms such as association and movement, but also generates resources to provide, uphold, and enforce the full array of human rights. It is processes such as these, in which the poor realise their rights and reap the benefits of new opportunities, which enable the fruition of citizenship—in short, legal empowerment.[116]

---

from existing rights related to doing business of the individual, newly bundled together under this term on the basis of their vital instrumentality in the livelihoods of the poor.' Empowerment Commission, *Making the Law Work*, vol. II, *supra* note 113, at 5.

114. Empowerment Commission, *Making the Law Work*, vol. I, *supra* note 112, at 20. See also *ibid*, at 8.

115. The relevant passage (Empowerment Commission, *Making the Law Work*, vol. I, *supra* note 112, at 7) is ambiguous. The principal point receives little support in the working group study upon which it is based: Empowerment Commission, *Making the Law Work*, vol. II, *supra* note 113, at 85.

116. Empowerment Commission, *Making the Law Work*, vol. I, *supra* note 112, at 3.

In this passage, and in the report from which it is taken, the rule of law *subject* finally appears in all her glory: as a market-citizen for whom fundamental rights are market rights, in a state dedicated to upholding those rights.

5. Dénouement: Global Integration

Rule of law literature speaks often of 'global integration', holding out the promise to poorer countries to 'join the club'. While the expression usually arises in reference to trade liberalisation, there are other relevant rule of law modes of 'integration' too, notably the growing transnational security network constructed through the efforts to promote rule of law as part of the recent 'war on terror'. The latter involves shared judicial and criminal methodologies, shared information gathering and disseminating techniques, and a shared narrative of conflict (previously centred on narcotics).[117] The former aims, in the language of a Bush-administration era National Security Strategy, to 'ignite a new era of global economic growth through free markets and free trade'.[118] This translates into USAID policy commitments to pursue 'bilateral investment treaties that open new markets, support job creation in the United States, and provide important protections to U.S. investors' as well as 'state-of-the-art free trade agreements that open new markets for U.S. agriculture, goods, and services and extend strong U.S. investment, transparency, and intellectual property protections abroad.'[119] The World Bank shares these goals: 'trade and integration' has long been one of three Bank 'metathemes'. In the literature of both the Bank and the US government, free trade benefits everyone, but it is particularly good for poorer countries—and, within them, for their poorest members. 'As the world moves into the

117. See Humphreys, *Theatre of the Rule of Law*, *supra* note 2, at ch. 5.

118. *US National Security Strategy 2006*, *supra* note 76, at 25–30. The themes of trade and security blend in the US National Security Strategies of 2002 and 2006. The latter, having discussed the importance of the rule of law in contributing to peace and security turns to trade, under the header 'Opening markets and integrating developing countries': 'We will continue to work with countries such as Russia, Ukraine, Kazakhstan, and Vietnam on the market reforms needed to join the WTO. Participation in the WTO brings opportunities as well as obligations—to strengthen the rule of law and honour the intellectual property rights that sustain the modern knowledge economy, and to remove tariffs, subsidies, and other trade barriers that distort global markets and harm the world's poor' (*ibid*, at 28).

119. See USAID, *Policy Framework for Bilateral Foreign Aid: Implementing Transformational Diplomacy Through Development* (USAID, 2006) at 11, 27–28. US Department of State, *Congressional Budget Justification, Foreign Assistance, Fiscal Year 2009* (Department of State, undated [2008]) at 120.

twenty-first century', an early Bank strategy document on Africa proclaimed, 'the consensus is greater than ever that markets, private initiative and integration into the global marketplace are the cornerstones of economic success'.[120] USAID's 2008 'economic growth strategy' claims that 'the current world trading system provides the greatest opportunity for global integration and poverty reduction the world has ever seen'.[121]

The rule of law lies at the heart of these visions in a two-way relation. On one hand, rule of law is considered a necessary precursor for a country's integration into the global economy; on the other, joining free trade regimes itself helps entrench the rule of law in signatory states. Reformers therefore promote accession to international trade mechanisms and use accession processes to further rule of law goals.[122] To encourage 'integration'—touted as a repository of investment and employment opportunities, and of heightened productivity standards, as well as a harbinger of pluralism and tolerance in recipient countries—certain groundrules must be in place. Foreign investors must be reasonably confident about what to expect.[123] Barriers to trade, both direct and indirect, must not only be removed but their removal must be enforced.[124] Judicial independence in this light also involves freedom

120. World Bank, *Africa Can Compete! A Framework For World Bank Group Support For Private Sector Development in Sub-Saharan Africa* (World Bank, 1998) at vii.

121. USAID, *Economic Growth Strategy: Securing the Future* (prepublication edition, 2008) at 9.

122. For illustration, the State Department's request for funding trade liberalisation in Vietnam: 'A top U.S. priority in Vietnam is to support a dynamic and expanding economic environment conducive to reform, legal transformation, and development of a vibrant private sector. USAID programs will assist Vietnam's World Trade Organization (WTO) and Bilateral Trade Agreement (BTA) implementation, comprehensive reform of laws and policies related to trade and investment, and creation of a business enabling environment that fosters private sector development and enhances competitiveness … Expanding technical assistance is imperative to develop institutional capacity and human resources for implementation of reforms and best practices, and to ensure that regulatory oversight keeps pace with integration into the global economy.' (US Department of State, *Budget Justification FY 2009*, *supra* note 119, at 394). See also, for the World Bank, Kikeri, Kenyon and Palmadem, 'Reforming the Investment Climate', *supra* note 43, at 11.

123. See, for example, World Bank, *World Development Report 2005: A Better Investment Climate for Everyone* (World Bank, 2004) at 36.

124. The State Department lists the following target indicators for FY 2008: 'Free Trade Agreements (FTAs) with South Korea, Malaysia, Thailand, Panama and United Arab Emirates enter into force. Two additional Bilateral Investment Treaties (BITs) enter into force; initiate additional BITs. Enter into Open Skies civil air transport agreements with Libya, Brazil, South Africa and Australia.' US Department of State, *Fiscal Year 2008 Performance Summary* (Department of State, 2009) at 99.

from nationalist pressures and protectionist bias. The courts must understand and respect private and commercial rights and interests in host countries, and must be familiar with the relevant international law. Global integration requires that a host state's legal institutions are in synch with outside markets; that a shared procedural framework governs the handling of goods and processes; that partners on both sides of a given transaction are acquainted with the procedures; and that they can be reasonably confident that transactions will follow expectations.[125] These 'rules of the game' reflect the World Bank's earliest definition of the rule of law: there are rules, the rules are known, they are actually enforced, independent adjudication exists in cases of dispute, and there are known procedures for changing the rules.[126]

It is thus a common objective of rule of law reform to 'assist', as one USAID project put it, 'development of the legal framework necessary to support Tajikistan's accession to the World Trade Organization and its participation in the global economy'.[127] Reformers therefore promote accession to international trade mechanisms and use accession processes to further rule of law goals. According to a World Bank study:

> Trade and product market reforms proved to be a major driver of other reforms in virtually all our case studies. By increasing competition, such reforms helped shift the incentives of incumbents once opposed to reform while creating new constituencies for change. In Mexico trade liberalization through the North American Free Trade Agreement (NAFTA) induced business associations to lobby the government for reductions in the regulatory burden to help them compete … And in Colombia greater openness and competition led employers to become vocal supporters of reforms aimed at increasing labor market flexibility … That an

125. See, for example, USAID, *Foreign Aid in the National Interest, supra* note 49, at 61.
126. Shihata, 'The World Bank and "Governance" Issues', *supra* note 11, at 85. According to the Bank: 'Differences in the quality of economic institutions—broadly understood as the "rules of the game"—have been found to be the most significant source of sustained economic growth in both cross-country research and case studies.' World Bank, *2004 Annual Review of Development Effectiveness, supra* note 100, at 51; generally, USAID, *Handbook on Legislative Strengthening* (USAID, 2000). See also Mamadou Dia, *Africa's Management in the 1990s and Beyond: Reconciling Indigenous and Transplanted Institutions* (World Bank, 1996) at 105; Cheryl Gray and Kathryn Hendley, *Developing Commercial Law in Transition Economies: Examples from Hungary and Russia*, (World Bank, 1995) at 1. The term is from Douglass North, *Institutions, Institutional Change, and Economic Performance* (Cambridge University Press, 1990) at 4.
127. ARD Inc. and Checchi & Co. Consulting, *Legal and Institutional Framework for a Market-Based Economy, supra* note 47, at 2–3. See too Booz Allen Hamilton, *Cape Verde WTO Accession, supra* note 46.

economy's openness is significantly associated with institutional change is among [our] main findings.[128]

The theme of global commercial integration drives a vision of a global legal architecture, provided and maintained by monadic public actors, along which (certain) private actors can move as frictionlessly as possible. The optimum arrangement is outlined in numerous Bank documents, and comprises the main subject of the 2005 World Development Report ('A Good Investment Climate for Everyone') and the IFC's *Doing Business* reports: the elimination of constraints on the movement of goods and capital, the minimisation of taxes on capital and investment, regulative ease of starting and closing businesses and flexible labour laws.[129] This architectural vision in turn guides rule of law promotion in-country—the protection of the rights and property of foreign investors, the elimination of discriminatory practices favouring domestic investors, and the secure enforcement of property and contract.[130]

6. Conclusion

The insistence and comprehensiveness of the rule of law narrative impresses. As a guiding motif, it points to something higher than local politics or sentiment—to a higher good. Indeed, the source of the 'law' that is to 'rule' remains ambiguous and somewhat mystical. And yet it is difficult to contest: who could argue against the rule of law? In this way, rule of law discourse tends to close down the space for political contestation—and the various

128. Kikeri, Kenyon and Palmadem, 'Reforming the Investment Climate', *supra* note 43, at 11.
129. World Bank, *World Development Report 2005*, *supra* note 123.
130. On this, see Stephen Knack and Philip Keefer, 'Institutions and Economic Performance: Cross-Country Tests Using Alternative Institutional Measures', 7 *Economics and Politics* (1995) 207–27; Rafael La Porta, Florencio Lopez-de-Silanes, Andrei Shleifer and Robert W. Vishny, 'Law and Finance', 106 *The Journal of Political Economy* (1998) 1113–55; Simeon Djankov, Rafael La Porta, Florencio Lopez-de-Silanes and Andrei Shleifer, 'The Regulation of Entry', 117 *The Quarterly Journal of Economics* (2002) 1–37; Simeon Djankov, Rafael La Porta, Florencio Lopez-de-Silanes and Andrei Shleifer, 'Courts: the Lex Mundi project', Revised Draft funded by the World Bank (World Bank, 2002); Simeon Djankov, Edward L. Glaesar, Rafael La Porta, Florencio Lopez-de-Silanes and Andrei Shleifer, 'The New Comparative Economics', The World Bank Policy Research Working Paper No. 3054 (World Bank, 2003); Juan C. Botero, Simeon Djankov, Rafael La Porta, Florencio Lopez-de-Silanes and Andrei Shleifer, 'The Regulation of Labour', 2004 *The Quarterly Journal of Economics* (2004) 1339–82; Robert Danino, 'Reforming Legal and Judicial Systems', *supra* note 52.

other concepts and institutions associated with it in donor literature are rapidly assimilated into the general soup of 'development' aid.

Nevertheless, this work is fraught with paradoxes. For one, despite an insistent suspicion about 'central planning' and indeed 'planning' of any kind in economic affairs, the programs to make all this happen are themselves centrally planned by a small group of large organisations based in a handful of world capitals, and (notwithstanding some inter-agency jockeying) working in close coordination. Second, the existence and pursuit of a procedurally rigorous legislative process grounded in a representative legislature is generally regarded as fundamental to most conceptions of the rule of law. However, funders are typically impatient with these processes, preferring to push through legislative templates developed elsewhere with the help of 'reform-minded' executives, bypassing legislative process where possible.

A third niggling paradox is more unsettling. There is a striking contrast between the state-bounded nature of 'the public' as ordinarily (and historically) conceived, and of the government tasked with responsiveness to it, on one hand, and the *essentially* transnational nature of the public as it consistently appears in rule of law program literature, on the other: a public composed of 'domestic and foreign investors'. Who is this transnational public? Presumably it is the aggregate of private interests with an identifiable stake in how a given government organises policy—which would seem to mean, as rule of law literature indeed clarifies, private firms and investors large enough to operate in multiple states. Can the interest of these relatively powerful actors really be understood as equivalent to, or indispensable to, the 'public interest' of host countries?

Ultimately, there seems to be at least one way in which rule of law promotion has been a clear if qualified success—and that is precisely in its performative or pedagogical dimension, in the dissemination of rule of law language itself, and of the morality tale it transmits, at least at the rhetorical level. There seems little doubt that the turn to rule of law language has consolidated its hold in international relations, in international development assistance, and in the shared discourse of public authorities and civil society organisations everywhere. Adopted now by all the major international actors, extending to bilateral and UN-based agencies as well as private funders, the language has also, unsurprisingly, become increasingly common among government bodies who must perforce deal with and respond to these agencies. Governments are evaluated on their adherence to this notional rule of law, investment flows towards it, funding is made conditional upon it. And NGOs too find themselves having to invoke this register to expedite funding applications.

Rule of law promotion is frequently criticised—by defenders and detractors alike—as having failed in its objectives. But to have near-universalised a particular vocabulary in regard to fundamental concerns of state and society is no mean feat. Perhaps the question is not so much whether all this rhetoric is leading to 'improved rule of law' 'on the ground', as the literature often wonders—but rather, what sort of international and transnational transactions are facilitated by this widely shared language, and who benefits from them?

Revolution or Regression? Retracing the Turn to Rights in 'Law and Development'

Florian Hoffmann

1. Taking Stock: The Law and Development Movement at (Roughly) Sixty-Five

A good ten years ago, a long-term observer of 'law and development' exclaimed that systematic interest in law and development was back on the agenda of academics and practitioners alike, reborn, as it were, after its untimely initial demise in the 1970s.[1] Since then, a sizeable literature has built up that both reflects and inspires new practices of law(s) of and in development and, at this juncture, the assertion that law is highly relevant to the development process has firmly entered the mainstream.[2] Indeed, law *as* development has become a mantra of development discourse now deeply entrenched in the programming of the multilateral financial institutions, international development agencies, and civil society organisations, so much so that rule of law promotion has, to an extent, become synonymous with development policy itself.[3] Yet, behind

1. David Kennedy, 'Laws and Developments', in John Hatchard and Amanda Perry-Kessaris (eds), *Law and Development: Facing Complexity in the 21st Century* (Routledge-Cavendish: London, 2003) 17–26.
2. The term 'development' is, of course, heavily charged and problematic itself; however, it will be employed as a working term in line with the general usage in the law and development literature; for a comprehensive overview of that literature, see David Trubek, 'The "Rule of Law" in Development Assistance: Past, Present, and Future', in David M. Trubek and Alvaro Santos (eds), *The New Law and Development: A Critical Appraisal* (Cambridge University Press, 2006) 74–94; this builds on earlier work such as David M. Turbek, 'Towards a Social Theory of Law: An Essay on the Study of Law and Development', 82 *Yale Law Journal* (1972) 1–50 at 1; or Brian Z. Tamanaha, 'The Lesson of Law and Development Studies', 89 *American Journal of International Law* (1995) 470–493.
3. Tor Krever, 'The Legal Turn in Late Development Theory: The Rule of Law and the World Bank's Development Model', 52 *Harvard International Law Journal* (2011) 288–319.

the celebratory chorus of legal scholars-turned-development experts who endorse law as a toolkit for nearly everything lurks considerable ambivalence about what law(s) and which development(s) are actually meant hereby. Many appear to endorse the rule of law merely as a necessary framework for the market economy, though some emphasise, instead, its inbuilt predisposition to be used for individual and collective empowerment, participation and accountability.[4] Some see modern law as a necessary epiphenomenon of capitalism, while others insist on its (relative) autonomy.[5] Some would query whether law's particular role in development has actually changed much over time, whereas others welcome its rise as a critical move against an earlier primacy of economics in development discourse.[6] Yet, besides the question of which side of development 'the law' is seen, the question of which substantive law(s) it actually refers to has also grown ever more complex. Initially it was mostly private law codes that were considered relevant to a development process geared towards generating economic growth, then the focus shifted to (public) constitutional law as a framework for economic and political transition, and then to human rights and administrative law as (legal) forms by which the development process itself could be reframed.[7] With this multiplication of legal fields (and experts), another question came up, namely from which disciplinary angle 'law and development' would be looked at. Many have focused on the international and transnational aspect of rule of law promotion and international lawyers, in particular, have shown a growing interest in 'development' as a corollary of the evolution of international law.[8] However, it were, arguably, comparative scholars of both private law transplants and of (domestic) constitutional rights who have provided most of the

4. Kennedy, 'Laws and Developments', *supra* note 1, and Srirak Plipat, 'Developmentizing Human Rights: How Development NGOs Interpret and Implement a Human Rights-Based Approach to Development Policy', <d-scholarship.pitt.edu/6392/1/Srirak_Plipat_2006_dissertation_all_chapters.pdf> (visited May 2014).
5. Lan Cao, 'Law and Economic Development: A New Beginning?', 32 *The Texas International Law Journal* (1997) 545–545; David M. Trubek, 'Developmental States and the Legal Order: Towards a New Political Economy of Development and Law', 1075 *University of Wisconsin Legal Studies Research Paper* (2008) 1–34.
6. Charles F. Sherman, 'Law and Development Today: The New Developmentalism', 10 *German Law Journal* (2009) 1257–1273, <www.germanlawjournal.com/pdfs/Vol10No09/PDF_Vol_10_No_09_1257-1273_Articles_Sherman.pdf> (visited May 2014).
7. Trubek, 'The "Rule of Law" in Development Assistance', *supra* note 2, at 84.
8. Luis Eslava and Sundhya Pahuja, 'Beyond the (Post) Colonial: TWAIL and the Everyday Life of International Law', 45 *Journal of Law and Politics in Africa, Asia and Latin America—Verfassung Und Recht in Übersee (VRÜ)* (2012) 195–221; see also and seminally, Sundhya Pahuja, *Decolonising International Law: Development, Economic Growth and the Politics of Universality* (Cambridge University Press, 2011).

empirical insights into how law interacts with development 'on the ground'.[9] Lastly, the 'law and development' debate is also cut across by an ethical divide between technocratic and political concerns, or, in other words, by a vision of law as a means to attain a predefined account of human welfare as against one of it as a field for political contestation about justice.[10]

By now, a growing body of critical scholarship has deciphered and exposed many of the paradoxes and the dark sides of the rule of law—and its promotion industry—, though even here, a strange ambivalence prevails about how the law's contribution to the development complex can ultimately be valued.[11] Development practitioners, many of whom come from a background of economics and other social sciences, often critique rule of law promotion and its spinoffs, such as 'good governance' or 'rights-based development', as naïve and lacking in substance and as re-directing significant funding away from the canon of (allegedly) tried and tested interventions.[12] Critical legal scholars, in turn, are adamant about the entanglement of the standard rule of law portfolio with a Eurocentric and capitalist development paradigm, but are nonetheless reluctant to divest themselves entirely from the idea of law as a development driver.[13] One response to these dilemmata from within the critical legal studies movement has been to rejoin the different strands and disciplinary perspectives of the debate on the level of structure, notably through a turn towards a broader perspective on the political economy of law *in* development.[14] By contrast, the response adopted in the present argument—and, particularly, in sections four and five—is to take a closer look at the ways in which specific legal forms interact with local contexts and at the outcomes this interaction generates. This empirical—but not empiricist—strategy is not set up against the structural narrative as such, but

9. Trubek, 'The "Rule of Law" in Development Assistance', *supra* note 2.
10. Kerry Rittich, 'The Future of Law and Development: Second Generation Reforms and the Incorporation of the Social', 26 *The Michigan Journal of International Law* (2004) 199–243.
11. David Kennedy, 'Law and Development Economics: Toward a New Alliance', in David Kennedy and Joseph E. Stiglitz (eds), *Law and Economics with Chinese Characteristics: Institutions for Promoting Development in the Twenty-First Century* (Oxford University Press, 2003) 19–70.
12. Summed up well in Peter Uvin, 'On High Moral Ground: The Incorporation of Human Rights by the Development Enterprise', 17 *Praxis: The Fletcher Journal of Development Studies* (2002) 1–11.
13. Stephen Humphreys, 'Prologue', in Stephen Humphreys, *Theatre of the Rule of Law: Transnational Legal Intervention in Theory and Practice* (Cambridge University Press, 2010) at xiii–xxvi.
14. David Kennedy, 'Law and the Political Economy of the World', 26 *Leiden Journal of International Law* (2013) 7–48.

it partially alters its plotline by adding to it the twist that the manifold usages of law 'on the ground' produce fundamentally unpredictable effects that irritate and, thereby, alter systemic logics. One phenomenon through which this can be observed is the turn to rights in development, and within it, the alleged constitutional rights 'revolution', which, later on, shall be examined as the latest twist in the unfolding 'law and development' saga. However, to this end, a brief tour de force of 'law and development' has to be first embarked upon.

2. Rewinding the Film: 'Law And Development' Up to the 'Rights Revolution'

Law and development was born jointly with 'development' itself in the post-WW II period when a Weberian understanding of modernity—and the central role of legal formalisation in it—was applied to the world at large, or, rather, to those places which had not yet developed to meet the standards of what 'the West' would call modernity.[15] Development, thus, encompassed three central (Weberian) elements, notably agency, change and value, which made it a process of induced movement towards a pre-defined state. The particular nature of that state remained variable and contingent upon the eyes of its respective beholders, it initially spanned a broad spectrum ranging from civilisation to either capitalism or socialism, though it was soon broken down to human welfare and, in particular, (national) wealth. Lack of it, both individually and collectively, defined development's main object, namely poverty, and the process whereby it would be attained would be economic and social development described as (economic) growth. This then set the agenda both for development-as-modernisation and for modern—i.e. Western—law as instrumental to it. The drivers of development discourse at this stage were, of course, the growing host of international organisations tasked with different aspects of economic governance, with the Bretton Woods organisations and their combined agenda playing a particularly prominent role.[16] Behind these lurked, arguably, the geopolitical interests of powerful states, with the latter, in turn, being partly driven and partly constrained by the competitive logic of the Cold War. Initially the focus of development would be on macroeconomic policy, with the rule of law merely in the background, but by the 1960s and

15. Chantal Thomas, 'Re-Reading Weber in Law and Development: A Critical Intellectual History of Good Governance Reform', 118 *Cornell Law Faculty Publications* (2008) 1–115.

16. Pahuja, *Decolonizing International Law*, *supra* note 8.

with not much to show as yet, development discourse spread out among academic disciplines and re-encountered in law its purported Weberian roots.[17] What in retrospect would be called the first 'law and development' movement (Law and Development (1.0)) then set out to promote law's intrumental relation to generating economic growth. On a substantive side, this implied introducing law(s) conducive to competitive market processes, on a procedural site it meant espousing the legal framework of liberal constitutional states. Overall it amounted to a massive project of legal transplantation, organised by Western governments and initially primarily by that of the United States through agencies such as USAID and the Ford Foundation.[18] Some have argued that Law and Development 1.0 was already an anachronism when it started, for in development discourse, modernisation theory had, by the late 1960s, already begun to be supplanted by dependency theory, a consequence of widespread decolonisation, the concomitant self-awareness of the global South and its economic predicament, and of the generalized spirit of critical rethink that marked this period.[19] On account of not rendering, or rendering the wrong, results on the ground, and under the theoretical impact of the structuralist undercurrents of the dependency model, 'law and development' notoriously self-critiqued itself out of existence for being, in essence, ethnocentric and naïve.[20] This coincided with the rise of 'critical legal studies' and the enterprise, ongoing to this day, of exposing liberal legalism as an epiphenomenon of the wider political ecomomy in which law is seen simultaneously as a function of the structural forces at play and as a cosmetic device to conceal their operation. Hence, while overt legal interventionism had gone out of fashion by the 1980s, a transmuted version of 'law and development' emerged through the legal academy's engagement with dependency theory,

17. David Trubek, 'Law and Development', in N. J. Smelser and Paul B. Baltes (eds), *International Encyclopedia of the Social & Behavioral Sciences* (Pergamon: Oxford, 2001) 8443–8446.

18. See, for instance, Philip Alston, 'Transplanting Foreign Norms: human rights and other international legal norms in Japan', 10 *European Journal of International Law* (1999) 625–633; R. L. Ajani, 'By chance and prestige: legal transplants in Russia and Eastern Europe', 43 *American Journal of Comparative Law* (1995); more recently Laurel E. Miller (ed.), *Framing the State in Times of Transition—Case Studies in Constitution Making* (United States Institute for Peace: Washington D.C., 2010); On the role of these governments and agencies, see Scott Cummings and Louise Trubek 'Globalizing Public Interest Law', University of Wisconsin Law School, Legal Studies Research paper Series, Paper No. 1073 (2009).

19. Tamanaha, 'The Lessons', *supra* note 2; Kennedy, 'Law and Development Economics', *supra* note 11.

20. See, inter alia, David Trubek and Marc Galanter, 'Scholars in Self-Estrangement: Some Reflections on the Crisis in Law and Development Studies in the United States', *Wisconsin Law Review* (1974) 1062–1102; and Tamanaha, 'The Lessons', *supra* note 2.

notably in form of the right to development. Conceived, originally, by the Senegalese jurist Keba M'baye in 1972, it was first articulated in the African Charter for Human and Peoples Rights adopted by the then Organization of African Unity (OAU) in 1981, and was subsequently brought to international prominence by the United Nations General Assembly's 1986 Declaration on the Right to Development (DRTD).[21] Despite never being uncontested, it was reaffirmed in the 1993 Vienna Declaration and Program of Action, in the 2000 Millennium Declaration, and in the 2002 Durban Declaration and Program of Action.[22] However, having gained currency in the debates around the 'New International Economic Order' (NIEO) in the 1970s, the right to development's primary objective was initially to strategically charge development discourse with the moral aura of rights language in order to change the terms on which the world economy and multilateral development aid were discussed.[23] It has since condensed into soft legality and played a significant role in internationalising 'law and development' in the 1980s.[24] However, its specific function has primarily been that of a punchy metonymy for dependency theory's argument for the historical injustice inherent in the global economy.[25] As such it has helped anchor the language of (in)justice into development discourse, and, by purporting to reframe development in terms of international rights and obligations, it has inscribed the idea of a common (international) responsibility into the multilateral development agenda. It also shifted the emphasis of 'law and development' from a private to a public law logic, which has come to dominate the discourse ever since.

It began doing this as the direct precursor—one might call it Law and Development (1.5)—of what would eventually become a second phase in the 'law and development' movement (Law and Development (2.0)), marked by the rise of the rule of law export industry that followed the democratic transitions of the 1980s and especially 1990s after the fall of the Berlin Wall. As with Law and Development (1.0), it were initially Western governments, which had quickly styled themselves into the echelons of a liberal—and liberal

21. A Res 41/128, 4 December 1986.
22. United Nations, *Durban Declaration and Plan of Action*, adopted at the World Conference against Racism, Racial Discrimination, Xenophobia and Related Violence (2002), <www.un.org/en/durbanreview2009/ddpa.shtml> (visited May 2014).
23. *Realizing the Right to Development—Essays in Commemoration of 25 Years of the United Nations Declaration on the Right to Development*, HR/PUB/12/4 (2013).
24. *Ibid.*
25. Thom Ringer, 'Development, Reform, and the Rule of Law: Some Prescriptions for a Common Understanding of the Rule of Law and its Place in Development Theory and Practice', 10 *Yale Human Rights & Development Law Journal* (2007) 178–208.

legalist—'new world order', that strongly promoted the adoption of the basic frameworks of liberal democracy and market capitalism in the transition countries. As is well documented in an immense body of literature on the state- and constitution-(re)building experiments that took place during this period, the emphasis of rule of law promotion then shifted to institutional design, particular in and through new constitutions and an evolving body of constitutional jurisprudence.[26] The aim was to manage transition so as to lead to the fastest possible attainment of liberal democracy and a market economy, not so coincidentally the same objectives as those of mainstream development discourse. Indeed, during this period, transition came to be merged semantically with development, the only difference being that the former implied a much shorter time horizon and, cocomitantly, a much more condensed development process. Economically, the Washington consensus set the script for transitional reform, not just in substance but also in pace. And legal liberalism saw a second coming when mostly Western constitutional designers once again set up a massive legal transplantation industry, this time focusing on out-of-the-box models of (liberal) constitutionalism.[27]

However, from this period onwards, the nexus between law *and* development would be subject to a host of parallel, if partly paradoxical conceptual innovations centered on the state as the necessary middle-term. The starting point was the mentioned shift of focus from private to public law or, at any rate, public legal institutions. Yet, while the focus on the state and state institutions was, thus, retained from the first 'law and development' movement, its sucessor shifted attention away from legislatures and executives to (constitutional) judiciaries and the judicial review process.[28] Although the constitution-builders of the 1990s had the implantation of Western-style liberal democracy in mind, their concern for strong judiciaries arbitrating a messy political transition process on the basis of globally recognized constitutional principles and fundamental rights already implied a growing distrust of politics, in general, and the state as (still) the primary space for political contestation, in particular. This corresponded, *grosso modo*, with a more differentiated view of the state—and state law—within (economic) development discourse. Hence, it was no longer the state as such that was seen as a potential impediment to economic growth, but legislative meddling and executive capture, which, however, could be balanced out by strong judiciaries and independent

26. Stephen Humphreys, *Theatre of the Rule of Law: Transnational Legal Intervention in Theory and Practice* (Cambridge University Press, 2010).
27. See David Trubek, 'Law and Development', *supra* note 17.
28. Kennedy 'Law and Development Economics', *supra* note 11, at 44.

regulatory agencies. The rise of new institutional economics and the consequent 'chasening' of the neoliberal paradigm cemented this view of state law and institutions as a crucial device to enable market functionality and repair dysfunctionalities.[29] It entered the economic mainstream, and with it the programming of the international financial institutions, as of the mid- to late 1990s and has since crystallized into a 'new developmentalism' in which the state is again seen in a proactive role as an enabler of markets and, thus, purportedly of growth.[30]

Yet, for the state to play this role, it has to be tightly disciplined and isolated from the sort of capture that 'law and development' identified as the primary obstacle to a functioning and (market) functional rule of law. Indeed, 'new developmentalism' can be seen as an attempt to re-balance the functional division of powers within the state in order to re-cast its very fabric along the lines of market functionality. It is, hence, the state itself that is the object and primary purpose of the state's apparent re-empowerment in this phase. The programme for such discipline emerged in form of the good governance agenda that arose in conjunction with Law and Development (2.0). Its focus on such overarching principles as transparency, accountability, participation, inclusiveness, responsiveness, and, of course, the rule of law, was meant to provide at once an ideal type for the new developmental state and a regulatory corset for its policy making. Its terms exude a universalist appeal to the (Weberian) values underlying modern statehood in abstraction of geography and historical trajectory and, as such, they have been deemed more acceptable to developing state governments than the reductive focus on corruption or human rights violations.[31] Good governance is also seen by the multilateral financial institutions as a key instrument for rule of law promotion that is itself neither legally formalised nor politically positioned. Hence, while the rise of good governance marks the shift away from macroeconomic structuralism to institutional design, it merely transcribes the neoliberal development paradigm into a different notation by helping to immunize the state against (re-)distributional politics.[32]

29. *Ibid*, at 38.
30. Trubek 'Developmental States', *supra* note 5; and Sherman 'Law and Development Today', *supra* note 6 at 1267.
31. Rittich 'The Future of Law and Development', *supra* note 10; Uvin, 'On High Moral Ground', *supra* note 12.
32. Gathii, 'Good Governance as a Counter Insurgency Agenda to Oppositional and Transformative Social Projects in International Law', 5 *Buffalo Human Rights Law Review* (1999) 107–174.

3. Revolutionary Empowerment or Counter-Revolutionary Conditioning?—The Turn to Rights in Development

The proliferation of good governance has, in turn, gone hand in hand with the judicial empowerment brought on by the latest wave of rule of law promotion, the general objective of which has been to enact and safeguard liberal public sector management.[33] While the state, albeit in a technocratised form, has, thus, reemerged in the development narrative with the turn both to institutions and to good governance, this turn has, simultaneously, also led to a gradual shift of emphasis away from the state and towards individuals and groups as the objects of development. This individualisation feeds from elements of the constitutional turn of 'law and development', from the citizen-as-stakeholder-oriented logic of good governance principles, and, perhaps most importantly, from a third conceptual step in form of the capabilities approach to development, pioneered by Amartya Sen in the 1980s.[34] Coming from the methodologically individualistic social choice theory, Sen sought to fuse the economic and the political aspects of development by individualising human welfare as the set of capabilities for 'achieving the kind of lives [people] have reason to value'.[35] This represented a shift of development's center of gravity from needs to an expanded conception of individual freedom, with the corollary that it is individuals—not states, societies, or cultures—who take center stage as primary agents of development.[36] While critics of the capabilities approach have argued that in its focus on (rational) individual choice, it still carries a liberal(ist) bias, it proved to be highly influential in creating the people-centered focus that has dominated development discourse for the past twenty years and that has, amongst others, resulted in yet another transformation of development discourse, notably into the concept of human security and its humanitarian offspring, the 'responsibility to protect'.[37] It also fed into a second major shift that ocurred roughly at the same moment, notably the rise of the rights-based approach to development—or Law and Development (3.0)—, which shall be looked at in the following.

33. Uvin, 'On High Moral Ground', *supra* note 12.
34. Amartia Sen, *Development as Freedom* (Oxford University Press, 1999); see also Pahuja, *Decolonising International Law*, *supra* note 8.
35. Sen, *supra* note 34, at 291.
36. Sakiko Fukuda-Parr, 'The Human Development Paradigm: Operationalizing Sen's Ideas on Capabilities', 9 *Feminist Economics* (2003) 301–17.
37. Hartley Dean, 'Critiquing Capabilities: The Distractions of a Beguiling Concept', 29 *Critical Social Policy* (2009) 261–278; for the 'responsibility to protect', see Anne Orford, *International Authority and the Responsibility to Protect* (Cambridge University Press 2011).

Prior to this new conceptual environment, the bringing together of human rights and development had not been easy, nor, indeed, was it particularly high on the international agenda. The reasons for this historical division were manifold, although two causes in particular stand out: the separation of international human rights into distinct civil and political, and economic, social, and cultural rights catalogues, on one hand, and the focus of development theory and practice on human welfare and objective needs, on the other hand.[38] The first cause had its roots in Cold War political dynamics, which led, contrary to the vision articulated in the Universal Declaration of Human Rights, to the drafting of two distinct treaties, and a consequent division of focus by both governmental and non-governmental actors.[39] This division was exacerbated by the fact that development theorists and practitioners did not generally view rights as a relevant concept for their problem field.[40] Hence, although, as would become clear in subsequent conceptual conjunctions, economic and social rights and development can be seen as two sides of the same coin, both circles did initially not mix or pool their resources. Behind these organisational divisions, there lay, of course, conceptual differences which informed the method and style with which the respective problem field was approached. Rights activism of either pedigree is generally focused on advocacy, i.e. on claiming what are held to be entitlements vis-à-vis those under an obligation to provide them, which, from a traditional legal perspective, can only be governmental actors; such advocacy is, therefore, closely linked to enforcement institutions, most notably national courts or international judicial or quasi-judicial mechanisms, and it is premised on governments being amenable to being taken before such bodies, as well as on their compliance with the decisions rendered by the latter. Moreover, rights advocacy is necessarily based on concrete actors and situations, namely individuals or identifiable groups, and on allegations of specific violations. By contrast, in the traditional needs-based development paradigm, governments, whether donor or recipient, are, in principle, seen as partners and not as adversaries, the focus is on policies rather than on remedies and aid is ultimately seen as a grant or investment rather than as an entitlement to be claimed by right.

38. See Paul Nelson and Ellen Dorsey, 'At the Nexus of Human Rights and Development: new methods and strategies of global NGOs', 31 *World Development* (2003) 2013–2026; see also Stephen Marks, 'The Human Rights Framework for Development: seven approaches', François-Xavier Bagnoud Center for Health and Human Rights, Working Paper (2003).

39. Notably the *International Covenant on Civil and Political Rights* and the *International Covenant on Economic, Social, and Cultural Rights*, both adopted in 1966, entering into force in 1976.

40. Kate Manzo, 'Africa in the rise of Rights-Based Development', 34 *Geoforum* (2003) 437–456 at 446.

However, by the second half of the 1990s, the conceptual rift between human rights and development began to be bridged as a result of the conjunction of several of the shifts described above. On the rights side, the impetus came from the triumphalist renaissance of rights discourse after the end of the Cold War.[41] Amongst others, this resulted in the re-emergence of the debate on development as a right and, more importantly, in the gradual transformation of economic and social rights from programmatic soft law to at least tentatively justiciable hard law.[42] This led to a graduation of economic and social rights to not just formal but, increasingly, operational parity with civil and political rights and a concomitant rise in their prominence on the international advocacy agenda. On the development side, the mentioned conceptual shifts towards a focus on institutional frameworks and their impact on individual welfare, the stakeholder-oriented logic of good governance, as well as the capabilities approach's turn towards individual empowerment set the scene for a new openness towards rights as instruments for development.[43] On the basis of these simultaneous conceptual moves, Law and Development (2.0), with its focus on courts and fundamental rights, can be taken to have laid the foundations for the bridge between rights and development, while it were the international development and financial institutions that subsequently pushed ahead this bridge-building process. Led by then Secretary-General Kofi Annan in conjunction with then High Commissioner for Human Rights, Mary Robinson, the United Nations began 'mainstreaming' human rights into its activities in 1997, with a particular emphasis on the UN's development activities, and with the United Nations Development Program (UNDP) and the United Nations Children's Fund (UNICEF) being pioneering organisations in this respect; the former, in particular, in its 1990 Human Development Report, used the fulfilment of human rights directly as a benchmark for development.[44] Likewise, the World Bank and, to a lesser extent, the International Monetary Fund (IMF)

41. Susan Marks, 'The End of History—Reflections on Some International Legal Theses', 8 *European Journal of International Law* (1997) 449–477.
42. Aoife Nolan, Bruce Porter, and Malcolm Langford, 'The Justiciability of Social and Economic Rights: An Updated Appraisal', 15 *Center for Human Rights and Global Justice Working Paper* (2009).
43. Philip Alston and Mary Robinson, 'The Challenges of Ensuring the Mutuality of Human Rights and Development Endeavours', in Philip Alston and Mary Robinson (eds), *Human Rights and Development: Towards Mutual Reinforcement* (Oxford University Press, 2005) 2–18.
44. See United Nations Development Programme (UNDP), *Human Development Report* (Oxford University Press, 1990); and Varun Gauri and Siri Gloppen, 'Human Rights-Based Approaches to Development: Concepts, Evidence, and Policy', 44 *Polity* (2012) 485–503.

have taken rights language on board around the same period, with the focus being on five interrelated processes, namely social development, economic growth, democratic governance, an equity-oriented grass-roots approach, and an international institutional design aimed at maximising world-market benefits for developing countries.[45]

Since then, the rights-based approach to development has had a stellar institutional career, becoming a dominant discourse in both development and human rights organisations. It is the subject of innumerous programmatic statements and operational guidelines within the development community and it is beginning to be applied by domestic policy-making and implementation agencies.[46] However, it has remained a controversial concept and its reception by traditional development actors as well as in academic literature has been mixed. To the former, it initially represented not much more than an usurpation attempt by the human rights community over such home grown concepts as 'pro-poor' development.[47] Within academic development studies, some even went so far as to regard the logic of rights as inimical to development work on account of its inherent antagonism to the state and state institutions.[48]

Considerable effort has since gone into clarifying the rights-based approach, though this has, for the most part, accompanied rather than preceded its operationalisation, so that it has remained a boat constructed while already at sea. Varun Gauri and Siri Gloppen provide a useful entry point by differentiating four 'analytic components' of rights based development which can be paraphrased as international legal precepts, donor-regulations and conditionalities, normative beliefs, and constitutional rights.[49] Arguably, to most adherents of the rights-based approach in both the human rights and the development community, the first two of these components are the start

45. Fukuda-Parr, 'The Human Development Paradigm', *supra* note 36.
46. Lisa Vene Klasen and Valerie Miller, 'Rights-Based Approaches and Beyond: Challenges of Linking Rights and Participation', 235 IDS Working Paper (2004); Srirak Plipat, 'Developmentizing Human Rights: How Development NGOs Interpret and Implement a Human Rights-Based Approach to Development Policy', Doctoral Dissertation, University of Pittsburg (2006); H.-O. Sano, 'Development and Human Rights: The Necessary, but Partial Integration of Human Rights and Development', 22 *Human Rights Quarterly* (2000) 734–752; and again, Uvin, 'On High Moral Ground', *supra* note 12.
47. Robert Archer, 'The Strengths of Different Traditions: What Can Be Gained and What Might Be Lost through Adopting a Rights-Based Approach to pro-Poor Development', 3 *Sur* (2006), <www.surjournal.org/eng/conteudos/artigos4/ing/artigo_archer.htm> (visited June 2014).
48. Uvin, 'On High Moral Ground', *supra* note 12; Krever, 'The Legal Turn in Late Development Theory', *supra* note 3.
49. Gauri and Gloppen, 'Human Rights Based Approaches' *supra* note 44.

and also the end point of rights based development. From this perspective, it essentially refers to the matching of development goals with international human rights obligations. Here, the shift to rights-based development means, essentially, a reframing of development as the process by which compliance with positivised international legal norms is achieved. International legal norms, most notably, though not exclusively, those laid down in the 'international bill of rights', are, hence, meant to assume the triple function of interpretation manuals for development goals, of regulatory frameworks for development processes, and of benchmarks for development outcomes.[50] There is, however, some divergence between human rights and development practitioners over whether these presumptively 'hard' legal norms merely represent a negative standard against which development policy must not contravene or whether they positively determine the substance and form of development. The mentioned rise of economic and social rights advocacy has certainly led to a more nuanced view on the (international) justiciability of 'second generation' rights, with, *inter alia*, the long negotiated adoption, by the UN Human Rights Council, of the Optional Protocol to the International Covenant on Economic, Social and Cultural Rights in 2008 marking a new phase.[51] However, despite the centrality of international human rights standards in rights-based development, international (legal) institutions have not played a significant role in the latter's unfolding. The continuing lack of institutional capacity and enforcement authority in the realm of social rights on part of international institutions have confined them, at best, to the role of avantgarde interpreters of test case situations far removed from

---

50. Examples include, again, the *Human Development Index* and the recent series of Guiding Principles, such as the *Guiding Principles on Extreme Poverty and Human Rights*, A/HRC/21/39, 27 September 2012; or the *Guiding Principles on Business and Human Rights*, A/HRC/RES/17/4, 6 July, 2011; see also Victor Abramovich, 'The Rights-Based Approach in Development Policies and Strategies', 88 *CEPAL Review* (2006) 33–48; Jennifer Chapman, 'Rights-Based Development: The Challenge of Change and Power', 27 *Global Poverty Research Group Working Paper Series* (2005); Shannon Kindornay, James Ron, and Charli Carpenter, 'Rights-Based Approaches to Development: Implications for NGOs', 34 *Human Rights Quarterly* (2012) 472–506.
51. See the Optional Protocol to the International Covenant on Economic, Social and Cultural Rights, A/RES/63/117, 10 December 2008; see also the Additional Protocol to the European Social Charter Providing for a System of Collective Complaints, CETS No. 158, 9 November 1995; the Additional Protocol to the American Convention on Human Rights in the Area of Economic, Social and Cultural Rights 'Protocol of San Salvador', A-52, 16 November, 1999; the African Charter on Human and Peoples Rights (CAB/LEG/67/3 rev. 5, 21 I.L.M. 58, 27 June, 1981) already contains in its body the (social) rights to work (Art. 15), health (Art. 16) and education (Art. 17).

the groundwork of (rights-based) development.[52] There is, however, some evidence that the greater prominence of the international social rights regime has given development actors advocacy tools to politically mobilise for greater international responsibility and for domestic policy change. [53]

Instead, it is on the operational level, which Gauri and Gloppen refer to as 'donor regulation and conditionalities', that rights-based development has really found its primary staging ground. Here it has become fused with the conceptual cornerstones of the contemporary development paradigm, notably the core good governance principles of accountability, empowerment, participation, equality and non-discrimination. On this level, rights provide the specific substance for these principles in the context of programme design, implementation and assessment. They function, in other words, as a policy framework. As such, their antagonistic character is largely muted and, therefore, their legal sting partially drawn by their conversion into (soft) administrative guidelines.[54] Indeed, donors and recipients alike have mastered the new language of rights-based governance in their mutually reinforcing reporting obligations.[55] This tête-à-tête between rights and development works because rights are framed as integral to the achievement of good governance. As was seen, the latter is geared not to concrete objectives, but to enhancing the agency of the recipients of development (aid), most notably the 'poor'. Rights language, thus, helps perform a subtle shift in development discourse away from objective need and towards subjective want—often expressed as an increase in choice—fulfilment of which is then deemed to result in 'empowerment'. It is, at least nominally, about increasing the control of specific constituencies over their own circumstances,[56] and it combines greater and more equitable access to socio-economic resources such as income, education, or health, with a subjective capacity for choice.[57]

52. Gauri and Gloppen, 'Human Rights-Based Approaches to Development', *supra* note 44, at 5.
53. Kindornay, Shannon Ron, and Carpenter. 'Rights-Based Approaches to Development, *supra* note 49.
54. Examples are, again, the *Guiding Principles on Extreme Poverty and Human Rights* or on *Business and Human Rights, supra* note 49.
55. See, for instance, United Nations Development Program (UNDP), *Indicators for Human Rights Based Approaches to Development in UNDP Programming: A Users' Guide*, (2006), or United Nations Development Program (UNDP), *Lessons Learned From Rights-Based Approaches in the Asia-Pacific Region* (2005); or Juliane Osterhaus and Folke Kayser, 'The Human Rights-Based Approach in German Development Cooperation', *Deutsche Gesellschaft für Internationale Zusammenarbeit* (GIZ) (2009).
56. Bina Pradhan, 'Measuring Empowerment: a methodological approach', 46 *Development* (2003) 51–57 at 52.
57. *Ibid*, at 54.

Empowerment, then, also implies the ability to claim both accountability in relation to all actors of the development process and participation in that process. The latter, in particular, potentially entails an active say in all stages of the development process, from the identification and prioritisation of needs to the planning, implementation and monitoring of programmes. This complex regime is safeguarded by claims, again articulated through rights, to equality and non-discrimination. In all, then, the reconstruction of good governance principles through rights language seems to provide an at once coherent and compelling narrative which appears to be compatible with contemporary development practice while containing the spark for a potentially revolutionary transformation of development agency.[58]

Yet, can rights-based development live up to this promise as the primary regulatory framework for development cooperation? While the open controversy between the human rights and the development community that marked the early phase of rights-based development has largely subsided, many critical points remain salient. Early critiques of rights-based development focused on two aspects, in particular: firstly, that this allegedly new approach did not add any significant value to either the re-focusing of development on disempowered and disenfranchised, i.e. poor, constituencies, or to the addressing of the needs of these constituencies through empowerment tools within the global governance agenda.[59] Secondly, that it represented nothing but a new type of aid conditionality, notably one which subsumed nearly all possible conditionalities under the comprehensive framework of international human rights, thereby creating a panoptical system of international surveillance over developing states which were, thus, reduced to mere duty bearers vis-à-vis individual and collective rights claimants.[60] Closely related to the latter critique is the more general point that, as already hinted, rights-based development is taken to be just the latest step in an essentially neo-liberal re-framing exercise which embroils the state in a paradoxical position. Rights-based development remains highly state-centric in its emphasis on state responsibilities, a necessary side-product of the focus on international human

58. Caroline Moser and Andy Norton, 'To Claim our Rights: livelihood security, human rights, and sustainable development', Overseas Development Institute (2001), <www.odi.org/sites/odi.org.uk/files/odi-assets/publications-opinion-files/1816.pdf> (visited June 2014).

59. Dzodzi Tsikata, 'The Rights-based Approach to Development: Potential for Change or More of the Same?', 35 *IDS Bulletin* (2004) 130–133; also, again, Uvin, 'On High Moral Ground', *supra* note 12.

60. Kate Manzo, 'Africa in the rise of rights-based development', 34 *Geoforum* (2003) 437–456 at 438; see also Gathii, 'Good Governance', *supra* note 32.

rights norms. States remain fundamentally responsible for both the creation of and compliance with international norms, with the trinitarian nature of their obligations, notably to respect, to protect, and to fulfil, ensuring that, indirectly, virtually all non-state actors continue to fall under their remit.[61] Hence, even though rights-based frameworks appear to address themselves to all stakeholders, it is ultimately states who have to ensure compliance, if only by underwriting a functioning rule of law as a necessary base condition for any rights regime. The ongoing transformation of a state from direct provider to regulator of public services within the paradigm of post-welfarist regulatory statehood changes the nature but not the scope of this responsibility.[62] Indeed, market failure itself, through the consequences it generates, is considered to fall into the functional obligations of the state. This continuing state-centeredness on the demand side is, however, increasingly unmatchable by the state's capacity to supply public service levels in accordance with international minimum standards either through its own financial intervention or through (market) regulatory authority. The current phase of global finance capitalism has reduced both the state's fiscal and, as a result of its own public sector reforms, its policy space, a situation that, arguably, applies to both industrialised and developing countries, the predicament of which is increasingly converging.[63] There is, hence, a clear mismatch between the demand for responsibility placed on a state by the logic of sovereignty and articulated through international law, and its factual capacity to supply this normative demand with material substance in (rights-based) development practice.

Yet, while the empirical state is thereby both overburdened and overdetermined, it is simultaneously sidelined by the promotion of good governance through rights. For these are, as was seen, essential instruments to discipline and constrain a state and its formal institutions in relation to individuals, groups and civil society in general. Empowerment and its derivatives accountability, participation and (formal) equality ultimately aim to make 'people' at least partially autonomous from state institutions and to capacitate them to appropriate to themselves their share of public goods. Through rights they endow development with the authority of global norms and thereby legitimate

61. See, generally, Andrew Clapham, *Human Rights Obligations of Non-State Actors* (Oxford University Press, 2006); Rittich 'The Future of Law and Development', *supra* note 10, at 217.

62. Colin Scott, 'Regulation in the Age of Governance: The Rise of the Post Regulatory State', 100 National Europe Center Paper (2003), <digitalcollections.anu.edu.au/bitstream/1885/41716/3/scott1.pdf> (visited June 2014).

63. Navroz K. Dubash and Bronwen Morgan, 'Understanding the Rise of the Regulatory State of the South', 6 *Regulation & Governance* (2012) 261–281.

the bypassing of formal state institutions. As such, rights-based development has been critiqued as an oxidant of sovereignty, even if, in many instances, that sovereignty may merely enshrine the authoritarian undercurrents of modern statehood.[64] The point here is not that rights-based development would challenge the state but that it continues to treat the state as the key problem while simultaneously relying on it as the only viable framework for a solution.

Besides being implicated in this fundamental paradox in relation to the role of a state, rights-based development has also been charged with being premised on a tautological linkage of rights and good governance. As Peter Uvin has pointed out, 'working out the relationship between development and human rights requires more than simply stating that one automatically implies, equals, or subsumes the other'.[65] A related critique concerns another paradox inherent in rights-based development, namely that between universal human rights, on one hand, and empowerment and its derivatives, on the other. Conceptually, this paradox has its roots in one of the core questions of political theory, notably how to relate rights with democracy, or, a fixed, *a priori* determination of the human being's essential characteristics with a mechanism by which those same human beings are meant to make relatively unconstraint choices about their personal circumstances. How, in other words, can a mandatory reference to one universal set of human rights be reconciled with its simultaneous premise to foster local individual and collective empowerment? Is there room for local variations? And how can a rights-based framework distinguish between freely-chosen 'inefficiencies' and those that result from local power-relations, lack of adequate information, and flawed decision-making mechanisms? How much top-down imposition is still compatible with local empowerment?

These questions can ultimately only be answered by looking at how rights-based development has played out in practice. Yet, although the new paradigm has implied a large-scale restructuring of programming frameworks, there is as yet only insufficient evidence of its impact and efficacy 'on the ground'.[66] What is clear is that it has placed rights discourse at the centre of

64. David Kennedy, 'International Human Rights Movement: Part of the Problem?', 15 *Harvard Human Rights Journal* (2002) 101–125.
65. Uvin, 'On High Moral Ground', *supra* note 12, at 3.
66. See 'The Impact of Rights-based Approaches to Development—Evaluation, Learning Process—Bangladesh, Malawi, and Peru', UK Interagency Group on Human Rights Based Approaches (2007), <www.crin.org/docs/Inter_Agency_rba.pdf> (visited June 2014); Hans Peter Schmitz, 'A Human Rights-Based Approach (HRBA) in Practice: Evaluating NGO Development Efforts', 44 *Polity* (2012) 523–541; and again Kindornay, Shannon Ron, and Carpenter, 'Rights-Based Approaches to Development, *supra* note 49.

the development policy-making process and that it has, indeed, become a dominant regulatory and conditionality framework, not least in conjunction with the overall shift towards (good) governance. However, to what extent this has actually empowered local communities and re-configured development agency, or even just led to tangible improvements in aid effectiveness remains an open question. Its eventual answer will, in equal measure, depend on the extent to which donors will have been willing to surrender control over both the objectives and the implementation of development to its stakeholders, and to what extent these stakeholders are able and willing to use rights to articulate alternative pathways. What is certain is that such empowerment will continue to require the institutional setting of a state from the vagaries of which it is, however, simultaneously meant to emancipate. Is rights-based development, hence, merely a paradox of wishful thinking or, indeed, as Uvin puts it, essentially 'fluff and power'?[67]

4. Another Plot: A 'Rights Revolution' by the (Domestic) Back Door?

While Uvin's statement might be a tempting critical conclusion apt to characterise rights-based development, along with most of other rights discourse, simply as 'part of the problem', it would fall short of the real life the concept has taken on.[68] That course has to do with the two other aspects of rights-based development that Gauri and Gloppen identify notably normative belief and constitutional litigation.[69] For beyond the confines of the 'aid industry', the idea of rights-based development has proliferated into wider civil society and has been picked up by a wide range of advocacy groups and grass-roots activists as a form of 'social accountability' for development processes.[70] Increasingly, stakeholders on the ground are adopting a rights optic to analyse local-level situations and articulate the resulting demands in terms of rights

67. Uvin, 'On High Moral Ground', *supra* note 12, at 10.
68. Kennedy, 'International Human Rights Movement', *supra* note 63; and David Kennedy, 'The International Human Rights Regime: Still Part of the Problem', in Ole Windahl Pedersen (ed.), *Examining Critical Perspectives on Human Rights* (Cambridge University Press, 2013) 19–34.
69. Gauri and Gloppen, 'Human Rights-Based Approaches to Development', *supra* note 44, at 11 and 15.
70. Siri Gloppen, 'Public Interest Litigation, Social Rights and Social Policy', in Anis A. Dani and Arjan de Haan (eds), *Inclusive States. Social Policy and Structural Inequalities* (World Bank: Washington D.C., 2008) 343–367.

claims. This does not, of course, mean that rights-consciousness would have become ubiquitous, nor that there would be formalised mechanisms in place everywhere through which such accountability demands could be fed into the relevant systems. But the specific interaction between activists and local constituencies has in some places crystallized into sustained political pressure or, indeed, systematic legal mobilisation 'from below'. This latter phenomenon, which emerged out in the field rather than having been designed on the drawing table of development policy, may represent the rights-based approach's real potential. As it is premised on a reasonably functioning rule of law and, within it, on the existence of legally enforceable rights catalogues, most commonly in form of constitutional bills of rights, it has been restricted to those (developing) countries to whom this applies.[71] In many of these, an impressive surge in fundamental rights litigation on development-related issues can be observed since at least the late 1990s. Hence, in a wide-range of low- and middle-income countries including, *inter alia*, the BRICS states Brazil, India and South Africa, but also Argentina, Colombia, Costa Rica or Venezuela, an exponential rise in individual and class-action type litigation on basic public goods such as education, housing, food, water and sanitation, or health has taken place.[72] This has led some to speak of a domestic 'rights revolution' that, however, is, for the most part, the product of a spontaneous legal evolution that has neither been centrally (or rationally) planned nor is entirely predictable in its effects.

A case in point is health rights litigation, which in many studies features as the initial catalyst for the 'rights revolution' and which, in turn, was mostly kicked off by well-organised HIV/AIDS NGOs pursuing highly targeted litigation strategies.[73] As critics have pointed out, this legal mobilisation did not emerge out of the blue but as a result of a convergence of interests and actors, including middle-class HIV/AIDS patients, the pharmaceutical industry, a socially reformist judiciary and intra-state political conflicts, all

71. Varun Gauri and Daniel M. Brinks, 'Introduction: The Elements of Legalization and the Triangular Shape of Social and Economic Rights', in Varun Gauri and Daniel M. Brinks (eds), *Courting Social Justice—Judicial Enforcement of Social and Economic Rights in the Developing World* (Cambridge University Press, 2008).
72. See, in particular, Charles R. Epp, *The Rights Revolution: Lawyers, Activists, and Supreme Courts in Comparative Perspective* (Cambridge University Press, 1998); and these recent empirical studies: Gauri and Brinks, *Courting Social Justice, supra* note 70; Alicia Ely Yamin and Siri Gloppen, *Litigating Health Rights: Can Courts Bring More Justice to Health?* (Harvard University Press, 2013).
73. Florian Hoffmann and Fernando Bentes, 'Accountability for Social and Economic Rights in Brazil', in Gauri and Brinks, *Courting Social Justice, supra* note 70.

embedded within a transnational flow of information and resources.[74] Yet, neither sophisticated legal liberalism nor the broader political economy of public interest litigation provide enough causal leads to fully explain why this 'rights revolution' happened and even less so what effects it has had. Indeed, besides the difficulty of clearly pinpointing its effects, it is even less straightforward to clearly assess them. The reason for this is that, following again Gauri and Gloppen, there are at least four variables involved in each case or set of cases that influence its trajectory and outcome. The first is access to justice which goes well beyond the mere presence of an independent judiciary but involves everything from the physical and personnel infrastructure of a legal system to the legal culture of both prospective litigants and the judiciary. Secondly, the amenability of the legal system to receive and process rights-based interventions into social policy, an aspect which involves the hazy process of doctrinal change as well as the shifting demarcation between the legal and political system. Thirdly, the elasticity of the political system in terms of legal interventions, or, in other words, the degree to which political actors and institutions are willing and capable to change broader policy in response to targeted litigation. And lastly, the enforcement capacity of litigants and, generally, the enforceability of judicial decisions. It is through highly variant combinations of these four factors that the overall outcome of social rights litigation is shaped.

An illustration is the case of health rights litigation in Brazil.[75] Since approximately 2002, there has been an exponential increase in successful individual access to medicines and treatment actions. Parallely, a highly independent-minded and proactive public prosecution service has used its administrative review powers as well as the threat of litigation to review and revise public health care management on municipal and state levels, and a network of public defenders, the public equivalent of pro bono advocates, has significantly expanded access to (health care-related) justice for those eighty percent of

74. Octavio Luiz Motta Ferraz, 'Harming the Poor through Social Rights Litigation: Lessons from Brazil', 89 *Texas Law Review* (2010) 1643–1686; Ran Hirschl, 'The New Constitutionalism and the Judicialization of Pure Politics Worldwide', 75 *Fordham Law Review* (2006) 721–754; Vanice Regina L. do Valle, 'Judicialization of Socio-Economic Rights in Brazil: The Subversion of an Egalitarian Discourse' (2012), <ssrn.com/abstract=2031719 2009> (visited May 2014).

75. The following section draws on material in Hoffmann and Bentes, 'Accountability for Social and Economic Rights', *supra* note 70; Ferraz, 'Harming the Poor', *supra* note 73; and Octavio Luiz Motta Ferraz, 'Brazil—Health Inequalities, Rights, and Courts: The Social Impact of the Judicialization of Health', in Alicia Ely Yamin and Siri Gloppen (eds), *Litigating Health Rights: Can Courts Bring More Justice to Health?* (Harvard University Press, 2013) 76–103.

Brazilians who exclusively rely on the country's public Unified Health System (*Sistema Unico de Saúde* [SUS]). The promise of the country's 1988 constitution, with its extensive bill of rights, including the right to public health (care), seemed, thus, to begin to be fulfiled not by the legislature nor the executive, but by the courts. What is more, the driving force of this judicialisation of health care seemed to come straight from civil society, starting with the ever increasing number of citizens across all social strata demanding the free dispensation of medicines and treatments as a constitutional entitlement and up to the thoroughly professionalised and highly effective HIV/AIDS movement systematically pushing litigation aimed at continuously updating 'highly active antiretroviral therapy' (HAART) dispensed by the Brazilian HIV/AIDS programme.[76]

However, upon a closer look, the effects of this particular rights revolution are puzzlingly ambivalent. While providing a remedy to a growing number of individuals in need of medical care otherwise unavailable to or unaffordable for them, the aggregate effect of litigation has also distorted the rationale of public health care management and has generated unintended and undesired consequences. Among these are, besides the mounting budgetary impact of judicially imposed health care costs, the partial conversion of public health care providers into mere administrators of judicial injunctions and the accompanying queue-jumping effects, the possible capture of health care litigation by a middle-class seeking to complement insufficient private coverage, and the increased indirect influence of the pharmaceutical industry in the judicial restructuring of specific health care fields.[77] The reasons for these supposedly negative effects are manifold. One aspect certainly has to do with a corporatist legal culture in which judges and prosecutors operate in relative isolation from policy-makers, seeing themselves as guardians of constitutional values rather than being encumbered by means-testing or complex cost-benefit analyses. This results in a judicial activism that, in aggregate, generates at least partly dysfunctional input into the public health system while subtly re-configuring the balance of powers between executive agencies and courts. In addition,

76. Amy Nunn, *The Politics and History of AIDS Treatment in Brazil* (Springer: New York, 2009); Jane Galvão, 'Brazil and Access to HIV/AIDS Drugs: A Question of Human Rights and Public Health', 95 *American Journal of Public Health* (2005) 1110–1116; Varun Gauri and Evan S. Lieberman, 'Boundary Institutions and HIV/AIDS Policy in Brazil and South Africa', 41 *Studies in Comparative International Development* (2006) 47–73; Rosalyn S. Park, 'The International Drug Industry: What the Future Holds for South Africa's HIV/AIDS Patients', 11 *Minnesota Journal of Global Trade* (2002) 125–154.

77. Hoffmann and Bentes, 'Accountability', *supra* note 70, at 140; and Ferraz, 'Harming the Poor', *supra* note 73.

the regulatory framework within which private health care providers operate has meant that the latter's principal clientele, namely the middle-class, has increasingly turned to the public system in order to complement their own partially insufficient coverage by means of litigation. Lastly, there is a significant enforcement gap, so that judicial remedies do not always lead to the actual provision of health care to litigant patients and tend to further involve the judicial machine.

The courts and (constitutional) rights are deeply entangled in this paradoxical system. Rights, insofar as they provide the basis for litigation, play a fourfold role. Firstly, they are inclusion devices by which clients-patients-citizens excluded from aspects of public or private health care (en)force their inclusion. Secondly, in some instances, they transcend inclusion and become instruments by which specific policies are framed or re-framed. Thirdly, they are also meant to enact formal and material justice, and it is this function that is often cited by activist judges as justification for ignoring policy constraints. Lastly and fourthly, insofar as rights are also used in litigation against private health care providers, they serve as structuration devices for health care business models. It is the courts—and, in some instances, quasi-judicial institutions—that enable this functionality; they link public health care administration with client-citizen-patients and intermediate their interaction. Yet, what the Brazilian case amply demonstrates is that this functional matrix operated by the courts is neither prescribed by the constitution nor is it pursued as a transparent strategy by any of the involved stakeholders, be they judges and prosecutors, client-citizen-patients, or health care administrators. Rather, it is the result of decentralised operational logics and processes which, in aggregate, result in a continuous string of unintended consequences. These imply non-linear outcomes that, consequently, are difficult to assess by a single standard. Puzzlement and critique have, thus, accompanied these domestic 'rights revolutions'. While successful (social) rights litigation does (re-)distribute public goods to individual litigants and thereby, arguably, represents a tangible empowerment, aggregate effects can be negative. There is, for instance and as hinted earlier, evidence in the Brazilian case that litigation is 'captured' by middle-class litigants enjoying greater factual access to justice and that, hence, the 'rights revolution' might effectively be re-distributing public funds and public goods from the poor to the non-poor. In addition, court-driven counter-majoritarian decision-making on the implementation of social policy is seen as lacking both legitimacy and functional rationality, as activist courts impinge into policy domains far beyond their expertise and accountability. One consequence—in Brazil and other places—has been administrative backlash and a questioning of the role judicially enforceable fundamental rights can play in pro-poor development.[78]

5. A Revolution in Development or a Regress to (Neo-)Liberal Legalism?

Does this zooming into the real life of rights in development, hence, impel one to somberly conclude that not only did the 'rights revolution' falter but also that 'law and development' has reached yet another potentially lethal impasse? To answer these questions, one needs to zoom out again to behold the broader contemporary picture. It has been aptly summed up by David Kennedy who concludes his comprehensive review of 'law and development' by stating that

> 'attention to the rule of law offers an opportunity to focus on the political choices and economic assumptions embedded in development policy-making. Unfortunately, however, those most enthusiastic about the rule of law as a development strategy have treated it as a recipe or ready-made rather than as a terrain for contestation and strategy.'[79]

This short declaration contains all the terms of the debate, notably substance versus form, top-down versus bottom-up, structure versus agency, politics versus anti-politics. It justly apportions blame for the methodological shortsightedness that accompanies the professionalization—and concomitant professional interest—of 'law and development', but it also remains open and non-committal as to underlying causes and desired effects. It also clearly refrains from dismissing law as a relevant factor of and in development and, thus, as an object of study and of (political) action. Indeed, Kennedy embeds this statement in a concluding section in which he articulates an opportunity for 'law and development' as an analytical framework to prolong its lease on life through 'critical and heterogeneous ideas'.[80] This does not sound like a revolutionary agenda, but neither like a reactionary one. Rights-based development, being 'law and development's' current incarnation, might as well be given the benefit of such ambivalence.

On the downside, one might argue, the fact that it has not (yet) delivered the fundamental transformations of multilateral aid and domestic social

78. Ferraz, 'Harming the Poor', *supra* note 73.
79. Kennedy, 'Law and Development Economics', *supra* note 11, at 19.
80. *Ibid*, at 63.

welfare it envisions raises the suspicion of inbuilt structural bias, or, simply put, of an ideological agenda. The tenets of the latter are easily traced to the plot of (neo)liberal hegemony; as has been shown earlier, the rights-based paradigm can be seen as going hand in hand with a wider good governance agenda meant to make the state safe for a globalised market economy. It aims to re-shape public administration into an instrument of technocratic governance and democracy into a strictly controlled mechanism for interest mediation. Rights, in this scenario, function as tools to keep politics at bay by fragmenting collective action and by re-orienting policy-making to process rather than to outcomes. As Ferraz has pointed out in his critique of the judicialisation of social policy in Brazil, the domestic 'rights revolutions' may actually direct attention away from the protracted questions of social justice and redistributive politics that lurk behind development on both the global and the domestic level.[81] From this perspective, the 'turn to rights' in development is neither politically neutral nor merely procedural; it re-allocates institutional power and resources to legal professionals and human rights experts and to those conversant with their idiom—which the genuine 'poor' are frequently not.[82] On his account, the politics of rights-based development has, thus, been a 'politics of politics denied'?[83]

Adherents of Law and Development (3.0) would, of course, contest this reading and point to some potential upsides. Critics of the critics have largely sought to rebuff the 'fluff and power' critique by turning to empirics. Hence, where the latter see the impact glass half empty, the former see it as half full; they argue that rights-based programming and domestic litigation have produced significant effects both in terms of individual empowerment and remedy and in terms of forcing upon traditional development discourse and practice logic of accountability, transparency and, to an extent, participation.[84] As one of the critics has himself pointed out, the 'turn to rights' initially represented the possibility of 'claims for absolute, non-negotiable rules to limit bureaucratic discretion (…) in a world whose complexity has created the danger of unfettered relativism and bureaucratic abuse'.[85] What is more, the

81. Ferraz, 'Harming the Poor', *supra* note 73.
82. Martti Koskenniemi, 'Human Rights Mainstreaming as a Strategy for Institutional Power', 1 *Humanity: An International Journal of Human Rights, Humanitarianism, and Development* (2010) 47–58; and Kennedy, 'International Human Rights Movement', *supra* note 63.
83. Kennedy, 'Law and Development Economics', *supra* note 11, at 70.
84. Malcolm Langford, 'Domestic Adjudication and Social and Economic Rights: A Socio-Legal Review', 6 Sur (2009) 98–133.
85. Koskenniemi, 'Human Rights Mainstreaming', *supra* note 81, at 48.

insertion of rights as both an analytical framework and (enforceable) claims vis-à-vis development policy has produced wider ripples in the political landscape; it has introduced what could be termed 'human rights'isms' into the syntax and grammar of development policy-making. The net effects of such linguistic hybridisation is, of course, by no means uniform or uniformly positive, but it does produce additional expressive spaces which, arguably, were not there before and which can and have been used for emancipatory and, indeed, 'progressive' purposes.[86] Lastly, the critics' critics point to the empirical facticity of rights discourse in relation to imagined alternative strategies. Is the prevalence of rights in development necessarily the result of a more or less conscious hegemonic project or could it also be the outcome of successful experimentation in the face of policy deadlock?[87] Were alternative strategies of mass political mobilisation, of cross-societal dialogue, or, indeed, of a colloquial (international) law as the locus of non-violent political action really available, were they really sidelined or suppressed by the rights industry? Perhaps, rights simply occupied discursive spaces and went into action like a virus, infecting and modifying its host but itself also being subject to immune reactions in a complex cycle that produces divergent outcomes. If so, it would then be down to the question of whether viruses evolve spontaneously or as a result of some compelling environmental necessity—a question not answerable in the ambit of this paper.

In the end, it is submitted, whether the critics or the critics' critics have it remains to be seen. Rights-based development, as, indeed, 'law and development' and, generally, the 'ideology of the rule of law' are clearly part of a wider transformation of the very concept of development.[88] The rise of what David Trubek has called the 'new developmental state' implies a merger between the conditions and functionings of the regulatory state of the (so called) industrialised world with the developmental state of the developing world.[89] Development, thus, takes place in an environment in which traditional state-based government no longer enjoys a monopoly but is complemented by

86. Hugo Slim, 'A Response to Peter Uvin—Making Moral Low Ground: Rights as the Struggle for Justice and the Abolition of Development', 17 *Praxis* (2002) 1–5.
87. Charles Sabel and William Simon. 'Destabilization Rights: How public law litigation succeeds', 117 *Harvard Law Review* (2004) 1016–1101 at 1019.
88. Koskenniemi, 'Human Rights Mainstreaming', *supra* note 81, at 47.
89. Trubek 'Developmental States', *supra* note 5; see also Dubash and Morgan, 'Understanding the Rise', *supra* note 20; and David Levi-Faur, 'States Making & Market Building for the Global South: The Developmental vs. the Regulatory State', 44 *Jerusalem Papers in Regulation & Governance* (2012), <regulation.huji.ac.il/papers/jp44.pdf> (visited May 2014).

international, transnational, private, and hybrid regulatory regimes. As a result, stakeholders, including individuals, governments, private enterprises and organised civil society, are faced with a plurality of regulatory demands that are only partially transparent and accountable or amenable to participation and review. The servicing of markets does provide something of an overarching functional logic for such 'governance', and rights do play a role in keeping counter-hegemonic political projects at bay. Yet, the, perhaps, central characteristic of rights discourse is its inherently transgressive character and the unpredictability of the outcomes it produces. Rights can always be used for and against, to create the substantive path dependencies the critics bemoan and to counteract them. For the hidden utopia of rights in development is not the empowerment of human rights experts, judges, or the global aid industry, but a radical turning upside down of epistemic and political agency. It is hidden not because it would be concealed from all but a rarefied revolutionary avant-garde but because it is impossible to predict the precise moments and locations of its occurrence. For the instances of authentic empowerment, when Sen's 'freedom' momentarily frees itself from the constraints of (neo)liberalism and becomes an exercise in substantive [S]elf-determination, only emerge between the rigid lines of political economy and out of complex and non-linear interactions that resist schematisation. Hence, it is, indeed, the oft-critiqued indeterminacy of law itself that enables emancipatory action, even if this can only ever be part of a broader political militancy for global justice.[90] Rights as the privileged discourse for the articulation of claims to an ever expanding individual and collective identity and against (perceived) oppressions thereof remain important wedges that keep spaces for wider political contestation open, not least, as has been seen, in relation to that widest of fields, development.

90. Hence, China Miéville's thesis that 'the' law is too structurally biased to be useful for emancipatory purposes is here not adhered to; nor is, however, the progressive legalist assertion that it is a universal language game amenable to being used for 'progressive' purposes without further considerations of the users' politics; for the former, see China Miéville, *Between Equal Rights: A Marxist Theory of International Law* (Brill: Leiden, 2004); for the latter, inter alia, Martti Koskenniemi 'The Politics of International Law—20 Years Later', 20 *European Journal of International Law* (2009) 7–19.

Articles

'The Lack of Such a Common Approach'—Comparative Argumentation by the European Court of Human Rights

Maija Dahlberg*

1. Introduction

The European Court of Human Rights' (the Court or ECtHR) reasoning and method of interpreting the European Convention on Human Rights (the Convention or ECHR) have been at the focus of legal research for quite some time. There is extensive potential for comparative argumentation;[1] demonstrating uniformity and coherence, it has the ability to justify and legitimate Court judgments. This potential is, however, often wasted in practice, as uniformity or coherence arguments are not sufficiently explained by the Court.[2]

The use of the comparative method is closely linked to the general method of treaty interpretation used by the Court.[3] As an international treaty, the Convention's interpretation is subject to rules set out in Articles 31–33 of the Vienna Convention on the Law of Treaties (the Vienna Convention).[4] The Vienna Convention is mainly invoked by the Court when it takes into account other international treaties or instruments (such as UN Conventions

* PhD candidate and lecturer of constitutional law at the University of Eastern Finland Law School, maija.dahlberg@uef.fi. I wish to extend my sincere thanks to Prof. Jaakko Husa, Mirjami Paso and Prof. Toomas Kotkas and the anonymous reviewers for the valuable comments and guidance they gave. All mistakes and omissions remain my own responsibility.

1. Comparative argumentation is here synonymous with comparative legal reasoning. Both concepts are used interchangeably.
2. See, for potential in the European Union context, Mitchel de S.-O.-l'E. Lasser, *Judicial Deliberations: A Comparative Study of Judicial Transparency and Legitimacy* (Oxford University Press, 2004) at 351–52 and 356–59.
3. See, on the existence of comparative method Christopher McCrudden, 'Human Rights and Judicial Use of Comparative Law', in Esin Örücü (ed.), *Judicial Comparativism in Human Rights Cases* (United Kingdom Comparative Law Series: London, Volume 22, UKNCCL, 2003) 1–22 at 7.
4. UN Doc A/CONF.39/27; 1155 UNTS 331.

or praxis of the UN-treaty bodies).[5] It has been pointed out that the Court uses international texts and instruments as *interpretative guidance* in search of common ground.[6]

This paper argues that interpretative guidance does not fully describe the ways comparative reasoning is used by the Court. Consequently, the main research question of this article is: *How is comparative argumentation used in the judgments of the Court?* By 'comparative legal reasoning' I mean all Court decisions where a source or outcome of comparative legal analysis has been explicitly or implicitly cited. This article demonstrates that there are various ways of using comparative argumentation, though the role of such arguments differs greatly between judgments. One can identify many reasons for using comparative legal reasoning in interpreting the ECHR. It has been claimed that the legitimacy of the Court will be increased by more use of comparative consensus argumentation.[7] To acquire legitimacy through consensus argumentation is not, however, that simple. The legitimacy question is going to support, in its part, the main inquiry by explaining why the comparative method of the Court is worth analysing in more detail.[8]

In this article, comparative law refers both to national jurisdictions and to the international community in its various guises: the Council of Europe, the European Union, the United Nations family of organisations, the

5. See art. 31(3) of the Vienna Convention. See also how this Article has been used by the ECtHR, e.g. *Demir and Baykara v. Turkey*, Application no. 34503/97, Judgment (12 November 2008), Grand Chamber, Reports of Judgments and Decisions (ECHR 2008) at paras 65–68. *See more* on treaty interpretation and art. 31 of the Vienna Convention, e.g. Leena Grover, 'A Call to Arms: Fundamental Dilemmas Confronting the Interpretation of Crimes in the Rome Statute of the International Criminal Court', 21(3) *European Journal of International Law* (2010) 543–83; Lucas Lixinski, 'Treaty Interpretation by the Inter-American Court of Human Rights: Expansionism at the Service of the Unity of International Law', 21(3) *European Journal of International Law* (2010) 585–604.
6. George Letsas, 'Strasbourg's Interpretive Ethic: Lessons for the International Lawyer', 21(3) *European Journal of International Law* (2010) 509–41 at 521–2. See also how the Court strongly argues in favour of the use of international texts and instruments for the interpretation of the Convention, *Demir and Baykara v. Turkey* (2008), *supra* note 5, at paras 69–86.
7. Kanstantsin Dzehtsiarou, 'Does Consensus Matter? Legitimacy of European Consensus in the Case Law of the European Court of Human Rights', *Public Law* (2011) 534–53 (He suggests that European consensus should be sufficiently persuasive and procedurally clear in order to enhance legitimacy, at 534).
8. See on argumentative means of generating judicial legitimacy examples of the argumentation from the European Court of Justice, French Cour de cassation and American Supreme Court, Lasser, *Judicial Deliberations*, *supra* note 2.

International Labour Organisation (ILO), and so on.[9] Comparative law in its traditional dimension, which tries to find similarities and differences between domestic legal systems, is not what this article urges.[10] It is however often the way comparative law is used in, for example, law drafting processes. By 'comparative law' I instead mean the wider international texts, instruments and law in both the Contracting and non-Member States.[11] The Court's practice of distinguishing between international and traditional comparative law[12] material varies. In some cases, the Court handles traditional comparative law and international law material together;[13] in others, they have been structurally separated.[14]

The assumption of the study is that comparative argumentation in the Court's case law is used wisely and for relevant reasons. By this I mean the Court should not deploy comparative argumentation if it did not play an actual judicial role. Yet it has been argued that the very existence of comparative law data in an informative manner (merely listing the comparative data)

9. See Paul Mahoney, 'The Comparative Method in Judgments of the European Court of Human Rights: Reference Back to National Law', in Guy Canivet, Mads Andenas and Duncan Fairgrieve (eds), *Comparative Law before the Courts* (BIICL: London, 2004) 135–50 at 136–7.
10. See comparative law in its traditional dimension, e.g., Konrad Zweigert and Hein Kötz, *An Introduction to Comparative Law* (3rd edn, Oxford Clarendon Press: Oxford, 1998) at 4 ('Comparative lawyers compare the legal systems of different nations.') at 32–47. There are multiple ways of understanding what comparative law is, see e.g. Esin Örücü, 'Developing Comparative Law', in Esin Örücü and David Nelken (eds), *Comparative Law a Handbook* (Hart Publishing: Oxford, 2007) 43–65 at 44–53.
11. I do not make a distinction between when the Court refers in its reasoning to international texts and instruments (such as UN Conventions or UN-organs) and when it refers to the law of the Contracting States. They all belong under the concept of 'comparative legal reasoning'. I recognise that there is a difference between giving survey of other international texts and instruments and analysis of the state of art in the different Contracting States. This difference is not, however, decisive for this research. The focus is to find out what kind of role comparative legal reasoning has, regardless of what source the comparative reasoning is based on.
12. By 'traditional comparative law' I mean an analysis of legislation and case law in the Contracting States.
13. The Court may flexibly combine traditional comparative law, international law and legal material from the European Union, Inter-American Court, African Union and from non-contracting states (e.g. the USA, New Zealand, Hong Kong, South Africa, Canada), see e.g. *Vinter and Others v. The United Kingdom*, Application nos. 66069/09, 130/10 and 3896/10, Judgment (17 January 2012), at paras 51–73.
14. The Court may, however, clearly separate international law and traditional comparative law material, see e.g. *Stanev v. Bulgaria*, Application no. 36760/06, Judgment (17 January 2012), Grand Chamber, Reports of Judgments and Decisions (ECHR 2012), at paras 72–87 and 88–95.

increases the legitimacy of the Court *per se* as it shows the audience the decision is well informed.[15] In order to gain the acceptance of the audience, however, it is not sufficient that comparative law data has been available for the judges—it should be used as a part of the argument itself rather than mere bare background data. Like any other legal argument, comparative arguments must fulfil the requirements of rationality. Rationality is required in order to ensure the judgment is legitimate and excludes the possibility of arbitrariness. The use of comparative reasoning should hence, at least in principle, be rational.

Situated at the crossroads of the forty-seven Contracting States, with many different legal cultures and traditions, the Court's judicature is by its very nature a 'comparative' institution. The use of comparisons is thus somewhat natural and obvious, and it is easy to state that comparative law has a clear footing in the Court's case law. The approach applied in this article is a case law study where the Court's judgments will be examined. The examined years are: 2002, 2007 and 2012. The article analyses comparative arguments by classifying them into four groups according to their functions. These categories are (1) cognitive, (2) decorative, (3) directional and (4) decisive function.[16]

The first way of using comparative law is for cognitive purposes: comparative material is present at the preliminary fact-finding stage, but no further references exist in the later reasoning of the Court. Secondly, comparative law can be used in a decorative way. This means that comparative law material is briefly referred to in the reasoning without going into further depth. Thirdly, comparative law can softly steer the interpretation in a certain direction. Here comparative material is directly referred to in the reasoning and there is therefore a link between the comparative material and the chosen interpretation. Fourthly, comparative material can play a decisive role, where the Court clearly states that the chosen interpretation is a direct result of the findings of the comparative material.

Section 2 of this contribution outlines generally the use of comparative legal reasoning in courts and in the ECtHR in particular. Section 3 surveys the case law and categorises the judgments into four groups. This categorisation reveals that there are many ways to use comparative material in the Court's

15. Kanstantsin Dzehtsiarou and Vasily Lukashevich, 'Informed Decision-Making: the Comparative Endeavours of the Strasbourg Court', 30(3) *Netherlands Quarterly of Human Rights* (2012) 272–98, at 278.

16. Comparative law arguments have been also categorised differently. See Dzehtsiarou and Lukashevich, 'Informed Decision-Making', *supra* note 15. In that study comparative law arguments were distinguished into two categories: for persuasive purposes and for informational purposes.

reasoning. Lastly, the possibilities for comparative reasoning to contribute to the legitimacy of the Court will be evaluated in Section 4.

2. Comparative Legal Reasoning: Why Bother?

2.1. Comparative Legal Reasoning in Courts

Practical comparative law is nowadays a rather common part of adjudication, both in domestic and international courts. After twentieth-century legal positivism's reinforcement of the marginal role of comparative legal reasoning, it was assumed that legal systems existed as a matter of fact, and that all legal systems could claim to be supreme.[17] There was an alleged inherent presumption that a system should not give effect to laws other than its own. Today, however, there are major doubts concerning the completeness of legal systems.[18] There is thus 'renewed interest in European legal theory in the use of comparative law before the courts'.[19] Individual legal systems can hardly be regarded as isolated from one another as legal questions are more or less similar across these systems. This gives fruitful basis for the use of comparative legal reasoning.[20]

The growing interest in comparative legal reasoning is in addition part of the greater philosophical notion that there cannot always be a 'single right answer' in contested cases. By recognising multiple solutions to the same legal question, the reasoning of the court can be deepened. This is especially true in human rights cases, due to their flexible, changing and complex nature. Comparative law gives a wider insight and range of plausible solutions to resolve the case in question. As Zweigert and Kötz have claimed, '[c]omparative law is an "école de vérité" which extends and enriches the "supply of solutions"'.[21]

---

17. See H. L. A Hart, *The Concept of Law* (2nd edn, Oxford Clarendon Press: Oxford, 1994) at v, 24; H. Patrick Glenn, 'Com-paring', in Esin Örücü and David Nelken (eds), *Comparative Law a Handbook* (Hart Publishing, Oxford, 2007) 91–108 at 97.
18. H. Patrick Glenn, 'Comparative Legal Reasoning and the Courts: A View from the Americas', in Guy Canivet, Mads Andenas and Duncan Fairgrieve (eds), *Comparative Law before the Courts* (BIICL: London, 2004) 217–27 at 218–9.
19. Glenn, 'Comparative Legal Reasoning', *supra* note 18, at 219.
20. See about the pragmatic aims of comparative law, H. Patrick Glenn, 'Aims of Comparative Law', in Jan M. Smits (ed.), *Elgar Encyclopedia of Comparative Law* (Edward Elgar Publishing: Northampton, 2006) 57–65; see arguments for and against the use of foreign law, Martin Gelter and Mathias M Siems, 'Citations to Foreign Courts—Illegitimate and Superfluous, or Unavoidable? Evidence from Europe', 62(1) *American Journal of Comparative Law* (2014) 35–85 at 37–42.
21. Zweigert and Kötz, *An Introduction to Comparative Law*, *supra* note 10, at 15.

Glenn underlines that the search for appropriate interpretation of law is too important for any potential external source to be eliminated *a priori*.[22] It has, notwithstanding, been emphasised that we should not expect more of the proof of comparative law than of adjudication in general.[23] Comparative reasoning does not mean that in every case the foreign law in question is to be followed or perceived to be binding; its relevance rests at the level of *persuasive* authority.[24]

Comparative law in human rights cases seems obvious for those who support the universality of human rights—it is after all the same human right that is being applied.[25] For those who support cultural relativism, however, the use of comparisons is pointless as rights are culturally determined.[26] Claimants of the universality of human rights have gone even further, arguing that 'if comparative human rights is to be the basis of some form of new *natural law*, then domestic courts, the European Court of Human Rights and the European Court of Justice must discover the true meaning of human rights not only by looking forward but by looking sideways, at each other and beyond'.[27] Moreover it is not seen to be enough that comparative law has been a part of the interpretation of the human rights cases; instead it must be 'at the heart of human rights cases'.[28] According to that view, human rights are to be regarded as embodying principles that are universal rather than purely domestic or even European.[29] Universal human rights seem however to be a rather unrealistic vision. The universalist argument can only work at the level of regional legal systems. At the European level for example it is more plausible to talk about regionally shared conceptions of human rights—that is, the *ius commune* of human rights.[30]

22. H. Patrick Glenn, 'Persuasive Authority', 32 *McGill Law Journal* (1987) 261–98 at 293.
23. See e.g. R. G. Fentiman, 'Foreign Law in National Courts', in Guy Canivet, Mads Andenas and Duncan Fairgrieve (eds), *Comparative Law before the Courts* (BIICL: London, 2004) 13–31 at 29.
24. Glenn, 'Persuasive Authority', *supra* note 22.
25. See Eva Brems, *Human Rights: Universality and Diversity* (Martinus Nijhoff Publishers: The Hague, 2001).
26. See US Supreme Court's judge Scalia refers in its dissenting opinion to the 'practices of the "world community", whose notions of justice are (thankfully) not always those of our people.' (*Atkins v. Virginia*, 563 US 304 at 348).
27. See Esin Örücü, 'Whither Comparativism in Human Rights Cases?', in Esin Örücü (ed.), *Judicial Comparativism in Human Rights Cases*, (UKNCCL: London, 2003) 229–42 at 230. Italics are by the author.
28. *Ibid.*
29. *Ibid.*
30. Christopher McCrudden, 'Judicial Comparativism and Human Rights', in Esin Örücü and David Nelken (eds), *Comparative Law a Handbook* (Hart Publishing: Oxford, 2007) 371–97, at 373.

Comparative law's central role, especially in human rights cases, has been emphasised by researchers.[31] Kentridge has sketched three reasons for why comparative reasoning is especially necessary in human rights cases. The first reason is the close family relationship between modern domestic bills or charters of rights in different countries. Instruments like the ECHR and the International Covenant on Civil and Political Rights can be traced back to the Universal Declaration of Human Rights as a common ancestor. As the basis of these human rights is the same, human rights conventions should thus be interpreted taking each other into account.[32] Secondly, many of the concepts found in a bill of rights are broadly stated. It is not easy to find judicial standards by which to assess the scope of, for example, the right to life, or freedom from cruel or inhuman treatment or punishment. The body applying the law should recognise the dangers of an entirely subjective approach. Finally, comparative law enables the judge to test his or her value-judgment against the judgments of other judges grappling with similar provisions. It has been emphasised that in particular Articles 9, 10 and 11 of the ECHR, which permit limitations on the rights stated, should be applied with a comparative law point of view.[33]

2.2. The Use of Comparative Reasoning by the ECtHR

The use of comparative legal argumentation in the ECtHR should mean much more than simply looking at the solutions to certain problems provided by the legal orders of the Contracting States. Some judges use comparative reasoning as part of the justification for a particular decision. In this way comparativism becomes a part of the process of reaching a more fully theorised result.[34] Comparison can essentially become one of the methods of interpretation of the Convention. Comparison can however also be used as a part of other methods of interpretation, for example as a part of dynamic interpretation. Furthermore, comparative reasoning may have a significant role to play when the Court is applying the margin of appreciation

31. See e.g. Anne-Marie Slaughter, 'A Typology of Transjudicial Communication', 29 *University of Richmond Law Review* (1994) 99–137, who sees that transjudicial communication is particularly potent in the human rights field (at 132).
32. See Christopher McCrudden, 'A Common Law of Human Rights? Transnational Judicial Conversations on Constitutional Rights', 20(4) *Oxford Journal of Legal Studies* (2000) 499–532 at 501.
33. Sydney Kentridge, 'Comparing Human Rights Jurisdictions', in Guy Canivet, Mads Andenas and Duncan Fairgrieve (eds), *Comparative Law before the Courts* (BIICL: London, 2004) 235–42 at 235–6.
34. McCrudden, 'Judicial Comparativism and Human Rights', *supra* note 30, at 374.

doctrine.[35] Comparative legal argumentation can also have functions other than an interpretative function: in the ECtHR's judgments, for example, it can have a purely cognitive function.

It has been pointed out that the ECtHR further uses comparative legal reasoning in an invisible way during the interpretative process.[36] Although a brief comparative survey may have been before the judges during proceedings, it is often entirely absent from the final judgment. In these cases the comparative survey does no more than confirm an interpretation already arrived at by the Court on the basis of other considerations.[37] Furthermore, it has been indicated that just because the judges in a certain court might never refer to a foreign case, piece of legislation, or doctrinal work, it does not follow that the comparison has no relevance or role for the Court.[38] This invisibility cannot, however, be seen as a positive outcome. Judicial decision-making should be based upon open and transparent reasoning if it hopes to attain greater legitimacy. Scarce resources cannot serve as an excuse for the invisible way comparative law is sometimes used. In these cases it is rather misleading to even talk about such use as comparative legal reasoning.

It is rather common for comparative law material to be provided before the Court by both the applicant and the respondent Government. Third-party interveners usually provide further comparative law material about the subject before the Court.[39] The Court itself rather regularly provides comparative law material in the case at hand.[40] However, the Court's preparatory work on the relevant comparative law aspects is not consistently done, and depends *inter alia* on the interest of the Chamber judges, time limits, and resources, as well as the availability of comparative law material.

What then is the legitimate way for the courts to use comparative reasoning? It has been stressed that great care must be taken when one talks

35. See Mahoney, 'The Comparative Method', *supra* note 9, at 143–5.
36. Dzehtsiarou and Lukashevich, 'Informed Decision-Making', *supra* note 15, at 274.
37. Mahoney, 'The Comparative Method', *supra* note 9, at 149.
38. Geoffrey Samuel, 'Comparative Law and the Courts', in Guy Canivet, Mads Andenas and Duncan Fairgrieve (eds), *Comparative Law before the Courts* (BIICL: London, 2004) 253–62 at 252.
39. See e.g. *Othman (Abu Qatada) v. The United Kingdom*, Application no. 8139/09, Judgment (17 January 2012), Reports of Judgments and Decisions (ECHR 2012). In this case both the respondent Government and the applicant as well as the third party interveners provided comparative law material before the Court.
40. See how the research division works Egbert Myjer, 'Pieter van Dijk and His Favourite Strasbourg Judgment. Some Remarks on Consensus in the Case Law of the European Court of Human Rights', in Marjolain van Roosmalen, Ben Vermeulen, Fried van Hoof and Marten Oosting (eds), *Fundamental Rights and Principles*, Liber Amicorum Pieter van Dijk (Intersentia: Cambridge, 2013) 49–72 at 69–70.

are chosen to demonstrate the potential change in the Court's reasoning regarding the emerging use of comparative arguments. The first year (2002) is chosen to demonstrate the then emerging trend of the use of comparative law in the reasoning of the Court.[50] The five-year period is seen as an appropriate period to illustrate the progression of the use of comparative reasoning within the Convention system: the final year (2012) demonstrates the now relatively established use of comparative reasoning by the Court. The years could easily have been others (e.g. 2001, 2006, 2011 *etc.*), but the choice of years is not decisive in this study. The research question concerns how comparative reasoning is used by the Court. In order to properly answer this question, I must first define the specific case law data which will be analysed. The study would be biased if I would take into account only cases which support my views.

The search term was 'comparative'. In total, 67 judgments were analysed.[51] In 2002 there were only four cases where comparative reasoning was used; in 2007 there were 18 judgments where comparative arguments could be found; and in 2012 the Court gave 45 judgments where comparative legal reasoning played a role. These cases will be analysed from the Court's point of view.

Four different methods of using comparative argumentation can be found in the judgments of the Court. It has been stated that the case law of the Court displays a coherent and consistent approach to comparative references to national law.[52] This study separates comparative arguments according to their *function* within the Court's reasoning.[53] The first way of using comparative law is for cognitive purposes: comparative material is present at the preliminary fact-finding stage, but no further references exist in the later reasoning of the Court. Secondly, comparative law can be used in a decorative

50. On the beginning of the use of comparative law before the courts, see Hart, *The Concept of Law*, *supra* note 17, at 24; Glenn, 'Com-paring', *supra* note 17, at 97.
51. Inevitably, the term 'comparative' used in the case search might leave some relevant cases out, and there again, take other irrelevant cases into account. This problem is, however, evident and unavoidable in all researches based on case law study: one can never be sure that the search covers all possible relevant cases. In 2012 there were 11 irrelevant cases out of 56 cases. In 2007 there were eight irrelevant cases out of 26 cases and in 2002 there were four irrelevant cases out of eight. In these cases, the word 'comparative' had another meaning. However, the search term 'comparative' can be seen as appropriate and justified, because it crystallises what is really looked at in the judgments. Two cases which were done only in French had to be left out of the study due to linguistic reasons. These were: *Flamenbaum et autres c. France*, Application nos. 3675/04 and 23264/04, Judgment (13 December 2012); *Ölan c. Turquie*, Application nos. 41445/04, 41453/04, Judgment (2 October 2012).
52. Mahoney, 'The Comparative Method', *supra* note 9, at 150.
53. See other categorisations of comparative arguments, Gelter and Siems, 'Citations to Foreign Courts', *supra* note 20, at 69–82.

The Grand Chamber did not use all the comparative material in its reasoning. There is no mention in the reasoning about the case law of the House of Lords, the US Supreme Court or the Court of Justice of the European Union. In addition, the extensive UN material is bypassed quickly: 'supervisory bodies of the United Nations treaties habitually accept statistics as evidence'.[68] More consideration could have been given to, for example, the Convention of the Rights of the Child in the instant case.

Cognitive function is problematic from the point of view of justifiability. It shows that comparative material had been available to the judges but was not used in the reasoning part of the judgment. It informs the reader that the judges were aware of the comparative aspects of the legal question at hand, but leaves unclear the extent to which the comparative data affected the chosen interpretation and why. These questions are relevant from the justifiability point of view.

3.2. Decorative Function

In the decorative manner comparative law's role may look undeniably narrow. In these cases, comparative reasoning pops up rather surprisingly and the argumentation is rather loose and short. In the Court's judgments, comparative reasoning is quite often used only as decoration in support of the chosen interpretation. The decorative use is, however, vulnerable to criticism. A short and loose use as only part of the chain of reasons can be seen to be neglectful or to underestimate the audience. More depth is required in order to be truly convincing.

It has been argued that references to comparative law are often no more than 'decorative'[69] or an 'accident'.[70] The point is well-founded but some caution should still be considered when making such criticisms. According to Nelken, criticising the decorative manner in comparative reasoning depends on how the institutional and constitutional roles of judges are perceived. Judges can be seen as bonded to the requirements of their own domestic legal culture.[71] Furthermore, in some cases the comparative aspect may appear as a decoration, but in reality may have played a decisive role in the judgment.

68. *D.H. and Others v. The Czech Republic* (2007), *supra* note 65, at para. 187.
69. See e.g. McCrudden, 'Judicial Comparativism and Human Rights', *supra* note 30, at 378.
70. See e.g. Ulrich Drobning, 'General Report', in Ulrich Drobning and Sjef van Erp (eds), *The Use of Comparative Law by Courts* (Kluwer Law International: London, 1999) 3–21 at 4.
71. See David Nelken, 'Comparative Law and Comparative Legal Studies', in Esin Örücü and David Nelken (eds), *Comparative Law a Handbook* (Hart Publishing: Oxford, 2007) 3–42 at 37.

A decorative reference to comparative law is seen in the case of *Yordanova*.[72] The case concerned removal of people of Roma origin from their makeshift houses. When evaluating whether the State's order to remove the inhabitants was justified under Article 8 paragraph 2, the Court paid attention to the Government's assertion that the applicants' removal was the appropriate solution. The Court did not accept the Government's claim of appropriateness of the removal as there was no proof that alternative methods of dealing with the risks had been seriously studied by the authorities.[73] The Court continued that there were a wide range of different options to be considered in respect of unlawful Roma settlements:

> Among those are legalizing buildings where possible, constructing public sewage and water-supply facilities and providing assistance to find alternative housing where eviction is necessary (see paragraphs … 73–83 … above).[74]

The paragraphs to which the Court refers consist of Council of Europe materials: a decision against Bulgaria delivered by the Council of Europe's European Committee of Social Rights, a resolution adopted by the Committee of Ministers of the Council of Europe, a recommendation adopted by the Committee of Ministers of the Council of Europe, as well as a resolution by the Parliamentary Assembly of the Council of Europe and a recommendation by the Council of Europe's Commissioner for Human Rights.[75] In addition, European Union documents are listed; namely, the comparative report by the European Union Agency for Fundamental Rights. Furthermore the General Comment concerning forced evictions and the right to adequate housing by the United Nations Committee on Economic, Social and Cultural Rights is contained in the section on 'Relevant international material'.[76]

This way of using comparative law material is far from comparative *reasoning*. It is a blunt use of comparative law in a purely decorative manner—a short reference to the paragraphs where comparative law material has been presented. It is, however, certainly possible and even highly likely that there was more discussion amongst the judges on the findings of the comparative material than the text suggests. This discussion is left absent from the final decision.

A short reference to comparative law material is made, for example, in the case of *Khodzhamberdiyev*.[77] Here the ECtHR concluded that the applicant

72. *Yordanova and Others v. Bulgaria*, Application no. 25446/06, Judgment (24 April 2012).
73. *Ibid*, at para. 124.
74. *Ibid*, at para. 125.
75. *Ibid*, at paras 73–79.
76. *Ibid*, at paras 80–83.
77. *Khodzhamberdiyev v. Russia*, Application no. 64809/10, Judgment (5 June 2012).

was no longer at risk of treatment in breach of Article 3 as the domestic court had already annulled the extradition order.[78] In the next paragraph, however, the Court points out that:

> [T]he Moscow Office of the United Nations High Commissioner for Refugees (UNCHR) Representation informed ... that the UNCHR had determined that the applicant met the criteria set out in its Statue in connection with the Article 1 A of the 1951 Convention relating to the Status of Refugees.[79]

This reference to a comparative authoritative source of law is rather surprising, considering that the ECtHR had already declared that a breach of Article 3 was not in question. The reference to the UNCHR is thus rather loose and serves only a decorative function.

In *Samsonnikov* the question was whether the expulsion of a second-generation immigrant violated the right to respect for private and family life under Article 8.[80] The Court concluded that in this context—where the applicant had several convictions for drug smuggling and violence—an absolute right not to be expelled could not be derived from Article 8, regardless of whether an alien entered the host country as an adult, at a very young age, or indeed even if he or she was born there.[81] After entering its conclusions, the Court added: 'Furthermore, according to the Recommendation Rec (2000) 15 of the Committee of Ministers of the Council of Europe, each member state should have the option to provide in its internal law'.[82] This addition seems superfluous as it only further supports the outcome already made.

In the case of *Aslakhanova* comparative reasoning was used in interpreting Article 46.[83] The substantial Articles in which the Court unanimously found violations were, *inter alia*, Article 2 (right to life), Article 3 (prohibition of torture or inhuman or degrading treatment) and Article 5 (right to liberty). Even though a long section was included in the judgment concerning international and comparative law on enforced disappearances, the interpretation of these Articles did not contain any comparative argumentation.[84]

78. *Ibid*, at paras 73–74.
79. *Ibid*, at para. 75.
80. *Samsonnikov v. Estonia*, Application no. 52178/10, Judgment (3 July 2012).
81. *Ibid*, at para. 90.
82. *Ibid*.
83. *Aslakhanova and Others v. Russia*, Application nos. 2944/06, 8300/07, 50184/07, 332/08 and 42509/10, Judgment (18 December 2012).
84. *Ibid*, at paras 60–68 (called 'III International and Comparative Legal Instruments in the Area of Enforced Disappearances') and at paras 69–79 (called 'IV International and Domestic Reports on Disappearances in Chechnya and Ingushetia').

Article 46 requires that Contracting Parties undertake to abide by the final judgment of the Court in any case to which they are party. Moreover, the Article says that the final judgment of the Court shall be transmitted to the Committee of Ministers, which shall supervise its execution. The Court can exceptionally take into consideration consequences which may be drawn from Article 46. The Court reiterated that Article 46, taken in conjunction with Article 1, imposes a legal obligation on the respondent state to implement appropriate general and/or individual measures to secure the rights of the applicant. The Court also made further general references to wider international law.[85]

The Court emphasised that this international principle has been consistently acknowledged by the Committee of Ministers in its supervision of the execution of the Court's judgments. The Court further observed that it is not its task to decide what measures of redress may be appropriate for a respondent State to take in accordance with its obligations under Article 46. The Court's concern is instead to facilitate the rapid and effective suppression of the shortcomings found within the national system.[86]

Under Article 46 the Court may find that there is a systemic practice incompatible with the Convention—an accumulation of identical breaches which are sufficiently numerous and inter-connected to amount not merely to isolated incidents or exceptions but to a pattern or system of incompatibility.[87] The Court repeated its findings of severe violations of Articles 2, 3, 5 and 13 by the Russian Government. The Court had regularly found violations of the same rights in similar cases: more than 120 such judgments had been adopted by September 2012. Moreover, more than 100 similar cases had been communicated to the Government and yet more were currently pending before the Court. As a result, it was easy for the Court to conclude that the situation in the present case must be characterised as resulting from systemic problems at national level, for which there was no effective domestic remedy.[88] Before coming to these conclusions, the Court referred to the comparative material: 'The widespread nature of the above-mentioned problems is attested by other relevant sources, including national and international bodies, and statements by various public officials'.[89]

85. *Ibid*, at para. 210.
86. 'The Contracting State's duty in international law to comply with the requirements of the Convention may require action to be taken by any State authority, including the legislature'. *Ibid*, at paras 210–211.
87. *Ibid*, at para. 212.
88. *Ibid*, at paras 216–217.
89. *Ibid*, at para. 218.

This kind of comparative reasoning would be more convincing if the content of these comparative authoritative sources was opened up. The Court ended up providing guidance to the Russian authorities in order to solve the systemic failure to investigate disappearances in the Northern Caucasus.

In the *Fáber* case there was only a short reference to the comparative material.[90] The section 'Relevant Domestic and International Texts' broadly presents reports of the European Commission against Racism and Intolerance on Hungary, UN Human Rights Committee's interpretation, a decision by the German Constitutional Court (*Bundesverfassungsgericht*), as well as recent case law from the US Supreme Court. The Court's reasoning, however, only makes one brief reference to this comparative material.[91]

This reference, to the European Commission (*not* Committee, as the Court wrongly claims) against Racism and Intolerance (ECRI), was used to help evaluate whether the display of the flag in question constituted a reprehensible act in the context of the applicant's right to freedom of expression. The referred ECRI's report contained evaluation of the extreme right-wing's movements in Hungary and their use of certain flags. After referring to the ECRI's report, the Court came to the conclusion that the applicant's decision to display that flag must be regarded as an expression of his political views.

As to the question of freedom of expression—when balanced against the counter demonstrators' right to protect against disruption of their assembly—there may have been a lot more relevant information to take from the comparative material, such as the practice of the UN Human Rights Committee and US Supreme Court praxis. It can also, however, be argued that it would have been better to forget entirely about this kind of comparative reasoning. There would have been more to cite in comparative law material than simply whether the display of a flag constituted a reprehensible act in the context of the applicant's right to freedom of expression, especially when it appeared the flags played no role in evaluating the danger which these members created.[92]

The right to adopt arose before the Court in the case of *Wagner*.[93] The Court made brief reference to the comparative material: '[T]he positive obligations that Article 8 lays on the Contracting States in this matter must be interpreted in the light of the Convention on the Rights of the Child'.[94]

90. *Fáber v. Hungary* (2012), *supra* note 46.
91. *Ibid*, at para. 52.
92. *Ibid*, at para. 56. There is an opposing view as to how comparative material should be used in the Court's reasoning, see dissenting opinion of Judge Keller in *Fáber v. Hungary* (2012), *supra* note 46, at para. 17.
93. *Wagner and J.M.W.L. v. Luxembourg* (2007), *supra* note 57.
94. *Ibid*, at para. 120.

Further, the Court took into account the comparative material when it considered how children's rights had been respected by the national authorities: '[T]he Court reiterates the terms of Recommendation 1443 (2000) of the Parliamentary Assembly of the Council of Europe'.[95] The references are again short, but make clear that the comparative material directly affected the interpretation.

In the *Evans* case the applicant complained that provisions of English law—requiring embryos to be destroyed once the man withdraws his consent to their continued storage—violated both the embryo's right to life (Article 2) and the applicant's right to respect for her private and family life (Article 8).[96] The Grand Chamber evaluated the balance of the applicant's rights against the rights of the man who withdrew his consent: '[T]his difficulty is also reflected in the range of views by the two panels of Israeli Supreme Court in *Nachmani* and in the United States case-law'.[97]

Comparative reasoning was present in the *D.H.* case, where Roma children were channelled to special schools.[98] The applicants maintained they had been discriminated against on the basis of their race or ethnic origin (alleged violation of Article 14 taken in conjunction with Article 2 of Protocol No. 1). First, the Grand Chamber emphasised the emerging consensus concerning the special needs of minorities: '[T]here could be said to be an emerging international consensus among the Contracting States … recognising the special needs of minorities and obligation to protect their security, identity and lifestyle'.[99]

The Court did not, however, develop this consensus argumentation any further. Nor is any further mention made in the rest of the Court's reasoning. The Court additionally referred to the comparative authoritative material:

> [S]ee also the general observations in the Parliamentary Assembly's Recommendation No. 1203 (1993) on Gypsies in Europe … and point 4 of its Recommendation no. 1557 (2002) on the legal situation of Roma in Europe … As is attested by the activities of numerous European and international organisations and the recommendations of the Council of Europe bodies … this protection also extends to the sphere of education.[100]

95. *Ibid*, at para. 126.
96. *Evans v. The United Kingdom*, Application no. 6339/05, Judgment (10 April 2007), Grand Chamber, Reports of Judgments and Decisions (ECHR 2007-I).
97. *Ibid*, at para. 80.
98. *D.H. and Others v. The Czech Republic* (2007), *supra* note 65. In this judgment some comparative material is used decoratively, while other sections are left cognitive purposes (these are dealt above).
99. *Ibid*, at para. 181.
100. *Ibid*, at para. 182.

The Court referred also to EU law material: 'In accordance with … Council Directives 97/80/EC and 2000/43/EC … and the definition provided by ECRI … such a situation may amount to "indirect discrimination"'.[101] Accordingly, the Court concluded (by thirteen votes to four) that there has been a violation of Article 14 taken in conjunction with Article 2 of Protocol No. 1.

These citations clearly show that comparative material is used in the Court's argumentation and does affect the interpretation of the ECHR. Even though reference to comparative material is brief and is often left unexplained as to the comparative material's input and weight on the interpretation, it still works to convince the audience. For this reason the decorative manner of comparative reasoning should not automatically be seen as bad argumentation.

3.3. Directional Function

Directional function means that comparative arguments play a role in *channelling the interpretation in a certain direction*. The comparative arguments do not, however, play a decisive role; only a directional one. In these cases decisive arguments come from other sources.[102]

In *Sitaropoulos* comparative material was centrally present in the judgment.[103] The question was whether Article 3 of Protocol No. 1 was violated when two Greek nationals were unable to vote in the Greek Parliamentary elections from abroad. The case was handled initially in the Chamber's First Section[104] and then, on the Government's request, in the Grand Chamber. The Grand Chamber operated with an extensive range of comparative material concerning the right to vote from abroad. The sections which go through the international and comparative material contain 15 paragraphs (from paragraph 21 to paragraph 45).

The comparative law material was taken into account in the Court's reasoning. First, the Court shaped the general principles relating to the

---

101. *Ibid*, at para. 184.
102. In the categories of directional and decisive functions it must be emphasised that the selection used in this article might leave some relevant cases aside; namely, comparison between two systems can clearly be made without using the word 'comparative'. Still, the word 'comparative' used in the search of directional and decisive arguments is well-founded, since usually a comparative material section is included in the judgment before leaning on them in the reasoning.
103. *Sitaropoulos and Giakoumopoulos v. Greece*, Application no. 42202/07, Judgment (15 March 2012), Grand Chamber, Reports of Judgments and Decisions (ECHR 2012).
104. *Sitaropoulos and Others v. Greece*, Application no. 42202/07, Judgment (8 July 2010).

right to vote. The Court reiterated the effect of possible consensus among Contracting States with regard to the interpretation of the Convention. It further emphasised that the existence or non-existence of common ground between Contracting States is one of the relevant factors in determining the scope of an authority's margin of appreciation.[105] The Court used the comparative survey from this consensus angle and stated:

> Furthermore, a comparative survey of the legislation of Council of Europe member States in this sphere shows that, while the great majority of them allow their nationals to vote from abroad, some do not ... However, as regards those States which do allow voting from abroad, closer examination reveals that the arrangements for the exercise of expatriates' voting rights are not uniform, but take a variety of forms.[106]

This conclusion is rather interesting. It was clear that there was a great majority of Contracting States that allowed voting from abroad. The Court then looked at *how* voting from abroad is arranged in these States. As a result, where arrangements for the exercise of expatriates' voting rights vary, the Court seemed to come to the conclusion that there was no consensus between the Contracting States on the matter at hand. The Court laconically concluded: 'As to the arrangements for exercising that right put in place by those Council of Europe member States that allow voting from abroad, there is currently a wide variety of approaches'.[107]

This takes us back to the question: what is actually meant by 'common ground' or 'consensus' amongst Contracting States? European consensus basically means there is a common understanding or clear trend of interpretation on a certain issue.[108] But it is rather misleading to state that the European consensus would demand that all the countries have similar arrangements on the issue at hand. On the contrary, European consensus arguably refers to a broader view on how Contracting States react to a certain issue, rather than how they technically solved it.

In this judgment the Court defined the European consensus by paying attention to the variable arrangements between the Contracting States and came to the conclusion that there was no consensus on the right to vote from abroad. This finding was not, however, decisive to the outcome of the

105. *Sitaropoulos and Giakoumopoulos v. Greece* (2012), *supra* note 103, at para. 66.
106. *Ibid*, at para. 74.
107. *Ibid*, at para. 75.
108. See e.g. *Konstantin Markin v. Russia*, Application no. 30078/06, Judgment (22 March 2012), Grand Chamber, Reports of Judgments and Decisions (ECHR 2012), at para. 126.

> of a letter ... by Mr Jacques Barrot, Vice-President of the European Commission, in which he stressed the importance of compliance with the principle of *non-refoulement* ... by Member States of the European Union.[127]

After this, the Court unanimously concluded that in the present case substantial grounds had been shown for believing there was a real risk that the applicants would be subjected to treatment in Libya contrary to Article 3. Consequently, there had been a violation of Article 3. The use of European Union authority is certainly a deliberate choice by the Court: the situation at hand touched both the EU and the ECHR institutions, and they are in line with each other in reminding States about the principles and boundaries of how to handle immigration situations.

Comparative reasoning played a directional role in the *Vinter* case, concerning life sentencing in relation to Article 3 (right not to be tortured or inhuman and degrading treatment).[128] The applicants complained that their whole life orders violated Article 3. The Court began by accepting that the sentence could violate Article 3 if it were wholly unjustified or grossly disproportionate to the gravity of the crime. The Court found support from comparative sources:

> The Court notes that support for this proposition can also be found in the comparative materials before the Court. Those materials demonstrate ... (see the Eight Amendment case-law ... the judgments of the Supreme Court of Canada ...).[129]

The Court further continued about the grossly disproportionate sentence and emphasised its restrictions:

> However, the Court also considers that the comparative materials set out above demonstrate that 'gross disproportionality' is a strict test and, as the Supreme Court of Canada observed in *Latimer* ... it will only be on 'rare and unique occasions' that the test will be met.[130]

While the attitude on life sentences in Europe was clearly against them, the Court did not see that this should affect the case.[131] The Court instead used Canadian case law to assess when such a sentence would be grossly disproportionate.[132]

---

127. *Ibid*, at para. 135.
128. *Vinter and Others v. The United Kingdom* (2012), *supra* note 13.
129. *Ibid*, at para. 88.
130. *Ibid*, at para. 89.
131. *Ibid*, at para. 55 where it is expressed that the majority of European countries do not have irreducible life sentences and some do not have life sentences at all.
132. *Ibid*, at para. 93.

Having thus decided the test of gross disproportionality must be interpreted strictly, the Court considered the circumstances of the particular convictions. The Court pointed out that, given the gravity of the murders for which they were convicted, the applicants' life orders could not be seen as grossly disproportionate. Secondly, the Court noted that none of the applicants had demonstrated that their continued incarceration served no legitimate penological purpose.[133] This was also decisive for the Court's reasoning. The Court thus held by four votes to three that there has been no violation of Article 3.

3.4. Decisive Function

Comparative reasoning may play a decisive role in the Court's reasoning. In this role, the comparative reasoning is the deciding factor for the chosen interpretation. Decisive argument is recognised by its wording and its placement immediately before the Court's conclusion. This is the strongest but also the most controversial function of comparative reasoning. Decisive comparative arguments are often based on the Court's findings on European consensus, widely accepted international treaties, or the opinions of powerful constitutional courts. In the decisive function the comparative reasoning and the outcome of the interpretation are directly connected: after the concluding comparative argument, the outcome is clear.

The case of *Hristozov* concerned access to unauthorised medical products.[134] The applicants complained of violations of Articles 2 (right to life), 3 (right not to be tortured or inhuman and degrading treatment) and 8 (right to private and family life) when the national authorities had prohibited their access to an experimental medical product. The judgment contains two comparative sections: 'Relevant European Union Law' and 'Relevant Comparative Material'.

First, the Court referred to European Union law when ruling that it was not the Court's task to pass judgment on the system of rules governing access to unauthorised medical products in Member States, nor to decide whether denial of access to medical products is in principle compatible with the Convention. The Court stressed its competence concerning EU law: it is not the Court's task to review compliance with other international instruments.[135]

Comparative reasoning was further present when the Court decided whether Article 2 could be interpreted as requiring access to unauthorised

133. *Ibid*, at para. 95.
134. *Hristozov and Others v. Bulgaria*, Application nos. 47039/11 and 358/12, Judgment (13 November 2012), Reports of Judgments and Decisions (ECHR 2012).
135. *Ibid*, at para. 105.

neglect by the authorities constituted the basis for the comparative reasoning to be decisive in the judgment.

The long and difficult *Othman* case, which concerned deportation of the applicant to Jordan, contained much comparative material and reasoning.[150] As concerned Article 6, the applicant complained he would be at real risk of a flagrant denial of justice if retried in Jordan. It is established in the Court's case law that an issue may exceptionally be raised under Article 6 by an expulsion or extradition decision in circumstances where a fugitive has suffered or risked suffering a flagrant denial of justice in the requesting country.[151] A flagrant denial of justice goes beyond mere irregularities or lack of safeguards in the trial procedures; it requires a violation of the principles of a fair trial guaranteed in Article 6 so fundamental as to amount to a nullification or destruction of the very essence of the right itself. The Court has always found that, since the *Soering* judgment, expulsion would be in violation of a fair trial under Article 6.

The question at hand concerned evidence obtained by torture. The Court relied strongly on international conventions, namely the United Nations Convention against Torture (UNCAT), when emphasising the fundamental prohibition against the use of evidence obtained by torture:

> Strong support for that view is found in international law. Few international norms relating to the right to a trial are more fundamental than the exclusion of evidence obtained by torture. There are few international treaties which command as widespread support as UNCAT. One hundred and forty-nine States are party to its provisions, including all Member States of the Council of Europe ... UNCAT reflects the clear will of the international community to further entrench the *ius cogens* prohibition on torture by taking a series of measures to eradicate torture and remove all incentive for its practice ... As United Nations Committee Against Torture has made clear.[152]

For these reasons the Court concluded that the admission of torture evidence was manifestly contrary not only to the provisions of Article 6, but to the most basic international standards of a fair trial.[153]

Turning to the instant case at hand and determining the sufficiency of the torture evidence, the Court used international reports which confirmed that torture was widespread and routine in Jordan. Accordingly, the Court decided that it would be unfair to impose any higher burden of proof on

150. *Othman (Abu Qatada) v. The United Kingdom* (2012), *supra* note 39.
151. That principle was first set out in *Soering v. The United Kingdom*, Application no.14038/88, Judgment (7 July 1989), ECHR Series A (1989) no. 161.
152. *Othman (Abu Qatada) v. The United Kingdom* (2012), *supra* note 39, at para. 266.
153. *Ibid*, at para. 267.

the applicant.[154] The Court turned to comparative arguments as to why the burden of proof must be at this level:

> [T]he Court does not consider that the Canadian and German case-law, which has been submitted by the Government … provides any support for their position … Finally, it is clear from Düsseldorf Court of Appeal's reasoning that it did not apply a balance of probabilities test to the requested person's allegations.[155]

Further, in evaluating the Jordanian State Security Court system, the ECtHR referred to international reports:

> In its conclusions on Article 15 of UNCAT, the Committee Against Torture expressed its concern at reports that the use of forced confessions in courts was widespread … The Special Rapporteur has described a system where the 'presumption of innocence is illusory' and 'primacy is placed on obtaining confessions' … The reports of Amnesty International and Human Rights Watch support this view.[156]

After these unequivocal international authority findings, the Court came to the conclusion that the applicant had discharged the burden of proof that could fairly be imposed on him. Consequently, the Court unanimously held the applicant's deportation to Jordan would be in violation of Article 6.

The Genocide Convention came before the Court in *Jorgic*, where it had to decide whether States had universal jurisdiction in genocide cases.[157] The applicant argued that there was a general rule of public international law, namely the duty of non-intervention, which in principle prohibited the German courts from prosecuting a foreigner living abroad for genocide purportedly committed by him in a foreign country against foreign victims. Universal jurisdiction over genocide cannot be found in the Genocide Convention. The ECtHR, however, reiterated that 'pursuant to Article 1 of the Genocide Convention, the Contracting Parties were under an *erga omnes* obligation to prevent and punish genocide, the prohibition of which forms part of the *jus cogens*'.[158]

The ECtHR was thus convinced by the respondent state's reasoning and took authoritative sources into decisive account. The respondent state's interpretation on universal jurisdiction for genocide:

> is widely confirmed by the statutory provisions and case-law of numerous other Contracting States to the Convention … and by the Statute and case-law of the

---

154. *Ibid*, at paras 272–273.
155. *Ibid*, at para. 275.
156. *Ibid*, at para. 277.
157. *Jorgic v. Germany*, Application no. 74613/01, Judgment (12 July 2007), Reports of Judgments and Decisions (ECHR 2007-III).
158. *Ibid*, at para. 68.

From the national system's point of view, the use of comparative reasoning and reliance on other States' or organisations' practices may be seen as undermining the respondent State's traditions and practices.[165] Supranational adjudication is often vulnerable to criticism: in the ECHR system there are forty-seven Contracting States, and to find a common understanding of interpretations, not to mention common acceptance, is challenging. It is not, however, always possible in human rights' questions to settle for middle-line interpretations. It is the main purpose of the ECHR system to protect the rights of the individuals. Finding appropriate interpretations with the help of comparative law is at least worth attempting in order to maintain the legitimacy of the ECHR system. At its best, comparative reasoning helps bolster the interpretation made by the Court as both justified and acceptable.

165. See reactions of the British audience on the questions of prisoners' right to vote, e.g. Nicolas Bratza, 'The Relationship between the UK Courts and Strasbourg', 5 *European Human Rights Law Review* (2011) 505–12.

Annulment in Action: How Does the Court of Justice of the European Union Explain Maintaining the Legal Effects of Annulled Instruments?

Samuli Miettinen

University of Helsinki
samuli.miettinen@helsinki.fi

ABSTRACT: Constitutional courts typically have some powers to determine the temporal effects of their judgments. The Court of Justice demonstrates a clear preference for *ex tunc* reasoning when deciding preliminary references. Interpretations and declarations of invalidity are effective from the date the measure entered into force, in some cases decades before the judgment itself. However, some judgments which concern direct annulment actions for EU instruments grant an effective annulment only *pro futuro*: The legal effects of the formally annulled instrument are maintained beyond even the date of the judgment, sometimes for an unspecified period of time into the future. This is unusual in a comparative context. A review of the lines of cases involving such decisions shows that the reasoning in this context is terse, and has strayed from the original need to ensure that the applicant was not in a worse position after annulment. It is not clear that these judgments are always confined to unique facts: they are linked to a past practice in similar contexts. In some cases, the decision also carries fundamental rights implications. The Court could increase legal certainty and the effective judicial protection of fundamental rights by developing its reasoning on when this is appropriate, especially when that decision is against the interests of the applicants.

1. Introduction

What happens when legislation is declared unconstitutional? This question is overdue for attention in the context of judicial review in the European Union. The European Union's constitutional treaties proclaim that the Union is founded on the rule of law.[1] A 2014 Communication from the European

1. Article 2 Treaty on European Union (TEU); The EU Charter of Fundamental Rights (CFR), preamble, second indent, TEU, preamble, second indent and fourth indent, Articles 21(1) and 21(2)(b) TEU, concerning the CFSP.

formally annulled instruments into the future, beyond the date of its judgment. In a few, it maintains them indefinitely. That it does so is not always clearly noted in literature.[15]

Second, the reasoning for such a controversial approach is not always clear or convincing. The Treaty provisions on temporal effects provide no basis for the constitutional value judgments that are implied when maintaining unlawful measures. What are the justifications for maintaining unlawful acts? How are they evaluated in the overall context of the 'complete system of protection' provided by the EU legal framework or the obligations to protect fundamental rights? Regardless of the substance of the dispute, the requirement of effective remedies in Article 47 of the Charter of Fundamental Rights calls for careful reasoning whenever the remedy provided in the form of annulment is curtailed.

Al Bakaraat International Foundation v Council and Commission (EU sanctions) [2008] ECR I-6351 at 373–376; Joined Cases C-14/06 and C-295/06 EP and Denmark v Commission (Electrical equipment directive) [2008] ECR I-1649 at 86; C-155/07 EP v Council (EIB Guarantees) [2008] ECR I-8103 at 87–89; C-166/07 EP v Council (International Fund for Ireland) [2009] ECR I-7135 at 73–75; C-370/07 Commission v Council (CITES Convention) [2009] ECR I-8917 at 64–65; C-40/10 Commission v Council (Staff regulations) [210] ECR I-12043 at 95. Before the European General Court, T-562/10 HTTS Hanseatic Trade Trust & Shipping v Council (EU Sanctions regime listing) [2011] ECR II-8087 at 41–43. These are listed in K. Lenaerts, I. Maselis, K. Gutman, and J. Nowak (eds), *EU Procedural Law* (Oxford University Press, 2014) at 414, fn 844. See also at least Joined Cases C-317 and 318/04 EP v Council and Commission (Passenger Name Records Agreement) [2006] ECR I-04721; Case C-355/10 European Parliament v Council (Border surveillance), Judgment of the Grand Chamber of 5 September 2012, not yet reported; Case C-566/10 P Italy v Commission, judgment of the Grand Chamber of 27 November 2012, Case C-137/12, Judgment of the Grand Chamber of 22 October 2013, not yet reported; Case C-490/10, EP v Council (Energy/Information legal basis), Judgment of 6 September 2012, Case C-414/04 EP v Council, [2006] ECR I-11279; Joined Cases C-317/04 and C-318/04 EP v Council (Passenger Name Record legal basis) [2006] ECR I-04721, as well as T-552/12 *North Drilling*, Judgment of 12.11.2013 not yet reported, T-133/12 Mehdi Ben Tijani Ben Haj Hamda Ben Haj Hassen Ben Ali v Council, Judgment of 2 April 2014 not yet reported, T-110/12, Iranian Offshore Engineering & Construction Co. v Council, Judgment of 6 September 2013 not yet reported, T-57/12 Good Luck Shipping LLC v Council, judgment of 6 September 2013, not yet reported; T-58/12 Nabipour and others v Council, Judgment of 12 December 2013, not yet reported; Joined Cases T-42/12 and T-181/12 Bateni v Council, Judgment of 6 September 2013, not yet reported.

15. See for example K. Lenaerts, I. Maselis, K. Gutman and T. Nowak (eds), *EU Procedural Law* (Oxford University Press, 2014) at 413–414, noting the 'attenuation of retroactive effect' and maintaining effects 'until the competent institution … has taken the necessary measures *to give effect to the judgment*'.

Literature has examined the stated reasons for delaying the effects of a preliminary reference in some detail.[16] It is a rare phenomenon also in the context of national constitutional courts.[17] Relatively little has, however, been said of the same practice in the context of annulment actions in the European Union. This discussion cannot be simply applied by analogy from the preliminary reference context, since the exceptional cases maintaining legal effects relate to *ex nunc* rulings, where the future invalidity of the act is not called into question. Just as the past is not the future, reasoning that is linked to questions of retroactivity in the *ex nunc* context may not be equally relevant in the *pro futuro* scenario. The historic lines of cases are explained in textbooks by a need to ensure that the successful party was not placed in a worse position following the annulment of an act that was beneficial.[18] However, modern rulings raise questions about the protection of applicants' individual rights.

2. Lines of Cases Modifying Temporal Effects in Annulment Proceedings

In principle, annulment should result in void legislation under Article 264 TFEU. When annulment actions concern legislative acts, the Court's monopoly on invalidity, the rules on standing in direct actions, and the practical safeguards that apply when an act is declared invalid all suggest that legality review, when it does take place in the context of annulment actions, should be taken rather seriously. This is not, however, always beyond dispute. First, the case law below demonstrates without question that successful annulment actions are not always

16. For preliminary rulings, see recently e.g. M. Broberg and N. Fenger, *Preliminary References to the European Court of Justice* (Oxford University Press, 2010) at 446–457; Donatas Murauskas, 'The Temporal Limitation by the Court of Justice of the EU: Dealing with the Consequences', (6) 2 *European Journal of Legal Studies* (2013) 78–95; Michael Lang, 'Limitation of Temporal Effects of CJEU Judgments: Mission Impossible for Governments of EU Member States', in Patricia Popelier, Sarah Verstraelen, Dirk Vanheule, and Beatrix Vanlerberghe (eds), *The Effects of Judicial Decisions in Time* (Intersentia: Cambridge, 2014) at 245–263.
17. Sarah Verstraelen, 'The Temporal Limitation of Judicial Decisions: The Need for Flexibility Versus the Quest for Uniformity', 14 *German Law Journal* (2013) 1687–1730 at 1690; Allan R. Brewer-Carías, *Constitutional Courts as Postive Legislators: A Comparative Study* (Cambridge University Press, 2011) at 95–102. See also the Venice Commission Study on individual access to constitutional justice, adopted by the Venice Commission at its 85th Plenary Session (Venice, 17–18 December 2010), Strasbourg, 27 January 2011, Study 538/2009, 102–110 for a list of provisions in CoE and observer states. In the US, See e.g. Marbury v. Madison, 5 US 137 (1803).
18. Case 81/72 [1973] ECR 575, discussed below, and Case C-41/95 EP v Council [1995] ECR I-4411 at 43–45. Paul Craig, and Grainne de Burca, *EU Law: Text, Cases and Materials* (5th edn Oxford University Press, 2011) 554.

successful in practice. The Court maintains the legal effects of unlawful decisions rather than declaring them void *ab initio*. Second, in most of these cases, the Court is not even ruling *ex nunc*, but *pro futuro*: it maintains the unlawful act *beyond the date of the judgment*. Two objections can be made. It does not protect the litigant's right to an effective remedy, since although they had standing and were successful, the unlawful act was maintained also as regards the litigated interest.[19] Where the litigant is an institution, they are arguably the protectors of the public interest even if they might consider it useful to maintain unlawful acts. When they request a temporal modification, the practice also enables the court to judicially resurrect acts that may not otherwise be promulgated in future legislative proceedings. Third, when the Court engages in this practice, its typical statement of reasons is insufficient. At best, the reasoning is based primarily on good faith, legal certainty, and serious economic consequences. This reasoning is merely transferred from *ex nunc* preliminary references and cases where a temporal modification is in the applicant's interest. This can be unconvincing or irrelevant in other cases, especially those with fundamental rights implications. It is particularly controversial when the temporal modification is not requested by the applicant. The reasoning also seems to value legal certainty over legality. In some cases, this controversial practice is not reasoned at all. Thus, it is not entirely clear that the Court is discharging its duty to give reasons for some constitutional rulings that are of great significance.

2.1. The Effectiveness of 'Restrictive Measures'

That the decisions are of a constitutional nature is amply demonstrated by the line of cases involving 'restrictive measures'. These involve an EU instrument listing persons subject to restrictive measures, with the result that the person 'can be stopped, their property can be controlled, their liberty taken away, their movement restricted, their businesses ruined, their family life inhibited or destroyed, and all without any kind of criminal charge[...]'.[20] A great deal has been written on this topic that will not be reiterated here.[21] The point to be made is that the practice of suspensory annulment is alive and well despite the *Kadi* saga.

The review must, however, begin with Kadi itself. Here, the Court of Justice found, on appeal from the Court of First Instance, that the inclusion of

19. Compare here the practice of allowing litigants to benefit from their own action where a preliminary reference grants only *ex nunc* effects.
20. Conor Gearty, 'In Praise of Awkwardness: Kadi in the CJEU', 10(1) *European Constitutional Law Review* (2014) 15–27 at 26–27.
21. See i.a. Christina Eckes, *EU Counter-Terrorist Policies and Fundamental Rights: The Case of Individual Sanctions* (Oxford University Press, 2009), and Cian Murphy, *EU Counter-Terrorism Law: Pre-Emption and the Rule of Law* (Hart: Oxford, 2012) at 115–146.

Kadi and Al Bakaraat on the list of persons who would be subject to restrictive measures[22] must be annulled.[23] The Court approved the practice of ex post notification in order to ensure the effectiveness of the sanctions regime. However, it noted that the rights of the defence and the right to be heard were not respected, because the instrument did not provide for a procedure for communicating the relevant evidence to the persons even after their inclusion on the list, and the Council had not taken steps to provide the evidence.[24] This was contrary to the principle of effective judicial protection under general principles of EU law, Article 6 and 13 of the European Convention on Human Rights, and Article 47 of the Charter of Fundamental Rights.[25]

In Kadi, The Court found that the annulment of the regulation with immediate effect 'would be capable of seriously and irreversibly prejudicing the effectiveness of the restrictive measures' because the listed persons could in the meantime take avoidance measures.[26] The Court found that it 'cannot be excluded that, on the merits of the case, the imposition of those measures' might prove justified even if the procedure was flawed.[27] Therefore it maintained the effects for up to three months from the date of the judgment[28] in order to allow the procedural infringements to be remedied.[29]

The *Kadi II* litigation[30] then demonstrated a subsequent failure to respect those procedural rights. Kadi received a limited statement of reasons, and was duly relisted.[31] However, as the Court concluded in *Kadi II,*

> 'none of the allegations presented against Mr Kadi in the summary provided by the Sanctions Committee are such as to justify the adoption, at European Union

22. Regulation (EC) No 881/2002 of 27 Mary 2002 imposing certain specific restrictive measures directed against certain persons and entities associated with Osama bin Laden, the Al-Qaeda network and the Taliban, and repealing council Regulation (EC) No 467/2001 prohibiting the export of certain goods and services to Afghanistan, strengthening the flight ban and extending the freeze of funds and other financial resources in respect of the Taliban of Afghanistan.
23. C-402/05 P and C-415/05 P *Kadi and Al Bakaraat International Foundation v Council and Commission (EU sanctions)* [2008] ECR I-6351 at 373–376.
24. C-402/05 P and C-415/05 P *Kadi and Al Bakaraat International Foundation v Council and Commission* at 334.
25. *Ibid,* at 335–337.
26. *Ibid,* at 373.
27. *Ibid,* at 374.
28. *Ibid,* at 376.
29. *Ibid,* at 376.
30. T-85/09 *Kadi v Commission* [2010] ECR II-5177; upheld on different grounds in Joined cases C-584/10 p, C-593/10 P and C-595/10 P *European Commission, Council, and UK v Kadi,* judgment of the Grand Chamber of 18 July 2013, not yet reported.
31. Commission Regulation (EC) 1190/2008.

level, of restrictive measures against him, either because the statement of reasons is insufficient, or because information or evidence which might substantiate the reason concerned, in the face of detailed rebuttals submitted by the party concerned, is lacking.'[32]

After a decade of wrongful listing, the UN Security Council lifted the measures.[33] The Court of Justice confirmed this would also have been required under EU law.[34] The Kadi annulment was originally modified in order to facilitate the objectives of the instrument, and to allow for a procedurally correct decision to be taken in circumstances where the law was unclear. However, the temporal modifications continue to be requested long after it should have been clear to the institutions what kinds of safeguards must have been available.[35]

2.2. Protecting 'The Smooth Functioning' of Agencies

Practical considerations also prevail where executive action is of doubtful constitutionality. In the *Schengen Border Code* case[36] the Court annulled a decision[37] concerning the Schengen Borders Code[38] on the grounds that the Commission had exceeded its implementing powers under the Code.

32. Case C-402/05 P and C-415/05 P *Kadi and Al Bakaraat International Foundation v Council and Commission*, at 163.
33. C. Gearty, 'In Praise of Awkwardness: Kadi in the CJEU', 10(1) *European Constitutional Law Review* (2014) 15–27 at 24.
34. The opposite was suggested in the Opinion of Advocate General Bot, 19.3.2013.
35. T-562/10 HTTS *Hanseatic Trade Trust & Shipping v Council (EU Sanctions regime listing)* [2011] ECR II-8087 at 41–43; T-552/12 *North Drilling*, Judgment of 12 November 2013 not yet reported, T-133/12 *Mehdi Ben Tijani Ben Haj Hamda Ben Haj Hassen Ben Ali v Council*, Judgment of 2 April 2014 not yet reported, T-110/12, *Iranian Offshore Engineering & Construction Co. v Council*, Judgment of 6 September 2013 not yet reported, T-57/12 *Good Luck Shipping LLC v Council*, judgment of 6 September 2013, not yet reported; T-58/12 *Nabipour and others v Council*, Judgment of 12 December 2013, not yet reported; Joined Cases T-42/12 and T-181/12 *Bateni v Council*, Judgment of 6 September 2013. Limitation may be necessary to facilitate the effectiveness of a successful appeal, or because other sanctions are valid and would be jeopardized, but this reasoning is not apparent in all of the judgments.
36. Case C-355/10 *European Parliament v Council (Border surveillance)*, Judgment of the Grand Chamber of 5 September 2012, not yet reported.
37. Council Decision of 26. April supplementing the Schengen Borders Code as regards the surveillance of the sea external borders in the context of operational cooperation coordinated by the European Agency for the Management of Operational Cooperation at the External Borders of the Member States of the European Union OJ L 11/20.
38. Regulation (EC) No 562/2006 of the European Parliament and of the Council of 15 March 2006 establishing a Community Code on the rules governing the movement of persons across borders (Schengen Borders Code), OJ 2006 L 105, p. 1, as amended by Regulation (EC) No 296/2008 of the European Parliament and of the Council of 11 March 2008, OJ 2008 L 97, p. 60.

According to the EP, the Commission's decision could, as a comitology decision, modify, or remove, or add new 'non-essential' elements, but could not modify 'essential' elements. It argued that the Commission's decision neither respected these essential elements, nor limited itself to the scope of the empowering legislation.[39] The changes were not merely 'flesh on the bones' of the original border code, but granted border authorities powers to take measures against ships and persons on the seas. In practice, this prevented persons on returned vessels from claiming asylum under the SBC.[40] Such rules were not 'surveillance' within the meaning of the empowering measure on which they were based.[41] They also went beyond the territorial scope of the implementing legislation, since they applied not only to territorial seas but also contiguous zones and the high seas.[42]

The annulment turned on the capacity to delegate 'essential elements' of legislation.[43] The Court of Justice noted that 'essential elements' were 'provisions which, in order to be adopted, require political choices falling within the responsibilities of the European Union legislature cannot be delegated'.[44] These could not be predetermined by the legislature itself, but were determined on a case by case basis in the context of judicial review.[45] Conferring enforcement powers on border guards entailed political choices,[46] and the conferral of those public authority powers meant 'the fundamental rights of the persons concerned may be interfered with to such an extent that the involvement of the European Union legislature is required'.[47] Nor did it matter that such otherwise 'essential'[48] rules were labelled 'guidelines', since they were clearly intended to have legal effects.[49]

In many respects, the ruling strengthens the constitutional legitimacy of EU delegated legislation. However, the reasoning for the annulment raises

39. Case C-355/10 *European Parliament v Council (Border Surveillance)*, at 43.
40. *Ibid*, at 49, referring to Article 13 Regulation (EC) No 562/2006 of the European Parliament and of the Council of 15 March 2006 establishing a Community Code on the rules governing the movement of persons across borders (Schengen Borders Code).
41. Case C-355/10 *European Parliament v Council (Border Surveillance)*, at 50.
42. *Ibid*, at 51.
43. For commentary, see Maarten Den Heijer, and Eljalill Tauschinsky, 'Where human rights meet administrative law: essential elements and limits to delegation', 9(3) *European Constitutional Law Review* (2013) 513–533; Merijn Chamon, 'How the concept of essential elements of a legislative act continues to elude the Court. *Parliament v Council*', 50 *Common Market Law Review* (2013) 489–860.
44. Case C-355/10 *European Parliament v Council (Border Surveillance)*, at 55.
45. *Ibid*, at 67.
46. *Ibid*, at 76.
47. *Ibid*, at 77.
48. *Ibid*, at 80.
49. *Ibid*, at 82.

some questions about the Court's decision to maintain the annulled provisions in force. As the Court pointed out, the measures were essential because they entailed political choices and affected fundamental rights. Nevertheless, the Parliament itself applied for the rules to be maintained, and the Court obliged. The 'smooth functioning'[50] of FRONTEX operations constituted 'important grounds of legal certainty'.[51] No specific time limit was given for the temporal restriction.[52]

2.3. Annulled Measures Achieve EU Objectives

Several lines of cases involve temporal modulation in order to achieve the aims of the annulled measure that are also aims of the Union. The interest of the institutional applicant, often but not always expressed by the applicant itself, is not in the complete annulment of an act but its replacement with a more advantageous act. In such circumstances, complete annulment would place the applicant in a worse position and its maintenance can be justified from that perspective. This can reveal some value judgments. Effectiveness of environmental objectives appears to prevail over procedural and legal basis concerns. Here, the precautionary principle, whilst unmentioned in the judgments, could provide further support for the practice.

The first of these cases concerns annulment against measures that protected the environment, but were brought on the incorrect legal basis of agriculture.[53] The EP brought an action against measures that extended the protection of forests against atmospheric pollution and fire[54] for a further five-year period.[55] The council could not, it seems, see the wood from the trees: the protection of forests pursued not only an agricultural but also an environmental purpose.[56] The agricultural aims were incidental, and therefore

50. Case C-355/10 European Parliament v Council (Border Surveillance), at 89.
51. *Ibid*, at 90.
52. See also point 2 of the operative part, where the Court 'Maintains the effects of decision 2010/252 until the entry into force of new rules within a reasonable time'. The new proposal COM(2013) 197 was formally approved in a Council vote on 13.5.2014: Council document 9814/14, 13 May 2014.
53. Joined Cases C-164/97 and C-165/97 EP v Council (Regulations protecting the forests, choice of policy legal bases) [1999] ECR I-1139.
54. Council Regulation (EC) No 307/97 of 17 February 1997 amending Regulation (EEC) No 3528/86 on the protection of the Community's forests against atmospheric pollution and Council Regulation (EC) No 308/97 of 17 February 1997 amending Regulation (EEC) No 2158/92 on protection of the Community's forests against fire.
55. Joined Cases C-164/97 and C-165/97 EP v Council (Regulations protecting the forests, choice of policy legal bases) [1999] ECR I-1139 at 3.
56. *Ibid*, at 13. See also 9–11 and 17–18 for the nomenclature debate on trees and forests.

the environment was the appropriate legal basis.[57] Since the choice of procedures meant the EP prerogatives, and therefore 'essential procedural requirements' had been violated, the measures were annulled.[58]

The Council requested, and Parliament agreed with, a temporal modification to suspend the effects of the annulment 'until such time as new rules have been adopted on the appropriate legal basis'.[59] It was appropriate because 'the full effect of … annulment might be seriously detrimental to the progress of action undertaken in the Member States, with the support of the Community, for protection of the environment.'[60] The court stipulated a 'reasonable' period for new regulations with the same subject-matter.[61]

In the second case, *EP and Denmark v Commission*,[62] the Court annulled provisions that prevented the use of particular hazardous substances in the Union.[63] The Commission had adopted these in a procedure which was contrary to the conditions set in the parent directive.[64] In this case, unlike most temporal modification cases, the applicants and interveners opposed the request that the effects of the provision should be maintained.[65] The defence had not included this in the written pleadings and should in any event have known that the substance had been prohibited by the EU legislature.[66] However, the temporal modification was at the complete discretion of the Court, which read Article 231 EC to allow it to make such a ruling ex officio.[67] It considered that the dispute concerned the drafting procedure of the parent directive, and the complexity of the drafting required that 'the effects of the annulled provision be maintained, on grounds of legal certainty'.[68] A specific end-date was provided.[69]

57. *Ibid*, at 16.
58. *Ibid*, at 20.
59. *Ibid*, at 21.
60. *Ibid*, at 22.
61. *Ibid*, at 24 point 2, operative part.
62. C-14/06 and 295/06 *EP and Denmark v Commission*, at 82–86.
63. Point 2 of the Annex to Commission Decision 2005/717/EC of 13 October 2005 amending for the purposes of adapting to technical progress the Annex to Directive 2002/95/EC of the European Parliament and of the Council on the restriction of the use of certain hazardous substances in electrical and electronic equipment.
64. C-14/06 and 295/06 *EP and Denmark v Commission* at 76; Directive 2002/95/EC of the European Parliament and of the Council on the restriction of the use of certain hazardous substances in electrical and electronic equipment, article 5(1).
65. C-14/06 and 295/06 *EP and Denmark v Commission* at 83.
66. *Ibid.*
67. *Ibid*, at 85.
68. *Ibid*, at 86.
69. The deadline was set as 30 June 2008, only three months from the date of the judgment. C-14/06 and 295/06 *EP and Denmark v Commission*, at 86.

2.4. Convenience Over Legality? The Formal Legal Basis Case Law

A conspicuous proportion of cases where an annulment action is successful but the temporal effects of the judgment are modified, involves legal basis litigation between the institutions. Here the institutions have long had a practice of requesting both annulment and the maintenance in force of the contested measure.[70] The court often obliges. The parties should, in many of these cases, have been well aware of the risk that the legal basis for measures was incorrect. The applicant institution typically inserts such a statement into the relevant legislative file, notes that its approval of the substance does not imply acceptance of a legal basis which it disputes, and later contests the measure before the Court of Justice. Thus, the argument that an institution or Member State should be allowed to rely on prospective validity are not always founded on particularly legitimate expectations.

Whilst the list of these cases is long, a sample of recent cases illustrates that they have constitutional implications. In *Commission v Council (Information exchange concerning road traffic offences)*,[71] the Grand Chamber took what may have been a decisive step in facilitating a broad range of police and judicial cooperation measures in the context of substantive policy legal bases. It found that a directive on information exchange on road traffic offences could be adopted on the basis of the Union's transport policy legal basis rather than the police cooperation provisions in Article 87 TFEU. This meant the applicability of the cooperation measure also to Denmark, the UK and Ireland. The Court found that 'the annulment of the directive without maintaining its effects could have negative consequences for European Union transport policy'.[72] It was also a mitigating circumstance that many Member states had already transposed the directive, and therefore legal certainty called for the maintenance of the unlawful obligation to do so.[73]

The consequences and circumstances of the legal basis temporal effects decisions vary somewhat, but the reasoning typically involves the effectiveness of the unlawful provisions and legal certainty for actors who have taken steps in furtherance of the measures. The case law includes relatively benign

70. See however C-271/94 at 37, where the applicant opposed this but the request was nevertheless granted in respect of measures taken on the basis of the annulled instrument which was *not* maintained.
71. C-43/12 *Commission v Council*, Judgment of the Grand Chamber of 6 May 2014, not yet reported.
72. 54. See also paragraph 2 of the operative part, providing a 12-month time limit.
73. 55–56.

cases on statistic collecting,[74] but also large financial commitments in the form of the International Fund for Ireland[75]and EIB guarantees cases.[76] Economic implications are often the main justification, and are considered separately below.

2.5. *Pacta sunt servanda?* International Agreements and the Union's Credibility

In the context of external action, the rationale for maintaining legal effects is time-honoured, and concerns protecting the credibility of the Union as an international actor. Unlike claims of certainty and legitimate expectations, a *pacta sunt servanda* argument could be based directly on the text of the Treaties: Article 216(2) TFEU provides that agreements concluded by the EU are binding on its institutions and Member States. International law governs the repudiation of agreements, and in this respect, the Court appears to recognize the legal force of those international obligations. Many of the cases have a formal procedural dimension, in that they are debates on the proper legal basis of measures which the applicant institutions accept in substance.

The judgment in the *Conditional Access Convention Signature* is one such case.[77] This involved the annulment of a Council Decision[78] on the signing of the Council of Europe Conditional Access Convention.[79] Here, the Commission and Council disagreed on the substantive legal basis that enabled the Union to participate. If it was the Common Commercial Policy, as the Commission and EP argued, then Member States would be precluded from participating on account of its exclusive nature. The Council argued that the appropriate substantive legal basis was instead Article 216(1) TFEU implied external dimensions of Article 114 (Internal market). The legal framework established by the Convention was substantively very similar to an internal

74. C-271/94 *EP v Council (Statistics on interstate trade and 235 EC)* [1996] ECR I-1689, at 40. But see a similar legal basis dispute revisited in C-490/10 *Parliament v Council*, Judgment of 6 September 2012, concerning statistics on the energy sector, at 91–92.
75. C-166/07 *EP v Council* (International Fund for Ireland), at 70–75.
76. C-155/07 *EP v Council EIB Guarantees*, at 86–89.
77. Case C-137/12 *Commission v Council (Conditional Access Convention)*, judgment of the Grand Chamber of 22 October 2013, not yet reported.
78. Council Decision 2011/853/EU: Council Decision of 29 November 2011 on the signing, on behalf of the Union, of the European Convention on the legal protection of services based on, or consisting of, conditional access.

    The European Convention on the legal protection of services based on, or consisting of, conditional access, 24 January 2001.
79. European Convention on the legal protection of services based on, or consisting of, conditional access.

market directive.[80] Exporting this to the entire European continent, and therefore facilitating trade in services,[81] was the primary aim of the Convention,[82] and therefore properly within the CCP.[83] Ancillary provisions, even where they went beyond the scope of the original directive, did not detract from that finding.[84]

The Grand Chamber declared the decision void, but maintained its effects for up to 6 months into the future to enable a new decision to be adopted.[85] In the circumstances of this case, maintaining the right of the Union to sign the agreement, as the temporal effects decision does, seems a sensible option since its powers to sign were not in doubt whereas the power of the Member States to do so as the incorrect legal basis implied, was lacking.

Not all of the decisions in this line of cases are obviously formalities.[86] The credibility of external undertakings was also at stake in the EIB Investment Guarantees and International Funds for Ireland case law, where the value of the undertakings was of national or international significance.[87] In Commission v Council (legal basis of external transport agreements),[88] the defect was not purely formal since a change in voting method, as required by the judgment, could affect the content of the act adopted.[89] Nevertheless, both the applicant (Commission) and the defendant (Council) requested a temporal limitation.[90] The Court noted that international agreements 'cannot

80. Directive 98/84 of the European Parliament and of the Council of 20 November 1998 on the legal protection of services based on, or consisting of, conditional access OJ L 320 p. 5457, based on ex-95 EC, the predecessor of 114 TFEU. C-137/12 *Commission v Council (Conditional Access Convention)*, at 59.
81. Case C-137/12 *Commission v Council (Conditional Access Convention)*, judgment of the Grand Chamber of 22.10.2013, not yet reported at paragraph 67.
82. *Ibid*, at 63.
83. *Ibid*, at 65.
84. *Ibid*, at 71. The provisions could in another context perhaps be classified as police cooperation requirements under legal bases found in the Union's Title on the 'area of freedom, security and justice'.
85. Case C-137/12 *Commission v Council (Conditional Access Convention)*, judgment of the Grand Chamber of 22 October 2013, not yet reported at 80–8. The statement in Case C-21/94 *European Parliament v Council (Road Taxes)* [1995] ECR I-01827, at paragraph 33, denying jurisdiction to impose a time limit in annulment actions, must be read as only preventing an injunction compelling the EU legislature to do so.
86. See also e.g. C-370/07 *Commission v Council (CITES Convention)* [2009] ECR I-8917, at 64–65, where the decision concerned an expression of common intent which had already been made.
87. See below, the 'economic interests opposed to annulment'.
88. C-211/01 *Commission v Council (legal basis of external transport agreements)* [2003] ECR I-8913, at 54–57
89. *Ibid*, at 52.
90. *Ibid*, at 54.

be amended unilaterally, without new negotiations being undertaken by the contracting parties'[91]. The parties did not, however, intend to renegotiate the agreement.[92] Therefore the effects of the contested decisions were maintained 'until the measures necessary to implement' the judgment were adopted.[93]

Some of the external agreements have direct fundamental rights implications. Thus, when the *Passenger Name Records* judgment annulled the PNR agreement with the United States but maintained its effects, it legitimated the transfer of data to security organizations without valid data protection arrangements. Here, too, the reasoning was based on the Union's international commitments: The unlawful agreement itself provided a 90-day renunciation period, which the court thought the Union could not avoid simply because the agreement was contrary to its own law.[94]

2.6. Significant Economic Interests Opposed to Annulment

Legal certainty, namely the protection of the economic interests of the parties who would suffer from annulment is explicitly at hand in many cases where temporal effects are modified. The specific circumstances are diverse: they have concerned external trade rules,[95] insufficient anti-dumping duties,[96] insufficient subsidies,[97] the legal basis of derogations from internal market measures,[98] as well as external payments to international funds[99] and the validity of European Investment Bank guarantees.[100] The annulment of EU budget items can also fall within this category.[101] A common thread uniting the case law is that a third party will already have relied on the unlawful measures, and its legitimate expectations or legal certainty is cited as a reason for

91. *Ibid*, at 55.
92. *Ibid*, at 56.
93. *Ibid*, at 57.
94. Case C-317/04 and 318/04 (Passenger Name Records) [2006] ECR I-04721, at para 73.
95. Case 275/87 *Commission v Council (temporary importation of containers based on 235 EC) (sum pub)* [1989] ECR 259; C-178/03 Commission v EP (Regulation concerning the export and import of dangerous chemicals) [2006] ECR I-107 at 64–65.
96. Case 264/82 *Timex v Council and Commission (anti-dumping duty)* [1985] ECR 849, at 32.
97. C-310/04 *Spain v Council (Cotton subsidies)*, at 140–141.
98. C-414/04 *EP v Council (legal basis of derogations from the EC electricity market)* [2006] ECR I-1129, at 58–59.
99. C-155/07 *EP v Council (EIB Guarantees)* [2008] ECR I-8103, at 87–89.
100. C-166/07 *EP v Council (International Fund for Ireland)* [2009] ECR I-7135, at 73–75.
101. Case C-106/96 *United Kingdom v Commission (combatting social exclusion)* [1998] ECR I-2729, paragraphs 39–42; Case 22/96 *Parliament v Council (Telematic networks funding)* [1998] ECR I-03231.

maintaining the effects of the measures.[102] In many, the legislature is asked to comply within a 'reasonable' time.[103]

Timex[104] illustrates the justification for maintaining these measures. The contested measure concerned anti-dumping duties which were imposed on competitors of Timex by a Regulation.[105] Timex raised arguments that the duties were determined incorrectly and were too low, that it was refused information that it was entitled to under the procedure, and that no adequate statement of reasons accompanied the refusal.[106] The failure to provide adequate information constituted a breach of essential procedural requirements laid down in the parent regulation.[107] However, as the aim of the action was not to annul the entire duty but to have a more strict duty imposed, the duty which was procedurally invalid was nevertheless maintained, 'until the competent institutions adopt the measures needed[…]'.[108]

In some cases, Member State budgets are also protected. In *Commission v EP and Council (Special non-contributory benefits)*[109] the court annulled the approval of specific provisions which prevented beneficiaries of EU-regulated social security benefits from 'exporting' those benefits.[110] However, it concluded that one of these could have been lawfully included in another list, and maintained this provision in force until such a time as it could be included in the EU legislation: Annulling this provision could lead to the grant of the

102. The Students' Residence directive case also focusses on rights granted to the beneficiaries of the annulled instrument, but these are third parties: C-295/90 *EP v Council (Students' Residence based on 235 EC)* [1992] ECR I-4593 at 22–24.
103. E.g. C-178/03 at 65, C-310/04, at 141.
104. Case 264/82 *Timex v Council and Commission (anti-dumping duty)* [1985] ECR 849.
105. Council Regulation (EEC) No 1882/82 of 12 July 1982 imposing a definitive anti-dumping duty on mechanical wrist-watches originating in the USSR.
106. Case 264/82 *Timex v Council and Commission (anti-dumping duty)* [1985] ECR 849, at 18.
107. Council Regulation 3017/79 of 20 December 1979 on protection against dumped or subsidized imports from countries not members of the European Economic Community, Article 7(4)(a). Case 264/82 *Timex v Council and Commission (anti-dumping duty)* [1985] ECR 849, at 31.
108. Case 264/82 *Timex v Council and Commission (anti-dumping duty)* [1985] ECR 849, at 32.
109. Case C-299/05 *Commission v Parliament and Council* [2007] ECR I-08695.
110. C-299/05 *Commission v EP and Council (Social security and special non-contributory benefits)* [2007] ECR I-8695, concerning point 2 of Annex I to Regulation (EC) No 647/2005 of the European Parliament and of the Council of 13 April 2005 amending Council Regulations (EEC) No 1408/71 on the application of social security schemes to employed persons, to self-employed persons and to members of their families moving within the Community and (EEC) No 574/72 laying down the procedure for implementing Regulation (EEC) No 1408/71 under the headings 'FINLAND', (b), 'SWEDEN', (c), and 'UNITED KINGDOM', (d) to (f).

benefit which could have been lawfully excluded 'to an unspecified number of recipient throughout the European Union'.[111] The temporal effects were modified 'for a reasonable period'.[112]

2.7. Staff Rules: Appointment and Pay for Classes of Persons

Staff remuneration case law is also linked to economic questions, but on the scale of individual civil servants, albeit entire classes of them, rather than economic entities. The first documented case where an annulment action resulted in prospective annulment involved staff pay regulations.[113] The Commission sought the annulment of a salary adjustment regulation for EU civil servants[114] that was not in line with a previous decision on the method of calculation[115] or the Staff Regulations' requirement to review remuneration each year in the light of a report on the development of pay and conditions in the Union.[116] The court found the Council was bound to observe its decision on the method of calculation[117] and failed to justify departing from it.[118] Thus, the more limited increase the Council had approved was declared void.[119] The Court then maintained the effects of the annulled regulation until a new regulation was passed 'to avoid discontinuity in the system of remuneration'.[120] Staff pay disputes continue to be litigated today, with similar circumstances and reasoning.[121]

111. C-299/05 *Commission v EP and Council (Social security and special non-contributory benefits)*, at 74.
112. *Ibid*, at 75.
113. Case 81/72 *Commission v Council (Staff regulations on remuneration)* [1973] ECR 575 at 15.
114. Council Regulation 2647/72 of 12 December 1973 adjusting the remuneration and pensions of the officials of the European Communities and other servants of those Communities.
115. Council Decision of 20 and 21 March 1972. Case 81/72 *Commission v Council (Staff regulations on remuneration)* [1973] ECR 575, at 4–5.
116. Regulation No 95/70 Staff Regulations of officials and the conditions of employment of other servants of the European Communities, Article 65.
117. Case 81/72 *Commission v Council (Staff regulations on remuneration)* [1973] ECR 575, at 9.
118. *Ibid*, at 11.
119. *Ibid*, at 14.
120. *Ibid*, at 15.
121. See i.a. C-40/10 *Commission v Council (Staff regulations)* [2010] ECR I-12043, C-63/12 *Commission v Council*, judgment of the Grand Chamber of 13 November 2013, C-66/12 *Commission v Council*, judgment of the Grand Chamber of 13 November 2013, C-196/12 *Commission v Council*, judgment of the Grand Chamber of 19 November 2013; C-453/12 *Commission v Council*, Action brought on 9 October 2012, pending; C-86/13 *Commission v Council*, Action brought on 20 February 2013, pending.

In one case, an entire class of appointments is called into question. *Italy v Commission (EPSO)*[122] is notable in that the court permanently kept in force a decision that was unlawful because it was not appropriately published in all of the languages. As is well-known, the Union has an official policy of linguistic diversity, resulting in over 20 equally authentic versions of legislative texts. However, it also has an unofficial policy of working languages, in practice widely spoken languages of some early large Member States.[123] This unofficial policy has been strengthened for example in the context of agencies, some of which may work in only one language. In recent years, Italy and Spain have queried why their official languages are not also among the working languages.[124]

In *EPSO*, Italy argued that it was wrong to publish full notices for competitions in only the three working languages of English, French and German, to require knowledge of at least one of these and then hold all of the selection proceedings in those languages.[125] The General Court had come to the conclusion that the practice was lawful.[126] This was not, however, in line with Regulation 1/58[127] which provided that the Official Journal is to be published in all the official languages.[128] Not publishing these in all the official languages granted an unfair advantage to some candidates.[129] Article 1 of Regulation 1/58 also provides that the Union's languages are not only official languages, but also working languages of its institutions.[130] It provides no grounds for derogation that would allow a choice of second language to be limited.[131] Vague arguments about the interests of the service[132] were not sufficient to constitute a statement of reasons that could be subject to judicial review.[133]

122. Case C-566/10 P *Italy v Commission*, judgment of the Grand Chamber of 27 November 2012.
123. See for example the Commission's own estimates of document drafting languages, reporting English as dominant over the distant but closest competitors French and German.
124. See e.g. the failed annulment action of Italy and Spain against the establishment of the European Patent Office: Joined Cases C-274/11 and C-295/11 *Italy v Council* and *Spain v Council*, Judgment of the Grand Chamber 16 April 2013.
125. Case C-566/10 P *Italy v Commission*, judgment of the Grand Chamber of 27 November 2012, at 15. Brief summaries were later published in all official languages.
126. *Ibid*, at 16.
127. Regulation 1/58 EEC Council: Regulation No 1 determining the languages to be used by the European Economic Community.
128. Case C-566/10 P, at 71.
129. *Ibid*, at 74–76.
130. *Ibid*, at 81.
131. *Ibid*, at 85.
132. *Ibid*, at 91.
133. *Ibid*, at 98.

In the case, the competitions had been concluded, and were first challenged, in 2007. By the time of the final judgment annulling the notices was issued, more than five years had elapsed. It is understandable that annulling the legal basis for hiring and maintaining the winners of that competition could be problematic. AG Kokott noted that the established line of analogous cases concerning staff competitions provided a solution: support the legitimate expectations of selected candidates, but make no decision on the effects for unselected candidates.[134] This solution was adopted by the Court.[135]

3. The Legal Framework for Temporal Effects

3.1. Textual Justifications in Treaty Provisions

The Court clearly has some constitutional authority to modify the temporal effects of its annulment actions. However, *pro futuro* decisions to extend the effects of unlawful acts into the future are not obviously based on literal readings of the relevant Treaty provisions. The question is whether 'definitive' effects can also be declared into the future. Before the Lisbon Treaty, Article 231 EC, concerning the temporal effects of annulment actions, read:

> 'If the action is well founded, the Court of Justice shall declare the act concerned to be void.
>
> In the case of a regulation, however, the Court of Justice shall, if it considers this necessary, state which of the effects of the regulation which it has declared void shall be considered definitive'.

Despite the text, annulment based on this provision could already during this period modify the temporal dimension of invalidity for instruments other than regulations.[136] The new provision in Article 264 TFEU approves this practice:

> 'If the action is well founded, the Court of Justice shall declare the act concerned to be void.
>
> However, the Court shall, if it considers this necessary, state which of the effects of the act which it has declared void shall be considered definitive'.

134. AG Kokott, at 115–116, citing referring to Case C-242/90 P *Commission v Albani and Others* [1993] ECR I-3839, at 13 and 14.
135. Case C-566/10 P, at 103.
136. E.g. Case C-295/90, *EP v Council (Student residence)* [1992] E.C.R. I-4193, at para. 8; referring to then Article 174(2) of the EEC Treaty. Here, too, the Court maintained the instrument 'for the time being'.

The change does little to provide greater support for the practice of maintaining annulled acts into the future, since the revised provision continues to refer to acknowledging 'definitive' effects. Articles 267 TFEU (on preliminary references), or 277 TFEU (the 'plea of illegality') give no further guidance on this point. Article 267 merely refers to jurisdiction to give rulings on 'the validity and interpretation of acts of the institutions [...]'. Article 277 only confirms the right of 'any party' to plead the illegality of a Union act on the same grounds as could apply to a direct annulment action regardless of whether a similar plea would be out of time for the purposes of a direct action, without stating the effects of that declaration.[137] Judgments on the annulment of regulations are not enforceable before they become final, but this set of provisions should not be interpreted as encouraging prospective legal effects beyond the context of the procedural provision.[138]

3.2. The General Rule: *ex tunc* Effects in Preliminary References

The general rule in preliminary reference cases is that the interpretation applies retrospectively. When national courts apply Union law, interpretations given by the Court of Justice in preliminary references are typically applied *ex tunc*, from the date the measure entered into force, rather than the later date at which that measure was interpreted.[139] In a small minority of cases, the judgment limits its own temporal effects.[140] That is also the case as regards declarations of invalidity made in the context of preliminary references, where *ex tunc* invalidity appears the rule.[141] Thus, a 2013 judgment may well develop an interpretation which is applied to facts from 1999, or

137. A plea of illegality can be raised in both types of procedures, illustrated by the judgment in Case C-583/11 P *Inuit Tapiriit Kanatami v EP*, Judgment of the Grand Chamber of 3 October 2013, not yet reported, at 93.
138. Rules of Procedure, Article 60, second paragraph, and Article 56, first paragraph.
139. For early applications and references see J Raitio, *The Principle of Legal Certainty in EC Law* (Kluwer: Deventer, 2003), 188–190 and 195–200.
140. The restriction must also be imposed in the same case where the interpretation is first made: Case C-262/96 *Sürül v Bundesanstalt für Arbeit* [1999] ECR I-2685, paragraph 109, criticised in W Alexander, 'Temporal Effects of Preliminary Rulings', 8(1) *Yearbook of European Law* (1988) 11–26 at 25. D. Anderson, and M. Demetriou, *References to the European Court* (2nd ed., Sweet and Maxwell: London, 2002), at 345. For a review of key authorities, K. Lenaerts, *Procedural Law of the European Union* (2nd edn, Sweet and Maxwell: London, 2006), at 196–199 or K. Lenaerts, I. Maselis, K. Gutman, and J. Nowak (eds), *EU Procedural Law* (Oxford University Press, 2014), at 248–249.
141. See also Case C-228/92 *Roquette Freres* [1994] ECR I-1445, para 17. M. Broberg and N. Fenger, *Preliminary References to the European Court of Justice* (Oxford University Press, 2010), at 446. See also A. Ward, *Judicial Review and the Rights of Private Parties in EU Law* (2nd ed, Oxford University Press, 2007), at 354, noting the default position of stating ex tunc effect has developed in the early 1980s, noting that in earlier case law, the

indeed 1973.[142] A declaration of invalidity can be retrospective even if the validity of that provision had previously been approved.[143]

3.3. Departing From *ex tunc* Effects in Preliminary References

Some Advocate Generals[144] and academic commentators[145] have argued for an *ex nunc* approach to declarations of invalidity. However, departures from the *ex tunc* approach remain rare in the context of preliminary rulings.[146] The Court of Justice itself views instances where it resorts to limiting the temporal effect of its judgments exceptional.[147] If a temporal exception is applied, two key conditions must be satisfied. Those concerned should have acted in good faith.[148] There should be a risk of serious difficulties.[149] Neither the financial consequences of a ruling for Member States[150] nor the long-standing perceived[151] or actual complicity of an EU institution in approving a practice

---

Court's lack of express statements to that effect made the temporal status of the annulled measure subject to debate. See e.g. Case 23/75 *Rey Soda v Cassa Conguaglio Zucchero* [1975] ECR 1279; Case 114/76 *Bela-Mühle Josef Bergmann KF v Grows-Farm GmbH* [1977] ECR 1211; Case 130/79 *Express Dairy Foods Limited v Intervention Board for Agricultural Produce* [1980] ECR 1887. Recently, Joined Cases C-293/12 *Digital Rights Ireland and Seitlinger and others,* Judgment of 8. April 2014, not yet reported.

142. See e.g. the saga leading to C-362/12 *Franked Investment Income III*, Judgment of the Third Chamber of 12 December 2013, not yet reported, especially Case C-446/04 *Test Claimants in the FII Group Litigation* [2006] ECR I-11753 and Case C-35/11 *Test Claimants in the FII Group Litigation* 13 November 2012, not yet reported (FII 2).
143. See in particular joined Cases C-293/12 *Digital Rights Ireland and Seitlinger and others,* Judgment of 8. April 2014, not yet reported.
144. Case 16/65, *Schwarze v Einfuhr-und Vorratstelle für Getreide* [1965] ECR 891, AG Gand at 899, arguing that giving wider effects would be contrary to the strict time limits for annulment actions.
145. G. Bebr, 'Preliminary Rulings of the Court of Justice: Their Authority and Temporal Effect', 18 *Common Market Law Review* (1981) 475–507 at 499–502.
146. See Donatas Murauskas, 'The Temporal Limitation by the Court of Justice of the EU: Dealing with the Consequences', 2(6) *European Journal of Legal Studies* (2013) 78–95 at 86–88 for some statistics. Muraskas considers six cases after Case 43/75 *Defrenne v Sabena II* [1976] ECR 455 where a preliminary ruling is not applicable ex tunc, most recently Case C-437/97 *EKW and Wein & Co* [2000] ECR I-01157.
147. For example C-263/11 *Ainārs Rēdlihs v Valsts ieņēmumu dienests*, judgment of the second chamber, 19.7.2012, not yet reported, at 59, and C-525/11, *Mednis SIA* Judgment of 18 October 2012, not yet reported, at 42.
148. Case 43/75 Defrenne, paragraph 73.
149. For example, C-313/05 *Maciej Brzeziński v Dyrektor Izby Celnej w Warszawie,* [2007] ECR I-00513 at 56, with references; in literature, K. Lenaerts, I. Maselis, K. Gutman, and J. Nowak (eds), *EU Procedural Law* (Oxford University Press, 2014) at 249–256.
150. C-263/11 at 59–61.
151. A lack of infringement proceedings does not imply legality: C-577/08 *Brouwer* [2010] ECR I-7489, para 39.

automatically leads to such a conclusion.[152] The temporal restriction must also be sought in the case where the interpretation is made: a later case turning on the same rule cannot be restricted to future facts.[153]

3.4. Temporal Effects of Annulment Actions: *ex tunc* and Exceptions

The same general approach to favour legality and immediate effect might be expected in the context of annulment actions. At first glance, this is so: complete *ex tunc* annulment is seen as the typical approach in annulment actions since at least the early 1970s.[154] However, the practice of extending the legal effects of unlawful acts[155] can also be identified nearly concurrently with the development of the main line of cases toward *ex tunc* effects.[156]

3.5. Relationship Between Invalidity and Follow-on Consequences

When considering the need for a temporal modification, it should be noted that annulment does not necessarily always call into question the validity of implementing national legislation.[157] In the simplest case involving the direct transposition of a directive by a discrete national measure, the directive obliges Member States to act but it is unusual for the directive to determine the authority of the legislature to act.[158] Taking away the obligation to act does not necessarily invalidate the power to do so, although as the fundamental rights case law shows, the same reasons can also call for the invalidation of the national acts.[159] The Court of Justice has generally upheld the finality of

152. Famously, Case C-415/95 *Bosman* [1995] ECR I-04921, where the Commission had approved a directly discriminatory 3+2 nationality rule in European league football.
153. Case C-292/04, *Meilicke and others,* [2007] ECR I-1835, at 32–41.
154. E.g. G. Bebr, 'Direct and Indirect Judicial Control of Community Acts in Practice: The Relation between Articles 173 and 177 of the EEC Treaty European Communities', 82 *Michigan Law Review* (1984) 1229–1249 at 1239, referring to Case 22/70 *Commission v Council (AETR/ERTA)* [1971] ECR 263.
155. For an early example, Case 81/72 *Commission v Council* [1973] ECR 575 at 13 and 15. This already involved indefinite effects.
156. Recently, K. Lenaerts, I. Maselis, K. Gutman, and T. Nowak (eds), *EU Procedural Law* (Oxford University Press, 2014) at 413, citing Case 22/70 *Commission v Council (AETR/ ERTA)* [1971] ECR 263 at 59–60 and Joined Cases 97, 193, 99 and 215/86 *Asteris and Others v Commission* [1988] ECR 2181 at 30.
157. Thomas Vandamme, *The Invalid Directive: The Legal Authority of a Union Act Requiring Domestic Law Making* (Europa Law: Groeningen, 2005).
158. See, however, instances where delegated regulations are made based on the combination of a national empowering law and the specific mandate provided in the EU instrument.
159. Look for example, at the effects of the Court's ruling in Joined Cases C-293/12 and C-594/12 *Digital Rights Ireland and Seitlinger* and Others, Judgment of 8 April 2014, not yet reported.

national judicial and administrative acts even where they are contrary to EU law.[160] Nor is it obvious that a national or Union authority that has acted in pursuit of an act which is later annulled has committed a 'sufficiently serious breach' that leads to liability.[161]

4. The 'Access to Justice' Case for *ex tunc* Annulment Actions

Ex tunc effects for annulment actions can be justified with the need to ensure access to justice. The Court of Justice of the European Union has in practice enforced its exclusive jurisdiction to examine the validity of EU measures. In order to have access to this legality review, an applicant's argument must reach the Court. Second, the possibility of doing so is extremely limited in direct actions. This means that the Union institutions and, much more rarely, Member States are the principal applicants when the validity of general legislative measures is challenged. Third, even where the CJEU does declare EU measures invalid, this does not always have direct impacts on a legal framework which relies on national implementing measures or separate legal acts such as judicial decisions. The access to justice case is most apparent in the context of fundamental rights protection, but can equally be made in the context of less sensitive legality review. A basic legality issue argues against *ex nunc* and *pro futuro* effects: Can there be a fair trial, or access to a court, under either the European Convention on Human Rights or the Charter of Fundamental Rights, if the applicant can never receive an effective legal remedy?[162]

4.1. Exclusive Jurisdiction of the Court of Justice

This difficulty exists principally because the Court of Justice of the European Union seeks to assert its own jurisdiction to determine the validity of EU legal acts, to the exclusion of other judicial recourse.[163] It alone is empowered

160. See the *Kapferer* line of cases, Case C-234/04, *Kapferer* [2006] ECR I-2585, at 20, recently C-221/10 P, Artegodan GmbH, Judgment of 19 April 2012, not yet reported, at 86.

161. Case C-224/01 *Gerhard Köbler v Republik Österreich* [2003] ECR I-10239, C-173/03 *Traghetti del Mediterraneo*, [2006] ECR I-5177.

162. See Article 6 and 13 ECtHR, Article 47 Charter of Fundamental Rights.

163. Jurisdiction is divided between the Court of Justice and the General Court under Article 256 TFEU and Article 51 of the Statute of the Court of Justice. For the rebukes when Member States' judicial systems attempt this, see e.g. Case C-314/08, *Krzysztof Filipiak v Dyrektor Izby Skarbowej w Poznaniu* [2009] ECR I-11049 and C-409/06 *Winner Wetten* [2010] ECR I-08015. However, recently C-41/11 *Inter-Environnement Wallonie*

to decide direct actions for annulment[164] and indirect pleas of illegality which arise in the context of a preliminary reference.[165] Under the *Foto-Frost* rule, a national court may not presume the invalidity of a Union act, but must refer any such question to the Court of Justice.[166] Nor, under the *TWD* rule, can an applicant that could undoubtedly have directly challenged an EU act later indirectly plead its invalidity.[167] For those actors, an immediate annulment action may be the only recourse. In almost all cases, national courts must disapply national law.[168] National courts typically tend to avoid direct conflicts with the Court,[169] preferring instead to question the validity of national implementing legislation where relevant.[170] Calls for national courts to review EU secondary legislation, particularly in order to ensure the effective protection of fundamental rights,[171] have mostly been ignored.

4.2. Direct Actions are Subject to Strict Conditions

Actions for annulment are further complicated by the strict conditions linked to time limits and standing. Article 263 sets a two-month time limit for actions. Those acts that are not challenged within the 2-month time limit cannot later

ASBL and Terre wallonne ASBL v Region wallone, Judgment of the Grand Chamber of 28 February 2012, not yet reported, at 62–63 for conditions applicable to the exceptional cases where the CJEU permits maintaining national measures contrary to EU law when they pursue the same objectives.

164. Article 263 of the Treaty on the Functioning of the European Union (TFEU).
165. Article 277 TFEU.
166. Case 314/85 *Foto-Frost v Hauptzollamt Lübeck-Ost* [1987] ECR 4199 at 11–20.
167. The 'TWD Deggendorf rule': Case C-188/92 *TWD Textilwerke Deggendorf GmbH* [1994] ECR I-833.
168. E.g. Joined Cases C-10/97 to C-22/97 *Ministero delle Finanze / IN.CO.GE.'90 and others*, ECR 1998 I-6307, concerning later national law. For a recent exception, where the CJEU permitted the national court to maintain a measure that was adopted contrary to EU law, C-41/11, noted above.
169. For a prominent exception, see Komárek, Jan, 'Czech constitutional court playing with matches: the Czech constitutional court declares a judgment of the court of justice of the EU ultra vires; judgment of 31 January 2012, Pl. ÚS 5/12, Slovak Pensions XVII', 8(2) *European Constitutional Law Review* (2012) 323–337.
170. See e.g. Georgios Anagnostaras, 'Activation of the Ultra Vires Review: The Slovak Pensions Judgment of the Czech Constitutional Court', 14(7) *German Law Journal* (2013) 959–973. Thomas Beukers, 'Case C-409/06, Winner Wetten GmbH v. Bürgermeisterin der Stadt Bergheim, Judgment of the Court (Grand Chamber) of 8 September 2010, not yet reported', 48(6) *Common Market Law Review* (2011) 1985–2004 at 1992–1993.
171. Dorota Leczyciewicz, 'Effective Judicial Protection of Human Rights After Lisbon: Should National Courts Be Empowered to Review EU Secondary Law?', 35 *European Law Review* (2010) 326–348.

be indirectly challenged by non-privileged parties[172] if it is 'beyond doubt'[173] that they had standing to bring a direct action.[174] Article 263 TFEU also provides the notorious 'direct and individual concern' test under which few non-institutional actors have standing to challenge legal acts.[175] The Court of Justice prohibits national courts from reviewing the validity of such acts, applies extremely strict time limits to annulment actions, and rarely finds that 'non-privileged' applicants have standing to directly challenge EU acts. The plea to take annulment seriously is all the more compelling since standing is so tightly controlled.

4.3. Who Protects Fundamental Rights?

The access to justice argument becomes most acute when the annulment action concerns a case with obvious fundamental rights concerns. Some authors have proposed that the complete lack of such protection calls for empowering national courts to carry out validity review of EU secondary law.[176] The call is no less compelling if the ineffectiveness is caused by temporal modifications in successful annulment applications rather than access to a court in order to plead that case.

5. How Should Decisions on Temporal Effects Weigh Competing Interests?

The lines of case law examined above demonstrate that unlawful instruments are maintained. Their effects are sometimes maintained not only *ex nunc* but

172. For privileged parties, actions against regulations are not limited: C-442/04 *Spain v Council* [2008] ECR I-3517 at 22. Roland Schwensfeier, 'The TWD principle post-Lisbon', 37(2) *European Law Review* (2012) 156–175 at 171–172.
173. On some doubts, see Case C-370/12 *Thomas Pringle*, Judgment of the Full Court of 27 November 2012, not yet reported, at 38–41.
174. Most famously, Case C-188/92 *TWD Textilwerke Deggendorf* [1994] ECR I-833, paragraph 13, and recently, Order of 15 November 2012 in Case C-102/12 P *Städter v European Central Bank*, Order of 15 November 2012, not yet reported, at 12.
175. See in particular the *Plaumann* test for individual concern: 'Applicants must show that the decision affects them by reason of certain attributes which are peculiar to them or by reason of circumstances in which they are differentiated from all other persons and by virtue of these factors distinguishes them individually just as in the case of the person addressed'. *Plaumann v Commission* 25/62 [1963] ECR 199, at 31. S. Peers and Marios Costa, 'Judicial review of EU acts after the Treaty of Lisbon', 8(1) *European Constitutional Law Review* (2012) 82–104 at 97–104 for the present context.
176. Dorota Leczyciewicz, 'Effective Judicial Protection of Human Rights After Lisbon: Should National Courts Be Empowered to Review EU Secondary Law?', 35 *European Law Review* (2010) 326–348.

pro futuro. Regardless of whether the legal framework facilitates sufficient review, the Court of Justice should consider expanding on its reasoning when ruling to maintain the effects of annulled instruments. The reasoning in the judgments explored above is without exception brief, and almost always includes an express consideration of only one interest in favour of the temporal modification. The Treaty does not provide clear criteria for such rulings. The court should therefore develop its reasoning more fully. At the very least, the court should define deadlines rather than refer to reasonable, or no, time limits. The need for these justifications is pressing now that the temporal modification is no longer always in the interest of the applicant or the public interests which they should protect.

5.1. Comparative Studies are Inconclusive

Where, then, should these reasons be identified if not in the Treaty text? Comparative studies are helpful, but inconclusive. Some guidance could be sought from the reasoning of national courts that allow declarations of temporary constitutionality, or pro *futuro* annulment.[177] Pro futuro appears unusual: as de Visser has noted, there is no uniformity in this respect decisions European constitutional courts.[178] Popelier and others have also suggested some criteria for making this decision in the context of a comparative study on interpretative rulings.[179] The current legal framework may not provide guidelines, but this could be an advantage rather than a flaw: the CJEU is relatively free to fashion a coherent doctrine based on the current needs of the Union rather than an inherited legal framework.

177. Maartje de Visser, *Constitutional Review in Europe: A Comparative Analysis* (Hart: Oxford, 2014), at 310–312 and 317–320.

178. *Ibid*, at 317–20: Belgian, French, German, Italian and Spanish Constitutional courts normally have ex tunc effects, whilst those from the Czech Republic, Poland and Hungary in principle invalidate ex nunc, whereas Belgian, German and French practice offers varying reasons for maintaining legal effects pro futuro and the Czech, Polish and Hungarian legal frameworks expressly permit this approach.

179. Patricia Popelier, Sarah Verstraelen, Dirk Vanheule, and Beatrix Vanlerberghe (eds), *The Effects of Judicial Decisions in Time* (Intersentia: Cambridge, 2014), at 5–6: The decision on modifying temporal effects should consider the impact of the rule, the foreseeability of the judicial decision, the special nature of the matter (in particular a fundamental rights connection or retroactive criminalization), whether the judgment departs from established practice or case law, and respect for the legislator's prerogative, i.e. 'the need to meet legitimacy requirements'. However, that study found that 'a recurrent theme [...] is the lack of both criteria and reasons given for deviations from the general rule regarding the temporal effect of a judicial decision.'

5.2. Preliminary Rulings on Invalidity are not Analogous

One obvious comparison should be approached with caution. It is tempting to reason by analogy from the case law where the temporal effects of preliminary rulings are modified. Murauskas has recently catalogued reasoning associated with the perceived consequences of a temporal effects ruling.[180] They are exceptional: the practical consequences of a ruling should not 'diminish the objectivity of the law and compromise its future application'.[181] The Commission's failure to initiate proceedings against Member States also militates in favour of limitation, as it may give rise to an impression of legality.[182] A party arguing for temporal limitation must be in good faith.[183] Previous, similar rulings on the same matter preclude a later temporal limitation.[184] The very large economic repercussions of a ruling have also been cited successfully.[185] Complex and cascading effects of a ruling were successfully raised to limit part of the *Bosman* judgment.[186]

Annulment actions and preliminary rulings involving questions of validity have previously been conflated i.a. in the context of deriving a right to modify temporal effects. It is however not clear that it is equally appropriate to apply this catalogue of reasons by analogy. First, preliminary rulings' modifications are not *pro futuro*, but *ex nunc*. Even then, proactive litigants are rewarded with the benefit of an interpretation even where its effects are otherwise limited *ex nunc*.[187] The very purpose of maintaining the effects of the decision is to avoid changing the position of the applicant. In cases concerning private applicants, this raises the access to justice question. Second, when individuals apply for direct annulment actions, they typically act on their own behalf and thus many of the same principles could be applied. However, the typical annulment action that involves a temporal modification is a case where the institutions or Member States are applicants. Can it really be said that they represent only an institutional, quasi-personal interest, or does their agency for the public benefit modify some of this reasoning? This calls for a stronger

180. Donatas Murauskas, 'The Temporal Limitation by the Court of Justice of the EU: Dealing with the Consequences', 2(6) *European Journal of Legal Studies* (2013) 78–95 at 88–93.
181. *Ibid*, at 89, citing Case 24/86 *Blaizot v Universite de Liege and Others* [1988] ECR 379.
182. Case 43/75 *Defrenne v Sabena II* [1976] ECR 455 and C-437/97 *EKW and Wein & Co* [2000] ECR I-1157. See, however, *Bosman*, where the Commission's express approval of the nationality rule did not lead to a temporal restriction.
183. Case C-288/05 *Stradasfalti* [2006] ECR I-8391, where the Member State evidently was not in applying a temporary derogation for several decades.
184. C-415/95 Bosman.
185. Case 43/75 *Defrenne.*
186. C-415/93 *Bosman.*
187. C-163/90 *Legros* [1992] ECR I-4625.

role for the court, as demonstrated by its ex officio powers to consider temporal effects in the context of annulment.[188]

5.3. Whose Interests Should be Protected?

In some cases, the applicant and indeed the entire class of beneficiaries of an annulment action is thereby placed in a better position than they had been in the case of unconditional and unrestricted annulment. This is so in the staff rules cases, but also annulment actions concerning economic interests and the legal basis of environmental measures. Those seem unproblematic. In other cases, the legitimate expectations of the applicant or third parties are at stake. Here, the reasoning of the court, never more than five paragraphs and rarely in the form of a balancing exercise, would benefit from additional dimensions. Greater discussion now could contribute to legal certainty later.

In the exceedingly rare cases where Member States bring annulment actions, they should be construed as also acting on behalf of persons who are not individually concerned and often cannot challenge the Union measure without first breaking it. Thus, they protect the public interest. So, too, when the Commission acts: it is arguable that the Commission's role as the guardian of the treaties should require it to take particular care to evaluate the public interest in the legality of acts based on the treaties. When a private individual brings a direct annulment action, they will have no recourse to other procedures under the rules developed by the Court of Justice. Here, too, the public interest in legality should be weighed carefully, since access to justice in other venues is limited.

In some cases, conducting this balancing exercise will reveal value judgments that may not be shared by the legislature. In order for the Union's commitments to be credible, it is necessary that its international partners can rely on agreements in most cases. However, when those arrangements have a fundamental rights dimension, it becomes less obvious that the international credibility of the union or the effectiveness of its instruments is always more important than the other, less often expressed, interests with which they should be balanced. Where, one might ask, is the effective legal protection of interests that run counter to such decisions? Credibility as an international actor, legal certainty, and the protection of legitimate expectations could all be cited as reasons *not to maintain* decisions that are unconstitutional. Should

188. That the litigant must also ask for the limitation, apparent in C-423/04 Richards [2006] ECR I-3585, C-57/93 *Vroega v NCIV* [1994] ECR I-4541, C-367/93 *Roders and Others v Inspecteur der Innoverrechten en Accijnzen* [1995] ECR I-2229, does not appear mandatory in the context of annulment: C-14/06 and 295/06 *EP and Denmark v Commission* at 85. The court has even validated daughter instruments that were not the subject of the annulment action: see C-271/94.

international credibility trump federal credibility? Should legal certainty, in many cases, the inertial mass of the existing legislative instrument, trump legality? This seems to emphasize secondary norms over the Union's constitutional structure. The threat of effective annulment could be seen as encouraging independent review of the Union's action. If illegality is a real, rather than only an imagined risk, could this encourage more careful decision-making?

5.4. Towards a Fundamental Rights Dimension?

There are some suggestions the Court of Justice is reconsidering the balance between fundamental rights and legal certainty when considering temporal effects. If so, that would accord with recent European Court of Human Rights jurisprudence. Although the European Court of Human Rights has occasionally recognised the need to maintain legal effects for a limited period,[189] it has recently noted in *Glien v Germany*[190] that this reasoning is more difficult to apply when the violations of human rights involve the right to liberty, as opposed to its earlier views in the context of discriminatory rules of pensions, insurance or tax law.

A similar change could now be underway at the Court of Justice of the European Union. Early signs were not encouraging.[191] However, the Data Retention Directive saga, culminating in the April 2014 *Digital Rights Ireland* judgment, suggests, that change is under way.[192] In this judgment, the Court relied on the Charter of Fundamental Rights to declare the data retention directive[193] invalid.[194] The directive imposed legislative requirements on Member States to ensure the retention of communications data since at the latest 2009,[195] so states that proceeded to amend or maintain

189. E.g. *P.B. and J.S. v Austria* Application 18948/02 Judgment 20 July 2010 at 49, and *Marckx v. Belgium*, 13 June 1979 at 58; on provisional future validity, *Walden v. Liechtenstein* (dec.), no. 33916/96, 16 March 2000; and *J.R. v. Germany* (dec.), no. 22651/93, Decisions and Reports 83-A.
190. *Glien v Germany* Application no. 7345/12 Judgment of 28 November 2013, at paras 101–103.
191. Consider for example the *Passenger Name Records, Kadi I* and *Schengen Border Code* cases, above.
192. Joined Cases C-293/12 *Digital Rights Ireland and Seitlinger and others,* Judgment of 8 April 2014, not yet reported.
193. Directive 2006/24/EC of the European Parliament and of the Council of 15 March 2006 on the retention of data generated or processed in connection with the provision of publicly available electronic communications services or of public communications networks and amending Directive 2002/58/EC.
194. See also Case C-301/06 *Ireland v EP and Council,* [2009] ECR I-00593, where the Court considered the same directive only on formal legal basis grounds.
195. 16 States made an optional declaration under Article 15(3) of the Directive to extend the implementation period from 15 September 2007 under 15(1) to 15 March 2009.

national legislation did so in contravention of the Charter and possibly pre-existing EU secondary legislation, in apparent compliance with the Court's 2009 judgment.[196] The 2014 judgment downplays many of the reasons that are typically cited when maintaining the legal effects of an annulled measure,[197] and ignores Advocate General Villalón's proposals to maintain the effects of the annulled directive.[198]

5.5. Time for a Debate on Temporal Effects?

The Court of Justice should consider explaining its reasoning in future cases that raise the issue of maintaining legal effects. International law and common law jurisdictions have experienced prominent discussions on temporal aspects of judicial decisions.[199] Temporal modification in the context of annulment actions raises some awkward questions that are unusual and also less problematic in other contexts. The practice in the context of annulment actions is not limited to acknowledging the past, but also shapes the future. This creates special constitutional moral hazards. These hazards are especially acute in the contexts of fundamental rights, and are aggravated by the restrictive conditions for bringing annulment actions. There are some encouraging signs that fundamental rights protection is viewed with special care in this context, as the Union's own 'access to justice' doctrine requires. However, that success is qualified. The Court of Justice could contribute greatly to legal certainty simply by elaborating, balancing and applying clear criteria for temporal modification in its case law.

196. Here, there is little doubt Member States were 'implementing' EU law as required under 51(1) CFR, even if this is broadly construed as in Case C-617/10 *Åklagaren v Akerberg Fransson*, Judgment of 26 February 2013, not yet reported.

197. Complete annulment leaves the Union and Member States potentially open to some unprecedented litigation, and creates some awkward situations: Sweden has already been ordered to pay a lump sum payment for failing to implement the directive, and an infringement action is maintained by the Commission against Germany for failing to implement the invalid directive.

198. Joined Cases C-293/12 *Digital Rights Ireland and Seitlinger and others*, Opinion of AG Villalón of 12 December 2013, at 155–158.

199. See e.g. Alan Rodger, 'A Time for Everything under the Law: Some Reflections on Retrospectivity', 121 *Law Quarterly Review* (2005) 57–79; Ben Juratowich, *Retroactivity and the Common Law* (Hart: Oxford, 2008); T.O. Elias, 'The doctrine of intertemporal law', 74 *American Journal of International Law* (1980) 285–307; R. Higgins, 'Time and the Law: International Perspectives on an Old Problem', 46 *International and Comparative Law Quarterly* (1997) 501–520; Alison L. Lacroix, 'Temporal Imperialism', 158 *University of Pennsylvania Law Review* (2010) 1329–1373; William Michael Treanor and Gene B. Sperling, 'Prospective Overruling and the Revival of 'Unconstitutional' Statutes', *Columbia Law Review* (1993) 1902–1955 for a discussion on perhaps the most complex situation where this type of decision is overruled, thus revalidating or reviving the unconstitutional statute.

Jean Monnet, Treaties and Peace in Europe

Ruth Donner[1]

1. Introduction

This article originated from a talk given at a closed Workshop in Vienna entitled 'The "Méthode Monnet" and the Future of Europe'.[2] More particularly, the life and work of Jean Monnet was taken as the common theme in order to pay tribute to a man who had devoted the greater part of his life to developing peaceful relations and cooperation between the States of Europe, so, *inter alia*, earning the title of 'the Father of Europe'. His life's work took many forms, but it must be remembered that Jean Monnet was also the first President of the High Authority of the first European Community, the Coal and Steel Community (ECSC) 1952, out of which developed the present European Union.

The Vienna Workshop is mentioned because Monnet was there quoted as saying he suggested the ECSC because he wanted 'to breach the bulwarks of national sovereignty to an extent that could gain the consent of the States, but would be deep enough to press them for unity.' As a Frenchman born less than two decades after the Franco-Prussian War of 1870–1871, and who had lived through the two devastating World Wars of 1914–1918 and 1939–1945 in Europe, though not always in Europe himself, he was throughout his life mindful of the need to create the conditions necessary for peaceful cooperation. His early training, however, was in marketing the family cognac business abroad and for this he travelled widely before 1914, gaining experience of other peoples and their ways of working with each other. With this background he took part between 1914–1918 in the inter-Allied Executives, confronting primarily the problems of economic organization and

1. M.A. Edinburgh, LL.B. Cantab., LL.M. Harvard, Jur.dr Helsinki. Formerly Adjunct Professor in Public International Law, Faculty of Law, University of Helsinki. Address: Pohjoisranta 12 A 1, FIN-00170 Helsinki.
2. This was organized by Professor Stefan Griller of the Vienna School of Economics and Business Administration. The participants represented a number of academic disciplines, yet all with a common theme, that of the life and work of Jean Monnet (1888–1975).

cooperation to further the Allied war effort. When he was sent to London, in 1914, there existed an International Supply Committee but as he pointed out, its 'title was ambiguous, its reality meagre.' He played an important part in establishing the Executives, starting with the Wheat Executive in 1915, the prototype of a series of inter-Allied institutions for the joint purchase of essential commodities.[3] By the end of 1917 he was the representative of France on all the Executives.

The emphasis here, on the other hand, is to link the three themes of the title in such a way as to look at how international treaties, tools of public international law, can serve to create a union of States Members, for it is through using their sovereign powers to enter into treaties that States consent to relinquish some of those powers, for the common good. This common theme linking the parts of this essay also excludes an exhaustive treatment of any one part. So, to begin with, I wish to show how by 1914 international treaties had developed to further inter-state relations. As especially peaceful such relations were of primary importance for Monnet, I recapitulate the part played by treaties in the peaceful settlement of international disputes. Secondly, I turn to some problems, and solutions, arising from international treaties concluded when Monnet himself was an active participant in international affairs. Thirdly, I return to the basic problem faced by the European Union today: is it to become a true union of States, akin to the United States of America, or is its character as a union of sovereign, equal, independent States in the classical connotation of public international law, and institutionalized in the Council of the European Union, to prevail. Here I limit myself strictly to some remarks connected to the life and work of Jean Monnet, referring back to my Introduction.

2. Treaties and International Co-operation *circa* 1800 to 1914

2.1. Multilateral Treaties in General

The early nineteenth century provided a turning-point in the history of treaties as instruments of international relations. Treaties as agreements between

3. Jean Monnet, *Memoirs* (Richard Mayne trans., Doubleday & Company: London, 1978) at Chapter 3, 1914–1918: Working Together, at 53 *et seq.* He stated: 'On my travels I had learned that economical forces were not blind and abstract, but could be measured and steered. Above all, I had come to realize that where there was organization there was real strength.' *Ibid*, at 61.

States, or earlier in history as between equals, have an ancient history, and the maxim of *pacta sunt servanda* that '[E]very treaty in force is binding upon the parties to it and must be performed by them in good faith'[4] is the most fundamental rule in customary public international law. Also, already in the early seventeenth century Grotius set out the principles of treaty interpretation, much as in the Vienna Convention on the Law of Treaties, 1969, and treaties of peace, in particular, had served to establish territorial settlements and delimit frontiers.

The importance of the Final Act of the Congress of Vienna, 1815, has been stated in different ways. Paul Reuter refers to the transformation of the treaty into multilateral treaties capable of establishing international organizations. He writes: 'The idea that a treaty which is binding upon different states by the same terms constitutes a single legal instrument first appeared at the Congress of Vienna.' And although the procedure is old it could 'be said that any multilateral treaty, in providing for a depositary, establishes an international organ.'[5] Reuter points out, however, that as a matter of procedure the Final Act summed up the transactions of the Congress of Vienna, which consisted of a number of bilateral treaties arrived at through collectively organized negotiations. The unity—or 'unicity'—of the actual treaty text is required for a depositary to function.

In his 'La Revolution française et l'Europe', 1904, Albert Sorel called the Final Act of June 9, 1815, 'the most comprehensive treaty which has ever been signed' and by basing general peace on a collective undertaking it began a 'new dispensation.'[6] The eight principal European powers recognized, and guaranteed, the rights and possessions of each European signatory. It is noteworthy too that the Final Act dealt with the Federal Constitution of Germany and that its Article 109 provided for the setting up of the Central Commission for the Navigation of the Rhine. Following on this, the Danube Commission was established at the Congress of Paris in 1856 to ensure free navigation on the Danube, as an international waterway.

The Austrian historian, Bittner, has estimated that between the Congress of Vienna Final Act and 1924, 16,000 treaties were concluded. The number of non-political treaties multiplied and they became more business-like

4. Article 26, Vienna Convention on the Law of Treaties, 23 May 1969, in force 27 January 1980, 1155 UNTS 331.
5. Paul Reuter, *Introduction to the Law of Treaties* (2nd edn, Kegan Paul International: London and New York, 1995) at 5–6.
6. Quoted in William Rappard, 'The Quest for Peace Yesterday and Today', *Annual Memorial Lecture* (David Davies Memorial Institute of International Studies: Aberystwyth University: Wales, 1954) at 4. 'The Concert' survived until the beginning of World War One.

and technical in nature.[7] Here I want only to look at two types of treaties in what is an overview of this period up to 1914: first, the growth of the international Unions; and, second, the development of international dispute settlement, principally treaties providing for arbitration.

2.2. Growth of the International Unions

The history of the international postal services in Europe dates back to the pre-Renaissance period, when messengers from royal and princely courts, monasteries, universities and guilds carried mail across national frontiers. In 1840 the service of the penny post was inaugurated in England and Germany. But it was in 1863 that the foundations were laid for the modern postal union.[8] At the suggestion of the United States, an International Postal Conference was convened in Paris, at which fourteen countries were represented. In 1874, a Postal Conference was summoned at Berne, and in 1875 the General Postal Union was set up, then re-christened the Universal Postal Union in 1878.

This Universal Postal Union (UPU) established a permanent organization, the International Postal Secretariat, housed in Berne. This was an administrative body and not recruited on the nationality principle of recruiting staff on the basis of their nationality. The staff of the secretariat were locally employed and numbered no more than some nine persons to begin with, functioning under the supervision of the Swiss Foreign Ministry, on behalf of the Swiss Government. But it was a permanent body that carried out the day-to-day work of the Union, providing information as well as making preparations for the sessions of the Congress, being the body, representing member States, that effectively governed the Union. Meeting every five years, the Congress arrived at its decisions by majority vote, the decisions coming into effect whether ratified or not. French was the only official language. This procedure thus put a limit, however modest, to the demands of State sovereignty in international relations. As the congresses were convened only every five years, Article 27 of the UPU Convention provided that any member of the administration, with the support of at least two other members, could

7. Arthur Nussbaum, *Concise History of the Law of Nations* (revised edn, The Macmillan Company: New York, 1954) at 196. He describes them as: 'treaties of commerce, consular treaties, treaties on extradition, on monetary matters on postal, telegraphic and railway communications, on fishing at sea, on copyrights, patents.' Note also, for example, the 1907 Paris Convention on the Creation of an International Office of Public Health.

8. Charles H. Alexandrowicz, *World Economic Agencies: Law and Practice* (Stevens and Sons: London, 1962) at 1. Here I am considering treaty-based unions as possible forerunners of the EU.

make proposals to be acted upon, with the exception of certain important proposals.

The territory of the UPU covered the world. A fundamental clearing principle for the functioning of the international postal service was that which allowed each Postal Administration to keep (subject to certain exceptions) all the charges collected by it from the general public. This system covered costs of transit. This, further, was based on an understanding of 'balance of interests' of addressor and addressee, together with acceptance of the 'gold franc', set at a fixed price for all. This was a forerunner of all proposals for a world currency.[9]

Non-discrimination in the treatment of foreign mail in transit was the rule. But member countries or their postal administrations were from the beginning permitted, by Article 8 of the UPU Convention, to make special arrangements among themselves for the mutual purpose of conceding conditions more favourable than those stipulated in the general convention. Conditions less favourable were not permitted. At the Centenary Symposium organized by the Commission of the European Communities at Brussels on 10 November 1988 in honour of Jean Monnet, it was pointed out in François Duchêne's Report that he introduced words such as 'non-discrimination' which have become standard 'European' principles.

The International Telegraphic Union, similarly to the UPU, was established by agreement between the representatives of States, in this instance numbering twenty, who met in Paris in 1865. They signed the multilateral convention by which the Union was established, with an International Bureau of Telegraphic Administrations as its central organization. As with the UPU, this was located in Berne.

Other agencies were set up by multilateral treaties in order to co-ordinate certain public utilities throughout the world. One such European agency was created by the International Convention on Railway Freight Traffic of 1890. In 1893 a Central Office of International Transport was set up at Berne for carrying out the informatory and executive tasks as defined by the Convention.

Thus before 1914 Leonard Woolf could write a book entitled *International Government* detailing the amount of international government that already existed. The use of the multilateral treaty, drawn up at a conference of representatives of States, for the purpose of breaking down the barriers of national sovereignty, was a fact of international life by 1914. But the pooling of sovereign power for the common good did not ensure co-ordination between the Unions, and the development of international agencies of a technical nature

9. *Ibid*, at 1–34, especially at 25.

remained sectorial. As late as at the UPU Congress in Cairo in 1934, it was suggested that as most post offices are at the same time telegraphic offices there should be arrangements for the joint functioning of the Bureaux of the UPU and ITU at Berne. This suggestion was not adopted by the Congress.[10]

2.3. Multilateral Treaties Providing for Third-Party Settlement of Disputes: Arbitration

The original UPU Convention of 1875 provided for the first time for compulsory arbitration of disputes between two or more members of an international agency concerning the interpretation or application of the Convention, or the Special Agreements or Regulations. In 1892, a permanent arbitral tribunal was created within the framework of the Union for International Transport by Rail. Acceptance of binding third-party settlement of inter-State disputes, here within the context of an international union as provided for in the constituent treaty, clearly enhances peaceful international relations. International treaties in general, by including such clauses, could thus be used as tools for limiting the excesses of State sovereignty.[11]

Arbitration is the oldest known means for settling disputes between equals, going back to the ancient world. Grotius, in the early 1600's advocated the use of arbitration as a method of settling disputes peacefully. But it was in the Jay Treaty between Great Britain and the newly independent United States of America, signed in 1794, and ratified in 1795, that the modern era of the peaceful settlement of disputes between States began. The Jay Treaty was concluded for the purpose of dealing with legal disputes that remained unsettled following the war that led to the independence of the United States of America. Three Mixed Commissions were established: first, the St. Croix River Boundary Commission reached a unanimous decision on a disputed frontier between Canada, which remained loyal to the British Crown, and the United States; second, awards were made on more than 500 claims arising out of maritime seizures; and the third Commission, to settle claims for pre-war debts owed to British subjects by debtors who had become U.S. nationals, had to be settled at a later date. By the Treaty of Ghent, terminating the war of 1812, Great Britain and the United States agreed to arbitration of

10. *Ibid*, at 20.
11. Count Mancini, Italian Deputy and later Foreign Secretary, played an important part for the introduction of jurisdictional, also known as compromissory, clauses in treaties in the later part of the nineteenth century. See Louis B. Sohn, 'Settlement of Disputes Relating to the Interpretation and Application of Treaties', 150 *Recueil des Cours* (1976) 195–294; also, Ruth Donner, *International Adjudication: Using the International Court of Justice* (Suomalainen Tiedeakatemia: Helsinki, 1988) at Chapter 4.

four further territorial disputes, following the success of the Jay Treaty. From this, between 1795 and 1900, one hundred and seventy-seven awards were rendered by arbitrators in inter-State boundaries and claims commissions disputes.

An example of such an international arbitration, of great national importance, was the *Alabama Claims* Arbitration of 1872.[12] During the America Civil War of 1860–1864 the Confederate ship, the 'Alabama', was fitted out in Liverpool docks as a cruiser. This then formidable warship sank, burnt and ransacked some 70 ships of the Union before being itself destroyed. The United States brought claims for, *inter alia*, alleged violations of its neutrality by Great Britain during the Civil War. By the Treaty of Washington of May 8, 1871, the two countries agreed to the setting up of an arbitral tribunal composed of five arbitrators: in addition to one appointed from the United States and one from Great Britain three others were appointed by Italy, Switzerland and Brazil, respectively. The importance of this arbitration lies not only in the rules regarding the duties incurred with neutral status laid down there, but also in the amount of the indemnity that Great Britain, at the height of its power, was obliged to pay the United States, that is, the sum of 15,500,000 U.S. dollars in the currency of that time. Britain paid within the time stipulated, of one year.

The most important developments for peaceful settlement of international disputes prior to 1914 occurred at the two Hague Peace Conferences, of 1899 and 1907.[13] Twenty-six States were represented at the First Conference and forty-four at the Second. The Convention for the Pacific Settlement of International Disputes, negotiated at the first conference and slightly amended at the second, codified the law of arbitration and established the Permanent Court of Arbitration. It also included definitions of good offices, mediation and commissions of inquiry. The procedure of international arbitration was clearly put on a legal basis, in answer to the claim put forward on occasion prior to 1899 that arbitration was a political process. Article 15 of the 1899 Convention and Article 18 of the 1907 Convention defined arbitration as follows: 'International arbitration has for its object the settlement of differences between States by judges of their own choice, and on the basis of respect for law.' Article 37 of the 1907 Convention added, 'Recourse to arbitration implies an engagement to submit in good faith to the Award.'

---

12. John B. Moore, *History and Digest of the International Arbitrations to which the United States has been a Party* (United States Government Printing Office: Washington D.C., 1898) Vol. I, at 755.
13. James Brown Scott, *The Hague Peace Conferences of 1899 and 1907* (The Johns Hopkins Press: Baltimore, 1909).

Yet, however far States had gone in relinquishing some of their sovereign rights in negotiated treaties by 1914, it was impossible to stop the outbreak of the First World War in 1914 and prevent the terrible tragedy in destruction of property and human lives that proved to be.

3. The Inter-War Period and to the Treaty of Paris, 1951[16]

The Peace Treaty drawn up at the Paris Peace Conference of 1919 included the Covenant of the League of Nations in its first 26 articles, and with the establishment of the League Monnet was an active participant in the post-war settlement in Europe. His experience during the war had been in economic organization but the success of the League depended on the organization to be set up and here his experience was of great value, or so he assumed: 'It was undoubtedly on account of this experience that Clemenceau and Balfour asked me to take on the job of Deputy to the League's Secretary-General, Sir Eric Drummond.' He points out that he had no part in the drafting of the League Covenant: 'Those who did draft it were careful to avoid setting up a genuine authority independent of the member States, or even a first nucleus of autonomous international power.'[17]

Monnet's position as Deputy to the Secretary-General lasted only until 1923, at which time he returned to Cognac to reorganize the failing family business. Having succeeded in that, he continued to head and run an international commercial bank, which took him on missions to Austria, Poland, Sweden and China, where he met General Chiang Kai-shek and helped to reorganize the finances of China. In 1936 the inevitability of war drew him back to public service for France. In 1938 the French Prime Minister, Edouard Daladier, sent him on a secret mission to the United States to order war-planes, a matter of great importance. In those few years at the League Secretariat, however, two treaties of especial importance in his work may be mentioned here. The first was the Versailles Treaty itself insofar as the German war reparations were concerned. The second was the Upper Silesia agreement. The first remained an unsolved problem, the second was at the time a success, as it was also for the Court of Justice established under the Treaty of Paris, 1951, setting up of the European Coal and Steel Community (ECSC). The Danzig question, touching on treaty relations, may be noted in a comparison with the Upper Silesia settlement before concluding with the Treaty of Paris, 1951, establishing the ECSC.

16. Entered into force 25 July 1952. Original text published in French. English translation published by the High Authority of the European Coal and Steel Community.
17. Monnet, *Memoirs, supra* note 3, at 80–81.

3.1. The Versailles Peace Treaty, 1919[18]

Two aspects of the Versailles Peace Treaty, as a treaty, may be noted. Firstly, Monnet considered the veto embedded in the functioning of the League Council was the cause and symbol of the inability to go beyond national self-interest. He added: 'The fault lay in the Treaty of Versailles: it was based on discrimination. From the moment I first began to be concerned with public affairs I have always realized that equality is absolutely essential in relations between nations.'[19] This was his first reaction to the Versailles treaty as a peace treaty because treaties, unlike civil contracts, are not voided by the use of force, at least not until the Vienna Convention on the Law of Treaties, 1969, article 52 provided: 'A treaty is void if its conclusion has been procured by the threat or use of force in violation of the principles of international law embodied in the Charter of the United Nations.'

Secondly, from the beginning, in the understanding of the financial clauses of the treaty, no account was taken of the Versailles treaty as a framework treaty. The Treaty of Versailles contained 440 articles, beginning with the Covenant of the League of Nations, and numerous annexes, including the constituent charters of several international organizations and territorial settlements. The contentious issue of particular importance here was that of the German war debt to the Allies (articles 231–249). Two main demands were made on Germany: payment of an indemnity to cover the war costs, at least payment towards the Allies' expenditure on the war; and reparations, as compensation for war damage, possibly including pensions and separate allowances where the family breadwinner was killed in the war. This was to pay for the damage and injuries which the enemy had inflicted on the Allied populations.

Professor Christian Tomuschat has recently reiterated the German criticism of the financial clauses of the Versailles Peace Treaty. He has compared 'The 1871 Peace Treaty between France and Germany and the 1919 Peace Treaty of Versailles'.[20] The seventeen articles of the Frankfurt Peace Treaty of 1871, he argues, imposed 'simple and straightforward' conditions on France.

18. Treaty of Peace between the Allied and Associated Powers and Germany (Treaty of Versailles), 28 June 1919, *British and Foreign State Papers* (HM Stationery Office: London, 1922) Vol. 112 at 1.
19. Monnet, *Memoirs, supra* note 3, at 97.
20. Christian Tomuschat, 'The 1871 Peace Treaty between France and Germany and the 1919 Peace Treaty of Versailles' in Randall Lesaffer (ed.) *Peace Treaties and International Law in European History from the Late Middle Ages to World War One* (Cambridge University Press, 2004) 382–396. Tomuschat makes no reference to Articles 233 and 248 of the Versailles Peace Treaty, as does Bernard Baruch, *infra,* note 28.

They were: (1) France renounced title over Alsace-Lorraine, and (2) France had to pay the sum of five billion French francs, reduced from the original claim for six billion, and which France was in a position to pay, and (3) certain issues of nationality. By contrast, he argues, the draft treaty of peace was handed over to the German delegation to the peace talks on 7 May 1919, and '[No] room for any subsequent negotiations was allowed.' The sum of reparations to be extracted from Germany was, he continues, exorbitantly high. Added to this, Article 231 of the Versailles Treaty put the blame for the war on Germany: 'The Allied and Associated Governments affirm and Germany accepts the responsibility of Germany and her allies for causing all the loss and damage to which the Allied and Associated Governments and their nationals have been subjected as a consequence of the war imposed upon them by the aggression of Germany and her allies.' Further, Tomuschat, who states that the First World War started in July 1914 with Austria's declaration of war on Serbia,[21] took issue with the wisdom of article 227 of the Versailles Treaty providing for the extradition of the German Kaiser. He argues that there was no precedent for attributing individual criminal responsibility in this manner.[22]

Counter to this is the argument that the Allies wished to try the Kaiser not as civilian Head of State, as indicated by Tomuschat, but as supreme military commander.[23] Further, Cassese, in his textbook, *International Law,*[24] places Article 227 laying down the responsibility of the German Emperor (Wilhelm II) for 'the supreme offence against international morality and the sanctity of treaties' under the heading of 'Past attempts' for international criminal justice.

Dissatisfaction with the reparations clauses of the Peace Treaty was expressed even as the treaty was being drafted. John Maynard Keynes' writings and actions are illustrative of both sides of the problem, although mostly critical of the treaty. In 1920 he presented the background causes of the war, stating,

21. *Ibid*, at 382, and thus not on the night of August 3, 1914, when Great Britain entered the war as a result of Germany's violation of the neutrality of Belgium, proclaimed by a treaty of 1837 to which Germany as successor State to Prussia was bound and to which Great Britain was a party. Gilbert Murray was in the House of Commons on August 3rd, 1914, and heard Foreign Secretary Grey's speech, 'ending with the terrible sentence "That unless the German army retired from Belgium we should be at war with Germany at 12 o'clock that night."' 'The League of Nations Movement: Some Recollections of the Early Days', in *Annual Memorial Lecture* (The David Davies Memorial Institute of International Studies, April 1955) at 3.
22. Tomuschat, 'The 1871 Peace Treaty', *supra* note 20, at 394.
23. Richard Overy, 'The Nuremberg trials and international law in the making', in Philippe Sands (ed.), *From Nuremberg to The Hague* (Cambridge University Press, 2003) 1–29 at 3.
24. Antonio Cassese, *International Law* (Oxford University Press, 2001) at 266.

was not a success. The animosity festered, leading to the election of a Nazi-majority government in Danzig in 1933 and open warfare at the beginning of September, 1939, and the start in Europe of what became World War II.

At the Peace Conference in Paris the Allied and Associated Powers determined to create an independent Poland. Poland, in turn, fearing weakness as a land-locked State situated between Germany and Russia, claimed its right, under President Woodrow Wilson's Fourteen Points of 8 January 1918 Point (or Article) XIII, to an outlet to the Baltic Sea. The German population of the port city of Danzig then objected to the prospect of being incorporated into Poland, together with a 'corridor' of territory connecting it to Poland. The creation of the Free City of Danzig under the protection of the League of Nations with a League Commissioner, the Swiss historian C. J. Burckhardt, and with self-government granted to the German population, was a compromise arrived at between the Allied Powers and incorporated in the Versailles Treaty, Articles 100–104. Provision was made for the rights of Poland vis-à-vis the Free City. No provision was made for the settlement of individual claims.[42]

Monnet's reaction made it clear that he feared for the future: 'The Constitution of Danzig, with which I was also concerned, could have become a model for international administration. But no one was thinking in terms of models: they were simply applying a peace treaty. So they established a Free City under a High Commissioner, and that was that.'[43] He had already recorded his concerns as regards the Peace Treaty of Versailles as one not based on the equality of the parties to it.

These treaties influenced Monnet's thinking on achieving peace in Europe through agreements on economic cooperation. It was with the Treaty of Paris, signed in Paris on April 18, 1951, establishing the European Coal and Steel Community, that Monnet took an active part, as the first President of its High Authority.

3.4. The Treaty of Paris, 1951, and the European Coal and Steel Community

While the advent of the ECSC was a culmination of earlier experience, both successful and unsuccessful, it represented at the same time something new in the history of European cooperation. First came the decisive political change. In a Note composed in Algiers on 5 August 1943, Monnet outlined a vision of a future Europe. He rejected a Europe 'reconstituted on a basis of national

42. Richard Overy and Andrew Wheatcroft, *The Road to War* (Penguin Books: London, 1999).
43. Monnet, *Memoirs, supra* note 3, at 91.

western European civil service. Britain had not favoured it, and Britain was not a party to the Treaty of Paris.[50]

Use of the term 'supranational' twice in Article 9 to describe the character of the functions of the members of the High Authority (Article 9) caused some consternation. Monnet used the term, but he also recorded his dislike: 'I disliked the word and always have.' What he found important was that the decisions of the High Authority were to be immediately binding in France, Germany and the other member countries.[51] By 1965, and the Merger Treaty between the European Communities, the term went out of use. In 1966, Emile Noël, Executive Secretary of the Common Market Commission rejected the argument that the Common Market Treaty was less supranational or more intergovernmental than the ECSC Treaty. He noted that although the implementing powers of the High Authority were laid down in full detail in the ECSC Treaty, in contrast, 'the powers of implementation of the Common Market Commission in all fields affected by the Rome Treaty will not be fully known until all the Community's common policies have been adopted.'[52]

Chapter IV of the ECSC Treaty, Articles 31–45, provide for the functioning of the Court of Justice, reminiscent of the jurisdiction of the Upper Silesia Tribunal. Article 31 provides, '[T]he function of the Court is to ensure the rule of law in the interpretation and application of the present Treaty and of the regulations for its execution.' This is not an inter-State court and its rulings were enforceable directly in the territory of the member States (Articles 44 and 92). Further, the Treaty included sanctions against member States who do not implement the judgments of the Court (Article 88). Contrast this with the Council of Europe,[53] set up by its constituent

50. Walter W. Rostow, *The United States in the World Arena* (Harper and Brothers Publishers: New York, 1960) at 213–216.
51. Monnet, *Memoirs, supra* note 3, at 297. Judge André (sic) Donner, of the Netherlands, first President of the European Court of Justice of the European Economic Community, describes the term 'supranational' as a rallying cry of a movement for European unity, and continues: 'But once people desired to understand what they felt and asked for a more detailed map of supranationality, the difficulties started. People turned to the lawyers, and the lawyers turned to their reports and their manuals for exact information on what is meant by a supranational organization and what might be its legal and political implications. And from that moment the term went into a decline.' André M. Donner, *The Role of the Lawyer in the European Communities* (Northwestern University Press and Edinburgh University Press, 1968) at 3–4.
52. Emily Noël, 'How the EEC's Institutions Work', 27 *Community Topics* (1966). This may explain why the Rome Treaty could be characterized by some as a framework treaty, but framework agreements do not envisage the redrafting of the original agreement. Cf. Bowman, 'The Multilateral Treaty Amendment Process', *supra* note 30.
53. Statute of the Council of Europe, London, 5.5.1949, European Treaty Series No. 1.

Statute in 1949 with ten founding States, that is, five of the ECSC members excluding the Federal Republic of Germany, plus Denmark, Ireland, Norway, Sweden and the United Kingdom. No court is established under that Treaty with binding jurisdiction as to its interpretation or application, and the European Convention for the Peaceful Settlement of Disputes of April 29, 1957, partly based on the statute of the ICJ, is a separate instrument and in reality of little practical importance[54]. Nor did the Schuman Declaration include reference to a Court.

4. Jean Monnet and the Future of Europe

Lastly, what relevance does Monnet's purported method of concluding agreements to create peaceful cooperation have for the future of Europe? Clearly, he was critical of certain aspects of treaty-making, such as what he saw as the inequality inherent in the Versailles Peace Treaty, perhaps even of treaties based on inter-State negotiations in general. Perhaps he underestimated the possibilities of framework conventions, although as we have seen these have their weaknesses too as being dependent on the success of future agreements. In 2008, Daniel Kalderimis argued that public international law is 'evolving ... to a decentralized system of specific, enforceable obligations, created through separate treaty-regimes.'[55] But can the problems facing the EU today be satisfactorily settled on the basis of a treaty regime?

54. It served as a jurisdictional basis for the Federal Republic of Germany's participation in the *North Sea Continental Shelf* cases before the ICJ in 1969 (*North Sea Continental Shelf* (Germany v Denmark and Germany v. the Netherlands), ICJ Reports (1968) 9 and ICJ Reports (1969) 3) when the Federal Republic was neither a member of the UN or the ICJ. However, on 17 June 2011 Greece requested permission to intervene in the case brought by Germany against Italy at the ICJ, claiming as the basis of the Court's jurisdiction Article 1 of the European Convention for the Peaceful Settlement of Disputes, 1957 (*Jurisdictional Immunities of the State* (Germany v. Italy: Greece Intervening), Judgment, ICJ Reports (2012) 99, para. 1). On the other hand, W. Ivor Jennings (later Sir Ivor) in his book *A Federation for Western Europe* (Cambridge University Press, 1940) included a 'Rough Draft of a Proposed Constitution for a Federation of Western Europe' of 23 articles one of which outlined 'The Federal Judiciary' with, *inter alia*, original and exclusive jurisdiction in all disputes between any two or more federated States.
55. Presentation to the Annual International Law Association (British Branch) Conference, 16–17 May, 2008. As for the Charter of the United Nations, the ICJ early on stated the problem: 'On the previous occasions when the Court has had to interpret the Charter of the United Nations it has followed the principles and rules applicable in general to the interpretation of treaties, since it has recognized that the Charter is a multilateral treaty, albeit a treaty having certain characteristics.' *Certain Expenses of the United Nations (Article 17, paragraph 2 of the Charter), (Advisory Opinion of 20 July, 1962)*, ICJ Reports (1962) 151 at 157.

The particular proposal of a treaty- Constitution for Europe was rejected by popular vote both in France and The Netherlands in the spring of 2005 and so the Treaty Establishing a Constitution for Europe was not proceeded with. Its successor, the Lisbon Treaty, was rejected in the first referendum held in Ireland in June, 2008, and accepted in the second referendum after Irish concerns were addressed. The European Union now has two basic treaties: the Treaty on European Union (TEU, amended) 2009, and the Treaty on the Functioning of the European Union (TFEU) as successor to the European Community Treaty, also of 2009.[56] This is not a constitution. Article 50 TEU now officially recognizes that 'Any Member State may decide to withdraw from the Union in accordance with its own constitutional requirements,' a right in accordance with the Vienna Convention on the Law of Treaties, 1969, Article 54. So, too, the Treaty on Stability, Coordination and Governance in the Economic and Monetary Union[57] has a formal intergovernmental structure even though it provides for wide powers to be used by the Union: it 'requires national budgets to be in balance or in surplus. This rule has to be incorporated into national law within one year of the entry into force of the treaty, using provisions that are guaranteed to be adhered to throughout the national budgetary processes ...' It has nineteen preambular paragraphs a loosely worded text and is subject to ratification.

Before turning for possible guidance to the experience of Jean Monnet, we may recapitulate briefly the proposition that the conclusion of international treaties furthers international cooperation by limiting sovereign powers.

4.1. Sovereignty

Much has been written in recent years of the dangers of the concept of sovereignty and the exercise of sovereign rights. Christof Schreuer has indicated the arguments, such as: 'The internal exercise of power has largely been insulated from the scrutiny of the larger community by such concepts as sovereign prerogative and internal affairs. The need to protect the national community from external danger frequently serves as a justification for internal repression.'[58] Sovereignty becomes associated with dictatorial power. It also

56. *Official Journal of the European Union*. Consolidated Versions of the TEU and the TFEU (2008/C 115/01).
57. Signed by the heads of State or government of all EU member States with exception of the UK and the Czech Republic on 2 March 2012.
58. Christoph Schreuer, 'The Waning of the Sovereign State: Towards a New Paradigm for International Law?', 4 *European Journal of International Law* (1993) 447–471. Similarly, Luzius Wildhaber, 'The European Convention on Human Rights and International Law', 56(2) *International Comparative Law Quarterly* (2007) 217–231 at 222.

becomes the cause of nationalism and economic protectionism, as Monnet found after 1918. But the attribute of 'sovereign' together with those of 'independent' and 'equal' to the States making up the community governed by international law does not have to mean arbitrary use of power.

Jean Bodin, who coined the use of the term in public international law, found that sovereignty, meaning supreme power, resided in the prince, but [T]ous les princes de la terre sont sujet aux lois de Dieu, de nature et à plusiers lois humaines commune à tous les peuples.'[59] We have been reminded of this in an article by Henri Legohérel of the University of Angers, the birthplace of Jean Bodin.[60] Professor Legohérel describes the night of St Bartholomew of 25 August 1572, when the Protestant (Reformed) elite of France was massacred by a mob. Henry of Navarre, who later, converted to Catholicism, became King Henry IV of France, escaped with his life and Bodin, a moderate Catholic, survived but his house was sacked. In this state of lawlessness some certainty had to be found, and Bodin found it, by analogy, in the 'souverain parlement' of Paris, the highest court of law from which there was no further appeal.

Wheaton describes sovereignty 'as the supreme power by which any state is governed.' When exercised internally it may be called constitutional law, when externally it 'may more properly be termed international law.'[61] To use the term 'constitutional law' implies adherence to a constitution rather than the use of arbitrary, repressive power. To equate sovereignty with irresponsibility may in part be the unfortunate consequence of the 'classic' law of State Responsibility, by which a State had duties to aliens, but not to its nationals. The law has since changed considerably: the requirement of 'fair and equitable' treatment in investment disputes, covered by Chapter 11 of the North American Free Trade Association (NAFTA), is not the same as the minimum standard for aliens in general international law in that the former does not intend more favourable treatment for investors from other countries. As Robert Schuman said in 1950: 'independence has never meant irresponsibility.'[62] The independence, sovereign independence, of States is not in itself an impediment to peace.

---

59. 'All the princes on earth are subject to the laws of God, of nature, and of the numerous laws common to all peoples.' Jean Bodin, *Six Livres de la République* (Paris, 1576).
60. Henry Legohérel, 'Jean Bodin et l'Europe de son temps', 1 *Journal of the History of International Law* (1999) 38–47.
61. Henry Wheaton, *Elements of International Law* (reproduced in the Classics of International Law, No. 19, 1866) at 27.
62. Monnet, *Memoirs, supra* note 3, at 332.

4.2. Treaties

If the exercise of sovereign powers has often recently been denigrated, it may, perhaps, be equally said that treaties are overrated as instruments of international relations. In the celebrated *S.S. 'Wimbledon'* Judgements of the PCIJ in 1923[63] the Permanent Court stated that the right of entering into international engagements is an attribute of State sovereignty. But the Court continued: 'The Court declines to see in the conclusion of any treaty by which a state undertakes to perform or refrain to perform a particular act as abandonment of its sovereignty.' There is, therefore, a certain contradiction in treaty-based organizations, not yet fully worked out. If the underlying strength of treaties is the customary rule of *pacta sunt servanda* then, as Professor Paul Reuter has written: 'In particular, the increasing intervention of international organizations means that the contractual framework of international conventions is left open to conflicting tensions.'[64] To continue his argument: whereas treaties are binding by virtue not of being treaties but of customary rules then 'if one were to speak of a 'Constitution' of the international community it would have to be a customary one.'

Monnet was well aware of the weaknesses of agreements negotiated between sovereign States. This is shown in what is one of the most interesting disclosures of his 'method'. Describing the Arbitral Tribunal of Upper Silesia, he wrote, '[I]t was a model institution: we had given it powers that at the time were very novel', and he refers to the independence of the arbitrators and the direct effect in national courts of the interpretations given by the Tribunal. He continues how the possibilities of this approach were not recognized until much later, because in Upper Silesia the problem was to stabilize the situation inherited from the war.

So, it may be asked, how would Monnet have reacted to the present state of the EU treaties, to the two treaties, the TEU and the TFEU as the heirs to the original treaty establishing the European Economic Community and to the ambitious constitution for Europe drawn up in the Convention on the Future of Europe under the chairmanship of ex-French President Valéry Giscard d'Estaing, as envisaged in the Laeken Declaration? Giscard d'Estaing, 'an elderly statesman with an ingrained intergovernmental approach' was chosen by the Laeken European Council in December 2001.[65] We have seen

63. PCIJ Series A, No. 1 (1923).
64. Reuter, *Introduction to the Law of Treaties, supra* note 5, at 28–29.
65. J. Shaw, P. Magnette, Lars Hoffmann and A. Vergés Bausili (eds), *The Convention on the Future of Europe. Working Towards an EU Constitution* (Kogan & Page: London, 2003) at 81.

how the Treaty establishing the ECSC was drawn up, not by negotiation between representatives of the States concerned but rather more on the basis of the proposals of Monnet and his colleagues, drafted by legal experts, and gone over point by point by them. Giscard's Convention worked differently. The Laeken Declaration established the Presidium of the Convention, composed of 13 members. Two of the important working groups were presided over by the Italian Vice-President, Giuliano Amato, who presented their conclusions in September 2002.[66] There is here a difference in the drafting procedure, although, it must be said, national representation was also present in the ECSC. Monnet, it is suggested, would have favoured a fresh look at the *method* of European cooperation.

4.3. Monnet and the Future of Europe

In his chapter on 'The European Community at Work (1952–1955)', Monnet comes with another highly significant comment. He writes: 'In the end, what I had to make clear to these men, still fresh from their national Parliaments, was simple, but it would be a long time before they felt it in their bones. Europe, that is, would be built by the same process as each of our national States—by establishing among nations a new relationship comparable to that which exists among the citizens of any democratic country: equality, organized by common institutions.'[67] And this new relationship among nations is clearly far removed from a 'treaty-regime' based on a treaty negotiated between governments.

In his interesting article, 'Is this a Constitution? Remarks on a Contested Concept', Professor Stefan Griller discusses whether it is correct to speak of a 'constitutional treaty', pointing out that avoiding any constitutional language in the Lisbon Treaty 'serves the purpose of avoiding similarities to constitutions of nation-States.' So Europe remains in part inter-governmental and in part communitarian, as in the two institutions of Council and Commission. He suggests that the 'borderline between a treaty under international law and a constitution would only be transgressed if future amendments would no longer be a prerogative of the Member States as the masters of the treaties, but a competence of the union organs.'[68] The Constitution of the United States of America improved on this, and also on their earlier, unsuccessful, Articles of

66. Valéry Giscard d'Estaing, *La Constitution pour l'Europe* (Foundation Robert Schuman/Albin Michel, 2003).
67. Monnet, *Memoirs, supra* note 3, at 383.
68. Stefan Griller and Jacques Ziller (eds), *The Lisbon Treaty: EU Constitutionalism Without a Constitutional Treaty* (European Community Studies Association of Austria, Publication Series: Wien and New York, 2008) 21–51 at 35 and 23.

Confederation: Article V of the Constitution provides for its own amendment by the people, in accordance with a constitutional process and not by direct popular vote. Article 48 TEU provides for amendments in accordance with an ordinary revision procedure where the Member States represented in the Council still control the procedure even though obliged to 'consult' and to 'notify'. The simplified revision procedures apply to Part Three of the TFEU relating to the internal policies and action of the Union. After consultations the 'European Council shall act by unanimity'.

Monnet's 'method' was many-faceted, as so many of his colleagues, friends, collaborators and employees have witnessed in a volume dedicated to his memory.[69] George Ball has written of his 'methods of operation'.[70] François Duchêne has written of his 'method, or methods', and of the 'method, or rather the approach.'[71] Rita Süssmuth points to how he was always in search of new forms of cooperation.[72] One aspect of his contribution to the development of European integration that runs through these reminiscences and appreciations was his willingness to listen to others, and not only to persons in position. In this, he would surely have taken seriously the views of the voters in France and The Netherlands, and in part Ireland, rejecting the draft constitution. He was also prepared to accept defeat, as with the French Senate's rejection of the European Defence Community in 1954. He was prepared to start afresh.

Accepting, then, that we have much to learn from Monnet's methods of working towards his goal of peaceful cooperation, there is one method that undoubtedly shaped his thinking, and that was from René Descartes' *A Discourse on Method*, first published in 1637, and familiar to him from his schooldays. One clear indication occurs in the Memoirs: 'how much simpler everything was if one tackled the difficulty itself, following the time-honoured maxim of Descartes and reducing it to its basic elements.'[73] Perhaps here

---

69. Henri Rieben (ed.), *Témoignages à la mémoire de Jean Monnet* (Fondation Jean Monnet pour l'Europe: Lausanne, 1989).
70. D. Brinkley and C. Hackett (eds), *Jean Monnet: The Path to European Unity* (St. Martin's Press: New York, 1991), Introduction.
71. *Ibid,* Chapter 7, 'Jean Monnet's Methods'.
72. Rita Süssmuth, 'Peut-on s'inspirer de Jean Monnet pour construire l'unité européenne aujourd'hui?', in Gérard Bossuat and Andreas Wilkens (eds), *Jean Monnet, l'Europe et les chemins de la Paix* (Publications de la Sorbonne: Paris, 1999) 463–468 ('Can we be inspired by Jean Monnet in the construction of European unity today?').
73. Monnet, *Memoirs, supra* note 3, at 350. The translator, Richard Mayne, has an asterisk by 'our Treatise on Method', on page 236 of the Memoirs: 'A tacit allusion to René Descartes's eponymous *Discours de la méthode* (1637).'

Monnet can encourage us to go back to Descartes, such as to near the end of Part II of his *Discourse*: 'And as a multitude of laws often only hampers justice, so that a state is best governed when, with few laws, these are rigidly administered.'[74]

In conclusion, not only was Monnet well aware of the limits inherent in treaty-based institutions, he also demonstrates to us Descartes' methods, such as, 'to cast aside the loose earth and sand, that I might reach the rock or the clay.'[75] Starting from this, and testing his propositions against the yardstick of reason and truth, Descartes made an invaluable contribution to the development of modern science. Monnet, surely, wished to do the same for the development of international, first European, cooperation by reconsidering the methods used to achieve it.

74. René Descartes, *A Discourse on Method* (Everyman's Library: London and New York, 1949) at 15.

75. *Ibid*, at 23.

The Law of Market Society

A Sociology of International Economic Law and Beyond

Sabine Frerichs

ABSTRACT: International economic law is dominated by 'international law' and 'economic law' perspectives. Socio-legal perspectives do gain ground at the margins of the field, but a sociology of international economic law, which addresses not only the subject matter but also the disciplinary dynamics of the field, has so far been missing. Drawing on Polanyi's *The Great Transformation* and recent work in the economic sociology of law, this article puts the 'law of market society' centre stage in developing a genuine sociology of international economic law. This includes a sociology of law and economics, which exposes how the discipline (power structure) of international economic law is articulated with the discipline (knowledge structure) of law and economics.

The law of market society includes all types of law that constitute or regulate the market, be it public or private law, national, international or even transnational law. Taking off from Polanyian ideas, law is conceived as a social institution 'embedding' the economy, but also as a 'fictitious commodity' which is itself subject to market forces. The tension between law's commodifying and decommodifying functions, which these concepts illuminate, is reflected in legal discourse. Moreover, it seems to drive 'law's great transformation' from its universalist origins in the nineteenth century to its national closings in the twentieth century, and to its transnational openings in the twenty-first century. In this sense, the law of market society follows itself a 'double movement'.

KEYWORDS: law, sociology, economics, market society, Polanyi, cognitive embeddedness, fictitious commodities, economic sociology of law

Table of Contents

Introduction: 'Polanyian' Agendas in International Economic Law

The aim of this article is to outline a sociology of international economic law, which draws on Karl Polanyi's historically oriented economic sociology as well as on recent developments in the 'economic sociology of law'.

Taking account of the core institutions of the international political economy, Polanyi naturally entered the field of international economic law. Moreover, he was not only interested in the normative and factual elements of the international economic order, but also in its cognitive underpinnings, namely, its embeddedness in the 'philosophy of economic liberalism', or what became the mainstream of the economic discipline. In fact, liberal economics had a great influence on the development of international economic law, both as a subject matter and a scholarly discipline. The self-regulating market, which Polanyi considers a chimera of economic liberalism, has been 'instituted' through fictitious commodities, which would ideally circulate on a global scale. A Polanyian sociology of international economic law would therefore have to start from the regulation of land, labour, and money in the context of the international political economy (including its national and transnational underpinnings).

Polanyian research agendas in international economic law are indeed on the rise. A pioneer in this respect is Christian Joerges, for whom Polanyi's study of the 'rise and fall' of the market economy in its national and international context is not only a source of inspiration, but a necessary complement to thinking about law in the 'postnational constellation'.[1] Important signposts in taking Polanyi to the law are his co-edited volumes 'Economy as a polity: The political constitution of contemporary capitalism'[2] and 'Karl Polanyi, globalisation and the potential of law in transnational markets'.[3] The latter volume exemplifies how international economic law can be 'reconstructed' from a Polanyian point of view: while the theoretical contributions discuss the applicability of Polanyi's analytical framework to the law of transnational markets, the empirical contributions focus on the regulation of different fictitious commodities on the European or global scale.

1. Jürgen Habermas, *The Postnational Constellation: Political Essays* (MIT Press, 2001).
2. Christian Joerges, Bo Stråth and Peter Wagner (eds.), *Economy as a Polity: The Political Constitution of Contemporary Capitalism* (UCL Press, 2005).
3. Christian Joerges and Josef Falke, Josef (eds.), *Karl Polanyi, Globalisation and the Potential of Law in Transnational Markets* (Hart Publishing: Oxford, 2011).

Similar 'Polanyi-inspired'[4] agendas in international economic law include Amanda Perry-Kessaris's edited volume 'Socio-legal approaches to international economic law: Text, context, subtext'[5] and Bettina Lange and Dania Thomas's edited volume 'From economy to society? Perspectives on transnational risk regulation'.[6] A systematic account of the law of the (globalised) market society has, however, as yet been missing. In order to fill this gap, this article lays ground for a sociology of international economic law, which draws on Polanyi's classical work, namely *The Great Transformation*,[7] but which also connects it with contemporary research interests in the 'economic sociology of law'. As a sociological sub- or, rather, meta-discipline, the latter aims to reconnect thinking about law, economy and society beyond the limits of the established disciplines of law, economics, and sociology. More specifically, the economic sociology of law can be understood as a complement to, or corrective of, law and economics, which replaces the latter's 'disembedded' view with a more 'embedded' view of law *and* economy *in* society. While a sociology of international economic law à la Polanyi would take the functional definition of international economic law seriously, which economists (or lawyer-economists) have come to use, it would also expose its disciplinary effects. In the 'economic law' perspective, it is not so much the origin of the norms than the object of regulation, which matters. The governmental premise as well as promise of this perspective is less the coherence of international law than the integration of global markets. A Polanyian sociology of international economic law would go beyond this functional imperative and highlight how the global economy is actually embedded in (law and) economics and, hence, shaped by highly selective economic theories. Not surprisingly then, international economic law increasingly lends itself to 'economic law' descriptions.

The argument is structured as follows: Section 1 introduces the disciplines of international economic law, focusing on the 'international law' approach, the 'economic law' approach, and the 'socio-legal' approach, which draw inspirations from law, economics, and sociology, respectively. Compared to the first two approaches, which share the disciplinary sensibilities of law, on the one hand, and economics, on the other, the third approach can be considered more interdisciplinary and pluralistic in character. Its critical interest

4. Sally Randles, 'Issues for a Neo-Polanyian Research Agenda in Economic Sociology', 13 *International Review of Sociology* (2003) 409–434 at 409; emphasis omitted.
5. Amanda Perry-Kessaris (ed.), *Socio-Legal Approaches to International Economic Law: Text, Context, Subtext* (Routledge: London, 2012).
6. Bettina Lange and Dania Thomas (eds.), 'Special Issue: From Economy to Society? Perspectives on Transnational Risk Regulation', 62 *Studies in Law, Politics and Society* (2013) 1–22.
7. Karl Polanyi, *The Great Transformation* (Beacon Press: Boston, 1957 [1944]).

in how international economic law is actually 'constituted' in normative as well as cognitive terms takes us to an understanding of the sociology of international economic law as a meta-discipline which reflects upon the very disciplines that dominate the field.

Section 2 draws on a fresh reading of *The Great Transformation* and reconstructs the role of law therein. After introducing Polanyi's historical approach and considering the legal and economic developments which the market society was premised upon, the law of market society will be systematised in two complementary ways: as the 'fifth' institution, or the missing link, between the key institutions of the international political economy (gold standard, balance-of-power system, liberal state, and self-regulating market), and as the 'fourth' fictitious commodity, which is—other than land (nature) and labour (humans)—lacking a clear substance, but which mediates—similarly as money—between economic and political functions and may itself take embedded or commodified forms.

Section 3 draws on contemporary legal discourse in order to reconstruct the history of the law of market society until today. The major lines of development are framed in Polanyi's terms of a 'movement' and 'counter-movement', which arguably matter as much on the academic level as on the political level. The development of the law of market society is retraced from its 'universalist' origins in the nineteenth century to its national 'closings' in the twentieth century, and to its transnational 'openings' in the twenty-first century. Tensions are highlighted between the divergent rationalities of liberalism and nationalism, formalism and instrumentalism, privatisation and politicisation, and overall between 'the economic' and 'the social', which are manifest in the law and rationalised in legal discourse.

1. The Disciplines of International Economic Law: Law, Economics, Sociology

This article is concerned with the question what the sociology of economic law is—or rather, what it could or should look like in a Polanyian spirit. At first consideration, the sociology of international law may be understood as one of the disciplines, or sub-disciplines, of international economic law, next to law (and political science) on the one hand and economics on the other. As such, it puts the subject matter of international economic law in a sociological perspective. However, as will be argued below, sociology can also be understood as a meta-discipline of international economic law, which goes beyond—and behind—both law and economics. If understood as a meta-discipline, the subject matter of the sociology of international economic law is the *discipline* of international economic law itself. Far from being beyond sociological interest, the definition and delimitation of international economic law both as a subject matter and as a field of study is, therefore, the first thing to analyse. Hence: 'What is international economic law?'[8]

If one starts from this relatively unpretentious question, one is immediately faced with ambiguities. Not being able to find a concordant definition, Charnovitz breaks the subject matter of international economic law down into its components: accordingly, 'international' refers to all cross-border matters; 'economic' to 'the economy itself (and perhaps also to economic analysis)'; and 'law' to hard law as well as soft law.[9] What comes out is 'a very broad body of law'—if not 'too broad'.[10] The potential scope of international economic law is illustrated in the following: assuming that '[i]n its broadest sense, international economic law includes all national and international legal norms that affect transnational movements of goods, services, capital and labor',[11] Paul arrives at a lengthy list of pertinent fields and subjects, including

> international business transactions, private international law, international trade law, immigration law, European Communities law, comparative law, transnational litigation, international arbitration procedure, and aspects of banking, competition, employment, environmental, intellectual property, securities, tax, and telecommunications laws that regulate transnational transactions.[12]

As an academic discipline, international economic law is 'a relative newcomer, bursting out as an autonomous field of law only in the last decades'.[13] Hence, one could suppose that its boundary lines are not fully established yet. While it is often considered part of public international law, international economic law is, in the eyes of leading scholars in the field, actually much more than that. Petersmann feels reminded of the 'story of the blind men touching different parts of an elephant and describing the same animal in contradictory ways': likewise, 'private and public, national and international lawyers continue to perceive [international economic law] from competing

8. Steve Charnovitz, 'What Is International Economic Law?', 14 *Journal of International Economic Law* (2011) 3–22.
9. *Ibid*, at 4–5.
10. *Ibid*, at 6.
11. Joel R. Paul, 'The New Movements in International Economic Law', 10 *American University Journal of International Law and Policy* (1995) 607–617 at 609, footnote 9.
12. *Ibid.*
13. David Kennedy, 'The Disciplines of International Law and Policy', 12 *Leiden Journal of International Law* (1999) 9–133 at 38.

perspectives', without ever getting a grip on the whole.[14] As will be shown in the following, international economic law may be ambiguous, but it is not amorphous. It is not 'undisciplined', but simultaneously confined to different disciplines. Most significant for the present discussion is the systematic difference between international law and economic law perspectives, which draw on law and politics and law and economics, respectively.

1.1. Disciplinary Perspectives of International Economic Law

To explore the difference between international law and economic law perspectives, we can start with David Kennedy's comparison of the 'disciplines' of public international law and international economic law. A short synopsis of the diverging 'world views of participants in the field', here in the US context, is given in the following:

> *Public international lawyers* look at the world and see states. They worry about how law will be possible among sovereigns; they remember wars and understand their history as progress from sovereign autonomy to international community, from formal rules to pragmatic principles and institutions. They look to political science for inspiration, and they want improved global governance.
>
> *International economic lawyers* look out and see buyers and sellers hoping to trade. They worry about the myriad risks of transacting internationally, particularly those caused by governments; they remember the Great Depression and understand their history as progress toward ever lower tariff barriers and an ever more flexible legal/institutional structure for trade bargaining. They look to economics for disciplinary inspiration and they want an ever more reliable free trade regime.[15]

In terms of the distinctive 'governmental sensibilities' of the two disciplines,[16] public international law is more about 'regime construction' whereas international economic law follows first and foremost the 'spirit of trade liberalization'.[17] One is about law and politics in international relations, the other about law and economics in the global market.

Ortino and Ortino approach the discipline of international economic law from a slightly different point of view, which helps to clarify its hybrid nature between law on the one hand, and economics on the other. For that purpose,

14. Ernst-Ulrich Petersmann, 'Methodological Pluralism and Its Critics in International Economic Law Research', 15 *Journal of International Economic Law* (2012) 921–970 at 935.
15. David Kennedy, 'The Twentieth-Century Discipline of International Law in the United States', in Austin Sarat, Bryant Garth and Robert A Kagan (eds.), *Looking Back at Law's Century* (Cornell University Press, 2002) 386–433, at 388; original emphasis.
16. Kennedy, 'Disciplines of International Law', *supra* note 13, at 16.
17. *Ibid*, at 46.

they distinguish between international law and economic law, both of which include a 'branch' called international economic law.[18]

As a (sub-)discipline of international law, international economic law deals with the 'international law of the economy'.[19] In other words, it looks only at those sections of the economy, which are 'governed by international law',[20] putting the legal origin of the respective rules first. As a (sub-)discipline of economic law, international economic law is 'not defined by its legal sources but rather by its object: the global economic system'.[21] It is the 'law of the global economy',[22] which encompasses not only international law but also 'national norms regarding transnational economic relations, as well as rules of private and public law concerning the ordering of cross-border economic relations'.[23] Moreover, besides 'formal laws', it also includes 'informal laws, such as non-legally binding customs and practices influencing economic behaviours'.[24] Most importantly, however, economic law builds on the 'laws' of economics, which closely links it to the economic discipline.

In terms of its disciplinary inspiration we can thus distinguish between international economic law as a legal discipline, which preserves the preoccupations of lawyers with legal sources (i.e. the origin of norms), and an economic discipline, which serves the interests of economists in efficient transactions (i.e. the object of norms). In line with the economic law approach, Ortino and Ortino define international economic law as 'the study of the legal rules regulating economic actors and activities that cross or have impacts across the boundaries of a single legal and economic system, and thus operate in or impact the global economic system'.[25] Thus understood, the economic law approach 'cuts across the boundaries between *legal systems* (e.g. national, regional, international and trans-national) and across those between traditional *fields of law* (e.g. constitutional, commercial and procedural law)'.[26]

Similarly, Petersmann distinguishes between a 'prevailing conception' of international economic law 'as "public international law regulating the

18. Federico Ortino and Matteo Ortino, 'Law of the Global Economy: In Need of a New Methodological Approach?', in Colin B. Picker, Isabella D. Bunn and Douglas W. Arner (eds.), *International Economic Law: The State and Future of the Discipline* (Hart Publishing: Oxford, 2008) 89–106.
19. *Ibid*, at 92.
20. *Ibid*, at 92.
21. *Ibid*, at 94.
22. *Ibid*, at 94.
23. *Ibid*, at 90.
24. *Ibid*, at 93.
25. *Ibid*, at 89.
26. *Ibid*, original emphasis.

economy"', and a 'competing conception' of international economic law 'as "multilevel economic regulation"'.[27] As to the prevailing (international law) perspective, he speaks of '[s]tate-centered "top-down conceptions"',[28] which are also marked as 'Westphalian conceptions' of international economic law.[29] As to the competing (economic law) view, this is understood to form part of 'citizen-oriented "bottom-up conceptions"' of international economic law'.[30] 'Multilevel economic regulation' can be considered an economic law perspective in that it 'focuses on the "functional unity" of private and public, national and international regulation of the economy'[31] and conceives international economic law as 'interdependent "social practices", which regulate economic activities and transactions such as the "private ordering" of the international division of labor among billions of producers, investors, traders and consumers in 192 UN member states'.[32] This 'international' division of labour is also referred to as '*transnational* division of labour'[33], bringing cross-border transactions between individuals into focus.

In his work, Petersmann promotes a third, 'cosmopolitan conception' of international economic law, also dubbed '"multilevel constitutionalism"', which re-interprets international economic regulation in the framework of generally accepted human rights.[34] In doing so, he builds on the economic law perspective but also goes beyond. Bringing, at least prospectively, the 'constitutional rights' of global citizens to the fore,[35] Petersmann enriches the economic law perspective of international economic law with normative premises of a different legal pedigree: international human rights. More generally, his aim is to complement the conventional understanding of international (economic) law as 'international law among states' with an advanced understanding of a 'cosmopolitan law among individuals' and an 'international law among peoples'.[36]

With regard to international economic law, we can thus distinguish between an international law perspective which is related to political science,

27. Ernst-Ulrich Petersmann, 'The Future of International Economic Law: A Research Agenda', in Christian Joerges and Ernst-Ulrich Petersmann (eds.), *Constitutionalism, Multilevel Trade Governance and International Economic Law* (Hart Publishing: Oxford, 2011) 533–575 at 571.
28. *Ibid*, at 544.
29. Petersmann, 'Methodological Pluralism', *supra* note 14, at 946.
30. Petersmann, 'Future of International Economic Law', *supra* note 27, at 544.
31. *Ibid*, at 536.
32. *Ibid*, at 537.
33. *Ibid*, at 573; original emphasis.
34. *Ibid*, at 572.
35. Petersmann, 'Methodological Pluralism', *supra* note 14, at 927.
36. Petersmann, 'Future of International Economic Law', *supra* note 27, at 574.

namely the subfield of international politics, but which also takes a legal-doctrinal approach, and an economic law perspective which is inspired by the discipline of economics and, first and foremost, interested in the regulatory framework of the economy (both as it *is* and as it *ought* to be), but which may also adopt other, distinctly legal perspectives, as is evident in Petersmann's approach.

Now, what would a sociological approach to international economic law look like? Hirsch notes a general 'scarcity of sociological analysis' in the field.[37] More specifically, he finds that the literature on regional trade agreements and their relations to the World Trade Organization, which is the focus of his research, is 'dominated by abundant economic and political analyses' while the 'relevance of socio-cultural factors is under-emphasized'.[38] What Hirsch then develops is, in fact, a *sociology* of international economic law in that he extensively draws on sociological theories. Moreover, it is also inspired by the *sociology of law* as a discipline that goes beyond legal norms in the strict sense (hard law) and also includes social norms (soft law), or, as Hirsch puts it, that takes the 'normative role of non-formal norms in the international system' seriously.[39] However, in his version, the sociology of international economic law is still stuck with the international law side of the field while it neglects its economic law side.

Having first elaborated on the sociology of international law, Hirsch's starting point is indeed in international law, and not in economic law.[40] Likewise, what is *classically* known as the sociology of international law seems firmly rooted in international law (and politics) and to reflect its state-centeredness, such as in the work of Max Huber.[41] Early notions of a 'world society' notwithstanding,[42] this type of sociology is preoccupied with the 'relationships between the state (the basic unit in the current international system) and various forms of international governance (prominently, international institutions)'.[43] In Hirsch's work, the position of the state in the

37. Moshe Hirsch, 'The Sociology of International Economic Law: Sociological Analysis of the Regulation of Regional Agreements in the World Trading System', 19 *European Journal of International Law* (2008) 277–299 at 277.
38. *Ibid*, at 287.
39. Moshe Hirsch, 'The Sociology of International Law: Invitation to Study International Rules in Their Social Context', 55 *University of Toronto Law Journal* (2005) 891–939 at 894.
40. *Ibid.*
41. Max Huber, 'Beiträge zur Kenntnis der soziologischen Grundlagen des Völkerrechts und der Staatengesellschaft', 4 *Jahrbuch des öffentlichen Rechts der Gegenwart* (1910) 56–134.
42. Hirsch, 'Sociology of International Law', *supra* note 39, at 935.
43. *Ibid*, at 931.

international system is equated with the position of the individual in society. This allows him to directly apply sociological theories about the relations between individual and society to the relations between state and international system.

The fact that different sociological theories—here systematised alongside the 'structure-agency divide' and the 'consensus-conflict divide'[44]—'lead to different conceptions regarding the nature and goals of [international economic law]',[45] yields relevant insights for Hirsch's own research but also accounts for its limitations. This can be illustrated with his analysis of international economic law, which is concerned with 'the extensive powers of some international economic institutions *vis-à-vis* sovereign states (notably with regard to the IMF and the WTO)'.[46] Drawing on micro-sociological theories, which emphasise individual agency, social interaction, and role- and rule-making 'from below', Hirsch makes a case for state autonomy in pluralistic settings. More specifically, he defends 'socio-economic pluralism' against 'socio-economic integration',[47] conceding that this may decrease 'legal coherence and certainty' and increase 'legal inconsistency and instability'.[48]

But even though Hirsch's view of states is anything but reductionist (as he does not rely on their 'realist' or 'rational' interests only but also points to their 'socio-cultural' identities), and even though he even mentions 'international economic relations among states *and individuals*',[49] he falls short of considering the economic law perspective on international economic law in any systematic way. Moreover, he also misses the opportunity to explore the perspective of economic sociology, which he briefly mentions,[50] to any sufficient extent: this could have taken him beyond Granovetter,[51] a representative of new economic sociology, who has little to do with international economic law, to Polanyi, who was actually much concerned with it. In this sense, Polanyi's *The Great Transformation* can not only be read as a classic of economic sociology but also as an outline of the sociology of international economic law.[52]

44. *Ibid*, at 896.
45. Hirsch, 'Sociology of International Economic Law', *supra* note 37, at 290.
46. Hirsch, 'Sociology of International Law', *supra* note 39, at 937; reference omitted.
47. Hirsch, 'Sociology of International Economic Law', *supra* note 37, at 297.
48. *Ibid*, at 299.
49. *Ibid*, at 280; emphasis added.
50. *Ibid*.
51. Mark Granovetter, 'Economic Action and Social Structure: The Problem of Embeddedness', 91 *American Journal of Sociology* (1985) 481–510.
52. Polanyi, *Great Transformation*, *supra* note 7.

In his sociology of international economic law, Hirsch technically equates the state with *homo sociologicus* (preferring its micro-sociological variant to its more prominent macro-sociological variant). In this respect, there is a striking parallel to the more established discipline of 'public international law and economics',[53] or the 'economic analysis of international law'.[54] If this is the international law version of international law and economics, its economic law version could, perhaps, better be termed the law and economics of international *economic* law: this would emphasise the functional unity of economic law across borders and preserve the reference to individuals, and not states, as its primary actors. Public international law and economics actually seems to do the opposite: 'In search of international *homo economicus*'[55] it falls into the same methodological trap as its sociological cousin: 'the focus that was before on the individual turns now upon the state'.[56] By equating states with individuals, it not only loses sight of the latter but also of the transnational network of economic and legal relations that underpins international economic law as the law of the globalised market society.

The only difference between the two accounts is that, this time, the state is not identified as *homo sociologicus* but as *homo economicus*. In both cases, we can speak of a move from methodological individualism to methodological nationalism, or rather, to 'methodological statism' (granting that the sociological account is less individualist and more interactionist than the economic account). At the same time, the economic law variant of international economic law seems predestined to bring individuals back in. After all, a distinction between 'domestic and international' law and economics[57] would be at odds with the proclaimed functional unity of its subject matter, not to mention assertions of 'disciplinary unity' within mainstream economics. In the end, the question of the right 'level of analysis: states or individuals'[58] for international economic law would best be answered with: both. Even in its international law variant, private actors can no longer be ignored, with

53. Anne Van Aaken, Christoph Engel and Tom Ginsburg, 'Public International Law and Economics: Symposium Introduction', *University of Illinois Law Review* (2008) 1–4.
54. Andreas L. Paulus, 'Potential and Limits of the Economic Analysis of International Law: A View from Public International Law', 165 *Journal of Institutional and Theoretical Economics* (2009) 170–184.
55. Rene Urueña, *No Citizens Here: Global Subjects and Participation in International Law* (Centre of Excellence in Global Governance Research: University of Helsinki, 2008) at 50.
56. *Ibid*, at 61.
57. *Ibid*, at 57.
58. Paulus, 'Potential and Limits', *supra* note 54, at 175.

international investment law serving as a prime example of new forms of 'subjectivation'[59] that put states and firms side-by-side as 'legitimate' legal subjects.

So far we have focused on the international law approach and the economic law approach to international economic law, which draw on the disciplines of (international) law and politics and (international) law and economics, respectively. In addition, we have considered a sociological approach to international economic law, which is more interested in the sociology of *international* law than in the sociology of *economic* law. However, in order to account for the law of the globalised market society, a focus on public international law seems not sufficient. Instead, emphasis has to be put on international and transnational, public and private economic regulation alike. Moreover, if the sociology of international economic law is not only conceived as a sub-discipline which studies the normative framework of the market society, but also as a meta-discipline which studies the market society as an artefact of law and economics, the 'disciplines' of international economic law become a subject matter in their own right. Before elaborating on this ambivalent position of sociology 'within' and 'above' the field, we will explore what is referred to as the socio-legal approach to international economic law.

1.2. The Socio-Legal Approach to International Economic Law

Perry-Kessaris takes the multiplicity of international economic law as a starting point to explore 'what [...] it mean[s] to take a socio-legal approach'.[60] Accordingly, '[i]nternational economic law is not a discipline. It is a field of study. So it falls to each of us individually to decide how to approach it'.[61] She suggests mapping the differences between socio-legal perspectives and other approaches to international economic law (including the international law and the economic law approach) in analytical, empirical, and normative terms—which would yield much variety also *within* socio-legal scholarship.[62]

> The 'analytical' components of an approach are the *concepts* and *relationships* it deploys to organise the field of study. The 'empirical' components of an approach are the *facts* and *methods* that may be used to confirm the real-life existence, or

59. Urueña, *No Citizens*, *supra* note 55, at 69.
60. Amanda Perry-Kessaris, 'What Does It Mean to Take a Socio-legal Approach to International Economic Law?', in Amanda Perry-Kessaris (ed.), *Socio-Legal Approaches to International Economic Law: Text, Context, Subtext* (Routledge: London, 2012) 3–18.
61. *Ibid*, at 3.
62. Victoria Nourse and Gregory Shaffer, 'Varieties of New Legal Realism: Can a New World Order Prompt a New Legal Theory?', 95 *Cornell Law Review* (2009) 61–137.

absence, of concepts and relationships. The normative components of an approach are the *values* and *interests* that it foregrounds or privileges.[63]

Perry-Kessaris's baseline definition of 'the' socio-legal approach is 'that it is interdisciplinary and sociologically attuned',[64] which does not say much in the positive but implies at least two things in the negative. The first attribute—interdisciplinary—distinguishes it from doctrinal legal work, which is conceived as an 'in-discipline approach' that builds analytically, empirically, and normatively on the legal discipline.[65] The second attribute—sociologically attuned—distinguishes the socio-legal approach, first of all, from the economic analysis of law, which takes economics to the law. Paradoxically, law and economics likewise comes close to an 'in-discipline approach' in that it imports its 'normative, analytical and empirical frame' from the economic discipline, and only applies it to a new subject matter: law.[66] In contrast to the relatively 'unitary' character of legal and economic approaches to international economic law, the socio-legal approach is not only more open to different 'disciplinary sensibilities'[67] but also more pluralistic as to how to 'balance' theory, reality, and morality.[68]

Hence, in its interdisciplinarity and plurality, socio-legal research in international economic law clearly differs from the much more coherent international law and economic law approaches prevailing in the field. To explore the wealth of scholarship outside these disciplines, one could start from the four constitutive elements which socio-legal research in international economic law generally combines: the 'legal' element, the 'social' element, the 'economic' element, and the 'global' element (here going beyond 'international').[69] While the socio-legal approach may, at first, appear to be under-theorised and over-specialised, it actually stands in the tradition of much more encompassing ('holistic') projects in the history of socio-legal thinking, which aim to bring law, economy, and society together, and not to isolate them in different scholarly disciplines.[70]

63. Perry-Kessaris, 'Socio-legal Approach', *supra* note 60, at 4; original emphasis.
64. *Ibid.*
65. *Ibid.*
66. *Ibid*, at 14.
67. Kennedy, 'Disciplines of International Law', *supra* note 13, at 14.
68. Perry-Kessaris, 'Socio-legal Approach', *supra* note 60, at 10.
69. Sabine Frerichs, 'Law, Economy and Society in the Global Age: A Study Guide', in Amanda Perry-Kessaris (ed.), *Socio-Legal Approaches to International Economic Law: Text, Context, Subtext* (Routledge: London, 2012) 36–49.
70. Sabine Frerichs, 'Studying Law, Economy, and Society: A Short History of Socio-legal Thinking', 19 *Helsinki Legal Studies Research Paper* (2009) 1–80.

In the present context, it may suffice to point to actual developments in international economic law, which suggest rethinking the classic legal-doctrinal and legal-political approach. According to Tan, regulation in this field has witnessed a 'movement away from hard coercive power as a mechanism of enforcing compliance towards a subtle, more reproductive form of persuasive power', which can best be depicted as a 'transition from hierarchical, inter-state law to plural, transnational law'.[71] Arguably, the 'discernible shift in the disciplinary apparatus of international economic law',[72] that is, in how 'power is institutionalised',[73] also affects the preferred disciplinary (or inter-disciplinary) approaches to international economic law: implying a shift from law to economics or to more 'sociologically attuned' approaches.

A similar argument is made by Petersmann, who sees a 'need for interdisciplinary research challenging state-centred methodologies underlying Westphalian conceptions' of international (economic) law.[74] To cure this deficit, he refers to the 'economic analysis of law' as well as to '[p]olitical and legal philosophy'.[75] In a different context—thinking about regulatory failure—he also comes to speak of socio-legal perspectives:

> The dangerous gap between the "law in the books" and the "law in action" (e.g. in terms of the incapacity of UN and WTO institutions to protect international public goods and cosmopolitan rights) not only prompts "new legal realist scholars" to call for multidisciplinary and comparative analyses of the "new legal pluralism" of multilevel governance regimes and of the increasing interactions between national and international rules and institutions.[76]

The two movements, or developments, mentioned in this quote—new legal realism and new legal pluralism—deserve further attention as they illustrate the benefits of taking a socio-legal approach to international economic law. While new legal realism has to do with the 'social' element, new legal pluralism has to do with the 'global' element of socio-legal research in international economic law. We will address both aspects in turn.

'The social' became a central reference of twentieth century legal thinking, with law being increasingly understood as a part of social engineering,

71. Celine Tan, 'Navigating New Landscapes: Socio-legal Mapping of Plurality and Power in International Economic Law', in Amanda Perry-Kessaris (ed.), *Socio-Legal Approaches to International Economic Law: Text, Context, Subtext* (Routledge: London, 2012) 19–35 at 33.
72. *Ibid*, at 32.
73. *Ibid*, at 33.
74. Petersmann, 'Methodological Pluralism', *supra* note 14, at 936.
75. *Ibid*, at 936.
76. *Ibid*, at 947.

that is, as a regulatory means to further social progress.[77] Legal realism was a central driving force in this respect. By furthering social scientific approaches to the law, realist scholarship brings the social context of the law back into a discipline which has come to be dominated by formalist and positivist legal reasoning. Both the law and society (L&S) movement and the law and economics (L&E) movement, which developed in the second half of the twentieth century, inherited their '"scientific outlook"' and their 'consequentialist' (means-end oriented) concept of law from legal realism,[78] but they have taken different turns as to how they approach the social context and the social function of law. The L&S movement can be understood as a truly interdisciplinary movement, which even includes 'lesser bits of economics'.[79] Nevertheless, sociological theories and methods do play a decisive role in guiding socio-legal research.[80] In contrast, the L&E movement is strongly linked to mainstream economics and, hence, much more 'disciplinary' in orientation. Its standard method is the rational choice approach.

What distinguishes L&S scholars from L&E scholars, then, is that L&S scholars are interested in the interrelations between 'the economic' and 'the social', and how the one came to dominate the other, whereas L&E scholars approach 'the social' usually through the lens of 'the economic' only. Against this backdrop, a division of labour between L&S and L&E scholarship, which leaves the 'the social' to the former and 'the economic' to the latter, would result in a loss of analytical and critical capacities. Instead, L&S scholars can and should include the economy in their research and approach it with their own distinctive methodologies and theoretical frameworks.

This point was made by Edelman in her 2004 Presidential Address to the American L&S Association, in which she discusses the relationship between L&S and L&E scholarship and the 'contested terrain' between the two.[81] As to the L&E movement, she argues that this has been 'extremely influential in the policy realm, so much so that concepts of law and justice are increasingly *defined* in economic terms and understood through the lens of market efficiency'.[82] In her view, the political (and cultural) impact of the L&E

77. Duncan Kennedy, 'Three Globalizations of Law and Legal Thought: 1850–2000', in David M. Trubek and Alvaro Santos (eds), *The New Law and Economic Development* (Cambridge University Press, 2006) 19–73 at 22.
78. Marc Galanter and Mark Alan Edwards, 'Introduction: The Path of the Law *Ands*', 72 *Wisconsin Law Review* (1997) 375–387 at 377.
79. *Ibid*, at 379.
80. John Hagan, 'Review: The Law & Society Movement Comes of Age', 17 *Contemporary Sociology* (1988) 648–650 at 648.
81. Lauren B. Edelman, 'Rivers of Law and Contested Terrain: A Law and Society Approach to Economic Rationality', 38 *Law and Society Review* (2004) 181–197.
82. *Ibid*, at 182; original emphasis.

movement calls for critical commentary on the part of L&S scholars, whose perspectives are understood to have 'important, if largely unexplored, implications for the nexus of market rationality and justice', that is, at the interface of law and economy.[83] Edelman highlights, in this respect, the concept of economic rationality, which is an unproblematic assumption in L&E (at least in its mainstream) but regarded as a highly contingent social phenomenon in L&S scholarship. Accordingly, 'L&S scholars would call attention to the social, political, and legal construction of rational economic behaviour', and not simply take it as given.[84]

With such enquiries we are entering the realm of 'new' legal realism: a rather heterogeneous current of contemporary socio-legal research, which is presented as a critical response to law and economics.[85] It namely takes issue with the neoclassical mainstream of law and economics, which is no longer considered a legitimate representative of legal realism, even though this is what it once emerged from.[86] Instead, law and economics is charged with furthering a new legal formalism, which has replaced legal principles with economic assumptions but is, otherwise, as axiomatic as the old legal formalism: the 'self-enclosed' type of legal scholarship which 'old' legal realism sought to overcome. By 'over-emphasising theory to the exclusion of empirics', law and economics has indeed developed into a type of 'armchair social science'.[87] In contrast, new legal realism—including the '"new legal realist" orientation in international economic law'[88]—is not only identified by its empirical orientation but also qualified by a normative interest in countering

> the re-triumphalism of market laissez-faire [...], a cynicism toward an unresponsive state, and the hollowing out of traditional conceptions of law in light of new governance challenges from below and the challenges of new global and transnational institutions from above—in sum, the new world order before us.[89]

This description of the new (economic) world order resonates with Petersmann's above reference to the '"new legal pluralism" of multilevel

83. *Ibid*, at 182.
84. *Ibid*, at 184; emphasis omitted.
85. Nourse and Shaffer, 'New Legal Realism', *supra* note 62.
86. Frerichs, 'Studying Law, Economy, and Society', *supra* note 70.
87. Joel P. Trachtman, 'International Economic Law Research: A Taxonomy', in Colin B. Picker, Isabella D. Bunn and Douglas W. Arner (eds.), *International Economic Law: The State and Future of the Discipline* (Hart Publishing: Oxford, 2008) 43–51 at 51.
88. Gregory Shaffer, 'A New Legal Realism: Method in International Economic Law Scholarship', in Colin B. Picker, Isabella D. Bunn and Douglas W. Arner (eds.), *International Economic Law: The State and Future of the Discipline* (Hart Publishing: Oxford, 2008) 29–42 at 29; Paul, 'New Movements', *supra* note 11.
89. Nourse and Shaffer, 'New Legal Realism', *supra* note 62, at 128–129.

governance regimes'.[90] This takes us to the 'global' element of the socio-legal approach.

It has become trivial to state that we are living in a 'global age',[91] and notions of 'globalisation' have recently been used in such an inflationary way that they may actually work to conceal continuities in transnational interdependencies and exchange, which go well beyond the last few decades. However, references to 'the global' also help to overcome the methodological nationalism which has long been prevalent in the social sciences: a preoccupation with the nation and the nation state in all 'sciences of the state', including jurisprudence and political science as much as economics and sociology. To emphasise the global element in socio-legal research means to take the dynamics of the modernisation process seriously, which does not end at national borders but brings about a highly interdependent 'world society'.[92] Even criticisms of this trend, and related countermovements, are, in many ways, globalised. While it can be questioned if economic, legal, and social practices are *really* global today (the bulk of it is not), the effects of globalisation—or of a global frame of reference—can be perceived (almost) everywhere, and long before we are all 'going global'.

While there is an increasing literature on the globalisation of law, we will here focus on a phenomenon which has been referred to as 'global legal pluralism'. Global legal pluralism combines something old (legal pluralism) with something new (the global) and, hence, falls nicely into the realm of socio-legal scholarship. Legal pluralism has long been perceived as a rather marginal, sociological or anthropological discourse which deals not only with official but also unofficial law, and has only lately found its way into the strongholds of legal thought. Michaels depicts the global comeback of legal pluralism as follows: 'The irreducible plurality of legal orders in the world, the coexistence of domestic state law with other legal orders, the absence of a hierarchically superior position transcending the differences—all of these topics of legal pluralism reappear on the global sphere.'[93]

Tamanaha distinguishes between six systems, or categories, of 'normative ordering', which are 'commonly discussed in studies of legal pluralism'.[94]

90. Petersmann, 'Methodological Pluralism', *supra* note 14, at 947.
91. Martin Albrow, *The Global Age: State and Society Beyond Modernity* (Polity Press: Cambridge, 1996).
92. Georg Krücken and Gili S. Drori (eds.), *World Society: The Writings of John W. Meyer* (Oxford University Press, 2009).
93. Ralf Michaels, 'Global Legal Pluralism', 5 *Annual Review of Law and Social Science* (2009) 243–262 at 244.
94. Brian Z. Tamanaha, 'Understanding Legal Pluralism: Past to Present, Local to Global', 30 *Sydney Law Review* (2008) 375–411 at 397.

Besides official legal systems, these include various cultural normative systems, namely, customary systems (made up by shared customs, norms, and institutions), religious systems (often merged with customary systems), and community systems ('imagined communities' of any scale, be it local, national, or global). In addition, Tamanaha also mentions functional normative systems (which regulate specific social spheres or sectors) and singles out economic normative systems (namely the capitalist market economy).[95] He thus lists a number of normative orders which do interact or conflict with official law, but which are, by themselves, not confined to state borders. One of his claims is 'that, riding on the tidal wave of economic globalisation, the most powerful contemporary impetus, momentum, and penetration of new norms is taking place through the economic/capitalist normative system'.[96] It is this process which also affects the form and contents of international economic law as the law and economics of globalisation.

Both of these developments—new legal realism and new legal pluralism—help to define the role and to understand the added value of socio-legal research in international economic law. They point beyond state-centred legal-doctrinal (and legal-political) approaches, which have shaped the international law approach to international economic law; but they also put the economic law approach into perspective. Instead of being preoccupied with the functional normative system of the economy only, they make conflicts between this and other systems of normative ordering visible and open the subject matter of international economic law to multiple perspectives. Instead of rendering the principles of economic analysis absolute, they expose the contingencies of economic reasoning and its effects in constructing and confining ('disciplining') the subject matter of international economic law in just another one-sided way. These *inter*disciplinary sensibilities can be harvested in a sociology of international economic law, which understands sociology not only as a sub-discipline but as a meta-discipline.

1.3. Outlining a Critical Sociology of International Economic Law

The sociology of international economic law can be understood both as sub-discipline and a meta-discipline of international economic law. As a sub-discipline it puts the subject matter of international economic law in a sociological perspective. As a meta-discipline its subject matter is the discipline of international economic law itself. In the following, we will go beyond the more conventional, or more agreeable, perspective of sociology as a

95. *Ibid*, at 397–399.
96. *Ibid*, at 406.

(sub-)discipline of international economic law next to international law and politics and international law and economics.

Drawing on the 'interdisciplinary and sociologically attuned' research orientation of the socio-legal approach[97] elaborated above, we may claim that a sociological approach to international economic law is neither bound to the international law perspective, nor to the economic law perspective, even though it can align itself with either of these. But it can also bring in a third perspective, such as that of new legal realism or global legal pluralism, or even transcend all these perspectives, by making the 'perspectivism' of different approaches to international economic law its very subject matter. In this article, we start from the economic law perspective, but articulate it with the perspective of the economic sociology of law. In so doing, we subject the discipline of (law and) economics, the driving force behind the economic law perspective, to a sociological critique.

The move from a sub-discipline to a meta-discipline of international economic law brings the relation of power and knowledge into focus. Both are involved in the 'confrontation of disciplines':

> [I]f disciplines are understood as social constructs [...] a confrontation of disciplines will never be a confrontation of "pure" knowledges or methodologies with its outcome determined by intellectual criteria such as methodological rigour, sophistication of theoretical analysis, or depth of empirical reference. Such a confrontation will always ultimately be a *social* conflict (in certain aspects, a political conflict in the sense of a competition for power or an attempt to exercise power).[98]

While Cotterrell speaks about the disciplines of law and sociology, he could also be referring to the disciplines of international economic law. The perspective of the sociology of international economic law as a meta-discipline can be derived from the following specification of academic disciplines as subject matter of sociological enquiry:

> In so far as intellectual disciplines and structures of power in society are closely interconnected, sociology is necessarily eventually drawn by its concern in understanding social structure to make the knowledge-claims of other disciplines part of its subject-matter (and so merely social data rather than "truths") so as to examine the contribution of these disciplinary knowledges to the maintenance, organization, and transformation of patterns of power relationships and social structure generally.[99]

97. Perry-Kessaris, 'Socio-legal Approach', *supra* note 60, at 4.
98. Roger Cotterrell, *Law's Community: Legal Theory in Sociological Perspective* (Clarendon Press: Oxford, 1995) at 48; original emphasis.
99. *Ibid*, at 62–63.

The sociology of international economic law—and of any other academic field or discipline—thus includes the aim to understand the intellectual force *of* the discipline as well as the social forces *behind* the discipline, in short: its theoretical implications and practical effects. These 'power-knowledge effects' (Foucault) can be conceived on a more abstract, structural level or on a more concrete, individual level.

For David Kennedy, disciplines provide the 'argumentative, doctrinal, and institutional materials' through which scholars pursue their 'personal, professional, political' projects.[100] Broude emphasises, in this respect, that international economic law scholars have mostly acted as 'advocates of universal economic liberalism'.[101] In fact, the discipline of international economic law seems to have its 'paradigmatic roots' in the 'Ricardian-Smithian traditions of liberal economic theories of market economics and international free trade'.[102] In this sense, international economic law 'enables the discipline of economics to transform itself from theory to practice'.[103]

From a sociological perspective, the definition of international economic law is not only a question of principles which can be settled theoretically (*a priori*), but also a question of practices to be studied empirically (*a posteriori*): the actual subject matter of international economic law. It is not only about picking the right conceptual framework and knowledge base, but also about capturing the real state of affairs as regards the normative authority and enforcement power of different economic regimes. Broude notes that, in reality, international economic regimes include 'Keynesian allowances for limited public and national manipulations of trade', which go beyond the ideals of 'liberal economic theory'.[104] Considering this 'pragmatic' side of international economic law, he argues that it can, perhaps, better be understood as '"political economy" than economics',[105] which manifests itself in 'embedded' forms of liberalism.[106]

These practical concessions notwithstanding, our starting point is the law of market society as it is shaped by the mainstream of the economic discipline,

100. Kennedy, 'Disciplines of International Law', *supra* note 13, at 14.
101. Tomer Broude, 'At the End of the Yellow Brick Road: International Economic Law Research in Times of Uncertainty', in Colin B. Picker, Isabella D. Bunn and Douglas W. Arner (eds.), *International Economic Law: The State and Future of the Discipline* (Hart Publishing: Oxford, 2008) 15–28 at 18.
102. *Ibid*, at 17–18.
103. *Ibid*, at 20.
104. *Ibid*, at 18.
105. *Ibid.*
106. *Ibid*, at 19.

or by what Polanyi refers to as the 'philosophy of economic liberalism'.[107] It is for this reason that a sociology of international economic law may find the economic law definition of the field analytically and empirically more adequate than the international law definition. However, if sociology is understood as a meta-discipline, this perspective would not be treated as normatively superior but it would be exposed in its disciplinary effects. Accordingly, the discipline (power structure) of international economic law is justified in terms of the discipline (knowledge structure) of law and economics—and vice versa.

Thus defined, the sociology of international economic law is part and parcel of the 'economic sociology of law': a field of research, which has recently attracted increasing scholarly attention.[108] Our above definition—or outline—of the sociology of international economic law is in line with how to conceive of the economic sociology of law, more generally. Accordingly, the economic sociology of law is located in the midst of three established disciplines (economics, sociology, jurisprudence) and three interdisciplinary research fields (economy and society, law and society, law and economy). Like the sociology of international economic law, the economic sociology of law could be understood as a relatively narrow sub-discipline; but, again, it can also be framed as a meta-discipline which reflects on the normative and performative effects of the existing interdisciplinary division of labour at the intersection of law, economy, and society.

While the economic sociology of law generally emphasises the 'embeddedness' of law and economy in society, its more specific task is to complement and contextualise law and economics (broadly understood) from a sociological point of view. Embeddedness is considered the core concept, or lowest common denominator, of economic sociology, and first of all connected with Polanyi's work. The embeddedness approach distinguishes economic sociology, which is 'institutionalist' by its very nature, from economic theory,

107. Polanyi, *Great Transformation*, *supra* note 7, at 269.

108. Richard Swedberg, 'The Case for an Economic Sociology of Law', 32 *Theory and Society* (2003) 1–37; Richard Swedberg, 'Max Weber's Contribution to the Economic Sociology of Law', 2 *Annual Review of Law and Social Science* (2006) 61–81; Sabine Frerichs, 'The Legal Constitution of Market Society: Probing the Economic Sociology of Law', 10(3) *Economic Sociology—European Electronic Newsletter* (2009) 20–25; Sabine Frerichs, 'Re-embedding Neo-liberal Constitutionalism: A Polanyian Case for the Economic Sociology of Law', in Christian Joerges and Josef Falke (eds.), *Karl Polanyi, Globalisation and the Potential of Law in Transnational Markets* (Hart Publishing: Oxford, 2011) 65–84; Diamond Ashiagbor, Prabha Kotiswaran and Amanda Perry-Kessaris (eds.), 'Special Issue: Towards an Economic Sociology of Law', 40 *Journal of Law and Society* (2013) 1–6.

which furthers, in its neoclassical mainstream, a 'disembedded' view of the (market) economy. At the same time, the idea of embeddedness links economic sociology to general sociology and its manifold theories of integration and differentiation. If understood in its most encompassing sense, economic sociology thus includes all levels of sociological analysis: the micro-level of actors, the meso-level of relations, the macro-level of regimes, and the meta-level of rationalities.[109] It goes without saying that different approaches emphasise different levels of analysis. For example, 'new' (American) economic sociology, as launched, amongst others, by Granovetter, who was briefly mentioned above,[110] puts emphasis on the micro- and meso-levels, whereas 'old' (European) economic sociology, which includes Polanyi's work, aims at the macro- and meta-levels of sociological analysis.

The economic sociology of law can be understood as an extension of economic sociology (and as a specification of general sociology), but it can likewise be seen as an extension of legal sociology. In fact, the dissociation of economic theory and economic sociology in thinking about the economy seems to be reflected in an analogous dissociation of legal theory and legal sociology in thinking about the law. In other words, the leading theories in both disciplines—economics and jurisprudence—have come to reflect the autonomy and separateness of economic and legal spheres rather than their social embeddedness. Both law and economics are thus dominated by 'disembedded' views of the economy and the law respectively. Moreover, much of today's economic and legal sociology seems preoccupied with the micro- and meso-levels of actors and relations, at the expense of a broader understanding of regimes and rationalities at the macro- and meta-levels of sociological analysis. Similarly, what has been reduced to law and economics (or, more precisely, the economic analysis of law) lacks a sociological framing which would shed light on the interaction of law and economy in society.

In response to these shortcomings, economic sociology not only includes a 'sociology of economy', but also a 'sociology of economics':[111] hence, a sociology of the economic discipline, and of scientific knowledge more generally. Likewise, the sociology of law includes a 'sociology of jurisprudence', that

109. Frerichs, 'Legal Constitution', *supra* note 108; Frerichs, 'Re-embedding Neo-liberal Constitutionalism', *supra* note 108.

110. In the context of Hirsch's sociology of international (economic) law; see Hirsch, 'Sociology of International Economic Law', *supra* note 37, at 280; Granovetter, 'Economic Action', *supra* note 51.

111. Milan Zafirovski, 'Sociology of Economics or Sociology of Economy? Theoretical-Methodological Arguments for Sociological Economics', 31 *Forum for Social Economics* (2001) 27–58.

is, a critical interest in legal scholarship, which it shares with critical legal studies. As regards the economic sociology of law, the cognitive turn from the *subject matter* of the law and the economy to the *disciplines* constructing and reproducing these spheres of reality, takes the form of a criticism of law and economics, or of any positive (or normative) theory that describes (or prescribes) how legal and economic rationalities are (to be) mediated.

What the following reconstruction of Polanyi's work and of the role of law therein emphasises is not only 'normative embeddedness' on the level of regimes but also 'cognitive embeddedness' on the level of rationalities.[112] On the one hand, the idea of the social embeddedness of the economy—which is considered the 'normal' case throughout history—is taken as a normative standard to pinpoint processes 'disembedding' or 're-embedding' the market in modern society. On the other hand, we can also emphasise the cognitive dimension of the market society, which relies, by and large, on the 'embeddedness of economic markets in economics'.[113] Moreover, market society as such seems to be embedded in the concepts and visions of the economic discipline. Arguably, this also affects the law of market society, and—with law and economics as a mediator—the legal discipline.

With regard to cognitive embeddedness and, more specifically, the 'legal construction of economic rationalities',[114] Lang recently characterised the agenda of the (new) economic sociology of law as follows:

> [I]n what ways, if any, are the cognitive infrastructures of markets—and therefore the particular forms of calculative rationality characteristic of such markets—created, entrenched, and mobilized through law and legal practices? What, in other words, is law's role in the construction, maintenance, and transformation of frameworks of knowledge and their associated practices of economic rationality in particular market contexts?[115]

While Lang's main interest is in the legal construction of economic rationalities, the economic sociology of law, as it is understood here, takes an equal interest in the economic construction, or transformation, of legal reasoning. This dual move, first, from economics to law and, then, from law to economics is already implied in Edelman's above observation that 'concepts of law and justice are increasingly *defined* in economic terms and understood

112. Frerichs, 'Re-embedding Neo-liberal Constitutionalism', *supra* note 108.
113. Michel Callon, 'Introduction: The Embeddedness of Economic Markets in Economics', in Michel Callon, Michel (ed.), *The Laws of the Markets* (Blackwell, Oxford, 1998) 1–57.
114. Andrew T.F. Lang, 'The Legal Construction of Economic Rationalities', 40 *Journal of Law and Society* (2013) 155–171.
115. *Ibid*, at 170.

mercantile conditions was there [...] a separate economic system in society. Nineteenth century society, in which economic activity was isolated and imputed to a distinctive economic motive, was, indeed, a singular departure.'[136] In spatial terms, Polanyi's analysis goes, from the outset, beyond national economies and polities, and suggests a global frame of reference instead. This is already clear at the beginning of his book where he postulates that nineteenth century civilisation—the first market society in history—rested likewise on national and international institutions.[137] Moreover, in Polanyi's view, the international political economy had become subject to '[t]he global sweep of economic liberalism'.[138] Accordingly, '[n]othing less than a self-regulating market on a world scale could ensure the functioning of this stupendous mechanism', which resulted in unprecedented global interdependencies.[139] Polanyi considered the market society as unsustainable and, at least in the long run, doomed to failure. Consequently, he recognises in the social countermovements of the late nineteenth and early twentieth century the 'self-protection of society'[140] against the 'satanic mill' of the market.[141] His vision of a liberal socialism, which strives for 'a society [that] can afford to be both just and free',[142] is itself rooted in the embeddedness paradigm and completes Polanyi's holistic approach. Like the historical scholars which he drew inspiration from, Polanyi studied the history of the modern market society not least in moral terms.

2.2. Economic Law in the Shadow of Speenhamland

Before turning to the role of institutions and commodities in Polanyi's approach, which help to understand the ambiguities of the law, it seems useful to briefly summarise the ideal-typical stages of the great transformation, which his book is about and which can also be depicted in legal terms.[143]

According to Polanyi, the social organisation of pre-market societies is characterised by institutional patterns of symmetry, centricity and/or autarchy, which are supported by behavioural principles of reciprocity, re-distribution and/or householding. More generally speaking, the default state before the great transformation is characterised by social embeddedness, which includes

136. *Ibid*, at 71.
137. *Ibid*, at 3.
138. *Ibid*, at 138.
139. *Ibid*.
140. *Ibid*, part II.2.
141. *Ibid*, part II.1.
142. *Ibid*, at 256.
143. Frerichs, 'Re-embedding Neo-liberal Constitutionalism', *supra* note 108, at 82.

the law: market exchange is still embedded in law, and law is embedded in society, underpinned by a strong collective conscience. Polanyi speaks of an (undifferentiated) complex of 'custom and law, magic and religion' in this respect, which kept the gain motive in check.[144]

The institutional pattern that distinguishes market society from pre-market societies is the market as predominant form of social organisation, which is supported by the behavioural principle of '[b]arter, truck, and exchange'.[145] Polanyi emphasises that market institutions and market behaviour are not confined to the modern market society only; instead, they may very well 'take a subordinate place in a society in which other [patterns and] principles are in the ascendant'.[146] What the great transformation starts with, then, is a gradual but radical 'disembedding' of the market, that is, its liberalisation and prioritisation in modernizing economies. Normatively speaking, market exchange is then no longer restricted by 'human laws'[147]—or by a natural law of divine origin—but left to 'the laws of Nature'.[148] Put differently, man-made law starts mimicking quasi-natural laws, which are rationalised and popularised by liberal economics. This includes the new norm of profit-seeking behaviour in markets of whatever kind, which is normalised and legitimised under the principle of *laissez-faire*. Just as the market, the law thereby becomes disembedded.

With regard to the 're-embedding' move, which completes the dialectics of the great transformation, Polanyi discusses contemporary efforts to re-regulate 'self-regulating markets' according to over-riding social needs. At the height of the Second World War he was faced with the blatant alternative of fascism or socialism, both of which he considered to be 'rooted in a market society that refused to function'.[149] However, Polanyi was as clear in his critique of the market society as he was in his rejection of totalitarian regimes. His vision of a re-embedded post-market society can best be described as a liberal form of socialism, which directly challenges the presumptions and pretensions of economic liberalism. Presumably, the naturalist and axiomatic language of the latter would then be replaced with an agenda that includes law as a means of progressive politics. In other words, law would be understood as a social instrument rather than as the (in-)visible hand of the market. In this regard, Polanyi's position resonates with legal realism.

144. Polanyi, *Great Transformation*, *supra* note 7, at 55.
145. *Ibid*, at 56.
146. *Ibid.*
147. *Ibid*, at 125.
148. *Ibid*, at 114.
149. *Ibid*, at 239. The 'collectivist' countermovement' is also framed in terms of socialism and nationalism; *Ibid*, at 145.

whose 'powerful social instrumentality' was premised on the gold standard.[174] Polanyi characterises international finance as 'an institution *sui generis*, [which was] peculiar to the last third of the nineteenth and the first third of the twentieth century, [and which] functioned as the main link between the political and the economic organization of the world'.[175]

Hence, through the gold standard, and the disciplining influence of international finance, '[t]rade had become linked with peace'.[176] In other words, the political (or peace) organisation of the world became anchored in its economic organisation and, hence, contingent on a reliable system of foreign trade and currency exchange. At the same time, the international monetary system was no longer a 'purely economic institution' but had itself developed a 'political function'.[177] The effects of this regime of the gold standard and international finance are depicted in terms that seem as topical today as they were in the late nineteenth century:

> By the fourth quarter of the nineteenth century, world commodity prices were the central reality in the lives of millions of Continental peasants; the repercussions of the London money market were daily noted by businessmen all over the world; and governments discussed plans for the future in light of the situation on the world capital markets.[178]

In short, the power and wealth of the nations ultimately became 'functions of currency and credit'.[179] When the gold standard collapsed, the whole system became obsolete. In Polanyi's words, '[t]he snapping of the golden thread was the signal for a world revolution'.[180]

2.4. From Rule of Law to Fictitious Commodities

The second step will be to recapitulate Polanyi's argument in the main part of the book with a view on the liaison of the self-regulating market and the liberal state, which was somewhat neglected in the introductory part. Bearing in mind that the liberal state was characterised above as a 'creation' of the self-regulating market, Polanyi's enquiries into 'The rise and fall of market economy'[181] should also yield insights into the fate and fortune of its political

174. *Ibid*, at 9.
175. *Ibid*, at 10.
176. *Ibid*, at 15.
177. *Ibid*, at 20.
178. *Ibid*, at 18.
179. *Ibid*.
180. *Ibid*, at 27.
181. *Ibid*, part two.

counterpart. The liberal state is typically seen as wedded to the 'rule of law', which is one entry-point for the law in Polanyi's argumentation. Ebner summarises in this respect: 'the rise of the market as a set of hegemonic institutions which shape the modern exchange economy coincides with the rule of law, which implies a reduction of social relations to the regulation of property and contract'.[182] Another option is to study the interface between the self-regulating market and the liberal state in terms of Polanyi's 'fictitious commodities', notably labour, land, and money, which can also be conceived as legal fictions. Both avenues will be explored in the following.

In order to do so, we can start from the chapter entitled 'The self-regulating market and the fictitious commodities',[183] which introduces the market economy as 'an economic system controlled, regulated, and directed by markets alone'.[184] Accordingly, 'order in the production and distribution of goods is entrusted to this self-regulating mechanism' only.[185] At first, market exchange appears to be a self-contained economic institution that is detached from all politics. In fact, the market economy rests on assumptions of political non-interference into the formation of markets and, notably, the price mechanism.[186] In positive terms, 'only such policies and measures are in order which help to ensure the self-regulation of the market by creating conditions which make the market the only organizing power in the economic sphere'.[187]

This paradox is also expressed in the policy of '*laissez-faire*', which was 'enforced by the state'.[188] Accordingly, the nineteenth century was not only characterised by 'an outburst of legislation repealing restrictive regulations' but also by 'an enormous increase in the administrative functions of the state'.[189] Polanyi highlights that 'the introduction of free markets, far from doing away with the need for control, regulation, and intervention, enormously increased their range'.[190] In the end, this means that the liberal state is 'liberal' only in its aims but not necessarily in its means—which can, according to Polanyi, reach from law to war: 'The economic liberal can, therefore, without any inconsistency call upon the state to use the force of law; he can even appeal to

182. Alexander Ebner, 'Transnational Markets and the Polanyi Problem', in Christian Joerges and Josef Falke (eds.), *Karl Polanyi, Globalisation and the Potential of Law in Transnational Markets* (Hart Publishing: Oxford, 2011) 19–40 at 22; reference omitted.
183. Polanyi, *Great Transformation*, *supra* note 7, chapter 6.
184. *Ibid*, at 68.
185. *Ibid*.
186. *Ibid*, at 69.
187. *Ibid*.
188. *Ibid*, at 139.
189. *Ibid*.
190. *Ibid*, at 140.

the violent forces of civil war to set up the preconditions of a self-regulating market.'[191] Following this argument, the 'rule of law' is less to be understood as a formal prerequisite of the market economy than as a powerful instrument for its implementation. The transformation of certain aspects of (economic) life into commodities appears to play a central role in this respect. Moreover, within the process of commodification the law can both act as a 'commodifier' and become itself a commodity. In order to make this point, we will first have a look at the (other) fictitious commodities.

Even though Polanyi distinguished somewhat inconclusively between economic and political institutions at the outset of his study, he was well aware of the novelty and artificiality of the institutional separation of economic and political spheres. Moreover, he was convinced that the market society, which resulted from subjecting everything to the laws of the market, was anything but self-sufficient. His argument is 'substantivist' in that it builds on 'the human beings [...] of which every society consists and the natural surroundings in which it exists'.[192] This is where the fictitious commodities come into play, which Polanyi considers 'fictitious' in that they are traded on the market but have not been produced for the market in the first place. In other words, the productive potential of human beings and their natural environment is turned into land and labour by an act of commodification, which is typically sanctioned by the law. Certain intrinsic aspects of social and natural life are thus singled out to be traded on the market. As to the production factors of land and labour, Polanyi argues that 'labor is only another name for a human activity which goes with life itself' and 'land is only another name for nature, which is not produced by man'.[193]

Due to his frequent references to nature, Polanyi is sometimes seen as a pioneer of the environmental movement. Even though this only took shape a generation later, it can easily be recognised as one of the social countermovements that Polanyi described and anticipated in his book. Polanyi's understanding of land and nature is quite comprehensive, including not only its 'economic function' but also its 'vital functions', which he specifies as 'the conditions of safety and security attached to the integrity of the soil and its resources'.[194] These are understood to encompass, amongst others, 'the vigor and stamina of the population, the abundance of food supplies, [...] even the climate of the country which might suffer from the denudation

191. *Ibid*, at 149.
192. *Ibid*, at 71.
193. *Ibid*, at 72.
194. *Ibid*, at 184.

of forests, from erosions and dust bowls'.[195] Considering the incisive consequences that the commodification of nature could entail for the livelihood of the people, it comes as no surprise that it eventually provoked a strong social reaction. Historically, this is reflected in the reintroduction of 'land laws and agrarian tariffs', which Polanyi explains 'by the necessity of protecting natural resources and the culture of the countryside against the implications of the commodity fiction in respect to them'.[196]

With regard to labour, Polanyi argues that this is a human activity which cannot 'be detached from the rest of life, be stored or mobilized'.[197] Subjecting labour to market forces, that is, the laws of supply and demand, would directly affect 'the human individual who happens to be the bearer of this peculiar commodity'—'the physical, psychological, and moral entity "man" [or "human"] attached to that tag'.[198] For the workers, the commodification of labour ultimately resulted in an 'extreme instability of earnings, utter absence of professional standards, abject readiness to be shoved and pushed about indiscriminately, complete dependence on the whims of the market'.[199] In order 'to protect industrial man from the implications of the commodity fiction in regard to labor power',[200] the social countermovements of the twentieth century found it necessary to interfere 'with the mobility of labor and the flexibility of wages' and to further 'social legislation, factory laws, unemployment insurance, and, above all, trade unions'.[201]

Compared to the substance of land (nature) and the substance of labour (human beings), the substance of money seems harder to define. On the one hand, Polanyi distinguishes between money as mere purchasing power and money as a marketable commodity. According to this, 'actual money' is 'merely a token of purchasing power which [...] comes into being through the mechanism of banking or state finance'.[202] On the other hand, Polanyi relates money to 'productive organization'[203] and 'capitalistic production'.[204] He thus seems to replicate the well-known distinction between real capital (or productive investment) and money capital (or speculative investment).

195. *Ibid.*
196. *Ibid*, at 132.
197. *Ibid*, at 72.
198. *Ibid*, at 73.
199. *Ibid*, at 176.
200. *Ibid*, at 132.
201. *Ibid*, at 177.
202. *Ibid*, at 177 and 196–197.
203. *Ibid*, at 130.
204. *Ibid*, at 132.

It seems that for Polanyi the question ultimately was who is in control of the money: the state or the market.[205] As long as governments could manage the money supply according to the needs of the national economy, it was mainly a political instrument. Under conditions of the international gold standard—a 'self-regulating mechanism of supplying credit'—money increasingly became a matter of the (world) market.[206] The mere existence of the gold standard thus furthered the commodity form of money (i.e. its exchange function), whereas national central banking was still premised on the 'manipulation' of currency exchange and money supply (i.e. its payment and investment function).[207] As Polanyi explicates, 'central banking and the management of the monetary system were needed to keep manufactures and other productive enterprises safe from the harm involved in the commodity fiction as applied to money'.[208] Against this backdrop, international economic law can be understood to strike a balance—however skewed—between economic self-regulation, that is, 'the organization of world commodity markets, world capital markets, and world currency markets under the aegis of the gold standard',[209] and political regulation in the context of central banking.

2.5. Between Commodification and Decommodification

The third step is to systematise the claims made above and to illustrate how the law, by instituting the economy, may itself become commodified. This time, our point of departure is Polanyi's essay on 'The economy as instituted process'.[210] Under this title, he advances a 'substantivist' approach to the economy, which acknowledges 'the transcending importance of [its] institutional aspect'.[211] Whereas liberal (classical or neo-classical) economics adheres to a 'formalist' understanding of frictionless markets, Polanyi conceives of the economy in terms of its 'institutional embeddedness'.[212] In this perspective, law would only be one of the institutions which provide the

205. Sabine Frerichs, 'From Credit to Crisis: Max Weber, Karl Polanyi, and the Other Side of the Coin', 40 *Journal of Law and Society* (2013) 7–26; Sabine Frerichs, 'Money Matters: The Heads and Tails of Conflict Constitutionalism', in Christian Joerges and Carola Glinski (eds.), The European Crisis and the Transformation of Transnational Governance: Authoritarian Managerialism versus Democratic Governance (Hart Publishing: Oxford, 2014) 1–19.
206. Polanyi, *Great Transformation*, *supra* note 7, at 195.
207. *Ibid.*
208. *Ibid*, at 132.
209. *Ibid*, at 76.
210. Polanyi, 'Economy as Instituted Process', *supra* note 161.
211. *Ibid*, at 35.
212. *Ibid*, at 36.

economic process with '[u]nity and stability, structure and function, history and policy'.[213] But, again, the legal institutedness of economic life is not specifically mentioned. Instead, money—the third fictitious commodity in *The Great Transformation*—is explicitly introduced as an institution in the substantivist meaning of the term.[214] As such, it can also be defined independently of markets, and of the modern market economy in particular. Polanyi distinguishes in this respect between different functions, or uses, of money, including the 'payment use', the 'standard, or accounting use', and the 'exchange use'.[215] As to the latter, he claims that '[i]n the absence of markets the exchange use of money is no more than a subordinate culture trait'.[216] However, in a market economy which works according to the price-mechanism this specific function becomes predominant.

Money is a means of exchange which has—in the commodified state—itself a price. As a 'quantifiable unit for indirect exchange', which consists in 'mere verbalizations or written symbols',[217] it can be considered the fictitious commodity par excellence. Law usually does not have a price but it is certainly a means of exchange. As 'symbolically generalised' media of exchange, both law and money condense an otherwise very complex sequence of communications. Importantly, the notion of 'exchange' is here not reduced to market exchange but also encompasses other forms or contexts of communication. From a Polanyian point of view, both law and money also 'mediate', in different ways, between political regulation and economic self-regulation, and thus play a pivotal role in the market society. By qualifying (by means of law) and quantifying (through money) what can be sold on markets, both take part in the process of commodification. In other words, both law and money are constitutive in bringing about fictitious commodities, and the market society as such.

As to the law, our argument is the following: while it would make sense to start with the role of the law in the decommodification of land, labour, and money, it seems to make even more sense to start with its role in the commodification process. If the fictitious commodities are basically legal artefacts on which the 'reality' of the market society is based, law is a commodifier and potential decommodifier at the same time. This idea is not entirely original but derived from Marxian lines of thinking, which have also inspired Polanyi's work. In linking one Karl to the other, we can claim that

213. *Ibid.*
214. *Ibid*, at 32.
215. *Ibid*, at 45.
216. *Ibid*, at 46.
217. *Ibid.*

the relationship between the 'economic structure of society' and its 'legal and political superstructure' resurfaces, in Polanyi's approach, in the ways that fictitious commodities 'institute' the self-regulating market. Supiot speaks of the 'dogmatic foundations' of the market in this respect—notably its foundation in *legal* dogmas.[218] In other words, the process of commodification works on the grounds of economic fictions that are translated into legal fictions. The relationship between law and economics is thus twofold: the market is shaped by legal institutions, but the law is also shaped by economic thinking. Not surprisingly then, lawyers and economists do share certain concepts—such as 'person' (subject), 'property' (object)', 'contract' (exchange)—which are all fundamental in enforcing the market society.

This constructivist reading of *The Great Transformation* is supported by a short piece entitled 'Our obsolete market mentality',[219] where Polanyi explicitly argues that the 'machinery' of self-regulating markets has also transformed our 'consciousness'. Accordingly, economic notions of humanity and society have 'gained the status of axioms' and, as such, come to 'constrict our minds and souls'.[220] In Polanyi's view, the 'delusion' of market society has too long dominated our thoughts and values, and only in the wake of a devastating crisis—namely the two world wars—'we begin to doubt the truth of some of these thoughts and the validity of some of these values'.[221] While these statements pertain to the embeddedness of the market society in economics, the economic embeddedness of the law of market society, its freedoms and obligations, is best captured in the following statement: 'In market society alone did the economic mechanism lay down the law.'[222] Varying this idea, Steiner speaks of 'a society in which law and morals are increasingly overwhelmed by the market mentality'.[223]

Somewhat paradoxically Polanyi's notion of the instituted economy thus includes not only the embedded but also the disembedded market, which is instituted with the help of the commodity fiction. The substance (humans, nature) and symbols (law, money) of economic life—its material values as well as its means of exchange—are then reduced to mere numbers in cost-benefit calculations. Hence, we are left with two conflicting roles of the

218. Alain Supiot, *Homo Juridicus: On the Anthropological Function of the Law* (Verso: London, 2007) at 94.
219. Polanyi, 'Market Mentality', *supra* note 159.
220. *Ibid*, at 147.
221. *Ibid*, at 146.
222. *Ibid*, at 154.
223. Philippe Steiner, 'Who Is Right About the Modern Economy: Polanyi, Zelizer, or Both?', 38 *Theory and Society* (2009) 97–110 at 105–106.

law: as commodifier and decommodifier. In its commodifying function, law itself becomes cognitively embedded in economics. It then turns into a means that serves the ends of the market: of creating competition, increasing efficiency, and furthering growth. Under these conditions, law appears as a production factor just like labour, land, and money (or capital) and ultimately comes with a 'price tag'. This means nothing less than that the law turns itself into a fictitious commodity next to land, labour and money—and other 'fourth' commodities, which have been suggested by Polanyi-inspired scholars, such as knowledge[224] or culture.[225]

We can speak of law as a commodity first of all in the macroeconomic sense: when the law of the market is enshrined in the form of a liberal economic constitution (again, functionally understood). On the international level, this includes, most prominently, the European economic constitution. Whenever regulatory competition allows a 'law market' to arise,[226] the commodity character of law also materialises in the microeconomic sense, and it becomes a variable factor in individual production or consumption functions. A certain legal rule or regime can then be marketed and shopped for at the national, regional or global level, with regulatory choices being taken for economic rather than political reasons, as customers and not as citizens. In Polanyian terms, an international economic regime which furthers regulatory competition imitates the logic of a self-regulating market.

If this is the commodity form of the law, which can be more or less pronounced in practice, but which is intrinsic to thinking about the law in terms of economics (or law and economics), its original substance may be found in the essence of social obligations. Indeed, for Durkheim law was but a symbol of social solidarity,[227] which is embedded in a community of interdependent and mutually committed individuals. This argument is taken up by Cotterrell, who has gone a long way to find 'law's community' also in transnational networks of a more instrumental, or economic, kind.[228] However, in this case, social solidarity seems to be reduced to a rather rudimentary substance—say,

224. Bob Jessop, 'Knowledge as a Fictitious Commodity: Insights and Limits of a Polanyian Perspective', in Ayse Bugra and Kaan Agartan, Kaan (eds.), *Reading Karl Polanyi for the Twenty-First Century: Market Economy as a Political Project* (Palgrave Macmillan: Basingstoke, 2007) 116–133.
225. Timothy Macneill, 'The End of Transformation? Culture as the Final Fictitious Commodity', 12 *Problématique* (2009), <www.yorku.ca/problema/Issues/Problematique1202.pdf> (visited 3 April 2014).
226. Erin A. O'Hara and Larry E. Ribstein, *The Law Market* (Oxford University Press, 2009).
227. Emile Durkheim, *The Division of Labour in Society* (Macmillan: Basingstoke, 1984).
228. Cotterrell, *Law's Community*, *supra* note 98; Roger Cotterrell, 'A Legal Concept of Community', 12 *Canadian Journal of Law and Society* (1997) 75–91; Roger Cotterrell,

of abiding by contracts—which even economists cannot do without. In a nutshell, the market society turns the bonds of community into an exchange of commodities, from which the law is not exempt.

3. Law's Great Transformation: A Short History of the Law of Market Society

Law's ambivalent—enabling and restricting—role in the market society has been framed in terms of an inherent tension between commodifying and decommodifying functions. This translates into a dialectical principle of development, which Polanyi describes as a 'double movement' of 'movement' and 'countermovement',[229] without yet applying it to the law. According to Polanyi, the double movement 'can be personified as the action of two organizing principles in society, each of them setting itself specific institutional aims, having the support of definite social forces and using its own distinctive methods'.[230] What is not mentioned here, but can be derived from the overall argument, is that these different principles of organisation also find their support in different scientific theories and disciplines; they are rationalised and justified, debated and contested in academic discourse. Polanyi contrasts the two 'organizing principles' as follows:

> The one was the principle of economic liberalism, aiming at the establishment of a self-regulating market, relying on the support of the trading classes, and using largely *laissez-faire* and free trade as its methods; the other was the principle of social protection aiming at the conservation of man and nature as well as productive organization, relying on the varying support of those most immediately affected by the deleterious action of the market—primarily, but not exclusively, the working and the landed classes—and using protective legislation, restrictive associations, and other instruments of intervention as its methods.[231]

The principle of economic liberalism is characterised as 'utopian'[232] and a 'peril to society',[233] the principle of social protection is considered as 'realistic'[234]

'Transnational Networks of Community and International Economic Law', in Amanda Perry-Kessaris (ed.), *Socio-Legal Approaches to International Economic Law: Text, Context, Subtext* (Routledge: London, 2012) 133–149.

229. Polanyi, *Great Transformation*, *supra* note 7, at 130.
230. *Ibid*, at 132.
231. *Ibid*.
232. *Ibid*, at 141.
233. *Ibid*, at 150.
234. *Ibid*, at 141.

in that it defends the 'interests of society as a whole'.[235] In scholarly terms, one is reminded of the dispute between (neoclassical) law and economics, including its adaptation to international economic law, and new legal realism, which feeds into the socio-legal approach to international economic law. Taking the cognitive dimension of embeddedness into account, it seems justified to conceive of the double movement not only in terms of social movements but also in terms of scholarly movements, which likewise pursue a political cause. Our focus in the following will be the dynamic of movement and countermovement in the law of market society, including law as an academic discipline that also shapes politics. In doing so, we do not mean to distract from the 'really existing social struggles',[236] but to follow them through to academia.

From a Polanyian point of view, the law of market society includes all types of law that constitute or regulate the (allegedly) self-regulating market. It cuts across different legal fields and disciplines, namely public and private law, national and international law (including transnational and supranational law). It encompasses both 'market-constitutive' and 'market-regulative' forms of law. Mirroring Polanyi's interest in the 'organisation' of the international political economy, it seems suitable to subsume these different fields and forms of law under the (broad) label of international economic law. Going beyond its functional definition put forward by lawyer-economists, a Polanyian approach to international economic law has to expose the conflicting rationalities which law adopts in constituting and containing the market society, and which also structure legal discourse. Interestingly, Polanyian categories have come to be explicitly used in legal scholarship in order to qualify certain forms of (transnational) legal regulation as disembedding or re-embedding. Again, such arguments also fulfil a political function in justifying or criticizing new pathways of the market society.

In the following, we will reconstruct the history of the law of market society from its formation in nineteenth century civilisation, the first market society in history, to its reformation in contemporary society, that is, the market society of the (early) twenty-first century. Combining different perspectives from different legal fields, a historical narrative emerges, which offers a legal supplement to, and update of, Polanyi's socio-economic approach. In line with the cited literature, we will schematically distinguish between three stages of the law of market society: its universalist origins in the nineteenth century, its

235. *Ibid*, at 162.
236. Nancy Fraser, 'A Triple Movement?', 81 *New Left Review* (2013) 119–132 at 127.

national closings in the twentieth century, and its transnational openings in the twenty-first century.

3.1. Nineteenth Century: Universalist Origins

Our reconstruction of the history of the law of market society begins with the nineteenth century: the timeframe that Polanyi originally set for his study. David Kennedy—albeit critical of the stories lawyers tell each other about this century (and about how they have made a leap ahead since then)—characterises its dynamic in the following terms:

> If the century has a direction, it is simultaneously from Europe outwards and from politics to commerce. The move to commerce brings a move from public to private order, and foreshadows a move from the imperial capitals of Paris, London and Berlin to the financial centers of London and New York.[237]

If this 'direction' indicates the liberal movement in Polanyi's terms, the countermovement soon becomes evident in 'explosions of nationalism',[238] which were triggered by the same dynamic. Whereas the beginning of the 'long' nineteenth century is given with the year 1789, the conventional legal narrative focuses on its last few decades only—'from roughly 1870 (the Franco-German war of 1871 will do) until 1914'.[239] In other words: 'For international law, as for much of the rest of twentieth century legal thought, it is really only the last five minutes of the nineteenth century that counts.'[240] What is referred to here is namely the 'triumph' of positivism over naturalism,[241] or the 'classic synthesis of the late nineteenth century'.[242]

Similarly, Duncan Kennedy begins his narrative of the 'Three globalizations of law and legal thought'[243] with an account of 'the rise of Classical Legal Thought between 1850 and 1914',[244] which he sees connected to 'the liberal attack on mercantilist or 'early modern' economic and social policy making'.[245] The social response—or countermovement—is reflected in the rise of 'socially oriented legal thought between 1900 and 1968',[246] which

237. David Kennedy, 'International Law and the Nineteenth Century: History of an Illusion', 65 *Nordic Journal of International Law* (1996) 385–420 at 391.
238. *Ibid.*
239. *Ibid.*
240. *Ibid.*
241. *Ibid*, at 398.
242. *Ibid*, at 397.
243. Kennedy, 'Three Globalizations', *supra* note 77.
244. *Ibid*, at 19.
245. *Ibid*, at 20.
246. *Ibid*, at 19.

already concerns the legal characteristics of the twentieth century. Whereas Kennedy's overall focus is on the latter, socially oriented law, he classifies the former, classical conception, not least in terms of 'the creation of a first global system of international economic law, based on free trade, the gold standard, and private international law (often applied by arbitrators) to settle disputes'.[247] Moreover, he explicitly points to the 'process of social transformation' brought about by this political-economic regime, and refers to Polanyi's work in this respect.[248] However, another name seems much more important in reconstructions of nineteenth century legal thinking: Friedrich Carl von Savigny. Kennedy attributes 'his seminal importance' to the paradoxical 'combination [...] of a universalizing legal formalist will theory with the idea that particular regimes of state law reflect diverse [...] societal normative orders'.[249] Von Savigny could thus become a patron of both: the liberal movement and its nationalist countermovement within the legal discipline.

Moreover, he can not only be considered the founding father of German historical jurisprudence but also of private international law, or the modern conflict-of-laws methodology. This is emphasised by Rödl, who reconstructs the (dialectical) development of the 'law of conflict of laws'.[250] Rödl distinguishes between 'universal free-trade law' in the nineteenth century[251] and '(national) private international law' in the twentieth century,[252] and divides the latter into two distinctive periods of 'nationally-organised capitalism'[253] and '"embedded liberalism"'.[254] To account for the 'long' nineteenth century in the timeframe mentioned above, we can speak of a development from universal free-trade law in the international political economy to national private international law under the regime of nationally-organised capitalism. As Rödl points out, von Savigny was not yet preoccupied with national interests but propagated a systematic (rationally deduced) form of conflicts-law instead, which would serve the interests of all nations in a world of free

247. *Ibid*, at 29.
248. *Ibid*.
249. *Ibid*, at 27.
250. Florian Rödl, 'Democratic Juridification without Statisation: Law of Conflict of Laws Instead of World State', in Christian Joerges and Tommi Ralli (eds.), *After Globalization—New Patterns of Conflict and Their Sociological and Legal Re-constructions* (RECON Report No. 15 ARENA: Oslo, 2011) 17–46 at 31; for a more comprehensive account see Florian Rödl, *Weltbürgerliches Kollisionsrecht: Über die Form des Kollisionsrechts und seine Gestalt im Recht der Europäischen Union* (European University Institute, 2008).
251. *Ibid*, at 32.
252. *Ibid*, at 34.
253. *Ibid*, at 35.
254. *Ibid*, at 38.

trade. Hence, von Savigny's methodology, which dates back to the year 1849, clearly supported the agenda of economic liberalism. In Rödl's terms, '[h]is push for a universalistic form of law of conflict of laws was an adaptation to the prevailing theoretical conceptions and hegemonic practical endeavours towards the desired international integration of national economies'.[255] This early universalism notwithstanding, von Savigny's reference to the 'spirit of the people' also paved the way for more nationalist interpretations.[256] In the end, 'national-particular and international-universal creeds' within the discipline could thus draw on the same legacy.[257]

The 'domestication of private international law' is also the focus of Muir Watt's history of the field.[258] The 'domestication' of the law of conflicts of law precisely consists in framing its contents in national, private, technical terms and separating it from the international, public, political sphere. For Muir Watt, this means leaving the transnational market, or the 'informal economic empire',[259] largely unattended—as it would then remain outside of both public and private international law. One of her historical reference points is 'the middle of the nineteenth century',[260] when von Savigny developed his 'universalist' methodology, which is also labelled as 'multilateralism' or 'monism'. Muir Watt points out that the legal universe, within which this conflict-of-laws methodology could be applied in a more or less technical manner, was the 'Romanist legal community' only and not the wider world society.[261] In contrast, a 'minoritarian methodology'[262] which existed side-by-side with von Savigny's 'Roman' multilateralism, could also deal with '"true conflicts"', that is, culturally or politically particularly sensitive issues.[263] This alternative methodology, which allows 'opening the legal order to other normativities on their own terms',[264] is labelled 'unilateralism' or 'pluralism'.[265] The paradox is that it is more universalist (going beyond Roman law nations) and particularist (emphasizing domestic legal perspectives), at the same time. However, this

255. *Ibid*, at 33.
256. *Ibid*, at 34–36.
257. *Ibid*, at 37.
258. Horatia Muir Watt, 'Private International Law Beyond the Schism', 2 *Transnational Legal Theory* (2011) 347–427 at 356.
259. *Ibid*, at 406, footnote 274.
260. *Ibid*, at 413.
261. *Ibid*, at 414.
262. *Ibid*, at 413.
263. *Ibid*, at 414.
264. *Ibid*.
265. *Ibid*, at 413.

'pluralist counter-narrative, left over from the era, before the nation-state'[266] also reminds us of a more political and potentially cosmopolitan function of conflicts-law. To 'reappropriate' this function[267] is what Muir Watt understands as a 're-embedding' countermovement, both now and then.[268]

Another, even older reference point of hers is the *ius gentium*, which preceded the separation of public and private international law and is notably introduced as 'as an overarching system of legality and morality, integrating relations as between both princes and merchants'.[269] This brings us back to the two Kennedies. Duncan Kennedy links nineteenth century legal thinking both to von Savigny's idea of a universalist Roman legacy and to the universalist ideal of *ius gentium*: '[Classical Legal Thought] affirmed that every country with a Western legal heritage shared the Roman legacy along with Savigny's Germans, [...] and that every nation that participated in the global order of commerce and finance participated in the *ius gentium*.'[270] David Kennedy explains how princes and merchants ended up in different, yet analogically structured legal orders. Accordingly, '[i]nternational legal positivism is simply the working out of the private law metaphor of contract for a public legal order'.[271] In other words, the positivist understanding of sovereignty, whose development is attributed to nineteenth century legal scholarship, mirrored private law relations: 'By the end of the century, sovereignty described a relation to territory parallel to the contemporaneous understanding of the relationship between individuals and their property, and the analogy became ever more explicit.'[272] While public international law owes its methodological individualism to private law, private international law owes its 'domestication' to the methodological nationalism of its public counterpart, which came to be dominant in the late nineteenth and early twentieth century.

Altogether, the nineteenth century exhibits a tension between universal legal forms, which are supportive of the agenda of liberalism, and national specifications (or exceptions), which rather serve protective means. Moreover, public international law came to mimic private law relations, and private

266. *Ibid*, at 406. Muir Watt's sentence continues: 'when it was in effect the only governance instrument available to mediate the conflicting regulatory claims of the medieval cities and ensure the fair resolution of disputes between merchants hailing from diverse origins'.
267. *Ibid*, at 426.
268. *Ibid*, at 420.
269. *Ibid*, at 361.
270. Kennedy, 'Three Globalizations', *supra* note 77, at 30; original emphasis.
271. Kennedy, 'International Law and the Nineteenth Century', *supra* note 237, at 398.
272. *Ibid*, at 408.

international law was adjusted to the national/territorial differentiation of public law. How this affects private law more generally will be discussed in the next section.

3.2. Twentieth Century: National Closings

Nineteenth century civilisation was characterised by classical legal thinking that reflected—in its universalism, formalism, and positivism—the ideological and institutional requirements of classical economic liberalism. However, towards the end of the 'long' nineteenth century, the international political economy increasingly moved from liberalism to nationalism. This conflict inherent to the normative and factual organisation of the world is also handed over to the twentieth century. The story of the twentieth century is the continuation of the market society with different legal means but similar political-economic tensions.

For the new law of the market society, we can draw on Duncan Kennedy's characterisation of the second 'globalisation' of law and legal thought. Accordingly, legal thinking '[b]etween 1900 and 1968' has become preoccupied with 'the social', that is, with reinventing the law 'as a purposive activity, as a regulatory mechanism that could and should facilitate the evolution of social life in accordance with ever greater perceived social interdependence at every level, from the family to the world of nations'.[273] Kennedy equates the new mainstream of legal thinking with the social reform movement, 'leaving out only Marxist collectivism at one extreme and pure Manchesterism at the other'.[274] In contrast to the '"conflict ideology"' of Marxism, and to the competitive rationality of laissez-faire liberalism, 'the social' is characterised as a '"harmony ideology," preaching a function for each organised interest, and the existence of a "public interest" in the coordination of their interdependent activities in order to maximise social welfare'.[275] Hence, in contrast to *laissez-faire*, there is now a clear perspective of social engineering. And other than radical Marxists, 'the social people' did not want to replace capitalism with socialism, in Kennedy's account, but 'to save liberalism from itself'.[276]

To highlight the discontinuities between nineteenth and twentieth-century legal thinking, but also to reflect on the continuities in the law of market society, we will dwell on Kennedy's picture of the new legal consensus a little longer. The end of the 'long' nineteenth and the beginning of the twentieth

273. Kennedy, 'Three Globalizations', *supra* note 77, at 22.
274. *Ibid*, at 39.
275. *Ibid*, at 42.
276. *Ibid*, at 38.

to nationalist countermovements: 'If we choose pragmatism over formalism, we will have chosen the international over the national, the modem over the classical, order over chaos, exactly as we have moved from the nineteenth to the twentieth century.'[295] This can also be understood as a (relative) move from 'rule' to 'policy'. With regard to the US context, Kennedy claims that, compared to their public international law colleagues, '[t]he inheritors of the private international law tradition—conflicts of law, international business transactions, comparative law, and international economic law—are all policy embracers'.[296] In this regard, the economic law paradigm only reflects the spirit of the time.

To complement this picture, and to follow up on the idea that 'the private is political', we will finally turn to national private law in the European context. Joerges summarises the history of private law in Germany with a view on the relationship of 'the science of private law and the nation state'.[297] Accordingly, the twentieth century is marked by three different periods, or generations, of private law scholarship, which are related to 'three aspects of nation-statehood'.[298] The first is the 'private law of the Volksnation',[299] which reflects the instrumentalisation of private law in the name of the (racially defined) 'national community' by National Socialism. The second is the 'private law of the Staatsbürgernation',[300] which refers to more enlightened ideas of a 'nation of citizens' conceived as an open civil society and based on a strong, liberal and democratic constitution. The third is Europeanised private law, or a private law 'beyond the nation state',[301] which already marks the transition from the twentieth to the twenty-first century.

On Joerges's account, one problem of twentieth century (German) scholarship was to come to grips with the nationalist heritage of the discipline. At the same time, it could not simply return to the—discredited—legal formalism and economic liberalism of the previous century but also had to cope with its new, regulatory role in the social welfare state (not yet mentioning the downscaling of the latter towards the end of the century). These characteristic tensions are illustrated by the fact that 'the programmatic idea of the

295. Kennedy, 'International Law and the Nineteenth Century', *supra* note 237, at 419–420.
296. Kennedy, 'Disciplines of International Law', *supra* note 13, at 27.
297. Christian Joerges, 'The Science of Private Law and the Nation-State', in Francis Snyder (ed.), *The Europeanisation of Law: The Legal Effects of European Integration* (Hart Publishing: Oxford, 2000) 47–82.
298. *Ibid*, at 50.
299. *Ibid.*
300. *Ibid*, at 63.
301. *Ibid*, at 74.

social market economy [...] seemed open to a variety of contents'.[302] To wit, the idea could equally be embraced by a new movement and a new countermovement whose 'models of "materialised" private law'[303] were far from identical. On the one hand, the ordoliberal theory of private law considered 'a State-guaranteed competitive constitution', which would bring about a well-functioning 'private-law society', 'an attractive model for the reconstruction of the economic and legal system'.[304] On the other hand, the emergence of the national welfare state motivated 'an alternative social model of private law', which starts from a 'theoretical, sociologically oriented reconstruction of the social functions of private law itself'.[305]

Hence, in the twentieth century, national and international economic law embraced 'the social' as an ingredient of 'embedded liberalism', which reflects the magic formula of the 'social market economy'. The domestication of private international law is complemented by the 'materialisation' of substantive private law. However, the harmony ideology of 'the social' cannot conceal the tensions underneath. In private law, the conflict inherent to the law of market society takes the new form of an ordoliberal movement, which strives for a 'private law society', and a more interventionist countermovement, which takes the social (and public) function of private law seriously.

3.3. Twenty-First Century: Transnational Openings

As to the situation in the late twentieth and the early twenty-first century, Duncan Kennedy speaks of an 'unsynthesized coexistence of transformed elements of [classical legal thought] with transformed elements of the social'.[306] This lack of an integrative—or hegemonic—consensus could still be framed in terms of pragmatism, which David Kennedy found to be characteristic of twentieth century legal thinking. In order to explore what seems to be new about the twenty-first century, we will begin with Rödl's account of recent developments in private international law, which suggest less that the private is political than that the political increasingly tends to be privatised. This is referred to as the 'privatisation of the function of law'.[307]

Accordingly, the new challenge after the nationalisation and 'materialisation' of private (international) law is its transformation 'into a framework

302. *Ibid*, at 50.
303. *Ibid*, at 56.
304. *Ibid*, at 57.
305. *Ibid*, at 67.
306. Kennedy, 'Three Globalizations', *supra* note 77, at 63.
307. Rödl, 'Democratic Juridification', *supra* note 250, at 40.

law in which private actors should be able to choose as freely as possible which national legal norms should, in each case, apply to the private legal relations that concern them'.[308] This implies not only the de-politicisation of the nation state—or, to speak with Muir Watt, of the federalist (US) or quasi-federalist system (EU) in question[309]—but, more specifically, its subjection to private economic choices, which may then undermine the political choices of a collective. What was a 'nation of citizens'—as Joerges depicted German constitutional democracy in the second half of the twentieth century—would then dissolve into a world of 'buyers and sellers'[310] which handle law as a commodity.

This privatisation of the political by means of regulatory competition is, as Rödl points out, 'diametrically opposed to our venture here'.[311] The reconstruction of conflicts-law in terms of its decommodification and re-politicisation, which Joerges and Rödl (amongst others) pursue, can be understood as the latest countermovement to an on-going trend in private international law. Both the privatisation of conflicts-law on the one hand, and its re-politisation on the other, take place in the 'postnational constellation',[312] that is, a markedly trans- and supranational context. This context also shapes the development of substantive private law, the 'Europeanisation' of which we will turn to next.

In a terminology which appears to be compatible with the present argument, Michaels distinguishes between 'the two rationalities of European private law'.[313] One is the formal, 'juridical' rationality[314] exemplified by classical legal thought and the *ius commune*. The other is the functional, 'instrumentalist' rationality[315] which is characteristic of 'materialised' private law, including its competing 'ordoliberal' and 'social' interpretations. The respective regulatory context does not have to be given by the nation state only but can also be defined by the European Union. Michaels's version of a 'European private law history'[316] gives an intriguing account

308. *Ibid*, at 41.
309. Muir Watt, 'Private International Law', *supra* note 258, at 379.
310. Kennedy, 'Disciplines of International Law', *supra* note 13, at 45.
311. Rödl, 'Democratic Juridification', *supra* note 250, at 31.
312. Habermas, *Postnational Constellation, supra* note 1.
313. Ralf Michaels, 'Of Islands and the Ocean: The Two Rationalities of European Private Law', in Roger Brownsword, Hans-W. Micklitz, Leone Niglia and Stephen Weatherill (eds.), *The Foundations of European Private Law* (Hart Publishing: Oxford, 2011) 139–158.
314. *Ibid*, at 142.
315. *Ibid.*
316. *Ibid*, at 149.

Another Polanyian interpretation of legal integration, or rather legal innovation, in the European context locates the countermovement not in 'hard law', that is in the triad of legislation, adjudication, and enforcement, but in 'soft law', or so-called new modes of governance. Marc Amstutz namely interprets 'European efforts [...] to establish a viable [Corporate Social Responsibility] model'[331] as an instance of 'world law', which is considered 'the [spontaneous] medium from which the Polanyian counter-movement to globalisation arises'.[332] In his view, the countermovement is 'no longer a matter of political communication, but one of *legal* communication'.[333] Law is here considered part of the functionally differentiated world of systems, while being disconnected from anything like a life world (which can be understood as a background condition for *social* movements). Reflecting the systems-theoretical emphasis on the cognitive or adaptive orientation of both world society and world law, Amstutz emphasises that 'in establishing the European Alliance for [corporate social responsibility], the [European] Commission created a legal institution that produces *cognitive resources*'.[334] These learning opportunities were capable to inform, irritate, and influence corporations (notably via the effects of 'market, reputation, public opinion'),[335] without imposing formal legal restrictions or sanctions. In the end, Amstutz claims that 'world law is civil society law' and, as such, 'not the product of any (state or other) organisational will, but the fruit of blind evolution, what von Hayek terms a spontaneous order'.[336]

Joerges agrees with Amstutz's account and also with Caporaso and Tarrow's approach only inasmuch as law is understood as a (possible) site, or means, of a Polanyian countermovement which seeks to re-embed European market-building in social policies, purposes, and responsibilities. However, as an instance of the 'discourse theory of law', Joerges's three-dimensional conflicts-law is committed to the principle of a democratic rule of law and complementary deliberative arrangements within and beyond nation states. Conflicts-law is thus understood as a *legal* countermovement, which nevertheless brings politics—and even the state—back in: 'Indeed, the state

331. Marc Amstutz, 'Globalising Speenhamland: On the Transnational Metamorphosis of Corporate Social Responsibility', in Christian Joerges and Josef Falke (eds.), *Karl Polanyi, Globalisation and the Potential of Law in Transnational Markets* (Hart Publishing: Oxford, 2011) 359–393 at 377.
332. *Ibid*, at 365.
333. *Ibid*, at 363; original emphasis.
334. *Ibid*, at 384; original emphasis.
335. *Ibid*, at 392.
336. *Ibid*, at 391; emphasis omitted.

has to remain present as a forum and organization form of democratic processes and a democratically legitimate law.'[337] Accordingly, political and legal communication remain closely linked and backed up with the legitimating potential of the (rationalised) life world. At the same time, Joerges indicates that it would be misleading to interpret Polanyi's 'spontaneous' countermovement—as Amstutz did—in a Hayekian sense of 'blind evolution' only. The key difference between the two accounts can be found in the envisioned form of the law. For Amstutz, the source of re-embedding is a 'self-validating global law'.[338] For Joerges, this is a new type of conflicts-law which is adjusted to the 'postnational constellation', but which requires nevertheless the 'organization form' of the state: in order to 'constitutionalise' governance arrangements, such as the corporate social responsibility practices studied by Amstutz, but also to rectify the 'de-coupling of [European] economic and [national] social constitutions',[339] which the recent case law of the European Court of Justice only laid bare.

'Globalising Speenhamland':[340] the title of Amstutz's study suggests that, in the global age, the social question requires other than national solutions which are based on hard law and public intervention. If self-regulating markets for labour were the nineteenth century answer to the paradoxes of social protection of Speenhamland, a 'self-validating global law' is expected to take labour relations into the twenty-first century, using corporate social responsibility both as incentive and corrective. What is interesting about this 'Hayekian' solution is that law is actually adapted to the market logic—and decoupled from politics.

By and large, the early twenty-first century is characterised by new efforts in the privatisation of the law, which would give more weight to a private choice of law under conditions of regulatory competition. Indubitably, the mere idea of a 'law market' fuels the commodification of law. The cosmopolitan counter-project combines, instead, the denationalisation of the form of

337. Christian Joerges, 'Alles nur *Marleasing*? Über Kollisionsrecht und Interlegalität, über Evolution und das Entdeckungsverfahren der Praxis im Angesicht der Krisen Europas', in Stefan Keller, Stefan and Stefan Wiprächtiger (eds), *Recht zwischen Dogmatik und Theorie: Marc Amstutz zum 50. Geburtstag* (Nomos Verlag: Baden-Baden, 2012) 53–73 at 73; my translation.

338. Amstutz, 'Globalising Speenhamland', *supra* note 331, at 367.

339. Christian Joerges, 'Integration Through Conflicts Law: On the Defence of the European Project by means of Alternative Conceptualisation of Legal Constitutionalisation', in Rainer Nickel (ed.), *Conflict of Laws and Laws of Conflict in Europe and Beyond: Patterns of Supranational and Transnational Juridification* (RECON Report No. 7 ARENA: Oslo, 2009) 531–561 at 538.

340. Amstutz, 'Globalising Speenhamland', *supra* note 331.

the law with a re-politicisation of its substance. With regard to the European level, the liberalisation and integration of markets through law can easily be framed as 'disembedding' them from their social and national context. As to the legal 're-embedding' of transnational markets, the question debated by (more or less) Polanyi-inspired scholars is basically *if* and *how* to decouple the law from economics and to re-couple it to politics. Suffice it to say that likening Polanyi's to von Hayek's approach seems taking the liberty of interpretation a little too far.[341]

3.4. The Example of European Regulatory Private Law

The outlined development of the law of the market society culminates—at least pars pro toto—in 'European regulatory private law', which seems suitable to summarise the present argument. Let us briefly resume: If a universalist private law with a 'juridical' rationality was characteristic of formal legal thought in the nineteenth century, the hallmark of the twentieth century was socially-oriented legal thought as expressed, not least, in the 'instrumentalist' rationality of 'materialised' private law. Whereas the former was constitutive of the liberal movement, the latter can be understood as a result of a re-embedding countermovement, which laid the foundations for the social market economy in liaison with the national welfare state. At the same time, one can already distinguish between a regulatory (efficiency-based) and a redistributive (equality-based) orientation of 'social law' in the most general sense—movement and countermovement *within* the regime of 'embedded liberalism'. If the early twenty-first century is now characterised by a heightened role of European 'regulatory' private law, this means that a specific type of regulation has been generalised on the European level: namely market regulation, including the law of 'regulated markets' as one of its key examples. Within the realm of private law, this shift of emphasis is expressed in what Micklitz calls a 'transformation of European private law from autonomy to functionalism in competition and regulation'.[342]

Micklitz clarifies that European regulatory private law, thus understood, 'may contain both elements, establishing market freedoms, therefore increasing private autonomy, while at the same time providing for rules that set boundaries to the newly created market autonomy'.[343] In this regard, he also

341. Frerichs, 'Re-embedding Neo-liberal Constitutionalism', *supra* note 108.
342. Hans-W. Micklitz, 'The Visible Hand of European Regulatory Private Law: The Transformation of European Private Law from Autonomy to Functionalism in Competition and Regulation', 28 *Yearbook of European Law* (2009) 3–59 at 6; emphasis omitted.
343. Hans-W. Micklitz and Dennis Patterson, 'From the Nation State to the Market: The Evolution of EU Private Law', 15 *EUI Working Paper Law* (2012) 1–19 at 12.

distinguishes between its 'negative variant', which stems from the effects of the four freedoms (free movement of goods, services, capital, and persons), and its 'positive variant', which includes 'the bulk of EU rules that have been adopted in the aftermath of the Single European Act outside Consumer and Anti-discrimination Law'.[344] However, his point is not so much a tension between negative and positive variants of European regulatory private law, but the latter's distinctiveness and apparent 'self-sufficiency': 'This private law is different from national private legal orders which [are] based on private autonomy and free will, it is a private law which takes its form, its procedure and its content from being instrumentalised for building and shaping markets.'[345]

A Polanyian perspective on European regulatory private law would have to question and contextualise this very assumption of self-sufficiency. This analytical step will be illustrated, in the following, with regard to one special objective of European market regulation: the creation of regulated network markets and their integration into 'a single market for network services (such as electricity, gas, waters, telecoms, transport and retail banking)'.[346] Due to the externalities of these network industries, and the resulting oligopolistic or even monopolistic market structures, they were typically organised by the government sector in the twentieth century. A precondition of the new regulatory arrangement is the commodification of the respective government activities: their redefinition and reorganisation as marketable 'network services'.

Hence, there are two points to be considered: the *commodification* of network services by means of (private) law, and the *self-sufficiency* of the new branch of regulatory (private) law. As to the commodification of 'services of general interest', which then become subject to (transnational) market competition, we can draw on Krajewski's and Batura's respective studies of the liberalisation of health services and telecommunications services, which are both framed in Polanyian terms. Krajewski points out that 'the commodification of an activity requires a fundamental change in the ideas underlying that activity, its legal and institutional framework, and the actual modalities of its production and consumption'.[347] While the first step implies a redefinition

344. *Ibid.*

345. *Ibid*, emphasis omitted.

346. Jordi Gual, 'Integrating Regulated Networks Markets in Europe', in George Gelauff, Isabel Grilo and Arjan Lejour (eds.), *Subsidiarity and Reform in Europe* (Springer: Berlin, 2008) 157–175 at 161.

347. Markus Krajewski, 'Commodifying and Embedding Services of General Interests in Transnational Contexts: The Example of Healthcare Liberalisation in the EU and

Rhetoric and Realpolitik: Interrogating the Relationship Between Transitional Justice and Socio-Economic Justice

Padraig McAuliffe*

ABSTRACT: In the last decade, theorists and scholars of transitional justice have not only explored avenues for the field to address the socio-economic roots of conflict, but have increasingly argued that success in this regard is the metric by which it should ultimately be judged. However, the record of the field in identifying or remedying violations of economic, social and cultural rights is underwhelming at best. While one might agree that the roots of conflict and authoritarianism are structural and that such deprivations *do* lend themselves to judicial or quasi-judicial action, neither the mechanisms of transitional justice nor the context in which they apply are apt to significantly catalyse beneficial change. As regards the former, the temporary, exceptionalist and extra-governmental nature of the mechanisms leave them unsuited to tackle structural abuses. In terms of the context in which transitional justice applies, advocates of a greater role in addressing root causes of conflict need to acknowledge that political transition from less to more democratic regimes is a relatively superficial phenomenon. The very real sense of civil-political possibility that transitions from war or authoritarianism to peace and democracy present is rarely accompanied by a transition in the shape of economic power. Transitional justice can take advantage of the period of flux to redress or temper political power imbalances symbolically, historically and jurisprudentially. These achievements are now dismissed by some as merely cosmetic outcomes of an overly liberal-legalist approach, but simultaneous opportunities to redress socio-economic imbalances simply may not exist. A more realistic appraisal of transitional justice's merits is possible only if we accept the relative superficiality of its mechanisms and context of application. Addressing structural injustice is the task of the transitional government and development agencies—schemes for transitional justice can at best form just one of many valid sources of advice, but assuming they can catalyse, dominate or contribute substantially to re-ordering horizontal inequalities is to set expectations too high.

KEYWORDS: transitional justice, peace-building, horizontal inequality, socio-economic justice

---

* Senior Lecturer, School of Law and Social Justice, University of Liverpool. E-mail: p.g.mcauliffe@liverpool.ac.uk. With thanks to the anonymous reviewer for a number of useful suggestions.

'*For every complex problem there is an answer that is clear, simple, and wrong.*' H. L. Mencken

1. Introduction

There is a growing belief among advocates, practitioners and policy-makers in transitional justice that the field needs to transcend its liberal-legalist origins in addressing violations of the civil and political rights of individuals. It is now argued with increasing frequency that policies in the area should demand wider systemic reform of those socio-economic structures in society that cause, exacerbate, and are produced by authoritarianism and conflict. As Miller outlines, the justifications for including issues of structural violence and inequality within the remit of transitional justice are pragmatic (only with attention to root causes can peace be sustainable), philosophical (an ethical preference for distribution and equity) and sociological (it is the concept of justice the population concerned most prefers).[1] This new emphasis has largely been compelled by the acknowledgment that while transitional justice can succeed to a greater or lesser degree in acknowledging or punishing the evil that flowed from abuse of political power, many of the economic advantages enjoyed by the *ancien* regime or portions of the population it represented remain in place to potentially sow the seeds of future conflict.[2] The precise nature of the claims that transitional justice can significantly impact socio-economic structures in post-conflict and post-authoritarian societies will be explored in greater detail in Sections 2 and 3, but it should be noted at this juncture that the arguments made for transitional justice's potential in addressing problems of under-development and inequality are distinctly ambitious. African scholars have argued transitional justice can and must 'elaborate remedial actions that comprehensively address grievances in societies emerging from conflict.'[3] Others contend that transitional justice measures should 'actively reverse the systems and attitudes that discriminate and dehumanize' across the entire society.[4]

1. Zinaida Miller, '(Re)Distributing Transition', 7 *International Journal of Transitional Justice* (2013) 370–380 at 377.
2. Robert Meister, *After Evil: A Politics of Human Rights* (Columbia University Press, 2011) at 27.
3. Japan International Co-Operation Society & International Center for Transitional Justice, 'Workshop on Transitional Justice and Development in Africa: Enhancing Socio-Economic Justice in Societies in Transition: Case Studies on the African Continent' (2008), <http://ictj.org/sites/default/files/ICTJ-JICA-Africa-Justice-Development-2008-English.pdf> (References to online sources are accurate as of 27 February 2015) at 7.
4. Matthew Mullen, 'Reassessing the Focus of Transitional Justice: The Need to Move Structural and Cultural Violence to the Centre', 26 *Cambridge Review of International Affairs* (2013) 1–18 at 16.

of formerly governmental activities in commercial terms, the second step involves a change in the law governing these 'services', such as a shift from mandatory to voluntary contractual relationships. 'The final and third stage of the commodification process is reached with the actual establishment of markets as systems of voluntary exchanges of products [or services].'[348] Batura emphasises, in turn, that '[t]ransnational telecommunications services markets were a legal construction in which a (competitive) market was created from scratch by using a holistic concept of what such a market had to look like'.[349] Accordingly, the liberalisation of telecommunications services was less about European market integration in the sense of removing national barriers between already existing service markets. Instead, it was an unprecedented 'market-building project which started at [the] international level', with Japan, the UK, and the US acting 'as its initiators'.[350]

So far, liberalisation and commodification seem to follow familiar patterns. At the same time, the 'regulated' network markets appear to be at odds with the 'self-regulating' markets that Polanyi had in mind. Nevertheless, they do rely on the commodity fiction, which can only be upheld with massive regulatory intervention.[351] In this respect, they only replicate the paradox of self-regulation already pointed out by Polanyi: just as the introduction of free markets by so-called *laissez-faire* polices entailed 'an enormous increase in the administrative functions of the state',[352] the essence of European regulatory (private) law is the active management of (network) markets, which cannot be left alone. Instead, there is a permanent 'need for control, regulation, and intervention'.[353] It seems the emphasis has only shifted from 'self-regulating markets' two centuries ago, to 'self-sufficiently regulated markets' today.

If the law of the market society of the twenty-first century is exemplified by European regulatory (private) law, which appears to be increasingly self-sufficient—what can be said about the underlying dynamic of movement and countermovement? We will consider two alternative interpretations. The

the WTO', in Christian Joerges and Josef Falke (eds.), *Karl Polanyi, Globalisation and the Potential of Law in Transnational Markets* (Hart Publishing: Oxford, 2011) 231–254 at 237.

348. *Ibid*, at 238.
349. Olga Batura, 'Embedded Transnational Markets for Telecommunications Services', in Christian Joerges and Josef Falke (eds.), *Karl Polanyi, Globalisation and the Potential of Law in Transnational Markets* (Hart Publishing: Oxford, 2011) 255–275 at 258–259.
350. *Ibid*, at 258.
351. Gual, 'Integrating Regulated Network Markets', *supra* note 346, at 166.
352. Polanyi, *Great Transformation*, *supra* note 7, at 139–140.
353. *Ibid*, at 140.

first interpretation would be that the countermovement is already expressed in the social objectives of the law in question. In fact, European regulatory private law was introduced above as combining both market-making and market-shaping functions. If social purposes and responsibilities already form part of the law of regulated markets (e.g., by granting vulnerable consumers access to commercial network services), this may appear as formally or substantively (relatively) self-sufficient. In this regard, both Krajewski and Batura point to aspects of decommodification in the regulation of services of general interest in the EU.[354] The question remains how this social-policy content made its way into the law (supranational anticipation or national resistance?).

The second, more critical interpretation builds on the above argument of law as a commodifier or even commodity. The point is here that 'social inclusion' is in the context of regulated markets not an end in itself (decommodification) but a means to uphold the commodity fiction and, thereby, to bolster the respective market activities. As Krajewski rightfully emphasises, the third and decisive step in the commodification process is that consumers and suppliers of network services 'are not only able to choose, but also exercise this choice to a considerable extent, and create opportunities for competition on markets'.[355] In other words, only when there is enough activity or exchange on the markets (however fictitious or regulated they are), the market forces can properly work and bring about the desired 'efficiency'. Inasmuch as European regulatory (private) law assumes this activating function, it acts as a production factor in bringing about a competitive network economy. Its 'self-sufficiency' is derived from this overarching economic goal, which disconnects it not only from other forms or branches of law but also from non-economic social or political concerns. In this view, the countermovement has been far from 'internalised'; it would, instead, question the direct connection of social rights to marketable services and oppose the market logic of the system as a whole.

Conclusion: Transformation of the Law, Reformation of the Market?

A historical sociology of international law, which would 'connect the development of normative systems to macro-level economic and social developments'

354. Krajewski, 'Commodifying and Embedding', *supra* note 347, at 241–242; Batura, 'Embedded Transnational Markets', *supra* note 349, at 261.
355. Krajewski, 'Commodifying and Embedding', *supra* note 347, at 238.

and which would also address the question: 'To what extent has the law influenced such developments, to what extent has it been influenced by them?',[356] has been found to be missing. The sociology of international *economic* law outlined above can be understood as a contribution to such an undertaking, even though it is 'historical' only in a secondary way: it reconstructs the history of the law of market society as it is implied in Polanyi's *The Great Transformation*, and as it is reflected and reconstructed in contemporary legal discourse.

In this article, the question of how the law is influenced by 'macro-level economic and social developments' has been approached not only in terms of law's embeddedness in the *economy* as a field of relations between actors and of 'regulations' from below and above, but also of law's embeddedness in the discipline of *economics*, which provides the field with its distinctive economic rationality. Academically speaking, law's embeddedness in economics is epitomised by the economic law approach to (or the law and economics of) international economic law. For an economic sociology of law, which emphasises the cognitive dimension of embeddedness, the disciplines of international economic law—namely law and economics—therefore become a subject matter in their own right.

Polanyi found the rise and fall of the market economy in the long nineteenth century to follow the patterns of a 'double movement' which develops around the two organizing principles of economic liberalism and social protection. The conflict between these divergent rationalities can be considered inherent to the normative and factual organisation of the international political economy (around the gold standard, the balance-of-power system, the liberal state, and the self-regulating market), which we equated with the rules and practices of international economic law. In this political-economic context, the law acts as a 'commodifier', which institutes and imposes the self-regulating market, and can itself become a commodity: an economic good which is priced and privatised. But it can also act as a 'decommodifier', which draws limits to the market sphere and contains the logic of commodification. This underlying tension, or ambiguity, in the constitution of the market society is reflected in the changing forms and functions that the law has taken over time: from its universalist origins in the nineteenth century to its national closings in the twentieth century, and to its transnational openings in the twenty-first century. Speaking of 'law's great transformation', we can claim that law's development over the last two centuries has contributed

356. Martti Koskenniemi, 'Why History of International Law Today?', 4 *Rechtsgeschichte—Zeitschrift des Max-Planck-Instituts für europäische Rechtsgeschichte* (2004) 61–66 at 66.

as much to the containment as to the 're-formation' of capitalism.[357] This can be illustrated as follows.

Other than Polanyi's notion of the rise and fall of market economy seemed to suggest, the market economy has not come to end in the two world wars, but was reinvented as a more 'social' type of market economy in the post-war decades. Streeck's study of the German political economy—which is the model case, in this respect—can be read as an extension of Polanyi's original argument, which traces the rise and fall of the *social* market economy.[358] In a nutshell, Streeck's argument is that the 'social reform' of the market economy could not prevent the reformation of capitalism at its core. In other words, however 'instituted' or regulated the *social* market economy was at the beginning or at its heyday, it remained a *market* economy after all.

In this context, non-contractual institutions that impose social obligations from above (as part of the public order, or authoritative forms of organisation) tend to be replaced by privately contracted institutions that result from individual choices from below (as part of systems of private ordering that facilitate voluntary coordination). Streeck refers to the former as 'Durkheimian institutions' and to the latter as 'Williamsonian institutions', thus linking them to old and new forms of institutionalism in sociology and economics. Accordingly, the 'slowly grinding force' of private interest[359] also gnaws at the law of market society. The 'legal embeddedness of the market' may thus end up as 'economic embeddedness of the law'. Streeck points out that '*Polanyian institutions* that are market-breaking rather than market-making probably need to be Durkheimian in character: public rather than private, obligatory rather than expedient, and political instead of economic'.[360] The result of the 'free' interplay of the law and the market often appears to result in the opposite: law becomes private, voluntary, and economic.

Streeck's distinction between old, Durkheimian and new, Williamsonian institutionalism is worth a second look. While his emphasis is on how institutions work in the real world, and not in the mind of scholars, his analysis can also be used to illustrate a shift from old to new institutionalism in the *conception* of institutional embeddedness. Rephrasing Polanyi's famous dictum about the market society, we could thus claim: 'Instead of economy being

357. Wolfgang Streeck, *Re-forming Capitalism: Institutional Change in the German Political Economy* (Oxford University Press, 2009).

358. *Ibid*; Sabine Frerichs, 'Review of Wolfgang Streeck: Re-forming Capitalism: Institutional Change in the German Political Economy', 50 *Management International Review* (2010) 827–832.

359. Streeck, *Re-forming Capitalism, supra* note 357, at 146.

360. *Ibid*, at 252; original emphasis.

embedded in social (i.e. Durkheimian) institutions, society is embedded in economic (i.e. Williamsonian) institutions.' In cognitive terms, new institutional economics and, to a certain extent, also new economic sociology, are thus concomitant with the 're-formation' of capitalism itself.[361]

To understand this dynamic, which shapes the law of market society, one has to combine the macro-level of regimes and the meta-level of rationalities, which has been one of the key motives in developing a Polanyian economic sociology of law, and of international economic law, in particular.

361. Frerichs, 'Re-embedding Neo-liberal Constitutionalism', *supra* note 108, here with reference to 'Hayekian' and 'Granovetterian' perspectives.

As Section 3 examines, the presumption among many in the literature is that the sheer fact of transition to peace and/or democracy automatically conduces to a revision of systemic inequalities. Implicit in this presumption is a further supposition that the transitional justice mechanisms available are capable of addressing economic inequalities and development issues with at least some degree of efficacy and all that prevents them modifying inequitable social structures (or mitigating their ill-effects) is the overly-narrow, liberal-legalist lens transitional justice habitually employs. However, this article contends that the problem is not that justice has been defined too narrowly or that civil and political rights have been elevated to a higher plane than socio-economic ones. The problem is instead the transition itself, regrettably but invariably a matter of elite bargaining over political and institutional reforms. As Payne, Reiter and Olsen demonstrate through controlling for old and new regime types, conflict type, duration, democratic history and the presence of a negotiated regime change, transition-type is ultimately the key deciding factor in determining how far and how expansively transitional justice can be pursued.[5] Many transitions end political repression but progress in this regard is often implicitly dependent on the pre-transition economy going unreformed or unpunished.

Because transitional justice is generally presented in very idealistic terms, scholars in the field have begun to acknowledge that its virtuous effects are more easily presumed than proven.[6] Amongst advocates and activists in particular, one sees in the literature an emotional commitment to expanding transitional justice that generally eschews doubts about its overall efficacy. Mobekk's warning that the 'expectations of truth commissions have tended to be exaggerated, and their challenges minimised' is one that applies across the board in transitional justice.[7] Indeed, the underestimation of costs, exaggeration of benefits and hyperbole in discussing pros and cons of proposals that blights humanitarian policy-making is particularly prevalent in transitional justice.[8] A fear has developed among practitioners and theorists about the damage to the credibility of transitional justice from exaggerated claims, and

5. Tricia Olsen, Leigh Payne and Andrew Reiter, *Transitional Justice in Balance: Comparing Processes, Weighing Efficacy* (U.S. Institute of Peace: Washington, DC, 2010).
6. Hugo van der Merwe, 'Delivering Justice During Transition: Research Challenges', in Hugo van der Merwe, Victoria Baxter and Audrey R. Chapman (eds), *Assessing the Impact of Transitional Justice: Challenges for Empirical Research* (USIP Press: Washington, DC, 2009) 115–142 at 121.
7. Eirin Mobekk, *Transitional Justice and Security Sector Reform: Enabling Sustainable Peace* (Geneva Centre for the Democratic Control of Armed Forces, 2006) at 77.
8. David A. Kennedy, *The Dark Sides of Virtue: Reassessing International Humanitarianism* (Princeton University Press, 2004) at 112.

concern has long been expressed that transitional justice advocacy 'claims too much.'[9] Some in the field now fear the 'overselling'[10] of transitional justice can encourage unrealisable public expectations of what it can achieve, ultimately causing unfair assessments that the mechanisms employed have failed:

> Governments, societies, and international actors have high expectations for transitional justice—so high, in fact, that it seems to be overloaded with goals … Regardless of how comprehensive its programs, transitional justice could not possibly fulfil all these goals.[11]

If the increasing ambition of transitional justice's goals were merely an academic question, there would be little cause for concern. However, its mechanisms must compete with ongoing peace-building processes like democratisation, demobilisation, development, rule of law reconstruction and land reform that donors also fund. Given that as much as 5% of development aid to a country can take the form of assistance to transitional justice initiatives,[12] it is necessary to question the extent to which this may lessen the availability of funding for other social reconstruction projects. As Hurwitz notes, 'there is often a high demand to include more activities in the peace-building equation, yet these demands are not often met with the funding or national or international capacity necessary to implement the dizzying array or activities.'[13] Pressure from donors who have funded transitional justice thus far has forced the movement to think more critically about the claims it makes and the ends it pursues.[14] Indeed, the management of expectations has now emerged as one of transitional justice's key challenges.[15]

---

9. Laurel E. Fletcher and Harvey M. Weinstein, 'Violence and Social Repair: Rethinking the Contribution of Justice to Reconciliation', 24 *Human Rights Quarterly* (2002) 573–639 at 601.
10. Kieran McEvoy, 'Beyond Legalism: Towards a Thicker Understanding of Transitional Justice', 34 *Journal of Law and Society* (2007) 411–440 at 426; Rachel Kerr and Eirin Mobekk, *Peace & Justice: Seeking Accountability After War* (Polity Press: London, 2007) at 181.
11. Olsen, Payne and Reiter, *Transitional Justice in Balance, supra* note 5, at 131.
12. For example, it constituted 5% in both Guatemala and Rwanda (Roger Duthie, 'Introduction', in Pablo de Greiff and Roger Duthie (eds), *Transitional Justice and Development: Making Connections* (Social Science Research Council: New York, 2009) 17–27 at 21.
13. Agnes Hurwitz and Kaysie Studdard, *Rule of Law Programs in Peace Operations* (International Peace Academy: New York, 2005) at 11.
14. Christine Bell, 'Transitional Justice, Interdisciplinarity and the State of the "Field" or "Non-Field"', 3 *International Journal of Transitional Justice* (2009) 5–27 at 11.
15. Office of the United Nations High Commissioner for Human Rights, 'Rule of Law Tools for Post-Conflict States: Prosecution Initiatives', <www.ohchr.org/Documents/Publications/RuleoflawProsecutionsen.pdf> at 3.

Bearing this in mind, this article examines the potential for transitional justice to significantly impact on patterns of distribution, development and inequality. It argues that the lack of progress in reducing inequality or poverty is less the result of 'ideological preoccupations'[16] of those administering justice or pursuing reconciliation and reparations than the product of doubts based (i) on practicality and (ii) on the law of unintended consequences. The first, practical, doubts flow from the belief that current transitional justice mechanisms, alone or in combination, are unsuited professionally, organisationally and conceptually to resolving issues of structural injustice. The apparent faith in the transitional justice literature that its mechanisms can or should operate generally as a simple mechanical lever for pursuing economic justice in deeply divided peace-building ecologies conspicuously lacks any reference to political economy literature on post-conflict reconstruction. This vast literature examines the distribution of political authority and economic reward, the politics embedded in the everyday operations of economic life and, in transitional societies, explores how institutions and policies can be crafted to channel patterns of illicit accumulation in the direction of sustainable development and structural change. However, if one looks beyond the aspirational language, one gets little sense in transitional justice literature how corrupt authoritarian or wartime accumulation can be transformed into fruitful and egalitarian structural change, how the degree to which a centralised bureaucratic state was degraded prior to transition impacts on the potential for developmental resource mobilisation, or how prospects for broad-based development is affected by GDP per capita levels. This new frontier in transitional justice is comprised of laudable but generic aspirations for a more equitable society, but there are no generic transitions. Each period of dramatic political change in each country will endure its own idiosyncrasies and institutional legacies which must inevitably make the aspirations for a beneficial structural impact of transitional justice more or less feasible. However, there appears to be little awareness in the literature of what the most relevant idiosyncrasies (e.g., duration and type of war/authoritarianism, extractive capacity of state, legitimacy) might be.[17]

The second, consequentialist, basis for doubt about the wider emancipatory potential of transitional justice stems from fear of jeopardising the transition by alienating those who stand to lose from fairer distribution of opportunities and wealth. On this basis, as Holmes argues, the greater attention given

16. Zinaida Miller, 'Effects of Invisibility: In Search of the 'Economic' in Transitional Justice', 2 *International Journal of Transitional Justice* (2008) 266–291 at 271.

17. This is, of course, a critique which extends more generally to the field of transitional justice.

to civil and political rights deprivations in transitional justice overall that is increasingly criticised is 'neither impartial nor random' (nor, it might be added, biased), but determined by the exigencies of transition:

> The selectivity of our attention to injustice is governed by asymmetries of political power. We ignore one injustice and focus on another depending on who has more political power or a more audible political voice.[18]

If, as critics of the hitherto-dominant liberal-legalist view of transition so correctly point out, the causes of the initial conflict endure beyond transition, so too will opposition to any amelioration of them. As Section 6 explores, the opposition of narrow but immensely powerful sectoral interests can stymie the developmental potential of transitional justice, but this essential factor of *transition* has received far less attention in the literature than the narrowness of the concept of *justice*. Kennedy's warning that the human rights professional's vocabulary 'encourages an overestimation of the distinction between its own idealism and the hard realpolitik of those it purports to address' is particularly apt in these circumstances.[19] Even in the most benign conditions, changing the imperatives of a domestic economy is a protracted and conflictual process. So too, it might be said, is altering the political landscape, but at the time when transitional justice projects are being mooted, the fact of a transition from conflict to peace and/or from authoritarianism to democratic rule implies some distribution of political power has already taken place, however superficially. However, after conflict or authoritarianism, struggles between the political leadership and those they replace or exclude over resources endure and may intensify even if the contest for political power is resolved.

Section 2 begins by recapitulating the links between socio-economic deprivation and conflict, and goes on to examine the perception in much of the literature that transitional justice's narrow focus on civil and political rights abuses has marginalised issues of development and redistribution. Section 3 examines how this critique, initially focused on the omission of the field to address parallel exploitations, has now degenerated into a rhetorical battle which pitches transitional justice as an actively harmful, neo-liberal project which calls into question the legitimacy of existing modalities of truth commissions, trials and reparations. Section 4 assesses the extent to which the marginalisation of socio-economic issues can be ascribed to ideological bias and the extent to which the practical limitations of traumatic political

18. Stephen Holmes, 'Concluding Remarks', in Morten Bergsmo *et al* (eds), *Distributive Justice in Transitions* (Torkel Opsahl: Oslo, 2010) 421–430 at 423.
19. Kennedy, *Dark Sides of Virtue*, *supra* note 8, at 28–29.

unequal power relationships which lead to unequal life chances, harming people by preventing them from meeting their basic needs.[44] The wrongs pursued were those gross human rights violations committed against individuals or collectivities (eg crimes against humanity, torture, murder) which were motivated by gaining or retaining political control, as opposed to social or economic abuses.[45] Likewise, the targets of transitional justice were perpetrators for whom criminal justice was the appropriate response, as opposed to beneficiaries of a systematically unfair economy where a more distributive conception of justice would be more opportune.[46] Criminal trial tends to cast conflict in terms of identifiable criminal acts against the victim's bodily integrity, formalising an attitude that the conflict was primarily about physical violence.[47] It singles out the instigators and actual perpetrators of violence 'while leaving to broader initiatives in rule of law, humanitarian assistance, democracy building, and economic development the task of resuscitating a "sick society."'[48] TRCs also focused initially on a narrow range of extreme forms of human rights abuse, as opposed to more mundane socio-economic deprivations like land dispossession or ethnic/religious/gendered discriminations. Even the widely valorised Latin American and South African TRCs have been criticised for merely revealing a 'diminished truth,' defining victimhood too narrowly, ignoring the political economies of repression, and, in the latter, eclipsing the racialised relationships between the beneficiaries of white power and deprived black citizens.[49] As van der Merwe put it, transitional justice is thus a concept 'that can be criticised as superficial for addressing only the excessive use of oppressive power or the ravages of collective violence rather than the basic nature of an exploitative system.'[50] Though it is argued the gains of transitional justice might be lost[51] or not fully realised if the

44. John Galtung, 'Violence, Peace and Research', 6 *Journal of Peace Research* (1969) 167–191 at 167.
45. Hugo van der Merwe, Victoria Baxter and Audrey Chapman, 'Introduction', in van der Merwe, Baxter and Chapman (eds), *Assessing the Impact, supra* note 6, 1–12 at 8.
46. John Torpey, 'Introduction: Politics and the Past', in John Torpey (ed.), *Politics and the Past: On Repairing Historical Injustices* (Rowman & Littlefield: Lanham, Md., 2003) 1–35 at 1, 7–8 and 10.
47. Colm Campbell and Catherine Turner, 'Utopia and the Doubters: Truth, Transition and the Law', 28 *Legal Studies* (2008) 374–395 at 376.
48. Fletcher and Weinstein, 'Violence and Social Repair', *supra* note 9, at 580.
49. Mahmood Mamdani, 'A Diminished Truth', in Wilmot James and Linda Van de Vijer (eds), *After the TRC: Reflections On Truth and Reconciliation in South Africa* (Ohio University Press, 2001) 58–61 at 58.
50. Van der Merwe, 'Delivering Justice', *supra* note 6, at 117.
51. Carranza, 'Plunder and Pain', *supra* note 16, at 329.

structural causes of repression or conflict are left unaddressed,[52] the field's concentration on consequences instead of structural causes was deemed to leave it ill-equipped to influence or inform any broader structural reform project.[53] Transitional justice's failure to examine the structural reasons for violence, amend injurious development policies or foster redistribution meant old grievances would inevitably morph into new ones.[54]

Transitional justice scholarship began to acknowledge that structural change in the state was more important than any of its individual processes in assuring the success of transition.[55] Many now argue it is imperative to permanently integrate structural issues and socio-economic justice into the transitional justice architecture. Scholars now routinely argue that addressing mass poverty should be recognised as an object of justice[56] and that the mechanisms of transitional justice should be applied to transforming oppressive economic arrangements that disenfranchise and exclude vulnerable and resentful segments of society.[57] Transitional justice would now connect with broader social justice projects, and in particular pursue a conception of development oriented not around the dangers of pursuing growth simpliciter through economic liberalisation but rather around equitable forms of growth geared ultimately towards welfare, securing minimum levels of income, and human dignity.[58] The most forceful advocacy of this shift in transitional justice from a limited concept of conflict prevention to societal metamorphosis is found in a widely-cited speech in 2006 by the then-UN High Commissioner for Human Rights Louise Arbour who argued that transitional justice 'must' have the ambition of assisting the transformation of oppressed societies into free ones by exposing discriminatory practices and violations of

52. Pablo de Greiff, 'Articulating the Links Between Transitional Justice and Development: Justice and Social Integration', in de Greiff and Duthie (eds), *Transitional Justice and Development, supra* note 12, 28–75 at 33.
53. Ruti Teitel, 'Transitional Justice in a New Era', 26 *Fordham International Law Journal* (2002) 893–906 at 894.
54. Lisa Laplante, 'Transitional Justice and Peace Building: Diagnosing and Addressing the Socioeconomic Roots of Violence through a Human Rights Framework', 2 *International Journal of Transitional Justice* (2008) 331–355 at 334.
55. Laurel E. Fletcher, Harvey M. Weinstein and Jamie Rowen, 'Context, Timing and the Dynamics of Transitional Justice: A Historical Perspective', 31 *Human Rights Quarterly* (2009) 163–220 at 205–206.
56. Carranza, 'Plunder and Pain', *supra* note 16, at 315.
57. Ismael Muvingi, 'Sitting on Powder Kegs: Socio-Economic Rights in Transitional Societies', 3 *International Journal of Transitional Justice* (2009) 163–182 at 181.
58. Naomi Roht-Arriaza and Katherine Orlovsky, 'A Complementary Relationship: Reparations and Development', in de Greiff and Duthie (eds.), *Transitional Justice and Development, supra* note 12, 170–213 at 175.

transition provide a complementary or superior explanation. Section 5 analyses the practical limitations of trials, truth commissions and reparations in catalysing development, fostering social justice and stimulating redistribution, arguing that the historical record and the inherent potential of these mechanisms offers far less scope for optimism than the rhetoric examined in Sections 2 and 3 would suggest. Section 6 argues that the fundamental premise underlying this rhetoric, namely that the freedom transition offers in the political-democratic sphere is equal, comparable or analogous to that in the economic, social or cultural spheres, is flawed.

To reduce the field to its composite words, the article concludes by arguing that there is less to be gained from questioning the *conception of justice* in transitional justice than there is from questioning the *potential of transition*. Much of the dissatisfaction with transitional justice in the literature in fact reflects the shortcomings of transition and not the amalgam of theories, individuals and institutions that apply in context-specific iterations of transitional justice. Applying these generalised one-aspiration-fits-all expectations to post-conflict states like Somalia or the Ivory Coast reveals what Colvin describes as the naïve technicism of transitional justice in assuming 'that societies can be understood and manipulated, and people behave rationally or at least predictably.'[20] Transitional justice consistently makes unrealistic conjectures about the malleability of social and political processes. Indeed, the need to separate utopian dreams from practical possibilities is seen by some as the most pressing challenge for the field overall.[21] Increased concern with issues of socio-economic justice in the field is welcome, necessary, and can highlight modest but beneficial ways in which post-conflict societies can be made more equitable. However, transitional justice's greatest impact will generally be in the area of civil and political rights. There is a danger that the socio-economic critique of transitional justice risks stigmatising advances in this area as unduly modest or even as impediments to greater reform.

2. Socio-Economics, Conflict and Transition

It borders on the truistic to argue that poverty is deeply intertwined with the dynamics of both conflict and authoritarianism. Though political, psychological and cultural stimuli may drive human rights abuses, they are usually

20. Christopher J. Colvin, 'Purity and Planning: Shared Logistics of Transitional Justice and Development', 2 *International Journal of Transitional Justice* (2008) 412–425 at 423.
21. Brandon Hamber, Liz Sevenko, and Ereshnee Naidu, 'Utopian Dreams or Practical Possibilities? The Challenges of Evaluating the Impact of Memorialisation in Societies in Transition', 3 *International Journal of Transitional Justice* (2010) 397–420.

conditioned by deeper socio-economic factors and pathologies of power that determine types of harm and who should suffer it. Poverty, inequality and absence of means for redress are among the primary causes of violence in conflicted societies.[22] Low-income states are estimated to be 15 times more prone to internal conflict than those in the Organization for Economic Cooperation and Development.[23] The inextricable linkage of underdevelopment with a high risk of violent conflict has long been a core assumption in development discourse.[24] The problem where there is an economic source to conflict is often less the scarcity of resources (though this is of course contributory), but rather horizontal inequality between groups and the impossibility of rectifying these socio-economic injustices through political channels:

> The cause is not so much lack of resources, per se, as injustice: social, economic and political structures that maintain the dominance of an in-group at the centre of power over an out-group at the periphery to the extent of denying the most basic economic, social and political rights.[25]

Even conflicts that are ostensibly cultural or ethnic are strongly associated with lower levels of economic well-being.[26] Even where inequality and poverty did not cause conflict, they may have constituted an aggravating factor or flowed from the conflict.[27] It is something of a commonplace that war can be a sustainable system of economic organisation. Conflict is often driven as much by the opportunity for a group to enrich itself through loot or control of natural resources as it is by grievance.[28] Authoritarianism is even more lucrative. When they died, the DR Congo's Mobutu Sese Seko and Indonesian dictator President Suharto amassed US$12bn and US$9bn respectively in assets,[29] while Chad's Hissène Habré left office taking the national treasury

---

22. Cynthia J. Arnson and I. William Zartman (eds), *Rethinking the Economic of War: The Intersection of Need, Creed and Greed* (Johns Hopkins University Press, 2005).
23. Stuart E. Eizenstat, John Edward Porter and Jeremy M. Weinstein, 'Rebuilding Weak States', 84 *Foreign Affairs* (2005) 134–146 at 140.
24. Mark Duffield, *Global Governance and the New Wars* (Zed Books: London, 2001) at 115.
25. Linda Agerbak, cited in Rama Mani, *Beyond Retribution—Seeking Justice in the Shadows of War* (Polity Press: Cambridge, 2002) at 128–129.
26. E.g., Philip Verwimp, 'An Economic Profile of Peasant Perpetrators of Genocide: Micro-level Evidence from Rwanda', 77 *Journal of Development Economics* (2005) 297–323.
27. E.g., Susan L. Woodward, 'Do the Root Causes of Civil War Matter? On Using Knowledge to Improve Peacebuilding Interventions', 1 *Journal of Intervention and State-Building* (2007) 143–170; Lars-Erik Cederman, Kristian Skrede Gleditsch and Halvard Buhaug (eds), *Inequality, Grievances and Civil War* (Cambridge University Press, 2013).
28. Paul Collier, Anke Hoeffler and Dominic Rohmer, 'Beyond Greed and Grievance: Feasibility and Civil War', 61 *Oxford Economic Papers* (2009) 1–27.
29. Carranza, 'Plunder and Pain', *supra* note 16, at 312.

with him.[30] Collaborators, kin and supporters will benefit commensurately. Internal conflict or repression operates as a form of 'development in reverse,'[31] eviscerating the economy at a macro-level by destroying or corrupting state institutions, infrastructure and resources, and at a micro-level by obliterating employment, welfare provision (if any) and public services.[32] Even when war or authoritarianism ends, pre-existing inequalities can endure to structure the life experiences of the survivor population, while displacement, disease and wide availability of weaponry can exacerbate these difficulties. Most civic unrest and violence which follows ostensibly successful transitions stem from socio-economic grievances that catalysed or flowed from pre-transitional conditions.[33]

2.1. The Narrow Lens of Transitional Justice

Though the types of states dealing with post-conflict legacies of deprivation and inequality are those to which transitional justice actors typically deploy, issues of socio-economic justice have until very recently played a marginal role in transitional justice, defined herein as 'the full range of processes and mechanisms associated with a society's attempts to come to terms with a legacy of large-scale past abuses, in order to ensure accountability, serve justice and achieve reconciliation.'[34] The most familiar examples of transitional justice like trials, truth commissions and lustration have paid minimal attention to issues of structural inequality. Because the conception of transition was typically a limited one implying a progression from war or authoritarianism to liberal democracy (defined in its most basic forms by Teitel as 'the move from less to more democratic regimes'[35] or by Smiley as one from a regime 'whose norms are bad to one whose norms are good'),[36] the conceptual and philosophical dimensions of economic injustice were not deeply analysed by those within and outwith transitioning societies attempting to make the emergent peace sustainable. The over-riding concerns were stability, reconfiguration of

30. Luc Huyse, *All Things Must Pass Except the Past* (Van Halewyck: Kessel-Lo, 2009) at 69.
31. Paul Collier *et al*, *Breaking the Conflict Trap: Civil War and Development Policy* (Oxford University Press, 2003) at i.
32. Jane Alexander, *A Scoping Study of Transitional Justice and Poverty Reduction* (DFID: London, 2003) at 6.
33. Rama Mani, 'Editorial: Dilemmas of Expanding Transitional Justice, or Forging the Nexus between Transitional Justice and Development', 2 *International Journal of Transitional Justice* (2008) 253–256 at 262.
34. U.N. Secretary-General, *The Rule Of Law And Transitional Justice In Conflict And Post-Conflict Societies*, UN Doc. S/2004/616 (3 August 2004) at para. 8.
35. Ruti Teitel, *Transitional Justice* (Oxford University Press, 2001) at 5.
36. Marion Smiley, 'Democratic Justice in Transition', 99 *Michigan Law Review* (2001) 1332–1347 at 1336.

state institutions and popular participation in politics. While the political universe changed, the poverty, inequality and under-development that characterised the earlier conflict consistently persist in the new liberal democratic dispensation, as illustrated by a random sample of states which undertook transitional justice to at least some degree. Four years after the end of *apartheid* in South Africa, 61% of blacks lived in poverty while only 1% of whites did.[37] The prime beneficiaries of apartheid famously retired into luxury holiday homes, their accrued wealth untouched.[38] Today, inter-race inequality remains high while intra-race inequality increases dramatically.[39] Even after democratic transition, Brazilian and Filipino land-ownership continued to be dominated by large *latifundia*, continuing to impoverish dependant rural communities.[40] The discredited militaries of Chile and Indonesia retained control of important enterprises within the state like copper mining and food distribution respectively, even where they lost political control.[41] Transition to Maoist rule in democratic Nepal did little to diminish the wealth of the deposed king.[42] Though Guatemala's peace accords established an increased target ratio for tax-to-GDP in order provide basic services and infrastructure for the indigenous groups whose deprivation led to war, the landed elite resist tax reform of any sort.[43]

Transitional justice appeared to concentrate on the civil-political tip of the iceberg and hence ignored vast structural issues beneath the waterline which formed the background or catalyst for the abuses it reckoned with. Its mechanisms concerned themselves more with physical violence attending past civil and political rights violations than with past or present structural violence, defined herein as the phenomenon whereby the structure of society manifests

37. Kora Andrieu, 'Transitional Justice: A New Discipline in Human Rights' *Online Encyclopedia of Mass Violence* (2010), <www.massviolence.org/IMG/article_PDF/Transitional-Justice-A-New-Discipline-in-Human-Rights.pdf> at 18.
38. Hennie Van Vuren, *Apartheid Grand Corruption: Assessing the Scale of Crimes of Profit in South Africa from 1976 to 1994* (Institute for Security Studies: Cape Town, 2006) at 16.
39. Mullen, 'Reassessing the Focus', *supra* note 4, at 11.
40. John H. Hertz, 'An Historical Perspective', in Justice and Society Program of the Aspen Institute (ed.), *State Crimes: Punishment Or Pardon* (Aspen Institute: Queenstown, Md., 1989) 19–38 at 22.
41. Tony Addison, 'The Political Economy of the Transition from Authoritarianism', in De Greiff and Duthie (eds), *Transitional Justice and Development*, *supra* note 12, 110–142 at 114 and 123.
42. Daniel Aguirre and Irene Pietropaoli, 'Gender Equality, Development and Transitional Justice: The Case of Nepal', 2 *International Journal of Transitional Justice* (2008) 356–377 at 361.
43. Tony Addison, Abdur Chowdhury and S. Mansoob Murshed, 'Financing Reconstruction', in Gerd Junne and Willemijn Verkoren (eds), *Post-Conflict Development: Meeting New Challenges* (Lynne Rienner Publishers: Boulder, 2005) 211–222 at 212.

economic, social and cultural rights before and during conflict.[59] This turn in transitional justice fits with an increased willingness in the field to embraces holistic, integrated strategies that combine retributive, restorative and reparative justice.[60] Transitional justice also embraces other disciplines such as peace-building and security sector reform which are increasingly conceptualised by the UN and INGOs in terms of human security.[61] Since 2011's World Bank Development Report identified a correlation between recurrent political violence and enduring poverty, the prevention of political violence has become a key goal of development assistance generally.[62]

This altered focus may have flowed from, and certainly accorded with, the perceptions of those whose lives international and domestic transitional justice actors tries to ameliorate. As victimisation was studied in greater depth came the realisation among scholars that it occurs on the level of gender, wealth and class, paving the way for a greater insistence on the indivisibility of rights in the literature that was not always appreciated in the hitherto predominant liberal-legalist paradigm.[63] Polls of survivor populations overwhelmingly demonstrate that socio-economic concerns trump the desire for criminal justice or truth in transitions. For example, Corkalo *et al* found that all communities in Bosnia deemed economic reconstruction and social justice more imperative than accountability.[64] In a survey of 2585 adults in Uganda in 2005, less than 1% believed justice was the most pressing priority after conflict, a figure dwarfed by the need for food (33%), education (5%) and health (6%).[65] In Nepal, only 3% of respondents thought punishing perpetrators was a priority, in contrast to compensation (24%), education (17%) and basic needs (16%).[66] Similar conclusions have also been drawn in the Democratic

59. Louise Arbour, 'Economic and Social Justice for Societies in Transition', 40 *NYU Journal of International Law & Policy* (2007) 1–27 at 3.
60. Paul Gready, 'Reconceptualising Transitional Justice: Embedded and Distanced Justice', 5 *Conflict, Security and Development* (2005) 3–21 at 7.
61. UN Development Programme, *New Dimensions of Human Security: Human Development Report* (1994) at 23.
62. World Bank, 'World Development Report 2011: Conflict, Security, and Development', <http://wdr2011.worldbank.org/>.
63. Laplante, 'Roots of Violence', *supra* note 54, at 346.
64. D. Corkalo *et al*, 'Neighbors Again? Intercommunity Relations after Ethnic Cleansing', in Eric Stover and Harvey M. Weinstein (eds), *My Neighbor, My Enemy: Justice and Community in the Aftermath of Mass Cleansing* (Cambridge University Press, 2004) 143–161 at 143.
65. Phuong Pham & Patrick Vinck, *Transitioning to Peace: A Population-Based Survey on Attitudes About Social Reconstruction and Justice in Northern Uganda* (University of California Human Rights Center, 2010) at 25.
66. Carla Fajardo and Warisha Farasat, 'Nepali Voices: Perceptions of Truth, Justice, Reconciliation, Reparations and the Transition in Nepal', International Center for Transitional

Republic of the Congo[67] and in Kenya.[68] East Timor's Commission for Reception, Truth and Reconciliation acknowledged violations of bodily integrity but went on to affirm that 'the impact of conditions in which [the Timorese people] lived, while often less remarked upon, was equally damaging and possibly more long-lasting.'[69] Laplante observes that widespread protests and riots in post-transitional Chile, South Africa and Guatemala arose from the same types of socio-economic grievances that underpinned earlier periods of human rights violations in these states.[70] A study of victims in Rwanda, Cambodia and East Timor demonstrated that the failure of their societies to secure their basic needs constituted significant impediments to peace and reconciliation, notwithstanding the apparent stability of the respective transitions.[71] While Latin American societies have been observed to tolerate violations by authoritarian regimes in the pursuit of public order, the revelation that the juntas and caudillos were corrupt (most notably the Pinochet Riggs Bank and tax fraud scandals) have proven far more damaging to their historical reputations than civil and political rights abuses.[72] Black South Africans in particular perceive the beneficiaries of apartheid as having escaped much-needed scrutiny.[73] As Oomen argues, '[e]ven if the input and output of justice mechanisms are perceived as fair, they will still lack legitimacy if they operate within a context of ongoing discrimination and deprivation.'[74]

Justice and Advocacy Forum (2008), <ictj.org/sites/default/files/ICTJ-Nepal-Voices-Reconciliation-2008-English.pdf>.

67. Patrick Vinck and Phuong Pham, 'Ownership and Participation in Transitional Justice Mechanisms: A Sustainable Development Perspective from Eastern DRC', 2 *International Journal of Transitional Justice* (2008) 398–411.
68. Simon Robins, '"To Live as Other Kenyans Do": A Study of the Reparative Demands of Kenyan Victims of Human Rights Violations' International Center for Transitional Justice and Advocacy Forum 28 (2011), <www.ictj.org/sites/default/files/ICTJ-Kenya-Reparations-Demands-2011-English.pdf> .
69. Commission for Reception, Truth and Reconciliation, *Chega! The Report of the Commission For Reception, Truth And Reconciliation* (2005), Chapter 7(9) at 2.
70. Laplante, 'Roots of Violence', *supra* note 54, at 331.
71. Wendy Lambourne, 'Transitional Justice and Peace-building After Mass Violence', 3 *International Journal of Transitional Justice* (2009) 28–48 at 42.
72. James Cavallaro and Sebastian Albuja, 'The Lost Agenda: Economic Crimes and Truth Commissions in Latin America and Beyond', in Kieran McEvoy and Lorna McGregor (eds), *Transitional Justice From Below: Grassroots Activism and the Struggle For Change* (Hart Publishing: London, 2008) 121–142 at 131–137.
73. Yasmin Sooka, 'The Politics of Transitional Justice', in Chandra Lekha Sriram and Suren Pillay (eds), *Peace Versus Justice?: The Dilemma of Transitional Justice in Africa* (James Currey: Suffolk, 2010) 21–43 at 33.
74. Barbara Oomen, 'Justice Mechanisms and the Question of Legitimacy: The Example of Rwanda's Multi-layered Justice Mechanisms', in Kai Ambos, Judith Large and Marieke

2.2. Towards an Expanded Focus

Until recently, these complaints about transitional justice's shortcomings and the potential for a more holistic response were merely 'Sunday beliefs,' conceptions of (in)justice that commanded subjective assent without actually inducing action to bring about an improved state of affairs.[75] The UN's seminal *Rule of Law and Transitional Justice Report* in 2004 acknowledged the need to repair the material damage of conflict or authoritarianism, but neglected to outline even a basic blueprint for tackling structural roots of conflict.[76] Practice on the ground offered little by way of example. However, in the last five years different suggestions have emerged as to how the field can address its past derelictions.[77] Lambourne conceives of a relatively wide form of 'socioeconomic justice' divided into historical justice (compensation, restitution, reparation) for past abuses and prospective distributive justice to minimise structural violence in future.[78] Andrieu asserts that the transformation of transitional justice should develop collective recognition procedures as the new rationale for social redistribution,[79] echoing Mani's and Alexander's earlier proposals of an explicitly distributive approach geared towards equity in resources and power in addition to pre-existing legal and rectificatory forms of justice.[80] Pillay similarly contends that a redistributive approach 'might enable the creation of lasting peace by addressing the material discrepancies and psychological legacies of conflict.'[81] Kalmanovitz would prefer transitional justice to prioritise social minima like education, nutrition,

Wierda (eds), *Building a Future on Peace and Justice: Studies on Transitional Justice, Peace and Development, The Nuremberg Declaration on Peace and Justice* (Springer: Berlin, 2009) 175–202 at 197.

75. Jon Elster, *Closing the Books: Transitional Justice in Historical Perspective* (Cambridge University Press, 2004) at 81.
76. UN Secretary-General, *supra* note 34, at para. 54.
77. A significant milestone was the International Journal of Transitional Justice's 2008, volume 2 special issue on transitional justice and development where a number of the contributors argued for an expansion of the transitional justice field. A sizeable literature has followed, most notably de Greiff and Duthie (eds), *Transitional Justice and Development, supra* note 12; Gaby Oré Aguilar and Felipé Gomez Isa (eds), *Rethinking Transitions: Equality and Social Justice in Societies Emerging from Conflict* (Intersentia: Cambridge, 2011); Bergsmo *et al* (eds), *Distributive Justice, supra* note 18; Paul Gready, *The Era of Transitional Justice* (Routledge: New York, 2011).
78. Lambourne, 'Transitional Justice and Peace-building', *supra* note 71, at 41.
79. Andrieu, 'New Discipline', *supra* note 37, at 20.
80. Mani, *Beyond Retribution, supra* note 25, at 10; Alexander, *Scoping Study, supra* note 32, at 48.
81. Suren Pillay, 'Conclusion', in Sriram and Pillay (eds), *Peace Versus Justice?, supra* note 73, 347–356 at 353.

education and health for the survivor population before attempting more corrective forms of justice.[82] Miller argues the field should aspire towards what she calls 'economic justice' which would address the economic roots of conflict, temper economic liberalisation with redistribution and impact on the transitional government's development plans.[83] Most ambitiously of all, Selim and Murithi assume transitional justice 'should be about expanding not only the choices, but also the options and blueprint for society and individuals to improve their livelihoods and wellbeing.'[84] Aguirre and Pietropaoli contend that it should assure outcomes based on the third generation right to development.[85] Perhaps more modestly, Duthie argues transitional justice measures are not a development strategy but should be designed in ways that are 'development sensitive,'[86] but this is an unusually circumspect vision of transitional justice's potential effect on post-conflict or post-authoritarian society. These distributive/egalitarian/developmental approaches would address the causes of poverty as well as its symptoms, conceptualising justice as equality in addition to the traditional transitional justice preoccupation with liberty.[87] The presumption is that virtuous circles would emerge wherein justice, development and democracy would mutually reinforce each other.[88]

In considering this presumption, it is imperative to note that development discourse and literature has largely neglected to engage with transitional justice, [89] though the UNDP has committed to strengthening the linkages between the two areas.[90] Development practitioners in the field are frequently unaware or uninterested in parallel transitional justice activities, a

82. Pablo Kalmanovitz, 'Corrective Justice versus Social Justice in the Aftermath of War', in Bergsmo *et al* (eds), *Distributive Justice*, *supra* note 18, 71–96 at 76–77.
83. Miller, 'Effects of Invisibility', *supra* note 16, at 267.
84. Yvette Selim and Tim Murithi, 'Transitional Justice and Development: Partners for Sustainable Peace in Africa?', 6 *Journal of Peacebuilding and Development* (2011) 58–72 at 64.
85. Aguirre and Pietropaoli, 'The Case of Nepal', *supra* note 42, at 356.
86. Roger Duthie, 'Towards a Development-sensitive Approach to Transitional Justice', 2 *International Journal of Transitional Justice* (2008) 292–309.
87. Muvingi, 'Sitting on Powder Kegs', *supra* note 57, at 166.
88. De Greiff, 'Articulating the Links', *supra* note 52, at 28; Lisa Hecht and Sabine Michalowski, 'The Economic Dimensions of Transitional Justice', University Of Essex Transitional Justice Network Concept Paper (2012), <www.essex.ac.uk/tjn/documents/TheeconomicandsocialdimensionsofTJ.pdf>.
89. Markus Lenzen, 'Roads Less Travelled: Conceptual Pathways (and Stumbling Blocks) for Development and Transitional Justice', in de Greiff and Duthie (eds), *Transitional Justice and Development*, *supra* note 12, 76–109 at 77 and 85.
90. United Nations Development Programme, 'Strengthening the Rule of Law in Conflict and Post-Conflict Situations: A Global UNDP Programme for Justice and Security 2008–2011' (2011), <www.unrol.org/files/rol_final_apr09.pdf> at 9.

phenomenon that reflects less the professional balkanisation that attends all peace-building than a belief that the mechanisms and insights of transitional justice are of limited application in conjuring a sustainable socio-economic agenda into being. If the international development community largely discounts transitional justice as being of anything more than tangential importance and if the record for transitional justice in addressing the structural roots of conflict by this point is negligible, why are there such large expectations? The novelty of focus may provide one explanation. Another answer may lie in the traditional optimism of scholars in the field regarding the potency of transition to redefine the norms on which a conflict-ridden society is based. The presumption of many is that periods of transition are times when 'everything is up for grabs all at once.'[91] Aguirre and Pietropaoli, for example, assert that transitions are rare periods of rupture 'that offer opportunities to reconceive the social meaning of past conflicts in an attempt to reconstruct their present and future effects,'[92] while Bergsmo *et al* see transition as a transformative constitutional moment where the distribution of poverty and wealth, land reform and the economy may be publicly addressed.[93] It is suggested that truth commissions may have greater purchase because they take place in times when significant decisions about the future course of the state will be adopted.[94] It is assumed that states should feel a greater compulsion to redress conditions of socio-economic deprivation in the transitional period, especially if they are presented as rights violations.[95] Arbour's optimism is explained by her faith that '[s]ocieties in transition present unique opportunities for countries to equip themselves appropriately to ensure respect for human rights and human dignity.'[96] Even the very narrow criminal remits of the ICC's interventions in Africa have been viewed as 'windows of opportunity' for restructuring the state and reducing poverty (albeit without any concrete proposals for how it should do so).[97] Given that development actors

91. Francois DuBois and Adam Czarnota, 'The Transitional Rule of Law', 24 *Alternative Law Review* (1999) 9–19 at 10.
92. Aguirre and Pietropaoli, 'The Case of Nepal', *supra* note 42, at 357.
93. Morten Bergsmo *et al*, 'Introduction', in Bergsmo *et al* (eds.), *Distributive Justice*, *supra* note 18, 1–14 at 2.
94. Rolando Ames Cobián and Felix Reátegui, 'Toward Systemic Social Transformation: Truth Commissions and Development', in de Greiff and Duthie (eds), *Transitional Justice and Development*, *supra* note 12, 142–169 at 145.
95. Laplante, 'Roots of Violence', *supra* note 54, at 331 (Preamble) and 341.
96. Arbour, 'Economic and Social Justice', *supra* note 59, at 26.
97. Christine Bjork and Juanita Goebertus, 'Complementarity in Action: The Role of Civil Society and the ICC in Rule of Law Strengthening in Kenya', 14 *Yale Human Rights and Development Law Journal* (2011) 205–230 at 226 and Wanza Kioko, 'The Place of Transitional Justice in Kenya's Political Transition', in Lawrence M. Mute, Kichamu Akivaga and

also generally use periods of political change to foster systemic changes in the structure of society, transition may appear an unusually propitious time for ambitious projects.[98] This faith is shared to varying degrees by some development actors,[99] anti-corruption theorists[100] and political economists who argue that egalitarian structural change is most feasible where antagonistic interest groups have temporarily or permanently lost power.[101]

Of course, critics of the emancipatory rhetoric of human rights have argued that humanitarians make arguments 'they know to be less persuasive than they claim' when activists and advocates attempt to revamp its tools (like transitional justice) to correct critical shortcomings (like a perceived narrowness of focus).[102] Notwithstanding the ostensibly immense confidence scholars have in transitional justice, even optimistic works are studiously opaque about what their conceptions of distributive, developmental or socio-economic justice will ultimately look like on the ground. Elements of a broad-based, development-friendly recovery like inflation policy, currency reform, bank regulation and even taxation go unaddressed in the literature. Advocates of a role for transitional justice in fundamentally altering the structures of divided societies acknowledge that thus far all we have are a series of hypothetical connections to be further researched,'[103] points of possible interconnection,'[104] 'a starting point for a broader conversation'[105] and underdeveloped concepts and boundaries.[106] Suggested activities ('exposing' discriminatory practices,[107] 'reaching' for deeper justice,[108] 'making connections')[109] exist in the realm of the exhortatory, at some causal remove from concrete betterment of peoples' lives. Though these developments in transitional justice ostensibly represent a welcome change from the traditional humanitarian reluctance identified

---

Wanza Kioko (eds), *Building an Open Society: The Politics of Transition in Kenya* (Claripress: Nairobi, 2002) 330–350 at 331.

98. Cobián and Reátegui, 'Toward Systemic Social Transformation', *supra* note 94, at 145.
99. Alexander, *Scoping Study*, *supra* note 32.
100. Christine Cheng and Dominik Zaum, 'Key Themes in Peace-Building and Corruption', 15 *International Peacekeeping* (2008) 301–309 at 307.
101. Donald Snodgrass, 'Restoring Economic Functioning in Failed States', in Robert I. Rotberg (ed.), *When States Fail: Causes And Consequences* (Princeton University Press, 2004) 256–268 at 264.
102. Kennedy, *Dark Sides of Virtue*, *supra* note 8, at 28.
103. Colvin, 'Purity and Planning', *supra* note 20, at 414.
104. *Ibid.*
105. Miller, 'Effects of Invisibility', *supra* note 16, at 291.
106. Hecht and Michalowski, 'Economic Dimensions', *supra* note 88, at 1.
107. Arbour, 'Economic and Social Justice', *supra* note 59, at 3.
108. Tafadzwa Pasipanodya, 'A Deeper Justice: Economic and Social Justice as Transitional Justice in Nepal', 2 *International Journal of Transitional Justice* (2008) 378–397 at 397.
109. De Greiff and Duthie (eds), *Transitional Justice and Development*, *supra* note 12.

civil and political violations over economic abuses in the South African TRC, the 'result has been entrenched, even increasing, inequality.'[139] On the basis of these arguments, transitional justice isn't merely failing to address socio-economic justice, it appears to exacerbate it by serving to protect the interests of the privileged at the expense of the poor,[140] actively perpetuating the position of existing economic elites instead of empowering the marginalised,[141] and serving as an enabling context for the ravages of the free market.[142] Lost amongst the stridency of these claims is the fact that these are essentially arguments from omission and temporal correlation. Because transitional justice has not addressed socio-economic justice and is located within broader trends of peace-building and democratisation that exacerbate or at least fail to mitigate socio-economic inequalities, it is argued that the field must therefore automatically support or conduce to marketisation and liberalising growth.

Ignatieff is convincing in arguing against this mechanical conflation of free market globalists and human rights internationalists. Though the moral individualism that traditionally characterises human rights and its transitional justice variant has some 'elective affinity with the economic individualism of the global market', the two cannot be presumed to march hand in hand as the relationship between the two is more usually antagonistic.[143] Because humanitarians presume institutions like transitional justice are inherently benign and effective, when they fail to realise their assumed potential claims tend to arise that policy-making has been 'captured,' distorted or misused.[144] In this case, transitional justice is assumed to have been commandeered by agents sympathetic to, or actively supportive of, globalising capital. However, as Section 4 goes on to argue, it is difficult to find any scholars or activists or policy-makers in the field supportive of neo-liberal economics or the idea that transitional justice should facilitate capitalism. Even if transitional justice does not act as a brake on simultaneous processes of economic liberalisation, it cannot be assumed to facilitate these processes. It may be entirely neutral. The prosecutor exploring the role of blood diamonds in the Sierra Leone conflict or the truth commissioner listening to rape testimony in Guatemala would be astonished to discover their work provided an 'enabling context for free markets'[145] purely because the scope of their enquiry didn't expand as far

139. Gready, 'Embedded and Distanced Justice', *supra* note 60, at 5.
140. Muvingi, 'Sitting on Powder Kegs', *supra* note 57, at 182.
141. Aguirre and Pietropaoli, 'The Case of Nepal', *supra* note 42, at 367.
142. Gready, 'Embedded and Distanced Justice', *supra* note 60, at 5.
143. Michael Ignatieff, *Human Rights as Politics and Idolatry* (Princeton University Press, 2001) at 7.
144. Kennedy, *Dark Sides of Virtue*, *supra* note 8, at 121.
145. Gready, 'Embedded and Distanced Justice', *supra* note 60, at 5.

is somewhat more generous when he accepts that widespread labour abuses and private sector exploitation in El Salvador 'are not entirely attributable' to the mandate of its Commission on Truth, which again focused more on individuals than broader systems.[132] Though rhetorically compelling, these arguments appear to conflate a failed operation (transitional justice) with the pre-existing disease (inequality). The best example of this tendency towards hyperbole is Miller's assertion that by ignoring the deeper roots of conflict, transitional justice mechanisms in explicitly causal terms "may actively contribute to new outbreaks of violence.'[133] The extension of this argument, that ignoring inequalities will inevitably lead to a recurrence of conflict,[134] appears to ignore the plethora of transitions in states like Mozambique, Angola, Guatemala and Sierra Leone which appear highly durable notwithstanding the absence of any real distributive justice.[135]

Others go further rhetorically to argue that transitional justice as currently practiced is effectively the handmaiden of neo-liberal structural adjustment programs. Certainly, economic liberalisation tends to accompany political transition, though few states will be untouched by it beforehand—it may after all have been a contributory factor to war or authoritarian rule. Numerous scholars argue that transitional justice must be understood as an integral part of the liberal peace-building model and therefore automatically promotes neo-liberal market-based economic models antithetical to redistribution of wealth or economic equality.[136] Makau Wa Mutua, for example, sees transitional justice as reproducing the assumption in global human rights of the naturalness of the market and the inevitability of capitalist relationships.[137] Nagy contends that transitional justice is open to the accusation of attempting to 'produce subjects and truths that align with market democracy and are blind to gender and social justice.'[138] Gready contends that by privileging

132. Mullen, 'Reassessing the Focus', *supra* note 4, at 14.
133. Miller, 'Effects of Invisibility', *supra* note 16, at 288.
134. *Ibid*, at 287.
135. As Holmes reminds us, since de Tocqueville progressive politics has had to grapple with the fact that many extremely unequal societies have manifested stability and immunity from class-based revolution (Holmes, 'Concluding Remarks', *supra* note 18, at 422).
136. Sandra Rubli, *Transitional Justice: Justice by Bureaucratic Means?* (Swiss Peace Working: Berne, 2012) at 3; Chandra Lekha Sriram, 'Justice as Peace? Liberal Peacebuilding and Strategies of Transitional Justice', 21 *Global Society* (2007) 579–591 and Patricia Lundy and Mark McGovern, 'The Role of Community in Participatory Transitional Justice', in McEvoy and McGregor (eds), *Transitional Justice From Below*, *supra* note 72, 99–120 at 104.
137. Makau Mutua, 'A Critique of Rights in Transitional Justice: The African Experience', in Aguilar and Gomez Isa (eds), *Rethinking Transitions*, *supra* note 77, 31–45 at 36–37.
138. Rosemary Nagy, 'Transitional Justice as a Global Project: Critical Reflections', 29 *Third World Quarterly* (2008) 275–289 at 275–276.

then refuse to accept sharply redistributive taxation?'[125] These are valid, some might say unavoidable, criticisms of transitional justice as currently practiced. It is also reasonable to suggest transitional justice may seem an empty gesture to those victims who benefit only indirectly from democratisation and establishing the rule of law or to those whose children and grandchildren will be the ultimate inheritors of any long-term transitional dividend.[126]

3.2. Transitional Justice as an Aggravator of Socio-Economic Injustice

However, there is another, more antagonistic strain to this position that significantly ups the rhetorical ante, going beyond merely cataloguing the regrettable omissions of the field to argue transitional justice as currently practiced is actively harmful in socio-economic terms. The most prevalent example is a zero-sum game argument already familiar in wider human rights debates to the effect that pursuing civil and political rights represents an acquiescence to the dominant neo-liberal economic order and an implicit renunciation of social justice issues like health, welfare and poverty. For example, Miller argues that the standard set of debates on transitional justice (truth versus justice, what works, etc.) have erected an artificial binary separation between the realms of economics and justice, a deliberate 'constructed invisibility' that consciously or unconsciously fosters an aggressively liberalising post-transition politics.[127] Carranza similarly argues that the field deliberately 'looks away' when it sees socio-economic injustices.[128] Teitel vaguely suggests that transitional justice 'has, in large part, displaced broader reform projects, and appears to represent a move away from progressive politics' without suggesting what those broader reform projects might be.[129] Wilson is more direct in contending that the South African TRC's narrow focus on extreme violence 'actually obstructed' a wider search for social justice there.[130] On this view, transitional justice appears a deliberate mechanism for ideological obfuscation to divert attention from the economic beneficiaries of the predecessor regime.[131] Mullen

125. Miriam J. Aukerman, 'Extraordinary Evil, Ordinary Crimes: A Framework for Understanding Transitional Justice', 15 *Harvard Human Rights Journal* (2002) 39–98 at 83.
126. Andrieu, 'New Discipline', *supra* note 37, at 15.
127. Miller, 'Effects of Invisibility', *supra* note 16.
128. Carranza, 'Plunder and Pain', *supra* note 16, at 330.
129. Teitel, 'New Era', *supra* note 53, at 901.
130. Richard A. Wilson, 'Justice and Legitimacy in the South African Transition', in Alexandra Barahona De Brito, Carmen González-Enríquez and Paloma Aguilar (eds), *The Politics of Memory: Transitional Justice in Democratising Societies* (Oxford University Press, 2001) 190–217 at 207.
131. Van der Merwe, 'Delivering Justice', *supra* note 6, at 117.

by Kennedy to make distributional choices, current advocacy is still slow to identify winners and losers, how much the winners stand to benefit, or how the losers might react.[110] The apparent progress in redefining transitional justice, therefore, is more rhetorical than programmatic or policy-based. Because these exhortations have yet to be acted upon, there is no established theoretical or empirical base on which to build.[111] Even a rudimentary 'lessons learned' stage that could serve as a generic template for activities to this end has yet to be arrived at. The generalised arguments made are inspiring but lacking in even the most minimal concrete detail if considered in the context of particularised transitions.

3. Transitional Justice and Rhetoric

If the potential of transitional justice to transform social and economic organisation of the state is as self-evident as its proponents suggest, the question remains as to why socio-economic justice has been pursued so infrequently in times of significant political change. In answering this question, the answer is found to lie not with the inadequacy of trials, truth commissions or reparations as catalysts for macro-economic reforms, nor the often painfully negotiated nature of transition, but in the conception of justice within the field. Arguments to the effect that more egalitarian social change is impaired by the narrowness of the concept of justice presuppose a wide latitude for transitional justice actors to define their fields of action and a high degree of efficacy once they act.

3.1. Transitional Justice as the Marginaliser of Socio-Economic Injustice

Aside from the startlingly ambitious nature of the propositions made about transitional justice's potential to thoroughly transform unjust arrangements in a manner that war, democracy, development and aid have not, what is most notable about this line of argumentation is the firmness with which it rejects transitional justice's existing modes of practice. As noted above, all arguments asserting a hitherto-unrealised distributive/developmental potency in transitional justice begin by deprecating the narrowness of the existing conception of justice. This narrowness is viewed as an inevitable consequence of the liberal paradigm which dominates the field, elevating legalism and

110. Kennedy, *Dark Sides of Virtue*, *supra* note 8, at xxiii–xxiv.
111. Colvin, 'Purity and Planning', *supra* note 20, at 414.

as the roots of all social division. Advocates of a wider role for transitional justice must remain alive to the possibility that neither a 'conspiracy of interests' nor a 'coherence of blindness' explain its lack of impact on unjust societal structures.[146]

A few other less common rhetorical strategies have been employed to criticise existing modalities of transitional justice. The first is the dramatic reorientation of the metrics by which transitional justice should be judged. For example Villa-Vicencio contended the South Africa TRC should be judged not on the basis of who went to prison but on whether the quality of everyday life was better,[147] while Alexander argues that transitional justice was 'critical' and 'vital' to poverty reduction (before somewhat contradictorily noting it rarely has this role).[148] Another line of argument is that transitional justice, with its focal points of retribution and restoration, is pointless if it doesn't make everyday life better or reduce poverty. The argument of Boraine, on the one hand, and Selim and Murithi, on the other, that reconciliation without economic justice 'is cheap and spurious', or merely symbolic, is implicitly or explicitly commended in much of the literature.[149] Another rhetorical strategy is to juxtapose transitional justice with other projects. Mani's position that transitional justice represents a costly luxury in a highly-constrained environment is reasonable, but she too appears to accept the zero-sum game interpretation when she further asserts that transitional justice 'often comes to represent a trade-off of sorts between justice or development.'[150] Though there is a legitimate concern that costly transitional justice projects are pitched financially against justice sector reform activities,[151] neither Mani nor anyone else manages to cite specific examples of money being diverted from development projects to transitional justice. Funding for transitional justice and development tend to come from different sources, while financial support for development dwarfs that of transitional justice.[152]

The trend in transitional justice scholarship towards addressing structural, socio-economic issues is welcome, and the critique of the limitations of its

146. Miller, 'Effects of Invisibility', *supra* note 16, at 272.
147. Conference speech cited in Mani, *Beyond Retribution*, *supra* note 25, at 125.
148. Alexander, *Scoping Study*, *supra* note 32, at 3 and 47.
149. Alex Boraine, *A Country Unmasked: Inside South Africa's Truth and Reconciliation Commission* (Oxford University Press, 2000) at 357; Selim and Murithi, 'Transitional Justice and Development', *supra* note 84, at 61.
150. Mani, 'Editorial', *supra* note 33, at 253, repeated at 257.
151. Muna B. Ndulo and Roger Duthie, 'The Role of Judicial Reform in Development and Transitional Justice', in de Greiff and Duthie (eds), *Transitional Justice and Development*, *supra* note 12, 250–281 at 265.
152. Lenzen, 'Roads Less Travelled' *supra* note 89, at 86.

existing modalities is a welcome antidote to the exaggerated claims that it forms the centre-piece of social repair.[153] It becomes counter-productive, however, when the existing valuable work trials, truth commissions and reparations programs do is devalued in the strident demands for a re-orientation of the field. If, as has been suggested, transitional justice, as a whole, risks losing credibility unless it improves overall living conditions for citizens in the transitional state, the field itself might be in danger.[154] In driving the field from non-existence to peace-building mainstream in less than two decades, transitional justice scholars formulate the issues, but also define how those issues are resolved, using their moral appeal, investigative missions and national NGO partners to pressure states to comply with their conceptions of how justice should be pursued.[155] Historically, ideas outlined in papers, conferences or the field about how transitional justice can be practiced often amount to self-fulfilling prophecies of what will be done in future, even if the success anticipated does not follow as inevitably. Kritz exaggerates only slightly when he contends that a government's transitional justice policy 'often depends less on well-grounded and proven policy considerations than on whether the junior member of staff writing the policy memo has some experience with the South African TRC or another transitional justice process,'[156] but he highlights the very salient fact that how scholars, advocates and practitioners think about and experience transitional justice can have a large impact on how it is practiced and its relationship to other socio-political phenomena. The parameters of transitional justice are often defined by what international donors at supranational, bilateral or INGO levels are willing to pay.[157] If mere accountability, or truth, or purges or lustration are held to be worthless by those within the field, then external support from donors and peace-builders may be jeopardised. Some rather large babies risk being thrown out with the bathwater if this perception that transitional justice as currently constituted unduly narrows the potential for thoroughgoing social transformation becomes an article of faith. It is worth therefore considering whether transitional justice has these wider, egalitarian and developmental potentials, both in terms of the mechanisms employed and the context in which they are used.

153. Fletcher and Weinstein, 'Violence and Social Repair', *supra* note 9, at 577.
154. Mani, 'Editorial', *supra* note 33, at 253–254.
155. Kathryn Sikkink, *The Justice Cascade: How Human Rights Prosecutions are Changing World Politics* (W.W. Norton & Co.: New York, 2011).
156. Neil J. Kritz, 'Policy Implications of Empirical Research on Transitional Justice', in van der Merwe, Baxter and Chapman (eds), *Assessing the Impact, supra* note 6, 13–21 at 14.
157. Barbara Oomen, 'Donor-Driven Justice and its Discontents', 36 *Development and Change* (2005) 887–910.

4. The Circumspection of Transitional Justice: Pragmatism or Ideology?

The foregoing criticisms of transitional justice have proceeded on the basis that the field has resisted claims for structural justice because its liberal-legalist framework and (unspoken) sympathy for market economics denies the legitimacy of these aims[158] or because transitional justice actors fear the dilution of the field's purposes.[159] However, while it is clear that the traditional debates on stability, truth and criminal justice have operated to overshadow the importance of economic factors in transition, it is questionable the extent to which this trend can be explained by any acceptance of the rightness of the neoliberal free market paradigm. On the basis of a survey of writings on transitional justice since the late 1980s, it is hard to discern any theorist in the field explicitly or implicitly arguing in favour of neo-liberal capitalist economics. It is significant that none of the writers mentioned earlier who disdain the liberal-legalist limitations of the conception of justice in transition can cite any scholars in the field who do so. For over a decade, mainstream transitional scholars have willingly accepted that reconstructing the socio-economic bases of society can exert a greater beneficial impact than accountability or truth without attracting principled dissent.[160] Even the architects of the now-maligned South Africa TRC fully accepted at the time that the reversal of apartheid economic policies was more important than seeing PW Botha behind bars, but regretted that the need to avoid alienating right-wing elements who could prevent the transition to democratic rule made this impossible.[161] Though the UN *Transitional Justice and the Rule of Law Report* (2004) neglected economic injustice, the UN Office of the High Commissioner for Human Rights' influential *Rule of Law Tools* series subsequently acknowledged that structural violence can have even more deleterious effects for the public than civil and political rights violations[162] and recommended that transitional justice mechanisms address it.[163] Numerous

158. Arthur, 'How "Transitions" Reshaped Human Rights', *supra* note 122, at 326 and 355.
159. Miller, 'Effects of Invisibility', *supra* note 16, at 267.
160. Robert Meister, 'Human Rights and the Politics of Victimhood', 16 *Ethics & International Affairs* (2002) 91–108; Fletcher and Weinstein, 'Violence and Social Repair', *supra* note 9, at 603.
161. Kader Asmal, 'Truth, Reconciliation, and Justice: The South African Experience in Perspective', 63 *Modern Law Review* (2000) 1–24 at 16 and 11.
162. Office of the United Nations High Commissioner for Human Rights, 'Rule of Law Tools for Post-Conflict States: Truth Commissions', <www.ohchr.org/Documents/Publications/ RuleoflawTruthCommissionsen.pdf> at 9.
163. *Ibid*, at 16.

truth commissions, the indictments in the Charles Taylor and Darfur trials, and the aforementioned polling of survivor communities constantly emphasise the inter-relation of bodily integrity abuses and economic injustice. Far from constituting a marginal position, the thesis that economic policies in authoritarianism and war are more permanent and damaging than civil and political abuses is something of an article of faith in transitional justice. No significant dissent is to be found in the literature on the universality of economic, social and cultural rights, on the one hand, or the indivisibility of all three generation of rights, on the other. Few would quibble with the assertion that traditionally parsimonious views of transitional justice risk limiting its potential, even if estimations of that potential exist on a wide spectrum from minimalist to utopian.

None of this should be surprising. Transitional justice invariably rallies 'reformist forces' and progressist elements that might be expected to support socio-economic justice.[164] As this section goes on to examine, the very few scholars who explicitly oppose a role for transitional justice in directly addressing socio-economic wrongs do so not on the basis of opposition to economic justice, development or redistribution, but on the basis that the available mechanisms of transitional justice are unsuited to doing so. What one instead sees in traditional transitional justice discourse is a concentration on how transitional justice can facilitate progress towards a liberal agenda of electoral politics, the rule of law, responsive governance and constitutionalism which opens the political space, essentially demonstrating ambivalence about the economic order. Transitional justice aspires towards a stable society, but not necessarily a capitalist one. Transitional justice is certainly guilty of under-analysing its potential in stimulating socio-economic reform, a matter which is slowly being redressed. However, under-analysis of the potential to catalyse socio-economic reform should not be confused with opposition to it. Much of the rhetoric surrounding transitional justice and structural injustice takes place on the basis of an unhelpful 'those who are not with us are against us' view of the field.

If policy-makers in transitional justice hold development or redistribution as legitimate aims in peace-building generally, then the palpable lack of enthusiasm for a developmental or redistributive role for transitional justice is better explained by the yawning gap between the ends proposed and the

164. Godfrey M. Musila, 'Accountability Debate in Kenya in Near Policy Vacuum and Ethnic Tension', in Phil Clark (ed.), *Oxford Transitional Justice Research: Debating International Justice in Africa* (Foundation for Law, Justice and Society: Oxford, 2010) 104–107 at 105.

means available than any ideological bias. As Cobián and Reategui put it, any significant developmental or redistributive project

> operates in the arena of massive and anonymous policies directed to whole categories of the population and is aimed at designing a general institutional framework, [while] transitional justice usually takes as its starting point the domain of the particular and the concrete: bringing justice to bear in relation to serious human rights violations suffered by specific individuals.[165]

By comparison to what critics of transitional justice argue it *should* pursue, the finite, targeted, traditional ambitions of the field of some truth and some accountability thus far appear mere micro-projects unsuited to grappling with widespread patterns of abuse, astronomical numbers of victims and complex consequences. Of course, one can argue that transitional justice can and must expand beyond this narrow remit, but the required change is not simply a technocratic expansion of institutions. Transitional justice needs new conceptual and philosophical foundations beyond the negative self-critique examined thus far or the largely unelaborated pleas for distributive, developmental or socio-economic justice. On the terms of the existing self-critique of transitional justice and in the absence of even the most rudimentary overall policy framework, the field must outline solutions based on different combinations of public and private legal norms (affirmative action, expropriation, taxation policy, investment, (de)nationalisation) to the most fundamental questions of distribution of wealth, allocation of capital, control of production and standard of living, as well as other practical-philosophical problems like how far back to address root problems or whether the new government can be held responsible for all or some of the depredations of the regime they removed. All of this must take place at a time when the state is rebuilding its constitutional institutions, creating a functioning civil service, imposing civilian control over the military and stabilising a currency, to name but a few of the vast plethora of state-building activities, all of which make acute economic demands. In addition, existing post-conflict or post-authoritarian institutions are dysfunctional or corrupted. Transitional justice typically occurs in what de Greiff labels 'very imperfect worlds.' By this, he means a society characterised not just by the massive and systematic violation of norms, but by the fact that there are enormous disadvantages implicated in any attempt to enforce compliance.[166] Finally, these societies must grapple with the paradox of transitional justice that the states with the greatest need for economically transformative justice will often be those with the fewest available resources.

165. Cobián and Reátegui, 'Toward Systemic Social Transformation', *supra* note 94, at 147.
166. Pablo de Greiff, 'Theorising Transitional Justice', in Melissa Williams, Rosemary Nagy and Jon Elster (eds), *Transitional Justice* (New York University Press, 2012) 31–77 at 35.

Given the dearth of concrete proposals from those who urge a more expansive role for transitional justice and the complexities of the post-conflict or post-authoritarian ecology, it is not that surprising that even those who acknowledge the shortcomings of the field are less than sanguine about its practical possibilities. Discussions about the relationship of transitional justice to wider reform need to acknowledge in practical terms 'the weakness of agency, actors, and organisational forms that could bring about profound change.'[167] Though enjoying a highly visible public profile and a degree of legal and/or moral authority, truth commissioners, like those who administer lustration or reparation schemes, merely constitute a corps of temporary public servants.[168] Transitional justice mechanisms are generally interdisciplinary and well-equipped to draw attention to injustices, to define the discourse of violation and perhaps to propose general outlines for reform. However, this is something quite far removed from the inherently conflictive and highly technical expert processes by which proposals are budgeted, designed and implemented. The apparent timidity of transitional justice is less the product of ideological bias than the commonly observed preferences within the field for clearly defined, mutually coherent and projectisable objectives.[169] With the exception of prosecutorial initiatives, transitional justice institutions are traditionally more reliant on the mobilisation of shame than on any enforcement capability they might possess. This circumspection better explains the perceived failure of the field to expand than an unspoken desire to obscure conflict's economic or resource-based origins.[170]

Much like 'a comprehensive anticorruption strategy ends up looking like a comprehensive peacebuilding or state-building strategy,'[171] the most aspirational claims sketched in Section 3 resemble something of a Borgesian map of desired outcomes so multi-dimensional that they reproduce the entire scope of peace-building in one-to-one facsimile. To take but one example, the forms of reparation usually proposed (ranging from employment and property guarantees to compensation and guarantees of non-repetition) 'could easily be read as the stuff of modern governance in its entirety, rather than as a special case of the requirements of governance in transitional societies.'[172] The UN Officer of the High Commissioner for Human Rights accepts that poverty, homelessness, education policy failures and other social ills are critically

167. Cobián and Reátegui, 'Toward Systemic Social Transformation', *supra* note 94, at 146.
168. *Ibid*, at 146.
169. Alexander, *Scoping Study*, *supra* note 32, at 55; Lenzen, 'Roads Less Travelled', *supra* note 89, at 83.
170. As argued in Miller, 'Effects of Invisibility', *supra* note 16, at 268.
171. Alix Boucher et al, 'Mapping And Fighting Corruption In War-Torn States', Stimson Center Report No.61 (2007) at 57.
172. Asmal, 'South African Experience in Perspective', *supra* note 161, at 16.

important subjects, but argues that incorporating them within the scope of transitional justice could risk expanding the mandate of a truth commission so broadly that it may be impossible to reasonably complete its tasks.[173] Even transitional justice scholars on the more expansive wing of the discipline like Roht-Arriaza warn that 'broadening the scope of what we mean by transitional justice to encompass the building of a just as well as peaceful society may make the effort so broad as to become meaningless.'[174] Building peace and building social justice should be inseparable processes,[175] but it does not necessarily follow that the institutions that work towards these ends must be inseparable also. In recognising the complementarity between development and transitional justice, the need to respect the integrity of the two fields is forgotten in much of the more optimistic scholarship.[176] Much of the foregoing has assumed that transitional justice mechanisms can formulate comprehensive strategies for a fairer society, but practitioners on the ground traditionally defer upwards to the state and downwards to smaller units that supply the want of expertise or on-the-ground knowledge that transitional justice mechanisms typically manifest.

To begin with the former, it is clear the even the weak apparatus of the transitioning state has far greater functionality and reach than any transitional justice mechanism alone or in combination. This is all the more so when intrusive peace-building missions like UNTAET or UNAMSIL or UNMIK are on the ground. Though Miller regrets that '[b]y leaving economic development, issues of resource distribution or inequality of power or wealth to separate courts or to executive control, transitional justice institutions implicitly tell society that development and conflict may be separated in a fair fashion,'[177] in the radically imperfect conditions of transition, a division of labour may actually be welcome.[178] The areas of economic injustice that the literature points to as key to a revitalised transitional justice are really all sectors of governance; as such they are inextricably interdependent. Practitioners appreciate that transitional justice is not necessarily the most conducive to taking into account the complexities of such governance. Adequate recompense for

173. Office of the High Commissioner for Human Rights, *supra* note 162, at 9.

174. Naomi Roht-Arriaza, 'The New Landscape of Transitional Justice', in Naomi Roht-Arriaza and Javier Marriezcurrena (eds.), *Transitional Justice in the Twenty-First Century: Beyond Truth Versus Justice* (Cambridge University Press, 2006) 1–16 at 2.

175. Nagy, 'Transitional Justice as a Global Project', *supra* note 138, at 277.

176. Lenzen, 'Roads Less Travelled', *supra* note 89, at 84.

177. Miller, 'Effects of Invisibility', *supra* note 16, at 3.

178. De Greiff points out that any beneficial connection of development to transitional justice also means preserving the integrity of the things that are being connected and that 'effective synergies depend on sensible divisions of labour' (De Greiff, 'Articulating the Links', *supra* note 52, at 29).

lost employment opportunities, forced displacements or resource deprivation would tie up entire national budgets for years to come of governments.[179] Transitional justice bodies on the ground are far less bullish about their prospects than external critics of transitional justice. For example, Peru's Integral Reparations Plan Group (*Grupo sobre el Plan Integral de Reparaciones*-GPIR) was at great pains to delimit their work from the macro-economic role of the state:

> [The] PIR does not seek to resolve poverty, exclusion and inequality, which have a structural character and respond to the overall functioning of a political and economic system. While some of its programs can and should contribute to improving the quality of life of victims and their families, its central objective is reparation and recognition of the victims as human beings, whose fundamental rights have been violated. This does not mean that the State should not also carry out a policy of social development aimed at attacking the roots of poverty and inequality, and the TRC provides, in other parts of this Report, concrete proposals of necessary institutional reforms, but the PIR has another purpose.[180]

Peace agreements, constitutions and programs for government could reach many of the same conclusions as a truth commission in a much faster time, with greater enforcement power and arguably with far greater democratic legitimacy. Indeed, Waldorf argues that because of the sensitivity of local political factors and the need for some form of democratic accountability, a short-term intervention like transitional justice is less apt to address structural injustice than whatever state structures emerge in the longer-term.[181] Beyond this, some dilemmas like the movement of capital and goods in globalised markets or conflicting private demands in the black economy, labour and production lie largely beyond the grasp of even highly functional states, let alone temporary bodies in dysfunctional ones.

The standard institutions of transitional justice also rely on smaller units to remedy the lack of capacity they typically manifest. The best-funded truth commission ever was that in South Africa, which nevertheless needed 1888 days to process requests for amnesty, and only published its report five years after ending hearings. Giving additional tasks to truth commissions will severely test already-strained competencies. The Liberian Truth and Reconciliation Commission acknowledged it could provide only limited recommendations to remedy issues over land tenure and redistribution,

---

179. Asmal, 'South African Experience in Perspective', *supra* note 161, at 16.
180. Comisión Verdad Y Reconciliación, *Informe Final De La Comisión Verdad Y Reconciliación Vol. IX* (2003), Part 4, Ch. 2.2, at 148.
181. Lars Waldorf, 'Anticipating the Past: Transitional Justice and Socio-Economic Wrongs', 21 *Social and Legal Studies* (2012) 171–186 at 179.

and so proposed a specific land commission to review the complexities of the land tenure system, which commenced work in 2010.[182] Tunisia hived off the anti-corruption remit from its commissions on human rights abuses and political reforms,[183] as did Bangladesh and Ghana.[184] South Africa and Rwanda similarly devolved issues of land to bodies other than their main transitional justice institutions. One can of course argue that it is regrettable that the truth commission and, to a lesser extent, trials in both countries could not influence the procedures of these land commissions on the basis that they might generate lessons about the use and abuse of land,[185] but this does remind us that transitional justice mechanisms operate best in terms of exercising influence (the mobilisation of shame) than defining policy (which needs both wide-ranging expertise, enforcement capacity and democratic legitimacy). Reasonable qualms about the adaptability of transitional justice mechanisms to the universe of post-conflict injustice are a more convincing explanation for their perceived under-performance in relation to economic justice than fears about their dilution or neo-liberal capture.

5. The Limitations of Transitional Justice Institutions

Scholars like Duthie or Hecht and Michalowski have suggested that the relative neglect of economic justice might owe to the complex nature of socio-economic rights and the various interlinked causes for their deprivation which the mechanisms of transitional justice might not be able to reckon with adequately on account of their limited resources, skills, size or capacity.[186] Certainly, it is easier for transitional justice to deal with civil and political abuses like torture or a murder in terms of identifying a violator (the physical perpetrator and the government/military figure who gave the order), the violated person(s) and a remedy (criminal punishment, guarantee of non-repetition by the democratising state) than it is diagnose the reasons for, and ways to rectify, the unequal macro-level economic organisation of society.[187] However, examples like the bills of rights in South Africa, Nepal

182. Selim and Murithi, 'Transitional Justice and Development', *supra* note 84, at 65–66.
183. Christopher Lamont and Hela Boujneh, 'Transitional Justice in Tunisia: Negotiating Justice During Transition', 49 *Politicka Misao-Croatian Political Science Review* (2012) 32–49 at 39.
184. Andrieu, 'Dealing With a "New" Grievance', *supra* note 115, at 548.
185. Miller, 'Effects of Invisibility', *supra* note 16, at 286–287.
186. Duthie, 'Towards a Development-sensitive Approach', *supra* note 86, at 306; Hecht and Michalowski, 'Economic Dimensions', *supra* note 88, at 5.
187. Kenneth Roth, 'Defending Economic, Social and Cultural Rights: Practical Issues Faced by an International Human Rights Organization', 26 *Human Rights Quarterly* (2004) 63–73.

and India demonstrate that socio-economic rights can be enforceable by law, while truth commissions in the likes of Sierra Leone, Liberia and South Africa have wrestled credibly (if not entirely successfully) with structural causes of conflict.

On similarly practical lines, Addison[188] and Elster[189] suggest that the dearth of resources available to transitional justice limit its distributive impact, while Waldorf argues the short life-spans of transitional justice mechanisms undermine their potential.[190] These organisational explanations are also unconvincing—if transitional justice could deliver on even a fraction of the promise advocates hold out for it in redressing socio-economic wrongs, any resource impediments could surely be overcome by international aid, while the case for extending, or even making permanent, mechanisms so obviously beneficial would be inarguable. The Limburg Principles that guide interpretation of the ICESCR accept the progressive realisation of rights over time and over the course of evolving national economic strength.[191] An extended timeframe for transitional justice would fit comfortably within the progressive realisation paradigm if states and donors were convinced of its developmental merit. The suggestion that expansive views of transitional justice are vague or utopian is also unconvincing.[192] The traditional aspirations of transitional justice have always existed on a spectrum of the immediately realisable (identifying those responsible for abuses, punishing them) to the nebulous (reconciliation at all levels of society) and quixotic (preventing all human rights abuses).

The most reasonable qualms over adaptability of transitional justice to issues of socio-economic justice are made clear on an examination of the three most commonly-used institutions, namely trials, truth commissions and reparation, in ascending order of assumed potential.

5.1. Trials

The litany of economic crimes that take place in the course of authoritarian rule is wearily familiar—corruption, tax evasion, customs evasion, fraud, misappropriation of public funds and exploitation of illegal or migrant labour. In situations of military conflict, war crimes like appropriation of

188. Addison, 'Political Economy of Transition', *supra* note 41, at 114.
189. Jon Elster, 'Introduction', in Jon Elster (ed.), *Retribution and Reparation in the Transition to Democracy* (Cambridge University Press, 2006) 1–14 at 1.
190. Waldorf, 'Anticipating the Past', *supra* note 181, at 6–7.
191. Commission on Human Rights, *The Limburg Principles on the Implementation of the International Covenant on Economic, Social and Cultural Rights,* U.N. Doc. E/CN.4/1987/17/Annex (1987) at paras 21–24.
192. A risk suggested, but not accepted, in de Greiff, 'Articulating the Links', *supra* note 52, at 40.

property, pillage and starvation can be added.[193] They are as much a part of an indivisible system of crimes on the part of the government or non-state grouping as torture and persecution. The clandestine nature of many of these activities is usually a reflection of their illegality, and most will be justiciable as crimes. Criminal trial remains the most familiar and most symbolically potent avenue for transitional accountability. As noted earlier, trials for economic abuses have sometimes proven far more damaging to reputations than those for civil and political rights abuses. Notable examples include the Pinochet tax fraud proceedings in Chile and the trials of Todor Zhivkov (Bulgaria) and Ramiz Alia (Albania) for embezzlement,[194] while Argentina's prosecutors probed the junta's liability for property theft.[195] Tunisia and Egypt prioritised the prosecution of Presidents Ben Ali and Mubarak for embezzlement in the aftermath of the Arab spring over crimes relating to physical abuse. However, these represent the exception rather than the rule—it is clear that transitional criminal accountability has more often ignored economic crimes on account of its primary concern with bodily integrity abuses.[196] Scholars now argue that criminal tribunals should approach economic crimes the way they undertake civil and political trials in the expectation that this can aid recovery of assets amassed by perpetrators and disclose information about the economic practices of the regime.[197] However, while trial can be successful in punishing economic malfeasance, it has much greater limitations in terms of the pedagogical or discursive role usually claimed for criminal prosecutions. Though economic crime is the product of social, economic and political factors, the individualist model of accountability in trial invariably struggles to expose or condemn wider patterns of conduct or structural conditions underlying the crime.[198] Furthermore, even where a conviction is secured, recovery is extremely difficult given the porosity of international financial borders and the trans-boundary activities of transnational corporations.

International criminal law and the ICC's complementarity regime increasingly sets the priorities for criminal accountability in many transitional states, but the law on economic crimes is far less developed than that relating to war crimes or crimes against humanity. One proposed solution has been to

193. Rome Statute of the International Criminal Court (adopted 17 July 1998, entered into force 1 July 2002) 2187 UNTS 901002.
194. Teitel, *Transitional Justice*, *supra* note 35, at 42.
195. Mark Osiel, *Mass Atrocity, Collective Memory and the Law* (Transaction Publishers: New Brunswick, 1997) at 95.
196. Carranza, 'Plunder and Pain', *supra* note 16, at 310.
197. De Greiff, 'Articulating the Links', *supra* note 52, at 34 and 35.
198. Andrieu, 'Dealing With a "New" Grievance', *supra* note 115, at 543.

designate and define large-scale corruption as a crime against humanity,[199] but there is much fear that international criminal tribunals or hybrid courts could be overloaded if given such a remit.[200] Restitution was not granted at the ad hoc tribunals or the hybrid courts of the previous decade. Indeed, if anything, international criminal justice has operated to jeopardise development—the extraditions of Slobodan Milosevic and Charles Taylor to The Hague were facilitated by the threat of withholding aid to Serbia and Liberia.[201] The UN Convention against Corruption criminalises corruption and prioritises asset recovery as its 'fundamental principle.'[202] While states parties are legally obliged to incorporate its measures into national legislation, most of the measures therein lie in the realm of civil law.

5.2. Truth Commissions

Truth commissions offer valuable advantages over trials in terms of reckoning with the anonymous catalysers and beneficiaries of structural violence as they employ less individualistic models of accountability, enjoy more lenient standards of proof, have a more explicitly pedagogical role and have demonstrated infinitely more pliability in terms of abuses covered, remedies awarded and agents employed. Nevertheless, when these commissions were being mainstreamed in the late 1980s and 1990s, their understanding of wrongdoing during the prior regime was limited to a 'dominant script' narrowly focused on civil and political rights abuses.[203] It was estimated that only three out of 34 truth commissions between 1974 and 2004 expressly engaged with economic crimes.[204] Abuses which could not be characterised as criminal (i.e. most socio-economic rights deprivations) were generally ignored, reinforcing a narrative of conflict that violence was political, ideological, ethnic or religious, and not economic.[205] Everyday life was largely ignored, limiting the 'truth' a given mechanism could reveal and consequently impeding its transformative potential. Latin American truth commissions typically noted the polarisation between left and right, the depredations of police and military, the corruption of the rule of law and the weakness of state institutions, but consciously

199. Ilias Bantekas, 'Corruption as an International Crime and Crime against Humanity: An Outline of Supplementary Criminal Justice Policies', 4 *Journal of International Criminal Justice* (2006) 466–484.
200. Andrieu, 'Dealing With a "New" Grievance', *supra* note 115, at 543.
201. Olsen, Payne and Reiter, *Transitional Justice in Balance*, *supra* note 5, at 86–87.
202. United Nations Convention against Corruption, 31 October 2003, entered into force 14 December 2005, 2349 UNTS 41.
203. Cavallaro and Albuja, 'The Lost Agenda', *supra* note 72, at 125.
204. Carranza, 'Plunder and Pain', *supra* note 16, at 315.
205. Campbell and Turner, 'Utopia and the Doubters', *supra* note 47, at 377.

omitted the socio-economic reasons underlying repressive behaviour.[206] The El Salvadorian truth commission focused on non-derogable breaches of the Geneva Conventions, the ICCPR and the American Convention on Human Rights.[207] Chile's influential Truth and Reconciliation Commission similarly focussed on bodily integrity violations like disappearances and torture, admitting that even though it recognised the 'crisis has deep roots, of a socio-economic character, it would go beyond its mandate to explore them.'[208] Notwithstanding its statutory remit to establish 'as complete a picture as possible of the causes, nature and extent of gross violations of human rights,' the South African TRC ignored corruption, employment patterns and access to resources as these matters were outside its mandate, though it did refer damningly to the role of business in sustaining apartheid rule, albeit only after the Commission's solitary hearing on issues of economic violence.[209] The sustained criticism of the South African body for its neglect of everyday living conditions was highly influential.[210] In its aftermath, policy-makers slowly began to accept that without attention to the enabling environment of structural violence, the work of truth commissions would be undermined and their impact weakened.

Most subsequent truth commissions have been more expansive in their approach. Guatemala's Commission on Historical Clarification scrutinised the systemic sources of cyclical state violence, and went on to make recommendations relating to social participation of Mayan communities, employment and integration into state agencies, and the use of indigenous forms of conflict resolution.[211] The Sierra Leone TRC examined patterns of social injustice and their interaction with conflict. It made recommendations on issues like discriminatory inheritance, skills training, economic empowerment, micro-financing schemes and the need to improve opportunities for women in the economy.[212] The Liberian Truth Commission listed greed and corruption as being among the root causes of conflict surrounding the Taylor regime and implicated the international community's hunger for raw materials

206. Laplante, 'Roots of Violence', *supra* note 54, at 335.
207. Thomas Buergenthal, 'The UN Truth Commission for El Salvador', 27 *Vanderbilt Journal of Transnational Law* (1994) 497–507.
208. Comisión Nacional de Verdad y Reconciliación, *Informe De La Comisión Nacional de Verdad y Reconciliación, Vol. 1* (1991) at 38.
209. Wilson, 'Justice and Legitimacy', *supra* note 130, at 208.
210. Eg Mamdani, 'Reconciliation without Justice', *supra* note 123.
211. Commission for Historical Clarification, *Guatemala: Memory of Silence; Report Of The Commission For Historical Clarification* (1999).
212. Sierra Leone Truth and Reconciliation Commission, Witness to Truth: Report of the Sierra Leone Truth and Reconciliation Commission, Vol. 2 (2004), Chapter 3, at paras 107–111 and 316–376.

as a contributory factor in conflict.[213] The Peruvian Truth and Reconciliation Commission examined how horizontal inequalities fed, and were exacerbated by, political violence and the role of social exclusion in the recruitment of Shining Path guerrillas, and integrated this analysis into a wider critique of national economic structures.[214] The report of East Timor's Commission for Reception, Truth and Reconciliation incorporated the international coffee trade, environmental degradation, forced displacement and famine.[215] The mandate of Kenya's Truth, Justice and Reconciliation Commission extended far beyond 2007's electoral violence to include corruption, displacements and irregular acquisitions of land.[216] Chad's truth commission was tasked with investigating the finances of former president Hissène Habré and his cronies but went on to highlight corruption, economic mismanagement and discrimination within important state institutions.[217]

In light of these successes, a number of scholars now recommend that truth commissions go beyond analysing the structural roots of war or repression to propose detailed, feasible solutions to the economic problems raised that would be acceptable to the public and actionable by the executive.[218] Truth commissions are seen as the cornerstone of justice, a triggering device for reforms and the measure 'best placed to take on the role of "spokesperson" for the changes sought by transitional justice' because of their moral standing and because they provide the largest factual context for legacies of socio-economic exploitation.[219] Perhaps most valuably, Laplante argues truth commissions can diagnose the state's failure to provide core minimum socio-economic conditions as rights violations[220] and 'can help initiate a longer-term reform process by creating the possibility for viewing underlying socio economic conditions not as unchangeable facts of life but as consequences of conscious policy decisions that fail to protect fundamental rights.'[221]

213. Truth and Reconciliation Commission of Liberia, *Consolidated Final Report Vol. 1* (2009) at 300–308 and 322–323.
214. Truth and Reconciliation Commission of Peru, *Final Report of The Truth And Reconciliation Commission, Vol. VIII* (2003), Part 2.
215. Commission for Reception, Truth and Reconciliation, *supra* note 69, at Chapter 7.
216. *National Dialogue and Reconciliation Agreement on Truth, Justice and Reconciliation Commission* (14 February 2009).
217. Alexander, *Scoping Study*, *supra* note 32, at 51.
218. Selim and Murithi, 'Transitional Justice and Development', *supra* note 84, at 66; Mani, 'Editorial', *supra* note 33, at 256; Laplante, 'Roots of Violence', *supra* note 54 at 333.
219. Cobián and Reátegui, 'Toward Systemic Social Transformation', *supra* note 94, at 148 and 151.
220. Laplante, 'Roots of Violence', *supra* note 54, at 352.
221. *Ibid*, at 342.

However, even where truth commissions meet the four generally-accepted criteria for success (independence, adequate resources and subpoena power, public hearings and the ability to name accused publicly),[222] advancement does not depend purely on technocratic expansion of a truth commission's remit and expertise. Truth commissions are undoubtedly valuable as diagnostic tools in uncovering what conditions permitted past violations and outlining broad general conclusions. However, to make the type of impact some suggest transitional justice should aim for requires complex and technical understandings of how government, economies and poverty interact if their recommendations are to bridge the gap between comprehension and correction. Unfortunately, the operations of truth commissions are far removed from the governance world of painful budgetary choices, prioritisation and macro-economic impact. Truth commissions are generally made up of a moral elite chosen for their integrity, not a technocratic elite chosen for expertise.[223] Genuine socio-economic justice will require the input of housing, education, health and finance ministries whose knowledge and skills will surpass those of the truth commission. Truth commissions may have representative legitimacy to identify past violations, but not necessarily the democratic legitimacy to dictate the disbursement of tax revenue or co-ordinate the activities of ministries. The South African TRC recommended reparations be paid to individual victims, but the elected government countered that the money should be spent on generic community needs like education, food and roofs for the homeless.[224] Even advocates of a more socio-economic slant to transitional justice accept that truth commissions lack both the professional competences and the authority to make technical specifications[225] or to make informed, strategic recommendations on areas like education.[226] If recommendations are posited at broad levels of generality, they risk utopianism or vagueness.[227] The best a truth commission may be able to do in macro-economic terms is to recommend that a certain policy or target should be prioritised,[228] but it cannot be presumed this should trump the considered opinion of civil servants and elected political representatives.

222. Priscilla Hayner, *Unspeakable Truths: Confronting State Terror and Atrocity* (Routledge: New York, 2001).
223. Teitel, *Transitional Justice, supra* note 35, at 81.
224. Neil J. Kritz, 'Where We Are and How We Got Here: An Overview of Developments in the Search for Justice and Reconciliation', in Alice H. Henkin (ed.), *The Legacy of Abuse: Confronting the Past, Facing the Future* (Aspen Institute: Washington DC, 2002) 21–45 at 44.
225. Cobián and Reátegui, 'Toward Systemic Social Transformation', *supra* note 94, at 160.
226. Gready, *Era of Transitional Justice, supra* note 77, at 215.
227. De Greiff, 'Articulating the Links', *supra* note 52, at 40.
228. Cobián and Reátegui, 'Toward Systemic Social Transformation', *supra* note 94, at 160.

Though truth commissions can be improved technically to compensate for these weaknesses by expanding their scope and employing more experts, their eventual success is ultimately reliant on the state's political will. The presumption of the optimists is that because truth commissions are a democratic channel, their proposals would not be 'rejected as disruptive and thus made susceptible to repression.'[229] However, just as states ratify human rights treaties that they do not abide by, time and time again governments are content to reap the reputational rewards of establishing a truth commission without using their reports as a blueprint for change.[230] As Mani notes, because executive commitment to implement truth commission recommendations is frequently lacking, the potential of truth commissions to catalyse institutional and structural reforms is 'still-born.'[231] The East Timorese CAVR report was handed over to the Parliament on 28 November 2005 by the then-President Xanana Gusmao at the direction of the Parliament, but since that time legislators have never debated its content or recommendations.[232] The Peruvian TRC was commended earlier for its breadth, but its recommendations on structural reform were ignored at the implementation stage.[233] The ANC government disregarded the vast majority of the TRC's recommendations, especially those relating to monetary reparations.[234] In Haiti, the recommendations of both the National Truth and Justice Commission and its Follow-Up Committee were rejected by the government.[235]

Explanations for what de Greiff identifies as the persistent gap between insight and transformation in truth commissions[236] have been sought in weak legal traditions[237] and lack of economic growth.[238] Though these factors are certainly contributory, the weakness of transition overall (of which weak rule of law and slow economic growth may be symptomatic) may best explain

229. Laplante, 'Roots of Violence', *supra* note 54, at 334.
230. Fletcher, Weinstein and Rowen, 'Context, Timing and Dynamics', *supra* note 55, at 194.
231. Rama Mani, 'Rebuilding an Inclusive Political Community After War', 36 *Security Dialogue* (2005) 511–526 at 518.
232. Heather Castel, 'Maximising Transitional Justice Opportunities: The Case for East Timor's CAVR', in Deborah Mayersen and Annie Pohlman (eds), *Genocide and Mass Atrocities In Asia: Legacies And Prevention* (Routledge: London, 2013) 68–85 at 81–82.
233. Lisa J. Laplante, 'On the Indivisibility of Rights: Truth Commissions, Reparations and the Right to Development', 10 *Yale Human Rights and Development Law Journal* (2007) 141–177 at 170.
234. Miller, 'Effects of Invisibility', *supra* note 16, at 282.
235. Amnesty International, 'Haiti: Still Crying Out for Justice' (1998), <www.amnesty.org/en/library/asset/AMR36/002/1998/en/2662abc8-dab1-11dd-80bc-797022e51902/amr360021998en.pdf> at 7.
236. De Greiff, 'Articulating the Links', *supra* note 52, at 36.
237. Fletcher, Weinstein and Rowen, 'Context, Timing and Dynamics', *supra* note 55, at 194.
238. Olsen, Payne and Reiter, *Transitional Justice in Balance*, *supra* note 5, at 75.

their consistent failure to make a positive impact. It has been demonstrated statistically that negotiated transitions are most strongly associated with truth commissions[239] and that truth commissions are correlated with negative effect on human rights.[240] This correlation does not prove that the modalities of truth commissions are misguided or counter-productive, but does tend to suggest that truth commissions are often established in weak or precarious transitions to provide reassurances to still-powerful 'losers' in transitions (like the erstwhile beneficiaries of war or repression) that their losses will be limited. As Arthur admits, the main actors in transition are 'elites who enter into a series of bargaining arrangements with one another as a means of managing their interests. The main focus of these actors is legal-institutional reform, rather than transformation at the socio-economic level.'[241] Truth commissions are often established as a result of these negotiations not to alter society but rather to limit retributive justice (and, it might be added, redistributive justice) in an internationally palatable way, even if assertive and ambitious commissions attempt to transcend these limitations.[242] Fear of destabilisation by alienated but powerful groups and the weak position of new regimes (a phenomenon that is examined in greater detail in the next section) is reflected globally in the lack of implementation of truth and reconciliation commission recommendations.[243] Longer-term impact is also limited by the fact that truth commissions do nothing to affect the local power relationships that impose restraints on the possibilities for justice.[244] Many truth commission recommendations are implemented only partially or not at all:

> [T]ruth commissions often exist in a sort of tension between, on the one hand, their objectives and results and, on the other hand a reality external to them over which they exercise no direct control.[245]

Given these limitations, which all but the most propitious of transitions will struggle with, the ultimate role of truth commissions will be beneficial but far removed from the transformational aspiration for transitional justice canvassed earlier. The legacy of even a quite successful truth commission will be less the sea-change in the national economic structure the rhetoric would suggest than a series of broad recommendations hostage to numerous political fortunes it has no control over. The translation of a report into the

239. *Ibid*, at 55.
240. *Ibid*, at 6.
241. Arthur, 'How "Transitions" Reshaped Human Rights', *supra* note 122, at 347.
242. Hayner, *Unspeakable Truths*, *supra* note 222, at 30.
243. Mobekk, *Enabling Sustainable Peace*, *supra* note 7, at 43.
244. Roht-Arriaza, 'The New Landscape', *supra* note 174, at 5.
245. Cobián and Reátegui, 'Toward Systemic Social Transformation', *supra* note 94, at 153.

improvement of everyday lives may remain chimerical. The impact of a truth commission will always be far more indirect and tentative than the sanguine expectations of its more optimistic advocates. What are left are more circumscribed, limited but undoubtedly beneficial tasks. Truth commissions can recommend a transparent budgetary structure to ensure state revenues are put to best use, but may not be able to define the precise shape of it. They can, like the South Africa TRC, propose a wealth tax where beneficiaries of apartheid can contribute to poverty reduction or reparations[246] but the tax itself and its parameters would remain subject to the give-and-take of parliamentary agreement. Truth commissions can recommend the removal of state personnel with records of corruption as development blockers even if they cannot dictate state policy to their replacements.[247] They can identify national ideals even if their concrete elaboration becomes the role of the executive, and operate as a powerful lobbying tool against government resistance even if they never become program designers.[248] Furthermore, the value of truth commissions in establishing a contextual background for trials, compensation, restitution and reparations cannot be gainsaid (for example, the Chilean government provides a monthly pension, school tuition and medical coverage to thousands of victims of dictatorial rule as a result of TRC recommendations). One of the reasons why truth commissions are criticised for delivering less than they promise is because this promise is pitched at an unreasonable, virtually 'magical' level that cannot be attained in the conditions of transition.[249] Scholars of truth commissions have long accepted that they can help create conditions in which reconciliation might occur, but cannot be tasked with generating that reconciliation.[250] Similarly, it might be wise to accept that truth commissions can help create an atmosphere conducive to a more just economy, but may lack the political support or institutional capacity to directly advance the process.

5.3. Reparations

Reparations are possibly the best example of how socio-economic justice in transitional justice has been mainstreamed. Overshadowed by trials, truth commissions and lustration in the earliest debates, reparations received

246. David Goodman, 'Why Killers Should Go Free: Lessons from South Africa', 22 *Washington Quarterly* (1999) 169–181 at 180.
247. De Greiff, 'Articulating the Links', *supra* note 52, at 36.
248. Laplante, 'Roots of Violence', *supra* note 54, at 350.
249. Mark Freeman, *Truth Commissions and Procedural Fairness* (Cambridge University Press, 2006) at 13–14.
250. Campbell and Turner, 'Utopia and the Doubters', *supra* note 47, at 395.

noticeably less attention within the field.[251] One prominent objection was the fact that no financial measures could be commensurate with violations suffered.[252] Some contested the moral propriety of a new government and successor generations not implicated in prior wrongdoing (and often defined by opposition to it) having to pay for the crimes of the *ancien regime*.[253] The scholarly fear that reparations would unacceptably monetise atrocity by 'elevating things over persons'[254] was made apparent by the Argentine *Madres de la Plaza de Mayo*'s rejection of compensation as blood money to silence legitimate victim complaints that might arise in the future.[255]

However, over time it became apparent that this principled stance could not be replicated by all survivors of conflict or authoritarianism who might endure poverty, hunger or homelessness. Increasingly in international human rights law the state is made liable for human rights violations either as the violator, on the grounds of omission to prevent, or as the subsidiary agent of compensation when the actual perpetrator cannot be identified or is unable to compensate. The entitlement of victims of grave human rights violations to reparations as rights-holders was recognised in a number of human rights instruments and conventions, but found its most comprehensive expression in the General Assembly's *Declaration of Basic Principles and Guidelines on the Right to a Remedy and Reparation for Victims of Gross Violations of International Human Rights Law and Serious Violations of International Humanitarian Law* in 2005.[256] The Principles outline that the victim is entitled to remedies that guarantee (*a*) equal and effective access to justice, (*b*) adequate, effective and prompt reparation for harm suffered, and (*c*) access to relevant information concerning violations and reparation mechanisms, though these as yet remain mostly in the realm of moral duty than enforceable legal obligation.[257] Reparations are no longer regarded as empty promises, temporary stopgap measures, or attempts to buy the silence of victims.[258]

---

251. Arthur, 'How "Transitions" Reshaped Human Rights', *supra* note 122, at 356.
252. Martha Minow, *Between Vengeance and Forgiveness: Facing History after Genocide and Mass Violence* (Boston: Beacon Press, 1998) at 104.
253. Teitel, *Transitional Justice*, *supra* note 35, at 139.
254. Raised but not necessarily endorsed in Minow, *Between Vengeance and Forgiveness*, *supra* note 252, at 131–132.
255. Laplante, 'Indivisibility', *supra* note 233, at 167.
256. *Basic Principles and Guidelines on the Right to a Remedy and Reparation for Victims of Gross Violations of International Human Rights Law and Serious Violations of International Humanitarian Law*, GA Res. 60/147, UN Doc. A/RES/60/147 (16 December 2005).
257. *Ibid*, Principle 11.
258. Lisa Magarrell, *Reparations in Theory and Practice* (International Center for Transitional Justice: New York, 2007) at 2.

Reparations are popular for a number of very obvious reasons. They can be justified intrinsically (victims deserve reparations) and instrumentally (they are needed to stabilise the transition).[259] They are less abstract than truth or justice, the most tangible proof of a state's willingness to make amends.[260] Consequently, reparations are assumed to have the greatest potential to make a difference in the lives of victims.[261] They can be faster to arrive than truth or justice as it is generally quicker and easier to identify a victim than to establish the guilt of a perpetrator. The material benefit of monetary support is obvious (though rarely, if ever, adequate), but reparations transcend their compensatory role to enable some less tangible rewards. Reparations can 'meet burning needs for acknowledgement, closure, vindication and connection.'[262] By demonstrating the seriousness with which the state now treats violations of rights, they promote civil trust.[263]

The *Basic Principles* distinguish four categories of reparation, namely restitution, compensation, rehabilitation and the guarantee of non-repetition.[264] In states like South Africa and Chile, violations of civil and political rights were chosen as the 'point of entry' for reparations, as opposed to economic, social and cultural rights.[265] This tended to favour individualised reparations such as compensation in the form of cash payments or pensions, and restitution in the form of returning property. However, it became apparent that the number of victims would always outstrip the finance available for reparations. As Kritz points out, while states like Chile, with a relatively healthy economy and a small, defined class of victims of state violence, could offer equitable and extensive compensation to individuals, this becomes impossible in a state like Rwanda where the handful of victims compensated satisfactorily (to the extent this can be said about any genocide reparations) would deplete the available funding for the vast majority of victims.[266] Comprehensive individual restitution programs run the obvious risk of burdening national budgets indefinitely, stripping the government of the funding needed to rebuild

259. Jon Elster, 'Land, Justice and Peace', in Bergsmo *et al* (eds), *Distributive Justice*, *supra* note 18, 15–24 at 17.
260. Roht-Arriaza and Orlovsky, 'A Complementary Relationship', *supra* note 58, at 173.
261. Pablo de Greiff, 'Transitional Justice, Security and Development: Security and Justice Thematic Paper', 6 *World Bank World Development Report Thematic Paper* (2011), <openknowledge.worldbank.org/bitstream/handle/10986/9245/WDR2011_0015.pdf?sequence=1> at 6.
262. Minow, *Between Vengeance and Forgiveness*, *supra* note 252, at 106.
263. De Greiff, 'Articulating the Links', *supra* note 52, at 59.
264. Basic Principles, *supra* note 256, Principle 18.
265. Laplante, 'Indivisibility', *supra* note 233, at 144.
266. Kritz, 'Where We Are', *supra* note 224, at 44.

the economy and state. Even if adequate resources were available, civil and political violation-based criteria for eligibility left communities that suffered serious forms of social and economic exclusion unsatisfied and created divisions within communities between the compensated and those who received little or nothing.[267]

As the scope of inquiry of TRCs expanded, it became undeniable that the same state and sub-state structures that led to bodily integrity abuses and seizure of property also led to unjust deprivation of jobs, of educational opportunities, healthcare and infrastructural investment. In keeping with the generational change in transitional justice from an intrinsic, backwards-looking concern with punishment and truth to a more forward-looking, state-building perspective, the fact that compensation and restitution were not in themselves sustainable nor did much to address poverty sustainably called into question the instrumental value of traditional modes of reparation. Consequently, there is an observable redirection towards reparations programs of greater complexity where a public good is distributed to a specific victim community, incorporating structural and sustainable collective benefits like reconstruction of destroyed public buildings, religious sites, education or health facilities, and symbolic measures such as public apologies, memorials and the re-naming public spaces.[268] Rubio-Marín, perhaps more accurately, uses the terminology of corrective reparations (i.e., giving adequate redress to victims) and transformative reparations (advancing the consolidation of a more inclusive democratic system).[269] Truth commissions nowadays typically propose a mix of the individual and collective, the corrective and the transformative.

The problem that has arisen is that this transformative approach to collective reparations is often indistinguishable in practice from development funding. In theory, the two should be separate in conception and delivery. In conceptual terms, development is the province of sustained, concerted actions to improve the economic, political, and social well-being of all people in a state or defined local area dominated by metrics like need and sustainability. While reparations also take need and sustainability into account, they uniquely address actual damage suffered by a defined set of people acknowledged as victims. This conceptual distinction between improving well-being generally and repairing harm more narrowly has traditionally been reflected in

267. Alexander, *Scoping Study*, *supra* note 32, at 42 and 52.

268. De Greiff, 'Articulating the Links', *supra* note 52, at 37.

269. Ruth Rubio-Marín, 'Gender and Collective Reparations in the Aftermath of Conflict and Political Repression', in Ruth Rubio-Marín (ed.), *The Gender Of Reparations: Unsettling Sexual Hierarchies While Redressing Human Rights Violations* (Cambridge University Press, 2009) 381–402 at 384.

the means of delivery—as Roht-Arriaza and Orlovsky point out, reparations are the domain of human rights courts, claims commissions and administrative programs while development subsumes a much wider array of agencies like INGOs, aid agencies and financial institutions.[270] The reason for the growing conflation of reparations with development is a simple economic one—in post-authoritarian and post-conflict situations, extreme poverty is the norm and the available resources are extremely limited. Money for reparation generally comes from general taxation, as opposed to re-appropriated loot. Compensating all the victims of socio-economic deprivations like those who suffered unemployment, corruption etc. would be beyond most reparations programs, which tend to be drastically under-funded. In this context, the estimated US$385m set aside for apartheid victims in South Africa or the US$45–60 per annum ring-fenced for Peru's 200,000 victims of human rights violations are both pitifully small in relation to the overall number of victims and rather large in terms of the national budget.[271] Reparations may take up a significant proportion of available funds but be too small or scattergun to make any appreciable impact on growth or redistribution.[272]

The consistent response of transitional states has been to prefer using finite resources for general development than particularised reparations. Just as collective reparations maximise the effectiveness of existing resources better than individual reparations, so too does subsuming collective reparations within development:

> [G]overnments tend to prefer the use of collective reparations, often for pragmatic reasons. Collective reparations may allow them to funnel programs into existing ministries, seem more efficient and less likely to be politically sensitive, require less new bureaucracy, and seem more acceptable to budget-conscious managers and creditors. Nonexclusive reparations also avoid problems associated with singling out victims or creating new resentments.[273]

There is in this approach an implied recognition that reparations are an imperfect vehicle for restoring losses as complex as careers, opportunities and health, and that more forward-looking reforms are better public policy.[274] For example, the Haitian government has decided to use the US$5.8bn repatriated from Swiss Bank accounts on Baby Doc Duvalier's return for improving

270. Roht-Arriaza and Orlovsky, 'A Complementary Relationship', *supra* note 58, at 171.
271. Figures taken from Olsen, Payne and Reiter, *Transitional Justice in Balance*, *supra* note 5, at 61.
272. De Greiff, 'Articulating the Links', *supra* note 52, at 39.
273. Roht-Arriaza and Orlovsky, 'A Complementary Relationship', *supra* note 58, at 192.
274. Vojtech Cepl, 'A Note on Restitution of Property in Post-Communist Czechoslovakia', 7 *Journal of Communist Studies* (1991) 367–375 at 375.

national living standards for all instead of awarding it to identified victims or victim communities.[275] Though the Peruvian TRC recommended a comprehensive slate of reparations such as healthcare, educational opportunities and restitution, the government made clear it preferred a more general social development program.[276] Victim-survivors there have been shunted into pre-existing development and poverty-alleviation programs, while the government attempted to distribute the funds for collective reparation programs through competition.[277] The general perception is that the government's reparations program does not correspond with specific damage caused by war and is instead more akin to development.[278] The Guatemalan truth commission sat somewhat on the fence, recommending both individual and collective reparations but stating that the latter should 'also favour the entire population, without distinction between victims and perpetrators.'[279] In the seminal *AZAPO* case, the South African constitutional court acknowledged that because the new constitutional state was tasked with reconciling and reconstructing the country, it would inevitably at some point have to choose whether to deploy national resources through reparations or to use available finances for food relief, housing and education. It held that parliament was justified in adopting a wide concept of reparations that would be communally balanced against the state's other obligations.[280]

This approach has divided opinion, once more illustrating the gap between transitional justice as traditionally understood and the more expansive hopes held out for it by some. Roht-Arriaza contends that equating collective reparations with development more generally 'conflates two separate obligations of government: to make reparation for wrongs it committed, and to provide essential services to the population.'[281] Victims believe that development is a pre-existing duty of the government, feel that incorporating reparations within development gives insufficient recognition to the violations they have suffered, and resent it when non-victims benefit from such programs.[282] Some argue that collective reparations have less trust-building power than

275. Andrieu, 'Dealing With a "New" Grievance', *supra* note 115, at 550.
276. Laplante, 'Indivisibility', *supra* note 233, at 160.
277. *Ibid*, at 163.
278. *Ibid*, at 163 and 164.
279. Commission for Historical Clarification, *supra* note 211, Part III, Reparatory Measures, at para. 10.
280. *AZAPO and Others v President of the Republic of South Africa and Others* (1996) 8 BCLR 1015 (CC) at 39, 25 July 1996.
281. Naomi Roht-Arriaza, 'Reparations Decisions and Dilemmas', 27 *Hastings International and Comparative Law Review* (2004) 157–219 at 188.
282. Laplante, 'Indivisibility', *supra* note 233, at 145 and 162.

individualised reparations derived from the recognition of responsibility by the perpetrator or the state would have.[283] Others question whether the undifferentiated envelopment of reparations within development may violate their essential character as acts of atonement for past harms.[284] By contrast, Kalmanowitz and Miller respectively argue that the focus on certain groups for certain violations erases the needs of the wider population from view[285] and makes structural factors 'doubly invisible.'[286] As the former puts it:

> [T]he more widespread and extensive the destruction caused by war, the weaker the rights [should be] to receive reparations. In the limiting case of a war that affects directly a large majority of the population (for example, Mozambique), rights and obligations of social justice should trump all rights of corrective justice.[287]

He recommends the mass pooling of all compensatory payments into a collective reconstruction fund to be dispersed in a forward-looking way according to broader principles of justice than have hitherto underpinned debates over reparations.[288]

The problem with changing from the traditional reparative allocation of resources based on entitlements to an allocation based on present or future needs is that it risks becoming completely uninformed by anything distinctly recognisable as transitional justice. Sceptics legitimately question is whether such measures would 'really still be part of transitional justice.'[289] Key questions that a transformative reparations policy would have to ask like whether citizenship in the violator state alone entitles one to indemnification, to what extent general taxation should be used, the liability of foreign governments and how much this liability can be encompassed within aid, how compensatory amounts should be decided or whether to compensate whole villages (or valleys, or provinces) would be dominated by state politicians or development actors given the relative paucity of reparations. The tail is unlikely to wag the dog—though useful in rebalancing power relations at a local level, reparations have little macro-economic impact[290] and do not radically redistribute power or wealth,[291] while no direct correlations can be drawn between the largesse of

283. Pablo de Greiff and Marieke Wierda, 'Reparations and the ICC: A Prospective Role for the Trust Fund for Victims', International Center for Transitional Justice (2004), <ictj.org/sites/default/files/ICTJ-Global-ICC-TrustFund-2004-English.pdf> at 8.
284. Roht-Arriaza and Orlovsky, 'A Complementary Relationship', *supra* note 58, at 173.
285. Kalmanovitz, 'Corrective Justice versus Social Justice', *supra* note 82, at 6.
286. Miller, 'Effects of Invisibility', *supra* note 16, at 278.
287. Kalmanovitz, 'Corrective Justice versus Social Justice', *supra* note 82, at 72.
288. *Ibid*, at 92.
289. Andrieu, 'Dealing With a "New" Grievance', *supra* note 115, at 550.
290. Roht-Arriaza and Orlovsky, 'A Complementary Relationship', *supra* note 58, at 173.
291. Miller, 'Effects of Invisibility', *supra* note 16, at 284.

a reparations program and the degree of socio-economic development of the state in question.[292] Far from steering debates on the socio-economic future of the state or tackling poverty, the more reparations become intermingled with state reconstruction and development, the more they have to plead for their own distinctiveness or relevance. As with trials and truth commissions, while reparations can make significant, targeted impacts, it would appear the wider potential for reparations to significantly impact poverty and development are greatly over-stated.

5.4. Summary

None of the foregoing analysis of the limitations of trials, truth commissions and reparations is to argue that all claims based on practicality have merit. While all the institutions of transitional justice have immense practical shortcomings, there can be very valuable synergies between transitional justice and development or poverty reduction, particularly the diagnostic role of truth commissions and compensatory role of reparations. However, even with a more realistic appraisal of their technical potential, the socio-economic legacy of transitional justice bodies may be minimal. Though they criticise the liberal-legalism of transitional justice, the following section illustrates that advocates of an expanded role for transitional justice fall into the same trap as legalism of overestimating the impact of normative change and underestimating the influence of external political factors.

6. The Political Economy of Transition

If the conception of *justice* does not explain the lack of impact of transitional justice on socio-economic structures, development or inequality, it is worthwhile switching attention to the other composite element of the concept, namely the *transitional*. As argued earlier, believers in the distributive potential of transitional justice rely on the presumption that the sheer fact of transition constitutes a window of opportunity 'not only for returning to a previous state of order but for deeply reforming it and dismantling old structures of economic crime, structural violence, and oppression.'[293] This greater ambition springs from a welcome critique of the liberalising impetus of the transitional political order, most notably the recognition that the field's concentration on the legal and political machinery of the new regime would benefit from a re-orientation towards economic and social conditions. However,

292. De Greiff, *Transitional Justice, Security and Development*, *supra* note 261, at 6.
293. Andrieu, 'Dealing With a "New" Grievance', *supra* note 115, at 538.

economic justice—transitions are typically more about modifying the existing order politically than any thoroughgoing process of social transformation. Cession of political power may therefore not be accompanied by cession of property or resources. As Mani puts it, 'faced with powerful lobbies resisting economic distribution, peacebuilders may turn to political 'redistribution' by way of elections as a stopgap measure.'[302]

The two decades of accelerated norm diffusion since transitional justice was mainstreamed have done little to alter the transitional stability calculus—the strength of the transition relative to the power of the *ancien* regime remains far more influential than the normative influence of international criminal law, international human rights law or civil society. For example, through analysis and coding of the pace of numerous transition types, Olsen, Payne and Reiter find that since the 1970s, a 'clean break with the past' such as overthrow, collapse or military defeat remains far more conducive to trial (the usual proxy employed for extensive transitional justice) than a negotiated transition, with trials being twice as frequent.[303] Furthermore, negotiated transitions are most strongly associated with truth commissions or no transitional justice at all.[304] Optimistic accounts of transitional justice's distributive potential exaggerate the ability of transitional justice to 'set the tone' for future governance[305]—political transition is continuously negotiated by dynamic, non-teleological relations of control and consent, power and authority among multiple power poles, some of whom will be the inevitable (and extremely reluctant) losers in any distributive process and therefore resist it.[306] Transitional justice therefore is a game of relatives not absolutes: the prospects for goals like land reform, return of ill-gotten profits by corporations and higher tax-burdens to rebalance the distribution of wealth should be determined not merely by the mechanisms available but also the opposition to be faced in a mediated state.[307]

The conviction that transitional justice can and should impact significantly on the macro-economic structures of all transitional states everywhere can be sustained only if the internal dynamics of the populations for which they were intended are disregarded, a recurring problem that bedevils the field.[308] Space

302. Mani, *Beyond Retribution*, *supra* note 25, at 183–184.
303. Olsen, Payne and Reiter, *Transitional Justice in Balance*, *supra* note 5, at 54.
304. *Ibid*, at 55.
305. E.g. Aguirre and Pietropaoli, 'The Case of Nepal', *supra* note 42, argue it can do this, at 375.
306. Tobias Hagmann and Didier Péclard, 'Negotiating Statehood: Dynamics of Power and Domination in Africa', 41 *Development and Change* (2010) 539–562 at 542–545.
307. E.g. Kalmanovitz, 'Corrective Justice versus Social Justice', *supra* note 82, at 92.
308. Pierre Hazan, 'Measuring the Impact of Punishment and Forgiveness: A Framework for Evaluating Transitional Justice', 88 *International Review of the Red Cross* (2006) 19–47 at 46.

precludes a detailed examination of the political economy of transitional states generally, which in any event will display infinite variation. Nevertheless, it is possible to briefly outline four salient limitations transitions impose on the prospects for economic justice that will lie largely outside the control of transitional justice institutions regardless of the extent to which the field re-imagines its principles and practices:

1. The transitional stability calculus which leaves economic structures intact
2. The complexity of patterns of accumulation under authoritarian rule and war economies
3. Democratically expressed preferences
4. The influence of global neo-liberalism

6.1. The Transitional Stability Calculus

It is something of a commonplace that transitional justice's role in accounting for past wrongdoing lies in tension with its role in establishing stability. As Addison argues, while some transitions from authoritarianism to democracy have been successful, 'others remain tentative, and some have been reversed with either a relapse into full dictatorship or with the trappings of democracy used to cloak semi-authoritarianism.'[309] Carothers argues that most post-authoritarian transitions are to a political 'gray zone' between liberal democracy and authoritarianism that maintains attributes of democratic life while the government disregards the law.[310] Periods of transition in partially democratised countries are those when risk of state failure is greatest.[311] Post-conflict states are even more insecure—44% of post-war states see a resumption of conflict within five years and 50% revert back to war in their first decade.[312] The war/peace distinction is increasingly viewed as a misleading one that obscures the sometimes dysfunctional nature of the peace. Peace may be more a reluctant hiatus in conflict born of fatigue than a process that results in genuine pacification between antagonistic groups.[313] Transition is also a time marked by unemployment, external debt, underdevelopment

309. Addison, 'Political Economy of Transition', *supra* note 41, at 111.
310. Thomas Carothers, 'The End of the Transition Paradigm', 13 *Journal of Democracy* (2002) 5–21 at 9–10.
311. Jack Goldstone *et al*, 'It's All About State Structure: New Findings on Revolutionary Origins from Global Data', 21 *Homo Oeconomicus* (2004) 429–455 at 438–439.
312. Gerd Junne and Willemijn Verkoren, 'The Challenges of Post-Conflict Development', in Junne and Verkoren (eds) *Post-Conflict Development, supra* note 43, 1–14 at 1.
313. Philippe Bourgois, 'The Continuum of Violence in War and Peace: Post-Cold War Lessons from El Salvador', in Nancy Scheper-Hughes and Philippe Bourgois (eds), *Violence In War And Peace: An Anthology* (Wiley-Blackwell: New York, 2003) 425–433.

and hyperinflation, which themselves are destabilising. Consequently, many transitions are marked by a conservative approach to economic structures. The more assertively states flex their muscles against those who benefitted materially from conflict or authoritarianism, the greater the risk may be of undermining economic activity or even the political settlement outlined in a peace deal.[314]

This risk is best illustrated by examples of the choices made even in relatively stable transitions. In Guatemala, those who signed the peace agreement (the liberal-conservative ruling party and the rebels) and those who supported it (civil society) were vastly outweighed in political-economic influence by the outgoing armed forces of the regime and the business elites who profited from past structural violence.[315] While progress on issues of identity and civil-political rights like cultural diversity, education reform, participation and political reform could be conceded, socio-economic reform aimed at reducing horizontal inequalities stalled.[316] Though the UN-brokered peace agreement stipulated democracy and reform of both army and governmental institutions, El Salvador's ARENA government resisted socio-economic redistribution in negotiations with leftist rebels lest it undermine its power-base in the business community.[317] Wood argues the peace agreement there reflected an explicit exchange of political inclusion for the rebels for the economic elite's continued control of assets, thereby preventing significant economic redistribution, even if there was ultimately some re-allocation of land.[318] The economic power of whites in South Africa was allied to the risk of collapsing the transition to democratic rule to foreclose an expansive conception of transitional justice.[319] National reconciliation in Namibia and post-Smith Zimbabwe was similarly dictated by the need to avoid antagonising the white community politically and economically.[320]

In more precarious transitions, political change is often to a form of belligerent power-sharing where those formerly in power try to maximise their economic gains even if political power is conceded. This should come as no

314. Cramer, 'Trajectories of Accumulation', *supra* note 300, at 135–136.
315. Graham K. Brown and Corinne Caumartin, 'Horizontal Inequalities in Post-Conflict Reconstruction: Guatemala and Nepal', in Aguilar and Gomez Isa (eds), *Rethinking Transitions*, *supra* note 77, 101–170 at 114.
316. *Ibid*, at 107.
317. Mani, *Beyond Retribution*, *supra* note 25, at 151.
318. Elisabeth Wood, 'Agrarian Reform, Land Occupation, and the Transition to Democracy in El Salvador', in Bergsmo *et al* (eds), *Distributive Justice supra* note 18, 141–176 at 175.
319. Elster, *Closing the Books*, *supra* note 75, at 197.
320. Mani, *Beyond Retribution*, *supra* note 25, at 92–93; Huyse, *All Things Must Pass*, *supra* note 30, at 119.

surprise—oppressive regimes install themselves in order to pursue certain economic policies that sustain their rule. If the violent suppression of underprivileged groups to safeguard economic power led to pre-transitional war or repression, the threat of its renewal remains pertinent in anything but the rare case of total defeat. Where internal or global power relations compel the removal of that regime, their economic interests and investments might endure long beyond the return to democracy. Jean-Bertrand Aristide's first radically egalitarian government in Haiti was overthrown after only seven months by the business community and upper echelons of the military who feared redistribution of wealth.[321] The economic power of regional warlords in Afghanistan was such that observers feared prosecuting them would boil down to a choice between justice and development. As Giustozzi put it, such an option would rule out any concept of 'transitional justice' in Afghanistan, which would target many if not all leading strongmen.'[322] Perhaps the most dramatic example of the sacrifice of economic justice to stability is in the persistent disparity between international aid given to security sector reform (and in particular disarmament, demobilisation and reintegration) and that given to reparations:

> The realities of aid flows and of local expenditures reflect this asymmetry regarding 'security' and 'justice' concerns: of the 22 countries with ongoing DDR programs in a recent global study, programs involving 1.25 million beneficiaries and the expenditure of more than 2 billion dollars, only a few have discussed the possibility of establishing reparations programs, but none of these countries has implemented one.[323]

Of course, one can argue that states should take greater risks in transition, but the general practice of new democracies is to move cautiously and resist testing the stability of transition.[324] States are more likely to adopt an initial 'weak state perspective' emphasising transitional stability, realistic goals for the state and incremental institutional development than choose risky confrontations with powerful groups. De Greiff, for example, argues that if expanding the scope of justice leads entrenched, powerful economic elites to oppose or block transition, it might be favourable to postpone dealing with these issues until more favourable times.[325] This appears to be the implicit position in many transitions.

---

321. Alex Dupuy, *The Prophet and Power: Jean-Bertrand Aristide, the International Community, and Haiti* (Rowman & Littlefield: Lanham, MA, 2007).
322. Antonio Giustozzi, 'War and Peace Economies of Afghanistan's Strongmen', 14 *International Peacekeeping* (2006) 75–89 at 86.
323. De Greiff, *Transitional Justice, Security and Development, supra* note 261, at 20.
324. Olsen, Payne and Reiter, *Transitional Justice in Balance, supra* note 5, at 5.
325. De Greiff, 'Articulating the Links', *supra* note 52, at 41.

may have been weakened in conflict or authoritarianism, the government's ability to engage constructively in the economy may be significantly weakened, making market-oriented policies attractive.[348]

As a result, many transitions are to popularly-elected centrist or centre-right governments whose policies are markedly different to the redistributive and developmental policies truth commissions and reparations programs will recommend or attempt. In Africa, for example, instead of a focus on systematic redistribution and equality of opportunity, civil society and political parties typically embrace a limited social compact framed by the precepts of the liberal tradition like rule of law, political freedoms, property rights and separation of powers.[349] Committed advocates of wider reform are usually a minority and struggle to marshal enough political resources to overcome the residual power of *ancien regime* figures.[350] There is a presumption in the transitional justice literature that governmental legitimacy 'is inextricably linked to redistribution and redress of patterns of discrimination.'[351] However, this is open to the criticism that development is being examined through an overly Western lens in which welfare ranks much higher on the list of priorities than it does when viewed through the lens of the domestic political culture of the transitional society itself, where no such expectation may ever have attached to the state.[352] Redistributive or welfarist states are the product of unique historical and social processes. By contrast, in many states where the state has behaved in a predatory or abusive manner in the past, basic security and local autonomy may top the hierarchy of goods the state is expected to provide. Though many scholars (the author included) might conclude that such minimalist policies risk reinforcing pre-transitional equalities, it is necessary to remember that the government itself might disagree, imposing significant limitations on what even the most immaculately calibrated truth commissions or reparations programs can achieve.

Even transitions to ostensibly social-democratic governments rarely see considerations of equality trump power politics or discourses of entitlement based on participation in the pre-transitional struggle. Formal democratisation in Mozambique and Angola has seen the leftist Frelimo and MPLA build single-party systems to tightly control state resources through and for their own structures.[353] Democracy itself can have adverse implications

348. *Ibid.*
349. Mutua, 'Critique of Rights', *supra* note 137, at 34–35.
350. *Ibid*, at 42.
351. Aguirre and Pietropaoli, 'The Case of Nepal', *supra* note 42, at 371; Kalmanovitz, 'Corrective Justice versus Social Justice', *supra* note 82, at 94.
352. Junne and Verkoren, 'Challenges', *supra* note 312, at 9–10.
353. Hagmann and Péclard, 'Negotiating Statehood', *supra* note 306, at 548–549.

for development by providing systematic, long-term incentives to purchase state influence, collect rents to finance campaigns and distribute resources to supporters.[354]

6.4. The Influence of Global Neo-Liberalism

Though the previous section argued that many transitional states will prioritise growth over redistribution or the immediate securing of social minima, not all liberal economic programs are freely adopted. Neo-liberal globalisation provides the inescapable background against which all peace-building activities take place. As noted above, transition is also a time marked by unemployment, external debt, underdevelopment and hyperinflation. States urgently require international financial assistance, but to secure it must agree to conditional loans or structural adjustment policies that emphasise rapid market de-regulation, reductions in expenditure on welfare, a small state and privatisation of national resources to avoid economic chaos.

The pernicious impact of the neo-liberal cure in terms of the long-term stability of the state is well understood in transitional justice literature,[355] but the relative ability of states to resist it does not appear to be. Loans and structural adjustment policies may undermine state capacity or the pursuit of development in the medium- and long-term, but are extremely tempting in the short-term as they may bolster political stability by mitigating or overcoming financial crises.[356] Transitional justice must grapple with the regrettable reality that the imperatives of the global economy significantly limit the agency of the state to reform the economy for the benefit of the socially excluded, let alone transitional justice institutions. Privatisation, austerity and economic liberalisation tend to eliminate discretionary expenditure. These policies are often not chosen by the transitional government, but rather are imposed on states by the threat to withhold loans or demand interest at a time when economies are vulnerable and financial support is needed to prevent economic crisis.[357]

Given the neoliberal-capitalist demands of the world economy and Bretton Woods institutions if the state is to receive funding or participate in

354. O'Donnell, 'Corruption', *supra* note 327, at 241.
355. The most frequently cited work is Roland Paris, *At War's End: Building Peace after Civil Conflict* (Cambridge University Press, 2004) which succinctly describes the most common harms, especially at 166–169 and 99–205.
356. Nicolas van de Walle, 'The Economic Correlates of State Failure: Taxes, Foreign Aid, and Policies', in Rotberg (ed.), *When States Fail, supra* note 101, 94–115 at 112.
357. Irwin P. Stotzky and Carlos Nino, 'The Difficulties of the Transition Process', in Stotzky (ed.), *Transition to Democracy in Latin America, supra* note 333, 3–20 at 6.

7. Conclusion

In the terms outlined by Karl Popper, the attempt to expand the scope of transitional justice can be seen as a move from piecemeal social engineering in the sense of fighting against the greatest and most urgent evil of society like crimes against humanity and torture to more utopian social engineering in the sense of fighting for a greatest ultimate good, in this case equality and welfare.[364] It is a significant evolution, from furthering an incremental change in a political sphere that is already undergoing regeneration to attempting to fundamentally transform a socio-economic sphere that may not. The enthusiasm and beguiling simplicity with which scholars contend that transitional justice can and should go further are intellectually attractive and intuitively appealing. However, these arguments are based on two questionable premises—firstly, that political transition opens significant opportunity for structural transformation, and secondly, that the mechanisms of transitional justice have the competence and legitimacy to help effect this transformation. This article has questioned both premises.

To begin with the first, it is clear that for a number of reasons political transition does not necessarily conduce to a fundamental re-evaluation of unjust economic structures. The preservation of an unequal economy may be the implicit or explicit bargain underpinning political liberalisation, the transitional state may lack the extractive capacity to redress the perverse incentives to maintain a weak state that flow from the war economies or authoritarian systems, the dictates of global neo-liberalism may exert greater influence than any national actor in government or transitional justice, and the mandates of democratically elected leaders might follow suit. Much, though certainly not all, of the socio-economic self-critique of transitional justice misdiagnoses the problem—the obstacle to fairer transitional justice is not the narrowness of the conception of justice, it is the narrowness of transition. One sees in the literature a type of cognitive dissonance—scholars observe on the one hand that transition rarely yields better socio-economic outcomes, but yet assume transition is automatically propitious time for reform.[365] A more realistic assessment of the prospects for addressing unfair societal structures might flow from a recognition that the factors that compel a more distributive or developmental approach to transitional justice also impair it. For example, as Holmes observes about Colombia:

> If part of the purpose of the original confiscations was to reduce the power of the peasants, and if this strategy was successful, would-be land reformers today do not

---

364. Karl Popper, *The Open Society And Its Enemies, Vol. II* (Routledge: London, 1992) at 145.
365. E.g., Aguirre and Pietropaoli, 'The Case of Nepal', *supra* note 42, at 372.

> have well-organized peasant allies who can help them put land reform into effect. The reason why restitution is needed, in other words, is the same reason why restitution is so devilishly difficult. Justice requires that the Colombian peasantry be given back the power they have lost; but justice alone does not give them the power they need to reestablish their political role in the country.[366]

The impetus towards social justice, development and/or redistribution is welcome, but cannot escape the 'moral dilemmas versus practical solutions' divide which has characterised the field since its earliest days.[367]

Even if a more benign transition obtains, there must be some doubt that transitional justice, for so long concerned with individual conduct and the stabilisation of society after the bargains of political elites, can impact significantly on the comparatively agent-less, macro-social structures and collective processes which underlie poverty and inequality. Even strong advocates of a shift from the time-bound and projectisable to an essentially limitless role for transitional justice in alleviating the structural causes of conflict accept that the direct developmental impact of trials or truth commissions or reparations on growth or distribution of national resources is either minimal or untraceable in purely economistic terms.[368] Baldly put, because of its temporary, exceptional and often wholly/partly external nature, transitional justice exists at a considerable remove from the capture by states, individuals or groups of surpluses from production or exchange and the consequent use of those surpluses in the service of health, literacy, education, income and employment. In particular, there is little to suggest those citizens and professionals who administer criminal justice, lustration or truth commissions are in any better position than development actors, parliamentarians or civil servants to examine the fundamental issue of whether a state's developmental or redistribution policy should be based on past suffering, present needs or future efficiency. Kerr and Mobekk have argued that the goals of transitional justice are too ambitious, often 'imposed from elsewhere and not in the power of those working within such processes to deliver them.'[369] This becomes apparent on the ground. Peru's Integral Reparations Plan Group made a conscious decision to renounce the ambition to remedy the causes of the civil conflict, eschewing an impossible attempt 'to achieve the goals of the whole transitional process' and preferring instead to address 'just an important piece

366. Holmes, 'Concluding Remarks', *supra* note 18, at 427.
367. Alexandra Barahona de Brito *et al*, 'Introduction', in De Brito, Carmen González-Enríquez and Paloma Aguilar (eds), *The Politics of Memory*, *supra* note 130, 1–39 at 35.
368. De Greiff, 'Articulating the Links', *supra* note 52, at 39.
369. Kerr and Mobekk, *Peace & Justice*, *supra* note 10, at 181.

of it.'[370] It is a choice many truth commissions, reparation programs and prosecutors will be forced to reach by the pressure of circumstances, and one armchair critics might do well to understand more sympathetically.

As in many areas of human rights, the norms in question in this debate are so fundamental that commitment to equality and poverty alleviation 'may dull an appropriately sceptical attitude' to what transitional justice can do.[371] The belief transitional justice can significantly impact the distribution of wealth and opportunity in an economy if only practitioners understand justice in a more holistic sense exemplifies the field's technocratic and utopian imperative, relying heavily on a logic of project management in which the right combination of technique and planning will accomplish the goals set for any given mechanism.[372] This 'toolbox' approach tends to assume the universality of the norms underlying transitional justice as applicable in all contexts, an optimism that inevitably disregards local political, social, cultural and historical contexts and purports to operate immune to local power struggles and political instrumentalisation.[373] In this manner, the types of 'vague statements' and 'received wisdom' canvassed in Section 3 and 5 'are produced about what transitional justice is and how its aims can be achieved.'[374] Broad generalised aspirations about how transitional justice as a concept can achieve socio-economic justice (or heal the traumatised, or end centuries-old cycles of violence) have achieved widespread acceptability within the field without any attention to the inevitably idiosyncratic and difficult conditions it will be applied in.

The idea that law can displace politics and resolve conflict is tempting and one that has animated transitional justice from the beginning.[375] The humanitarian tendency to assume tools like transitional justice conduce to humanitarian outcomes like poverty eradication and socio-economic reform is one all policy-makers should be wary of.[376] Because even the most noble intentions can fail, scholars and practitioners in the field should be rigorous about what

370. Lisa Magarrell, 'Reparations for Massive or Widespread Human Rights Violations: Sorting Out Claims for Reparations and the Struggle for Social Justice', 22 *Windsor Year Book of Access to Justice* (2003) 85–98 at 94.
371. Andreas Follesdal, 'Methods of Philosophical Research on Human Rights', in Fons Coomans, Fred Grunfeld and Menno T. Kamminga (eds), *Methods Of Human Rights Research* (Intersentia: Antwerp, 2009) 233–246 at 233.
372. Colvin, 'Purity and Planning', *supra* note 20.
373. Rubli, *Justice by Bureaucratic Means?*, *supra* note 136, at 9.
374. *Ibid.*
375. Ruti Teitel, 'Humanity's Law: Rule of Law for the New Global Politics', 35 *Cornell International Law Journal* (2002) 356–387 at 385.
376. Kennedy, *Dark Sides of Virtue*, *supra* note 8, at 119.

transitional justice can and cannot do. The best transitional justice strategies are those that are clearly defined and realistic, while those that are overtasked will dash artificially elevated expectations and disillusion the public. Scholars now warn that the overpromising regarding transitional justice's transformative macro-economic impact can only lead to unfair assessments that the institutions have failed, with a consequent loss of support for transitional justice overall.[377] Much of the rhetoric in this debate is unsupportable, and the absolutism of the claims makes traditional approaches to truth, justice and reparations look like craven betrayal when they may in fact be all political conditions and institutional competences allow for. Posner and Vermeule note that the literature in the field either condemns transitional justice for failing to reach unrealistic ideals of justice or dismisses any effort at transitional justice because it falls short of them.[378] The danger is not that transitional justice remains unduly limited in its outlook, but rather that overzealous proponents of an expanded practice make the perfect the enemy of the good.

It is worthwhile, therefore, considering what developmental goods transitional justice delivers independent of any direct attempt to fundamentally alter economic structures. First and foremost, to the extent that transitional justice helps stabilise and legitimise the national political community through truth, criminal accountability and reparations, it may help inoculate society against re-inflammation of the passions that led to conflict or repression and can then be said to have a developmental impact. Above all else, preventing further conflict is the fundamental precondition for achieving poverty reduction.[379] In more positive terms, transitional justice can foster the basic conditions in which development can occur by fostering a more participatory and inclusive environment, on the one hand, and good governance on the other. The primary connection between transitional justice and development flows from the former's ability to establish the rule of law and affirm the currency of rules and norms. This traditional focus on civil and political rights has two main impacts. The first is that it tends to develop public civic trust, an assumption that strangers or institutions comply with abstract and general values and norms, which tends to facilitate cheaper, faster and fairer economic transitions in economies that go on to enjoy better growth and investment.[380] The second is the establishment of rights as justified

377. Addison, 'Political Economy of Transition', *supra* note 41, at 111; Duthie, 'Towards a Development-sensitive Approach', *supra* note 86, at 306.
378. Eric A. Posner and Adrian Vermeule, 'Transitional Justice as Ordinary Justice', 117 *Harvard Law Review* (2004) 762–825 at 768.
379. Alexander, *Scoping Study*, *supra* note 32, at 48.
380. De Greiff, 'Articulating the Links', *supra* note 52, at 46.

claims that trigger remedies for violation instead of fixing them merely as aspirations for future conduct.[381] Transitional justice can buttress rule of law values like accountability, culpability and duty, potentially creating a culture where all rights (civil, political, economic, social and cultural) are enforceable and subject to remedies where violated.[382] Given that macro-level social and economic development is thought by some to be impossible without a functioning legal system,[383] transitional justice can highlight that functionality in a most publically visible manner.

If human development is conceived in terms of enlarging peoples' choices as Sen famously proposed, even a relatively conservative approach to transitional justice can help establish the courts and state as defenders of rights, helping the socio-economically marginalised to see themselves as full members of the political community.[384] The South African judge Albie Sachs argues that while dignity, land, jobs and education are the 'real reparation' people want, there is still much value in apology, shame and humanising the relationship between perpetrator and victim.[385] It should not be assumed that a concentration on the latter impedes realisation of the former, but much of the more enthusiastic rhetoric canvassed earlier does just that. Finally, transitional justice may contribute to better practice on the part of development actors by making them more aware of the effect of human rights violations on everyday life. It can empower state and non-state actors with a tool to pressure government toward ensuring equitable development. However, scholars should be readier to acknowledge that there will be countervailing pressures.

Establishing the rule of law and the currency of civil and political rights is a necessary condition for development and redistribution, even if it is far from sufficient. Bearing this and the relative inability of transitional justice mechanisms to directly effect macro-level economic change in mind, it is not necessarily be fatal to hopes for economic equality to postpone highly contentious, *potentially* transformative transitional justice policies lest they undermine the delicate balance of power and compromise that the transition represents. Development and socio-economic justice are not matters of one-off intervention, but are rather continuous processes of critical dialogue with an expanding set of groups and interests to ensure that engagements

381. *Ibid*, at 55.
382. *Ibid*, at 52.
383. Stephen Toope, 'Legal and Judicial Reform through Development Assistance: Some Lessons', 38 *McGill Law Journal* (2003) 357–417 at 363.
384. Amartya Sen, *Development as Freedom* (Knopf: New York, 1999).
385. Cited in Lyn S. Graybil, *Truth and Reconciliation in South Africa: Miracle or Model?* (Lynne Rienner Publishers: Boulder, 2002) at 155.

undertaken reflect the needs and interests of at least some of these groups, including those who benefitted from past injustice. As Waldorf contends, 'the reduction of longstanding inequality is necessarily "post-transition"—something to be accomplished as part of creating an new and hopefully more democratic order,'[386] though critics are certainly correct to argue that development of socio-economic rights cannot be assumed to flow automatically from positive developments in terms of democratisation and rule of law.[387]

Andrieu contends that it is the existence of boundaries to transitional justice that make it an actual theory. Attempts to turn transitional justice into a 'catchall formula' risk enchanting transitional justice unfairly with 'magical powers' to transform and regenerate societies, when in reality it is better suited to merely addressing individual social ills in the hope that it may ultimately contribute to the solution of the state's wider problems.[388] This is a position with which this paper concurs. The boundaries of transitional justice may benefit from some stretching, and few would quibble with more prosecutions for kleptocracy or corruption, a more structural remit for truth commissions or a more ambitious approach to reparations, but socio-economic metamorphosis and poverty reduction should not be the metric by which transitional justice should be judged. It may be necessary to compromise or abandon some of the undoubtedly laudable principles, assumptions and ideals inherent in the expansionary position for the sake of retaining the coherence, saleability and reputation of transitional justice.

Without attention to the dynamics of transition and the weakness of the state, arguments that transitional justice practitioners should 'turn the majority of their attention and resources to efforts that directly target existing structural and cultural violence'[389] or formulate a 'holistic and comprehensive settlement addressing the foundational problems' that unleashed conflict[390] risk re-hashing the simplistic rhetoric and sloganeering advice that mar debates on the protection of socio-economic rights.[391] This conclusion is not to counsel hopelessness about the prospects of redressing long-term patterns of inequality in transitional states, but rather modesty about what can be achieved in the radically imperfect ecology of weak, impoverished and divided states.

386. Waldorf, 'Anticipating the Past', *supra* note 181, at 9.
387. Arbour, 'Economic and Social Justice', *supra* note 59, at 10; Peter Uvin, *Human Rights and Development* (Kumarian Press: Boulder, 2004) at 155.
388. Andrieu, 'Dealing With a "New" Grievance', *supra* note 115, at 553.
389. Mullen, 'Reassessing the Focus', *supra* note 4, at 10.
390. Mutua, 'Critique of Rights', *supra* note 137, at 39.
391. Roth, 'Defending Economic, Social and Cultural Rights', *supra* note 187, at 63 and 65.

The Radical Use of History in the Study of International Law

Henry Jones[1]

"History as inspiration and ideology has a built-in tendency to become self-justifying myth. [...] It is the business of historians to try and remove these blindfolds"—Eric Hobsbawm, *What Can History Tell Us about Contemporary Society?*

"To learn from the past ... the distinction between what is necessary and what is the product merely of our own contingent arrangements, is to learn the key to self-awareness itself"—Quentin Skinner, *Meaning and Understanding in the History of Ideas*

"People know what they do; frequently they know why they do what they do; but what they don't know is what what they do does."—Michel Foucault, *Madness and Civilization: A History of Insanity in the Age of Reason*

Abstract: In this paper I look at the use of history in international law, starting with specific historical studies of the subject. I then go on to consider why history is useful; with particular reference to ideas of what is contingent and what is necessary. This leads to a detailed consideration in the majority of the paper of different approaches to history, all with a shared desire to use history to address the present. I look at the broad approaches of Marxist, Contextualist and Postmodern history, with the focus on key exponents of these positions; Eric Hobsbawm, Quentin Skinner and Michel Foucault. In conclusion, I argue that we must study the history of international law to understand and change its present. This work will be more productive with a proper consideration of historical method.

Keywords: international law, history, historiography, contingency, necessity

1. Introduction

A radical approach to something is commonly understood as being a thorough, far reaching proposal for change, in practice or understanding, addressing the

---

1. Lecturer in Law, Durham University.

fundamental nature of something. The etymology of the word is in physical science; radical refers to the most fundamental natural processes. In its common political use it is a term denoting a desire for large scale change, usually but not essentially, associated with the left and with revolutionary change. As Raymond Williams notes, the term in twentieth century political use arose out of difficulties in the use of the terms communist or socialist: '[r]adical seemed to offer a way of avoiding dogmatic and factional associations while reasserting the need for vigorous and fundamental change'.[2]

This last sense captures why I have used the word. I want to examine different approaches to histories, which I argue have a shared radical character, but which often fall into different dogmatic camps. I will not attempt to give any sort of complete radical history here, a task obviously beyond one paper, or even one person. I simply set out to explore different approaches to history, and in particular the history of ideas, which I find useful in understanding the history of international law. The potential radicalism of my approach lies in the use of historical study to question the present. This *use* of history, which may be termed political but is free of specific demands and conclusions, is to demonstrate the contingency of the present. I ask the twin questions of why things are the way they are and how could they have been different.

The history of International law has grown exponentially as an area of interest in recent years. The history of international law was the 'most neglected'[3] part of international law for some time, but this is no longer the case. There is a wealth of study which can be generally classed historical, both in mainstream and critical or theoretical scholarship. I want to argue in part that a weakness of much of this work comes from a lack of reflection on history itself. Whether the work is a history *of* international law, *within* international law, or international law *in* history,[4] the method of historiography is often unclear. I am not attempting to represent 'the state of the field', merely to re-emphasise the potential in the use of history for political ends, rather than simply for its own sake.

2. Raymond Williams, *Keywords: A Vocabulary of Culture and Society* (Revised edition, Oxford University Press, 1983) at 252. For a recent and provocative discussion of the idea of radical international law, see Bill Bowring, 'What is Radical in "Radical International Law"?', 22 *Finnish Yearbook of International Law* (2011) 1–29.
3. Lassa Oppenheim, 'The Science of International Law: Its Task and Method', 2 *American Journal of International Law* (1908) 313–356. This sentiment was echoed by Wilhelm Grewe, *The Epochs of International Law* (Trans. M. Byers, De Gruyter, 2000) at 1.
4. These terms are taken from Matt Craven, 'Introduction: International Law and Its Histories', in Matt Craven, Malgosia Fitzmaurice and Maria Vogiatzi (eds.), *Time, History and International Law* (Martinus Nijhoff: Leiden, 2007) at 7.

The question of method is a very simple one; an historical method is simply how we choose our data. The question of what goes in and what is left out of a history leads to a lot of complicated issues, some of which I discuss below, but is at root this simple. Depending on what we want to say about the present, we choose different historical materials. After all, it should not be so controversial to suggest that a truly accurate history is either impossible or useless. As Paul Ricoeur very nearly says, a truly accurate history would be as useful as Lewis Carroll's one-to-one scale map.[5] A choice of scale is made, and this requires the inclusion and exclusion of material. But also a political choice is made. History which confirms the necessity of the present and the legitimacy of contemporary global arrangements does exist, and is consistently popular.[6] Simply doing history is not radical, but a radical disaffection with the present inspires and demands a historical method to support it.

So, what is wrong with the present that would lead to this sort of search through the data of history? More specifically, what is wrong with the present of international law? Poverty is one familiar example of the gap between the promise of international law and the actual conditions imposed by regulation through international. As Susan Marks, for one, has demonstrated, international law is involved in both the promise of a better future through development, and the creation of so called poverty 'traps'.[7] Poverty is 'something certain groups of people do to others'.[8] In a search for a way to expose this relationship, and do something to oppose it, history offers a basis for argument. The objection to poverty is the political aim which inspires the choice of historical material.

The three historical methodologies or approaches which I am interested in are the Marxist, Cambridge School, and Postmodern. These broad terms are insufficient to cover the variety of methods which they contain. For a Marxist historian who has regularly explained and defended his methodology I will look at Eric Hobsbawm.[9] One of the key academics in developing the

5. Lewis Carroll, *Sylvie and Bruno Concluded* (MacMillan, 1893). This is sometimes referred to as the paradox of the complete map. Ricoeur discusses different scales of history, and their uses, in Paul Ricoeur, *Memory, History, Forgetting* (Trans. K. Blamey & D. Pellauer, University of Chicago Press, 2004) 209–216.
6. The popular history writing of Niall Ferguson is one obvious example.
7. Susan Marks, 'Human Rights and the Bottom Billion', 1 *European Human Rights Law Review* (2009) 37–49.
8. *Ibid*, at 48.
9. My starting point for Hobsbawm's discussion of the practice of history is Eric Hobsbawm, *On History* (Abacus: London, 1998) I am aware of alternative statements of Marxist methodology, but have chosen to focus on Hobsbawm's for purposes of space and clarity.

Cambridge School approach to the history of ideas is Quentin Skinner,[10] and he too has published widely and repeatedly on the subject of method and in defence of his method. Postmodern is perhaps the least useful term, and certainly does not help much in its unifying of diverse approaches to a variety of subjects under one label. I will be looking at the historical method and work of Michel Foucault.[11]

The shortcomings of these labels must be highlighted from the start. Marxist and Postmodern are highly loaded terms, easily used in a tone of mocking chastisement.[12] Furthermore, and in common with Cambridge School, they do not serve to easily demarcate an area or type of study, referring to a wide variety of practices and political viewpoints. However, they do suggest a general approach to history, and are at least useful for this. I use the terms knowingly, and after considering their shortcomings, as still the best label for the work I am interested in.

Alongside this discussion of different radical approaches to history, I want to briefly look at one historical subject in international law; the work of Hugo Grotius. Specifically, I am interested in how the history of Grotius can be told in several different ways, each true to their own standards, each satisfying the most basic conditions of historical practice. However, that a variety exists tells us something about the practice of history in international law, and what it is for. In Hersch Lauterpacht's classic text, 'The Grotian Tradition in International Law',[13] he describes a pragmatic tradition of international

---

Particularly notable is E. P. Thompson, *Poverty of Theory and Other Essays* (Merlin Press: London, 1978).

10. Skinner has published a variety of works on historical method, as a starting point see Quentin Skinner, *Visions of Politics Volume One: Regarding Method* (Cambridge University Press, 2002).
11. Foucault's reflections on methodology are dispersed throughout his works, but a good place to start is Michel Foucault, 'Questions of Method' in *Power: Essential Works of Foucault 1954–1984 volume 3* (James D. Faubion ed., Penguin: London, 2002) at 223; and Paul Veyne, 'Foucault Revolutionises History' in *Foucault and his Interlocutors* (Arnold I. Davidson ed., University of Chicago Press, 1997) at 146.
12. For example, Terry Eagleton uses the term postmodern critically in *The Illusions of Postmodernism* (Blackwell: Oxford, 1996), and with scorn in his earlier work 'Capitalism, Modernism and Postmodernism', I (152) *New Left Review* (1985) 60–73. Marxism and Marx are given similar treatment by a variety of postmodernists; particularly relevant are Foucault's comments, dealt with later, in various interviews, lectures and books. Postmodern may be regarded as redundant following Sokal's Hoax, and Marxism rejected as the failed ideology of the Cold War.
13. Hersch Lauterpacht, 'The Grotian Tradition in International Law', 23 *British Yearbook of International Law* (1946) 1–53. This is discussed under The Historical Turn in International Law, below.

law scholarship which draws its origin from Hugo Grotius. In the work of Richard Tuck, we find a very different Grotius, one who is writing to justify the imperial practices of the Dutch Provinces.[14] In Benjamin Straumann's work we find a third Grotius, one who is deeply involved in the Roman philosophical arguments which fill his work, and from which his originality is drawn.[15] This variety of interpretations is not explored to set up which is 'better' history, or which is more or less true, but simply to demonstrate the different aims and intentions which produce different histories.

In conclusion I argue that history can be used as a radical tool. Indeed, history used to demonstrate the contingency of current arrangements, 'history that *might have gone another way*',[16] is a radical revisiting of the study of international law. By doing this I want to open up new possibilities for considering political action in international law. The classic history sustains a system of international law which continues to allow global inequality and catastrophic poverty.[17] A radical history, under whatever methodological banner we might choose, can and should demonstrate the contingency of this present understanding of international law.

2. The Historical Turn in International Law

In the last few years there have been a number of attempts to sum up the 'state of the field' of the history of international law. George Galindo has argued that '*The Gentle Civilizer of Nations* represents a historiographical turn in the work of Koskenniemi and paves the way for the same in the field of international law.'[18] Koskenniemi himself has offered an overview of current

14. Richard Tuck, *The Rights of War and Peace* (Oxford University Press, 1999). This is discussed under Contextualism, below.
15. Straumann's main work is currently only available in German, *Hugo Grotius und die Antike. Römisches Recht und römishe Ethik im frühneuzeitlichen Naturrecht.* A selection of papers drawn from this work are available in English, see in particular Straumann, 'Is Modern Liberty Ancient? Roman Remedies and Natural Rights in Hugo Grotius' Early Works on Natural Law', 27 *Law and History Review* (2009) 55–85. For a general introduction to Straumann's work on Grotius see Randall Lesaffer's review essay 'On Roman Ethics, Rhetoric and Law in Grotius', 10 *Journal of the History of International Law* (2008) 343–347. This work of Straumann is discussed in the Conclusion, below.
16. Martti Koskenniemi, *The Gentle Civilizer of Nations* (Cambridge University Press, 2001) at 5 (italics in original).
17. See Susan Marks, 'Human Rights and the Bottom Billion' *supra* note 7; and Margot Salomon, *Global Responsibility for Human Rights: World Poverty and the Development of International Law* (Oxford University Press, 2007).
18. George Galindo, 'Martti Koskenniemi and the Historiographical Turn in International Law', 16 *The European Journal of International Law* (2005) 539–559.

historical study of international law,[19] particularly the work of German scholars and the Max Planck Institute's works in the history of international law in Germany.[20] Koskenniemi offers some explanations for the increased interest in the history of the discipline, particularly a 'sense of increased political possibility connected with the end of the Cold War'[21] and the new opportunities connected with a postmodern outlook which thinks against the old grand narratives. He also outlines three areas of history of international law which need developing; the intellectual history of international law, the focus on the west and its "Other", and an historical sociology of international law. In intellectual history, Koskenniemi favours a contextualist outlook, drawing on the methodological work of the Cambridge school.[22] The relationship of the West with the non-European world in the history of international law is also under-researched, although there is important work from critical and postcolonial scholars, as well as other studies by third world lawyers and some significant treatment of colonialism.[23] The third and most open category of historical sociology includes the need to study the interplay of different types of international society and normative systems, as well as the connection between international law and other social developments, such as economics. Finally, sociology could also include the history of international law as a professional practice, again something Koskenniemi himself has engaged with.

Also written in the style of addressing the state of the field and most useful here as a starting point is Matt Craven's introduction to the edited collection *Time, History and International Law*.[24] Craven splits the histories of international law in to three groups; histories *of* international law, histories *within*

19. Martti Koskenniemi, 'Why History of International Law Today?', 4 *Rechtsgeschichte* (2004) 61–66. This article develops, along with 'Histories of International Law: Dealing with Eurocentrism', 19 *Rechtsgeschichte* (2011) 152–176, many concerns about the practice of history of international law first raised in the introduction to *The Gentle Civilizer of Nations*.
20. An overview and electronic copies of much of the research group's work can be found at <www.rg.mpg.de/en/forschung/voelkerrechtsgeschichte/> (visited 19 February 2015). It should also be added that the Erik Castrén Institute in Helsinki has, under Koskenniemi, produced a huge amount of historical research. For a more detailed overview of the study of the history of international law, again with the focus firmly in Germany, see Ingo Hueck, 'The Discipline of the History of International Law—New Trends and Methods on the History of International Law', 3 *Journal of the History of International Law* (2001) 194–217.
21. Koskenniemi, 'Why History of International Law Today?', *supra* note 19, at 64.
22. Which I deal with in some detail below.
23. Koskenniemi himself has recently reiterated the need to write a non Euro-centric history of international law in Koskenniemi, 'Dealing with Eurocentrism', *supra* note 19.
24. Craven, 'Introduction: International Law and Its Histories', *supra* note 4.

international law and international law *in* history. The history of international law is the grand history which Oppenheim hoped for. Instances of this sort exist, such as Nussbaum's *A Concise History of the Law of Nations*[25] or Grewe's *Epochs*[26] but are rarely and perhaps even ill advisedly undertaken. The problem of telling the history of international law is that a singular, unified history requires a grand narrative which 'somehow captures "international law" on a broad canvass as a singular idea or set of ideas tied together in some coherent manner.'[27] This approach then demands a set of assumptions about what constitutes international law, and who is involved in making its history. This shuts out any opposing voices, and ultimately denies the possibility of any other history.

One type of history of international law written in this style is Lauterpacht's. Writing in the immediate aftermath of the Second World War, Lauterpacht uses Grotius' work as the basis of a call to return to 'principle … against makeshifts'.[28] A Grotian international lawyer is one 'who has found a workable synthesis of natural law and state practice'.[29] This is a pragmatic approach, which seeks to construct a functioning system of positive law while not being afraid to call on natural law to fill the gaps. On this basis, Grotius was not a Grotian, in Lauterpacht's terms, as he failed to provide 'a workable synthesis of natural law and state practice'.[30] While Lauterpacht is dismissive of Grotius' method, which has 'no redeeming feature',[31] he does approve of Grotius aim, the humanisation of the conduct of war. He then sets out to redescribe the content of Grotius' work according to the need for it in contemporary international society, focusing on Grotius' work on sources, practice, and the goals of international law. Lauterpacht's is a history of law's struggle against politics.

Iain Scobbie tells us that Grotius is used as 'essentially a conceit upon which Lauterpacht hangs his own argument'.[32] Lauterpacht was himself writing in the aftermath of the Second World War, and clearly was expressing his own concerns for the humanisation of war and the need to secure peace. While this is true, I want to highlight two aspects of Lauterpacht's use of

25. Arthur Nussbaum, *A Concise History of the Law of Nations* (MacMillan: New York, 1947).
26. Grewe, *The Epochs of International Law, supra* note 3.
27. Craven, 'Introduction: International Law and Its Histories', *supra* note 4.
28. Lauterpacht, 'The Grotian Tradition', *supra* note 13, at 1.
29. *Ibid*, at 5.
30. *Ibid.*
31. *Ibid*, at 4.
32. Iain Scobbie, 'The Theorist as Judge: Hersch Lauterpacht's Concept of the International Judicial function', 2 *European Journal of International Law* (1997) 264–298 at 266.

Grotius which I think demonstrate a problematic and unsatisfactory use of history, his argument for Grotius' importance, and his discussion of 'reason of state'. Lauterpacht accepts Grotius' 'pre-eminence' unquestioningly despite all the shortcomings of his work, for two simple reasons. Firstly, everyone else generally accepts the central importance of Grotius,[33] and secondly, his work is so often referred to by both his successors, and those making arguments in international law.[34] In a central section of Lauterpacht's article he blames the 'unprecedented ascendancy of the ideas of 'reason of state'[35] for the horrors of war in the first half of the Twentieth Century. Lauterpacht, as an international lawyer writing in 1946 wants international law to exist as a final end to such arguments, as a limit to absolute state sovereignty. He roots this in Grotius, and finds it to be Grotius' argument, and it does have to be found. Grotius never once mentions 'reason of state', as it is 'so obvious and so fundamental that … he regards it as below the dignity of his work to engage with … the subject'. Grotius also makes no mention of Machiavelli, his 'disapproval is one of silence'.[36] From these silences, Lauterpacht finds an absolute rejection of 'reason of state' thinking, and a strong and principled opposition to Machiavelli and his followers.

I do not think this is acceptable as a treatment of an historical text. The work of Grotius exists in a particular time, for a particular purpose. Lauterpacht's arguments are strong and noble, but the question must be asked; why are they hidden behind Grotius? The answer must be that by adopting a starting point which everyone agrees on, that Grotius is the Father of International Law, then by putting his arguments in Grotius' mouth they are more persuasive. This is true, but this is history in the rhetorical mode, used to tell a persuasive story, it hides a great deal about what international law does and has done. Lauterpacht never acknowledges that it is even possible to tell a different, but still accurate, history. This history shuts down debate and excludes politics. Any radical history must acknowledge that *all* history is ideological, and oppose Lauterpacht's claim of absolute truth.

The point I am trying to make is similar to that which Susan Marks makes when discussing the 'falseness' of false contingency.[37] Her point is that things are false not because they do not match reality, but because of what they exclude. Lauterpacht's history is 'generally true *so far as it goes*, but false as to

33. Lauterpacht, 'The Grotian Tradition', *supra* note 13, at 19.
34. *Ibid*, at 15.
35. *Ibid*, at 33.
36. *Ibid*, at 30.
37. Susan Marks, 'False Contingency', 62(1) *Current Legal Problems* (2009) 1–21 at 15–19.

what it excludes'.[38] The discussion of Grotius' contribution to international law, for example, stops at the positive. It excludes alternative narratives which highlight, for example, Grotius' deep engagement with Dutch colonialism. This is not to say that Lauterpacht did not know this, but he acted as if he did not. He acted as if no other narrative were possible. Lauterpacht was seeking to bolster a form of international law to which he was fully committed. This is the political position which directed his choice of method when he came to write history.

In Craven's account, there are histories of international law written primarily in opposition to the possibility of a unified history. These are the histories Koskenniemi described as made possible by a postmodern rejection of grand narratives. Craven draws attention to the work of Nathaniel Berman as an example, and the inspiration that he derives from the historical work of Foucault. *The Gentle Civilizer of Nations* also fits in to the position of being chiefly written *against* a traditional unified form of history, rather than necessarily for an alternative. This Koskenniemi sets out in his introduction, where he declares his 'non-rigorous' and 'experimental' method, mixing biographical and contextual history to present a narrative of the profession and its 'sensibility'.[39] As Craven points out, there are tensions within Koskenniemi's method, which he fails to resolve.[40] Koskenniemi does not succeed in writing either a non Eurocentric history of international law, or one which does away with the story of great men and their deeds. His history remains essentially 'Whiggish', in spite of his attempts to avoid this with talk of the 'sensibilities' of international lawyers. These criticisms, and others, were developed more fully by Galindo.

In an excellent, critical review of *The Gentle Civilizer of Nations*,[41] Galindo argues that while the book is an important and brilliant contribution, it leaves many questions in need of answer. Most of these questions concern Koskenniemi's historiography, or the lack of it. Firstly, the book is supposed to answer some of the questions left by *From Apology to Utopia*, in particular the criticism that understanding law as a set of argumentative practices does not tell us enough about what international lawyers do. The main objective of *The Gentle Civilizer of Nations* is to 'understand why international lawyers take certain positions and support certain arguments at different times and places'.[42] The need for history in this task is that only 'investigation of international law as it

38. *Ibid*, at 17.
39. Koskenniemi, *Gentle Civilizer, supra* note 16, at 1–10.
40. Craven, 'Introduction: International Law and Its Histories', *supra* note 4, at 12–13
41. Galindo, 'The Historiographical Turn', *supra* note 18.
42. *Ibid*, at 541.

was practised in the past can heighten the self-understanding of international lawyers today'.[43] Koskenniemi then consciously unites his theoretical and historical projects as directly related; an important step in bringing together historical and theoretical work more generally.

Koskenniemi certainly succeeded improving the understanding of the development of professional international law. The book has been hugely inspirational to many, a number in which I would humbly include myself. However, his work lacks a clear engagement or discussion of the practice of history. He describes his work as a history of ideas but, apart from some references to the historical concerns of Foucault, he does not elaborate. As Galindo notes, Koskenniemi has referred positively to the Cambridge school elsewhere, and I disagree with Galindo's dismissal of this work as having nothing in common with Foucault. Certainly some of the familiar criticisms of Foucault as a historian may cross over in to the work of Koskenniemi, such as the disappearance of opposing continuities in the focus on discontinuities, but more crucial is this lack of open reflection on method. This is most apparent as a problem when Koskenniemi talks of spirit and sensibilities which unite his subject. The *esprit d'internationalité* of the international lawyers in this period is put forward as an *a priori* fact, and Koskenniemi does not go to any great lengths to demonstrate that it did not or could not have existed anywhere else.

Again the problem of the dialectic of necessity and contingency emerges. What in this narrative is necessary and what contingent? How could things have 'gone another way', and what would it have looked like? Ultimately, *why* did events not progress in that other way? This is the problem with not openly discussing and reflecting on method, and in not exploring why the history is written. *The Gentle Civilizer of Nations* says something important about the missed potential for a better world through international law, but it does not tell us why international law failed.

Finally, Koskenniemi describes his historiography as a 'narrative' one, again without reflection on what this might mean. Two obvious engagements with this issue spring to mind from works on historical method; Skinner's work arguing against 'the Cult of the Fact'[44] and Hayden White's work.[45] I will develop both of these positions later. Ultimately, all of these criticisms concern Koskenniemi's lack of discussion of historiography as a

43. *Ibid.*
44. Quentin Skinner, 'The Cult of the Fact', in *Visions of Politics, supra* note 10, at 8–26.
45. Hayden White, *The Content of the Form: Narrative Discourse and Historical Representation* (John Hopkins University Press, 1987) in particular Chapter 2, at 26. See more generally *Metahistory* (John Hopkins University Press, 1973).

major shortcoming in an otherwise brilliant work. Galindo, by questioning Koskenniemi's historiography, raises a similar issue to that which I address here: that a proper and open consideration of the methods of history must be engaged in to properly understand and even achieve the political possibilities of historical work. Koskenniemi does declare that his history is written to allow for action in contemporary international law, and that history is in this sense a political act.[46] However, the subtle way he describes his methodology, and the absence of a clear historiography, means that we are still left with a question of what this history is for, and how exactly it might be different.

It is not possible to write a history of everything and everyone who might be included in the history of international law. The presentation of a unified history is always partial, and the critical historical responses to this tradition have highlighted many alternative versions of the same sort of history. History *within* international law, as an approach, involves the focus on the history of an aspect of international law, such as an idea, a theme or an institution. This is by far the most common form of history of international law. This sort of history starts from the simple observation that all lawyers are, to some extent, engaged in history,[47] and can include such diverse studies of the same object as Neff's *War and the Law of Nations: A General History*[48] or Kochi's *The Other's War*.[49] This sort of history has its own attendant shortcomings. Firstly, there is a risk of presuming that the object or idea under investigation has at all times remained the same. The meaning of concepts, such as territory or sovereignty, has changed over time. However, acknowledgement of this can lead to further difficulties, for what is the point of telling the history of sovereignty if the thing under consideration is not always the same? Alternatively, when telling a history of the evolution of a concept, the story quickly becomes yet another progress narrative and a lapse back in to a grand narrative dictated by teleology of 'progress'.[50]

Craven's third category, international law in history, is the history of international law as a social phenomenon, and its relation to others, such as

46. Koskenniemi, *Gentle Civilizer, supra* note 16, at 10.
47. Craven highlights the surprising places recognition of this can be found, giving examples from Ian Brownlie and David Kennedy. Craven, 'Introduction: International Law and Its Histories', *supra* note 4, 6 at footnote 40.
48. Stephen Neff, *War and the Law of Nations: A General History* (Cambridge University Press, 2005).
49. Tarik Kochi, *The Other's War: Recognition and the Violence of Ethics* (Birkbeck Law Press: Oxford, 2009).
50. Such history was addressed decisively and in general by Karl Popper, *The Poverty of Historicism* (Routledge: London, 1957). Specifically in the area of international law, see Thomas Skouteris, *The Notion of Progress in International Law Discourse* (Cambridge University Press, 2010).

politics, economics or sociology. International law is here seen as either taking a role within or against some other social force; international law as a *part of* politics, or as a corrective or restraint upon politics. An example of this sort of history is found in much of the critical history of international law and its role in imperialism. It is also present in a mainstream version, in the simplistic account of practice forming law, or in the many answers to the realist challenge passed downed by Austin and Morgenthau.

It is in part as a solution to these various problems and shortcomings that I propose to draw greater attention to the methods of history. Hayden White first wrote about the political potential of historical study in a 1966 article entitled 'The Burden of History'.[51] In this work, White declared that 'we require a history that will educate us to discontinuity more than ever before; for discontinuity, disruption and chaos is our lot. [...] If human beings learn to see themselves as disconnected from the past … they may come to realize what an enormous amount of freedom they enjoy'.[52] The historian's role must be to 'participate positively in the liberation of the present from the burden of history.'[53] At this stage his approach is a little crude, but the political intention is plain to see.

In later work, studying what he came to call 'metahistory',[54] White stressed the contingency of different historical narratives, and the impossibility of one true account. Instead, he argued that many different and contradictory accounts could be equally true, and what mattered was the intention behind the history writing, or the mode it was written in. *Metahistory*[55] sets out a complex structuralist account of different forms of historical discourse, the detail of which is not important here. Instead it is the focus on the politics inherent in history writing, and the intention to make this visible, which I want to emphasise. In his other essential monograph, *The Content of the Form*,[56] White moves away from some of these structuralist limitations and the focus on 'tropes',[57] and instead discusses history as narrative, as a form more suited to literary criticism than scientific. History is written as narrative to make it comprehensible, but life is not lived according to a narrative. This imposition of an invented narrative on to past events hides the chaos and

51. Hayden White, 'The Burden of History', 5 *History and Theory* (1966) 111–134.
52. *Ibid*, at 134.
53. *Ibid*, at 124.
54. The term is first used in 'The Politics of Contemporary Philosophy of History', *3 Clio* (1973) 35–54, but is most associated with the book *Metahistory, supra* note 45.
55. White, *Metahistory, supra* note 45.
56. White, *The Content of the Form, supra* note 45.
57. Historical tropes were central to *Metahistory*, but the term appears only once in *The Content of the Form.*

chance of lived reality, the 'meaninglessness which alone can goad the moral sense of living human beings to make their lives different for themselves and their children, which is to say, to endow their lives with a meaning for which they alone are fully responsible'.[58] White's politics may be a little too individualist for some tastes, but they are clear and presented openly. History writing is always a political act, and it is most useful for any radical political purpose if this is acknowledged and presented.

Are politics and method related? Yes, method is how we embody our politics. The political position I am putting forward here is very simple. International law is deeply involved in the ordering of the contemporary world. This is a world in which 'six million children under five years old die annually of malnutrition by causes that could be prevented by existing economic and technical resources'.[59] It is a world where 'the terrorism that shall be branded as the enemy of humanity [is not] the intellectual property system that allows hundreds of thousands of Africans to march into early death by sexually transmitted disease'.[60] These are the simple facts which are to be opposed. These are taken directly from Koskenniemi's work. These are the problems of contemporary reality that he opposes. Presumably, these are the political issues which drive his radical history. I do not claim that he does not have politics, or a method, but that they are at best obscure in his historical writing. In *From Apology to Utopia*, structural biases direct the otherwise indeterminate structure of legal arguments.[61] These are unacknowledged in the operation of the law. By acknowledging and exposing them, Koskenniemi argues they can easily be undermined.[62] This is the same work that a radical history does, and can contribute to. It is in revealing and undermining these biases and certainties that history is useful. This is the value of an open and clear method.

3. False Necessity and False Contingency

Before I begin to address the methods of history which I am interested in, I must address the issue of contingency specifically. I said I want to look

58. Hayden White, *The Content of the Form, supra* note 45, at 72.
59. Martti Koskenniemi, 'What is International Law for?', in Malcolm Evans (ed.), *International Law* (2nd edition, Oxford University Press, 2006) at 63.
60. Martti Koskenniemi, '"The Lady Doth Protest Too Much" Kosovo, and the Turn to Ethics in International Law', 65 *The Modern Law Review* (2002) 159–175 at 172.
61. Martti Koskenniemi, *From Apology to Utopia: The Structure of International Legal Argument* (Reissue with new epilogue, Cambridge University Press, 2005) 600–615.
62. For an excellent discussion of *From Apology to Utopia* more generally, and structural bias in particular, see Jason Beckett, 'Rebel Without a Cause? Martti Koskenniemi and the Critical Legal Project', 7 *German Law Journal* (2006) 1045–1088.

at history which in some way demonstrates the contingency of the present. The idea of contingency in international law, and law in general, is familiar, and obviously prompts reference to the ideas of necessity and contingency, and their 'false' corollaries. These ideas and their importance were dealt with by Susan Marks in her important paper: 'False Contingency'.[63] Marks uses the idea of false contingency 'as a complement and corrective'[64] to false necessity. False necessity is most well known as a key idea in the thinking of Roberto Unger,[65] and Marks elaborates this work excellently. The problem Marks identifies with this idea, whilst acknowledging its power and influence on herself and others, is that 'the idea appears to have taken root that to investigate "necessary factors"—limits, pressures, systemic constraints, and so on—is to commit yourself to determinism in the fatalistic sense.'[66]

Marks' article also concerns historical study. She begins with reference to the famous line from Marx that '[men] make their own history, but they do not make it just as they please in circumstances they choose for themselves; rather they make it in present circumstances, given and inherited'.[67] The idea of false necessity is in part an historical one. The claim that the present is *necessary*, that things have to be as they are and that historical development led inexorably to this situation, is what is to be criticised and undermined as *false*. However, this falsification of necessity should not, as Marks argues, lead to a situation where everything is seemingly possible in a world of chance and chaos. Everything may well be possible, but only certain things actually happen. The limits placed on the possibility of historical development must not be forgotten. There are various things which may be looked at that demonstrate false contingency, and the super-structures which Marx was interested in are a prominent one. Marks wants us to remember that while individuals do indeed make their own history, and that the present is contingent, the circumstances of making history are often determined. The point bears quotation in full:

> 'I believe it is quite right to hammer the point that history is a social product, not given but made. For if it has been made, then it can be remade differently. [...] The worry I want to explore here, however, is that we may be undertaking this work in a way which causes us to neglect the equally important progressive point that possibilities are framed by circumstances. While current arrangements can indeed

63. Marks, 'False Contingency', *supra* note 37.
64. *Ibid*, at 11.
65. Roberto Unger, *False Necessity* (2nd edn., Verso: London, 2004).
66. Marks, 'False Contingency', *supra* note 37, at 11.
67. Karl Marx, 'The Eighteenth Brumaire of Louis Bonaparte', in Terrell Carver (ed.), *Marx: Later Political Writings* (Cambridge University Press, 1996) at 32.

> be changed, change unfolds within a context that includes systematic constraints and pressures. In general terms what I wish to re-evoke is the idea that things can be, and quite frequently are, contingent without being random, accidental or arbitrary.'

To do this, Marks asks for a return to considering the determination of events. Rejecting both that things are inevitable, and that the range of outcomes is infinitely malleable, we are left with an historical exploration of what is possible. Marks calls her position 'anti-anti-Marxism',[68] that is it is not a defence of Marxism, but a resistance to rejections of Marxism. It is following this that I start with a consideration of the Marxist historical method, below.

There is an obvious absence from Marks' article; the work of Koskenniemi. As discussed above, Koskenniemi's historical work addresses exactly the issue of what to do after establishing the contingency of legal arguments. In particular, if *The Gentle Civilizer of Nations* is taken as a follow up to *From Apology to Utopia*, as Galindo suggests, then it is best read as an answer to exactly Marks' questions. *From Apology to Utopia* famously puts forward what is known as 'the indeterminacy thesis'. Koskenniemi, as much as anyone, is synonymous with highlighting the indeterminacy of international law. However he rejects, in terms similar to Marks', that this leads to 'an "anything goes" cynical scepticism, the giving up of political struggle and the adoption of an attitude of blasé relativism'.[69] This is to misunderstand the purpose of deconstruction, and to view it as an end in itself. Deconstruction leads in Koskenniemi's work, as in many others, on to a reconstruction.[70] The reconstruction is the historical study, the demonstration of 'a history that might have gone another way'.[71]

Koskenniemi's work in this area does not make Marks' article unnecessary or flawed however. This is because Koskenniemi's history does not fulfil Marks' project, if it even seriously engages with it. While Koskenniemi states that his historical study seeks to 'infuse the study of international law with a sense of historical motion and political, even personal, struggle',[72] as discussed earlier the methodology, or lack of one, leaves his study politically vague and uncommitted. By not setting out his own political struggle, and how he has

68. Marks, 'False Contingency', *supra* note 37, at 21.
69. Martti Koskenniemi, 'Letter to the Editors of the Symposium', 93 *American Journal of International Law* (1999) 351–361.
70. For an excellent discussion of post-structuralism in international law, and particularly the idea of renewalism, see Akbar Rasulov, 'International Law and the Poststructuralist Challenge', 19 *Leiden Journal of International Law* (2006) 799–827.
71. Koskenniemi, *Gentle Civilizer, supra* note 16, at 5 (italics omitted).
72. *Ibid*, at 2.

engaged in it, Koskenniemi does not allow us to decide if we want to join him. There is no opportunity to judge the value of his history, because we don't know what he is struggling against, or how. The necessary factors are absent; the sense of "anything goes" lingers on.

Paavo Kotiaho has described this as the 'contradiction between the appearance and essence of Koskenniemi's work'.[73] Koskenniemi's work appears as a challenge to the liberal international legal system; but the culture of formalism 'is still embedded in the traditional structure of international legal argumentation … within the same liberal theory of politics'.[74] This supposedly empty form of law is in fact 'complicit in the perpetuation of the current status quo.'[75] Thus the essence of Koskenniemi's work and in particular the historical project, remains in support of the status quo, since the culture of formalism ignores any necessary factors in the practice of legal argumentation. As Akbar Rasulov has compellingly put it;

'International legal argument almost never works like a coin … it acts more like buttered toast: released in a free fall, it may flip over several times, but it will almost always land the same side down. (And the question must then become: why?) Any suggestion that 'that is just what toasts do' would give toasts "way too much credit".'[76]

There are necessary conditions which dictate certain outcomes, even where others are or were possible. The history of international law must address this, to address the possibility of radical change.

To finish with Koskenniemi then, whom I have attempted to use as an interlocutor, not as a target, a few points need to be made. Koskenniemi, under what he calls 'instrumentalism', demonstrates a full and subtle awareness of the structural bias of international law. The content of the rules is indeterminate, but the focus of them is biased. As he puts it; 'it is never Algeria that will intervene in France or Finland in Chechnya'.[77] There is a reality outside the formalism of international law which dictates its operation. These are the necessary conditions which limit international law. The point of

73. Paavo Kotiaho, 'A Return to Koskenniemi, or the Disconcerting Co-optation of Rupture', 13 *German Law Journal* (2012) 483–496 at 485.
74. *Ibid*, at 494.
75. *Ibid.*
76. Akbar Rasulov, 'Review: From Apology to Utopia: The Structure of Legal Argument', 16 *Law and Politics Book Review* (2006) at 590 (Quoting Duncan Kennedy, 'A Semiotics of Critique', 22 *Cardozo Law Review* (2001) at 1185). Rasulov also employs the same metaphor excellently to address post structuralism and international law more generally in Akbar Rasulov, 'International Law and the Poststructuralist Challenge', *supra* note 60, at 806.
77. Koskenniemi, '"The Lady Doth Protest Too Much"', *supra* note 60, at 172.

formalism, as Jason Beckett has put it, is *empathy*.[78] It allows an appreciation for others. Under such conditions 'the inner anxiety of the Prince is less a problem to resolve than an objective to achieve'.[79] It was with this aim that Koskenniemi embarked on history. This is Koskenniemi's radicalism. I now turn to the methods of history to suggest how this radicalism could be joined and built upon by others.

4. Three Methods of Historical Research

4.1. Marxism

To delimit the method of historical research generally considered 'Marxist' is a difficult task. Marx's *The Eighteenth Brumaire of Louis Bonaparte*[80] is a fantastic piece of historical writing, and an excellent exemplar of the method of research. In this text Marx writes of how Louis Bonaparte's *coup d'état* demonstrated that tragedy repeats as farce, how historical processes are at once open and determined, and how unexpected outcomes may be explained through an analysis of conditions. In this one text we find a complex demonstration of dialectical materialist history, which never the less remains hugely readable, comprehensible and entertaining. This text is a demonstration of Marx's own method when writing history. To understand how this same work may be done today I turn to Eric Hobsbawm's work *On History*,[81] and in particular the chapters which address the Marxist approach to history.

The role of Marx as an inspiration is a clear unifying element of different research which we might label as Marxist, but the existence of one label does not demonstrate one approach. The Marxist approach can be more or less nuanced. Hobsbawm calls the un-nuanced Marxism 'vulgar-Marxism'.[82] He gives seven main elements of vulgar-Marxism, worth quoting as a guide of what *not* to do;

(1) The 'economic interpretation of history', that is the belief that 'the economic factor is the fundamental factor on which the others are dependent' (to use R. Stammler's phrase); and more specifically, on which phenomena hitherto not regarded as having much connection with economic matters, depended. To this extent it overlapped with

78. Beckett, 'Rebel Without a Cause?', *supra* note 62, 1070–1072.
79. Koskenniemi, '"The Lady Doth Protest Too Much"', *supra* note 60, at 175.
80. Marx, 'The Eighteenth Brumaire of Louis Bonaparte', *supra* note 67.
81. Hobsbawm, *On History*, *supra* note 9.
82. Hobsbawm, 'What do Historians owe to Karl Marx?', in *ibid*, at 192.

(2) The model of 'basis and superstructure' (used most widely to explain the history of ideas). In spite of Marx and Engels' own warnings and the sophisticated observation of some early Marxists such as Labriola, this model of dominance and dependence between the 'economic base' and the 'superstructure' mediated at most by

(3) 'Class interest and the class struggle'. One has the impression that a number of vulgar-Marxist historians did not read much beyond the first page of the Communist Manifesto, and the phrase that 'the [written] history of all hitherto existing societies is the history of class struggles'.

(4) 'Historical laws and historical inevitability'. It was believed, correctly, that Marx insisted on a systematic and necessary development of human society in history, from which the contingent was largely excluded, at all events at the level of generalisation about long-term movements. Hence the constant preoccupation of early Marxist writers on history with such problems as the role of the individual or of accident in history. On the other hand this could be, and largely was, interpreted as a rigid and imposed regularity, for example in the succession of socio-economic formations, or even a mechanical determinism which sometimes came close to suggesting that there were no alternatives in history.

(5) Specific subjects of historical investigations derived from Marx's own interests, for instance in the history of capitalist development and industrialisation, but also sometimes from more or less casual remarks.

(6) Specific subjects of investigation derived not so much from Marx as from the interest of the movements associated with his theory, for example in the agitations of the oppressed classes (peasants, workers), or in revolutions.

(7) Various observation about the nature and limits of historiography, derived mainly from no. 2 and serving to explain the motives and methods of historians who claimed to be nothing but impartial searchers after truth, and prided themselves on establishing simply *wie es eigentlich gewesen* [what actually happened].[83]

These elements of vulgar-Marxist history had their uses. Hobsbawm allows that such simplified approaches to history attracted more attention because they were instantly utilisable to re-examine history. Furthermore, the desire to address pressing and obvious current issues directed interest to some elements of Marxism instead of others. However, Marxist history must be more than simply a general emphasis on economic and social factors. Elements of Marx's own work can be set aside, such as the teleology of his history, the

83. *Ibid*, at 192–193.

specific hierarchy of levels and modes of interaction in the theory of basis and superstructure, and his thoughts on Oriental societies.

So what should a Marxist approach to history consist of, after avoiding the vulgarity already discussed? Firstly, Marxism is an opposition to empiricism, which is the attempt to assimilate the study of the social sciences to the natural sciences. Societies are 'systems of relations between human beings, of which the relations entered into for the purpose of production and reproduction are primary for Marx'.[84] Marxism is about analysing the structure and functioning of these systems as self maintaining entities, both in their internal relationships and their relationships with the outside environment, both human and non-human. In this study Marxism insists on a hierarchy of social phenomena, base and superstructure, and on the existence of internal tensions, contradictions. The final point is that social systems must be viewed historically, and analysis must be aimed at the internal dynamic of change in social structure. While Marx's specific teleology may be rejected, the idea of history, or society, progressing cannot. What is needed, what must be constructed, and what must be used is a dialectical model, that is a model which accounts for 'the simultaneous existence of stabilising and disruptive elements'.[85]

Marx himself wrote very little history, or what might be easily recognised as history. His most obviously historical works address current political situations with some historical consideration, as seen in *The Eighteenth Brumaire of Louis Bonaparte*[86] or *Class Struggles in France*.[87] The core of this is the materialist conception of history, and this idea, in Marx's own writing, is clearly explored in the *The German Ideology*.[88] It can be reduced to a single sentence; 'it is not consciousness that determines life, but life that determines consciousness.'[89] This is Marx's own Copernican revolution in philosophy, and as important to his thinking as any categorical imperative.

Marx elaborates on the materialist conception of history in the same text;

'This conception of history thus relies on expounding the real process of production—starting from the material production of life itself—and

84. *Ibid*, at 196.
85. *Ibid*, at 202.
86. Marx, 'The Eighteenth Brumaire of Louis Bonaparte', *supra* note 67.
87. Karl Marx, 'Class Struggles in France', in Karl Marx, *Political Writings Volume Two: Surveys From Exile* (David Fernbach ed., Penguin: London, 1973) 35–143.
88. Karl Marx and Friedrich Engels, 'The German Ideology', in *Collected Works of Karl Marx and Friedrich Engels Volume 5* (International Publishers: London, 1976).
89. Hobsbawm giving his own translation from *The German Ideology*. Hobsbawm, 'Marx and History', in *On History*, *supra* note 9, at 211. His reference is to page 24 of *The German Ideology*.

comprehending the form of intercourse connected with and created by this mode of production, i.e., civil society in its various stages, as the basis of all history; describing it in its action as the state, and also explaining how all the different theoretical products and forms of consciousness, religion, philosophy, morality, etc. etc., arise from it.'[90]

Hobsbawm stresses that process of production is not simply the material production of life, but 'the complex set of mutually dependent relations among nature, work, social labour and social organisation'.[91] Furthermore production is from both hand and head. This is the programme of research Marx set down, and the programme followed by Marxist history.

So, crudely, Marxism in history is a decision that '[a]nalysis of any society, at any moment of historical development, must begin with analysis of its mode of production'.[92] This is a radical approach to history, prioritising a particular determinative factor in human social development. Marx himself was interested in current political problems. When using historical methods, he started from contemporary society and worked backwards. History helped explain the present, and the key element was the mode of production, in all its many and complicated forms. It is this use of history, to help understand the present, and most importantly how to change it, that I call radical. Quoting the famous aphorism; 'the philosophers have only *interpreted* the world in different ways; the point is to *change* it'.[93]

When approaching the history of international law from a radical perspective, seeking to address fundamental issues, this focus on material elements challenges the image of law being created for the solution of purely political problems, out of humanitarian goodness, to fix problems suffered by all humanity. This is history with a conservative agenda, a history which reassures us that 'all is for the best, in this best of all possible worlds'.[94] As Hobsbawm, from his Marxist perspective, put it '[h]istory as inspiration and ideology has a built-in tendency to become self-justifying myth. […] It is the business of historians to try and remove these blindfolds'.[95] Of course, it is actually only the business of *radical* historians to remove these blindfolds. The writing of

90. Marx and Engels, 'The German Ideology', *supra* note 88, at 53.
91. Eric Wolf, *Europe and the People without History* (Berkeley, 1983) at 74.
92. Hobsbawm, 'Marx and History', *supra* note 76 at 214.
93. Karl Marx, 'On Feuerbach', in Joseph O'Malley (ed.), *Marx: Early Political Writings* (Cambridge University Press, 1994) at 118.
94. This famous paraphrasing of the lessons of Pangloss in Voltaire's *Candide* is used by Susan Marks, 'False Contingency', *supra* note 37, at 3.
95. Hobsbawm, 'What can History tell Us About the Present?', in *On History*, *supra* note 9, at 47.

different histories is a conflict, and there are plenty who happily write history as self-justifying myth.[96] Hobsbawm asserts the need to use history to understand the present as a first step towards political change. This is a radical aim, and it is an aim common to other approaches to history to which I now turn.

4.2. Contextualism

Contextualism is a general term for an approach to history which was pioneered by a group of historians of ideas at Cambridge University in the 1960s, taking inspiration from the works of Peter Laslett and Morrice Mendelbaum.[97] Laslett's edition of Robert Filmer's *Patriarcha*[98] in 1949 demonstrated that the work was written long before it was first published, written perhaps as early as 1630 and not published until 1679. His edition of Locke's *Two Treatises of Government*[99] discovered a similar time lapse, that Locke had most likely written the work in 1681, although it was published in 1690. These two discoveries undermined traditional interpretations of why the texts were written and how they were received. It also raised questions about what the publishers were trying to do with the text by issuing them at this later date. This raising of questions about what was intended in the writing of a text, and how it was received by its audience, started the investigation of the context of famous works of political thought. The approach, as with that in the previous section, begins with an exploration of what not to do.

In 1969 Quentin Skinner published an essay which quickly came to serve as a manifesto for this new approach; 'Meaning and Understanding in the History of Ideas'.[100] In this Skinner attacked, even ridiculed, a wide variety of received historical understanding of political thinking. His basic argument was that much of the activity termed the history of ideas 'suffered from a

96. Again, the work of Niall Ferguson seems the most appropriate example.

97. For a useful discussion of the emergence of this school, see J. G. A. Pocock, 'Quentin Skinner: The History of Politics and the Politics of History', 10 *Common Knowledge* (2004) 532–550. Other sources of inspiration sometimes referred to include Wittgenstein and Isaiah Berlin. Thinkers associated with the Cambridge School who have written on aspects of international political thinking include Richard Tuck, James Tully, Anthony Pagden and David Armitage. There are others, and the impracticality of assembling a complete list further demonstrates that it is inappropriate to talk of a 'school' in any strict sense.

98. Robert Filmer, *Patriarcha and Other Political Writings* (Peter Laslett ed., Oxford: Blackwell, 1949).

99. John Locke, *Two Treatises of Government* (Peter Laslett ed., 2nd edn., Cambridge University Press, 1967).

100. Originally published as Quentin Skinner, 'Meaning and Understanding in the History of Ideas', 8 *History and Theory* (1969) 3–53. The essay was revised and included in Skinner, *Visions of Politics, supra* note 10. My references are to the original publication.

leading to the ultimate explanation of a theory. This is the reading of, in Skinner's example, Machiavelli as the father of modern political thought, or as in the example of Lauterpacht, Grotius as the father of international law. This may be true as a statement of an author's historical significance, but it contributes nothing to understanding the text itself. Worse, it leads to the reading of the text looking for the signs of anticipating the next generation, and the sowing of the seeds for the final outcome. This is again the reading of historical texts for what they say about the present, and as contributions in the construction of a necessary present. This is apologetic history. Ultimately, the reception of a work at any time, and any renewal of interest, raises the question again of why the work is being read, and how it is being understood.

Skinner's solution is a modification of the approach of reading the text in its context. The contextual approach is not free of problems itself. While clearly holding advantages over this study of the history of ideas for contributions to timeless and universal debates, a narrow insistence on reading a text in its context has its own problems. Skinner argues that this practice rests on 'a fundamental mistake about the nature of the relations between action and circumstance.'[115] Put briefly, the problem is that an insistence on the explanation of actions is grounded exclusively in the conditions of the action. This rules out many considerations which may be useful in understanding what an author was trying to do. Intention to do something is part of causation and prior to an act, but intention *in* doing something is not, it is concurrent with the action and cannot be a cause. A study purely of the context which caused an action misses this out. Secondly, looking only at the cause of an action misses the way a text was understood. This is the difference between the meaning which an author puts in to a text, and the understanding with which it is received. The reception of a text must be taken in to account to gain a full appreciation of it.

Skinner's method for the history of ideas is that to know what an author was doing we must know what he intended to do and what he was understood as doing. His intentions can be, and must be, informed by the present historical context, but we must also take account of how the text was understood, and also what the authors themselves thought they were doing. The context does not determine what is said; rather it is the framework for understanding what is said and what it might have been possible to say in the given context. The radical intention of this method is then made clear in Skinner's conclusion;

> '[I]t has I think become clear that any attempt to justify the study of the subject in terms of the "perennial problems" and "universal truths" to be learned from the

115. Skinner, 'Meaning and Understanding', *supra* note 100, at 42.

> classic texts must amount to the purchase of justification at the expense of making the subject itself foolishly and needlessly naïve. Any statement, as I have sought to show, is inescapably the embodiment of a particular intention, on a particular occasion, addressed to the solution of a particular problem, and thus specific to its situation in a way that it can only be naïve to try to transcend. [...] [T]here simply are no perennial problems in philosophy: there are only individual answers to individual questions, with as many different answers as there are questions, and as many different questions as there are questioners.'[116]

This absolute focus on contingency as an attack on the majority of work done in studying the history of ideas does not lead to a desperate conclusion however. This contingency does not render the study purely academic and ultimately impossible, although it may seem to. Instead, by discovering for example what Locke's questions were, and what his answers were for himself, and how he was received, it should be possible to see how different his society was from ours. Locke should not be read to find what Jeremy Waldron has slightly foolishly called 'as well-worked-out a theory of basic equality as we have in the canon of political philosophy'.[117] Locke should be read to discover what Locke meant by equality, and what he was trying to do. This way we can be free to think about what we might desire by the term equality, or whether we desire it at all.[118] There exists the possibility to think again unburdened by the 'great texts', since they have been put in their proper place.

The historian of this school most often referred to by international lawyers is Richard Tuck. *The Rights of War and Peace*[119] is an engagement with the history of international law by a historian. It prioritises the analysis of texts, as discursive acts, in their context. I will also pay particular attention to Tuck's version of Grotius, as the second example of a history. Firstly, I want to look at this work as an example of contextual history.

Tuck argues that, read in their context, which is as they were intended and understood as speech acts, the famous liberal works from Grotius and Hobbes to Rousseau and Kant could not argue for a sovereign individual without also arguing for a sovereign state. The emergence of the sovereign individual is inextricably linked to the emergence of the sovereign state, both of which are made possible by new ways of thinking demanded by European

116. *Ibid*, at 50.
117. Jeremy Waldron, *God, Locke, and Equality: Christian Foundations in Locke's Political Thought* (Cambridge University Press, 2002) at 8.
118. As Tzvetan Todorov argues, 'the prejudice of equality ... consists in identifying the other purely and simply with one's own "ego ideal" (or with oneself)'. Tzvetan Todorov, *The Conquest of America* (Harper Perennial, 1985) at 165.
119. Tuck, *The Rights of War and Peace, supra* note 14.

expansion. As Weber put it, 'the historical origin of modern freedom has had certain unique preconditions which will never repeat themselves',[120] that is, the discovery and conquest of new worlds. The invention of freedom and democracy was made possible by this expansion. Without any new worlds to discover, their existence ceases to be possible 'under the domination of highly developed capitalism'.[121] This use of the context in which ideas of individual liberty were created leads to a questioning of the philosophical foundations upon which that liberty rests. Ultimately, in a world where the free sovereign state has largely ceased to exist, and the language of international affairs refers more often to the police action of the international community, the opportunity to even think about the free individual has passed.[122] This creates space for a re-examining of the origins of these ideas and demands a new account of how people might live morally.

Tuck's Grotius, as opposed to Lauterpacht's, is a writer completely situated in his time.[123] Grotius is writing primarily about the private war being waged by the Dutch East India Company against the Portuguese crown. Grotius is also concerned with the war for independence between the United Dutch Provinces and Spain, and in *The Law of War and Peace* particularly, the ongoing Thirty Years War. This history of Grotius emphasises his 'strong version of an international right to punish and to appropriate territory which was not being used properly by indigenous people'.[124] Tuck also situates Grotius as starting the modern liberal rights discourse, with 'a far reaching account of what agents can do to one another, both in the state of nature and in the international arena'.[125] His successors then had to struggle with these 'brutal implications'.[126]

This contextual approach produces a fundamentally different story to the traditional history offered by Lauterpacht. Grotius is no longer the Father of an international law which seeks to limit the excesses of state behaviour, to humanise and ultimately end war. Instead he launches a rights discourse which is hugely permissive, and focused on punishment and appropriation.

120. Max Weber, *From Max Weber: Essays in Sociology* (H. H. Gerth and C. Wright Mills trans. and ed., Routledge: London, 1948) at 71–72.

121. *Ibid.*

122. Or rather, it has become a circular argumentation and recitation of the same questions and answers. See for example Thomas Franck, *The Empowered Self: Law and Society in the Age of Individualism* (Oxford University Press, 2001).

123. Richard Tuck, *The Rights of War and Peace, supra* note 14, Chapter 3.

124. *Ibid*, at 108.

125. *Ibid.*

126. *Ibid.*

Tuck uses history to consciously attack these traditional narratives, and offer a radical alternative. This alternative Grotius not only gives us an argument that the origins of international law were explicitly imperial, but it also reveals the politics behind Lauterpacht's writing. This Grotius would not be such a suitable candidate for Lauterpacht's tradition, and Lauterpacht's arguments do not fit quite so comfortably in this mouth. This critique provides the opportunity to challenge and oppose the politics behind a history such as Lauterpacht's.

Anne Orford has very recently dismissed the radical potential of contextual history: 'the self-imposed task of today's contextualist historians is to think about concepts in their proper time and place—the task of international lawyers is to think about how concepts move across time and space.'[127] This discards too much that can be useful in the contextualist study of history. I also find it curious that Orford takes this position, since her own preferred method of description seems to fit in with the historical method I am discussing here. Orford has recently argued for 'a turn to description as a mode of legal writing'.[128] Emerging from various attempts to understand the concept of the Responsibility to Protect, Orford, rather than seek 'what the … concept really meant at some deeper level' instead approaches 'the concept as an articulation of international authority's "consciousness of itself"'.[129] Or, to quote Foucault, Orford sets herself the task to 'make visible precisely what is visible … to make us see what we see'.[130]

It strikes me that this is exactly the same task that a radical history undertakes. By removing grand narratives, the myths of doctrine and coherence, the contextual approach to history as set out by Skinner and practiced by Tuck, does help us see what we see. History can be freed to explore again what is contingent, and what is necessary, in contemporary social reality. Furthermore, it demonstrates why this is so, and opens space to ask what is to be done about it. Orford's approach is largely inspired by Foucault. However, before turning my attention to him, I want to introduce a third Cambridge school historian who has most obviously engaged with Foucault's work and attempted to adopt some techniques from his methodology.

127. Anne Orford, 'The Past as Law or History? The Relevance of Imperialism for Modern International Law', IILJ Working Paper 2012/2 (History and Theory of International Law Series) at 2, finalized June 2012, <www.iilj.org/publications/2012-2.Orford.asp> (visited 17 August 2013).

128. Anne Orford, 'In Praise of Description', 25 *Leiden Journal of International Law* (2012) 609–625.

129. *Ibid*, at 612, quoting Foucault, *The Birth of Biopolitics*.

130. *Ibid*, at 617, quoting Foucault, 'La philosophie analytique de la politique'.

James Tully first attempted a 'Foucauldian' history in *An Approach to Political Philosophy*,[131] and continued his reading of Foucault in *Strange Multiplicity*[132] and most recently in the two volumes of *Public Philosophy in a New Key*.[133] Tully, drawing inspiration from Wittgenstein, Skinner and Foucault, prioritises practices of governance as an area for study, with the aim of disclosing 'the historically contingent conditions of possibility of this historically singular set of practices of governance and of the range of characteristic problems and solutions to which it gives rise'.[134] This Tully calls 'practical philosophy', which is practical in two senses; firstly because it has a *use* and secondly because it *engages* with 'concrete struggles'. The use of history in addressing these problems of governance is 'as an object of comparison and contrast', which shows 'the practices and their forms of problematisation as a limited and contingent whole'. This historical and critical relationship with the present is then used to engage with 'concrete struggles, negotiations and implementations of citizens who experiment with modifying practices of governance on the ground'.[135] Foucault provides a synopsis of the approach which Tully favours;

> 'The critical ontology of ourselves must be considered not, certainly, as a theory or a doctrine; rather it must be conceived as an attitude, an *ethos*, a philosophical life in which the critique of what we are is at one and the same time the historical analysis of the limits imposed on us and an experiment with the possibility of going beyond them.'[136]

In *An Approach to Political Philosophy*, Tully's Foucauldian approach begins with a discussion of the emergence of the new governance problems which arose out of European expansion in the 16th and 17th centuries.[137] This new mercantilist system is the system of governance which Tully argues Locke was writing in and about. Locke is revisited as writing about the problems of the juridical way of governing which was created in this period. In *Strange Multiplicity* Tully's focus is on struggles of cultural recognition, but in *Public Philosophy in a New Key* the focus is widened to recognition more

131. James Tully, *An Approach to Political Philosophy: Locke in Contexts* (Cambridge University Press, 1993), Chapter 6.
132. James Tully, *Strange Multiplicity: Constitutionalism in an Age of Diversity* (Cambridge University Press, 1995).
133. James Tully, *Public Philosophy in a New Key* (Two volumes, Cambridge University Press, 2008 & 2009).
134. *Ibid*, Volume 1, at 16.
135. *Ibid*, at 16–17.
136. *Ibid*, at 19, quoting Foucault 'What is Enlightenment?', in *The Politics of Truth*, at 33.
137. Tully, *An Approach to Political Philosophy*, *supra* note 131, Chapter 6.

generally. For Tully, the scope of recognition is co-extensive with governance. Recognition concerns the way individuals or groups are recognised as part of a governance system, by other members of that system. By then exploring a variety of historical issues attached to the recognition of people for governance, most obviously imperialism[138] and Indigenous peoples,[139] but also questions of cosmopolitanism,[140] constitutionalism,[141] mass communications[142] and globalisation.[143] Tully questions and undermines the notion of unified public, and instead prioritises the struggle over recognition itself. Tully then uses a contextual history, while considering governance and power after Foucault, to try and increase the opportunity and space for struggle. In conclusion, he suggests a practical identity engaged with these free, open and pluralistic struggles, and that solidarity to this engagement is a source of peace in a conflicted society.[144]

I disagree then with Orford's charge that contextual history is not an engagement with contemporary reality. I will discuss later more general criticisms of the contextual approach, but for now I think it is enough to say that while people can still ask what Grotius thinks about the invasion of Iraq,[145] the lessons of contextual history are yet to be learnt in international legal scholarship. These lessons start with what not to do, but also provide positive instructions on what to do. They allow the construction of historically defensible arguments in the history of ideas. Skinner's politics may not be our politics, but he is involved in a political struggle over meaning and understanding. This is the struggle of any engagement in an argument, and it can be usefully taken on.

The purpose of the contextual study of famous texts is to better understand the present, to understand 'the distinction between what is necessary and

138. Tully, *Public Philosophy in a New Key: Volume 2, supra* note 133, Part 2.
139. *Ibid*, Part 3.
140. *Ibid*, Chapter 1.
141. *Ibid*, Chapter 4.
142. *Ibid*, Chapter 6.
143. *Ibid*, Part 1.
144. *Ibid*, Conclusion.
145. Some examples include Ove Bring and Per Brostrom, 'The Iraq War and International Law: From Hugo Grotius to George W. Bush', in Jan Hallenberg and Håkan Karlsson (ed.), *The Iraq War: European Perspectives On Politics, Strategy And Operations* (Routledge: New York, 2005) 118–141; Noel Cox, 'International Law After Iraq—An Ethical or Historical Approach to Justification of Self-Defence', in Satyanarayana Prasad (ed.), *Right of Private Defence—Expanding Horizons* ((The Icfai University Press: Hyderabad, India, 2008) 214–243; and for an imagined consultation with Grotius on the legality of the war, see Dean Flavy, 'What would Grotius Do? The Founder of International Law Speaks Out on Iraq', <writ.news.findlaw.com/commentary/20030403_falvy.html> (visited 17 August 2013).

to trace the battles which were fought and the victories which were won to make it so. This is not a traditional historical way of speaking, but is instead a historico-political discourse. This is a history which is directed by political struggle. There is no neutral position, the 'truth' of history is 'a truth that can be deployed only from its combat position, from the perspective of the sought-for victory and ultimately … of the survival of the speaking subject himself'.[161] By accepting this link between truth and force, Foucault reveals that the claim of truth is *always* used as a weapon in a struggle. Taking a side, being against something, is to move away from a position which accepts the truth and instead to challenge it. It reveals the ways that we are made to 'believe we are living in a world in which order and peace have been restored'.[162] Foucault's history reignites a struggle which has been hidden and obscured by a more traditional form of history, the history which tells us that all is for the best.

The other vital aspect of Foucault's work is that it is 'history of the present'.[163] Foucault's approach is both historical and critical. He writes history consciously from his present, and he is ultimately the focus in an attempt to understand the limits on present consciousness. That is to say that when Foucault asks why other historians wrote the history they did, he does not hide from the implied question of why he writes the history he does. History addresses the present by exposing the limits to our understanding and experience that are historically constructed. Critical history study is an attempt to break these limits.[164] As Foucault puts it: 'It's a matter of shaking this false self-evidence, of demonstrating [the object's/practice's] precariousness, of making visible not its arbitrariness but its complex interconnection with a multiplicity of historical processes'.[165]

Roth pushes the idea that Foucault is writing from a present of epistemic shift.[166] The episteme begun by Kant, in which knowledge was governed,

161. *Ibid*, at 52.
162. *Ibid*, at 53.
163. Michael Roth, 'Foucault's "History of the Present"', 20 *History and Theory* (1981) 32–46.
164. This project of exposing the structures which control knowledge are the subject of Michel Foucault, *The Order of Things: An Archaeology of the Human Sciences* (Tavistock Publication: New York, 1970).
165. Foucault, 'Questions of Method', *supra* note 11, at 225.
166. Roth, 'Foucault's "History of the Present"' *supra* note 163, at 32–46. On the concept of episteme see Michel Foucault, *The Order of Things: An Archaeology of the Human Sciences* (Tavistock Publication: New York, 1970) and Michel Foucault, *Aesthetics, Method, Epistemology: Essential Works of Foucault 1954–1984 Volume 2* (James D. Faubion ed., Penguin: London, 2002), for another view, and a good discussion of the causes of epistemic shift, see Alasdair MacIntyre, 'Epistemological Crises, Dramatic Narrative and the Philosophy of Science', 60 *The Monist* (1977) 453–472.

fundamentally, by anthropology, is coming to an end. The new episteme, or *a priori* in Roth's preferred term, is begun by removing man as the limit on what is and can be known. Foucault explicitly compares himself to Kant:

> 'Anthropology constitutes the fundamental arrangement that governed and controlled the path of philosophic thought from Kant until our own day. This arrangement is essential, since it forms part of our history; but it is disintegrating before our eyes, since we are beginning to recognise and denounce in it, in a critical mode, both the forgetfulness of the opening that made it possible and a stubborn obstacle standing obstinately in the way of an imminent form of thought.'[167]

This is obviously radical. But it is also, I believe, a position not so far from what I have already discussed. This again is a use of history to question the present, without ignoring the structures limiting possibility. Foucault, partly as described by Veyne, gives us a series of things to do and not to do, as have the Marxists and the Contextualists. Objects are dismissed, truth is made contingent, ideology is forgotten, along with all '-isms', as merely reified rationalities. This might make things complicated, and I think the commentary on Foucault is sometimes over complicated, but it does leave something very useful. It demands the exploration of all the surrounding factors of any historical question. This Foucault calls 'eventalization', and his aim is to remove the burden of explaining causality by constructing all the different ways of understanding a singular event.[168] Nothing is left out, nothing is necessarily prioritised. This may be contingency with all falseness forgotten, but I don't think so.

Foucault was not interested in the outrage he might cause in the traditional study of the penal system, or psychiatry, or whatever else. For him '[t]he only important problem is what happens on the ground'.[169] By 'shaking' the faith in the usual answer to the question of what is to be done about prisons, the question of 'what is to be done' is put back in to the hands of the people actually affected by imprisonment. Foucault's critique takes the authority to propose reform away from those who govern, and also away from himself or any other commentator. This is crucial in understanding Foucault's usefulness, and challenging the rejection of his work as not useful for not proposing any serious reform. In challenging and revealing structures of domination and control, and the on-going nature of political struggle, Foucault argued as much against leaders or philosophers as any other target. It is absolutely and demonstrably *not* the purpose of political philosophy or critical thinking to

167. Foucault, *The Order of Things*, *supra* note 164, at 342.
168. Foucault, 'Questions of Method', *supra* note 11, at 227.
169. *Ibid*, at 235.

propose reform. But that does not mean there is nothing constructive here. Foucault constructs the very possibility of resistance and struggle, in revealing the nature and form of control and subjugation. Critique:

> 'Should be an instrument for those who fight, those who resist and refuse what is. Its use should be in processes of conflict and confrontation, essays in refusal. It doesn't have to lay down the law for the law. It isn't a stage in a programming. It is a challenge directed to what is.'[170]

Or as Marx once described his project; 'ruthless criticism of everything existing'.[171]

Foucault wrote 'I would like my books to be a kind of tool-box which others can rummage through to find a tool which they can use however they wish in their own area. [...] I don't write for an audience, I write for users, not readers.'[172] Foucault allows us to understand better the construction and control of the present. This is clearly a fecund area for political action, if not a political project in and of itself.

4.4. Don't be Vulgar

In these three authors or approaches I have sought to draw a unifying line of using the past to question the present. History can and should be employed in political argument, as a tactic against the crushing use of ideology founded on a (wilful?) misreading or misappropriation of history and of the present. I now want to briefly deal with some of the problems of putting these three groups together, and some of the attacks made by or on behalf of each group. I keep in mind the imperative 'don't be vulgar' after Hobsbawm's characterisation of 'vulgar Marxism'. Ultimately, I think many of the conflicts between different approaches are based on a 'vulgar' reading of the method.

The vulgar Marxism Hobsbawm attacked was set out earlier, and was an attack on an oversimplified reading of Marx, which focused exclusively on certain big ideas whilst failing to pay attention to the subtleties of the approach proper. In two other essays in the same collection, Hobsbawm looks at postmodernism, and the failings of this new approach to history, and even the dangers of doing it.[173] Foucault answers some of Hobsbawm's

170. *Ibid*, at 236.
171. Karl Marx, 'For a Ruthless Criticism of Everything Existing', in Robert C. Tucker (ed.), *The Marx-Engels Reader* (Norton: London, 1978) 12–15.
172. Michel Foucault, 'Prisons et asiles dans le mécanisme du pouvoir [1974]', in *Dits et Ecrits vol. 11*. (Gallimard: Paris, 1994) 523–524.
173. Eric Hobsbawm, 'Postmodernism in the Forest' and 'Identity History is not Enough' both in *On History*, *supra* note 9, at 254–265 and 351–366 respectively.

complaints, as does Skinner. I contest that his use of 'postmodern' is itself vulgar, over simplified and putting certain eye-catching statements in the foreground whilst ignoring the subtleties.[174]

Written as a review essay of Richard Price's *Maroon Societies*,[175] 'Postmodernism in the Forest' has plenty of praise for the content of the work while criticising the author's 'doubts about the possibility of objective knowledge or unified interpretation, that is to say, about the legitimacy of research as hitherto understood.'[176] Price's book does not follow these traditional practices, according to Hobsbawm, instead attempting to satisfy 'the requirements of postmodernism'.[177] The book, it seems, is full of useful information, presented in an incomprehensible way. In particular, it tells Hobsbawm nothing about the most important questions of slavery, ownership of people and ownership of land. The study of alien peoples is what history has often done, accepting that the past is a different country, without the invention of postmodernism.[178] Ultimately Hobsbawm feels that this was better, and told us more of what he has decided we need to know.

Identity History is not Enough[179] raises more clearly Hobsbawm's complaints against 'postmodernism'. Here Hobsbawm focuses the discussion on the experience of Nazi retreat in 1944 in southern France, particularly the slaughter of the men of the villages and towns. These events raise many questions for historical understanding of universality, identity, past and present, lived historical memory and detached academic research. History is a product used and misused by non-historians. It is an historian's duty to seek truth and point out fiction. However, the 'fashion' for 'postmodernism' is based on a sceptical approach to the enlightenment project and rationality.[180] This leads to, amongst other things, the return of fiction as equally valid, the disavowal of the importance of truth and a very dangerous space for reckless invention and misuse of history. Hobsbawm's emotive example of fact is the Holocaust, and apparently a postmodern approach allows the denial of the Holocaust's

174. There are a large number of such arguments, the most well-known being Terry Eagleton, *The Illusions of Postmodernism* (Blackwell, 1996); Alex Callinicos, *Against Postmodernism: A Marxist Critique* (Polity Press, 1989); and David Harvey, *The Condition of Postmodernity* (Blackwell, 1990). In my limited experience, such rejections of postmodernism seem to be peculiar to British Marxism, but this is not the place for an exploration of this issue.
175. Richard Price, *Maroon Societies: Rebel Slave Communities in the Americas* (John Hopkins University Press, 1979).
176. Hobsbawm, 'Postmodernism in the Forest', *supra* note 173, at 258.
177. *Ibid*, at 263.
178. *Ibid*, at 263–264.
179. Hobsbawm, 'Identity History is not Enough', *supra* note 173, at 351–366.
180. *Ibid*, at 357–358.

historical truth.[181] To be fair, Hobsbawm is not seeking a return to any form of scientific positivist truth, but instead believes the value of history and the public responsibility of historians, to be undermining ideological fictions by producing truth. Historians are 'myth-slayers'.[182]

This is, I argue, a vulgar reading of postmodernism. Firstly, on the question of 'facts', I want to turn to Skinner to clarify. In attacking an extreme proponent of positivist history, much stronger than Hobsbawm's claims, Skinner characterises Geoffrey Elton and his insistence on the purity of historical method as 'the cult of the fact'.[183] The cult of the fact believes that 'by uncovering the facts of history, the historian can aspire to discover "the true reality of the past"'.[184] This assumes that what is *fact* is self evident, and that the truth is recognisable from the assembly of facts. Again, Hobsbawm claims nothing like this, and would probably join Skinner in rejecting this image of history. However, Hobsbawm does cling to the idea of facts.

Skinner demonstrates how difficult it is to say what a fact is. His example is in cataloguing the art which has been owned or displayed in Chatsworth House.[185] To assert this as fact requires an answer to what a work of art it is, a definition which is hardly uncontested but which is required instantly for the historian to do any work. The dismissal of facts as absolute things is here dealt with at a higher level than saying that something was or wasn't in Chatsworth House. It is a problem of definition, of concepts, and of perceptions. This is the subtlety which is at the heart of any move away from facts and the search for truth.

Secondly, and more generally, I think that Hobsbawm's complaints misconstrue Foucault's work, as a leading example of what he terms postmodern. Hobsbawm makes no reference to Foucault as a historian, but does note that '[Price] is to be congratulated for deliberately avoiding references to Barthes, Bakhtin, Derrida, Foucault *et al.*'[186] I want to briefly draw on two writers who have tried to reconcile Foucault and Marx, so as to better contest current political struggles.

Foucault wrote that 'Marxism exists in the nineteenth century like a fish in water: that is, it is unable to breath anywhere else',[187] but his work is filled

181. *Ibid*, at 358–359.
182. *Ibid*, at at 363.
183. Quentin Skinner, 'The Cult of the Fact', in *Visions of Politics*, *supra* note 10, at 8.
184. *Ibid*, at 12. Skinner's reference is to Geoffrey Elton, *The Practice of History* (Collins: London, 1969) at 79.
185. *Ibid*, at 19.
186. Hobsbawm, 'Postmodernism in the Forest', *supra* note 173, at 261.
187. Foucault, *The Order of Things*, *supra* note 164, at 262.

with allusions and references to Marx, particularly some of the collections of lectures:

> 'I often quote concepts, texts and phrases from Marx, but without feeling obliged to add the authenticating label of a footnote with a laudatory phrase to accompany the quotation. As long as one does that, one is regarded as someone who knows and reveres Marx, and will be suitably honoured in the so-called Marxist journals. But I quote Marx without saying so, without quotation marks, and because people are incapable of recognising Marx's texts I am thought to be someone who doesn't quote Marx. When a physicist writes a work of physics, does he feel it necessary to quote Newton and Einstein? He uses them, but he doesn't need the quotation marks, the footnote and the eulogistic comment to prove how completely he is being faithful to the master's thought.'[188]

I think it is revealing, but should not be over stated, that Foucault put Marx in such a position in his thinking. Similarly to Kant, Marx is accepted as a master, who has to be learnt from and used, but also addressed critically, and surpassed. Part of the tension between a Foucauldian study and a Marxist study is that Foucault places Marx in this previous episteme, the one he is trying to escape. This is why he can say that Ricardo and Marx are the same, they both look at society in the same way, looking at economics and wage relationships, and the conflicts between them as merely 'storms in a children's paddling pool'.[189] However, whilst this epistemic distinction continues, Foucault's attitude to Marx changes, or at least softens in later work. These two highly critical engagements with Marx take place in a book which is filled with aggressive attacks on Marxism, and written perhaps with a conscious effort to distance the author from the particular form of French Marxism then prevalent.[190]

Alan Hunt writes an autobiographical story of his own struggle to reconcile his interests in both Marx and Foucault. He finds value in the very different focuses of Marx and Foucault, and believes that both can be held in mind when addressing his interests in law. The two come closest together in this reading on the question of practices. While Foucault clearly states his interest in practices, Hunt argues that Marx also held practice as a central focus, quoting from *The German Ideology*:

> 'The social structure and the state are continually evolving out of the life process of definite individuals ... as they actually are, i.e. as they act, produce materially, and

188. Michel Foucault, 'Prison Talk', in Colin Gordon (ed.), *Power/Knowledge: Selected Interviews and Other Writings 1972–1977* (Pantheon: New York, 1980) at 52.
189. Foucault, *The Order of Things, supra* note 164, at 199.
190. Sartre's review of *The Order of Things* captures this well. The original review appears in 30 *L'Arc* (Oct. 1966) at 87–88.

> hence as they work under definite material limits, presuppositions and conditions independent of their will.'[191]

This shared interest provides a starting point for reconciliation, and hope that there is some legitimacy in using both authors. Ultimately, Foucault reminds us of contingency and Marx of process and determinacy.

Simon Springer offers a more thorough attempt to use Foucault and Marx together, and a demonstration of what is to be gained.[192] By looking at neoliberalism through the methodology of Foucault and Marx, Springer finds neoliberalism as a discourse, but a discourse which is constituted by and constitutive of material forms.[193] It is neither best understood as 'top-down ideological hegemony' or 'bottom-up, as in post-structuralist notions of governmentality'.[194] The discourse is instead rooted in the material, with primacy given to both structure and agency. His project is not complete, and he does not claim success, but finds that anything useful in destabilising neoliberalism's rationalities is useful in itself. This sentiment is very Foucauldian.

A couple of further points need to be made concerning Foucault's relationship with Marxism. Firstly, there is a context which might explain some of the scorn Foucault directed towards Marx and Marxism; the French Communist Party (FCP). In an interview with Duccio Trombadori in 1978 Foucault discussed Marxism and his own experiences at length.[195] He joined the FCP in 1950, like many of his contemporaries, in search of 'an utterly different reality'.[196] He left the party in 1953, after the party had supported the fictitious and anti-Semitic 'Doctors' Plot' against Stalin.[197] He also felt excluded because of his homosexuality, and that the Communist Party upheld the traditional bourgeois conceptions of normal life.[198] Foucault had joined the party under the influence of Althusser, one of his tutors at the École Normale, and they remained friendly for the rest of Althusser's life, despite Foucault's

191. Karl Marx and Friedrich Engels, *The German Ideology*, as quoted in Alan Hunt, 'Getting Marx and Foucault into Bed Together!', 31(4) *Journal of Law and Society* (2004) 592–609 at 605.
192. Simon Springer, 'Neoliberalism as Discourse: between Foucauldian Political Economy and Marxian Poststructuralism', 9 *Critical Discourse Studies* (2012) 133–147.
193. *Ibid*, at 143.
194. *Ibid*, at 135.
195. Michel Foucault, 'Interview with Michel Foucault' in *Essential Works*, *supra* note 11, at 239–297.
196. *Ibid*, at 249.
197. *Ibid.*
198. James Miller, *The Passion of Michel Foucault* (Anchor Books: London, 1993) at 58.

rejection of Marxism and the FCP, in which Althusser played a prominent role. His time in the party, Foucault claimed, at least taught him something about the pliability of truth; 'the fact of being obliged to maintain something that was radically opposed to what one could believe was also part of that exercise of dissolution of the self and the search for the entirely other'.[199]

Christopher Chitty has recently produced a new English translation of a text which is absent from any current English language collections of Foucault's work; 'Les Mailles de Pouvoir'—'The Mesh of Power'.[200] Chitty argues that Foucault's growing interest in power as a subject of study coincides with a renewed interest in Marx.[201] The 'Mesh of Power' text is the most obvious engagement with Marx by Foucault. In it Foucault claims that his theory of power is, at least in part, derived from the second volume of *Capital*;[202]

> 'What we may find in the second volume of *Capital* is that *one* power does not exist, but many powers. Powers, this means forms of domination, forms of subjugation that function locally, for example in the workshop, in the army, on a slave plantation or where there are subservient relations.'[203]

He also attributes to Marx the local functioning of power existing first, and only later forming a State;

> 'These powers cannot and must not simply be understood as the derivation, the consequence of some kind of overriding power that would be primary. The schema of the jurists, whether those of Grotius, Pufendorf, or Rousseau, amounts to saying: "In the beginning, there was no society, and then society appeared when a central point of sovereignty appeared to organise the social body, which then permitted a whole series of local and regional powers"; implicitly, Marx does not recognise this schema. He shows, on the contrary, how, starting from the initial and primitive existence of these small regions of power—like property, slavery, workshops, and also the army—little by little, the great State apparatuses were able to form.'[204]

199. Foucault, 'Interview with Michel Foucault', in *Essential Works*, *supra* note 11, at 249.
200. Michel Foucault, 'The Mesh of Power', 2 *Viewpoint Magazine* (September 2012), <viewpointmag.com/the-mesh-of-power/> (visited 17 August 2013).
201. Christopher Chitty, 'Towards a Socialist Art of Government: Michael Foucault's "The Mesh of Power"', 2 *Viewpoint Magazine* (September 2012), <viewpointmag.com/towards-a-socialist-art-of-government-michel-foucaults-the-mesh-of-power/> (visited 17 August 2013).
202. Foucault is making a reference here to the second volume of Capital, but he does not mean Volume Two, but the edition published by Editions Sociales in France. This second volume comprises Sections, 4, 5, and 6 of Volume One of Capital, the sections on the production of relative and absolute surplus value.
203. Foucault, 'The Mesh of Power', *supra* note 200, at 3.
204. *Ibid*, at 3–4.

related political choices, each united by wanting to use history to change the present. This task can be more successfully undertaken by reflecting on the method of history which is being used. If we want to change the world, we must understand why things are the way they are, and how they could have been different. I finish on White's own understanding of why history is important in any political project;

> 'One can never move with any politically effective confidence from an apprehension of "the way things actually are or have been" to the kind of moral insistence that they "should be otherwise" without passing through a feeling of repugnance for and negative judgement of the condition that is to be superseded.'[210]

210. *Ibid,* at 73.

The 1948 Recognition of the State of Israel by the USA and the USSR and International Law

Patrick C. R. Terry*

Abstract: On November 29, 2012, the UN General Assembly decided to upgrade the status of the State of Palestine from "entity" to "non-member-state." Israel opposed that decision also on the basis that Palestine did not fulfil the criteria of statehood.

This article, in contrast, will examine whether the State of Israel itself fulfilled those criteria when it was recognized as a state by the USA and the USSR in May 1948 immediately after the Israeli Declaration of Independence had been proclaimed.

Following a brief summary of the contentious customary international law rules on state recognition, these will then be applied to Israel as it was on May 14, 1948. This will necessitate a discussion of the question of where sovereignty resided in territories mandated under the Covenant of the League of Nations. Based on the conclusion that sovereignty rested in the inhabitants, albeit in suspended form during the Mandate, it will be shown that Israel, by declaring its independence on May 14, 1948, actually seceded from the independent State of Palestine. It will then be explained why Israel at that time failed to meet any of the criteria of statehood so that there can be no doubt that, irrespective of GA Resolution 181 (II), both the Soviet and the American recognitions of Israel were premature, and therefore inconsistent with international law.

The fact that Israel has managed to establish itself as a viable state since then allows the article to conclude on a tentatively positive note: there is at least some hope for the recently recognized State of Palestine.

Keywords: Recognition of states, secession, mandate system, Palestine, Israel

* Patrick C. R. Terry is a Professor of law at the University of Public Administration in Kehl, Germany. He holds a Ph.D. in public international law (Kent, UK), a LL.M. in international law with international relations (Dist) (Kent), and two German law degrees (Stuttgart and Tübingen).

All URLs were last accessed on 15 February 2015.

1. Introduction

On November 29, 2012, the UN General Assembly (GA) decided to upgrade the State of Palestine, which had been proclaimed on November 15, 1988,[1] from an "entity" to a "non-member-state",[2] thereby granting it "implicit recognition as a sovereign state."[3] This move had been vehemently opposed by the USA and Israel. Israel's Representative to the UN described the decision as "affixing a seal of approval onto an entity that does not meet the basic criteria of statehood."[4]

More than 64 years earlier, on May 14, 1948, Israel had declared its independence. While the entity was immediately recognized as a new state by the USA[5] and the USSR,[6] Britain, the former mandatory for Palestine, refused to follow suit. The UK declared that Israel did not fulfil the "basic criteria of an independent state."[7]

This article will examine whether Britain's assertion was correct. After outlining the rules on state recognition in customary international law, these will then be applied to Israel. This will necessitate a discussion of the question where sovereignty resided in territories mandated under the Covenant of the League of Nations, such as Palestine. It will be argued that sovereignty rested in the inhabitants, albeit in suspended form during the Mandate. Therefore Israel, when it declared its independence at the end of the Mandate on May 14, 1948, actually seceded from the then independent State of Palestine.

1. Declaration of Independence, Annex III, <unispal.un.org/UNISPAL.NSF/0/6EB54A389E2DA6C6852560DE0070E392> (References to online sources are accurate as of 15 February 2015).
2. General Assembly (GA) Resolution A/67/L.28 (2012), passed in a 138:9:41 vote.
3. Louis Charbonneau, 'Palestinians win implicit recognition as sovereign state', <http://www.reuters.com/article/2012/11/29/us-palestinians-statehood-idUSBRE8AR0EG20121129>.
4. Israel's Permanent Representative to the UN Ron Prosser, Address to the UN Security Council, 15/10/2012; Statements by Israeli Leaders, Israeli Ministry of Foreign Affairs, 'Unilateral Declaration/Premature Recognition of a Palestinian State', <www.mfa.gov.il/MFA/Palestinian+State/Statements-by-Israeli-Leaders-29-Jun-2011.htm>.
5. Michael Ottolenghi, 'Harry Truman's Recognition of Israel', 47 *The Historical Journal* (2004) 963–988 at 963–964; Stephen Kinzer, *Reset Middle East, Old Friends and New Alliances: Saudi Arabia, Israel, Turkey and Iran* (I.B. Tauris & Co. Ltd.: London, 2011) at 154; 'No Time to Hesitate', *TIME Magazine*, 24/05/1948, <www.time.com/time/magazine/article/0,9171,794348,00.html>.
6. 'Russian Recognition of Israel', *The Times*, 18/05/1948, 4.
7. Philip Marshall Brown, 'The Recognition of Israel', 42 *American Journal of International Law* (1948) 620–627 at 620 (quote); 'British Caution', *The Times*, 18/05/1948, at 4; 'Britain is aloof to the New State', *New York Times*, 15/05/1948, at 2.

Despite at that time failing to meet any of the criteria of statehood Israel was immediately recognized by the USA and USSR. This leads to the conclusion that these recognitions were both premature and unlawful.

The controversial creation of the State of Israel in 1948 within the territory of the Palestine Mandate is an excellent example of the act of recognition being used as a tool to create facts on the ground irrespective of international law. As subsequent recognitions of Bosnia-Herzegovina or Kosovo have shown, major powers will disregard legal criteria, while at the same time confirming their validity, when wanting to achieve a particular resolution of a conflict. The recent recognition of Palestine expresses the international community's wish for a peaceful two-state-solution to this decades-old conflict in the Middle East, a goal the recognition of Israel was already meant to achieve more than 65 years ago.

It should be pointed out that this article only deals with the recognition of Israel against the backdrop of the situation in Palestine in mid-1948 and has no implications for Israel's current status as a state.[8]

2. The Recognition of the State of Israel in May 1948

2.1. The Recognition of States

Before examining whether the American and Soviet recognitions of Israel in May 1948 were lawful, the rules of international law on the recognition of states need to be explained.

The recognition of states is governed by customary international law. Generally applicable rules have not been codified and attempts at doing so have failed. The International Court of Justice (ICJ), in its recent Advisory Opinion on Kosovo, also declined to address the topic.[9] Against this backdrop it is not surprising that the recognition of states has always been very

8. John Dugard, *Recognition and the United Nations* (Grotius Publications Limited: Cambridge, 1987) at 62; John Quigley, *The Statehood of Palestine, International Law in the Middle East Conflict* (Cambridge University Press, 2010) at 120–121.
9. ICJ, *Accordance with International Law of the Unilateral Declaration of Independence by the Provisional Institutions of Self-Government of Kosovo*, Advisory Opinion of October 22, 2010, at para. 51; the ICJ declared it had not been asked 'whether or not Kosovo has achieved statehood', nor had it been asked 'about the validity or legal effects of the recognition of Kosovo by those States which have recognized it as an independent state'.

controversial. Some have even argued that extending recognition is a purely political decision[10] while others disagree on the effects of and criteria for granting recognition.

Nevertheless, many states' past and recent declarations, which evidence *opinio juris*, indicate that states feel compelled to judge an entity against specific criteria before granting recognition,[11] itself an act they view as merely declaratory of the fact that a new state exists.[12] State practice—where, despite inconsistencies, most like cases have been treated alike—, seems to confirm this.

10. This is illustrated by the different approaches taken in the late 1940s: Hersch Lauterpacht in his *Recognition in International Law* (Cambridge University Press, 1947) at V states: 'There are only few branches of international law which are of greater, or more persistent, interest and significance for the law of nations than the question of Recognition of States … Yet there is probably no other subject in the field of international relations in which law and politics appear to be more closely interwoven'. At about the same time Brown, 'The Recognition of Israel', *supra* note 7, argued (621) that 'in spite of the comments and theories of the writers on the subject of recognition the simple truth is that it is governed by no rules whatever … the act of recognition is political in nature'. Even in 1999 Thomas D. Grant, in his *Recognition of States, Law and Practice in Debate and Evolution* (Praeger Publishers: Westport, 1999) at 168, makes the point that 'whether recognition is a subject of law or of politics is indeed one of the centers of debate over recognition today'; regarding Yugoslavia, see Hurst Hannum, 'Self-Determination, Yugoslavia, and Europe: Old Wine in New Bottles?', 3 *Transnational Law & Contemporary. Problems* (1993) 57–69 at 60; Marc Weller, 'The International Responses to the Dissolution of the Socialist Federal Republic of Yugoslavia', 86 *American Journal of International Law* (1992) 569–607 at 587.
11. Certainly the USA viewed the recognition of states as governed by the 'law of nations' as far as the recognition of Israel was concerned. In a memo of May 13, 1948, written by the Legal Advisor to the Under Secretary of State, the Legal Advisor states: 'The present memorandum is limited to the legal question, and does not deal with the political question whether the existence of a new state ought to be recognized'; *Memorandum by the Legal Adviser (Gross) to the Under Secretary of State (Lovett), Recognition of Successor States in Palestine*, May 13, 1948, United States Department of State, Foreign Relations of the United States (FRUS), 1948, The Near East, South Africa and Africa, Volume V (Part 2, 1948) 960–965 at 960; Roland Rich, 'Recognition of States: The Collapse of Yugoslavia and the Soviet Union', 4 *European Journal of International Law* (1993) 36–65 at 55; J. J. Lador-Lederer, 'Recognition—A Historical Stocktaking (Part I)', 27 *Nordisk Tidsskrift Int'l Ret.* (1957) 64–92 at 80; he quotes a British Government note to the United Nations of August 24, 1948: '… the recognition or non-recognition of States is a matter of legal duty and not of policy'.
12. Article 3 Convention on Rights and Duties of States (1933), US Treaty Series 881; Article 9 Charter of the Organisation of American States (1948), 119 UNTS 47; Opinion No. 1, Arbitration Commission, EC Conference on Yugoslavia, 29/11/2001; *Report of the International Committee of Jurists Entrusted by the Council of the League of Nations with the Task of Giving an Advisory Opinion upon the Legal Aspects of the Aaland Islands Question*, League of Nations O.J., Special Suppl. 3, October 1920, 8; *Deutsche Continental*

Viewing the recognition of states as declaratory, of course, means it is necessary to establish the criteria an entity must meet before recognition as a state is extended. Notwithstanding the many critics, states have for a long time been remarkably consistent in re-iterating the same statehood criteria as basis for assessing whether an entity merits recognition as a state, despite not always adhering to them: the so-called "Montevideo criteria".[13]

Gas-Gesellschaft v. Poland (1929), 5 Ann. Dig. ILC, 11, 15; *Tinoco Arbitration* (United Kingdom v. Costa Rica; Chief Justice Taft as sole arbitrator), 18 *American Journal of International Law* (1924) 147–174 at 154 (governments); William Edward Hall, *A Treatise on International Law* (Clarendon Press: Oxford, 1924) 19–20; Amos S. Hershey, *Essentials of International Public Law and Organization* (Macmillan Company: New York, 1927) at 199; Herbert W. Briggs, 'Recognition of States: Some Reflections on Doctrine and Practice', 43 *American Journal of International Law* (1949) 113–121 at 117; Quincy Wright, 'Some Thoughts about Recognition', 44 *American Journal of International Law* (1950) 548–559 at 557; Lador-Lederer, 'Recognition', *supra* note 11, at 78. He believes the declaratory theory dates back to a statement by US President Monroe in 1823 regarding former European colonies; James Crawford, *The Creation of States in International Law* (Oxford University Press, 2006) 22–26; José Maria Ruda, 'Recognition of States and Governments', in Mohammed Bedjaoui (ed.), *International Law: Achievements and Prospects* (UNESCO: Paris, 1991), Ch. 12, 449–465 at 454; John O'Brien, *International Law* (Cavendish Publishing Limited: London, 2001) at 172; Hilary Charlesworth & Christine Chinkin, *The boundaries of international law, A feminist analysis* (Manchester University Press, 2000) at 140; Jorri Duursma, *Fragmentation and the international relations of Micro-States* (Cambridge University Press, 1996) at 115; Stephanie Baer, *Der Zerfall Jugoslawiens im Lichte des Völkerrechts* (Peter Lang GmbH: Frankfurt am Main, 1995) at 323–324.

13. *Deutsche Continental Gas-Gesellschaft v. Poland*, 5 Ann. Dig. ILC, 11; the *Permanent Mandates Commission*, in September 1931, enumerated prerequisites regarding the termination of a mandate (it examined the issue in connection with Iraq's prospective independence). These principles were subsequently approved by the *Council of the League of Nations*; 12 *League of Nations Official Journal* (1931) 2044–2057 at 2057; Theodore D. Woolsey, *Introduction to the Study of International Law, Designed as an Aid to Teaching, And in Historical Studies* (Scribner, Armstrong & Co.: New Haven, 1874) at 49 (§ 36); T. J. Lawrence, *The Principles of International Law* (D. C. Heath & Co.: Boston, 1923) at 85; Hall, *A Treatise, supra* note 12, at 19–20; Hershey, *Essentials, supra* note 12, at 158–159; Briggs, 'Recognition of States', *supra* note 12, at 171; Brown, 'The Recognition of Israel', *supra* note 7, at 620–621; he also cites a supportive 1936 *Institut de Droit International* resolution; Thomas D. Grant, 'Defining Statehood: The Montevideo Convention and its Discontents', 37 *Columbia Journal of Transnational Law* (1998–99) 403–457 at 414–418; Bengt Broms, 'States', in Mohammed Bedjaoui (ed.), *International Law: Achievements and Prospects* (UNESCO: Paris, 1991), Ch. 1, 41–65, at 43–44; Charlesworth, Chinkin, *The boundaries, supra* note 12, at 125–126; Duursma, *Fragmentation, supra* note 12, at 112; Crawford, *The Creation of States, supra* note 12, at 45–46 (although he does argue for some variation); Stefan Talmon, 'The Constitutive versus the Declaratory Theory of Recognition: *Tertium Non Datur?*', 75 *British Yearbook of International Law* (2004) 101–181, at 109–111, 125.

These criteria are derived from Article 1 of the 1933 *Convention on Rights and Duties of States (Montevideo Convention)* and were reaffirmed by, among others,[14] the United States as recently as 2009:

> '… Second, based on its assessment of Kosovo's development during the period of UNMIK administration, the United States was satisfied that Kosovo's viability as a state was not in doubt and that it met the criteria of statehood outlined in Article 1 of the 1933 Montevideo Convention: … Consideration of these criteria had likewise been a cornerstone of U.S. recognition of other states seeking independence in the former Yugoslavia in the early 1990s.'[15]

The Israeli Ministry of Foreign Affairs, in response to a possible unilateral declaration of independence by the Palestinians after May 4, 1999, enumerated these criteria as follows:

> 'International law has established a number of criteria for the existence of a state: effective and independent governmental control, possession of defined territory; the capacity to freely engage in foreign relations; and control over a permanent population.'[16]

These criteria, which are generally accepted, are defined as follows:

> "***Permanent population***" refers to an undefined number of people living permanently in a specific area. Usually, nationality makes the relevant group of people easily identifiable, although nationals need not be a majority. There is no minimum number required, and the group of people living in the entity do not necessarily have to be bound to each other by race, religion, or culture. The population must, however, form a stable community.[17]

14. ICJ, *Kosovo, supra* note 9, Written Statement by the Government of Japan (April 17, 2009) 2; Written Statement by the Federal Republic of Germany (April 2009) 31; Written Statement of the Kingdom of Norway (April 16, 2009) 4; as for the UK, the Minister of State at the Foreign Office declared in 1986: 'The normal criteria which the Government apply for recognition as a State are that it should have, and seem likely to continue to have, a clearly defined territory with a population, a Government who are able of themselves to exercise effective control of that territory, and independence in their external relations. Other factors, including some United Nations resolutions, may also be relevant'; as quoted by O'Brien, *International Law, supra* note 12, at 173; Colin Warbrick in 'Recognition of States', 41 *International Comparative Law Quarterly* (1992) 473–482 at 473; points out that British practice has mostly adhered to these criteria.
15. *Ibid*, ICJ, Written Statement of the United States of America (April 17, 2009) 34; see also: Statement by the US Department of State in 72 *American Journal of International Law* (1978) at 337.
16. 'May 4, 1999–Some frequently asked questions', Israeli Ministry of Foreign Affairs, <www.mfa.gov.il/MFA/MFAArchive/1990_1999/1999/4/May+4-+1999+-+Some+Frequently+Asked+Questions+-+19.htm>.
17. Duursma, *Fragmentation, supra* note 12, at 117; Charlesworth, Chinkin, *The Boundaries, supra* note 12, at 126–128; Broms, 'States', *supra* note 13, at 44; Crawford, *The Creation of States, supra* note 12, at 52–55.

"***Defined territory***" requires a specific area in which the entity can exercise what is commonly regarded as the functions of state to the exclusion of others. Based on state practice it is assumed that border disputes do not usually impair an entity's recognition as a state, but that an undisputed core of territory is required.[18]

"***Government***" is generally assumed to mean "effective government". It is widely seen as the most important and most contentious criterion. The entity's leadership must be able to enforce law and order, and guarantee a certain degree of stability within a given area. The state organs must be able to govern effectively, if possible on the basis of some organizational structure, without having to resort to third parties.[19]

"***Capacity to enter into relations with other states***" mainly requires the ability to conduct foreign relations independently. State practice implies that formal independence (independence in the legal sense) is sufficient. "Real" independence, meaning economic or military independence, is not required.[20] Jellinek's "Drei-Elemente-Lehre" differs here by arguing that a government is only "effective", if it can potentially conduct its foreign affairs independently.[21]

State practice evidences two cases when entities meeting these criteria are nevertheless not recognized as states: (i) states where the principle of internal self-determination is fragrantly violated,[22] and (ii) states that were created by illegal use of force.[23] Because both exceptions are, as will be shown, not applicable to the situation in Palestine in 1948, they will not be discussed here.

Although the decision whether to recognize another state is still widely seen as being the prerogative of the individual recognizing state, there is agreement that extending recognition before the entity fulfils the statehood criteria is unlawful.[24] Premature recognition becomes especially pertinent in cases of secession. A state that recognizes a seceding entity before it fulfils the

18. Duursma, *Fragmentation, supra* note 12, at 116–117; Charlesworth, Chinkin, *The Boundaries, supra* note 12, at 128–132; Broms, 'States', *supra* note 13, at 44; Crawford, *The Creation of States, supra* note 12, at 46–52.
19. Duursma, *Fragmentation, supra* note 12, at 118–120; Charlesworth, Chinkin, *The Boundaries, supra* note 12, at 132–133; Baer, *Der Zerfall, supra* note 12, at 49–50; Broms, 'States', *supra* note 13, at 44–45; Danilo Türk, 'The Dangers of Failed States And a Failed Peace in the Post Cold War World', 27 *New York University Journal of International Law & Politics* (1994–95) 625–630 at 625–626; Crawford, *The Creation of States, supra* note 12, at 55–62; Talmon, 'The Constitutive', *supra* note 13, at 110–111.
20. Duursma, *Fragmentation, supra* note 12, at 120–127; Charlesworth, Chinkin, *The Boundaries, supra* note 12, at 133–135; Talmon, 'The Constitutive', *supra* note 13, at 111–116.
21. Talmon, 'The Constitutive', *supra* note 13, at 109–110.
22. Talmon, 'The Constitutive', *supra* note 13, 122–124, 146–147, 171–179.
23. O'Brien, *International Law, supra* note 12, at 185; Talmon, 'The Constitutive', *supra* note 13, 124, 144–146, 171–179.
24. Briggs, 'Recognition of States', *supra* note 12, at 171; Ruda, 'Recognition of States', *supra* note 12, 451; O'Brien, *International Law, supra* note 12, at 186–187; Baer, *Der Zerfall, supra* note 12, at 318–323; Wright, 'Some Thoughts', *supra* note 12, 556 and fn. 17.

statehood criteria is guilty of interference in the domestic affairs of the parent state.[25] It also undermines the *uti possidetis* principle, which the ICJ views as a "general principle" of international law.[26]

Long before the UN Charter came into force there already was widespread agreement that premature recognition was unlawful.[27] In 1874 Theodore Woolsey had declared that

> *If the question is still one of armed strife, as between a colony and the mother country, or between a state and a revolted portion of it, to take the part of the colony or of the revolted territory by recognition is an injury and may be a ground of war; …*[28]

William Hall, writing in 1924, also maintained that

> *Until independence is so consummated that it may reasonably be expected to be permanent, insurgents remain legally subject to the state from which they are trying to separate. Premature recognition is therefore a wrong done to the parent state; in fact it amounts to an act of intervention.*[29]

Hall goes on to describe American and British reluctance to recognize the South American "Spanish" Republics' independence from Spain between 1810 and 1825 as based on their wish to avoid violating international law.[30] A report before the *Senate Foreign Affairs Committee* on the question of their recognition stated:

> *The political right of the United States to acknowledge the independence of the Spanish American Republics, without offending others, does not depend upon the justice but on the actual establishment of that independence.*[31]

---

25. Ruda, 'Recognition of States', *supra* note 12, at 451; O'Brien, *International Law, supra* note 12, 186–187; Baer, *Der Zerfall, supra* note 12, at 318–323; Wright, 'Some Thoughts', *supra* note at 556–557; Lawrence, *The Principles, supra* note 13, at 85–86.
26. The *uti possidetis* principle has been described by the ICJ as demanding the 'intangibility of frontiers inherited from colonization' in order to 'secure respect for the territorial boundaries which existed at the time when independence was achieved'. The ICJ concluded that this principle 'accorded pre-eminence to legal title over effective possession as a basis of sovereignty'. Although its application could curtail 'the rights of people to self-determination', the principle's primacy was nevertheless the 'wisest course' because it ensured 'stability'; ICJ, *Case Concerning the Frontier Dispute (Burkina Faso v. Republic of Mali)*, Judgement, 22/12/1986, ICJ Reports (1986) at 554, 564–567 (paras. 19–26); EC Arbitration Commission on Yugoslavia, Opinion No. 3, reprinted in 3 *European Journal of International Law* (1992), 184; Article 6 of GA Resolution 1514 (1960).
27. H. Lauterpacht, *Recognition, supra* note 10, at 9–12; Lawrence, *The Principles, supra* note 13 at 85–86.
28. Woolsey, *Introduction, supra* note 13, at 55 (§ 40).
29. Hall, *A Treatise, supra* note 12, at 105; Hershey, *Essentials, supra* note 12, at 208; Lawrence, *The Principles, supra* note, at 85–86.
30. Hall, *A Treatise, supra* note 12, at 105–108.
31. Hall, *A Treatise, supra* note 12, at 106.

termination of the Mandate was not legally possible,[53] arguably resulting in a continuation of the Mandate after May 14, 1948.[54]

The *Covenant of the League of Nations* did not outline the procedure for termination. In the case of the Iraq Mandate all parties concerned (Iraq, Britain, and the League of Nations) had agreed to the termination.

Some have argued that unilaterally terminating the mandate violated Article 27 of the Palestine Mandate,[55] a provision contained in all mandates, which stated:

> *The consent of the Council of the League of Nations is required for any modifications of the terms of this Mandate.*

Based on this it could be argued that—after the dissolution of the League—UN agreement was necessary when terminating the Mandate. Others have argued that the mandate's character as an international agreement ruled out unilateral termination, except in cases of breach.[56]

Regarding "A"-Mandates, such as Palestine, this view is not convincing. Terminating an "A"-Mandate—after all, the League of Nations' goal—is clearly not a "modification."[57] Rather, Article 27 is a safeguard against abuses of

53. *The Times*: "U.S. Support for Partition of Palestine", 13/10/1947, 4; "Britain and Palestine, Firm Statement to U.N.", 17/10/1947, at 4. The Legal Adviser at the US State Department concluded in a memo: "British abandonment of the mandate may be a breach of Great Britain's international obligations.", *Memorandum by the Legal Adviser (Gross) to the Under Secretary of State (Lovett), Recognition of Successor States in Palestine*, May 13, 1948, FRUS, 1948, *supra* note 11, 960–965, at 962.
54. Julius Stone, *Israel and Palestine: Assault on the Law of Nations* (John Hopkins University Press, 1981) at 121–122 (only East Jerusalem, the West Bank and Gaza); D'Amato, 'The West Bank Wall', *supra* note 46, at 2–3; D'Amato argues that the Palestine Mandate continues: once Britain renounced the mandate it "devolved upon the United Nations", namely the GA and the ICJ. He seems to justify this by applying the English law on trusts. This argument is, however, unconvincing. There is near universal agreement that the mandates system was not identical to the English concept of trusts, but only contained elements of it (see, for example: ICJ, *International Status of South–West Africa, supra* note 48, 132: "It is therefore not possible to draw any conclusion by analogy from the notions of mandate in national law or from any other legal conception of that law"); Goudy, 'On Mandatory', *supra* note 49, at 177–182; he argues persuasively that the mandates system is "derived from Roman law", and that there are numerous differences to the English law on trusts; Berriedale Keith, 'Mandates', 4(3) *Comparative Legislation & International Law* (1922) 71–83 at 75.
55. See *supra* note 53.
56. Quincy Wright, 'Sovereignty of the Mandates', 17 *American Journal of International Law* (1923) 691–703 at 699.
57. Quincy Wright, 'The Proposed Termination of the Iraq Mandate', 25 *American Journal of International Law* (1931) 436–446 at 440 (referring to Iraqi independence in 1932, he states: "not a modification … but fulfilment of a mandate").

power by the mandatory, but not intended to prohibit it "giving notice". It was always possible for a different mandatory to take over.

It is therefore more convincing to assume that unilaterally terminating an "A"-mandate was possible simply because their termination, once the people concerned were able to stand on their own, was the mandates system's *raison d'être.*[58] Some even believed that the mandatory may lawfully "weary of well-doing and renounce his mandate".[59]

As far as Palestine is concerned it must be reiterated that all the relevant parties wanted Palestine to become independent—albeit in very different forms, and in some cases after a short transition period. The termination of the Mandate was thus a foregone conclusion. Against this backdrop the assumption that Britain did have the right to unilaterally terminate the Mandate seems compelling. There was agreement that the people of Palestine were now able to stand on their own, so that the mandate's aims had been achieved, irrespective of the fact that the British offered a different justification.

Britain's termination was also not seriously challenged as unlawful by the international community. The United Nations acknowledged the British withdrawal as evidenced by Resolution 181 (II). Its preamble stated: "… takes note of the declaration of the mandatory Power that it plans to complete its evacuation of Palestine by August 1, 1948." The resolution even demanded termination of the mandate "as soon as possible, but not later than by August 1, 1948", and established a Commission which was to deal with the transfer of power.[60] Although it could be argued that the ICJ, in its Advisory Opinion on the *International Status of South–West Africa,* demanded the GA's consent when a mandate was terminated, Resolution 181 (II) thus granted it.[61]

58. Keith, 'Mandates', *supra* note 54, at 81; Wright, *ibid*, at 440 (in favour of "automatic termination" in this case; he even doubts whether the mandatory's consent is necessary).
59. Arnold D. McNair, 'Mandates', 3 *Cambridge Law Journal* (1927–28) 149–160 at 160.
60. GA Resolution 181 (II).
61. ICJ, *International Status of South–West Africa, supra* note 48, at 141–142; the court—referring to the South–West Africa Mandate—states: "Article 7 of the Mandate required the authorisation of the Council of the League for any modification of its terms … the Court said that those powers … now belong to the General Assembly … By analogy it could be inferred that the same procedure was applicable to any modification of the international status of a territory under Mandate which would not have for its purpose the placing of the territory under the trusteeship system." Although dealing with South African plans to annex the mandated territory, the ruling could imply that granting independence to a mandated territory/terminating a mandate also requires UN consent. Similarly, the *Permanent Mandates Commission*, in September 1931, enumerated the general prerequisites regarding the termination of a mandate (which it examined the in connection with Iraq's prospective independence): these principles were approved by the *Council of the League of Nations; 12 League of Nations Official Journal* (1931) 2044–2057. The procedure

Furthermore, the Security Council also implicitly accepted the termination of the mandate and there is no evidence that any state regarded Palestine as still being under British mandate as of May 15, 1948. Britain's role as mandatory for Palestine therefore ended on May 14, 1948.

b) Resolution 181 (II) as Legal Basis for Israeli Independence

It has often been claimed that GA Resolution 181 (II) provides the legal basis for the subsequent partition of Palestine.[62] This assertion is based on the assumption that the resolution was binding on the international community, and the population of Palestine. Israel's "Declaration of Independence" was consequently merely executing the international community's binding decision.[63]

---

in 1931 could imply that the Council viewed its consent as essential when a mandatory wanted to terminate a mandate. This view is, however, not convincing. Granting independence to dependent nations is the fulfilment of the UN's goal of realizing the right of self-determination and of the League of Nations' aim of full independence, at least in respect of "A"-Mandates. Creating obstacles in that respect would be contradictory. Also, UN consent was not obtained when Transjordan was granted independence, without any questions of legality—as far as UN participation was concerned—being raised. Similarly, Syria was a founding member of the UN (although many argue the country only became independent in 1946), without consent having been obtained from an international organization.

62. Alexander, 'Israel in Fieri', *supra* note 49, at 427; implicitly Yehuda Z. Blum, 'The Missing Reversioner: Reflections on the Status of Judea and Samaria', 3 *Israel Law Review* (1968) 279–301 at 287; implicitly Lador-Lederer, 'Recognition', *supra* note 11, at 84; and Sol. M. Linowitz, 'Analysis of a Tinderbox: The Legal Basis for the State of Israel', 43 *A.B.A. Journal* (1957) 522–525 at 525; Ilan Dunsky, 'Israel, The Arabs, and International Law: Whose Palestine Is It, Anyway?', 2 *Dalhousie Jorunal of Legal Studies* (1993) 163–200 at 174 (although his arguments are not very clear; while arguing the Resolution "authorized Israel to declare legally its independence", he goes on to claim that the "Arabs were entitled to reject" it); Howard Grief, 'Legal Rights and Title of Sovereignty of the Jewish People to the Land of Israel and Palestine under International Law', 2 *NATIV Online* (2004), <www.acpr.org.il/English-Nativ/02-issue/grief-2.htm>; his arguments are also contradictory. On the one hand he argues that the "State of Israel" was "brought into existence" by the resolution, while on the other hand he argues the resolution was "illegal" due to an illegal abrogation of Jewish rights; Dugard, *Recognition*, *supra* note 8, at 60.
63. In December 1948 the USSR Representative at the UN declared, during the debate on the admission of Israel, that "the State of Israel has been created and exists in accordance with a resolution passed in the General Assembly … its territory is clearly defined by an international decision of the United Nations"; cited by Crawford, *The Creation of States*, *supra* note 12, 426, fn. 198; Israel declared that the resolution was "the only internationally valid adjudication on the future of the government of Palestine"; Letter dated 5 July 1948 addressed to the United Nations Mediator by the Minister for Foreign Affairs of the Provisional Government of Israel, U.N. Doc. A/648 (1948), Annex I, Document 4, at para. 1, <unispal.un.org/UNISPAL.NSF/9a798adbf322aff38525617b006d88d7/ab14d4aafc4e1bb985256204004f55fa?OpenDocument>.

> *April 1 … indicates that the Security Council was not prepared to accept or implement the General Assembly's Resolution of November 29.*[72]

This interpretation was in line with what the US Representative at the United Nations, Austin, had already declared before the Security Council on February 24, 1948:

> *The Security Council's action, in other words, is directed towards keeping the peace and not to enforcing partition.*[73]

In another memorandum of May 13, 1948, prepared by the Legal Adviser at the State Department, the creation of a Jewish State was viewed as having received "moral sanction" in the GA's "Partition Plan", which is obviously not the same thing as "legal sanction".[74] The Acting US Representative at the UN at the time of Israel's recognition later stated that "like most General Assembly Resolutions, it [the Partition Resolution] was merely a recommendation."[75] By subsequently even advocating a temporary solution contrary to the resolution,[76] the USA reaffirmed that it viewed Resolution 181 (II) as non-binding.

Lastly, neither the Arab nor the Jewish leadership in Palestine adhered to the resolution.[77] The Palestinian Arabs and the Arab states expressly stated that they viewed the resolution as not binding.[78]

While the Jewish leadership in Palestine officially declared their acquiescence to the resolution, and even referred to it in the Israeli "Declaration of Independence", it, in truth, ignored the resolution's content where it did not suit them:[79] no preparations were ever made for the economic union

72. *Action on the General Assembly's Resolution of November 29, 1947, on the Palestinian Question*, 3; Memo by Fraser Wilkins (Department of State), <www.trumanlibrary.org/whistlestop/study_collections/israel/large/documents/newPDF/2-20.pdf#zoom=100>.
73. *Statement made by the United States Representative at the United Nations (Austin) before the Security Council on February 24, 1948* (Extracts), FRUS, 1948, *supra* note 11, 651–654 at 653.
74. *Memorandum by the Legal Adviser (Gross) to the Under Secretary of State (Lovett), Recognition of Successor States in Palestine*, May 13, 1948, FRUS, 1948, *supra* note 11, 960–965 at 962.
75. Jessup, *The Birth*, *supra* note 66, at 264.
76. *Ibid*, at 265–279; Weiß, 'Die Entstehung', *supra* note 68, at 804.
77. Halderman, 'Some International', *supra* note 66, at 82.
78. Elaraby, 'Some Legal Implications', *supra* note 66, at 103; Dunsky, 'Israel' *supra* note 62, at 174.
79. Simha Flapan, *The Birth of Israel, Myths and Realities* (Pantheon Books: New York, 1987) at 33; Crawford, *The Creation of States*, *supra* note 12, at 432; Quigley, *The Statehood*, *supra* note 8, at 104; Kattan, *From Coexistence*, *supra* note 66, at 232.

envisaged by the GA,[80] and its timetable for conferring independence on both states step-by-step was not followed by the Jewish Agency or the other Jewish groups. Actions like the attack on Deir Yassin—an Arab village that was, after all, outside the territory of the prospective Jewish state—, and *Plan Dalet*—which explicitly called for offensive military action beyond the Jewish state's envisaged borders—strongly suggest that the Jewish Agency was never prepared to accept the territorial boundaries and the population mix anticipated in the resolution.[81]

Jewish non-adherence to the resolution is sometimes justified on the grounds that Arab rejection had freed the Jewish population from the obligation to respect its content.[82] That argument is unconvincing. If Resolution 181 (II)—a decision by a world body, not a contract between Arab and Jewish Palestinians—was indeed a binding resolution, then any form of non-compliance would have been a question of enforcement. Arab non-compliance would therefore not have resulted in Jewish freedom of action, but in the world body having to enforce its decision. Except in the case of self-defence, post-WW II international law does not allow individual states, let alone non-state actors, to unilaterally resort to the use of force in response to a wrongful act.[83] Jewish action anyway went way beyond enforcement of the resolution, the Jewish state in the end being about 50 % larger than envisaged, a sequence of events that can only be reconciled with the view that the resolution was non-binding.

80. Flapan, *ibid*, at 41; Moshe Naor, 'Israel's 1948 War of Independence as a Total War', 43 *Journal of Contemporary History* (2008) 241–257 at 248–249.

81. Judah L. Magnes, 'Toward Peace in Palestine', 21 *Foreign Affairs* (1942–43) 239–249 at 240; Flapan, *The Birth*, *supra* note 79, at 22 and 42; Jeremy Salt, *The Unmaking of the Middle East, A History of Western Disorder in Arab Lands* (University of California Press, 2008) at 142–144; Quigley, *The Statehood*, *supra* note 8, at 104; Kattan, *From Coexistence*, *supra* note 66, at 189–203; Shlaim, *Israel and Palestine*, *supra* note 52, at 58–61; Peter Mansfield, *A History of the Middle East* (2nd ed., London: Penguin Books Ltd., 2003) at 235.

82. Letter dated 5 July 1948 addressed to the United Nations Mediator by the Minister for Foreign Affairs of the Provisional Government of Israel, U.N. Doc. A/648, Annex I, paras. 4.2 (borders), 4.4 (economic union), 4.6 (Jerusalem), <unispal.un.org/UNISPAL.NSF/9a798adbf322aff38525617b006d88d7/ab14d4aafc4e1bb985256204004f55fa?OpenDocument>.

83. Antonio Cassese, *International Law* (Oxford University Press, 2005) 241–277; Nigel White, Ademola Abass, 'Countermeasures and Sanctions', in Malcolm D. Evans (ed.), *International Law* (Oxford University Press, 2010), Ch. 18, at 531–558 and 534–545; see also: Article 50 of the International Law Commission's *Draft Articles on State Responsibility for Internationally Wrongful Acts*.

International and local reactions also invalidate the argument that—though initially not binding—the resolution reflected international *opinio juris* and therefore immediately became binding.[84] International reaction, just outlined, in fact contradicts this assertion. Furthermore, 23 states (of 56 voting) did not support the resolution. There is therefore no evidence that by 1948 the resolution had attained more legal value than a mere recommendation.

It follows that the contentious question of whether the GA acted *ultra vires* by approving the plan of partition is not legally relevant due to the recommendatory nature of the resolution.

c) Secession

aa) Sovereignty[85]

In order to be able to judge whether Israel seceded from Palestine it is necessary to examine where sovereignty actually resided in mandated territories, such as Palestine. This was and is one of the most contentious issues surrounding the mandate system.[86] The Covenant does not provide an explicit answer,[87]

---

84. Jean Allain, *International Law in the Middle East, Closer to Power than Justice* (Ashgate: Aldershot, 2004) at 97.
85. The precise meaning and scope of the term "sovereignty" in international law need not be examined in this context. It should, however, be pointed out that the concept is much contested. See, for example: Antony Anghie, *Imperialism, Sovereignty and the Making of International Law* (Cambridge Univeristy Press, 2005); Matthew C. R. Craven, *The Decolonization of International Law: State Succession and the Law of Treaties* (Oxford University Press, 2007) esp. 7–92; Karen Knop, *Diversity and Self-Determination in International Law* (Cambridge University Press, 2002) esp. 109–211.
86. Mark Carter Mills, 'The Mandatory System', 17 *American Journal of International Law* (1923) 52–64 at 54; Mills points out that, during the peace negotiations, US Secretary of State Lansing repeatedly (and unsuccessfully) tried to bring the fact that it was unclear where sovereignty would reside to President Wilson's attention; E. Lauterpacht, 'The Contemporary', *supra* note 66, at 514; Leeper, 'International Law', *supra* note 46, at 1204; McNair, 'Mandates', *supra* note 59, at 158–159; Lawrence, *The Principles*, *supra* note 13 at 80–82; Hall, *A Treatise*, *supra* note 12, at 162–163; Quigley, *The Statehood*, *supra* note 8, at 66–75; Kattan, *From Coexistence*, *supra* note 66, at 56–58; Anghie, *Imperialism*, *supra* note 85, at 125–127, 133, 147–156.
87. The fact that the issue of where sovereignty resided was not explicitly regulated in the Covenant should, perhaps, not be surprising. Many contemporary lawyers would not have been unduly perturbed by this. As Craven has explained, a vast array of different arrangements existed in the 19th century: "sovereign" and "semi-sovereign" states, vassals, unions, protectorates, etc.; by the middle of the century a minimum of eleven different categories of states was recognized; Matthew Craven, 'Statehood, Self-Determination, and Recognition', in Malcolm D. Evans (ed.), *International Law* (Oxford University Press, 2010), Ch. 8, at 203–251, 210–214.

which has led to a proliferation of theories on the topic,[88] further complicated by the different categories of mandate.

Some concluded that the old-fashioned concept of sovereignty was ill-suited to the legal novelty of the mandate system. They maintained that the question could not be answered or that sovereignty was "in abeyance".[89] Others argued that sovereignty lay with the mandatory as evidenced, for example, by its control of the mandated territories' foreign relations.[90] It was also argued that the League of Nations retained sovereignty and the mandatory was simply acting on its behalf, as evidenced by the former's supervisory role.[91] Another school of thought adhered to the notion that sovereignty rested in the inhabitants of the mandated territories, albeit temporarily exercised by others.[92]

Many others argued that assuming shared sovereignty (in various combinations) was the correct solution, and others again argued that the answer to the question where sovereignty rested was dependent on the category of mandate

88. Blum, 'The Missing', *supra* note 62, at 282; Lawrence, *The Principles, supra* note 13, at 80–82 (he believed there should be a case-by-case evaluation of where sovereignty resided based on the individual mandates); Hall, *A Treatise, supra* nota 12, at 162–163 (he believed sovereignty over the mandates to be divided between the mandatory and the League of Nations); Quigley, *The Statehood, supra* note 8, at 66–75; Anghie, *Imperialism, supra* note 85, at 147–156.
89. Blum, 'The Missing', *supra* note 62, at 282; Leeper, 'International Law', *supra* note 46, at 1208; ICJ, *International Status of South–West Africa, supra* note 48, Separate Opinion Judge Sir Arnold McNair, at 150.
90. Lord Balfour, 'Statement, 18th Session of the Council, 1922', 3 *League of Nations Official Journal* (1922) 547.
91. Norman Bentwich, 'Mandated Territories: Palestine and Mesopotamia (Iraq)', 2 *British Yearbook of International Law* (1921–22) 48–56 at 48; seems to agree, when he states that the "League of Nations becomes the general guardian of three infant nations" who "delegates the care of the minor to a Power who is termed the Mandatory". In later articles he seems more doubtful, especially regarding Palestine: he repeatedly points out that the "Mandatory exercises full power of legislation and administration" ('Nationality in Mandated Territories Detached from Turkey', 7 *British Yearbook of International Law* (1926) 97–109 at 100).
92. ICJ, *Legal Consequences for States of the Continued Presence of South Africa in Namibia (South–West Africa) notwithstanding Security Council Resolution 276 (1970)*, Advisory Opinion, 21/06/1971, Separate Opinion Vice-President Ammoun, ICJ Rep. 1971, 69; Judge Ammoun refers to Stoyanovsky's view "of virtual sovereignty residing in a people deprived of its exercise by domination or tutelage" as the "more accurate view"; Anghie, *Imperialism, supra* note 85, at 179–180; Percy E. Corbett, 'What is the League of Nations?', 5 *British Yearbook of International Law* (1924) 119–148 at 129–130 (limited to "A" mandates).

of "C"-Mandates, rejected the assumption that sovereignty was "transferred" to the mandatory. With the exception of South Africa, no mandatory ever claimed sovereignty.[102]

The League of Nations' role regarding the mandated territories was certainly significant.[103] It is, however, doubtful whether that role amounted to sovereignty over the mandated territories.[104] The mandatories were to provide "tutelage" to the mandated territories "on behalf of the League", and the League was to perform considerable supervisory functions. The *Permanent Mandates Commission* certainly took its supervisory tasks very seriously and adopted "the widest possible interpretation" of its rights. The importance of these supervisory functions has also repeatedly been stressed by the ICJ.[105]

Nevertheless, it is very difficult to sustain the argument that sovereignty over the mandated territories rested in the League: firstly, the official goal of the mandates system envisaged all mandated territories becoming independent states at some point in the future; secondly, the question of who would become mandatory had already been decided by the Allies prior to the League taking up its functions: and, thirdly, the mandatory, in the case of "A"-Mandates, was only permitted to provide administrative assistance on behalf of the League.[106] When Iraq's future independence (Mandate for Mesopotamia/Iraq) was discussed in 1931, the question of a transfer of sovereignty from the League—for example by way of a treaty—was thus never discussed.[107]

102. Leeper, 'International Law', *supra* note 46, at 1207.
103. E. Lauterpacht, 'The Contemporary', *supra* note 66, at 514; Lewis, 'Mandated Territories', *supra* note 95, at 474.
104. An implicit rejection by the ICJ of the idea that the League of Nations retained sovereignty over the mandated territories (*International Status of South–West Africa, supra* note 48, at 132) could be in seen in the court's statement, after having rejected the notion that the League of Nations' function amounted to that of a "mandatory": "It [the League of Nations] had only assumed an international function of supervision and control"; this was affirmed by the ICJ in *Namibia (South–West Africa), supra* note 92, at 29; Leeper, 'International Law', *supra* note 46, at 1205; he points out that the League never claimed sovereignty; Wright, 'Sovereignty', *supra* note 56, at 697.
105. ICJ, *International Status of South–West Africa, supra* note 48, at 136.
106. E. Lauterpacht, 'The Contemporary', *supra* note 66, at 514–515; Wright, 'Sovereignty', *supra* note 56, at 697; Quigley, *The Statehood, supra* note 8, at 66.
107. The *Permanent Mandates Commission*, in September 1931, enumerated the general prerequisites regarding the termination of a mandate (which it examined in connection with Iraq's prospective independence). These principles were subsequently approved by the *Council of the League of Nations*; a transfer of sovereignty was not mentioned; 12 *League of Nations Official Journal* (1931) 2044–2057.

The correct view of the mandates system would therefore seem to be that sovereignty already rested in the nations under mandate but was exercised on behalf of these nations by the mandatory under the League of Nations' supervision.

Early statements made by officials in the Foreign Office regarding Britain's aims confirm this. In December 1918 a future member of the delegation to the Peace Conference in Versailles described it as the "foundation" of British policy regarding Palestine that there should be "a Palestinian State with Palestinian citizenship for all inhabitants, whether Jewish or non-Jewish."[108] Accordingly, citizens of "A"-Mandates, including Palestine, not only had a nationality separate from that of the mandatory, but actually had their own nationality.[109]

Furthermore, once the mandates were in place, the mandatories and third states tended to treat the mandated territories as future states, even though governmental functions may have been exercised by the mandatory. Among other things, the mandatories concluded treaties with third states for the mandated territories.[110] In the case of Palestine, even the UK itself concluded a bilateral treaty with the mandated territory in 1922.[111]

Third states took a similar view of the relationship between the mandatory and the mandate. In 1932 the British government sought to grant Palestine trade concessions, and enquired of states it was bound to in Conventions of Commerce as to their response.[112] Spain disapproved and declared that, as far as Palestine was concerned, "the territory in question could in no way

108. Arnold Toynbee (Political Intelligence Department, British Foreign Office); Minutes of December 2, 1918; reprinted in Doreen Ingrams, *Palestine Papers 1917–1922, Seeds of Conflict* (John Murray Publishers Ltd.: London, 1972) 43 (Public Record Office, Foreign Office 371/3398); furthermore, Article 30 of the *Treaty of Lausanne* with Turkey (concluded after the *Covenant of the League of Nations* had come into force) stated: 'Turkish subjects habitually resident in territory which in accordance with the provisions of the present Treaty is detached from Turkey will become *ipso facto*, in the conditions laid down by local law, nationals of the State to which such territory is transferred."

109. Quigley, *The Statehood*, *supra* note 8, at 54–58; Kattan, *From Coexistence*, *supra* note 66, at 137.

110. Quigley, *The Statehood*, *supra* note 8, at 53–54 (providing many examples, mainly of treaties concluded between Palestine and Egypt).

111. *The Agreement between the Post Office of the United Kingdom of Great Britain and Northern Ireland and the Post Office of Palestine for the Exchange of Money Orders*; the treaty was signed in London on January 10, 1922, and in Jerusalem on January 23, 1922; it was also registered at the League of Nations and published in the League of Nations Treaty Series; Quigley, *The Statehood*, *supra* note 8, at 54.

112. Quigley, *The Statehood*, *supra* note 8, at 61–64.

be considered as imperial territory, but solely as a foreign country ... From this point of view, it was in a situation with regard to the mandatory power analogous to other sovereign states."[113] In their responses the United States and Italy also both insisted that Palestine was a "foreign country" in relation to the United Kingdom, and went on to point out that this, in their view, also applied to all the other territories under British mandate.[114]

These reactions can also be easily reconciled with the *Permanent Mandates Commission's* view, expressed in 1937, that the "Palestinians formed a nation, and that Palestine was a state, though provisionally under guardianship."[115]

This understanding of the mandates system is only compatible with the notion that sovereignty already rested in the inhabitants of the mandated territory. Its exercise was, however, suspended to a varying degree according to the class of mandate until such a time as the peoples concerned "were able to stand by themselves".[116] During this interim period the functions of sovereignty were to be exercised by the mandatory under the supervision of the League of Nations.

113. *The Ambassador in Spain (Laughlin) to the Secretary of State*, October 28, 1932; United States Department of State, FRUS, Diplomatic Papers, 1932, The British Commonwealth, Europe, Near East and Africa, at 36–37.

114. *The Secretary of State to the British Chargé (Osborne)*, August 27, 1932; *The Chargé in Italy (Kirk) to the Secretary of State*, October 22, 1932; United States Department of State, FRUS, *ibid*, at 32, 35–36.

115. League of Nations, Permanent Mandates Commission, Minutes of the Thirty-Second (Extraordinary) Session, Devoted to Palestine, Held at Geneva from July 30th–August 18th, 1937, Tenth Meeting, <unispal.un.org/UNISPAL.NSF/0/FD05535118AEF0DE052565ED0065DDF7>.

116. ICJ, *Namibia (South–West Africa), supra* note 92, Separate Opinion Vice-President Ammoun, 69; very similar to this line of argument, as far as "A"-Mandates, especially Syria and Mesopotamia, are concerned: Corbett, 'What is the League of Nations', *supra* note 92, at 129–130; as far as "A"-Mandates are concerned: Leeper, 'International Law', *supra* note 46, at 1206; referring specifically to Palestine: Grief, 'Legal Rights', *supra* note 62, at 6. He, however, implausibly argues that sovereignty was vested only in the Jewish people; Wright, 'Sovereignty', *supra* note 56, at 696; his position is somewhat unclear; after having rejected the notion that sovereignty resided in the "mandated communities" he goes on to state that "communities under 'A' mandates doubtless approach very close to sovereignty"; Mansfield, *A History, supra* note 81, 183 ("A"-Mandates as "five new states"); Lewis, 'Mandated Territories', *supra* note 95, at 464; disagrees (he refers to the "A"-Mandates as "caricatures of independent states"); as does Alexander, 'Israel in Fieri', *supra* note 49, at 425. He bases his argument on the principles of the English concept of trusts. He, however, overlooks the fact that there is widespread agreement that the mandates system was not based on the English concept of trusts, but only included elements of it (see the discussion of this issue in note 54).

Regarding "A"-Mandates, described in Article 22(4) of the Covenant, such as Palestine, any other interpretation is untenable. After all, these peoples were already explicitly "provisionally" recognized as "independent nations" and their wishes were to be the "principal consideration" when choosing the mandatory.[117]

bb) Conclusions in Respect of Palestine

Based on the view that sovereignty in mandated territories rested in their inhabitants, even though its functions were exercised by the mandatory for the duration of the mandate, it must be assumed that this "suspension" automatically ended with termination of the mandate. Full sovereignty therefore rested with the people of Palestine, once the British role there had come to an end.[118]

This correct interpretation of the mandates system also invalidates the argument that the "Declaration of Independence" was justified on the basis that, once the British had left, sovereignty was "up for grabs"—a kind of *terra nullius* situation—and that Israel therefore had every right to assert its sovereignty.[119]

117. Hershey, *Essentials*, *supra* note 12, 187–191, esp.189, fn. 34; Hershey views mandated territories of the "A"-Class as comparable to the "most liberal" kind of "protectorate" and believes their status to be similar to that of Cuba. As far as Cuba (168, fn. 33) is concerned, Hershey claims that the US-Cuba treaty of 1903–04 imposes "legal limitations upon sovereignty", and that the US-Cuban relationship is therefore best viewed as a "Protectorate". It should be noted that Cuba was at that time already a member of the League of Nations (169, fn. 33 cont'd.). Nevertheless, according to Hershey, it is not a "fully sovereign state". His comparison allows the conclusion that Hershey believed the "A"-mandates to be states, although not yet "fully sovereign"; a view shared by Quigley, *The Statehood*, *supra* note 8, 26–31, 70–79.

118. The Foreign Office came to a similar conclusion. In a Minute dated May 14, 1948 (FO. 371/68664), addressed to the UK delegation at the UN in New York and prepared by the Legal Advisers at the FO, it was argued that once the Palestine Mandate had been terminated, sovereignty in Palestine "will probably lie in the people of Palestine"; quoted in Kattan, *From Coexistence*, *supra* note 66, at 189; It must also be pointed out that many insignia of an independent state were already in place in Palestine during the Mandate (flag, own citizenship laws, a system of criminal and civil laws, etc.); Kattan, *ibid*, 58–59, 137–138, 189; Grief, 'Legal Rights', *supra* note 62, at 7; he, however, argues that once the British Mandate ended, sovereignty rested only in the Jewish people regarding the whole of Palestine. He therefore views the creation of Israel not as a secession, but, implausibly, argues that the Arabs were "in illegal possession" of those parts of Palestine not under Israeli control. This is an extreme view which is wholly unconvincing and is not supported by the text of Israel's Declaration of Independence.

119. The ICJ would most likely reject any such argument; see *Western Sahara*, Advisory Opinion, 16/10/1975, I.C.J. Rep. 1975, 12, 38–39, at paras 79–81. When dealing with Spanish colonization of the Western Sahara in 1884, the ICJ declared: "In the view of the Court, therefore, a determination that Western Sahara was a *"terra nullius"* at the time of

It must therefore be concluded that at the moment Palestine achieved independence Israel seceded from it.[127]

The Israeli declaration of independence in itself was not contrary to international law. As the ICJ pointed out in respect of Kosovo, there is no rule in international law prohibiting an entity's unilateral declaration of independence.[128] This does, however, not apply to the decision of other states on whether to recognize this seceding entity as a state, a topic the ICJ explicitly did not address.[129]

d) Did Israel Fulfil the Criteria of Statehood in Mid-May 1948?

As will be shown Israel, in mid-May 1948, did not fulfil the criteria of statehood as accepted in customary international law. In fact, the new Jewish state did not meet any of the four necessary requirements.

aa) Permanent Population

Palestine, at the time, was in a state of civil war. At the time of the "Declaration of Independence" thousands of prospective Arab citizens of the new Jewish state were fleeing.[130] Because the boundaries were undetermined, it

now, with the termination of the Mandate, become established in fact, and maintain that the lawful inhabitants of Palestine are alone competent and entitled to set up an administration in Palestine for the discharge of all governmental functions without any external interference."; Cablegram from the Secretary-General of the League of Arab States to the Secretary-General of the United Nations, May 15, 1948, para. 10(e); UN Doc. S/745; also quoted in Quigley, *The Statehood*, *supra* note 8, at 105.

127. Crawford, *The Creation of States*, *supra* note 12, 427, 433; Quigley, *The Statehood*, *supra* note 8, at 103–104; to some extent this is also evidenced by the statements made by the Arab Higher Committee and by the Jewish Agency before the Security Council on May 15, 1948; the spokesman for the Arab Higher Committee referred to Palestine as an "independent nation" with a "rebellious minority", while the representative of the Jewish Agency explained that the State of Israel had been "established within Palestine"; both statements indicate that a secession was being attempted; UN Security Council, 292nd meeting, May 15, 1948, UN Doc. S/PV.292 (also quoted in: Quigley, *The Statehood*, *supra* note 8, at 103–104).
128. ICJ, *Kosovo*, *supra* note 9, at paras. 79–81.
129. *Ibid*, para. 51.
130. Naor, 'Israel's', *supra* note 80, 256; he states: "By the close of the war, 700000 Palestinian residents of Palestine (out of 1.1 million) had become refugees"; Tom Segev, 'Mohammed und Herr Cohen', 3 *Spiegel Geschichte* (2011) 82–85 at 84; Don Peretz, 'A Binational Approach to the Palestine Conflict', 33 *Law & Contemporary Problems* (1968) 32–43 at 33, fn. 8; Flapan, *The Birth*, *supra* note 79, at 81–118; Quigley, *The Statehood*, *supra* note 8, at 104; John Strawson, *Partitioning Palestine, Legal Fundamentalism in the Palestinian-Israeli Conflict* (Pluto Press: London, 2010) at 137; Shlaim, *Israel and Palestine*, *supra* note 52, at 28–29.

was unclear who would be a citizen of which entity at the end of the war. Therefore Israel could not claim to have a permanent population in mid-May 1948.

bb) Defined Territory

It is obvious that with war raging in Palestine and no agreed or obvious boundaries in existence, Israel did not possess a defined territory.[131] The war can also not be claimed to be a mere border dispute, but, as mentioned earlier, the Arab side denied the new state's right to exist. Due to its non-binding nature, Resolution 181 (II) did also not provide any firm borders for the new state as evidenced by the fact that both sides did not plan to adhere to it. Since the Jewish people formed a minority in Palestine, and the Arab population was dispersed right across Palestine, there was also no obvious "natural", or administrative[132] border Israel could lay claim to, a fact that distinguishes Israel's secession from many others.

cc) Effective Government

Although the Jewish Agency and the military groups supporting it were without doubt much more effective and much better organized than anything the Arab population had created and there were no all-Palestine institutions once the British had left,[133] the Jewish leadership in Palestine could not claim to provide an effective government in the sense of being able to enforce law and order in the prospective Jewish state.[134] As far as its prospective Arab citizens were concerned there was complete chaos. On the first day of independence,

131. Abba Eban, 'Israel: The Emergence of a Democracy', 29 *Foreign Affairs* (1950–51) 424–435 at 424 ("the year 1948 was characterized by a struggle for sheer physical survival ... these doubts were not resolved until the end of the year..."); Kattan, *From Coexistence, supra* note 66, at 235.

132. The existence of administrative borders in the case of Yugoslavia allowed the European Community to argue that the state of Yugoslavia was in the process of "dissolution" instead of having to assume that multiple sessions were taking place (Croatia, Slovenia, Bosnia, etc.); see: Opinion No. 1, Arbitration Commission, EC Conference on Yugoslavia, 29/11/2001.

133. Weiß, 'Die Entstehung', *supra* note 68, at 806.

134. Weiß, 'Die Entstehung', *supra* note 68, at 806; Quigley, *The Statehood, supra* note 8, at 104; Kattan, *From Coexistence, supra* note 66, 232, 234–235; he also points out there were still British troops in Palestine at the time of the Declaration of Independence, the last troops were evacuated on June 29, 1948; Strawson, *Partitioning, supra* note 130, at 132; he points out that the "Peoples Administration" set up by the Jewish Agency only voted by a small majority (6:4) in favour of the "Declaration of Independence". According to Strawson this was due "to the precarious military situation".

the Arab states—as expected—mounted an attack on the prospective new state. It must therefore be concluded that, although the Jewish authorities were the most effective institutions within Palestine, they could not claim to be able to provide an effective government.[135]

dd) Capacity to Enter into Relations with Other States

Based on the lack of effective government and the fact Israel was a part of Palestine in mid-May 1948, it was formally also not able to conduct its foreign affairs independently.

In summary therefore, Israel, in mid-May 1948, did not fulfil any of the "Montevideo" criteria.[136]

ee) Recognition *de Facto* or *de Jure*?[137]

The US statement is sometimes described as "only" being a *de facto* recognition, which is generally seen as a minus to the *de jure* recognition extended by the Soviet Union.[138] Regarding the State of Israel, the American statement actually is much closer to a *de jure* recognition, while being of a *de facto* nature as far as the provisional government is concerned. The State of Israel is mentioned in a matter-of fact-way as the "new State of Israel", as if there were no doubt regarding its existence and viability.[139] In a "proposed" telegram[140] from President Truman to Rabbi Wise, the President, in September 1948, explained:

> *In answer to your question, there is no question but that my action on May 14, 1948, constituted an unconditional recognition of the State of Israel. In addition, at that*

---

135. Naor, 'Israel's', *supra* note 80, at 243 ("in the eyes of the Yishuv's leadership, the war was perceived … as an existential struggle"). On May 19, 1948, the Israeli National Council was forced to declare a State of Emergency; Kattan, *From Coexistence*, *supra* note 66, 232, 234–235.
136. Naor, 'Israel's', *supra* note 80, 256; referring to the War of Independence as of May 1948 he declares: "in the course of the war, the transition from Yishuv to statehood began…"; Ottolenghi, 'Harry Truman's', *supra* note 5, at 973; he states that in May 1948 "the Yishuv … was moving towards statehood."
137. *De facto* recognition is seen as recognition of the current situation as to who is in effective control of a given territory, be that a particular government or an entity that claims to be a new state. Such recognition is provisional in nature and, more importantly, does not include legal sanction. *De jure* recognition, on the other hand, is full, including legal, recognition.
138. Kattan, *From Coexistence*, *supra* note 66, at 233; he, for example, takes this view.
139. This interpretation is supported by a statement the Acting US Representative Jessup made before the Security Council in December 1948; quoted by Jessup himself, *The Birth*, *supra* note 66, at 294–295.
140. According to the State Department, it is not clear whether the telegram was actually sent. Another version of the telegram was found in the "Clifford Papers", in which the word "established" had been substituted by "elected".

time, a provisional government had been established and de facto recognition was given the provisional government.[141]

The difference between *de facto* and *de jure* recognition is, however, not relevant in this case, as a *de facto* recognition of the State of Israel was, at the time, just as unjustified as a *de jure* recognition due to the non-fulfilment of any of the "Montevideo" criteria.[142]

e) Principle of Non-Recognition

The principle of non-recognition does not offer any further reasons for not recognizing Israel. The principle of non-recognition in cases of flagrant violations of self-determination had, by 1948, not yet become a part of customary international law.[143] The principle of non-recognition in the case of illegal use of force is also not applicable to the recognition of the State of Israel. The situation in Palestine was primarily one of civil war, not of outside military intervention. Whether it could be argued that the principle could or should be applied, as far as Israel's borders—based on the 1949 armistices, instead of Resolution 181 (II)—are concerned, is not relevant to the question of the recognition of Israel as this can be viewed as a "mere border dispute".

f) Premature Recognition

Both the American and the Soviet recognition were, however, premature.[144] This view was shared by the British government that declared that Israel did not "fulfil the criteria of an independent state".[145] The Israelis themselves describe the war between themselves and the Arabs as of May 15, 1948, as

141. *Proposed Telegram by President Truman to Rabbi Stephen S. Wise*; available at: FRUS, 1948, *supra* note 11, at 1432.
142. Lador-Lederer, 'Recognition', *supra* note 11, at 64; he argues that there is no "practical distinction" between *de facto* and *de jure* recognition but that the distinction was used as a diplomatic tool.
143. Crawford, *The Creation of States*, *supra* note 12, at 427 and 433; Kattan, *From Coexistence*, *supra* note 66, at 43; ICJ, *Kosovo*, *supra* note 9, at paras 79 and 82; the court pointed out that the right of self-determination had only "evolved" during "the second half of the twentieth century".
144. Crawford, *The Creation of States*, *supra* note 12, at 427; Kattan, *From Coexistence*, *supra* note 66, at 232–236.
145. See *supra* note 7; Kattan, *From Coexistence*, *supra* note 66, at 233–236; Miriam Haron, 'Britain and Israel, 1948–1950', 3 *Modern Judaism* (1983) 217–223 at 217; she points out that according to internal British documents the British Government still "had strong reservations about the viability of Israel" eight months after Israel's Declaration of Independence. The British minister in Tel Aviv arrived in May 1949 and reported that Israel was an "artificial creation" that only survived thanks to "American Jewry" (219–20).

is evidenced by the case of Somaliland, which declared its independence in 1991, and is widely seen as fulfilling the criteria of statehood at a time when there is no sort of effective government in Somalia. Nevertheless, Somaliland has not been recognized as an independent state by the international community.[158]

In recent times there have been exceptions where the *uti possidetis* principle was seen as secondary to the right of (external) self-determination in a non-colonial context.[159] That was, however, not yet the case in 1948,[160] and the exception's applicability to the situation in Palestine in 1948 seems doubtful.[161]

As Israel in mid-May 1948, however, did not fulfil any of the statehood criteria, this issue need not be further discussed. The recognition of Israel on

---

a "dissolution" of the state instead of as multiple secessions; Opinion No. 1, Arbitration Commission, EC Conference on Yugoslavia, 29/11/2001; see also Koskenniemi, 'National Self-Determination', *supra* note 154, at 256–257.

158. Craven, 'The Statehood', *supra* note 87, at 204; for further details, see Alison K. Eggers, 'When is a State a State? The Case for the Recognition of Somaliland', 30 *Boston College International & Comparative Law Review* (2007) 211–222.
159. ICJ, *Kosovo, supra* note 9, at para. 82; the ICJ did not decide whether there is such a "remedial right" of secession based on the right of self-determination (para. 83), but pointed out that this was a "subject on which radically different views were expressed by those taking part in the proceedings."; Collins, *supra* note 155, 148.
160. ICJ, *Kosovo, supra* note 9, at paras. 79, 82; the court pointed out that the right of self-determination had "evolved" only "in the second half of the twentieth century"; Dunsky, 'Israel', *supra* note 62, at 172; Kattan, *From Coexistence, supra* note 66, at 143; Strawson, *Partitioning, supra* note 130, at 88 and 108.
161. As Koskenniemi has pointed out, the GA's resolutions on Gibraltar and Mayotte in fact indicate that "the will of the population … may at least in a colonial context be overridden by the self-determination of a larger entity." (Koskenniemi, 'National Self-Determination', *supra* note 154, at 262–263). Transferred to the situation in Palestine, the view adopted by the GA would seem to suggest that the right of self-determination of Palestine's people—arising in a colonial context- might well have been judged to outweigh any Jewish right of self-determination there.

    Island of Mayotte: Despite a large majority of the island's inhabitants supporting French rule (in a 2009 referendum 95% of the population voted in favour of Mayotte becoming a French département), the GA has repeatedly "reaffirmed" the "Union of Comoros'" sovereignty over the island (see, for example, GA Resolution 37/65 (1982); GA Resolution 49/18 (1994); in 1976 a draft resolution of the Security Council, recognizing the "Union of Comoros'" sovereignty, received 11 affirmative votes, but was vetoed by France); for

    Gibraltar, see the 1964 "consensus" on Gibraltar adopted by the UN *Special Committee on Decolonization* (paras. 787–822, esp. 812), <legal.un.org/repertory/art73/english/rep_supp3_vol3-art73_e.pdf>; and GA Resolution 2070 (1965), passed in a 96:0:11 vote.

May 14 and May 17, 1948, was clearly premature,[162] so that there can be no doubt that the USA and the USSR violated international law.[163]

3. Conclusion

More than 64 years after Israel declared its independence, and the new state was recognized by the USA and the USSR, the State of Palestine was recognized as such by the General Assembly when it granted it the status of "non-member-state". This move was opposed by a number of states. Notably Israel argued that the State of Palestine did not fulfil the necessary criteria of statehood.

This article has argued that Israel, when it was recognized in May 1948 by the USA and the USSR, was in just such a position. Despite failing to meet any of the relevant criteria of statehood the super-powers immediately extended recognition of the new state.

It was shown that Palestine as a whole emerged into independence once the British had unilaterally terminated the Palestine mandate. It was then argued that Israel's immediate "Declaration of Independence" amounted to secession from Palestine. Based on an analysis of the rules in customary international law regarding state recognition it was explained that Israel, in May 1948, did not fulfil any of the relevant criteria of statehood, so that it must be concluded that the American and Soviet recognitions were premature and therefore inconsistent with international law.

More than sixty years later there can be no doubt that Israel has developed into a viable state. That surely offers some hope to the new State of Palestine.

162. Many of those who argue that US recognition of Israel was "plainly justified" also negate the existence of any legal rules on recognition (see, for example Brown, 'The Recognition of Israel', *supra* note 7, at 620–627); Lador-Lederer, 'Recognition', *supra* note 11, at 84; on the other hand argues that there is no reason to assume American recognition of Israel was premature, as the Declaration of Independence was issued "half a year after its [Israel's] establishment had been decided by the United Nations- but thirty years after the Balfour Declaration." This argument is not convincing. Even leaving aside the legal questions raised by Lador-Lederer's assertions relating to the UN and the Balfour Declaration, these "decisions" cannot obviate the necessity to establish whether an entity has fulfilled the criteria of statehood—criteria he himself supports, but which in the case of Israel he does not apply.

163. On the basic illegality of premature recognition as seen by the US Department of State, see: *Memorandum by the Legal Adviser (Gross) to the Under Secretary of State (Lovett), Recognition of Successor States in Palestine*, May 13, 1948, FRUS, 1948, *supra* note 11, 960–965 at 960.

The Container and the Septic Tank: Statism, Life, and the Geopolitics of Territoriality

Panu Minkkinen

Abstract: By way of a geopolitical analysis, the essay will suggest the necessity of a reinterpretation of state and territory that touches upon phenomena commonly perceived to be challenges brought about through globalization. Although globalization can be understood as a process that puts both the factual and conceptual boundaries of territory into question, perhaps those borders and boundaries were never as fixed and stable as traditional liberal theory would have us believe. Every boundary is an attempt to contain something that aspires to transgress, every container an exercise in confining an expansive vitalistic impulse: will to power.

Keywords: territoriality, state, globalization, geopolitics, Kjellén, Nietzsche, will to power

1. The Juridico-Political Assumptions

Otto Brunner's *Land and Lordship*[1] has, no doubt, already been sufficiently criticized to make it practically speaking obsolete, ranging from Brunner's own political escapades in the Third Reich and the Nazi reception of his claims to the sheer inaccuracy of his historical interpretations. Even so, the book has endured the damning evidence and remains a classic in the *opera omnia* of constitutional history.[2] What could explain such resilience?

Brunner's central thesis was that the legal history of his day—and this would be the first half of the 20th century—was so deeply rooted in the conceptual soil of the modern state that it was unable to account for the differences and nuances of other historical periods. He namely claimed that constitutional history had a tendency of presenting the historical development of

1. Otto Brunner, *Land and Lordship: Structures of Governance in Medieval Austria* (originally published 1939) (Howard Kaminsky and James Van Horn Melton trans., University of Pennsylvania Press, 1992).
2. The translators' introduction provides an excellent overview. See Brunner, *Land and Lordship*, *supra* note 1, at xiii–lxi.

the state as a gradual progression from designs that were 'not yet' the modern state—in a word, from 'society'—into its fully developed modern variant.

The evolutionary pairing of 'society' and 'state' allowed for the use of other binaries as well, such as 'private' and 'public', 'might' and 'right', 'illegal' and 'legal', and so on. All these binaries were allegedly inadequate for an accurate understanding of premodern constitutional phenomena.[3] But the binary vocabulary of the modern state was used despite its analytical shortcomings so that the findings could be better communicated to lawyers and law students in a professionally familiar environment. At the same time, historical research had to compromise its own ability to properly account for phenomena that did not conform to the modern template.

The topic of Brunner's research was medieval lordship and the various constitutionally relevant phenomena like the feud that were particular to it.[4] Brunner attempted to show how medieval rule could not be seen as an underdeveloped reflection of the modern state and its constitutional premises but as something quite unique and specific. So a medieval lord did not exercise his power in an environment of factual might that was 'not yet' framed by normative competences. But neither was he bound by any positive constitution in the modern sense of the word. Rather, the political world of the Middle Ages was governed by what Brunner called the 'Good Old Order', a sense of 'Right' that stood above both ruler and people and that would be defended if necessary:

> '... in the Middle Ages there is no secular power that exercised internal sovereignty in the sense of modern political theory. No jurisdiction could institute or administer positive law without being responsible to others—not merely God or conscience—regarding the justice of that law. Any individual affected by the actions and commands of a medieval lord or ruler could challenge their legitimacy. The ruler who acted unjustly, even in his capacity as judge, was always open to retribution.'[5]

In other words, the rule of the medieval lord was not framed by a state 'in the making', by a nascent idea of liberal democracy where the delimiting functions of normative competence were still underdeveloped. It was a

3. Brunner's critique is similar to how one might argue against Weber's account of what he calls 'Anglo-Saxon law' or 'law as craft'. By methodologically prioritizing the formal rationality that was specific to continental civil law, Weber's sociology 'colonizes' the common law and is unable to understand its unique features. See Max Weber, *Economy and Society: An Outline of Interpretive Sociology Vol 1 & 2* (Ephraim Fischoff et al. trans., University of California Press, 1978) at 785–88.
4. On the feud and Brunner's contribution, see e.g. Jeppe Büchert Netterstrøm and Bjørn Poulsen (eds), *Feud in Medieval and Early Modern Europe* (Aarhus University Press, 2007).
5. Brunner, *Land and Lordship*, *supra* note 1, at 120.

completely different type of order where each social actor, the ruler, the cleric, the serf, the landless peasant, all had rights that were as original as the other's. Hence no sovereign hierarchy, hence nothing state-like in any modern sense.

But why, then, this short prelude about the controversies of constitutional history? If the political applications of Brunner's allegedly 'German mentality' of Right have already shown their true sinister colours, and if even the accuracy of his historical description has been put into question, what is left? Surely not another claim about a return to the dark ages?

Perhaps there is still a lesson to be learnt here, a lesson that is neither historical nor 'epochal' but that, for want of a better word, one could call 'methodological'. It should be fairly easy to note how Brunner's general claim—that we, the moderns, are at pains to see into the past beyond certain historical ruptures—echoes of a certain Foucaultian position. Indeed, one can detect similarities in the conceptual history that Brunner and others like Reinhart Koselleck swore by,[6] and the French *Annales* School that Foucault's name is, rightly or wrongly, often associated with.[7]

But 'methodologically' speaking the historical problem that these schools of thought tried to address can be seen as a two-way street. If it was impossible to understand the premodern with the vocabulary of the modern—this would be Brunner's claim about Medieval lordship—then it would be equally impossible to understand our contemporary late modernity with the vocabulary of an earlier modernity that has already past us by. In many ways, this is why the king had to be beheaded,[8] why Foucault insisted that a juridico-political framework—a modern vocabulary—had left us quite helpless before the disciplinary and governmental technologies of the contemporary normalizing society. It is this 'methodological' idea, indebted to Brunner just as much as it is to Foucault, that will first be developed here.

In *Globalization and Legal Theory*, William Twining described the recent global challenges as a legal pluralism that did not fit comfortably with the traditional ways in which we understood law. Pluralism allegedly expressed itself in two ways. It could firstly be understood as the overlap of multiple legal orders in a single jurisdiction as in, for example, the application of both

6. See e.g. Reinhart Koselleck, *The Practice of Conceptual History: Timing History, Spacing Concepts* (Todd Presner et al. trans., Stanford University Press, 2002).
7. On Foucault and history, see e.g. Paul Veyne, 'Foucault revolutionizes history', in Arnold I. Davidson (ed.), *Foucault and His Interlocutors* (University of Chicago Press, 1978) 146–182. On the *Annales* School, see e.g. Michael Harsgor, 'Total History: the Annales School', 13 *Journal of Contemporary History* (1978) 1–13. On the two schools, see Irmline Veit-Brause, 'A Note on *Begriffsgeschichte*', 20 *History and Theory* (1981) 61–67.
8. Michel Foucault, *The History of Sexuality. Volume I: An Introduction* (originally published 1976) (Robert Hurley trans., Vintage Books: New York, NY, 1990) at 88–89.

religious and secular law in a single case or the co-existence of domestic and international law within the same geographical space. But a more radical interpretation of legal pluralism would include the political critique of what Twining called 'statism' or 'state centralism', that is, 'the idea that the state has a monopoly of lawful power within its own territory'.[9]

Twining's take on pluralism reveals how the new global challenges relate to space. Traditionally legal rule is thought to be confined to an area, and the challenge of globalization is essentially a dissolution of established and acknowledged borders, of the limits that both constitute the legitimate power of the state and contain it within its competence. Indeed, Anthony Giddens once famously noted that the nation-state is the 'pre-eminent power-container of the modern era.'[10] Or as Wendy Brown puts it in a much more eloquent and pertinent fashion:

> 'Containment within an increasingly boundaryless world is one kind of psychic longing animating the desire for walls; the fantasy of impermeability—perhaps even impenetrability—complements it. Sovereign power carries the fantasy of an absolute and enforceable distinction between inside and outside.'[11]

The uncontained power that comes with globalization turns out to be next to impossible to regulate because it crosses both factual and conceptual borders with such ease and so defies the socio-spatial rationality of the law.[12]

So globalization is not only a political arena on which hegemonic and counter-hegemonic strategies are played out,[13] but also the contrast against which the socio-spatial assumptions of statism—and by implication the whole juridico-political paradigm more generally—can be tested. As a legal phenomenon, the state is essentially territorially constituted. In Michael Mann's words:

> 'Only the state is inherently centralized over a delimited territory over which it has authoritative power. Unlike economic, ideological or military groups in civil

9. William Twining, *Globalization and Legal Theory* (Cambridge University Press, 2000) at 84. For a new take along these lines, see Hans Lindahl, *Fault Lines of Globalization: Legal Order and the Politics of A-Legality* (Oxford University Press, 2013).
10. Anthony Giddens, *The Nation-State and Violence: Volume Two of A Contemporary Critique of Historical Materialism* (University of California Press, 1987) at 120. See also Peter J. Taylor, 'The State as Container: Territoriality in the Modern World-System', 18 *Progress in Human Geography* (1994) 151–62.
11. Wendy Brown, 'Desiring walls', in Wendy Brown, *Walled States, Waning Sovereignty* (Zone: New York, NY, 2010) 107–33 at 119.
12. See also Gavin W. Anderson, *Constitutional Rights After Globalization* (Hart: Oxford, 2005). Anderson's development of the theme of spatiality is surprisingly weak.
13. See e.g. Boaventura de Sousa Santos, *Toward a New Legal Common Sense: Law, Globalization, and Emancipation* (Butterworths: London & Edinburgh, 2002) at 163–311.

society, the state elite's resources radiate authoritatively outwards from a centre but stop at defined territorial boundaries. The state is, indeed, a place—both a central place and a unified territorial reach.'[14]

But although social scientists have devoted much attention to the fallacy that John Agnew famously called the 'territorial trap',[15] in law much less work has recently been done on the concept of territory itself. If the territorial state functions as the spatial container of power as most liberal accounts continue to assume, then how enclosed a space are we actually dealing with? If globalization implies the dissolution of borders and limits that once demarcated a global surface into legally containable entities, then how impermeable were those borders to begin with? In short, what is territory? What are its borders? How should we understand the relationships between state, territory, and law?

What will follow will be based on three rather simple assumptions and a claim that I will try to substantiate with some admittedly esoteric readings, perhaps the sort of 'local idiosyncrasy'[16] that only this journal could host.

I will firstly assume that the statism on which public international law and constitutional theory (among others) are founded is a paradigmatic example of the type of modern juridico-political discourse that Foucault had in mind. It frames the state with a hierarchy of legally defined competences that have been established by a sovereign lawgiver either directly through legislation or by way of delegation. Further, its conceptual premise is a set of binary oppositions similar to the ones that Brunner identified in relation to constitutional history without which modern legal discourse would be rather meaningless: state and society, public and private, the factual and the normative, and so on.

Secondly, there is undoubtedly at least a sense that 'reality', whatever it may be, has run off and escaped our conceptual grasp of the world. The old juridical vocabulary of modernity is, if not obsolete, then at least inadequate. Often we use the rather tired and condensed metaphors of 'globalism' and 'globalization' to depict this new reality. And the terms are used either as possibly vain attempts to identify remnants of the juridico-political with which

14. Michael Mann, 'The Autonomous Power of the State: Its Origins, Mechanisms and Results', 25 *European Journal of Sociology* (1984) 185–213 at 198.

15. John Agnew, 'The Territorial Trap: The Geographical Assumptions of International Relations Theory', 1 *Review of International Political Economy* (1994) 53–80. See also Simon Reid-Henry, 'The Territorial Trap Fifteen Years on', 15 *Geopolitics* (2010) 752–56, and the articles that follow in this special issue.

16. Martti Koskenniemi, 'The Case for Comparative International Law', 20 *Finnish Yearbook of International Law* (2009) 1–8 at 8.

we could still recapture and harness something in our new political reality,[17] or as a celebration of the loss of control and the consequent possibility of realizing something completely new in the ruins.[18]

Thirdly, globalization implies the gradual dissolution of the borders and limits that formerly structured a legally constituted world. The new fuzziness of these limits affects the conceptual arsenal of law when, for example, the distinction between public and private, between the powers of the nation state and a globalized economy, have been lost in mutual interdependency. But globalization is also a challenge to the territorial premises of the state and law. Statism as a juridico-political discourse traditionally defined the public exercise of power through the socio-spatial characteristics of territory. The state ruled in a sovereign way over individuals within the bounds of its territory, and within those borders its rule was also protected from outside interference. But in a globalized world these territorial premises seem as hopelessly outdated as the attempts of public international law to temper abuses of power with the traditional language of human rights and state responsibilities. If it has become conceptually difficult to tell the states' public exercise of power apart from other more fluid expressions of power—WTO law comes to mind[19]—then in an analogous way the exercise of legal power is no longer territorially founded and bound in the same way as it once perhaps was.[20]

Following these three admittedly simplified assumptions—that statism is essentially a juridico-political discourse, that a globalized political reality is a challenge to the explanatory potential of the juridico-political, and that the challenge involves the gradual dissolution of borders and limits, both conceptual and territorial—this essay will make the following claim that I hope to be able to at least provisionally substantiate. The assumptions above imply a historical change, that we have gone through a gradual shift from a juridico-political world that was constituted with borders and territories into a globalized world of fluid governance that we are at pains to account for with the language of law, state and territory.

---

17. This would basically cover all attempts at the juridical (re)empowerment of fluid governance. For a good discussion, see Peter Fitzpatrick, '"The New Constitutionalism": Globalism and the Constitution(s) of Nations', 10 *Law, Democracy and Development: Journal of the Faculty of Law at the University of the Western Cape* (2006) 1–20, and the literature cited therein.
18. Primarily I'm referring to the doomsday polyphony that followed the publication of Michael Hardt and Antonio Negri, *Empire* (Harvard University Press, 2000).
19. See e.g. Andrew Lang, *World Trade Law After Neoliberalism: Re-imagining the Global Economic Order* (Oxford University Press, 2011).
20. See e.g. Neil Brenner, 'Beyond State-Centrism? Space, Territoriality, and Geographical Scale in Globalization Studies', 28 *Theory and Society* (1999) 39–78.

But moreover, what if our assumptions about territoriality were confused to begin with? What if—and this is essentially a Foucaultian conditional—we were able to constitute power with a juridico-political rationality even though the operational traces of its technologies should have always suggested something rather different? Perhaps that rationality was never even intended to *explain* territorial and statist phenomena but, rather, to merely reinforce the normative straps of its legal object. So what would a territory released from its juridico-political straight-jacket look like?

In a response to geographers who queried about his 'profuse use of spatial metaphors', Foucault argued that:

> '*Territory* is no doubt a geographical notion, but it's first of all a juridico-political one: the area controlled by a certain kind of power ... can you be sure that I am borrowing these terms from geography rather than from exactly where geography itself found them?'[21]

Foucault's response implies a difference between two spatial notions, namely between geographical territory and juridical territory. But even though he may here be criticizing geographers for their unacknowledged debt to the juridical, it could also suggest a possible common source for the two. So territory understood neither geographically nor juridically but as something that animates both.[22]

Perhaps such a common source could be a certain Nietzschean idea of geopolitical territory.

2. The Three-Element Doctrine

I would like to begin addressing the juridico-political with an iconic quote:

> 'In order to avoid legal fictions and to recognize the natural existence of the state that precedes all jurisprudence, it seems obvious to seek the objective essence of the state in one of its constituting elements that seemingly exists in reality. These elements are land [*Land*], nation [*Volk*] and sovereignty [*Herrscher*].'[23]

---

21. Michel Foucault, 'Questions on Geography', in Jeremy W. Crampton and Stuart Elden (eds), *Space, Knowledge and Power: Foucault and Geography* (Colin Gordon trans., Ashgate: Aldershot, 2007) 173–82 at 176–77.
22. Henri Lefebvre ties the two up with violence: 'every state is born of violence, and ... state power endures only by virtue of violence directed towards a space.... A founding violence, and continuous creation by violent means (by fire and blood, in Bismarck's phrase)—such are the hallmarks of the state'. Henri Lefebvre, *The Production of Space* (Basil Blackwell: Oxford, 1991) at 280.
23. Georg Jellinek, *Allgemeine Staatslehre* (originally published 1900) (3rd edn, Julius Springer: Berlin, 1919) at 144. All translations from the German are mine. Due to the

This is the truncated version of Georg Jellinek's so-called 'three-element doctrine' (*Drei-Elemente-Lehre*) that served as the starting-point for definitions of the state especially in constitutional theory over the course of the 20th century.[24] Although the doctrine itself was soon questioned from a number of different perspectives,[25] it remained a point of reference for much of the discussion that followed. So what can one infer even from this truncated version of the doctrine?

For one thing, setting up 'legal fictions' against 'reality' is Jellinek's attempt to criticize some of the shortcomings of a particular type of constructivist or early-positivistic public law represented in the work of, for example, Carl Friedrich von Gerber.[26] Moreover, the elements don't appear to be in a random order. Jellinek seems to progress from the seemingly most tangible element to the more abstract ones. Because a nation will always be more than a random collection of physical beings, and because state power will always be exercised in a very particular way, land without further qualifications would seem as the appropriate starting point.[27] Jellinek's constitutional theory is also 'two-sided' in a way that complements a normativist perspective with a factual one, and so it couples the *de jure* with the *de facto*:

> 'The state is firstly a social structure, and furthermore a legal institution. Accordingly the doctrine of state [PM: *Staatslehre*, i.e. constitutional theory] is divided

two-sidedness of Jellinek's doctrine, these three factual elements will have their juridical counterparts in territory, a constituted nation, and sovereign state power.

24. Taking into account Jellinek's prominence in constitutional theory, surprisingly little of his work has been translated into English. See Georg Jellinek, *The Declaration of the Rights of Man and of Citizens: A Contribution to Modern Constitutional History* (H. Holt & Co.: New York, NY, 1901) and Georg Jellinek, *The Rights of Minorities* (A. M. Baty and Thomas Baty trans., P. S. King & Son: London, 1912). See also Stanley L. Paulson and Martin Schulte (eds), *Georg Jellinek—Beiträge zu Leben und Werk* (Mohr Siebeck: Tübingen, 2000); Martti Koskenniemi, *The Gentle Civilizer of Nations: The Rise and Fall of International Law 1870–1960* (Cambridge University Press, 2001) at 198–208, and Martin Loughlin, *Foundations of Public Law* (Oxford University Press, 2010) at 216–221.
25. On e.g. recognition as a prerequisite of statehood, see James Crawford, *The Creation of States in International Law* (2nd edn, Clarendon Press: Oxford, 2006) at 12–27, and Stefan Talmon, 'The Constitutive versus the Declaratory Doctrine of Recognition: *Tertium non Datur*?', 75 *British Year Book of International Law* (2004) 101–81.
26. On Jellinek's intellectual environment, see e.g. Duncan Kelly, 'Revisiting the Rights of Man: Georg Jellinek on Rights and the State', 22 *Law and History Review* (2004) 493–530.
27. Jellinek's contemporary and friend Max Weber also noted that a formal characteristic of the state was an administrative and legal order that 'claims binding authority, not only over the members of the state, the citizens … but also to a very large extent over all action taking place *in the area of its jurisdiction.*' Weber, *Economy and Society*, *supra* note 3, at 56 [PM: my emphasis].

> into the sociological doctrine of state [*soziale Staatslehre*] and the juridical doctrine of state [*Staatsrechtslehre*].'[28]

In other words, Jellinek combines a sociological perspective with a legal one.[29] This methodological dualism—for a neo-Kantian 'socio' and 'legal' separately without the unholy 'socio-legal' fusion—also requires that each of the three elements has to be analyzed from two different perspectives, both *de facto* and *de jure*. In relation to land, Jellinek outlines its factual and sociological dimensions through an analysis of the pre-capitalist patrimonial state.[30] The patrimonial lord rules over his land as property through practices that are closer to private law than to public law. Jellinek calls this a 'pre-statist' (*vorstaatlich*) order, and therein lies its weakness:

> 'It [PM: the patrimonial theory] stands or falls on the recognition of a pre-statist order of property. It demonstrates clearly the arbitrariness that can follow from the position of such a putative legal order that without further explanation treats the territorial element of the state as the main thing and people as incidental.'[31]

The factual or sociological dimension of the state's relationship to land is, then, analogous to property, as something that one rules over as owner. Resorting to patrimonialism is, of course, exactly the sort of theoretical construction that Brunner criticized.[32] A 'pre-statist' order is quite clearly something that is 'not yet statist', a societal projection that brings with it all the binary fallacies typical of the juridico-political template that Brunner was opposed to: a society that is 'not yet' a state, private ownership that is 'not yet' under public rule, dominion that is 'not yet' *imperium*, factual power that is 'not yet' normatively contained, and so on.

28. Jellinek, *Allgemeine Staatslehre*, *supra* note 23, at 11. I am here deliberately trying to avoid a juridical definition of 'constitutional theory' although Jellinek's German vocabulary does not translate easily. See however Martin Loughlin, 'In Defence of *Staatslehre*', 48 *Der Staat* (2009) 1–28.
29. 'Sociological' is here shorthand for all non-normativist human and social sciences. For Kelsen its prerequisite would be a nation that is not constituted by law: 'The assertion that the State is not merely a juristic but a sociological entity, a social reality existing independently of its legal order, can be substantiated only by showing that the individuals belonging to the same State form a unity and that this unity is not constituted by the legal order but by an element which has nothing to do with law. However, such an element constituting the "one in the many" cannot be found'. Hans Kelsen, *General Theory of Law and State* (originally published 1945) (Anders Wedberg trans., Harvard University Press, 1949) at 183.
30. On the patrimonial state, see e.g. Weber, *Economy and Society*, *supra* note 3, at 1013–15.
31. Jellinek, *Allgemeine Staatslehre*, *supra* note 23, at 201.
32. See Brunner, *Land and Lordship*, *supra* note 1, at 124–26.

Later Jellinek dedicates separate chapters to the legal characteristics of each of the three elements. And once again, apparently making his way from the more concrete to the more abstract, he begins with land. The physicality of the land in which the bond of the body politic is rooted delineates the socio-spatial dimension of the state's rule. The legal definition of land in this sense is territory (*Gebiet*) which expresses its juridical aspect in two ways. Firstly, in a negative sense, only the state is permitted to exercise authority within the confines of its territory, but also secondly, in a positive sense, everyone within the state's territory is subjected to its authority.[33]

Territoriality is, Jellinek claims, a necessary prerequisite of the state's personhood, of its existence as a legal subject. It follows already logically from the fact that the members of a state are those who have settled within its territory, and through territoriality the state itself enables the settledness that makes membership possible to begin with. But social reality requires it as well:

> 'The development of a state and all activities of the developing state can only take place on the basis of a spatial unfolding. While corporations are otherwise spaceless, the existence of a state requires a spatial extension. Only this spatial extension of its authority and the exclusiveness that it implies give it the possibility of fulfilling its purposes completely.'[34]

In other words, Jellinek associates territoriality as the 'spatial extension' of the state to its purposiveness, to the state's ability, teleological purpose, and even moral duty to bring about political ends by appropriating a given physical space. The appropriation of a physical space as territory individualizes the state as a legal person. The spatial extension of the state establishes its territorial integrity, the negative function of its personhood that applies to international law:

> 'What brings about the requirement to respect a state's territory is that it is a state, not that it has something that belongs to it. Accordingly, in international law a territorial violation is not an infringement against ownership but a violation against the very personhood of the attacked state.'[35]

In its positive sense, territoriality is also the principle behind the authority of the state over the individuals, be they citizen or aliens, that find themselves within its borders. Jellinek goes to great lengths to show how the state's public rule over its territory should not be confused with private land ownership.

33. Jellinek, *Allgemeine Staatslehre*, *supra* note 23, at 394. One can think of the negative and positive senses of territoriality as spatial expressions of internal and external sovereignty.
34. Jellinek, *Allgemeine Staatslehre*, *supra* note 23, at 395–96.
35. *Ibid*, at 397–98.

To rule over territory in this public sense is *imperium*, not dominion, and the former is always a power to command individuals. Land as real property can only be the object of *imperium* in an intermediate way as effects that are produced by individuals under state rule. In other words, territorial rule is not based on a property right but on the authority of the state:

> 'The constitutional 'right to territory' is, then, nothing but a reflex of the rule by personhood [*Personenherrschaft*]. It is a reflex right, not a right in the subjective sense.'[36]

3. The Geopolitical Life of the State

Territory is, then, an extension of the 'imperial' power and the authority that the state exerts as a 'person'. The state does not rule over land like the patrimonial landowner but, rather, exercises its authority over individuals within the bounds of a given territory in spite of the ownership arrangements that may regulate the relationships between, say, lord, vassal and landless peasant. Although these juridico-political assumptions of territoriality have been tested and criticized often enough by, for example, political geographers,[37] legal scholars have been less than keen to let go of their juridical categories even if developments in the 'real world' would clearly seem to suggest it. Even Jellinek's attempt to couple the constructivist and positivistic starting-points of public law with a dash of sociological 'reality' was soon criticized by the positivists themselves.[38]

But some of the counterarguments have appeared in political theory and, intermediately, in certain variations of constitutional theory, as well. And Rudolf Kjellén, an early 20th century political theorist from Sweden, can at least partly take the credit. Kjellén was Professor of Political Sciences at the universities of Gothenburg and Uppsala and a Bismarckian conservative politician often accused of having inspired national socialist ideologies both in Germany and elsewhere. Kjellén's political legacy is, however, more

36. *Ibid*, at 401. A reflex right is not a subjective right in the proper sense but the reflexion of an obligation or other circumstances. See e.g. Hans Kelsen, *Pure Theory of Law* (originally published 1960) (Max Knight trans., University of California Press, 1967) at 128–29.
37. For a general introduction, see e.g. Kevin R. Cox, *Political Geography: Territory, State and Society* (Blackwell: Oxford & Malden, MA, 2002).
38. On Kelsen's critique of Jellinek's 'methodological dualism', see e.g. Stanley L. Paulson, 'Hans Kelsen's Earliest Legal Theory: Critical Constructivism', 59 *The Modern Law Review* (1996) 797–812.

complex than that. But perhaps he should be best known for coining the word 'geopolitics'.[39]

In terms of constitutionalism, Kjellén's input can, perhaps, best be described as an organic state theory insofar as he considers states to be 'sentient and rational beings.'[40] Kjellén constructs his overall theory around a perspective on territoriality that he describes as 'geopolitical'. Here geopolitics is defined as the synthesis of an 'old' juridical theory mainly represented by Jellinek and a 'new' geography that, for Kjellén, is inspired by the work of the German political geographer Friedrich Ratzel.[41] The main flaw of the juridical theory, with or without its two-sided realism, is allegedly its static nature and its inability to explain states in a genuinely historical way. And Ratzel's political geography, at least so Kjellén claims, provides the theory with the required historical dynamism:

> 'Geopolitics is the doctrine of the state as a geographical organism or a spatial phenomenon: in other words, the state as land, territory, area or, more precisely, as *Reich*.'[42]

Reich, *imperium*, a new dynamic of territoriality: this is what Kjéllen's geopolitics seemingly contributes to our understanding of the state. But what would this imply in practice? Within the overall organic theory, territory as land that is ruled over by the *imperium* of the state takes on a central meaning:

> 'One word tells us everything: the *Reich* is the *body* of the state. The *Reich* is not property like the peasant's farm; it belongs to the personhood of the state. It is the state itself.'[43]

---

39. Kjellén's major work is Rudolf Kjellén, *Staten som Lifsform* (Hugo Geber: Stockholm, 1916) where the term 'geopolitics' was first introduced. In the absence of an English translation I have used the German edition, Rudolf Kjellén, *Der Staat als Lebensform* (Margarete Langfeldt trans., 2nd edn, S. Hirzel: Leipzig, 1917). All translations from the German are mine. See also Ola Tunander, 'Swedish-German Geopolitics for a New Century: Rudolf Kjellén's "The State as a Living Organism"', 27 *Review of International Studies* (2001) 451–63; Ola Tunander, 'Swedish Geopolitics: From Rudolf Kjellén to a Swedish "Dual State"', 10 *Geopolitics* (2005) 546–66, and Ola Tunander, 'Geopolitics of the North: Geopolitik of the Weak', 43 *Cooperation and Conflict* (2008) 164–84.
40. Kjellén, *Der Staat als Lebensform*, *supra* note 39, at 30. The classic formulation of this theory is Herbert Spencer's 'organic analogy'. See Herbert Spencer, 'The Social Organism' (originally published 1860), in Herbert Spencer, *Essays: Scientific, Political and Speculative* (Williams and Norgate: London & Edinburgh, 1891) 265– 307.
41. On Ratzel's dubious heritage, see e.g. John Agnew, *Geopolitics: Re-Visioning World Politics* (Routledge: Abingdon, 2003) at 96– 99.
42. Kjellén, *Der Staat als Lebensform*, *supra* note 39, at 46, 32 and 43.
43. *Ibid*, at 57. The word *Reich* is, of course, notoriously difficult to translate with its troubling political implications.

Although Kjellén may well be underestimating the peasant's existential attachment to the land that he toils over, territory as *Reich* accounts for the body of a 'sentient and rational being'. In other words, Kjellén does not consider the state as an abstract juridical fiction as the 'old' theory would claim, but neither is it the more or less static object of a social science which would be the headway made in Jellinek's socio-legal dualism. For Kjellén, the state-person is a politically dynamic actor, and his main criticism concerns the inability of the juridico-political paradigm, singularly legal or dually socio-legal, to account for this political dynamism. In our more contemporary parlance, what Kjellén finds lacking in the 'old' theory is its inability to account for the factual power exercised by the state.

Territory is *Reich*, and *Reich* is body. Body, for its part, implies form and boundaries. Because the existence of a state is essentially a question of political power relations, natural borders cannot be decisive. The development of state power and the stability of the state system require, once again, dynamic rather than static borders.[44] Land as a natural phenomenon with its borders and limits provides a framework and the raw material, but for Kjellén it is up to the state to 'organize' it into its territorial *Reich*.[45] In other words, the territorial space of the state including its borders is not a static given but a dynamic socio-spatial body that is constantly reorganizing itself, even when the dimensions of the body remain physically the same at a given moment. On rare occasions we may actually see a state expand beyond its existing borders as it grows, but for the most part it merely maintains its territory holding out against what it perceives to be external threats. Normally our view about state territory and borders is like a cartographic snapshot of how things are at a single historical moment. But we can better understand Kjellén's analogy of how states 'live' like organisms if we look at a longer historical sequence in fast-forward and see how those 'bodies' change over time in size and dimension.

If the state is considered as something that is experienced rather than merely theorized, Kjellén identifies an internal and an external dimension that can only together explain the Janus-faced complexity that the traditional juridical theory has problems with. We can focus on the state's internal constituents, and consequently we will primarily associate the state with its legal personhood. As a legal person, the state will be experienced as both coercion and rights, as will and force. Being the Swede he is, Kjellén would also include in these internal constituents the numerous tasks that the state has committed itself to in order to promote social welfare. So the aim of Kjellén's theory would be to capitalize on the scientific advances that Jellinek's dualism

44. *Ibid*, at 77–78.
45. *Ibid*, at 79.

Nietzsche's Zarathustra equates life with will to power which the 'secret life' later confirms in a dialogue: 'Only where life is, is there also will; but not will to life, instead—thus I teach you—will to power!'[55]

In *Beyond Good and Evil*, Nietzsche then further specifies that to refrain from violence as a 'fundamental principle of society' is social decay because it negates life. Life is 'a process of appropriating, injuring, overpowering the alien and the weaker, oppressing, being harsh, imposing your own form, incorporating, and at least, the very least, exploiting …'.[56]

In Kjellén's geopolitical terms, this would mean that territory can never be completely confined within defined borders. At any frozen moment in time, a state may well be localized at the territory that it occupies there and then. But the will to power embedded in Kjellén's notion of 'life' implies that historically a state will always be looking out for opportunities to improve its conditions of existence. In terms of territorial borders, such improvements may include the possibility of expansion, of appropriating new resources, or of merely redefining geopolitical balances.

But perhaps will to power expresses itself in a 'defensive' way, as well. Because the whole terrestrial surface is covered with states bordering each other, coexistence is always caught in a tension where the wills of individual states collide. While one state may be expansively looking for opportunities to grow, its neighbour may be merely securing what it already has. And so the latter territorially established state is under the threat of annihilation by its neighbour, a potential 'death' that it must remain prepared for.[57]

But the most telling traces of Nietzsche's theory of the state can be found in *Twilight of the Idols* where Nietzsche once again criticizes liberalism's

---

See e.g. David T. Murphy, *The Heroic Earth: Geopolitical Thought in Weimar Germany, 1918–1933* (Kent State University Press: Kent, OH, 1997).

55. Friedrich Nietzsche, *Thus Spoke Zarathustra: A Book for All and None* (originally published 1883–85) (Adrian Del Caro trans., Cambridge University Press, 2006) at 90 ('On Self-Overcoming'). This Nietzschean take on life can also be traced in Deleuze's vitalism. See John Marks, *Gilles Deleuze: Vitalism and Multiplicity* (Pluto Press: London, 1998).
56. Friedrich Nietzsche, *Beyond Good and Evil: Prelude to a Philosophy of the Future* (originally published 1886) (Judith Norman trans., Cambridge University Press, 2002) at 153 (§ 259).
57. Elsewhere Nietzsche associates the life that appropriates the weaker with an instinct for growth and for an accumulation of force. Growth is a feeling of domination, of a will to assimilate the new to the old in an act of simplification that disregards or subsumes minor inconsistencies 'in its own interest'. See Friedrich Nietzsche, 'The Anti-Christ: A Curse on Christianity' (originally published 1898), in Friedrich Nietzsche, *The Anti-Christ, Ecce Homo, Twilight of the Idols, and Other Writings* (Judith Norman trans., Cambridge University Press, 2005) 1–67 at 6 (§ 6), and Nietzsche, *Beyond Good and Evil, supra* note 56, at 121–22 (§ 230).

self-contented idea of its own virtuous 'considerate morality'. For Nietzsche, the loss of hostile instincts represents a loss of vitality which is a sign of decline:

> 'Strong ages, *noble* cultures see pity, 'neighbour love', and the lack of self and self-feeling as something contemptible. Ages should be measured by their *positive forces* ... we moderns with our anxious self-solicitude and our neighbour love, with our virtues of work, modesty, lawfulness, and science—accumulating, economic, machine-like—we are a *weak* age.'[58]

The prerequisite of a strong age should be what Nietzsche calls the 'pathos of distance', that is, the conscious effort to stand out and to resist the movement towards equality that liberal theories represent. These undermine will to power by leveling differences in the name of morality. But Nietzsche puts a curious twist into his criticism. For even though equality may in itself represent a decadent form of existence under a state, the struggle for such a liberal institution does not:

> 'As long as they are still being fought for, these same institutions have entirely different effects and are actually powerful promoters of freedom. On closer inspection, it is the war that produces these effects, the war *for* liberal institutions which, being a war, keeps *illiberal* institutions in place.'[59]

So perhaps in the end Nietzsche is not the unequivocal critic of liberalism that he is often made out to be. It is more complicated than that. If the individual principles of a liberal state—human rights, equality, the rule of law, and so on—are still being fought for, the state is, in a manner of speaking, 'alive'. The struggle inherent in Nietzsche's idea of a 'war *for* liberal institutions' resembles the way in which Carl Schmitt would understand the political nature of a constitution.[60] 'Fighting for' the principles and institutions of a liberal constitution implies that they are in danger or under threat. Indeed, the mere fact that they have been constitutionally entrenched suggests some form of threat, for otherwise no act of constituting them would have been necessary. This acknowledged danger or threat that necessitates the protection of liberal principles or institutions by constituting them is what Schmitt means by enmity, a hostile 'opponent' that is also audible in Nietzsche's 'pathos of

58. Friedrich Nietzsche, 'Twilight of the Idols, or How to Philosophize with a Hammer' (originally published 1889), in Friedrich Nietzsche, *The Anti-Christ, Ecce Homo, Twilight of the Idols, and Other Writings* (Judith Norman trans., Cambridge University Press, 2005) 153–229 at 212.
59. Nietzsche, 'Twilight of the Idols', *supra* note 58, at 213.
60. On a Schmittian political constitutional theory, see Panu Minkkinen, 'Political Constitutionalism versus Political Constitutional Theory: Law, Power and Politics', 11 *International Journal of Constitutional Law* (2013) 585–610.

distance'. So long as the enmity continues to challenge constituted principles and institutions—and with Schmitt it never ceases to do so—the constitution remains alive and animated with will to power. Nietzsche continues:

> 'For there to be institutions, there needs to be a type of will, instinct, imperative that is anti-liberal to the point of malice: the will to tradition, to authority, to a responsibility that spans the centuries, to *solidarity* in the chain that links the generations, forward and backwards *ad infinitum*.'[61]

In other words, Nietzsche may not be critical of liberal states *per se*. But constituted principles and institutions, liberal, conservative, leftist or otherwise, that have been removed from the reach of political struggles and the will to power that animates them represent stagnation and the absence of life. And this is what political liberalism tends to do with the principles that it endorses: it universalizes them, human rights being the most obvious example.

In a similar way, a closed and contained territory, that is, the traditional territorial premise of the juridico-political paradigm, is like a septic tank that manages the struggles that are characteristic of politics until they become domesticated, stagnant and dead. In Foucaultian terms, a constitutionally fixed state area represents governmental rather than geopolitical territoriality.

But life tells Zarathustra: 'I am that *which must always overcome itself*.'[62] In its struggle for either political institutions or for geopolitically improved conditions of existence, will to power must keep itself alive by immediately denouncing whatever it may have achieved. Through self-overcoming, life as a vitalistic force overrides what it desires: 'Whatever I may create and however I may love it—soon I must oppose it and my love, thus my will wants it.'[63]

There are two ways to reconcile life's self-overcoming with territory. Firstly, the state's imperialistic appetite for new geopolitical conquests may well be insatiable, and this would certainly be true of what were once called 'great powers', the *Grossmächte* that characterized one half of the 20th century ideal of geopolitical power balance still audible in, for example, the 'great power unanimity rule' that applies to the permanent members of the UN Security Council.[64] But Nietzsche's idea of self-overcoming can also be reconciled with non-imperialistic aspirations. All space that is occupied as territory

61. Nietzsche, 'Twilight of the Idols', *supra* note 58, at 214.
62. Nietzsche, *Thus Spoke Zarathustra*, *supra* note 55, at 89.
63. Nietzsche, *Thus Spoke Zarathustra*, *supra* note 55, at 90.
64. For a classic study on great powers, see Leopold von Ranke, 'The Great Powers' (originally published 1833), in Leopold von Ranke, *The Theory and Practice of History* (Wilma A. Iggers trans., Routledge: London, 2011) 29–53.

remains incomplete. A state is constituted space, and it is constituted because a constituent subject like a nation considers that space worthy of protection. And a space requires protection only if it is under threat. The idea of self-overcoming implies, then, that even after it has been constituted, state territory remains under the threat of potential challenges. Will to power feeds off of the constant possibility of territorial disputes and political antagonisms, and so long as the potentiality of antagonisms keeps animating political practice, the territory of the state remains 'alive' in Kjellén's geopolitical sense.

5. Nietzsche and the Critical Conspiracy

So what to make of these esoteric vignettes of mainly 'dead German men'? Why would they be relevant for us today as critically minded academics working in areas like public international law and constitutional theory?

I have two proposals that I would like to conclude with.

Firstly and more generally, the lineage of Nietzschean and post-Nietzschean jurists and political thinkers, those mentioned earlier like Brunner and Schmitt, as well as others like Max Weber, Maurice Merleau-Ponty, perhaps even Walter Benjamin, represent a 'conspiracy', to borrow a wonderful expression from James Martel,[65] that is critical without being either Marxist in any conventional sense of the term or confusedly 'postmodern'. Working out the theoretical premises of this Nietzschean undercurrent would, for one thing, allow us to assess better the critical potential of, for example, cultural conservatives like Schmitt or Brunner without having to resort to apologetic denials about their personal politics.[66] But it could also provide a better understanding of the political ramifications of, say, Foucault, Georges Bataille, Gilles Deleuze or Sarah Kofman and a number of other more contemporary theorists working in that lineage.[67] Nietzsche is the common denominator—or at least one of them—who also functions like a watershed after which the premises of a politically relevant critique change radically.

But more specifically, a geopolitical take on territoriality and on the socio-spatial dimensions of law drawing on this Nietzschean lineage represents an

65. See James R. Martel, *Textual Conspiracies: Walter Benjamin, Idolatry, and Political Theory* (University of Michigan Press, 2011).
66. For highly relevant critical work along these Nietzschean lines, see Andreas Kalyvas, *Democracy and the Politics of the Extraordinary: Max Weber, Carl Schmitt, and Hannah Arendt* (Cambridge University Press, 2008).
67. Such a point is made, perhaps unnecessarily forcefully, in e.g. Alan Schrift, *Nietzsche's French Legacy* (Routledge: Abingdon, 1995).

important opportunity to find tangent points with critical research currently conducted in political and human geography. Excellent research pushing the limits of territoriality is, of course, already conducted in law. To name but a few examples, Andreas Philippopoulos-Mihalopoulos's Deleuze-inspired work on spatial justice is highly relevant here,[68] as are, of course, all elaborations on Rosi Braidotti's nomadic subjectivities.[69] Chris Butler has recently published a book on Henri Lefebvre and law that has already found such tangent points with geographers,[70] while Alison Kesby, another Australian, frames her analysis of the fluidity of borders in public international law with Étienne Balibar's work.[71]

But perhaps what we are still missing is more focused and engaged collaboration with geopolitically oriented geographers, and for very particular reasons. Critical legal geography[72] represents a more established and mainstream social-sciences-oriented critique of territory, and perhaps its contribution would not be much more than what socio-legal approaches already offer. But geographers such as Stuart Elden and Joe Painter have written on the more theoretical aspects of state, sovereignty, territory and security.[73]

What unites the geographers' preoccupations with ours—or what I assume to be ours—is putting into question the essentially modernist 19th century juridico-political paradigm of the state that, as I have earlier hinted,

68. See e.g. Andreas Philippopoulos-Mihalopoulos, 'Spatial Justice: Law and the Geography of Withdrawal', 6 *International Journal of Law in Context* (2010) 201–16 and Andreas Philippopoulos-Mihalopoulos, 'Law's Spatial Turn: Geography, Justice and a Certain Fear of Space', 7 *Law, Culture and the Humanities* (2011) 187–202.
69. See e.g. Rosi Braidotti, *Nomadic Subjects: Embodiment and Sexual Difference in Contemporary Feminist Theory* (2nd edn, Columbia University Press 2011) and Andrew Woolford and R.S. Ratner, 'Nomadic justice? Restorative Justice on the Margins of Law', 30 *Social Justice: Race, Security & Social Movements* (2003) 177–94.
70. Chris Butler, *Henri Lefebvre: Spatial Politics, Everyday Life and the Right to the City* (Routledge: Abingdon, 2012). See also Henri Lefebvre, *State, Space, World: Selected Essays* (Gerald Moore, Neil Brenner and Stuart Elden trans., University of Minnesota Press, 2009).
71. Alison Kesby, 'The Shifting and Multiple Border and International Law', 27 *Oxford Journal of Legal Studies* (2007) 101–19.
72. See e.g. Nicholas K. Blomley and Gordon L. Clark, 'Law, Theory, and Geography', 11 *Urban Geography* (1990) 433–46; Nicholas K. Blomley, *Law, Space, and the Geographies of Power* (Guilford Press: New York, 1994), and David Delaney, *The Spatial, the Legal and the Pragmatics of World-Making: Nomospheric Investigations* (Routledge: New York, 2010).
73. See e.g. Stuart Elden, *Mapping the Present: Heidegger, Foucault and the Project of a Spatial History* (Continuum: London, 2001); Stuart Elden, *Terror and Territory. The Spatial Extent of Sovereignty* (University of Minnesota Press, 2009), and Joe Painter, 'Rethinking territory', 42 *Antipode: A Radical Journal of Geography* (2010) 1090–18.

may never have been valid currency after all. We are still mesmerized by its mirage even if the factual world should convince us otherwise. For example, the critique of governmentality can hardly avoid a nostalgic longing for the territorially confined state that we may no longer have recourse to, and the concern for individualized rights, human rights or otherwise, by definition reinvokes the liberal framework of the rule of law. As soon as the withering-away of the state begins to look like a possible scenario, we fall back on our old statist premises.[74]

Because territory provides the conceptual foundation of the juridico-political paradigm, both state and law in their current senses would fall with it. There is no juridical state without territory. Globalization as a factual challenge to traditional territoriality is like the socio-spatial teaser to that collapse.

74. Neil Walker seems to be making a similar claim in Neil Walker, 'Taking Constitutionalism Beyond the State', 56 *Political Studies* (2008) 519–43.

The Juridical Nature of Unilateral Acts in International Law

Eva Kassoti*

ABSTRACT: This article explores the juridical nature of unilateral acts of States in international law, and particularly the question of whether and under which circumstances these acts may have binding force under international law. In order to do so, the author utilizes the, so far underdeveloped, theory of 'international juridical acts'. Irrespective of their bi/multilateral or unilateral origin, the theory gathers all acts within a broader context of juridical acts based upon the manifestation of intention by their author/s. To test the validity of this theory, the article examines the way in which the distinction between legal and non-legal instruments is made in practice in relation to both international agreements and unilateral acts. The article demonstrates that international courts apply the same criterion for determining the legal nature of international agreements and unilateral acts as well as the same means for determining the existence of that criterion. On this basis, it is argued that international adjudicative bodies treat unilateral acts and international agreements as belonging to the same genus of acts—thereby empirically confirming the validity of the juridical acts theory. The author concludes with a call to develop a coherent concept of 'international juridical acts' as a standard tool for ascertaining the binding character of all acts, irrespective of their contractual or unilateral character.

KEYWORDS: unilateral acts, juridical acts, international agreements, intention

1. Introduction

In his seminal 1983 article[1] Prosper Weil warned against the consequences of the proliferation of soft law instruments[2] for the 'normativity threshold' in international law, *i.e.* 'the line of transition between the non-legal and the

* Dr Eva Kassoti, Lecturer in Law, The Hague University. LL.B. Democritus University of Thrace; LL.M. University of Nottingham; Ph.D. University of Bristol.

1. P. Weil, 'Towards Relative Normativity in International Law?', 77 *American Journal of International Law* (1983) 413–442.
2. The term 'soft law instruments' is used here to denote instruments incorporating non-legal commitments. See A. Boyle, C. Chinkin, *The Making of International Law* (Oxford University Press, 2007) at 212.

legal, between what does not constitute a norm and what does.'[3] According to Weil, the wide-spread use of such instruments would lead to the blurring of the 'normativity threshold' beyond recognition.[4] Thirty years later, the question of the distinction between law and non-law has lost none of its significance. It is the need to maintain the identity of international law *qua* law (as a system of binding norms the breach of which would entail the responsibility of the subject that breached them) that ensures continued engagement with the topic.[5] International lawyers such as Weil,[6] Klabbers[7] and D'Aspremont[8] have convincingly argued that retaining the binary distinction between legal and non-legal is crucial if international law is to fulfill the essential functions of every legal system. Legal certainty, predictability and stability in international relations are predicated on the existence of a normative order in which *lex lata* is not conflated with *lex ferenda*.[9] Thus, soft law is problematic since it undermines the 'simplifying rigour of law'[10] by creating grey zones of normativity. As legal and non-legal instruments co-exist side by side, the boundaries between moral, political and legal obligations become harder to recognise.

The problem of distinguishing between legal and non-legal obligations especially pervades the discussion of unilateral acts of States. Forty years after the ICJ upheld the binding force of unilateral acts in the *Nuclear Tests Case*,[11] the legal nature of these acts still remains unclear. Some international lawyers,

3. P. Weil, 'Towards', *supra* note 1, at 415.
4. *Ibid*, at 415–416.
5. See generally H.L.A. Hart, *The Concept of Law* (3rd ed., Oxford University Press, 2012); G.J.H van Hoof, *Rethinking the Sources of International Law* (Kluwer Law: Deventer, 1983) at 20–28.
6. P. Weil, 'Towards' *supra* note 1, at 418–9.
7. J. Klabbers, 'Law-Making and Constitutionalism', in J. Klabbers, A. Peters, G. Ulfstein (eds.), *The Constitutionalization of International Law* (Oxford University Press, 2009) 81 at 81–85.
8. J. D'Aspremont, 'Softness in International Law: A Self-Serving Quest for New Legal Materials', 19 *European Journal of International Law* (2008) 1075–1093.
9. J. Klabbers, 'The Undesirability of Soft Law', 67 *Nordic Journal of International Law* (1998) 381–391 at 391. On the functions of international law see also R. Y. Jennings, 'What is International Law and How Do We Tell When We See It?', 37 *Schweizerisches Jahrbuch für Internationales Recht* (1981) 59–88.
10. J. Klabbers, 'International Courts and Informal International Law', in J. Pauwelyn, R. A. Wessel, J. Wouters (eds.), *Informal International Lawmaking* (Oxford University Press, 2012) 219–240 at 219.
11. *Nuclear Tests Cases (Australia v. France)*, ICJ Reports (1974) 253; *New Zealand v. France*, ICJ Reports (1974) 457. The Court's judgments in these two cases are almost identical. Hereinafter, for reasons of clarity all references made to the *Nuclear Tests case* will concern the case between Australia and France.

such as Rubin[12] and Thirlway,[13] consider the judgment a politically expedient means to avoid ruling on the vexed question of the legality of nuclear tests. At the other end of the spectrum, lawyers such as Pellet,[14] consider the binding nature of such acts to be well rooted in international law. The work of the International Law Commission on the subject[15] did not yield much clarity either. The final product of the Commission's decade long struggle with the topic, the 2006 Guiding Principles,[16] leaves much to be desired. Rather than providing a clear boundary between unilateral juridical and unilateral political acts, the Guiding Principles simply rehash the relevant case-law, and consequently add precious little to the debate. At the same time, unilateral acts have become a standard tool of modern State interaction and, as it will be shown below, the ICJ has repeatedly upheld their binding force in its subsequent case-law.

In this light, the present article aims to explore the question of the juridical nature of unilateral acts of States with a view to establish whether and under which circumstances these acts may create binding effects on the international plane. In doing so, the article will empirically test the validity of the, so far underdeveloped, theory of international juridical acts. This theory proposes that all acts—whether of unilateral or bi/multilateral origin–produce legal effects if they manifest the intention of their author/s to become bound. However, is the intention to be bound a valid criterion for distinguishing between political promises and unilateral juridical acts? And if so, how is intention, an element seemingly so intangible, to be determined objectively?

In order to answer these questions the article will begin by exploring the concept of juridical acts in national and international law. It will be shown that the doctrine in question is prevalent in countries following the civil law tradition, but it has largely remained underdeveloped in international law. Next, the focus will turn to the approach adopted by international courts to address the problem of distinguishing between legal and non-legal obligations in the field of international agreements and unilateral acts. It will be argued

12. A. Rubin, 'The International Legal Effects of Unilateral Declarations', 71 *American Journal of International Law* (1977) 1–30.
13. H. Thirlway, 'The Sources of International Law', in M. Evans (ed.), *International Law* (4th ed., Oxford University Press, 2014) 91–117 at 111.
14. A. Pellet, 'Article 38', in A. Zimmerman *et al.* (eds.), *The Statute of the International Court of Justice: A Commentary* (2nd ed., Oxford University Press, 2012) 731–870 at 762.
15. See the Analytical Guide to the work of the ILC on Unilateral Acts of States, <http://legal.un.org/ilc/guide/9_9.htm> (visited 15 June 2014).
16. Guiding Principles applicable to unilateral declarations of States capable of creating legal obligations with commentaries thereto, adopted by the ILC at its 58th session (2006), II *Yearbook of the ILC* (2006) at 369. Hereinafter referred to as the 2006 Guiding Principles.

include both contracts and unilateral acts,[21] juridical facts consist of 'conduct and or events to which the law attaches legal consequences.'[22] Principal examples of the former category would include contracts and unilateral promises, whereas of the latter, the birth or death of an individual.[23]

While not all civil law countries have adopted the same refined dichotomy of the sources of obligations as France, juridical acts are a common topos in the civil law tradition. Despite terminological differences, the term is used throughout the civil law world to connote acts that create legal effects based upon the manifestation of intention by their author/s.[24] Indeed, the element of intention lies at the very core of the concept: according to the Italian definition, juridical acts are 'declarations of will setting out the intended legal effects and to which the legal system attaches legal effects in accordance with the intended result,'[25] while under the Dutch Civil Code, juridical acts are declarations of will, to which the law gives binding effect to the extent that they manifest their authors' intention to become bound thereby.[26] Similar definitions that emphasise the element of intention are to be found in the civil codes of Germany, Greece, Belgium, Austria, Portugal, Slovenia, Slovakia, Bulgaria, Hungary and other civil law countries.[27] It is also important to note

21. *Ibid*, Art. 1101–1.
22. *Ibid*, Art. 1101–2.
23. B. Fauvarque-Cosson, Mazeud, *European Contract Law*, *supra* note 18, at 66–86.
24. C. von Bar, E. Clive, H. Schulte-Nölke, *Principles, Definitions and Model Rules of European Private Law, Draft Common Frame of Reference (DCFR)*, prepared by the Study Group on a European Civil Code and the Research Group on EC Private Law (*Acquis* Group 2009), <http://ec.europa.eu/justice/contract/files/european-private-law_en.pdf> (visited 15 June 2014) at 173–174.
25. B. Fauvarque-Cosson, D. Mazeud, *European Contract Law*, *supra* note 18, at 84. The concept of juridical acts, or *'atti giuridici'*, is the creation of doctrine and is not to be found in the Italian Civil Code (*Codice Civile*) or in any special legislation. However, *atti giuridici* are of paramount importance in the Italian theory of classification of obligations. See M. Cappelletti, J. H. Merryman, J. M. Perillo, *The Italian Legal system: An Introduction* (Stanford University Press, 1967) at 177–179.
26. Article 3:33 of the Dutch Civil Code (*Burgerlijk Wetboek*). See also J.M.J. Chorus, P.H.M. Gerver, E.H. Hondius, *Introduction to Dutch Law* (4th rev. ed., Kluwer: Deventer, 2006) at 151–153.
27. C. von Bar, E. Clive, H. Schulte-Nölke, *Principles*, *supra* note 24, at 173–4; B. Fauvarque-Cosson, D. Mazeud, *European Contract Law*, *supra* note 18, at 76–86. For instance, according to the German Civil Code (*Bürgerliches Gesetzbuch*), juridical acts (*Rechtsgeschäfte*), namely acts that express the intention to be bound, include both contracts and unilateral acts (*Einseitige Rechtsgesch äfte*). See Articles 104–111 of the German Civil Code. The Greek Civil Code (*Αστικός Κώδικας*), which was modeled after the German Civil Code, also embodies the concept of juridical acts and puts primary emphasis on the intention of the parties to create legal effects thereby (Article

that the 2009 Model Rules on European Private Law,[28] prepared by the Study Group on a European Civil Code and the Research Group on EC Private law under the auspices of the European Commission, expressly refer to juridical acts as a core common concept of EU private law. Model rule II.1:101(2) provides that a juridical act is 'any statement or agreement, whether express, or implied from conduct, which is intended to have legal effects as such. It may be unilateral, bilateral or multilateral.'[29] By way of contrast, legal systems based on the common law tradition have not adopted the concept of juridical acts—with the exception of the 'hybrid' Scottish system.[30]

A perusal of the relevant legislation, case-law and literature reveals that, although juridical acts of a bi/multilateral origin, *i.e.* contracts, are more commonly used, the civil law tradition has long accepted that legal effects may be borne out of acts of purely unilateral origin.[31] Indeed, the majority of States that have incorporated the concept of juridical acts into their legal systems have also expressly acknowledged the binding force of unilateral undertakings—without the need of any form of acceptance or reliance by the addressee.[32] Thus, the civil law tradition accepts the enforceability of

---

130 of the Greek Civil Code). See generally, M. Stathopoulos, *Contract Law in Greece* (2nd rev. ed., Kluwer Law International: The Hague, 2009) at 83–84. The concept of juridical acts, as manifestations of the intention of their author/s to be bound, is also prevalent in Belgian legal theory. See P. Van Ommeslaghe, 'L'engagement par volonté unilatérale en droit belge', *Journal des Tribunaux* (1982) 144–149. Under Article 34 of the Slovak Civil Code (*Občiansky Zakonnìk*), acts in law, or juridical acts, are manifestations of will aimed at the creation, modification or termination of rights and obligations. In a similar vein, Article 67 paragraph 1 of the Estonian Civil Code (*Tsiviilseadustiku Üldosa Seadus*) defines juridical acts as declarations of intention directed at bringing about a certain legal consequence. Scottish law also recognises that intention is central to the formation of voluntary obligations. The latter are divided in two categories, namely contracts and unilateral promises. See Scottish Law Commission, Memorandum No. 35, Constitution and Proof of Voluntary Obligations: Unilateral Promises, 10 March 1977, <http://www.scotlawcom.gov.uk/publications/discussion-papers-and-consultative-memoranda/1970-1979/> (visited 15 June 2014).

28. C. von Bar, E. Clive, H. Schulte-Nölke, *Principles*, *supra* note 24, at 170.
29. *Ibid.*
30. M. A. Hogg, 'Promise: The Neglected Obligation in European Private Law', 59 *International and Comparative Law Quarterly* (2010) 461–479 at 464. See also M. A. Hogg, *Promises and Contract Law: Comparative Perspectives* (Cambridge University Press, 2011) at 134–142.
31. B. Fauvarque-Cosson, D. Mazeud, *European Contract Law, supra* note 18, at 73–74, 82–84.
32. P. Lenner, 'Promises of Rewards in a Comparative Perspective', 10 *Annual Survey International & Comparative Law* (2004) 53–101 at 61–65; M. A. Hogg, 'Promise', *supra* note 30, at 463–464.

gratuitous promises, *i.e.* promises by which the promisor undertakes to do or refrain from doing something without receiving anything in exchange, such as public promises of rewards, gift promises or unilateral undertakings made in the context of business.[33] The binding effects of such gratuitous promises are expressly recognised in German, Austrian, Bulgarian, Slovenian, Estonian, Italian, Portuguese, Dutch, Belgian, Finnish, Swedish and Scottish law.[34]

However, short of deeds under seal, purely unilateral promises that have not been accepted or relied upon by the promisee are not enforceable against the promisor in common law legal systems.[35] This is not to say that the concept of unilateral undertakings is entirely foreign to the common law tradition. However, for such promises to create binding effects, some form of *quid pro quod* or reliance on behalf of the addressee is needed. As Judge Jessup noted in his Separate Opinion to the *South West Africa* cases: 'it is also generally recognised that there may be *unilateral agreements*, meaning agreements arising out of unilateral acts in which only one party is promisor and may well be the only party bound.'[36]

The main reason underpinning the difficulty of the common law tradition to recognise the binding force of gratuitous promises lies in the importance attached to the doctrine of consideration within that legal tradition. Although English law and American law adopt slightly different definitions, the doctrine of consideration insists on the existence of an element of exchange, or reciprocity, in the formation of contracts.[37] Thus, purely gratuitous promises are not considered enforceable in the absence of an element of reciprocity, *i.e.* in the absence of consideration. As Justice Parker stated in *Mills v. Wyman*:

> General rules of law established for the protection and security of honest and fair-minded men, who may inconsiderately make promises without any equivalent,

33. P. Lenner, 'Promises', *supra* note 32, at 61–62.
34. C. von Bar, E. Clive, H. Schulte-Nölke, *Principles, supra* note 24, at 180–181. See, for example, Article 111 of the German Civil Code (*Bürgerliches Gesetzbuch*); Article 3:32 of the Dutch Civil Code (*Burgerlijk Wetboek*); Article 44 of the Bulgarian Obligations and Contracts Act; Article 1989 of the Italian Civil Code (*Codice Civile*); Article 67 paragraph 2 of the Estonian Civil Code (*Tsiviilseadustiku Üldosa Seadus*); Section 1 of the Requirements of Writing (Scotland) Act 1995.
35. J. Beatson, A. Burrows, J. Cartwright, *Anson's Law of Contracts* (29th ed., Oxford University Press, 2010) at 91; J. Cooke, D. Oughton, The Common Law of Obligations (3rd ed., Oxford University Press, 2000) at 66–67.
36. *South West Africa Cases,* ICJ Reports (1962) 319, Separate Opinion of Judge Jessup, at 402. (Emph. added).
37. C. Larroumet, 'Detrimental Reliance and Promissory Estoppel as the Cause of Contracts in Louisiana and Comparative Law', 60 *Tulane Law Review* (1986) 1209–1230 at 1210–1211.

> will sometimes screen men of a different character from engagements which they are bound in *foro conscientae* to perform … The rule that a mere verbal promise, *without any consideration*, cannot be enforced by action, is universal in its application, and cannot be departed from to suit particular cases in which a refusal to perform such a promise may be disgraceful.[38]

Conversely, the civil law counterpart of consideration, cause or *causa*, is a much broader concept that focuses on the aims motivating each party to create obligations by means of a juridical act—rather than merely on the existence of an element of reciprocity of obligations.[39] Thus, in civil law jurisdictions, a juridical act without a cause—*i.e.* without an achievable aim—or with an unlawful cause is invalid.[40] The main rationale underpinning the concept of cause is the protection of individuals. Under normal circumstances, individuals do not enter into contractual or other obligations, unless they wish to pursue an aim. For example, when entering into a contract for sale, the buyer promises to pay the agreed amount of money *because* the seller promises to deliver the item and similarly, the seller promises to deliver the item *because* the buyer promises to pay the agreed amount of money. In this sense, 'for bilateral contracts, the *cause* of the obligation of each of the parties lies in the obligation of the other.'[41] The function of cause is to protect a party in cases where the pursued aim cannot be realized by allowing that party to be released from their respective obligations. Thus, in the abovementioned example, if the item for sale is destroyed and thus, the seller is unable to deliver it, the buyer is released from their obligation to pay the agreed amount

38. *Mills v. Wyman*, 20 *Mass.* (3 *Pick.*) 207 (1825) at 209–210 (Emph. added), <http://grammar.ucsd.edu/courses/lign105/student-court-cases/mills.pdf> (visited 15 June 2014).
39. C. Calleros, 'Cause, Consideration, Promissory Estoppel, and Promises under Deed: What Our Students Should Know about Enforcement of Promises in a Historical and International Context', 13 *Chicago-Kent Journal of International & Comparative Law* (2013) 83–120 at 96.
40. See for example Art. 1131 of the French Civil Code (*Code Civil*): 'An obligation without cause or with a false cause, or with an unlawful cause, may not have any effect.' <http://www.google.nl/url?sa=t&rct=j&q=&esrc=s&source=web&cd=4&ved=0CE4QFjAD&url=http%3A%2F%2Fwww.legifrance.gouv.fr%2Fcontent%2Fdownload%2F1950%2F13681%2Fversion%2F3%2Ffile%2FCode_22.pdf&ei=ujuPU7qLLIWqO9mOgdAG&usg=AFQjCNG9WyQsA6iRNF1YoH3CVOf73H6iXQ&bvm=bv.68235269,d.ZWU> (visited 15 June 2014). See also Art. 1261 of the Spanish Civil Code (*Código Civil*): 'There is no contract unless the following requirements are met: 1. Consent of the contracting parties. 2. A certain object that is the subject matter of the contract. 3. Cause of the obligation established.' <http://www.elra.eu/wp-content/uploads/file/Spanish_Civil_Code_%28C%C3%B3digo_Civil%29%5B1%5D.pdf> (visited 15 June 2014).
41. T. Kadner Graziano, *Comparative Contract Law: Cases, Materials and Exercises* (Palgrave MacMillan: Basingstoke, 2009) at para. 338.

of money: the existence of the buyer's *cause* of obligation has ceased to exist. However, as far as unilateral undertakings are concerned, the civil law tradition has accepted that the intention of the author to give something solely for the 'pleasure of doing something good' is a valid cause for the creation of legally binding effects.[42]

2.2. The Concept of Juridical Acts in International Law: An Underdeveloped Idea

The previous section provided a brief overview of the concept of juridical acts in national law. Against this background, this section will focus on the

42. *Ibid,* paras 338–349; C. Larroumet, 'Detrimentral Reliance', *supra* note 37, at 1220. It is worth noting that Hugh Thirlway discussed to some extent the interplay between consideration and *causa* within the context of unilateral acts in his Hague Academy Course in 2002. See H. Thirlway, 'Concepts, Principles, Rules and Analogies: International and Municipal Legal Reasoning', 294 *Recueils des cours* (2002) 265–406 at 269. Thirlway criticized the judgment of the Court in the *Nuclear Tests* cases and argued that the principle propounded by the Court in that case, namely that unilateral acts that evidence the intention of their authors to become bound may have legal effects, was based more on political expediency rather than sound legal principles. In his view, the Court simply wished to do away with the problem of having to rule upon the legality of nuclear tests. *Ibid,* at 337. In support of his thesis, Thirlway claimed that the *Nuclear Tests* judgment is an isolated one and, more importantly, that none of the sources enumerated in Art.38 of the ICJ Statute may be considered as the source of the binding force of these acts. Furthermore, Thirlway explored the possibility of extrapolating from municipal legal reasoning in order to justify the binding effects attributed to such acts by the Court. In this context, the learned scholar discussed the concepts of consideration and *causa* in relation to unilateral acts. In his view, consideration and *causa* are similar concepts and, irrespective of the legal system in which the question of the binding force of unilateral commitments may arise, such commitments are never binding in the case 'where an undertaking has been given upon which the potential beneficiary has no intention of relying.' *Ibid,* at 341. (Emph. added). It is respectfully submitted that this conclusion is erroneous both in the light of the consistent jurisprudence of the Court in relation to the binding force of unilateral acts and of the aforementioned discussion regarding the definition and function of the concepts of consideration and *causa*. First, the Court has, on a number of occasions, upheld the principle to the effect that unilateral acts may have binding force on the international plane—as it will be shown in due course. Secondly, although it is true that, as far as synallagmatic contracts are concerned, the differences between *causa* and consideration are minimal, the same is not true when it comes to unilateral acts. While the application of the concept of consideration does not allow legal systems that follow the common law tradition to consider unilateral commitments as binding in the absence of an element of *quid pro quod*, the application of the concept of *causa* leads to different conclusions. As it was shown above, cause is a much broader concept that inquires into the reasons behind the creation of obligations by means of a juridical act. Thus, legal systems that have accepted the intention to undertake an obligation without more as a lawful cause have had no difficulty to endow unilateral commitments with binding force-even in the absence of reciprocity or reliance on behalf of the beneficiary.

few attempts that have been made to transpose the concept of juridical acts into the international field. As remarked earlier, Verzijl's *International Law in a Historical Perspective* is one of the rare English-language works in which the question of international juridical acts is treated at length. More particularly, in the sixth volume of the aforementioned treatise, Verzijl attempted to provide a systematic exposition of all legally relevant facts, *i.e.* of all events or actions from which juridical relations may originate.[43] In his view, all juridical relations, namely the totality of rights and obligations between international legal persons, may be traced back to three main legally relevant, or juridical, facts.[44] These include the simple fact of the co-existence of States which entails compliance to and respect of certain fundamental obligations and rights;[45] natural events which may give rise to new international rights and obligations (such as the emergence of an island in the territorial sea); and actions undertaken by subjects of international law.[46]

As far as the latter category is concerned, Verzijl attempted to bring all the manifestations of a State's action at the international level into two broad categories, namely to lawful acts (international juridical acts) and to unlawful acts (international delicts).[47] According to Verzijl, State acts that are 'intended to produce specific legal effects on the inter-state level and in fact producing them under normal circumstances'[48] belong to the category of juridical acts or 'acts in law'. Regarding the typology of acts that make up the category of juridical acts, Verzijl argued that the main distinction to be found in practice is between unilateral and plurilateral acts.[49] Thus, Verzijl propounded a concept of international juridical acts in which the element of the intention to create legal effects was central. In his view, these acts, which may be of either unilateral or plurilateral origin, produce legal effects because they evidence the intention of their author State, or States, to become bound on the international plane.[50] Therefore, according to Verzijl's definition of international juridical acts, the intention to create legal effects is the key criterion for determining the legal status of an international act.

43. J. H. W. Verzijl, *International Law, supra* note 17. Note that the sixth volume is entitled 'Juridical Facts as Sources of International Rights and Obligations.'
44. *Ibid,* at 2.
45. *Ibid,* at 4 *et seq.*
46. *Ibid.*
47. *Ibid.*
48. *Ibid,* at 48.
49. *Ibid.*
50. *Ibid.*

Lauterpacht also maintains that intention is the main determinant of international rights and obligations.[51] As Fitzmaurice observed in his commentary on Lauterpacht's judicial pronouncements, although the latter did not develop a theory on international juridical acts as such, he emphasized the role of intention in establishing the juridical nature of instruments of either unilateral or treaty character.[52] One of the many examples offered by Fitzmaurice is Lauterpacht's Separate Opinion in the *Norwegian Loans Case,*[53] in which the latter noted that 'whether it is a treaty or a unilateral declaration, it is—if it is to be treated as a legal text…—a manifestation of intention to create reciprocal rights and obligations.'[54] Furthermore, Lauterpacht argued that, since both treaties and unilateral undertakings constitute legal acts, in the sense that both kinds of acts manifest the intention of States to create legal effects, the same rules of interpretation and invalidity applicable to treaties are also applicable *mutatis mutandis* to unilateral undertakings. More specifically, in his Separate Opinion in the aforementioned case, Lauterpacht examined the effects of the French Declaration made under Art. 36. 2 of the ICJ Statute that contained a reservation excluding issues of national jurisdiction—as understood by the French Government—from the compulsory jurisdiction of the Court.[55] In Lauterpacht's opinion, instruments purporting to

51. Note however that Lauterpacht, as a Special Rapporteur of the International Law Commission, was more reluctant about the binding nature of unilateral acts as such. More specifically, in discussing the creation of obligations by means of unilateral declarations, Lauterpacht supported that unilateral declarations following the pattern of offer and acceptance, such as unilateral declarations accepting an offer or accepting the terms of an already existing instrument, as well as unilateral declarations that have been accepted by the State to which they are addressed, constitute in essence treaty undertakings. Although not addressing the question directly, Lauterpacht admitted the possibility of binding unilateral acts that do not follow the abovementioned pattern of offer and acceptance. As an example thereof, he cited the *Free Zones Case*, in which a declaration made by the Swiss Agent was held to be binding, although no international agreement was concluded. (See the *Case of the Free Zones of Upper Savoy and the District of Gex, PCIJ Series* A/B, No. 46 (1932), at 170). While Lauterpacht admitted the limitations of adopting a contractual perspective towards all unilateral acts, he did not go as far as accepting unilateral acts as a separate genus of juridical acts. However, as it will be shown below, by 1957 Lauterpacht seems to have accepted the view that purely unilateral acts, in the sense of acts that by no stretch of interpretation may be brought within a contractual frame, are binding as such. See H. Lauterpacht, 'Report on the Law of Treaties', II *Yearbook of the ILC* (1953) 101.
52. G. Fitzmaurice, *The Law and Procedure of the International Court of Justice* (Vol. II, Grotius: Cambridge, 1986) at 822–829.
53. *Certain Norwegian Loans Case*, ICJ Reports (1957) 9.
54. *Ibid,* Separate Opinion of Judge Sir Hersch Lauterpacht, at 49.
55. *Ibid, Certain Norwegian Loans Case*, at 21.

create obligations but which, at the same time, contain an 'automatic' reservation, *i.e.* a reservation to the effect that the extent of the obligation contained therein shall be reserved for the exclusive determination of the author State, are not legal instruments at all.[56] In support of his argument, he adduced evidence to the effect that the rule regarding the invalidity of such instruments is present in all major legal systems and thus, constitutes a general principle of law.[57]

Most importantly for the present purposes, Lauterpacht argued that this rule is applicable not only to treaties, but also to instruments of unilateral character.[58] That both treaties and unilateral acts, in which a reservation of the 'automatic' type has been inserted, should be considered invalid was later reiterated in Lauterpacht's Dissenting Opinion in the *Interhandel Case*.[59] In that case, Lauterpacht repeated his opinion in the *Norwegian Loans Case* and added: '… it is not therefore necessary to repeat here the views there expressed, in particular those derived from general principles of law applicable to all legal instruments, whether bilateral or unilateral, *intended* to create legal rights and obligations.'[60]

Juridical acts have remained at the margin of contemporary international legal scholarship. One of the few modern international lawyers to engage with the topic is Jean D'Aspremont.[61] In a similar vein to Verzijl, D'Aspremont classified all legal obligations into two main categories: juridical acts and juridical facts. Juridical acts allow subjects of international law to create new rules to the extent that they manifest the intention of their author/s to be bound. In his own words: 'to enable it to qualify as legal act, the legal effect of the act in question must *directly* originate in the will of the legal subject to whom the behaviour is attributed and not to any pre-existing rule in the system.'[62] On the other hand, juridical facts are acts the legal basis of which may be found in a pre-existing rule in the system. Thus, the legal effects of juridical facts 'originate in the legal system itself, which provides for such an effect prior to the adoption of the act.'[63] The theory of juridical acts has been central to D'Aspremont's attack against soft law theorists. He argues that the

56. *Ibid*, Separate Opinion of Judge Sir Hersch Lauterpacht, at 39.
57. *Ibid.*
58. *Ibid.*
59. *Interhandel Case*, ICJ Reports (1959) 6, Dissenting Opinion of Judge Sir Hersch Lauterpacht.
60. *Ibid*, at 106 (Emph. added).
61. J. D'Aspremont, 'Softness', *supra* note 8.
62. *Ibid*, at 1078.
63. *Ibid*, at 1079.

problem of distinguishing between legal and non-legal obligations, namely the problem of 'soft law' vs. 'hard law', only arises in relation to obligations that stem from the will of the author State/s, *i.e.* from juridical acts, and not from any other pre-existing rule. Thus, according to him, the *problèmatique* of soft law cannot be properly understood 'short of a sound theory of the legal act.'[64] It is unnecessary to discuss in detail D'Aspremont's arguments against soft law. It has been clarified from the outset that I subscribe to the view that the distinction between legal and non-legal acts needs to be preserved if international law is to retain its distinctiveness and effectiveness. Irrespective of where one's sympathies might lie, the point made by D'Aspremont is still valid. In practice, the question of the binding force of an act does not normally arise in relation to acts that are based upon an established rule of customary law, or a general principle of law. It does, however, arise in relation to international agreements and unilateral acts.

On the basis of the above, it is evident that the concept of international juridical acts is far from adequately developed in theory. However, the few international lawyers who have touched upon the topic concluded that the criterion for establishing that acts of either unilateral, or bi/multilateral origin are to be considered as juridical acts—in contrast to mere political pledges—is the intention of their author to be bound.

3. Intention as the Criterion for Distinguishing Between Legal and Non-Legal Acts: The View from the Law of Treaties

As seen above, with few exceptions, legal literature offers limited input to the question of ascertaining the legal nature of international acts. Nevertheless, an area in which the problem of distinguishing between legal and non-legal acts is of utmost practical significance is that of the law of the treaties. In this field of international law, States, lawyers and international judicial bodies are often faced with instruments of controversial legal nature. At this point, an excursion to the law of treaties is considered essential since it will provide the necessary foundation upon which the argument of the next section will be built, namely that both types of legal acts share intention as the determinant of their legal character and that the same methodology can be applied to both in order to establish the presence of the requisite element of intention.

64. *Ibid*, at 1078.

3.1. Intention and the 1969 Vienna Convention on the Law of Treaties

Although it does not cover the whole spectrum of agreements under international law,[65] it is customary to make a reference to the 1969 Vienna Convention on the Law of Treaties as a starting point in every discussion relating to international agreements. According to the definition inserted in the Vienna Convention, an international treaty is 'an international agreement concluded between States in written form and governed by international law, whether embodied in a single instrument or in two or more related instruments and whatever its particular designation.'[66] Although the above definition does not make any direct reference to intention, the requirement that a treaty is 'governed by international law' is generally interpreted as encompassing the element of the intention to create legal effects. More particularly, an examination of the reports produced by the successive Special Rapporteurs of the International Law Commission on the Law of Treaties shows that the intention to create legal effects was consistently cited as the key criterion for ascertaining the legal character of an international agreement.

In his first report on the law of treaties, Lauterpacht defined international treaties as agreements concluded 'between States, including organisations of States, intended to create legal rights and obligations of the parties.'[67] In a similar vein, Lauterpacht's successor, Fitzmaurice inserted the requirement of the intention to create rights, obligations or, more generally, to establish relationships in international law in his definition of international treaties.[68]

---

65. See Article 3 of the Vienna Convention on the Law of Treaties, adopted 23/05/1969, <http://untreaty.un.org/ilc/texts/instruments/english/conventions/1_1_1969.pdf> (visited 15 June 2014).
66. Art. 2.1 (a) of the Vienna Convention on the Law of Treaties.
67. H. Lauterpacht, 'Report on the Law of Treaties', *supra* note 51, at 93. In the commentary following the definition of international agreements, Lauterpacht highlighted the problem of distinguishing between instruments of a legal character and mere declarations of policy in the field of international law. As examples of the latter category, he cited, *inter alia*, the 1941 Atlantic Charter and the Universal Declaration of Human Rights adopted by the General Assembly in 1948. The difference between such non-binding instruments and international agreements properly so called lied, in his opinion, in the fact that the latter instruments evidence the intention of their author States to create rights and obligations on the international plane. Thus, Lauterpacht concluded that 'in the event of a dispute on the subject it must properly be a question for judicial determination whether an instrument, whatever its description, is in fact intended to create legal rights and obligations between the parties and as such coming within the category of treaties.' *Ibid*, at 96–8.
68. G. Fitzmaurice, 'Report on the Law of Treaties', II *Yearbook of the ILC* (1956) 104, at 107. The relevant part of his 1956 Report on the Law of Treaties reads: '… a treaty is an

constitute an immediate commitment by the Greek and the Turkish Prime Ministers, on behalf of their respective governments, to accept unconditionally the unilateral submission of the present dispute to the Court.'[79]

Similarly, Judge Read in his Separate Opinion in the *Advisory Opinion on the International Status of South West Africa*[80] identified the intention to create legal obligations as one of the essentials of the juridical nature of international agreements. In his own words: 'It is unnecessary to discuss the juridical nature of an international agreement. It is sufficient, for present purposes, to state that an "arrangement agreed between" between the United Nations and the Union necessarily included two elements: a meeting of minds; and an intention to constitute a legal obligation.'[81]

3.3. The Problem of Establishing the Element of Intention in the Law of Treaties

The above sections have demonstrated that intention is the determinant factor in attributing legal effects to an international agreement. However, as Klabbers phrased it, intention is an 'awkward concept.'[82] This is so because intention, in the common sense of the term, refers to a psychological element—to the state of mind that an individual may have at a given moment in time. Undoubtedly, it is very hard to discern the intentions of individuals—as Cicero once said: 'There is nothing more obscure than human intentions.'[83] And if one considers that the task at hand is discerning not the intentions of individuals but that of abstract entities, such as States, then the difficulties are only multiplied. How is one to determine whether a particular instrument expresses the intention of its authors to become bound according to its terms?

The difficulties that are borne from the concept of intention have been addressed in theory by differentiating between the 'subjective' and the 'objective' intention of a State or, in other words, between the 'real' and the 'manifest' will of a State.[84] International lawyers, such as Klabbers[85] and

79. *Ibid*, at 44 (Emph. added). For a commentary of the judgment see H. Thirlway, 'The Law and Procedure of the International Court of Justice 1960–1989', 62 *British Yearbook of International Law* (1991) 13–170 at 14–5.

80. Separate Opinion of Judge Read in the *International Status of South West Africa Advisory Opinion*, *supra* note 76.

81. *Ibid*, at 170.

82. J. Klabbers, *The Concept*, *supra* note 72, at 65.

83. M. T. Cicero, *Pro Murena: Speech in defense of Lucius Licinius Murena*, 63 BC, at para. 36, <http://www.perseus.tufts.edu/hopper/text?doc=Cic.+Mur.+36&fromdoc=Perseus%3Atext%3A1999.02.0019> (visited on 15 June 2014).

84. J. Klabbers, *The Concept*, *supra* note 72, at 65.

85. *Ibid*.

Fitzmaurice,[86] have argued that, in the context of the law of treaties, the task of establishing the intention to be bound, is not an investigation into the motives and reasons, *i.e.* into the 'subjective' or 'real' intention of a particular State/s, but one of establishing the 'objective' or 'manifest' intention of the State/s in question. In other words, it has been suggested that what one is looking for in ascertaining whether a certain instrument is an international agreement or not is not the what the States really had in mind when they produced a particular instrument—something that would be impossible to fathom—but what was manifested to the outside world.

This objective reading of the criterion of intention is supported by the judgment of the Court in the *Maritime delimitation and territorial questions between Qatar and Bahrain Case*.[87] In this case, the International Court of Justice was faced, amongst others, with the question of the legal status of the agreed minutes of a discussion between the Foreign Ministers of Qatar and Bahrain that took place in Doha in December 1990.[88] According to Qatar, the 1990 Minutes amounted to an international agreement that enabled the ICJ to exercise jurisdiction over the dispute. Bahrain disagreed and argued that the minutes were a simple record of negotiations and did not rank as an international agreement.[89] Bahrain based its argument on a subjective interpretation of the element of intention claiming that, at the time that the discussion between the two Ministers took place, there was no intention on its behalf to create a binding instrument. In support thereof, Bahrain cited a statement made by its Minister for Foreign Affairs in 1992, in which he stated that: 'At no time did I consider that in signing the Minutes I was committing Bahrain to a legally binding agreement.'[90]

However, the Court did not accept Bahrain's contention. In the opinion of the Court, the 1990 Minutes 'do not merely give an account of discussions and summarize points of agreement and disagreement. They enumerate the commitments to which the Parties have consented. They thus create rights and obligations in international law for the parties. They constitute an international agreement.'[91] Thus, by rejecting Bahrain's argument and by focusing

86. M. Fitzmaurice, 'The Identification and Character of Treaties and Treaty Obligations between States in International Law', 73 *British Yearbook of International Law* (2002) 141–185 at 165–168.
87. *Maritime delimitation and territorial questions between Qatar and Bahrain Case,* ICJ Reports (1994) 112.
88. *Ibid,* at 118–9. The agreed minutes concluded between the disputing parties will be henceforth referred to as 'the Doha Minutes' or as the '1990 Minutes'.
89. *Ibid,* at 120.
90. *Ibid,* at 121.
91. *Ibid.*

on the actual content of the Minutes, the Court clearly favoured an objective interpretation of the element of intention.

Nevertheless, simply stating that what one is looking for in determining the legal character of an international instrument is the 'objective' or 'manifest' intention of its authors is not enough. The next question that naturally arises is whether there are any indicators of the manifest intention of a State/s to become bound by an international agreement. A review of the relevant case-law of international judicial bodies reveals that when confronted with the question of determining the legal status of an international instrument, these bodies have recourse to a number of indicators of the manifest intention of its authors.[92] These indicators relate to the actual terms used in the instrument and to the context surrounding it. Thus, on the basis of the pertinent case-law, Klabbers compiled a list of indicators of manifest intention including: whether the instrument in question specifically expresses consent to be bound, whether it contains provisions regarding entry into force and judicial settlement, whether it is registered under Art.102 of the UN Charter,[93] and whether any statements were made during the stage of negotiations that evidence the manifest intention of the authors of the instrument to become bound by it.[94]

Finally, it is worth commenting on the approach employed by the ICJ with regard to determining the legal nature of an international agreement on the basis of the above indicators of 'manifest intention.' A close examination of the line of argumentation of the Court in the *Aegean Sea Continental Self Case* and in the *Qatar vs. Bahrain Case* shows that the Court, in establishing the existence of the requisite element of intention, will first examine the actual terms of the agreement and, if no objective evidence of an intention to be bound can be inferred therefrom, then it will continue its investigation by scrutinizing the context surrounding the agreement.[95] As it was stated in the *Aegean Sea Continental Self Case*: 'In determining what was indeed the nature of the act or transaction embodied in the Brussels Communiqué, the Court must have regard above all to its actual terms and to the particular circumstances in which it was drawn up.'[96]

92. J. Klabbers, *The Concept, supra* note 72, at 72; J. Klabbers, 'Law-Making', *supra* note 7, at 118 *et seq.*; M. Fitzmaurice, 'The Identification', *supra* note 86, at 168.
93. Charter of the United Nations, signed on the 26th of June 1945, <http://www.un.org/en/documents/charter/index.shtml> (visited 15 June 2014).
94. J. Klabbers, *The Concept, supra* note 72, at 75–89.
95. *Ibid,* at 200; M. Fitzmaurice, 'The Identification', *supra* note 86, at 168.
96. *The Aegean Sea Continental Self Case, supra* note 75, at para. 96.

In that case, the Court, having examined the actual terms of the Communiqué, decided that the text of the agreement gave rise to a 'divergence of views'[97] and continued by investigating the context in which the Communiqué was drawn up[98]—only to conclude that the instrument in question was not intended to create any binding commitment.[99] By way of contrast, in the *Qatar v. Bahrain Case*, the Court considered that the 1990 Minutes clearly expressed the intention of the parties to become bound[100] and thus, there was no need to have recourse to the context surrounding their making. According to the judgment:

> The Court does not find it necessary to consider what might have been the intentions of the Foreign Minister of Bahrain, or, for that matter, those of the Foreign Minister of Qatar. The two Ministers signed a text recording commitments accepted by their Governments, some of which were to be given immediate application. Having signed such a text, the Foreign Minister of Bahrain is not in a position subsequently to say that he intended to subscribe to a "statement recording a political understanding", and not to an international agreement.[101]

3.4. Intention and its Discontents: D'Aspremont's Call to Move Away from Intention

The previous section showed that the element of manifest intention is the criterion for identifying the binding nature of acts of a contractual origin and that the ICJ has established its own methodology for deciding whether the requisite element of intention has been met. However, some international lawyers, such as D'Aspremont, have argued that, due to the hurdles associated with ascertaining intention, international law should do away with the criterion of intention altogether and replace it with a more tangible one.[102] Since intention lies at the core of the theory of international juridical acts, it would be worthwhile to assess at this point the merits of such criticisms. In his monograph, D'Aspremont laments the formidable difficulties of identifying the legal character of international agreements and unilateral acts. According to him, the problem lies in the very criterion upon which law—ascertainment is based on the international plane, *i.e.* the criterion of intention: 'Indeed,

97. *Ibid*, at para. 100.
98. *Ibid*, at paras 100–106.
99. *Ibid*, at para. 107.
100. *Maritime delimitation and territorial questions between Qatar and Bahrain Case, supra* note 87, at para. 25.
101. *Ibid*, at para. 27.
102. J. D'Aspremont, *Formalism and the Sources of International Law: A Theory of the Ascertainment of Legal Rules* (Oxford University Press, 2011) at 180.

such a criterion ultimately bases the identification of international legal acts on a fickle and psychological element.'[103] D'Aspremont argues that although the Court has made some attempts to provide a clear methodology for establishing intention in the context of law-ascertainment, these attempts have been rather inconsistent and in its more recent case-law, the Court seems to have abandoned these efforts.[104] In his view, the difficulties inherent in determining the existence of an element as intangible as intention necessitate the replacement of this criterion with another one that would provide much needed clarity and consistency. D'Aspremont then moves on to suggest that intention should be replaced with what he calls 'written linguistics indicators', namely with words or phrases contained in the instrument itself that would clearly indicate the binding nature of the instrument in question.[105] Such indicators 'should be as simple as possible to contain the indeterminacy inherent in ordinary language and leave as little doubt as possible as to the instrument of the nature concerned.'[106] As an example, D'Aspremont cites the practice of the Security Council when adopting legally binding decisions under Chapter VII of the UN Charter.[107] Indeed, when the Security Council seeks to impose legally binding obligations on the basis of Chapter VII, it uses very clear and consistent terminology adding the words 'decides' in the text of the resolution itself in order to demonstrate its binding character.[108]

Although D'Aspremont's arguments may be appealing in their mathematical simplicity, upon further consideration, it seems—in my opinion at least—that they are not convincing. First, D'Aspremont argues that the ICJ seems to have abandoned its efforts to provide for a clear methodology in establishing intention in its later case-law. The two examples mentioned are the 1975 Maroua Declaration in the context of the *Cameroon v. Nigeria Case*[109] and the press release of 31 May 2005 creating GTAN in the context of the *Pulp Mills Case*.[110] However, a close examination of these two instances does not lend support to the view propounded by D'Aspremont. In the *Cameroon v. Nigeria Case*, the Court was confronted *inter alia* with the question of the legal nature of the 1975 Maroua Declaration, a joint

103. *Ibid.*
104. *Ibid,* at 182–184.
105. *Ibid,* at 188.
106. *Ibid.*
107. *Ibid,* at 190.
108. *Ibid.*
109. *Case concerning the Land and Maritime Boundary between Cameroon and Nigeria,* ICJ Reports (2002) 303.
110. *Case concerning Pulp Mills on the River Uruguay,* ICJ Reports (2010) 14.

communiqué issued by the parties in which it was stated that 'the two Heads of state of Cameroon and Nigeria *agreed* to extend the delineation of the maritime boundary between the two countries from Point 12 to Point G on the Admiralty Chart No. 3443 annexed to this Declaration.'[111] Cameroon claimed before the Court that the Declaration constituted a binding agreement between the two States to the extent that its wording clearly '*manifested their intention* to be bound by the instrument they signed.'[112] Nigeria counter-argued that the Declaration was not an international agreement to the extent that it had not been approved by Nigeria's Supreme Military Council after having been signed by the Head of State.[113] Contrary to D'Aspremont's assertions, the Court followed its established methodology in examining the juridical nature of the instrument in question. It first scrutinised the actual content of the Declaration in order to determine whether it evidenced the manifest intention of the two States to be bound thereby. Having quoted the abovementioned part of the Declaration where it was expressly mentioned that the two States 'agreed' on a specific maritime boundary between them, the Court concluded that, in its view, the Declaration 'entered into force immediately upon its signature.'[114] The fact that the Court quoted the actual content of the Declaration before coming to a conclusion as to its juridical nature, verifies the Court's adherence to its previous methodology: where the actual terms of an instrument evidence the manifest intention of its authors to become bound, the Court has no need to have recourse to contextual indicators. This point is also supported by the arguments put forward by the parties in the case at hand. In their submissions, both Cameroon and Nigeria built their argumentation around the existence or validity of the intention to be bound by the 1975 Declaration—thereby confirming that, in their view as well, the element of intention was critical for the Court's determination of the juridical character of the Declaration.[115]

The second example given by D'Aspremont relates to the joint press release of 31 May 2005 by Uruguay and Argentina creating the GTAN, a joint commission for the study of the effects that the construction of paper factories would have on the ecosystem of the Uruguayan River.[116] In its submissions,

111. *Case concerning the Land and Maritime Boundary between Cameroon and Nigeria, supra* note 109, at para. 264 (Emph. added).
112. *Ibid,* at para. 253.
113. *Ibid,* at para. 258.
114. *Ibid,* at para. 264.
115. *Ibid,* at paras 253–258.
116. *Case concerning Pulp Mills on the River Uruguay, supra* note 110, at para. 132.

Uruguay argued that, on the basis of the joint press release, the two States 'decided to make the GTAN the body within which the direct negotiations between the Parties … would take place.'[117] On the other hand, Argentina considered that in creating the GTAN, the two States did not wish to substitute it for CARU—another joint commission that had been established earlier for the management of the shared river resources.[118] Having accepted that the press release in question 'sets out an agreement between the two States', the Court found in favour of Argentina and concluded that by establishing GTAN, the two States did not agree to derogate from obligations undertaken under earlier treaties.[119] However, this example does not support D'Aspremont's thesis to the extent that it does not relate to law-ascertainment at all. As the submissions of both parties evidence, the question put forward to the Court did not concern the juridical status of the joint press release of 31 May 2005; neither Uruguay, nor Argentina disputed that the instrument in question constituted an international agreement. Rather, what was in dispute was the scope of obligations undertaken thereby. If it is accepted that the identification of the juridical character of an instrument and its interpretation are two distinct operations—and D'Aspremont makes this distinction with some forcefulness[120]—then it stands to reason that an example of the latter may not be used to refute the validity of the Court's approach to the former.

Furthermore, D'Aspremont's thesis seems to suffer from a degree of internal inconsistency. In his critique of the Court's current approach to ascertaining the element of intention, he argues that the authors of an instrument may deliberately use ambiguous terms in its drafting—in order to benefit from that ambiguity later on and, possibly, deny that they ever intended to create legal effects thereby.[121] However, how would resort to 'written linguistics' assuage this particular problem? Even if we postulate that the threshold of law-identification changes from intention to written linguistics, the residual problem of deliberate ambiguity would still persist: if States consciously use ambiguous terms, having recourse exclusively to the language of the instrument itself would not yield much clarity either. Finally, it needs to be noted that the only example used by D'Aspremont to illustrate the benefits of

117. *Ibid*, at para. 133.
118. *Ibid*, at para. 90.
119. *Ibid*, at paras 138–150.
120. J. D'Aspremont, *Formalism*, *supra* note 102, at 180.
121. *Ibid*, at 183–184.

'written linguistics', *i.e.* the resolutions of the UN Security Council when acting under Chapter VII, is not truly representative of the types of instruments that raise problems in practice. Arguably, the framework within which the UN Security Council makes a decision to impose obligations upon Member States is fundamentally different to the one within which States undertake obligations by means of a treaty or a unilateral act. While the Security Council has a vested interest in making it abundantly clear to Member States that specific obligations are bestowed upon them, the same does not always hold true for States when they negotiate treaties or decide, for their own reasons, to commit themselves through unilateral acts.

All in all, it seems that criticism about the Court's inconsistent approach to intention is unwarranted. In its recent case-law, the Court has re-affirmed its previously established methodology of determining intention by having recourse both to the content of the act and to the context within which it was adopted. Furthermore, calls to move away from intention as a law-identification criterion fall short of convincing to the extent that alternative criteria, such as D'Aspremont's 'written linguistics' theory, suffer—when put to the test—from a greater degree of indeterminacy than intention.

3.5. Interim Conclusions

This section dealt with the question of distinguishing between legal and non-legal acts in the field of the law of treaties. On the basis of the 1969 Vienna Convention on the Law of Treaties and of the relevant case-law of the International Court of Justice, it was demonstrated that the decisive factor for attributing legal effects to an international instrument is whether the instrument in question evidences an intention to create legal effects. The section continued by inquiring into the element of intention and it was further established that, in the context of international agreements, intention is to be determined objectively with regard to the actual terms of the agreement and to the context surrounding it. It was shown that, when confronted with the task of ascertaining whether a given instrument expresses the manifest intention of its authors to be bound, the ICJ gives priority to the actual terms of the agreement and has recourse to context only if the actual terms of the instrument do not clearly express the requisite element of intention. Finally, the discussion turned to D'Aspremont's critique against the element of intention and to current theorizing on law-identification. It was shown that his criticism is, to a large extent, unfounded since alternative law-ascertainment criteria fail to offer more clarity. Against this background, the next section will examine the distinction between legal and non-legal acts in the field of unilateral acts.

4. Unilateral Acts as Juridical Acts

4.1. Intention as the Criterion for Distinguishing Between Unilateral Juridical Acts and Unilateral Political Acts

The previous section demonstrated that the element of the intention to be bound is what distinguishes binding acts from non-binding ones within the framework of the law of treaties. This section turns to unilateral acts and demonstrates that, both in judicial practice and in theory, the same criterion, *i.e.* the intention of the author to be bound, is used to differentiate between unilateral juridical acts and unilateral acts with no legal effects on the international plane.

In the *Nuclear Tests Case*,[122] the ICJ emphasised the importance of the element of the intention to create legal effects for the attribution of legal effects to such acts. In the words of the Court: 'When it is the intention of the State making the declaration that it should become bound according to its terms, that intention confers on the declaration the character of a legal undertaking, the State being thenceforth legally required to follow a course of conduct consistent with the declaration.'[123] In more recent case-law the element of intention has continued to play a major part in drawing the line between legal undertakings and mere political statements of unilateral origin. In the *Nicaragua Case*,[124] the US claimed that a resolution of the Nicaraguan Junta expressing its intentions of holding democratic elections was legally binding upon the latter.[125] The Court refused to share this opinion; instead, it declared itself unable to identify anything in the documents and communications transmitting the Junta's declaration from which it could be inferred that any legal undertaking was intended to exist. Thus, the Court concluded that 'it could not find an instrument with legal force, whether unilateral or synallagmatic, whereby Nicaragua has committed itself in respect of the principle or the method of holding elections.'[126]

Similarly, in the *Frontier Dispute Case*[127] the element of intention was central to the Court's decision. Here the act in question was a statement made by the Head of State of Mali who accepted in advance a report to be drawn by the Mediation Committee concerning the territorial dispute between Mali and

122. *Nuclear Tests Case*, *supra* note 11.
123. *Ibid.*
124. *Case concerning Military and Paramilitary Activities in and against Nicaragua*, Merits, ICJ Reports (1986) 14.
125. *Ibid*, at para. 257.
126. *Ibid*, at para. 261.
127. *Case concerning the Frontier Dispute*, ICJ Reports (1986) 554.

Burkina Faso. The Court, having cited both the *Nuclear Tests* and *Nicaragua* cases, asserted that such unilateral declarations might have the effect of creating legal effects for the State on whose behalf they are made.[128] The Court proceeded to emphasize that the intention of the declarant State is crucial in conferring on the declaration the character of a legal undertaking—in that respect, it was stated that 'it all depends on the intention of the State in question.'[129] Having considered the declaration of the Head of State of Mali, the Court finally concluded that there were not any grounds to interpret it as a unilateral juridical act.[130]

Apart from case-law originating from the ICJ, there are decisions from other international adjudicating bodies in which the intention to be bound also features as the main determinant in attributing legal effects to unilateral acts. More particularly, in the *Case concerning Sections 301–310 of the Trade Act of 1974*,[131] a dispute settlement panel of the World Trade Organisation dealt with the legal significance of unilateral statements made by the US representatives in relation to a complaint filed by the European Union claiming that certain US legislation was incompatible with WTO commitments.[132] In addressing the question of the legal nature of the statements the WTO panel cited the abovementioned passages of the *Nuclear Tests* judgment relating to the element of intention and stated that the criterion of the obligation was the intention of the State to become bound by its unilateral pronouncements.[133] Having examined the statements made by the US Trade Representative, the panel concluded that they constituted legal commitments binding on the US.[134]

Apart from the ICJ and the WTO dispute settlement panel, the arbitral tribunal in the *Dispute concerning Access to Information under Article 9 of the OSPAR Convention*[135] also highlighted the decisive importance of the intention to be bound in determining the legal character of a unilateral act. The arbitral tribunal in that dispute was asked to determine whether the UK had violated its obligations under the Convention for the Protection of the Marine

128. *Ibid*, at para. 39.
129. *Ibid.*
130. *Ibid*, at para. 40.
131. *Case concerning Sections 301–310 of the Trade Act of 1974*, WT/DS152/R, Report of the Panel (Dec. 22, 1999), <http://www.wto.org/english/tratop_e/dispu_e/cases_e/ds152_e.htm> (visited on 15 June 2014).
132. *Ibid*, at para. 1.4.
133. *Ibid*, footnote 692.
134. *Ibid*, at paras 7.125–7.126.
135. *Dispute concerning Access to Information under Article 9 of the OSPAR Convention*, (OSPAR Arbitration), Final Award, 02/07/2003, <http://www.pca-cpa.org/showpage.asp?pag_id=1158> (visited on 15 June 2014).

Environment of the North–East Atlantic[136] (OSPAR Convention) by failing to provide Ireland with certain information concerning the MOX plant (a mixed oxide plant) in Sellafield, UK, on coast of the Irish Sea.[137] Amongst others, the arbitral tribunal was faced with the question of assessing the legal effects of a statement made by the UK according to which no new commercial contracts would be accepted for reprocessing spent fuel at Dounreay, Scotland, with the result of future reductions in radioactive discharges in the maritime area.[138] The tribunal noted that 'unilateral declarations accompanied by an intention to be bound may create binding obligations'[139] and quoted the relevant dictum of the ICJ in the *Nuclear Tests Case*. Although the tribunal explicitly accepted the possibility that the statement may have created an obligation for the UK, it refused to rule upon its binding nature since it considered that the statement was not relevant to the question of access to information about activities at Sellafield and thus, to the dispute.[140]

Finally, it is important to mention that the element of the intention to be bound features heavily both in the reports prepared by the Special Rapporteur[141] and in the 2006 Guiding Principles adopted by the ILC.[142] According to Guiding Principle 1, 'Declarations publicly made and manifesting the will to be bound may have the effect of creating legal obligations.'[143] As far as the debate within the ILC is concerned, there was consensus amongst the members—who accepted unilateral acts as a legal institution in international law—that intention was the main condition for attributing legal effects to unilateral declarations.[144] Pellet, the most vociferous proponent of the Commission's project to codify unilateral acts, stated during the 2002 debate that:

> International law was not based entirely on the expression of the will of the States but it was plain that, insofar as they were bound by treaty obligations and by

136. Convention for the Protection of the Marine Environment of the North–East Atlantic, 22/09/1992, <http://www.ospar.org/content/content.asp?menu=00340108070000_000000_000000> (visited on 15 June 2014).
137. For a case-commentary, see T. L. McDorman, 'Access to Information under Article 9 of the OSPAR Convention (Ireland v. UK)', 98 *American Journal of International Law* (2004) 330–339.
138. *Dispute concerning Access to Information under Article 9 of the OSPAR Convention, supra* note 135, at para. 87.
139. *Ibid,* at para. 89.
140. *Ibid,* at para. 90.
141. See for example the First Report on Unilateral Acts, UN Doc. A/CN.4/486, 05/03/1998, <http://untreaty.un.org/ilc/guide/9_9.htm> (visited 15 June 2014).
142. See the 2006 Guiding Principles, *supra* note 16.
143. *Ibid.*
144. See for example the statements made by Brownlie, Pambou-Tchivoudva, Chee and Addo, Summary Record of the 2772nd meeting, I *Yearbook of the ILC* (2003) at 144–145.

> unilateral acts, it was by their own individual or collective wish ... Why were States bound under the treaty mechanism? It was because they wished to be bound and limit their freedom of action. The same was true when States formulated unilateral acts. It was indispensable to orderly relations between States that they should be bound by the expression of their will.[145]

4.2. The Problem of 'Subjective' vs. 'Objective' Intention in the Context of Unilateral Acts

The previous section demonstrated that, on a par with international agreements, the intention of the author State to be bound is widely accepted as the main criterion for distinguishing between unilateral juridical acts and unilateral political acts. However, intention in the context of unilateral acts creates the same problems as in the context of the law of treaties. Once again, the dilemma between 'subjective' or 'real' intention and 'objective' or 'manifest' intention rears its head. In other words, when called upon to establish the element of the intention to be bound, is one supposed to be looking for the real intention of the author State or for the intention that was manifested to the outside world?

The conundrum of 'subjective' versus 'objective' intention in the context of unilateral acts was intensely debated within the ILC. Koskenniemi adopted a subjective understanding of the notion of the intention to be bound and argued that unilateral acts did not constitute a legal institution because they lacked the necessary objectivity to qualify as such.[146] In his own words:

> The very concept of a unilateral act was fundamentally ambivalent ... It was a sociological description of States acting ... That process was impossible to describe in terms of a voluntary scheme in which States had the intention of creating legal effects and in which they formulated actions to that effect ... The expression of will could not be decisive ... : *it was impossible to know what the will of States was.*[147]

In Koskenniemi's opinion, the ICJ attributed legal effects to the French statements in the *Nuclear Tests Case*, not because it was France's intention to become bound by its unilateral statements, but because these statements had created expectations to other States. Thus, in his view, the only general rule that can be deduced from the *Nuclear Tests* judgment is that States sometimes 'behaved in a particular way and then found themselves bound because that was the logic of the situation.'[148]

145. See Summary Record of the 2722nd meeting, I *Yearbook of the ILC* (2002) 75, at para. 54.
146. See the statements by Koskenniemi in Summary Record of the 2722nd meeting, *Ibid,* at paras 42–46.
147. *Ibid.* (Emph. added).
148. *Ibid,* at para. 45.

However, Koskenniemi's position is flawed on two grounds. First, if we accept that unilateral acts are not a legal institution because the element of the intention to be bound cannot be objectively determined, then it is also necessary to accept that the same must be true for intention in the law of treaties. This would mean that international agreements, the legal character of which is also based on the existence of an intention to be bound, are not a legal institution. This is however not the case. In the previous section it was shown that the ICJ has, in its practice, interpreted the requirement of the intention to be bound objectively—according to the actual terms of the agreement and to the context surrounding it. Pellet also commented on the problems that Koskenniemi's conceptualisation of intention in objective terms would entail for the law of treaties: 'Mr. Koskenniemi had also pointed out that there was no point in codifying promise, for example, because, by definition, it expressed the will to be bound. However, the same could be said of a treaty and it was nevertheless very useful to codify treaties.'[149]

More importantly, this subjective reading of the element of the intention to be bound is not supported by judicial practice. A close examination of the ICJ's judgment in the *Nuclear Tests Case* reveals that the Court indicated that, as with international agreements, what one is seeking when ascertaining the legal nature of a unilateral act is the 'objective' or 'manifest' will of the author. Two points in the judgment corroborate this view. The first one relates to the rules stipulated by the ICJ regarding the method of ascertaining the intention to be bound and the second to the references made by the Court to good faith and to other States' reliance on a unilateral act.

First, the Court, having proclaimed the general rule that a unilateral declaration may be binding if it expresses the intention of its author to be bound by it,[150] proceeded to state that: 'intention is to be ascertained by interpretation of the act.'[151] In a later part of the judgment, the method of interpreting the act was clarified: 'It is from the actual substance of these statements and from the circumstances attending their making, that the legal implications of the unilateral act must be deduced.'[152] The fact that the Court referred to the actual terms of the unilateral instrument and to the context surrounding its making as the means for ascertaining the intention to be bound points to an objective construction of the criterion of intent.[153]

149. Summary record of the 2818th meeting, I *Yearbook of the ILC* (2004) 182 at para. 8.
150. *Nuclear Tests Case, supra* note 11, at para. 46.
151. *Ibid,* at para. 47.
152. *Ibid,* at para. 53.
153. G. Fitzmaurice, 'The Law and Procedure of the International Court of Justice 1951–4: Treaty Interpretation and other Treaty Points', 33 *British Yearbook of International Law* (1957) 202–293 at 230.

Another part of the judgment that supports this proposition is the part in which the Court made reference to the role of good faith and to other States' reliance on a unilateral act. Directly after quoting the dictum in the *Temple of Preah Vihear Case*[154] relating to the normative effect of intention: '... the sole relevant question is whether the language employed in any given declaration does reveal a clear intention...',[155] the Court added that:

> One of the basic principles governing the creation and performance of legal obligations, whatever their source, is the principle of good faith. Trust and confidence are inherent in international relations ... Thus interested States may take cognizance of unilateral declarations and place confidence in them, and are entitled to require that the obligation thus created be respected.[156]

By appealing to the principle of good faith and to the trust, confidence and reliance that other States may place in what was manifested to them by a unilateral act, the Court clearly supported an objective understanding of the requisite element of intention. Had the Court adopted the contrary view, *i.e.* that what matters is only what the author had in mind at the time of formulating the act, there would be no reason to refer to good faith and to other States' reliance. The same opinion, namely that intention in the context of unilateral acts refers to the objective intention of the author State to be bound, also finds widespread support in theory.[157]

4.3. Ascertaining the Intention to be Bound in the Context of Unilateral Acts

It was established in the previous section that, as with international agreements, the objective intention of the author State to be bound is the decisive factor in determining that a unilateral instrument gives rise to a binding legal obligation. However, how is one to ascertain that a given instrument of unilateral character does or does not express the objective intention of its author to create binding obligations?

It has already been mentioned that, as the Court enunciated in the *Nuclear Tests Case*, ascertaining the intention to become bound involves interpreting the intention of the author State in accordance with the actual content of the act and the context attending its making.[158] This is another similarity between

154. *Case concerning the Temple of Preah Vihear*, ICJ Reports (1961) 17.
155. *Ibid*, at 32.
156. *Nuclear Tests Case*, *supra* note 11, at para. 48.
157. A. Orakhelashvili, *The Interpretation of Acts and Rules in International Law* (Oxford University Press, 2008) at 466; C. Eckart, *Promises of States under International Law* (Hart Publishing: Oxford, 2012) at 208–211.
158. *Nuclear Tests Case*, *supra* note 11, at para. 53.

the law of treaties and the law governing unilateral acts. As established previously, ascertaining the intention to be bound in the law of treaties also involves interpretation of the act in accordance with its actual terms and the context surrounding it. Thus, both types of legal acts share the same method of determining the existence of the element of intention.

The only difference—in terms of interpretation—is the standard of interpretation to be applied to unilateral acts. According to the ICJ, the standard of interpretation applicable to unilateral acts is restrictive: 'Of course, not all unilateral acts imply obligation; but a State may choose to take up a certain position in relation to a particular matter with the intention of being bound … When States make statements by which their freedom of action is to be limited, a restrictive interpretation is called for.'[159] Adopting a more rigid standard of interpretation in the context of unilateral acts is understandable; the Court was anxious to ensure that obligations going beyond those intended by the declarant would not be opposable against it, thereby echoing a well-established principle of international law to the effect that States may not be bound against their will.[160] The same restrictive standard of interpretation was also adopted by the WTO Panel in the *Case concerning Sections 301–310 of the Trade Act of 1974*:

> Attributing legal significance to unilateral statements made by a State should not be done lightly and should be subject to strict conditions … A sovereign State should normally not find itself legally affected on the international plane by the casual statement of any of the numerous representatives speaking on its behalf in today's highly interactive and inter-dependent world … nor by a representation made in the heat of legal argument on a State's behalf.[161]

159. *Ibid*, at para. 47.
160. In the *Lotus Case*, the Permanent Court of International Justice stated that:

> International law governs relations between independent States. The rules of law binding upon States therefore emanate from their own free will as expressed in conventions or by usages generally accepted as expressing principles of law and established in order to regulate the relations between these co-existing independent communities or with a view to the achievement of common aims. *Restrictions upon the independence of States cannot therefore be presumed*". (Emph. added).

The Case of the SS Lotus, PCIJ Series A, No. 10 (1927) at 18. The restrictive standard of interpretation to be applied to unilateral acts is also mentioned in the 2006 Guiding Principles. According to Guiding Principle 7: 'A unilateral declaration entails obligations for the formulating State only if it is stated in clear and specific terms. In the case of doubt as to the scope of the obligations resulting from such a declaration, such obligations must be interpreted *in a restrictive manner*.' (Emph. added.) See the 2006 Guiding Principles, *supra* note 16.

161. *Case concerning Sections 301–310 of the Trade Act of 1974*, *supra* note 131, at para. 7.118.

However, it is important to highlight that, apart from the standard of interpretation, which is stricter for unilateral acts, the method of ascertaining the legal nature of the act is the same for both unilateral acts and international agreements. More recent case-law of the ICJ verified that the method of ascertaining the intention to be bound, first articulated in the *Nuclear Tests Case*, is still relevant today. In the *Armed Activities on the Territory of the Congo Case*, the Court was faced with the question of the legal effects of a unilateral statement made by Rwanda's Minister of Justice at the Sixty-first Session of the United Nations Commission on Human Rights, according to which, '[t]he few [human rights] instruments not yet ratified'[162] by Rwanda at that date 'will shortly be ratified' and reservations 'not yet withdrawn will shortly be withdrawn.'[163] The DRC argued that Rwanda, through that statement, had unilaterally committed itself to withdraw its reservation to Art. IX of the 1948 Genocide Convention[164]—a jurisdiction clause which allows the parties to the Convention to submit any disputes relating to its interpretation, application or fulfilment to the ICJ.[165] The Court considered that in order to determine the legal effects of the statement, it must 'examine its actual content as well as the circumstances in which it was made.'[166] The Court, having analysed the statement made by the Rwandan Minister, concluded that it did not create a binding obligation on Rwanda to withdraw its reservation.[167]

The same rule regarding the determination of the element of intention has been also enshrined in the 2006 Guiding Principles.[168] According to Guiding Principle 3: 'To determine the legal effects of such declarations, it is necessary to take account of their content, of all the factual circumstances in which they were made, and of the reactions to which they gave rise.'[169] Again, in Guiding Principle 7, it is stated that: 'A unilateral declaration entails obligations for the formulating State.... In interpreting the content of such obligations, weight shall be given first and foremost to the text of the declaration, together with the context and the circumstances in which it was formulated.'[170] In the

162. *Case concerning Armed Activities on the Territory of the Congo Case, New Application 2002*, ICJ Reports (2006) 6 at para. 45.
163. *Ibid.*
164. Convention on the Prevention and Punishment of the Crime of Genocide, adopted on the 9th of December 1948, <http://www.icrc.org/ihl.nsf/full/357?OpenDocument> (visited 15 June 2014).
165. See Article 9, *ibid.*
166. *Armed Activities Case, supra* note 162, at para. 49.
167. *Ibid,* at para. 52.
168. 2006 Guiding Principles, *supra* note 16.
169. *Ibid,* Guiding Principle 3, at 371.
170. Ib*id,* Guiding Principle 7, at 377.

Expressing an intention to be bound in clear and specific terms does not necessarily involve the use of particular phrases, such as 'our State undertakes to…' or 'we solemnly proclaim to…' Rather, the case-law of the ICJ indicates that it is sufficient that an intention to undertake a binding commitment can clearly be deduced from the text of the act. For example, the following statement, which was contained in a Communiqué issued by the office of the President of the French Republic, was found by the Court to clearly convey an intention to create legal effects in the context of the *Nuclear Tests Case*[175]—even though it fell short of a solemn proclamation:

> The Decree reintroducing the security measures in the South Pacific nuclear test zone has been published in the Official Journal of 8 June 1974. The Office of the President of the Republic takes this opportunity of stating that in view of the stage reached in carrying out the French nuclear defence programme France will be in a position to pass on to the stage of underground explosions as soon as the series of tests planned for this summer is completed.[176]

On the other hand, the use of broad terms and the absence of a precise time-frame for carrying out the commitment usually indicate a political act and not a binding undertaking. In the *Armed Activities case*, the Court found that the statement made by the Rwandan Minister regarding the future withdrawals of reservations to human rights treaties was not made 'in sufficiently specific terms' and lacked a 'precise time-frame for such withdrawals.'[177] Thus, it was concluded that the Rwandan statement was too indeterminate to be considered as a unilateral binding commitment.[178] Finally, the significance of clear and specific wording for ascertaining the existence of a legal commitment has also been enshrined in the 2006 Guiding Principles. According to Guiding Principle 7: 'A unilateral declaration entails obligations for the formulating State only if it stated in clear and specific terms.'[179]

B. Indicators of Manifest Intent to be Bound: The Context in which the Act took Place

i) The Publicity of the Act

Apart from the content of a unilateral act, the circumstances in which the act was made can also be indicative of the author's manifest intention to become bound. One such indicator is the publicity of the act. The ICJ, in

175. *Nuclear Tests Case*, supra note 11, at para. 51.
176. *Ibid*, at para. 35.
177. *Armed Activities Case*, *supra* note 162, at paras 50–51.
178. *Ibid*, at para. 52.
179. Guiding Principle 7, *supra* note 16.

ascertaining the binding effects of the French statements in the *Nuclear Tests Case*, repeatedly referred to the fact that those statements were made in public. For example, in paragraph 46 of the *Nuclear Tests* judgment it is stated that: 'An undertaking of this kind, if given publicly, and with an intent to be bound, even though not made within the context of international negotiations, is binding.'[180] The Court went on to add that:

> The unilateral statements of the French authorities were made outside the Court, publicly and *erga omnes* ... In announcing that the 1974 series of atmospheric tests would be the last, the French Government conveyed to the world at large, including the Applicant, its intention effectively to terminate these tests. It was bound to assume that other States might take note of these statements and rely on their being effective.[181]

The evidentiary value of publicity was also mentioned in the discussions within the ILC. In 1998, Brownlie noted that: 'The criterion of publicity ... was certainly relevant in terms of evidence and of the identification of those to whom the act was addressed.'[182] Publicity also features in the 2006 Guiding Principles as the main indicator of the intention of the author to assume obligations of a legal nature. According to Guiding Principle 1: 'Declarations publicly made and manifesting the will to be bound may have the effect of creating legal obligations.'[183] The commentary to Guiding Principle 1 explicitly states that the public nature of declarations represents an important indication of their authors' intention to commit themselves.[184]

ii) The Forum in which the Act was Made

Next, the focus turns to the forum in which a unilateral act is made as an indicator of the manifest intention of the author to become bound. Two judgments decided by the Permanent Court of International Justice, the *Mavrommatis Palestine Jerusalem Concessions Case*[185] and the *Certain German Interests in Polish Upper Silesia Case,*[186] are relevant here. A common feature of these cases is that they both concerned unilateral acts in the form of declarations made in the course of judicial proceedings. In both cases the Court

180. *Nuclear Tests Case, supra* note 11, at para. 46.
181. *Ibid,* at paras 52–53.
182. Summary Record of the 2527th meeting, I *Yearbook of the ILC* (1998) 59 at para. 15.
183. Guiding Principle 1, *supra* note 16, at 370.
184. *Ibid,* Commentary to Guiding Principle 1.
185. *Mavrommatis Jerusalem Concessions Case,* PCIJ Series A, No. 2 (1924) at 6.
186. *Rights of Minorities in Upper Silesia (Minority Schools) Case,* PCIJ, Series A, No. 15 (1928) at 4.

upheld the binding character of the declarations and was keen to stress the added significance that making such declarations before a court entailed.

The *Mavrommatis Palestine Concessions Case* involved a dispute between the United Kingdom and Greece; the latter was exercising at the time diplomatic action on behalf of one of its citizens, Mavrommatis. The facts of the case originated from a series of pre-war concessions granted to Mavrommatis by the City of Jerusalem. After the end of World War I, the administration of Jerusalem was given to Great Britain on the basis of the terms of the Mandate for Palestine.[187] Subsequently, the UK proceeded to grant a number of concessions to another constructor, in defiance of the pre-existing contracts with Mavrommatis. According to the Greek Government, this amounted to a violation of the international obligations accepted by the UK as the mandatory of the said territory and ultimately, to damage to Mavrommatis' interests.[188]

An issue closely related to the aforementioned question of damages concerned a clause in the contract between the UK and Rutenberg, according to which the latter had the right to request the expropriation of M. Mavrommatis' concessions. During the proceedings, the British agent made a declaration before the Court to the effect that even if a request of expropriation were received, the British Government would not comply with it.[189] More particularly, the British representative stated before the Court: 'That explicit declaration I, as such authorized representative of H.M. Government, and a member of it, here repeat that we intend to carry out whatever obligations, if any, the Court says are imposed upon us by the terms of the Lausanne Protocol. That being so, there can be no question of our acting upon any request to expropriate M. Mavrommatis.'[190] On the basis of this statement, which the Court considered as binding beyond any doubt, it was concluded that no question of expropriation of Mavrommatis' concessions could arise in the future.[191]

Another case, which involved a unilateral act in the form of a statement made during the proceedings of the Court, was the *Case concerning certain German Interests in Polish Upper Silesia*. In that case, the Permanent Court was called upon to adjudicate on the compatibility with international law

187. See the *Mavrommatis Case, supra* note 185, at 11 *et seq.*
188. *Ibid,* at 26–28.
189. In essence, the declaration made by the representative of the British Government endorsed a previous declaration by Rutenberg, according to which the latter renounced the right to ask for the expropriation of Mavrommatis and would not oppose his being allowed to proceed with his concessions. See *Ibid,* at 36–37.
190. *Ibid,* at 37.
191. *Ibid.*

of a Polish national decree, under which the properties of certain German nationals in Poland were to be expropriated.[192] At the beginning of the oral proceedings, the Polish representative declared before the Court that his Government did not intend to expropriate certain parts of the properties in question.[193] The Permanent Court, in a similar vein to the *Mavrommatis Case*, noted that it could be 'in no doubt as to the binding character of all these declarations.'[194]

Not only the PCIJ, but also the ICJ, has acknowledged the fact that a declaration made during judicial proceedings usually evidences the manifest intention of its author to become bound by it. In the *Case concerning Questions relating to the Obligation to Prosecute or Extradite*,[195] Belgium instituted proceedings against Senegal before the ICJ. In its application, Belgium claimed that Senegal had breached its obligations under the 1984 UN Convention against Torture[196] by failing to either prosecute Habre, the former President of Chad, or to extradite him to Belgium for the purposes of criminal proceedings.[197] At the time that the application was filled, Habre was under house arrest by Senegalese authorities.[198] On 19 February 2009, Belgium filed a request for the indication of provisional measures asking the Court to 'indicate, pending a final judgment on the merits, provisional measures requiring Senegal to take all steps within its power to keep Mr. Habre under the control and surveillance of the judicial authorities of Senegal.'[199] In its request, Belgium indicated that the reason for requesting provisional measures was a statement made by the President of Senegal regarding the possibility of lifting Habre's house arrest in case Senegal failed to find the budget necessary in order to hold his trial.[200] Lifting the house arrest would mean that Habre would have the opportunity to flee Senegal and that, in

192. *Rights of Minorities Case*, *supra* note 186, at 12.
193. *Ibid*, at 13.
194. *Ibid.*
195. *Case concerning Questions relating to the Obligation to Prosecute or Extradite*, Judgment, 20 July 2012, <http://www.icj-cij.org/docket/files/144/17064.pdf> (visited 15 June 2014).
196. United Nations Convention against Torture and other Cruel and Inhuman or Degrading Treatment or Punishment, adopted on the 10th of December 1984, <http://www2.ohchr.org/english/law/cat.htm> (visited 15 June 2014).
197. *Case concerning Questions relating to the Obligation to Prosecute or Extradite*, *supra* note 195, at para. 1.
198. *Ibid*, at para. 17.
199. *Case concerning Questions Relating to the Obligation to Prosecute or Extradite* (Order of 28 May 2009) at para. 15, <http://www.icj-cij.org/docket/index.php?p1=3> (visited 15 June 2014).
200. *Ibid*, at para. 13.

Belgium's opinion, would cause irreparable prejudice to its rights to bring criminal proceedings against him.[201]

During the hearings, the Senegalese representatives asserted on several occasions that the statement made by the President of Senegal was taken out of context and that Senegal was not contemplating lifting the house arrest imposed on Habre.[202] At the end of the hearings and following a question by a member of the Court, the representative of Senegal solemnly declared that: 'Senegal will not allow Mr. Habre to leave Senegal while the present case is pending before the Court. Senegal has not the intention to allow Mr. Habre to leave the territory while the present case is pending before the Court.'[203] The Court highlighted the fact that this formal assurance was given before it and concluded that, because of this assurance, there was no risk of irreparable damage to the rights claimed by Belgium.[204] The Court's decision verifies the importance placed upon the forum in which the act is made as a manifest indicator of a State's intention to become bound by a unilateral act.

By way of contrast, the written and oral assurances given by Australia in the context of the *Case concerning Questions Relating to the Seizure and Detention of certain Documents and Data* fell short of eliminating the risk of irreparable damage to Timor-Leste's rights. It is important to note at the outset that, as it will be shown below, the Court did not question that the undertakings were binding on Australia as a matter of international law; rather, they were deemed insufficient since the intention of the author State was qualified by certain temporal and substantive reservations. The dispute in question concerned the seizure in March 2013 and subsequent detention of certain documents and data from the Canberra-based office of a legal adviser to Timor-Leste by Australian agents, allegedly pursuant to a warrant issued under the 1979 Australian Security Intelligence Organisation Act.[205] The seized material includes documents, data and correspondence between Timor-Leste and its legal advisers relating to the pending arbitral proceedings between Timor-Leste and Australia under the Timor Sea Treaty of 20 May 2002.[206] On 17 December 2013, Timor-Leste filled an application

201. *Ibid.*
202. *Ibid,* at para. 68.
203. *Ibid.*
204. *Ibid,* at paras 72–73.
205. *Case concerning Questions Relating to the Seizure and Detention of Certain Documents and Data*, Order of 03 March 2014, at para. 1, <http://www.icj-cij.org/docket/files/156/18078.pdf> (visited on 15 June 2014).
206. *Ibid.* See also *Arbitration under the Timor Sea Treaty of 20 May 2002* (*Timor-Leste* v. *Australia*), Permanent Court of Arbitration, <http://www.pca-cpa.org/showpage.asp?pag_id=1403> (visited on 15 June 2014).

with the Court asking it, *inter alia*, to adjudge and declare that the seizure of the documents and data violated the sovereignty of Timor-Leste and its property rights under international law.[207] On the same day, it also submitted a request for the indication of provisional measures asking the Court, amongst others, to order Australia to deliver into the Court's custody all seized documents and data as well as 'a list of any and all documents and data that it has disclosed or transmitted ... to any person, whether or not such a person is employed by or holds office in any organ of the Australian State or of any third State.'[208]

During the course of the proceedings pertaining to the provisional measures request, Australia gave a series of written and oral assurances to Timor-Leste regarding the seized material, the most important of which (and the one that the Court discussed at length) being a written undertaking made by Australia's Attorney-General on 21 January 2014.[209] The following declaration by the Attorney-General was included therein:

> Until final judgment in this proceeding or until further notice or earlier order of the Court:
>
> 1. I will not make myself aware or otherwise seek to inform myself of the content of the Material or any information derived from the material; and
> 2. Should I become aware of any circumstance which would make it necessary for me to inform myself of the Material, I will first bring that fact to the attention of the Court, at which time further undertakings will be offered; and
> 3. The Material will not be used by any part of the Australian Government for any purpose other than national security purposes which include potential law enforcement referrals and prosecutions; and
> 4. Without limiting the above, the Material, or any information derived from the material, will not be made available to any part of the Australian Government for any purpose relating to the exploitation of resources in the Timor Sea or related negotiations, or relating to the conduct of:
>
>   *(a)* these proceedings; and
>   *(b)* the proceedings in the Arbitral Tribunal [constituted under the 2002 Timor Sea Treaty].[210]

It is also worthwhile to note that, in its oral pleadings, Australia repeated on a number of occasions that the undertaking was binding upon it as a matter of international law. According to Australia's Agent, Mr Reid: 'Allow me to repeat what I said yesterday for the benefit of our friends. The Attorney—General

207. *Ibid*, at para. 2.
208. *Ibid*, at para. 5.
209. *Ibid*, at para. 38.
210. *Ibid*.

of the Commonwealth of Australia has the actual and ostensible authority to bind Australia as a matter of both Australian law and international law. I need say no more. Again, as I said yesterday, Australia has made the undertakings. Australia will honour them.'[211]

The Court had no difficulty in drawing the conclusion that the undertaking of 21 January 2014 was binding upon Australia, since the latter had expressly and repeatedly manifested its intention to become bound thereby: 'The Court has no reason to believe that the written undertaking … will not be implemented by Australia. Once a State has made such a commitment concerning its conduct, its good faith in complying with that commitment is to be presumed.'[212] However, what was problematic for the Court was that the intention of Australia was qualified by two reservations. The first one was of a temporal nature; the Court noted that the commitment of Australia to keep the seized material sealed was only given until the Court's decision on the request for the indication of provisional measures.[213] Secondly, the Court was also concerned with the 'national security' reservation contained in paragraph 3 of the written undertaking. The reservation opens up a possibility of making use of the seized material for national security purposes, thereby not completely eliminating the risk of disclosure of the highly sensitive information in question.[214] On this basis, the Court, while considering it beyond doubt that the undertaking of 21 January 2014 made 'a significant contribution towards mitigating the risk of irreparable prejudice created by the seizure of the … material to Timor-Leste's rights', concluded that it did not remove the risk in its entirety.[215] Thus, the Court decided to indicate certain provisional measures including ordering Australia to ensure that the seized material will not in any way or at any time be used to the disadvantage of Timor-Leste until the case at hand has been concluded and to keep under seal the seized documents and data until further decision by the Court.[216]

iii) The Author of the Act

The authority that formulated the unilateral act on behalf of the author State is also relevant in establishing whether the act expresses a manifest intention

211. Statement by Mr Reid, public sitting held on 22 January 2014, CR 2014/4, at 27, <http://www.icj-cij.org/docket/files/156/17926.pdf> (visited on 15 June 2014).

212. *Case concerning Questions Relating to the Seizure and Detention of Certain Documents and Data, supra* note 205, at para. 44.

213. *Ibid,* at para. 46.

214. *Ibid.*

215. *Ibid,* at para. 47.

216. *Ibid,* at para. 55.

to become bound. The relevant jurisprudence of the ICJ makes it clear that declarations emanating from Heads of States carry a lot of evidentiary weight. In the *Nuclear Tests Case*, the Court stressed that: 'Of the statements made by the French Government now before the Court, the most essential are clearly those made by the President of the Republic.'[217] Furthermore, in its Order of 28 May 2009—in the context of the *Case concerning Questions relating to the Obligation to Prosecute or Extradite*—the Court indicated that it was understandable for Belgium to become concerned by the statement regarding the possibility of Habre leaving Senegal, since that statement came from the Senegalese Head of State,[218] before ruling that the statements made before it by the representatives of Senegal clarified the previous statement by the Head of State and unequivocally expressed Senegal's intention not to let Habre leave Senegal.[219]

The fact that statements made by Heads of States constitute an indicator of the manifest intention to become bound does not mean that declarations or acts stemming from other authorities are not valid unilateral acts. At this juncture, it is important to differentiate between the validity of a unilateral act and the question of proving the manifest intent to be bound thereby. As far as validity is concerned, the Court made it clear in the *Armed Activities Case* that not only Heads of States, but also Heads of Government, ministers for Foreign Affairs and other representatives of a State in specific fields may formulate binding unilateral acts in areas falling within their competences.[220] According to the Court:

> It is a well-established rule of international law that the Head of State, the Head of Government and the Minister for Foreign Affairs are deemed to represent the State merely by virtue of exercising their functions, including for the performance, on behalf of the said State, of unilateral acts having the force of international commitments … The Court notes, however, that with increasing frequency in international relations other persons representing a State in specific fields may be authorised by that State to bind it by their statements in respect of matters falling within their purview. This may be true, for example, of holders of technical ministerial portfolios exercising powers in their field of competence in the area of foreign relations, and even of certain officials.[221]

217. *Nuclear Tests Case, supra* note 11, at para. 51.
218. *Case concerning Questions Relating to the Obligation to Prosecute or Extradite*, Order of 2009, *supra* note 199, at para. 70.
219. *Ibid.*
220. *Armed Activities Case, supra* note 162, at paras 46–47.
221. *Ibid.*

The ILC's Guiding Principles on Unilateral Declarations repeat almost verbatim the above dictum of the Court.[222]

However, the fact that a number of State officials may legally bind the State through their unilateral declarations as a matter of law, does not negate the claim made here, namely that international courts and tribunals—in determining whether a unilateral act evidences a manifest intention to be bound—will attach more evidentiary value to statements made by the upper echelons of a State. The judgment of the Court in the *Nuclear Tests Case* and the Court's Order of 28 May 2009 in the context of the *Case concerning Questions relating to the Obligation to Prosecute or Extradite* verify this claim.

C. The Significance of Registration Under Art. 102 of the Charter of the United Nations

Art. 102 of the UN Charter imposes on Member States the duty to register the international agreements they have entered into with the UN Secretariat: 'Every treaty and international agreement entered into by any Member of the United Nations after the present Charter comes into force shall as soon as possible be registered with the Secretariat and published by it.'[223] According to the second paragraph of Art. 102, the sanction for failing to fulfil this registration duty is that the Member State will not be allowed to invoke the non-registered treaty before any organ of the UN. Art. 102 of the UN Charter essentially reproduces—with minor changes—the duty of registration enshrined in Art.18 of the Covenant of the League of Nations.[224] The latter was adopted in the aftermath of World War I in order to satisfy the public demand for 'open diplomacy'.[225] The need to avoid secrecy in international relations was also stressed at the San Francisco Conference prior to the

222. See Guiding Principle 4, *supra* note 16, at 372. Guiding Principle 4 states that:

> A unilateral declaration binds the State internationally only if it made by an authority vested with the power to do so. By virtue of their functions, heads of State, heads of Government and ministers for foreign affairs are competent to formulate such declarations. Other persons representing the State in specified areas may be authorized to bind it, through their declarations, in areas falling within their competence.

The commentary to Guiding Principle 4 expressly states that the Principle is directly inspired by the judgment of the Court in the *Armed Activities Case*. See Commentary to Guiding Principle 4, *ibid.*

223. Art. 102 of the UN Charter, *supra* note 93.

224. Covenant of the League of Nations, adopted in Paris on the 28th of June 1919, <www.yale.edu/lawweb/avalon/leagcov.htm> (visited 15 June 2014).

225. M. Hudson, 'The Registration and Publication of Treaties', 19 *American Journal of International Law* (1925) 273–292 at 273.

conclusion of the UN Charter. From a very early stage of the negotiations, it became apparent that the treaty registration system established under the Covenant of the League of Nations should be carried forward to the United Nations and thus, Art. 102 was adopted.[226]

On the face of it, Art. 102 has nothing to do with unilateral acts, since it expressly stipulates that it refers to international agreements. However, the fact that a well-known unilateral act, namely the 1957 Declaration made by Egypt on the Suez Canal and the arrangements for its operation,[227] was deposited and registered with the UN Secretariat under Art. 102 of the UN Charter raises the interesting question as to whether registration of a unilateral instrument could be considered as a reliable indicator of the manifest intention of the author State to be bound by it. This is so especially in light of the fact that registration under Art. 102 of the UN Charter is widely considered to be an indicator of the manifest intention of a State to be bound by an international agreement.[228]

In order to put the discussion in context, it is worthwhile to briefly revisit the 1957 Declaration and the circumstances surrounding its making. The Egyptian Declaration was made in the aftermath of the so-called 'Suez Crisis'. The 'Suez Crisis' was created after the decision of the Egyptian Government to nationalise the Suez Canal Company in 1956 and led to a failed military intervention by UK, France and Israel against Egypt.[229] The following year, the Egyptian Government issued a Declaration under which it re-affirmed its intention to abide with the 1888 Constantinople Convention[230] and to ensure free and uninterrupted navigation through the Canal.[231] Apart from re-affirming pre-existing obligations, Egypt—through the Declaration—also undertook some new ones, such as the obligation to ensure that the Canal is maintained and developed in accordance with the progressive requirements of modern navigation and that an autonomous Suez Canal Authority would

226. E. Hambro, L. Goodrich, A. Simons, *Charter of the United Nations: Commentary and Documents*, (3rd ed., Columbia University Press, 1969) at 610.

227. Declaration on the Suez Canal and the arrangements for its operation made by Egypt on 24 April 1957, Registr. No. 3821, 265 *UNTS* 299 (1957). Hereinafter referred to as the 1957 Declaration or the Suez Canal Declaration.

228. See for example the literature cited in D.N. Hutchinson, 'The Significance of Registration or Non-Registration of an International Agreement in determining whether or not it is a Treaty', 46 *Current Legal Problems* (1993) 257–290 at 258, fn.4.

229. A. Clapham, *Brierly's Law of Nations* (7th ed., Oxford University Press, 2012) at 212.

230. Constantinople Convention regarding the free navigation of the Suez Maritime Canal, adopted on 29 May 1888, in J. Allain, *International Law in the Middle East: Closer to Power than Justice* (Ashgate Publishing: Aldershot, 2004) at 277–280.

231. Art. 3 of the 1957 Declaration, *supra* note 227.

further atmospheric nuclear tests in the South Pacific.'[241] Furthermore, the ICJ emphasised in its judgment that the opinions expressed by the addressees of a unilateral act—regarding the scope and meaning of such an act—can in no way impinge upon its legal status and that it is up to the Court to form its own interpretation. According to the Court: 'The Court must however form its own view of the meaning and scope intended by the author of a unilateral declaration which may create a legal obligation, and cannot in this respect be bound by the view expressed by another State which is in no way a party to the text.'[242]

Similarly, in the *Frontier Dispute* and in the *Armed Activities* cases, instead of attaching weight to the reactions of the addresses, the Court made its own determination of the legal effects of the relevant unilateral acts taking into account the content of the act and the circumstances in which these were made. In both cases, the addresses of the acts argued that the acts were binding upon the author States;[243] however, the Court disagreed with them and found that the acts in question were not of a juridical nature.[244] In light of the relevant case-law, the claim that the reactions of the addressee of the act may serve as an indicator of the manifest intent of the author State to be bound seems misguided.

5. Conclusion

This article explored the question of the legal nature of unilateral acts in international law with a view to establish a criterion for distinguishing between unilateral acts with legal effects on the international plane and unilateral political acts. This question was examined through the lens of the 'juridical acts theory', a theory that brings all acts, irrespective of their contractual or unilateral origin, within a broader concept of juridical acts based upon the manifestation of an intention to be bound. It was shown that, while the theory of juridical acts is widely accepted in civil law countries, international law lacks a fully developed theory of international juridical acts and that only a handful of lawyers, such as Verzijl, Lauterpacht and D'Aspremont have dealt with the topic.

241. *Nuclear Tests Case (New Zealand v. France), supra* note 11, at para. 28.

242. *Ibid,* at para. 50.

243. *Frontier Dispute Case, supra* note 127, at para. 38; *Armed Activities Case, supra* note 162, at para. 45.

244. *Ibid, Frontier Dispute Case,* at para. 40; *Ibid, Armed Activities Case,* at para. 52.

The focus then turned to the law of international agreements since this is the field of law nearest to that of unilateral acts in which the problem of distinguishing between binding and non-binding instruments has arisen. It was demonstrated that, according to both doctrine and judicial practice, the manifest or objective intention of the author States to be bound is the criterion for distinguishing between binding agreements and mere political understandings. Furthermore, it was shown that, in the law of treaties, ascertaining the existence of the manifest intention to be bound involves interpretation of the agreement in accordance with its actual text and with the context surrounding it and that, in practice, a number of indicators of the manifest intent to be bound are used to facilitate the task of interpretation including, amongst others, registration under Art.102 of the UN Charter and the existence of provisions regarding entry into force and judicial settlement.

Next, the discussion turned to unilateral acts and it was established that, as with international agreements, the manifest intention to be bound features both in theory and in judicial practice as the criterion for distinguishing between unilateral juridical acts and unilateral political acts. Against this background, the article continued by inquiring as to whether any reliable indicators of the manifest intent of the author to be bound by a unilateral act may be deduced from the relevant judicial practice—a question that was not tackled within the work of the ILC on the topic. In this respect, it was argued that the content of the act, its publicity, the forum in which the act was made and the authority who made the act on behalf of the State may be relied upon in practice to facilitate the determination of the existence of a manifest intent to be bound. The analysis of the relevant case-law revealed that unilateral acts and international agreements have another similarity: the same method of ascertaining the manifest intent to be bound, namely interpretation of the act in accordance with its content and the context surrounding it, is applicable to both. In doing so, it was established that international courts, by applying the same criterion for determining their legal nature and the same means for ascertaining the existence of that criterion, treat unilateral acts and international agreements as belonging to the same genre of acts—thereby validating the theory of international juridical acts originally propounded by Verzijl and Lauterpacht. In this light, the usefulness of developing a coherent doctrine of international juridical acts becomes apparent. This doctrine could become a useful tool in establishing the threshold beyond which States may become bound by their behaviour, irrespective of the form—contractual or unilateral—in which that behaviour is manifested on the international plane.

Book Reviews

Edited by

Rain Liivoja

The Right to Self-determination under International Law 'Selfistans,' Secession, and the Rule of the Great Powers by Milena Sterio. Routledge, 2013. 222 pp. ISBN 978-0-415-66818-7

In this book, Milena Sterio, an Associate Professor of Law at the Cleveland-Marshall College of Law, carefully constructs a new theory to explain and account for recent results of secessionist self-determination struggles. The eternal battle between two fundamental international law principles, territorial integrity of states and the right to self-determination has been raging for about a hundred years already and neither of the competing argumentative sides seems to be tiring out. However, Sterio takes a third way in this book. Instead of turning to the existing legal doctrines and choosing sides, she argues that, after the end of the Cold War questions of self-determination have not been (and could not have been) effectively resolved through the application of traditional legal rules. The system changed with the dissolutions of Soviet Union and Yugoslavia, becoming much more unpredictable and non-legal, and making the two fundamental principles equally useless for solving particular secessionist cases. Actually between the years 1945–1991 there was only a single case of Bangladesh as a successful unilateral secession.[1] While the system was back then definitely more *predictable*, it was arguably outside the legal context as well, meaning that Bangladesh did not have any *special* right according to the general right of self-determination. In all the other cases outside decolonization context, territorial integrity simply won.

Sterio seems to be both an idealistic believer of the international legal order as a whole and, at the same time, very nihilistic about its current schizophrenic application in secessionist situations. Looking solely at the legal facts of the cases, everything seems to be happening at random—arbitrarily even. The Kosovars, East Timorese and South Sudanese are escaping deadlocks and have been (contestably) successful in their self-determination struggles while Chechens still live without autonomy and Georgian secessionist provinces are more or less in a legal vacuum and in a 'frozen state'. Kosovo's 'success' could be contested more than the others, since it is still lacking many attributes of a state. However Sterio is using Kosovo as a successful example and, compared to other cases mentioned, it is much closer to East Timor (with UN presence and nation-building efforts for instance) than Chechnya. Many

1. Bangladesh declared independence after the Indian occupation of East Pakistan on the 26 March 1971. The new self-declared state spent several years in the usual legal limbo resulting from the lack of recognition base and hostile relations with Pakistan. Finally, on a Commonwealth meeting on 22 February 1974 Pakistan recognized Bangladesh as an independent state and the rest of the world followed suit. The case of Bangladesh was exceptional and its circumstances were never repeated anywhere during the Cold War.

One may argue that the independence of Eritrea should be noted as the second successful example of Cold War secession. Sterio does not list it as such and I must agree with her. As with the case of Bangladesh, Eritrea declared unilaterally independence when it felt it had the sufficient military strength to do so, on 24 May 1991. However, this led to series of negotiations with the Addis Abeba government and its independence became *de jure* with the Ethiopian (and subsequent international) recognition, symbolically exactly 2 years from its declared *de facto* independence, on the 24 May 1993. The secession and recognition practices went through fundamental changes during these critical two years. Eritrea 'frozen' case would arguably prefer to have Kosovo's status to what they have now, their territory being treated by an overwhelming majority as under the sovereignty of the old parental state. Put bluntly, self-determination has been inconsistently applied on non-colonized or non-occupied peoples, and these applications have been lacking any solid legal base. The Montevideo statehood criteria, combined with scholarly suggestions of independence, sovereignty, permanence, willingness and ability to observe international law, a certain degree of civilization and, in some cases, recognition, do not really make much of a difference. Certainly Kosovo, East Timor and South Sudan do not outright stand out. Hence we need a theory that can explain why these examples are *sui generis*[2] and this is exactly what Sterio sets out to do.

Sterio's theory is constructed around four cumulative criteria that each people seeking for self-determination must fulfil in order to be successful in their quest for statehood. First, any group looking for recognition for the right to self-determination needs to demonstrate, in addition to normal statehood criteria, that they have suffered heinous human rights abuses. Secondly, it needs to prove the central government's relative weakness and consequent inability to properly administer the region in question. Thirdly, it needs to indicate that the international community has become involved in the administration of the area. Finally, the separatists need to confirm that they have the support and backing of the great powers. However, the first three criteria are only complementary to, and stem from, the last and the most important one. Underlining the significance of the last criterion, Sterio calls this theory the 'great powers rule'.

The great powers possess *de facto* decision-making authority and are, because of this fact, 'more' sovereign than other states in the world arena. By exercising their *de facto* powers in controlling the world media they may be able to affect the public opinion both within their country and globally, therewith manipulating the fulfilment of the first and second criteria. In addition, through their veto-wielding or otherwise disproportionate powers within international organizations, they are usually able to involve these organizations in the places of their own choosing, hence meeting the third requirement. Taken at face value these arguments show that actually secessionist struggles have all to do with politics and friends in high places. No legal criterion is in the end relevant or it can be distorted when convenient. Only the political will of the great powers will make or break all the self-determination claims, now and in the future. Being an international lawyer Sterio, while admitting this, does not like to highlight it and continues to make the proper legal distinctions between peoples and minorities, between internal and external self-determination and so on. In addition

resembles more a post-Cold War case, with the dissolution of Soviet Union influencing the outcome of its self-determination struggle in more ways than one. After 1991 international environment appeared to be a bit more favorable towards secessions and additionally with the disappearance of Soviet aid Mengistu's government was unable to continue the war.

2. The *sui generis* justifications went sometimes to extraordinary lengths with Kosovo. The recognition was a 'special, no-precedent creating exception to, rather than a qualification or abandonment of, the post-decolonization norm of territorial integrity'. Mikulas Fabry, *Recognizing States* (Oxford University Press, 2010) at 180.

she separates the contesting party's claim for statehood and need for recognition—the former being a legal construct which has legal criteria and the latter being a political act that has legal consequences. Under the great powers rule, however, this distinction becomes regrettably unnecessary: if an entity can get the support of the most important great powers, she argues that even matching the Montevideo criteria is not that important. While the author's politics-over-law bias is very clear from the outset, it does not detract from the high quality of her book and it only challenges the more idealist reader to disagree with the carefully crafted arguments.

Also, Sterio applies her theory reasonably convincible to case studies from the practice of the International Court of Justice (ICJ).[3] This being said, two complaints must be made. First; the case studies, while numerous enough, seem to have been chosen for the exact purpose of proving the author right while more inconvenient cases have been ignored to avoid inconsistencies in the application of the great powers rule. She herself admits 'perhaps regrettably' omitting the examples such as Eritrea and Namibia. I find it somewhat puzzling that she did not include in her examples the dissolution of Yugoslavia, which would have been desirable in both time wise since she is mostly concerned with the new practice after the Cold War and content wise since it would have included examples both successful (Croatia) and unsuccessful (Republika Srpska) cases of secession. Secondly, Sterio leaves the number and identities of 'great powers' surprisingly open so they can be adjusted to suit each case individually. She names the usual suspects[4] with a 'these can include' clause so she does not have to stand by all of them in all of the individual cases while also leaving the list open-ended.

Sterio is herself the first to admit that her theory is only semi-legal. She finds this unfortunate and points the blaming finger at the ICJ, especially their unprecedented and missed chance in the infamous Kosovo case.[5] Statehood is at the very centre of international legal order and is in itself of fundamental importance of the system. Therefore the questions of statehood should be carefully regulated by the international community to accomplish maximum predictability in the creation of states. Without a world parliament—and given that the current lack of rules is unsatisfactory—the ICJ would be the logical authority to regulate this contested subject, even with non-binding advisory opinions as it was given a perfect chance with the Kosovo case. It may be argued that the courts should not make law, even 'advisory law'

3. She goes through the ICJ cases of *East Timor (Portugal v. Australia)*, ICJ Reports (1995) 90; *Accordance with International Law of the Unilateral Declaration of Independence in Respect of Kosovo (Advisory Opinion)*, ICJ Reports (2010) 403; *Western Sahara (Advisory Opinion)*, ICJ Reports (1975) 12; and the *Legal Consequences of the Construction of a Wall in the Occupied Palestinian Territory (Advisory Opinion)*, ICJ Reports (2004) 136. She does not restrict herself to ICJ practice and looks at other examples to strengthen her theory, such as Chechnya and South Sudan.

4. G8, India, declared or undeclared nuclear powers such as Israel and Pakistan, and 'rogue' or politically more unpredictable states such as Syria, Iran, North Korea and Afghanistan. She could have also included 'regional great powers' such as Australia, which plays major part in one of her chosen cases, that of East Timor. To be fair, a closed list is all-nigh impossible to construct since the theory has its eye set on the future and power centers, especially regional power centers, of tomorrow are not known or are just plain speculative.

5. *Kosovo Advisory Opinion*, supra note 3.

through advisory opinions. However Sterio is arguing that since we need clear rules or principles for these types of situations it would be preferable to do so through the ICJ than, say to get a resolution out of the General Assembly. The necessary majority would be well-nigh impossible to get at any rate.

Sterio turns to the recent history of secessionist struggle to look for patterns. She seeks to demonstrate with the great powers rule why some groups have been able to form their own 'Selfistans' while others have failed. The rule should be able to predict when a certain group will be able to succeed in the self-determination bid and, take a seat in the General Assembly with a placard in front of them in some instances even contesting their parent state.

Sterio goes through the cases of East Timor, Kosovo, Chechnya, Georgia and South Sudan. She argues that while the great powers rule is applicable for all the cases, only with respect to South Sudan and East Timor was there both a solid legal base for independence—either through delayed decolonization or through remedial secession in the end accordingly approved by Khartoum or Jakarta—and the political backing from the great powers to make this particular independence happen. But these particular instances where international law and the great powers rule coincidentally point at the same outcome do not solve the real problem; that of international law failing to develop new normative rules on self-determination, through its political organs and especially through its courts. The resulting legal vacuum is filled by geopolitical visions of the great powers. Their will may coincide with the international law in particular instances but the backing of the great powers would have been sufficient even without the law. These great powers are the most relevant actors in this arena because of both their coercive capabilities and by the fact that law is not offering any counterbalance to their designs. Yet this particular area of international law is simply too important to be decided through a complex network of power-political visions and changing alliances.

Sterio makes an excellent comparison between the cases of Kosovo and Chechnya in terms of the people's right for self-determination through the remedial secession. She argues that Kosovars and Chechens can be considered peoples so they both have a general right for internal self-determination and may arguably have a special right for external self-determination if the parent state fails to provide them with the internal autonomy they deserve. While Chechnya has never had any substantial form of autonomy, Kosovo had a respectable one until 1989. Under the 'remedial right only' secession theory,[6] Chechnya had as strong a case for external self-determination as Kosovo in 1989 and definitely a much more convincing case for it in 2008. However, Kosovo has fulfilled its national aspirations in an independent republic and Chechnya has minimal autonomy with a puppet ruler installed by Moscow. Kosovo's claim to independence is not stronger than Chechnya's in any legal sense. Kosovo's history, while tragic and culminating in the war of 1998–1999, does not show any *sui generis* characteristics when compared to Chechnya's. Sterio is at her best when drawing

6. This theory has been strongly advocated by Allen Buchanan. His theory places significant constraints of secession, but Kosovo would still easily qualify in between 1989–1999. Allen. Buchanan, 'Theories of Secession', 26 *Philosophy & Public Affairs* (1997) 31–61.

these parallels, making it hard to disagree with her.[7] So, what should be made of the fact that Kosovo 'made it' while Chechnya did not? While Sterio succeeds convincing the reader with some cases I still would argue that she is oversimplifying things and disregarding international law to the extreme on the others. Additionally the numbers of cases chosen fail to convince, which is truly a shame since the theory could have yielded interesting perspectives on, inter alia, Tibet, Krajina and Palestine.

Sterio recognizes the undesirability of the great powers rule and lists its numerous negative consequences. The rule mixes law and politics, and makes the situation worse by giving the latter the upper hand. It promotes total inequality between states; not only by giving 'super-sovereign' status for the great powers—which is not that far-fetched according to realist view of international relations—but also because some potential states are able to achieve full statehood and all the advantages that it brings because of political reasons while just as justified potential states remain frozen in their limbo of *de facto* existence. In addition, since the criteria for the new states are not clear and in the end do not seem to be demanding much, the great powers rule produces only namely or partly independent states or just plain puppet-states. This is a big problem since it undercuts the concept of state sovereignty that the state-based international system is depending on. Would Kosovo or South Sudan be able to maintain themselves without the significant UN and other international organizations' assistance? Can South Sudan maintain itself even with current level of assistance? Is this only a transitional period or are these entities lacking solid ground for their own institution building? As a result of these dependencies regional instability can increase. There are two sides to this coin, however: while it is true that the declared independence of Chechnya clearly increased instability and violence in the region, the *de facto* secession of Abkhazia and *de jure* secession of East Timor have arguably decreased tensions in the short term. Sterio argues convincingly that in the end, no matter how they were created in the first place, all of these entities are totally dependent on the military support of the great powers and if the these powers would ever withdraw, the dependency in question would be powerless to defend itself by internal or external challenges to its sovereignty.

The existence of these new entities may not be grounded in a healthy and viable economic or political framework. Not only is their national cohesion[8] starting to

7. She quotes Russia's own *sui generis* justifications for denying Chechnya's independence, summarized in 1991 by Boris Yeltsin as following; 'Chechens don't have a constitutional right to secede (under Soviet constitution of 1977), their secession would stir other separatists within Russia, and Chechnya is a major hub in the oil infrastructure of the Russian Federation and thus vital to Russian economy and energy access'. While these are understandable arguments, none of them really addresses the Chechens right to self-determination under international law.

8. An '*Infra-review*', observed legitimacy of a new state by its citizens, as presented by Obiora Chinedu Okafor in his *Re-Defining Legitimate Statehood* (Martinus Nijhoff, 1999). Of course these are never black-and-white clear cut things to measure. Kosovo Serbs have very different feelings about the legitimacy of the Republic of Kosovo than their Albanian counterparts and so on. All in all Serbs have had a truly 'lesser' right to self-determination with the break-up of Yugoslavia than all the other peoples of that multinational entity. It is a pity that Sterio did not go through their experiences, except for the few pages in respect of Kosovo.

be created from scratch, but also they all now possess newly created and unhappy minorities. Despite these difficulties, it is arguable that ultimately there has been a positive response to the direction in which the new-born country is heading, for most of the people, most of the time. Therefore there is a great need for a *legal* based doctrine or solid legal practice by (preferably) the ICJ in order to achieve secessions that will prove more or less inevitable, in a more predictable and less violent atmosphere. The outcome of international law might be unjust in some cases, but it is absolutely preferable to plain international politics in all the cases. I think Sterio would agree.

Tero Lundstedt
University of Helsinki

Foreign Investment and the Environment in International Law by Jorge E. Viñuales. Cambridge University Press, 2012. 423 pp. ISBN 978-1-107-00638-6

Jorge E. Viñuales has made a comprehensive and timely contribution that, while focusing on foreign investment, brings together elements from two fields of international law, namely international investment law and international environmental law. Both of these fields of international law have developed quite rapidly and somewhat separately but they are in interaction, for example when foreign investments are targeted to the environment, natural resources and environment related fields, or when they (potentially) have environmental impacts. The book appears to be further developed from an article that Viñuales published in the *British Year Book of International Law* in 2009[1] and naturally goes much further in details and length.

Viñuales sets out to make a theoretical point that, as international investment law and international environmental law develop and become more precise and demanding, the interaction between them will intensify both in terms of synergies and conflicts. Furthermore he claims that this theoretical point has two important practical implications. The first one is that the operations of investors in several different sectors, such as extractive industries, energy production or waste treatment, will be affected. The second one is that the regulatory powers of State in the environmental sector are 'strait-jacketed' by investment disciplines.

When identifying and analysing main legal issues raised by the interactions of foreign investment and environmental protection in contemporary international law, Viñuales aims to produce an unbiased contribution, by taking the perspective of an environmental lawyer in Part II and that of an investment lawyer in Part III. According to him, the protection of the environment is a great challenge of the time, but that such protection is best served by disentangling law from hope. This expression and the employment of the term 'strait-jacket' as described above, suggest that he may lean slightly more towards international environmental law, but with a 'realistic twist'. This impression is of course backed up by Viñuales' professional and academic background, which includes a strong focus of international environmental law as the Harold Samuel Professor of Law and Environmental Policy at the University of Cambridge, Pictet Chair of International Environmental Law at the Graduate Institute of International and Development Studies in Geneva and Director of the Programme on Institutions for Sustainable Development at the Centre for International Environmental Studies. However, the author also has experience in international investment law, and such a combination of expertise is perfect to conduct this study.

The book is divided in three parts. While Part I sets the framework, Parts II and III address, respectively, two kinds of conflicts: normative conflicts and legitimacy conflicts. Normative conflicts refer to conflicts that might arise between international obligation stemming from international investment law and another international

1. Jorge E. Viñuales, 'Foreign Investment and the Environment in International Law: An Ambiguous Relationship', 80 *British Year Book of International Law* (2009) 245–332.

obligation from international environmental law. Legitimacy conflicts, on the other hand, arise between norms or measures stemming from different legal systems altogether. For example, a common type of a legitimacy conflict involves a regulation or a measure adopted by a host state for environmental protection or more broadly for environmental reasons, that adversely affects the interests of a foreign investor, who then claims that the measure or regulation is in breach of an international investment obligation of the host state.

This kind of division is particularly helpful when forming a picture of different fields of international law, as well as systems of national and international law surrounding a foreign investment having an environmental aspect and therefore relevant when considering which conflict norms might be applied into a particular case, thus adding clarity to the presentation of the topic. Then again, it may also be viewed as a bit limiting to categorically divide conflicts and their elements to legitimacy or normative conflicts, as a conflict may well contain both legitimacy and normative elements, sometimes even closely intertwined, making it not always so easy to distinct one from the other. In fact the style of presentation in general throughout the text is somewhat categorized, in the sense that under several headings and subheadings first an argument or statement is made and then it is further developed through a division into subcategories e.g. (i), (ii), (iii) and so on. Again some readers, could view this frequent division clarifying whereas others may find it systematically chopping down the text into quite small pieces.

Viñuales calls for the clarification of the link between international environmental norms and domestic environmental measures, in order to have a fuller understanding of the impact of international environmental norms. A clear link in his view would also demonstrate that collisions between environmental measures and investment disciplines would take the form of normative conflicts, which in turn, would call for a different treatment by investment tribunals, than that accorded to mere legitimacy conflicts.

To support his theoretical point that international investment law and international environmental law are developing and their interaction is intensifying, in Chapter 1 Viñuales points out three signs, namely, (1) conceptual evolution, containing a shift from a primary focus on environmental protection to one on sustainable (economic and social) development towards a green economy, indicating that the role of the private sector in global environmental governance has moved from marginal to central, (2) developments regarding integration of environment into investment treaties and (3) several investment disputes involving an environmental element. This also sets a clear context for the rest of the book. The chapter also includes a very useful listing of recent investment dispute cases which indicates in a clear and easy manner the environmental component in each case. In Chapter 2 the author continues backing up his theoretical point by demonstrating thorough examples how the trend of intensified interaction may be viewed as being synergetic or conflicting and succeeds in it very well.

Part II, which addresses normative conflicts, begins with a short presentation of possibly applicable conflict norms in Chapter 6. Then, Chapters 7, 8, 9 and 10 deal with certain substantial or specialized fields of international environmental law, namely freshwater, biological and cultural diversity, dangerous substances and activities, and climate change. This approach provides further support for the author's theoretical point that international environmental law is becoming increasingly specialized. However, one could also point out that international environmental law is not actually becoming more 'precise' as Viñuales claims: for example, the language of numerous multilateral environmental agreements, one of the main sources of international environmental law, may actually be very imprecise and leave a great deal of room for interpretation and different kinds of applications. This may even contribute to some investment disputes. In practice, the drafting of multilateral environmental agreements is often a result of intense negotiations and, if all goes well, followed by a compromise language in the agreement. Then again, one way or the other—be it precise or imprecise—it certainly leads to the remaining element of his theoretical point that international environmental law (as well as international investment law) indeed become more demanding.

Chapter 10 on climate change includes quite a bit of discussion of specific EU law, in particular in Section 10.2.2 ('Cap-and-trade systems'). While there is interesting case-law on the emission trading directive, this discussion appears to extend a bit beyond the scope of international law, which is the focus of this book.

Another point related to the scope of the book which could be raised in this context, is that there are several references to international human rights law. For example, in the useful list of cases in Section 1.3 ('The third sign—the environment breaks into investment disputes'), the environmental component of *Foresti et al. v. South Africa*[2] is described as 'Dispute concerning the effects of post-apartheid redistribution policies based on economic, social and cultural rights' (at 20). This catches the eye of the reader: How might this be an environmental component in an investment dispute? Similarly, in the same section, cases against the United States regarding minority rights are referred to without providing further clarification of the link to an environmental component (at 23). Interaction of international human rights law and international investment law would seem to be a separate topic.

The link that certain human right cases have to environmental questions (and investment issues) is better explained in Section 9.2.5 ('Protection of the rights of individuals and minorities'). For example, regarding *Lopez Ostra v. Spain*,[3] the author points out the view of the European Court of Human Rights that 'by allowing illegal waste-treatment plant to cause nuisance and health problems to local residents, Spain had failed to strike a fair balance between the interests of the effected individuals and the interest of the community to have the waste (from operation of tanneries) treated' (at 243).

The first practical implication of the theoretical point claimed by Viñuales—that the operations of investors in several different sectors, such as extractive industries, energy production or waste treatment, will be affected—is convincingly supported by arguments throughout the book that refer to several investment dispute cases.

2. *Piero Foresti, Laura de Carli and others v. Republic of South Africa*, Case No. ARB(AF)/07/1, International Center for Settlement of Investment Disputes, Award of 4 August 2010.
3. *Lopez Ostra v. Spain*, Application No. 16798/90, European Court of Human Rights, Judgment of 9 December 1994.

However, a few remarks could be made regarding the supportive arguments for the second practical implication—that the regulatory powers of State in the environmental sector are 'strait-jacketed' by investment disciplines. Indeed there are cases, such as those explored by Viñuales, which strongly support this implication. As Part III of the study well demonstrates, States have been ordered to pay compensation where they have, for example, breached the standard of fair and equitable treatment, or illegally expropriated property of an investor by an environmental regulation or other measure. However, as Chapter 15 on defence arguments based on environmental considerations and in particular in 15.1 on police powers doctrine reveal, a State may have room to manoeuvre if it legitimately employs its police powers. For example, a domestic environmental protective measure that conflicts with an international investment agreement providing for investment protection may not necessarily lead to state liability. There have been some investor-state arbitration cases where arbitration tribunals have taken the approach that deprivations of property, such as expropriation, resulting from environmental measures, may not result in compensation or even be regarded as expropriation as they may be considered to be within the police powers of a state. Viñuales points this out by reference to the cases of *Saluka Investments BV v. Czeck Republic*[4] and *Chemtura v. Canada*[5](at 125–126). However, as he also notes, other tribunals have taken a different approach to the matter, ruling that any taking must be compensated because the underlying reason is irrelevant—*CDSE v. Costa Rica*[6] and *Metalclad v. Mexico*[7](at 124–125).

Additional space for States to adopt domestic environmental measures has also been a topic of discussion within the context of contemporary international investment agreements. A report by the Organisation for Economic Co-operation and Development (OECD) published in 2011,[8] which Viñuales also refers to in the Chapter 1, indicates that language referring to environmental concerns, although rare in bilateral investment agreements (BITs), is common in 'non-BITs', namely regional or other international investment agreements (IIA). From the IIAs examined in this study, 8.2%[9] contained a reference to environmental concerns. All of the

4. *Saluka Investments BV v. The Czech Republic*, UNCITRAL, Partial Award of 17 March 2006.
5. *Chemtura Corporation v. Government of Canada*, UNCITRAL, Award of 2 August 2010.
6. *Compañia del Desarollo de Santa Elena SA v. Republic of Costa Rica*, Case No. ARB/96/1, International Center for Settlement of Investment Disputes, Award of 17 February 2000.
7. *Metalclad Corporation v. United Mexican States*, Case No. ARB(AF) 97/1, International Center for Settlement of Investment Disputes, Award of 30 August 2000.
8. Gordon Kathyrn, Pohl Joachim, 'Environmental Concerns in International Investment Agreements: a survey', *OECD Working Papers on International Investment*, No. 2011/1, May 2011, OECD Investment Division.
9. The study surveys the use of references to environmental concerns in a sample of 1,623 IIAs that the 49 countries that are invited to the—Freedom of Investment process have concluded with any other country. The survey assesses the extent, kind and frequency of such language in IIAs as well as the evolution of its use over time. The said countries were: Austria, Argentina, Australia, Belgium, Brazil, Canada, Chile, China, Czech Republic, Denmark, Egypt, Estonia, Finland, France, Germany, Greece, Hungary, Iceland, India, Indonesia, Ireland, Israel, Italy, Japan, Korea, Latvia, Lithuania, Luxembourg, Malaysia, Mexico, Morocco, Netherlands, New Zealand, Norway, Peru, Poland, Portugal, Romania, Russian Federation, Saudi Arabia, Slovakia, Slovenia, South Africa, Spain, Sweden, Switzerland, Turkey, United Kingdom, and United States.

examined non-BIT IIAs contained such references, but only 6.5% of BITs did. Then again, the references included in the IIAs (a category that includes all investment agreements in the international level, including BITs) varied greatly, but these did include reserving policy space for environmental regulation in general or for more specific limited subject matters (at 14–17).

As there are doctrines, such as the one on police powers, providing at least some level of flexibility and perhaps at least to some extent a trend regarding IIAs that may further increase flexibility in the future by integrating the environment into investment treaties, as explained in the paragraph above, instead of the expression 'strait-jacket' in the second practical implication, perhaps it could have been formulated e.g. that the regulatory powers of State in the environmental sector are *affected* by investment disciplines. This small difference in nuance, making it more neutral, would have brought the second practical implication closer to the wording of the first one—that the operations of investors in several different sectors, such as extractive industries, energy production or waste treatment, will be affected—and at the same time perhaps slightly better reflect his aim to produce an unbiased contribution, in which he actually succeeds well.

As the book is a general presentation to the topic, it necessarily has a limited scope and lacks detail on some points (although the analysis of case law is quite detailed). Nonetheless, it still would have been interesting to read slightly more on certain issues: What, for example, is included in the concept of a 'watch-dog' as a component of a contractually agreed accountability mechanism regarding an investment in extractive industries and what have been experiences with such mechanisms (at 72)?

In conclusion, the purpose set for the book is well achieved: Viñuales successfully present arguments for his theoretical point with its two practical implications. The book is a very welcome contribution to the field, as previously there has not been such a comprehensive study on the topic. Combining two different fields of international law is, of course, challenging but, with the proper limitation of its scope, possible and extremely interesting.

In general, the book is an excellent addition to the discussion of contemporary international law: it shows how important it also is to deal with its fragmentation or further specialization into different fields, as in practice international lawyers cannot really escape from it. It also serves as a very useful general guidance for further studies in the field, as many of the elements presented in the book and some left outside of its scope definitely spark ideas for further exploration. The combination of theoretical and practical points of view made the book a particularly enjoyable reading experience.

Maria Pohjanpalo
University of Helsinki

New Finnish Doctoral Dissertations in International Law

Lectio Praecursoria

Sir Custos, My learned Opponent, ladies and gentlemen, dear colleagues and friends. So it begins.

Where could I go, yet leave myself behind? These searching words were written by Saint Augustine in reflection of the human condition, never wholly autonomous, neutral or objective. He was reflecting thus in the late Roman Empire, an age stamped with elegant scepticism. Augustine's own scepticism had a target. It was the neo-platonist presumption that the universe is structured by order—order that is all-pervasive and accessible to understanding by human mind. Through reason, it was thought, humankind would come to understand the natural order, reach the perfection that was its *telos* (the end goal) and reap the reward of external peace and inner happiness. Not so, argued Augustine, for reason does not operate independently. Rather, it is subjected to the influence of the will. Whereas the reason (*ratio*) may be the cool, calm realm of order, the will (*voluntas*) is the realm of passions and, thus, potentially, the realm of disorder, for will is not an independent agent either. It is moved by love. It can be moved by the right kind of love—which for Augustine was the love of God—or it can be seduced by false loves, the love of self, lusts, the kind that will plunge humankind into a state of confusion. To achieve good, the will of the individual must be moved to seek it through the right kind of love. Now, as described by Augustine, the individual's heroic struggle with the chains of habit that restrain the will from wanting the good is no simple tug-of-war between good and evil, between reason and the appetites, but rather a tense and dynamic dialectic in which the will at one time drives reason toward and at another time diverts reason from the discovery, the acknowledgement, and the pursuit of the good. This dialectic constitutes nothing less than the human self. *Where could I go, yet leave myself behind?* Nowhere. Such is the paradox of human person.

In a further paradox of human existence, each individual being is a fundamentally social being. The universe of others shapes us and protects us. But at the same time it threatens us, even to the point of annihilation. This is because we have different and conflicting interests and passions and ideas of how to live. We are not the same but we nevertheless need to live together. Acknowledging the irredeemability of such irresolution is one of the controlling ideas behind liberal democracy. Accordingly liberal democracy accepts pluralism as a form of organizing human coexistence. With the plurality of equal voices the markers of certainty dissolve. With the end of any substantive idea of the good life, various conceptions of the good life prevail.

Such is the ambivalent world in which my thesis is situated: it is the liberal world, our world. My thesis seeks to offer a critical and yet sympathetic study of the conditions for and possibilities of practising and enforcing human rights—with violence if need be—in a world that is steeped in contradictions. To be sure, the all-pervasive ambivalence has important consequences for the way in which relations within liberal democracies are constituted, and governed. One such consequence is that there can be said to be two opposed attitudes to organizing human co-existence through legal rules. One is individualist, the other is altruist. The individualist approach quite prefers to organize communal life by sticking to the existing legal rules as long as they guarantee enough freedom to have different conceptions of the good life; the altruist approach, on the other hand, much favours to reach for the common good by applying equitable standards and adopting innovative and intrusive policies in accordance with the dictates of justice. Now, given that relations with other people are both necessary and incompatible with one's freedom, altruism and individualism both contradict each other and co-exist with each other. This constitutive dichotomy comes in various shapes and forms.

In part One of the thesis I examine some such mutually exclusive but jointly exhaustive paired concepts against the background of history. I use a historical narrative to illustrate how neither side in these paired concepts can be sustainable on its own: 'government and individual' (played out through the tension between the early liberal theories of Hobbes and Locke); 'universality and particularity' (analysed against the tumult of the great eighteenth-century revolutions); 'naturalism and positivism' (studied in the context of the Terror of the French Revolution and the subsequent criticism of natural rights); and 'international community' and 'sovereign states' (examined in the context of setting up the League of Nations and the United Nations). These various moves in history make up a storyline that is not any old historical narrative but, very specifically, the liberal story of rights—I use this particular narrative with the explicit aim of simultaneously examining and analysing the sequence of events that is usually presented as the triumphant course of development of the liberal ideal of human right, the 'rise and rise of human rights'. By recounting this story through dichotomies, I seek to demonstrate how the various instances of the individualism/altruism conflict have conditioned the thinking, the creation and the application of human rights. Indeed, the liberal ideal of human rights has also been shaped by the violence of antagonisms and revolutionary episodes, historical jumps and discontinuities that mark points of reversal from altruism to individualism, or vice versa. By foregrounding this, I seek to challenge the naturalness that attaches to human rights. That is to say, I seek to challenge the assumed certainty of the universally valid that especially in recent years has given liberal democracies the moral assurance to use social and military power to spread human happiness to those who are less fortunate. As human rights are as justifications for such operations used as the universal fundamental, they have been offered as apolitical, ahistorical factoids, the application of which is presumed to be automatic, axiomatic. And yet, as I demonstrate in my thesis, human rights are deeply historical, social, political, and cultural constructions, always riddled with dichotomies.

Because the various instances of the conflict between 'individualism' and 'altruism' now inhere in human rights, I argue, every instance of administering human rights will raise this fundamental dichotomy. That is to say, any given right will consist of two equally exhaustive but mutually exclusive approaches to the world, one individualist and the other altruist. Any right will speak for the individual as well as the government; particularity as well as universality; positivism as well as naturalism; sovereign states as well as international community. Importantly, do note, as neither of the two options in these pairs will be sustainable on its own, this leads to a continuous, contextual dialectic between the two. Given this ambivalence in rights and their inherent ambiguity as criteria of decision, it is impossible to move in a deductive fashion from the general concept of a right to application. There will have to be some other way to account for the process of practising and deciding human rights.

This is the claim of indeterminacy and it forms the subject matter of part Two of my thesis. As the claim is essentially an empirical one, I use the European Convention on Human Rights as a document through which to illustrate how rights cannot provide determinate answers to competing claims—not at the formation, not in the application. In the cacophony of different conceptions of the good life, I seek to demonstrate, liberal rights can only emerge as legislative compromises. They must be formulated so as to include the different, and at times conflicting, purposes of the drafters, and the assumptions they have about the society, the world and the future. Any application of a thus formulated right will consequently, inevitably, imply a choice among the various purposes. This compels a move to discretion and political preference in the application of rights. Discretion does not mean arbitrariness, however. As illustrated by the case-law of the European Court of Human Rights, decisions on human rights are both indeterminate and non-arbitrary in that they can be explained only by reference to criteria outside the scope of their formal justifications. By this I mean the legal culture of stabilizing conventions and 'shared understandings' of how to identify a rule and an exception, for example, or what the proper institutional role of a judge is, or how the prevailing societal structures should be altered, if at all. Such stabilizing conventions, while essential to the functioning of a legal system, are also problematic in the sense that those that have the power to decide on human rights will in the habitual, bonafide application of formal rights come to reproduce certain a priori commitments—certain values and structures, priorities and prejudices—that have, despite their contingency and inconclusiveness, come to seem natural and unavoidable. And here's the thing: such commitments may well work in favour of those that are privileged, against the downtrodden. They may even become a tool in the hands of the decision-maker. When one becomes alive to this, the indeterminacy of rights also offers a way out of the prevailing status quo to a better, more just world, as the indeterminate nature of rights makes them amenable to consciously purposeful interpretations by the decision-maker.

Because rights do not in themselves offer any clear guidance as to how to choose among the various competing priorities justifying them, then the decision-maker may effectively choose the justification that best fits her idea of a just world. Here, the possibility of abuse arises. After all, rights are indeterminate precisely because no substantive agreement can be reached on what constitutes a just world. A legal technique that reaches directly to (one of) the purpose(s) of the rule, either evokes moral naturalism or licenses the decision-maker to realize her own purpose. This is the second problem with the indeterminacy of rights: it will make rights amenable to consciously purposeful, instrumentalized interpretations by powerful actors. The point at which there is no distance between the decision-maker and her preferences is the point at which hope may turn into fear. With regard to rights, the fear is real because there is violence in human rights. I do not mean only the violence of exclusion and denial of rights. I mean the physical violence that may be needed for the rights to be.

In part Three of the thesis I examine the problem of humanitarian violence in a world steeped in ambivalence. I chart the theory and practice of humanitarian violence from the sixteenth century onwards to the present day to illustrate how, from the start, there has been the keenly felt need to act on behalf of the oppressed, on the one hand, and the fear, on the other, that any right to act on one's own moral impetus could too readily be abused. The tension between human rights and violence, I argue, cannot be resolved. This is because the constitutive indeterminacy of rights and rules cannot be gotten rid off, not even in extreme situations—especially in extreme situations. Instead, we are left with the continuous process of decision-making and reappraisal, and the collective, formal process of ascertainment. Humanitarian violence remains poised between necessity and proscription.

In all three parts of the thesis my central argument is that there can be no general solution to conflicts in which equal and yet different claims compete against each other. Accordingly, those who are in positions of power to decide are fundamentally at a loss and therefore fundamentally responsible. And so, the crucial question becomes whether they can remain responsible for the justice of their causes. *This* is where the hope and the fear of the liberal world reside. And *this* is where formal rules regain their importance. Even if impossible as clear-cut behavioural directives, formal rules are all-important in upholding a sense of the political accountability of those who are in positions of power and decide on such matters as the use of military force. The form of the legal statements is the thin wedge with which the decision-maker will be forced to take some distance to her own preferences. By force of the pure form of legal statements the decision-maker will have to follow a certain procedure and base her decisions on general principles. Instead of taking her own preferences and values as a given, she must argue and justify those preferences in a formal process through generally accepted standards. Crucially, formally, these rules are available to everyone.

This is what legal rules do, and this is especially what human rights do: they construe political opponents as equal members of the community and offer a space in which even the enemy is encountered within a universe of political antagonism instead of seeking to exclude it completely from view. In this way the formalism of human rights strives to keep open the possibility of universal community, beyond the irreducibility of difference. It is precisely because of their fundamental indeterminacy and the dichotomies that inhere in them, that human rights provide the terrain on which the never-ending struggle over the hope and the fear of the liberal world will be waged. They lead into a dialectic between the government and the individual, universalism and particularism, naturalism and positivism, international community and sovereign states—between altruism and individualism. What is more, human rights hold a promise of the universally good that is not reducible to time or place, they offer hope of a better and a more just world. This is where the power of human rights lies. Human rights, I argue, are the most powerful source of critique we have, *as long as* we do not lose sight of the critique of human rights. As I see it, this can be accomplished by understanding the indeterminacy of rights. It is through such understanding that we can take responsibility in the social order, for it makes us conscious of the Augustinian paradox of the human condition, and invites us to accept it without paralysis or cynicism. It beckons us to strike the ultimate pose in responsibility and commitment: 'Here I stand; I can do no other'.

With that, my learned Opponent, Professor Gearty, I now call upon you to present your critical comments on my dissertation.

REPORT ON JARNA PETMAN, 'HUMAN RIGHTS AND VIOLENCE'

Professor C A Gearty

Examination held on 28 April 2012

The Importance of the Field

The issues dealt with in HUMAN RIGHTS AND VIOLENCE are both important and very broad. It is well known how powerful the term 'human rights' is today. There is a vast array of scholarship on the subject, much of it rooted in international law but also much recently emerging from a diverse array of fields, among them international relations, sociology and political science/governance. Additionally there has also always been a strong philosophical dimension to the literature with issues of whether rights exist, their remit and foundational basis (if they have them) and so on having attracted the work of many academics. This breadth and depth of learning is not surprising; as I said in my oral report at the start of Jarna Petman's examination, the idea of human rights has 'replaced God in the eyes of many people as a source of certain ethics in these uncertain secular times. Its attractions are found not only among the post-theists. Old socialists feeling their way towards a new form of expression for their embattled sense of equality find in "human rights" a formula that preserves some at least of what was good about their past while being understood as well (at least to some extent) in today's capitalist world. Human rights give them a chance to talk about the rights to food, to hunger, to shelter, even if it means they also have to put up with rights to property and due process coming from the rich.' I would add here that it is a subject in which a wider range of inter-disciplinary thinkers and political activists feel at home than perhaps any other field of research that can also and at the same time command the attention of the academy.

The field of violence is equally broad and takes many scholarly shapes, not least in the form of studies of terrorism and of war. In the context of law, it has been most frequently seen as a topic best analysed under the rubric of the international law of armed conflict, though increasingly the fields of humanitarian intervention and counter-terrorism have also developed strong legal components. As with human rights there is as much vagueness as there is importance in the term, so it becomes essential to be clear about the focus of academic engagement in the field. Jarna Petman has presented her work on human rights and violence through the lens of an international lawyer with a strong grasp of philosophy and of the history of ideas. As such I have no doubts as to the importance of the field in which she has located herself for the purposes of her work.

The Thesis

Jarna Petman's thesis is divided into three parts. In Part One her concern is with the paradoxes that litter the field of human rights, and her ideas are developed through an historical engagement with her subject. As is well known in scholarship paradoxes are routes to better understanding rather than to confusion—understanding that they are there and then asking hard questions about why they are there helps the thinking academic to push past the obvious into the world of deeper structures. This is something that Jarna Petman achieves with great style.

This section on paradoxes is followed by Part Two, on the indeterminacy of rules. What is particularly valuable is Jarna Petman's location of her subject in the prior—and wider—question of the indeterminacy of rules viewed as a whole. Indeterminacy is as she says (p 11 of the mss) part 'of the nature of rules in general'. How the idea of human rights plays out here is an important theme which is dealt with very well—and rightly fore-grounded by Jarna Petman in much of this part of her work.

Part Three is concerned with violence in particular. I would observe that the relationship between human rights and violence is vastly under-explored in the literature so this section is a particularly welcome addition to learning. There is in far too much of the study of human rights a set of assumptions about non-violence which only a mind determined to avoid the obvious lessons of the past could persist in holding. In fact human rights are steeped in blood—the blood of tyrants; the blood of kings; the blood of colonial subjects made to genuflect either to Christian or (as we have now got into the habit of saying) 'Western' values. In this part of her work, Petman is particularly engaged with how this violence has played out in the course of the past decade—a time during which all of us have had less excuse than before not to make this connection with violence: human rights have played at least a part in the justifications provided for the invasions of, first, Afghanistan and then, secondly and mainly, Iraq. Some well-established human rights 'experts' have even written books about the need for a 'lesser evil' to confront and destroy the enemy without. I found Jarna Petman's third part of her thesis, which she calls in a cleverly disconcerting way 'humanitarian violence', particularly stimulating.

Application of the Examination Criteria

(i) Has the candidate demonstrated capacity for 'independent research'?

I have no doubt that the work is that of Jarna Petman and the capacity for independent research that it displays is self-evident. Her successful bringing to a conclusion of this project, the immensity of which would have defeated many lesser scholars, is a testimony to her ability to engage in independent work. This would be the case even if this had been Jarna Petman's sole activity over the past few years. In fact she has combined it with many professional duties in the University—and to have been able to combine her research with these duties is further evidence (if it were needed) of her capacity for independent research.

(ii) Has the candidate demonstrated her 'thorough knowledge of the field'?

Jarna Petman's learning is prodigious. The thesis ranges far and wide, dealing with the origins of the language of rights in Greek and Roman times through the medieval period and into the present. It covers the more recent emergence of the idea of international human rights law and the grip that the field has taken on international discourses of rights in recent decades. It locates the work that it does in a strong critical tradition (in which Jarna Petman moves with confidence) which roots the analysis of law in a wider sceptical debate about the indeterminacy of rules and about the implications of this for the study of law. The last part, on 'humanitarian violence', demonstrates a thorough understanding of the development of international law and of the emergence within that field of discourses of justice and of humanitarian intervention which have underpinned the use of violence for the end of human rights.

(iii) Has the candidate demonstrated her competence 'in the methodology of the research field'?

Jarna Petman has chosen as her approach a methodology which combines the strengths of historical research, critical thinking and legal analysis. From time to time the work displays something of a tension between the narrative form best suited to a text book and the more scholarly/critical engagement that fits well with an academic monograph. It was as though at these points the reader received the impression of there being here not one book, but two: the first a well-written account of the emergence of human rights law and its sister field of humanitarian law; the second a more scholarly and shorter book on the indeterminacy of rules and a set of reflections on how this indeterminacy plays out in the human rights/humanitarian law field. While this tension is never fully resolved—and indeed at the Oral Examination I wondered whether or not the answer might be to think about the project as having two potential off-springs in the literature rather than one—I have no doubts that the holding of the two together in the work as a whole is successful, at very least is done in a highly competent way.

(iv) Have the 'objectives, methods and results of research … been dealt with' with 'sufficient thoroughness in the dissertation'?

The answer is yes. The thoroughness of the dissertation is one of its very strongest features and is a reason for my unequivocal judgment about the 'thorough knowledge' of her field that Jarna Petman has displayed. In her introduction she sets her objectives in a clear way and then works them through the thesis in a manner that is consistent and effective. The thesis culminates in a clear recounting of what its original goals were and how these had been achieved in the pages that had gone before. There is little sense in this dissertation of a thesis drifting around in search of themes with which to fill its pages. Of course the task Jarna Petman has set herself is enormous and I need at this juncture to recall the remarks I have made above about the textbook aspect to some of what she has written: certainly sometimes the book sets out to cover large-scale narratives in a descriptive way but I never felt this was at the price of overall coherence.

(v) What is 'the scholarly value of the dissertation'?

The work is effective as a work of scholarship at two levels. First it is an important account of the emergence of international human rights and humanitarian law as elements of great importance in the field of international law. Second it is a meditation on the uncertainty of rules and of what the effect of such indeterminacy is for the scholar working in this field.

I would also suggest that there is a potential third scholarly dimension of the first importance, one that is latent in the dissertation but which could perhaps be foregrounded a little more in any subsequent development of the thesis for publication. This is the relationship between human rights and violence. I have already alluded to this, and referred to the way in which Jarna Petman deals with it, mainly in Part Three of the thesis. But as discussed in the Oral Examination—and anticipated above—it is clear that the theme of violence runs through the history of human rights and links very nicely not only with the historical treatment in Part One but with the reflections on indeterminacy in Part Two as well. This was the focus of much discussion at the Oral Examination and I will not repeat it at any great length here, except to say that many of the writers (eg Hobbes; Rousseau), events (Magna Carta 1215; America, 1776; France 1789) and legal developments (the Universal Declaration of Human Rights, 1948; common Article One of the Covenant on Civil and Political Rights and the Covenant on Economic, Social and Cultural Rights, 1966) discussed in the book reflect different types of engagements with the fact of political violence: the subjugation of the King in 1215; the fact of the danger of violence inherent in life producing Leviathan (Hobbes); the overthrow of the Ancien Regime producing the French Declaration of the Rights of Man and of the Citizen, 1789; and so on. Were the thesis to be revised for publication as a scholarly monograph, then space would open up for a reading of human rights in history which would be able to devote the right amount of attention to this neglected thread in human rights, the thread of violence. I think such a volume would be very scholarly—and much of the thinking and preparatory work for it has already been done in the course of this excellent thesis.

General Comment

I want as I draw these brief remarks to a close to make one point about substance and a second about style.

As to substance, there is a need for critical scholars to do what Jarna Petman has done so well in many parts of this work, and this is to wrestle with the issue of the 'bad-faith' use of words, of (in this context) the twisting of the language of rights to do harm not good. Why do I say this? It is easy for the facile promoters of the ersatz-truth promised by rights simply to assume their version of the world is right and criticise everybody around them for taking a different view. It is much harder for a critical scholar who is after all committed to indeterminacy, who has made uncertainty an article of faith. How do you criticise others when you yourself deny that there is a simple truth out there which you have got hold off (and others have yet to see)? It is to Jarna Petman's immense credit that she takes this issue on and addresses it honestly and imaginatively. Of course this produces a tension, the commitment to indeterminacy jostling with the passionate belief in right and wrong, but it is a creative tension—one that leads to a better understanding of her subject.

Now as to style. Jarna Petman is a truly excellent writer. Her English is clear, almost old-fashioned in its construction and, at times, quite formal in its structure. The thesis is marked by excellent phrase-making, sparkling ways of describing old things, new spins put on what you might have assumed were materials about which nothing fresh could be said. There is a passion driving the narrative too, a strong sense throughout of an author with something to say—and with a pleasing ability to say it. As a reader required to examine the thesis I was exceptionally grateful for the excellent prose style of Jarna Petman—it made her thesis not only easy to understand but a pleasure as well to read.

The Performance in the Public Examination

Finally so far as the criteria of evaluation are concerned, I am asked to comment on the candidate's performance in the public examination. This was excellent. Jarna Petman started in the correct way with a written account of her work which explained what she was seeking to do in a way that made sense to the people present, many of whom may well have been coming to the subject for the first time. After this opening presentation and my preliminary remarks there was for a very substantial period of time an intense discussion of the work and of the themes and ideas that underpinned it. The atmosphere was enlivened by the large number of people present (over 100, I would say) and while this made for quite an occasion I imagine it can only have added to the pressures on the examinee. Jarna Petman acquitted herself excellently, conceding what had to be conceded but knowing also when to stand her ground. I was particularly impressed by her ability to withstand some quite hostile questioning which while never undermining her thesis forced her to a justification of it in a sometimes quite fundamental way. This she did with great ability. It is clear that she is a very good speaker used to the public arena and no doubt this experience assisted her in the examination. It was all round a very impressive performance.

Recommendation

I recommend that Ms Petman be awarded the Doctorate Degree.

LSE 10 May 2012

A Science of Interests: The Project of 20th Century Positivist International Law*

Mónica García-Salmones

When I opened for the first time *Law as Fact*, by Karl Olivecrona, a well-known author in these latitudes, I was struck by one thing.[1] It was not so much the content of the book, which nevertheless constitutes an interesting case of positivist literature. The striking fact was rather what appears on the library card, inside the cover of the book. Among other things the card, probably inserted somewhere in the late 1930's or early 1940's, reads: '*Kirjoja ei saa lainata koteihin, joissa sairastetaan tarttuvia tauteja.*' In English: 'You may not borrow books if in your home someone has a contagious disease.' I do not think that this warning was meant particularly for Finnish readers. I can well imagine that in any European country, or indeed, in any country where in the 1930's there was a library, one could reasonably expect to find such a warning. We do not find these prohibitions in our books anymore, probably, because the spread of contagious diseases has been prevented, and with the wonderful advance of the natural sciences we can state today that contagious diseases in Finland, are an event, the exception, and not the rule.

There was an incredible development in natural sciences in the years between 1850 and 1950, the period roughly covered by the present research (the discovery of the DNA already in the 19th century, for instance). This dissertation analyses international legal positivists' desire to emulate the success of the empirical methods applied in the biological and physical sciences; their wish to work with law with the certainty that natural facts started to provide as the natural sciences method developed. On commencement of this project, the results to be obtained from it were not immediately clear, but these evolved slowly through the examination of many texts and historical narratives. I traced positivist lawyers' claim about the impossibility of knowing an objective reality and of recognising what is objectively good and just beyond the competition between individual interests. Positivists perceived their lack of the theoretical tools to predict and even understand the behaviour of individuals or states, and shifted their focus towards empiricism. The aim was then to provide a viable representation of the world, as hard sciences were already doing, for instance, in studies of the behaviour of atoms.

Positivism was the main school of international law during the 20th century. That this was the case was a matter facilitated by the coordinated efforts made by Western lawyers to present to the world the positivist legal theory as eminently separated from politics. International lawyers who took an emphatically realist approach described

* *Lectio praecursoria* held at the public examination of the doctoral dissertation at the University of Helsinki on 7 May 2012. Professor Joseph H. H. Weiler from New York University acted as opponent.

1. Karl Olivecrona, *Law as Fact* (Einar Munksgaard: Copenhagen and Humphrey Milford: Oxford, 1939).

law as a post-political moment, thus referring to the problematic issue they considered law had settled: conflict. In this manner, they demonstrated that they were not very far removed from theories about the state and the state of nature which arose in early modernity. Law was thus the outcome of politics or the consent of nations, as someone like Lassa Oppenheim would put it, and as such it was endowed with authority. The convention was, firstly, to highlight the legitimacy of the community of interests that international society was now viewed as comprising, on the basis that it was legal; and, secondly, to abstain from unpacking the normative substantial choices made by states in enhancing that community of interests through international law. If we take seriously the claim that 'law is the normative order governing politics'[2] and use it as an analytical tool to interpret a snapshot of the state of international law at the beginning of the 20th century, the image of a very thin international public sphere appears. The roughly common economic interests of powerful Western states constituted international politics in this sphere.

The first question this dissertation has set out to answer is whether positivist law merely refracted the reality of international politics during the 20th century; or whether it in fact contributed to the production of that reality, thus participating in a wider political project for a certain type of economisation of the legal-political world. The dissertation has also sought to explore whether norms in positivist international law were able to devise an empty normativity, as the positivists asserted; and therefore, whether they merely 'carried' the common interests of states.

The findings of this research situate the theoretical background of international economic-legal positivism within the philosophical tradition of interests and the impetus that that tradition gained from the following factors: (1) the rise of the British Empire, as a fundamentally economic empire; (2) the growing economic interdependence between countries that went hand-in-hand with a new understanding of the concept of 'civilisation' as a way to organise the economic exploitation of the territories of the world; and (3) the centrality acquired by international adjudication as a legal technique used to decide in relation to interests.

This study reveals an era of fascination and dazzle in the discipline of international law engendered by the use of the empirical scientific method and the discovery of the unifying virtues of economy. That era has now passed, not only because we look at the world today and see an economic crisis that is for the most part incomprehensible, but more fundamentally because we are now aware of the reality that material and spiritual wealth is not reaching large parts of the populations of the globe—a fact the scientific method is not able to address, let alone explain.

The analysis pursued throughout the dissertation demonstrates that international legal positivists condensed the new theoretical foundation of international public law into the concept of interests. The aim was to establish, as the basis of a new legal-global order, an uncomplicated system of law among various commercially interdependent nations interacting among themselves and with powerful private individuals.

2. Jan Klabbers, *The Concept of Treaty in International Law* (Kluwer Law International: The Hague, 1996) at 247; see generally on this question, Martti Koskenniemi, 'The Politics of International Law', 1 *European Journal of International Law* (1990) 4–32.

That system of law would satisfy the opposing economic interests of an elite group and, occasionally transform them into common interests. The preference for this new foundation for the production of the new international law was clearly a symptom of a wasted intellectual reservoir and a consequence of a pragmatic era.

Although taken to be equivalent with his or her interests, in 20th century positivism the individual does not appear at a natural level as the 'self-interested individual of the classic economists'—Adam Smith and others—and natural lawyers from Grotius onwards. Legal positivists of the last century viewed the nature of the individual as being instead biological; both instincts and struggle. Therefore, the paradigm of interests in positivist international law is even more foundational than being something 'natural' in human beings. The new positivist legal science regarded 'interests' as a pattern providing for order, which explained the world in economic terms: commonality of interests, competition of interests, balance of interests, solidarity of interests.

The specific meaning and content of the concept of interests varied within the tradition, but always had a fixed value of an economic nature. International legal positivists generally used interests as a term to describe commercial and economic activities. And while interests can also encompass political interests, they are always described in a relativistic sense and, as a result, as the object of exchange and competition. This finding lies behind the classification of the type of 20th century international legal positivism analysed in this book as economic-legal positivism.

Legal positivists rejected transcendence, and deliberately avoided producing an adequate theory of morality in law, or indeed any theory that reflected on what is to be a human being or considered the human being holistically: as part of a community, as a spiritual and social being. Using this standpoint, economic-legal positivism produced an isolated individual, who is, as it were, 'theoretically floating'. This is the 'economic individual'.

Notions like the reason of lawyers, morality and justice were labelled as unscientific, among other reasons, because they produced anarchic—i.e. unpredictable and uncertain—results. Law ought to be based on statistics and facts in order to be scientific—the facts of aspects of human behaviour should correspond with the facts of the content of law.

Just as in the international positivist project the universality of ancient legal orders was deprived of its political or moral core and thus made universally materialist, the mode of thinking about economic issues within a political world was turned into the opposite conundrum: how should politics be conducted in an economic world? The neoliberal politics of the project led to the establishment of a legal framework in which every individual can seek his or her own interests

Reaching beyond the previous analysis, my argument has been that if international law, or perhaps, if in particular international law, is thought to have been made by human beings—a key argument of positivists—and for human beings, then in order to produce good, scientific law, lawyers no longer need only possess economic expertise and a focus on interests, but should also return to the ideal of expertise in human beings. As has become clear, alterity is not only an expression of solidarity in times of crisis; but openness to others is a necessary means for producing international law with a foundation in the individual.

Individualism is an understanding of human beings that distorts reality, among other reasons, because it underestimates the political capacity of human beings. Due to this flaw, it is sterile in the project of further theorising on an international polity. Faithful to its ideological principles, the theory of individualism goes in the opposite direction to a theoretical foundation of international law on a common polity, on a theory of publicness, on the sociability of human beings, on the need for solidarity among countries—essentially, it stands against the idea of international law as a social phenomenon. Indeed, rather than promoting the sovereignty of international law by fostering its democratic aspects—representation, accountability and deliberation—20th century economic-legal positivists argued that the democratic political system of the nation state was in reality only an arena for the competition of interests—that the polity, the *demos*, was a fiction both in the national and international realms. In brief, they argued that the competition of interests was a universal political phenomenon.

Indeed, if one reduces international law to an economic paradigm which states that what unifies humanity is its economic aspects, both historical and ontological, it is likely that individualism will produce a functioning legal order.

For lawyers drawing on the materialist economic tradition of the classic economists and the Austrian Economic School, the objective standpoint of the legal order is established by an 'empty normativity'—a normativity without substance that functions as the mirror concept of interests, and unites private and public interests in a single concept of law. This empty normativity offers an objective stage for exchange and for channeling the conflict of interests, and is thus adapted to the conditions and philosophical foundations of modern capitalism.

Kelsen, one of the main figures of the project of positivism in international law and therefore the key figure in this book, devoted a large proportion of his 600 works to theorise on the standpoint that there is 'no right answer', but only ideologies trying to veil their particular interests.[3] However, although Kelsen's conviction to that effect was shared by the majority of legal positivists—which may be seen as an expression of their scepticism—they were theoretically ambitious. Thus, the key element of 20th century positivist international law is its universalism in, as we have seen, philosophical and epistemological terms: law becomes a legal medium.

But their universalism was also pragmatic. The ideal of the *civitas maxima* as an expression of universalism and community was embraced with a pragmatic twist. Because economic-legal positivism is not based on a transcendental principle, as we have seen, the universality of the legal order is to be achieved by promoting the empirical unity of the contents of the different legal orders, international law becoming a regulator of human behaviours. This has found expression, in particular, in the proliferation of international organisations since World War II and the consistent elaboration of a regulatory regime on a global scale (covering such areas as trade, asylum, finance, and the environment).

3. Hans Kelsen, 'Zur Theorie der Interpretation', 8 *Internationale Zeitschrift für Theorie des Rechts* (1934) 9–17, at 14.

This research approaches its subject on the basis of philosophical realism, an approach chosen due to its inherent complexity which facilitates a holistic take on nominalism and idealism, both of which being philosophies economic-legal positivism draws on. Furthermore, the epistemology of philosophical realism is based on human sociability, which offers a better representation of the real world than that provided, for instance, by the immanent philosophy of the 19th century that was also employed by economic-legal positivists.

The research had recourse to the geological method originally developed by Joseph H. H. Weiler. Using this method, this dissertation is a study of strata—layers of international legal theories and practices of the past with internally consistent characteristics. The method is useful because it allows the reader to isolate a single layer of the past and research its historical attributes and philosophical principles. This is the case because geology emphasises accretion and not change, thus facilitating the examination of a section forming a single, independent whole. The geological method has also contributed to the discovery of unexpected theoretical connections when one proceeds to the examination of a section. One such connection made in this book, significantly, is the link between economic-legal positivism and international administration.

Using the geological method one can state that economic-international legal positivism is an ever-expanding and, more importantly, theoretically deepening phenomenon of the 20th century. In the 21st century, we observe the difficulty of theorising concepts such as that of international polity or of international public law; and we also ascertain that international law is unable to address the question of solidarity among countries. In geological terms, this research claims that this problem is only the surface, under which rest a series of layers of philosophies and legal theories founded upon materialist economic principles.

The economic legal-positivists were diligent crafters of the new global order during the past century, and many may feel compelled to be grateful for that. Nevertheless, at various points in this book the reader might have felt invited to concur with the argument that 'interests prove a very fragile foundation for an international community'.[4]

Together with the list of conclusions enumerated above, the current running below the thesis's surface is an enquiry about the position in the discipline of international law occupied by the scientific method today. By describing economic-legal positivism's search for a scientific method during the 20th century, uncovering the political nature of that project—at once enveloped and facilitated by its method—and evaluating that political project are important purposes of this research. Probably one of the main discontinuities discernable between the international legal positivists of the 20th century and current authors advocating positivism is that the latter lack the former's sense of political urgency. The consciousness of being involved in a struggle

4. Kingsbury and Donaldson recently wrote what seems to me to be a project for the reconceptualisation of law, Megan Donaldson and Benedict Kingsbury, 'From Bilateralism to Publicness in International Law', in Ulrich Fastenrath, Rudolf Geiger, Daniel-Erasmus Khan, Andreas Paulus, Sabine von Schorlemer and Christoph Vedder (eds), *From Bilateralism to Community Interest: Essays in Honour of Bruno Simma* (Oxford University Press, 2011) 79 at 82.

against political conservativism and more traditional forms of liberalism, while at the same time living through the growing trend towards global economic unity gave economic-legal positivism great critical power at the beginning of the last century. That political project of uniting the global order through economy has evidently lost its freshness. However, no plausible substitute project has emerged and therefore nothing notable has changed in that (political) sphere in current international legal positivism. Of course, international law in general remains strongly positivist, and some argue that this might be a good thing.[5] But the fact that we are still bound up in a political project of the past also helps explain in historical terms that the key elements of the revival of theoretical positivism tend to be based on internal deliberations on how to maintain the formality of law. Perhaps inadvertently, this focus on 'only formality' carries forward the political premises of its predecessors by glossing over a discussion about those very premises; but in a more fundamental sense the attitude of some of current positivists seems to arise from an awareness of substantial problems and risks in the international legal order, which paradoxically (paradoxically, because the problems have been engendered through law)[6] now, only law can contain.[7]

By engaging with the fundamentals of positivist international law, the present dissertation uncovers a political theory about the role of law founded on an economic paradigm. It is for us to broaden that foundation in the project of making a more just world.

5. And in fact apparently necessary in order to put forward naturalist principles; for a helpful discussion see Jan Klabbers, 'Back to Front: Positivism, Constitutionalism, and Accountability' in Jean d'Aspremont and Jörg Kammerhofer (eds), *International Legal Positivism in a Post-Modern World* (Cambridge University Press, forthcoming in 2014).
6. See David Kennedy, 'Law and the Political Economy of the World', 26 *Leiden Journal of International Law* (2013) 7–48; Benedict Kingsbury, 'International Courts: Uneven Judicialization in Global Order', in James Crawford and Martti Koskenniemi (eds), *Cambridge Companion to International Law* (2011) 203–227; see especially Antony Anghie, *Imperialism, Sovereignty and the Making of International Law* (Cambridge University Press, 2005); also uncovering the structural bias of the system of international law against the Third World, Martti Koskenniemi, *From Apology to Utopia: The Structure of International Legal Argument.* (reissue, Cambridge University Press, 2005).
7. Two interesting and perhaps the most representative examples of this formalism are Jean d'Aspremont, *Formalism and the Sources of International Law* (Oxford University Press, 2011) and Jörg Kammerhofer, *Uncertainty in International Law: A Kelsenian Perspective* (Routledge, 2010).

A Science of Interests: The Project of 20th Century Positivist International Law by Mónica García-Salmones. University of Helsinki, 2012

I served as preliminary reader and then 'opponent' of the dissertation of Mónica García-Salmones. In the following I present my reflections and conclusions on the intellectual and scientific quality of the research, on the originality of the theses contained in the dissertation and on its contribution to the field. I also make a recommendation as to the 'grade' of the dissertation.

Doctoral traditions differ from country to country ranging from the term-paper-masquerading-as-a-doctorate of the Austrian tradition through the 1500-page Spanish tomes to the 15-year-research one sometimes sees in Denmark. One's judgment and assessment are conditioned by the influence of such diverse traditions on one's expectations and sense of quality. I should declare my own: my own sensibilities were forged in the European University Institute where I defended my own dissertation, and then at the Universities of Michigan, Harvard and NYU where at various times I directed the doctoral programs—I am currently the faculty director of the doctoral program at NYU. I have sat on thesis juries and examined dissertations throughout the Western world.

It is against this background that I have formed my opinion on *A Science of Interests: The Project of 20th Century Positivist International Law*, the title of the dissertation submitted and defended by Mónica García-Salmones.

It is, in a very literal sense of the word, an outstanding piece of work which confirms Helsinki not only as one of the most important centers for the study and research of international law, but as a distinguished 'doctoral school' of which this dissertation is an example.

The dissertation employs, impressively, several methodologies in the elaboration of its central theses: it is at one and the same time, an history and an historiography. It employs philosophical tools and makes a contribution to philosophy, notably notions of 'alterity'. It predicates a materialist notion of economics and political economy—and their alternatives—as foundational for understanding late 19th century international law and its alleged (alleged, since this is the core of the hypothesis/thesis) evolution/transformation in and through the 20th century, and in doing so it makes contributions to our understanding of political economy not so much as a science in and of itself, but as a refracting tool to understand law.

The overall and most impressive methodological contribution is holistic: the ability to employ these different perspectives as a method to understanding not only certain evolutionary decisive moves in international law, but international law as such. In this respect this work is, in the strict sense, second to none. I have not encountered a work that does this better. These were the words I used in my preliminary evaluation and this judgment is confirmed on the basis of the spirited defense which took place in Helsinki in May 2012.

It is important to understand the scope of the contribution that this dissertation makes. It is first a sustained analysis—at a level of detail and depth unknown hitherto—of the most dominant signifier of international law in modernity—positivism. It tracks it back to Grotius and carries through to the second half of the 20th century. It is only the delicacy of the author, that its scathing analytical tools are not turned on most contemporary international lawyers. The method of analysis is principally 'vicarious' and, thus, situated firmly in the critical 'school' established by the supervisor. By vicarious I mean that it does not examine—principally—the international legal phenomenon (or phenomena) directly but always refracted through its understanding, perception and articulation by other international lawyers, whose own work is understood, in a second vicarious move, as refracting the philosophers who shape these perceptions. One is, thus, always looking at things through someone else's spectacles.

In my preliminary reading I considered this a potential weakness of the dissertation—instead of discussing international law it discusses the discussion of international law. I raised this critique forcefully at the defense—but Ms. García-Salmones prevailed: her answers were more convincing than my critique and I became persuaded that what I perceived as a potential fundamental flaw was in fact one of the strengths of the thesis and that I myself was the 'victim' of a certain positivist bias rooted in a certain notion of reality.

Still addressing method, in this work one looks at international law through the eyes of principally Oppenheim and Kelsen. One cannot but comment on the intellectual audacity of this timid looking and sounding individual. Typically doctoral work of this nature will select some obscure theorist where 'originality' is guaranteed—the first cartographer is always original. Kelsen is arguably the most studied of legal philosophers of the 20th century. One would expect that any claim to originality would simply be a proxy to deficient research of the secondary literature. And yet she has a reading and a normative critique of Kelsen which is both respectful, original and devastating. As for Oppenheim, because his claim to fame was the leading treatise of international law in English, he has not been the subject of any in-depth philosophical investigation. I think it is fair to say that most readers will be discovering a new and substantially more important scholar than they had known or imagined before. To explain this is to understand one of the most important contributions of this dissertation. Since his principal work is a treatise of positivist law, the very positivism which Oppenheim advocated would lead to a degradation of his intellectual importance: after all, by its nature, ontologically speaking from a positivist perspective, a Treatise was but a photograph of extant international law demanding, to be sure, certain analytic and synthetic skills, but not any particular depth, and, more critically, being 'passive'"—simply reporting reality. How impressive can the intellectual endeavor be? Not so impressive. How important can it be? Not much beyond archeology of international law. García-Salmones explodes both analytically and, even more importantly, normatively this vision (and self-vision) of positivism. She shows not only its implicit material content, but also its pronounced ideological bias, and, as a 'science' that was predicated on 'interests' (rather than 'transcendence'—a phrase she uses liberally), she shows how and which real world economic interests it actually serves. How the building blocks of positivism determine what will be included or excluded from the positive content of international law and how those inclusions and exclusions serve certain economic (and political) interests. The analysis of how positive law reacted to, and legitimated, certain forms of colonialism is hugely convincing and hugely important.

The interesting conclusion which I base on her work—it is not her conclusion but I think one consistent with the burden of the dissertation—is that Oppenheim is far, far more important than one had appreciated and arguably, heresy or heresies, though naïve and altogether less profound, even more important from some perspective of shaping and impacting the history of the 20th century than the great Kelsen.

To return to method, one looks at Oppenheim and Kelsen as refracted through the works and approaches which shaped their way at looking at things. There is a deep irony and implicit breathtaking epistemic statement that the only way to understand an international law which makes a claim to 'objectivity' can be through such a subjectivist approach: for after all the ultimate 'view' of international law is as-seen-through-the-eyes-of-Oppenheim/Kelsen-as-seen-through-the-eyes-of-Laband-Jellinek-etc-as-seen-through-the-eyes-of-García-Salmones-as-seen-through-the-eyes-of-[her reader].

A 'direct' (as opposed to vicarious) history or historiography or any critical (non-descriptive) view of international law is implicitly dismissed as naïve and in any event impure since contaminated by the subjectivist view of the observer. There is, thus, a humility (when practiced well) or pretended humility (when practiced poorly) in the vicarious approach which prefers to examine the phenomena through other (important) eyes rather than directly through one's own. It is practiced well when there is a close listening to the voice of the protagonists through which one is refracting reality. It is practiced poorly when one is listening mostly to one's own voice.

García-Salmones' treatment is a *tour de force*: Though normatively critical, she reads her protagonist empathetically and even sympathetically. I could not find an instance of strained readings to serve her theses.

Substantively, the claims are extremely important, since they touch on the dominant school of international law. I have already alluded to the explosion of the classical myths of positivism to be in and of itself without a moral or normative bias. The bias is, in some ways predictably, the bias of capitalist economic interest. Allowing capital (of individuals) to enrich its owners without the responsibility of public power *et cetera*. I do not intend here to give a summary of all the substantive contributions of this dissertation, save to say that insights, one piled on the other, as if never ending, contribute to an understanding, in the most nuanced way, of some of the most important building blocks and tools, such as interest, or sovereignty, or imputation, or power with which we try to understand and give meaning to positive international law.

Two points are important to make. In her normative critique at times one could have the feeling that she herself has fallen in some way victim to the very malaise she has diagnosed, in other words though convincing in exploding the myth of normative neutrality, perhaps too monolithic in limiting the content of such normativity to the usual bogeyman of capitalism. Her treatment of human rights—another obsession of 20th century international law, at least in its second half—illustrates that she is aware of that danger and manages in some respects to counter it and acknowledge a broader normative concern. Though even there, quite brilliantly, she manages to show how the turn to the judge, adjudication, empowerment of the individual and all other artifacts which are often naïvely associated with the turn to human rights, also tend to serve individualistic economic interests.

The second point which is important to understand is that her normative critique is not a standard left-wing critique of right-wing capitalism masquerading as value-free science. The deeper normative critique—a soulful lament that runs through the dissertation—is not rooted in the common hearkening to a more just social order, and an elimination of the depredations of capitalism. It is not even at its deepest a lament of the turn to the economic from the political, interests rather than values. It is rooted at its deepest in the 'opportunity cost' of positivism, which throw asunder 'transcendence', natural law, and at times explicitly mostly implicitly God.

This is also the central weakness of the thesis. It is, appropriately, a hugely normative dissertation—appropriately since it is, after all, a critique of the conceits of positivism. But the alternative normativity is never spelt out and is left vague and employing underspecified terms such as 'transcendence'. If the basis of the normative critique were a standard, say, Marxist or Gramscian worldview, there would be much less of a problem. But since it is distinctly not that, a certain normative black hole hovers over the dissertation, especially given the classical critiques of natural-law-type explications of international law.

I want to be precise in explaining this point: one could not expect in a single dissertation to develop both a full-bodied analysis and critique of positivism and then to develop a full-bodied alternative of a 'transcendent' international law. So the black hole does not and cannot diminish from the huge intellectual achievement of the dissertation. But it is work to be done if one normative strand, the less common normative strand, of the dissertation is to be fully convincing.

It should be noted that though the focus is on Oppenheim and Kelsen, in effect the most important and some of the less important scholars and thinkers of international law and legal philosophy more generally are covered in this dissertation. Independently of the 'Thesis'—this is a work of very considerable learning form which any reader—any reader—will learn considerably. In conclusion, both methodologically and substantively this dissertation makes original and important contributions to the field. It is an outstanding piece of scholarship.

I come now to the question of the grade. This has to be left to the practices and no doubt very high standards of Helsinki. In my experience, if I take into account both the learning, the scope, as well as the original analysis and insights, it is comparable to the very best dissertations that I have seen.

J. H. H. Weiler
Professor
NYU School of Law

Birth of the European Individual: Outline of a Theory of Legal Practice*

Samuli Hurri

'Just before the collision it is essential you do not shut your eyes. You will feel that you are suddenly floating in the air. At that moment you will see your mother's face. Then, you are no more.' The quote is from the art installation 'Before the Collision', by the Swiss artist Thomas Galler.[1] Originally the text of the quote appeared in a military manual written during the Second World War for Japanese kamikaze pilots.

I was struck by the poetic quality of these few lines that are not only beautiful, but magnetic. This highly gentle agitation, it seems to me, appeals to the so-called death instinct: one's silent craving for a way back to mother's womb, one's repressed fight against the external reality in which one is forced to live. The death instinct is a will to destroy the order of the external world by destroying one's own existence in that world. Looking at this piece of text taken from the kamikaze manual, I felt the movements of the god of death and doom, Thanatos, the son of night and darkness.

Great part of the poetics of the kamikaze manual is due to its dreadful purpose of instructing pilots to sacrifice themselves. Even today, it exerts shocking power on its reader, but interestingly, despite being a piece of text, there seems to be no imposition of 'meaning' involved; it does not operate through ideological filters. Rather than those, this poetic power passes directly through the irrational element of human beings' psychic life: fears and desires, subliminal cravings and repulsions, lust and anxiety. It also works through what some have considered the fundamental human condition, *Unheimlichkeit*, the curbed but ineradicable sense of not belonging to this world.[2] There is much that is strange, but nothing surpasses humans in strangeness.

The theme of the book I present as a doctoral thesis is the birth of the European individual as a juridical problem in the 1970s. Unknown to the prevailing legal systems of Europe, but in a strange way prefiguring the later notion of the European citizen, a space between nationals and aliens had to be created for this peculiar subject-position. The book starts from the point where juridical practice—namely, the practice of the European Court of Justice—created this space and thus staged the conception of the European individual. Set off like this, the book presents the European individual at first as a literary character, appearing in the textual body of six legal case dossiers. Doctrinally these dossiers concern the legitimacy of European Community Member States derogating from the free-movement rights of workers. Yet, in the book, the cases constitute an electrifying laboratory for the study of law and society.

* *Lectio praecursoria* held at the public examination of the doctoral dissertation at the University of Helsinki on 28 October 2011. Professor Emilios Christodoulidis from the University of Glasgow acted as opponent.

1. Thomas Galler, 'Before the Collision' (installation, black-and-white laser copies, 2008) in *Why Do You Resist: Forms of Resistance in Contemporary Art* (Pori Art Museum, 11 June–5 September 2011).
2. Martin Heidegger, *An Introduction to Metaphysics* (Yale University Press: New Haven and London, 1987) 146–165.

The concrete individuals whose cases the book analyses are a scientologist, a dangerous gunman, a provocative trade-unionist, a rogue pimp, a drug dealer, and two prostitutes. These delinquent individuals, each expelled from one of the Member States, provide the raw material for constructing the European individual. With these ingredients available, the book embarks on a larger project that requires developing its own analytical tools. These tools may force the case-dossiers to open up their entrails, the nether region of juridical discourse. The book's aim is to explore that sub-textual region, not legal argumentation as such. The book depicts this region as 'a general field of power': rather than some fixed comprehensive structure, it is an unsettled contact surface, a network of active relations, between different social fields of practice. Yet the book's aim is not only to define and describe undercurrents and relations existing in that region, but also to expound on how juridical practice encounters those forces. This brings back elements of juridical argumentation but with a broader view of their social operation at the boundaries of the juridical field.

In the book, the law encounters two other practices of governing: the economic regime of market, competition and circulation; and the security regime of surveillance, precaution and control. The cross-border movement of workers produces a 'regime-collision' between these two: for the one, movement strengthens market functioning and thus gives more capacity to the overall system of production; whereas for the other, movement brings alien elements into the space of existing societies and thus threatens their order. The conflict between economy and security generates trials in which objective social structures confront each other just as much as individual litigants. In the cases studied, these structures emerge as certain types of knowledge, all of which are more or less outlandish from a purely legal perspective: secret knowledge pertaining to maintaining order and security in societies; psychological knowledge of the internal makeup of individuals that allows prediction of their future dangerousness; economic knowledge that sees people either as factors of production or as self-interested calculators.

The law's survival in the general field of power depends on its ability to confront these knowledges—that is, law's ability to translate languages of knowledge into the language of juridical power. To perceive these translation mechanisms, the book lays out the choice of basic elements that the legal field makes available to legal actors. Practice of these elements enacts the law in the general field of power, where its crucial function is to make power visible. In fulfilling that function, the practice of law—and its confrontation with practices of knowledge-power—produced the European individual.

Some of Michel Foucault's concepts are used to develop tools for analysing legal case dossiers. These include above all the concepts of *subjectivation*, *battle form* and *military order*, as well as the conceptual pair of *jurisdiction* and *veridiction*. Moreover, Foucault's concern with formations of knowledge-power has crucially influenced the book's design. Relationships between the law and knowledge-power—such as security administration and economic governing—give the book some of its basic structure. Yet the book draws on the work of Foucault in other ways, without which it could not deliver on its promise. Let me briefly outline these more vital ways.

(a) Foucault's idea was to anchor research in problems (uncertainties, difficulties) that constitute events in the living reality of practices. This, he says, 'allows entry to the field of thought'. Following that idea the book endorses a rather radical primacy of problems: only problems exist. The book also endorses another methodical postulate concerning problems: a worthy problem presents not merely some set of objects for study but limits to objectivity, fundamentally irresolvable antagonisms where intelligibility meets its edges. The problem of the book, the European individual, presents this type of antagonism between economy, security and the law. Catching on the European individual as a problem-event, the book opens a window on these antagonisms and through them also more generally on Europe's agonies on the underside of its integration.

(b) The book depicts as a 'general field of power' what for Foucault was a living reality of social practices. This reality consists of an ever-changing network where mechanisms of exercising power constantly connect and disconnect with each other. While antagonisms between fields of practice are irresolvable, problem-generative connections between their mechanisms constantly keep forming. In the book, mechanisms provided by the legal field and employed by its lawyer practitioners are called law's 'strategic action schemes'. Through actors' exercise of these mechanisms in individual cases, the juridical field connects with other fields of practice and thus enters the general field of power. The idea of the book is to use the problem of the European individual to show how the field of law, on the one hand, and the fields of economic governing and policing of security, on the other, were connected at a certain point. Materialising in the cases studied, this point of junction is where the European individual was born as a peculiar subject, actor and object.

(c) Foucault's life-long project was what he called the genealogy of the modern subject. In his mind, the modern subject is a self-subjecting individual whose governability depends on his 'self-knowledge'. Procedures for production of self-knowledge (*conscience*) have been developing through a very long history of networking power practices. In the book's design, this history grows into the background of the European individual, giving it a broader background canvas of historical meaning. Through a set of readings of Foucault's genealogies, the book achieves a basic understanding of the general field of power and creates instruments for analysis of cases. Yet the net result of these readings is something different: the event of the birth of the European individual becomes a hologram-like historical reflection of layers buried deep in the past. As a hologram, it allows a fleeting sight of two thousand years of European human-making—as if concurring in one single event!

(d) To achieve that result, a rough outline of Foucault's genealogy of the modern subject is embedded, element by element, in the structure of the book. Starting from modern economic and juridical systems of governing (in Part I), the book then proceeds backwards to early modern times formative of the state and the so-called *raison d'état* (in Part II), and finally ends with the Christian practice of confession developing from late antiquity onwards (in Part III).

> The pitch of this reconstruction is the resemblance of uses of desire in disparate practices of governing situated rather far-off from each other, both in social space and in historical time. One of these practices, Christian confession, is a thin but tremendously significant thread in the genealogical rhizome of the modern subject. Its significance is due to its intricate mechanism of simultaneous excitement and repression of desire. This peculiar mechanism is the historical germ of today's organisation of governing. Taken together, this organisation consists of two gigantic realities of power, vitalising societies through an interplay that carries out the same operations at macro-level as did confession at the level of each individual: economic governing excites desire, juridical power represses desire.

In her book on *The Psychic Life of Power*, Judith Butler defines subjection as 'the process of becoming subordinated by power as well as the process of becoming a subject'; subjection is a process where 'power that at first appears as external, pressed upon the subject, pressing the subject into subordination, assumes a psychic form that constitutes the subject's self-identity'.[3] Drawing on that definition, I present my clinical case studies, together with some exercises in genetic critique of law in society, as a work on legal subjection, that is, as a work on the psychic life of juridical power.

3. Judith Butler, *The Psychic Life of Power: Theories in Subjection* (Stanford University Press: Redwood City, CA, 1997) 2–3.

The Birth of the European Individual by Samuli Hurri University of Helsinki 2011

Samuli Hurri's work is a very ambitious and accomplished thesis, which provides evidence of serious, thorough and intelligent engagement with both legal cases and social and legal theory. The level of critical engagement is high and parts of the analysis are, in fact, exceptional. It was defended robustly and intelligently during the *viva voce* examination on October 28th, 2011, on which occasion the candidate was able to defend and further develop some of the more difficult and controversial arguments contained in the thesis. On this occasion the candidate showed an exceptional ability to capture and argue the points raised, and in that sense to do justice both to the questions and to his work.

My recommendation is that the dissertation be accepted on the grounds that it meets all the criteria stipulated by the University for the award of a doctoral thesis. The thesis is both highly original and highly ambitious. In terms of erudition and knowledge of the broader field it is one of the best I have read in nearly 20 years of examining doctoral theses. The methodology, placing its emphasis on the 'microscopic' examination of cases (and the micro-analytics of power effects), shows a profound reading and understanding of Michel Foucault's work in its full trajectory, from the 'archaeological' and 'genealogical' method and tactics, all the way to the later emphasis on 'pastoral' power and the mechanisms of the production of knowledge in his late work.

Foucault's influence is in fact stamped all over the method, structure and content of the work, but it is the critical engagement with Foucault rather than a straightforward application, that marks the work's novelty and significance. Finally., in what concerns the criteria stipulated, the presentation and defence of the thesis, as mentioned above, was first-class.

The title of the thesis is the 'birth of the European individual' and it might *prima facie* strike the reader as odd that several decades *after* the launch of the European community project, and in fact at a time of a profound crisis on the processes of integration, one might still be speaking of 'birth'. Could one not in fact go further, and talk of the risk at least, that we are witnessing a profound, if not fatal, 'sickness' of the European individual, strapped to a logic of deregulation running amok, thrown currently into one of Europe's most profound crises, stripped of welfare entitlements, social protection, the youth facing unprecedented levels of joblessness, and the rise of a security and policing apparatus that Europe had not witnessed before in peacetime. Reading about this strange 'birth' T S Eliot's poem comes to mind: 'Were we led all that way for/ birth or death? … I had seen birth and death / But had thought they were different; this birth was / Hard and bitter agony for us, like Death … / We returned to our places / But no longer at ease here in the old dispensation' ('Journey of the Magi').

So, why 'birth' at *this* historical conjunction? Hurri's interjection here, adapted from Foucault, is wonderfully revealing: For Hurri, the European individual *is born as a problem.* And a 'problem', following Foucault, 'is something that allows entry into the field of thought'. This is a profound point, and although no explicit reference is made to it, it points directly to the philosophical tradition of phenomenology. Phenomenology takes as its starting point *what appears* (the Greek 'phenomenon'), and what appears involves disturbing the flow of what remains un-thought. In that, to go back to Foucault and Hurri now, 'it is necessary for a certain number of factors to have made it uncertain, to have made it lose familiarity, or to have provoked a number of difficulties around it.' That is what attends the birth of the European individual, brought into question as a problem.

So if phenomenology concerns what appears, then a critical phenomenology concerns the conditions of *making perceptible*. With the help, therefore, of what questions is the European individual to be brought to presence, as a problem, and at the same time, perhaps, as a normative ideal? Can the notion of the European individual perform the 'gathering' work that we might wish it to do, to bring something of a distinctive identity to the fore? And this is a concern that becomes more difficult to sustain and more urgent to do so in the face of the onslaught of economic globalization and its harnessing of the notion of the European individual to the logic of the integration of capital.

Hurri's work is not particularly concerned with capitalist integration except in chapter 3 on the homo oeconomicus, to which we shall return. It does nevertheless help to pose the question, which is also his question, about what conditions the appearance (and disappearance) of the European individual. Hurri's emphasis here is on the conceptual work that the distinction between European 'national/alien' performs, as deployed in the reasoning of the Courts, and his method is to home in on decisions of national and European courts over how that distinction is deployed in their reasoning, tracking the minutiae of legal argument. As he puts it:

> The laboratory makes perceptible certain non-juridical forces, rationalities and powers that the dossiers themselves say not so much about. The vision of the way in which legal practice interlaces and counteracts these forces and powers is what the birth of the European individual puts forward as an object of research.

The ambition of the work is high, no less than a history of the present and genealogy of the European individual. What serves to contain this near-impossible task is the choice of methodology, or as the author prefers to put it, the 'laboratory of legal theory', situated in the European Jurisprudence of the 1970s and in particular in what he identifies as occurring at the interface of 'two sets of legal structure': the law of aliens and the law of natives. The mechanism for difference-making at the heart of this work consists of the provision for derogation from the right to free movement. This mechanism consists of two parts. The key part of the mechanism is that derogations are possible if the *ordre public* of a Member State would otherwise come under threat. If it is by probing the dynamics of that interface, in the reasoning of the Courts, that the author attempts to bring out not just a legal history of the emergence of the 'European individual' he also aims to make perceptible the '**non**-juridical forces, rationalities and powers … [given the law's] interlacing and counteracting these [other] forces'. He does this through a very interesting juxtaposition of knowledges, juridical contra 'anti-juridical' (psychological, economic, sociological etc) and the methodology he chooses.

If the 'juridical' is to do the work that the author intends it to do, there are two urgent questions that must be addressed first: (i) why will the legal story tell the broader story of the birth of the European Individual, if it is the case that the law 'interacts and interlaces' with other forces *only selectively*?; and (ii) why will the largely redundant jurisprudence ('these cases cannot be taken as the basis of the normative understanding of present controversies') of these largely unexceptional cases furnish a critique and 'history of the present' of such exceptional ambition and reach?

There are important points made in the book's introduction about the aspirations of universality and the messy judicial business of confronting both 'otherness' and 'other knowledges' and the revised thesis has gone a long way to redressing these. There is now also a good analysis of the balance of legality and equity in chapter 10, which goes some way to addressing the question of the application of law against the significant problem of what *balance* of particularity and universality the European demos presupposes and requires.

Generally, and true to its Foucauldian roots, the book is structured around three triptychs: 'the human form', 'power' and 'knowledge'. The birth of the human individual is then sequentially examined as a problem of legal form, of power and of knowledge. Occupying the centre of each triptych we have a legal problematisation, respectively around rights/decisions (triptych 1), rule of law/common good (triptych 2) and (the aforementioned) legality/equity (triptych 3). Flanking the legal middle section of each triptych we have economic and psychological conceptualisations of 'man' (triptych 1), 'war' and 'Reason of State' understandings of power (triptych 2) and 'scientific' and 'pastoral' knowledges of man, as instrumentalised in triptych 3. What this yields, in each case through painstaking analyses of the cases, is a profound account of veridiction and jurisdiction, the construction of dangerousness, and the tension between law and order. The complex architecture of the thesis brings these out extremely well and it is to the credit of the author that he uses the structure so intelligently to yield such dividends. What is also note- and praise-worthy is that the author resists by and large 'pigeon-holing' his work in a specific paradigm of legal theorising, a tendency very prevalent today, and although he is mainly addressing post-structuralist literature, he is also at home with figures as diverse as Jhering, Althusser and the nowadays highly unfashionable Comte, and he does an admirable job not only of bringing them into the debate, but of inter-relating their theories.

There are a number of arguments in the thesis worthy of further note:

(i) History / genealogy:

The account offered in the work is presented as an genealogy of the European individual. Drawing on the work of Foucault, this term has a very precise meaning that ties it to a 'strategic' excavation of the past, such that might allow a 'troubling' of the historical trajectory of the European subject. As Foucault puts it in the History of Sexuality, the genealogy involves the effort to think one's history in a way that frees thought from what it 'silently thinks' and so enable it to think differently. If history is how things have come to be thought of as objective, genealogy recovers contingency and with it carries the political history of struggles into the present. It is against what is silenced over that genealogy rails, and this impetus is what drives so much of the analysis in the thesis and grounds the idea of resistance and strategy.

(ii) Law as field of resistance and strategy

In each 'triptych', in each of the confrontations of the 'juridical' with the logics of the spheres that surround it and undercut it, the juridical is maintained as a sphere of resistance and strategy. The analysis of 'relative autonomy' frees it from the point-by-point determination of the economic; Jhering's 'battler' forever renews it; as contrasted to the logic of 'secutity', to the logic of the 'police' and the logic of State (Raison d'Etat), the juridical, it is argued, harbours alternative possibilities and interpretations. Its potential depends on the heterogeneous and on incongruous linkages, the setting of the context of 'battle'. 'Battle-form' is the analytical device that Hurri borrows from Foucault, to shape confrontation situations. There is, throughout the thesis, a firm commitment that the law can provide the leverage here, in strategic opportunities of argumentation, and much of the argument, and the careful analysis of the arguments in the cases, pivots on this dimension of the juridical. Law is open to be seized, is the message.

(iii) 'Homo Oeconomicus'/homo Juridicus

One of the less persuasive oppositions 'staged' in the book is that between the two 'latinised men', homo 'oeconomicus' and 'juridicus'. The first is meant to encapsulate desire, the second, the subject of the rights of man, to relinquish it. What is perhaps least persuasive in this contra-distinction is Foucault's insistence that economic man captures the 'free play of desire' and he has 'never been called on to relinquish those interests'. Unlike poor homo juridicus who relinquishes his rights to the rule of law and the social contract, the economic man relinquishes nothing. The opposition is unsustainable, perhaps due to the fact that Foucault's analysis of ordo-liberalism, on which the contradistinction draws, misses what is significant or essential about ordo-liberalism, and adopts a simplified picture of economic rationality similar to the one endorsed by economists of the neo-liberal turn in the late 70s and 80s. Karl Polanyi's words about Adam Smith, writing much earlier of course, nonetheless resonate here. *Never,* Polanyi said, *has **a misreading** of human nature proved more prophetic for the future.* The mis-reading—the free play of desire—is also Foucault's. And the ordo-liberals, Eucken and Roepke in particular, argued for a liberal interventionism that would subsume economic activity to the interests of community and values of society—motives that is *other* than self-interest—as essential components of what we might today call a 'social market.'

In any case the discussion of ordo-liberalism remains too reliant on Foucault single short lecture and while Foucault may be guilty of collapsing ordo-liberalism, with its specific economic rationality, into the rampant neo-liberalism of Hayek, it is advisable that, when published as a book, either Foucault be taken to task for his account, or that the analysis of homo oeconomicus opens out to a broader conceptualization.

(iv) Law and war

This analysis that contrasts law and war is much improved and makes some very significant points. There is perhaps some room to further integrate the important literature on executive exceptionalism and emergency legislation, and so much interesting work drawing on Benjamin and Schmitt, but the relevant chapter as it stands does some excellent work here in terms of linking it back to the 'battle form' but also of contrasting and comparing the two models, law and war, as principles or frameworks of intelligibility.

(v) Althusser, Jhering and Comte

I mention the three theorists only to commend the author for his exceptional analysis of all three and the success in integrating them as interlocutors in the debate without simplifying, treating them a-contextually or reducing their argument to fit his purposes. In relation to Jhering, Hurri explains that 'when individuals from their own point of view struggle for their own subjective rights only, from a point of view external to their subjective interests they struggle for the law in the objective sense as well.' The connection between the objective and the subjective dimension is what matters here and, this is the intelligent move, a grounding back of law to the materiality of practice. 'To avoid becoming illusory,' says the author, 'the objective legal system as a whole relies on concrete individual rights. *Reciprocity* between objective law and subjective rights is Jhering's new 'doctrine'. According to this doctrine, maintenance of the law is carried out, not only by the functionaries of the system, but also by individual persons asserting their rights: 'the person with legal rights returns to the law the service which he receives from it.'

The discussion is then linked forward, to another great theorist of the materiality of practices, Louis Althusser. Turning the discussion of ideology as 'false consciousness' on its head, the attention is instead on how ideology relates a conceptual device (*dispositif*) with the materially existent ideological state apparatuses (*appareils*) Hurri speaks here insightfully of a 'hinge' between that which pertains to ideas and that which pertains to the real: 'a hinge' is what 'enables the material and spiritual ways of existence of ideas to clasp hands: the idealist representation concedes that there is a material mode of existence…' At this point, he says 'Althusser makes the materialist move that dislocates the idealist primacy … a move [that] consists of the simple turning of the *if… then* conditional formula of action on its head. In their mutual relationship, Althusser now ushers action to the place of cause and condition, and ideas to the place of effects or derivatives. Action not only materialises ideas, but *precedes*, *conditions* and *generates* them. *If* action occurs, *then* an idea will follow.'

This is an insightful analysis. And it is finally coupled with the discussion of Comte, who is certainly not a theorist much *in vogue*. Given the author's familiarity with Luhmann's work I cannot help but think it something of a missed opportunity that Luhmann does not make an appearance here, given the emphasis on 'control phenomena' and 'pathological phenomena' but most importantly in the context of variation and its proper limits. Luhmann's reliance on the theory of evolution for social systems, his relevant chapter on variation, retention, and of course stabilization, in law in *Das Recht der Gesellschaft*, would have been a wonderful addition here. Also, the author might want to connect more tightly the notion of what is a 'pathological' and what a 'control' phenomenon to the idea that law is, as he puts it, explored through its breaches.' But in any case it is really refreshing to see such an intelligent and robust account of the 'sociological' knowledge that Comte offered to import into a discipline that he very much invented.

(vi) Legality and equity

The analysis of the difference between legality and equity, the *kata nomon* and that which follows the flexible logic of application in *epieikia* (a small correction: *epieikia* is the noun and *epieikes* the adjective) is both most suggestive and perhaps less accomplished that the rest of the thesis. There is important literature on equity and mercy (Nussbaum in particular, but also Simmonds, Detmold and others) which would be relevant here. Much of this discussion pivots on the distinction between universality and particularity, philosophically speaking a rather explosive topic, though the discourse-theory on application (notably the work of Klaus Gunther) bypasses some of the hurdles. As for *Antigone*, which is referred to in the text, the tragedy is not here relevant in its famous quoted clash of divine and secular law, but in the hubris of Creon, who refuses to yield, whose judgement shows no *epieikia.* I would recommend here, if this chapter is to be retained when submitted to a publisher, that this important literature is engaged with. This would also help answer the quandary that the author sets for himself with the wonderful phrase: 'When reality takes legality by surprise, the latter cannot but stand in awe.' (322) The point about the phrase is that it sets the bar high, and the analysis in the chapter does not match the height! Legality immunizes itself from surprise—that is in the nature of legal expectations. It can only be taken by surprise if it is somehow 'pierced', in a sense despite itself. A gap shows up, not because the *kata nomon* is 'silent' (p 273)—*Creon is anything but*—but because equity *forces* a space open *as a gap*. That is an emergent property, and it catches out legality by surprise. But all this is significantly more complex than what the thesis intimates as the problem.

Conclusion:

This is a highly accomplished thesis that works at a number of levels. It is to the credit of the impressive powers of synthesis of the author that he weaves so many voices into the discussion. There are, given the extraordinary ambition of the book, inevitably some moments of over-reach, and I have identified a couple of these weaknesses above. But this should not take away from the fact that this is an excellent thesis, combining an impressive level of erudition with a structure that delivers not only in its contrast of juridical and other knowledges, but in identifying the multiple facets of the function of the law in its 'interface' with this other knowledges (polyvalence, penetration, expulsion), and doing it through the 'micro-analytics' of careful dissection of legal argument rather than any sweeping statements and pronouncements.

To my mind this is clearly and excellent thesis and I have no qualms in recommending the award of the PhD and a high mark for it.

Emilios Christodoulidis
Professor of Legal Theory, University of Glasgow, UK
Glasgow, Nov 10th, 2011

Transformations in Trade Politics: West African Civil Society Participation in Economic Partnership Negotiations with the European Union*

Silke Trommer

Four years ago in July 2008, I stood on the shores of Lake Geneva. During a summer school on the World Trade Organisation, a lecturer asked me the most despised question for any new doctoral student: what was my PhD on? I explained my interest in the dynamics of trade negotiations between Europe and the African, Caribbean and Pacific countries. I wanted to know who had impact on what aspects of negotiations, through which mechanisms? To my horror, the lecturer announced that mine were non-questions that required no further study since the answer was self-evident. To illustrate this, I was asked: 'When a grandfather negotiates with a five-year-old, who do you think wins?'

Since today is a moment of truth, I admit that I was embarrassed and disheartened at the time, although I also felt on the basis of my own childhood experience that five-year-olds can mount considerable resistance, and that given the right conditions, a five-year-old can be very well capable of getting its way. Power, then, seemed to me a much trickier affair than was suggested during this brief exchange.

In the real world, by 2008, trade politics was frustrating expectations that trade policy outcomes mechanically follow from countries' market size and geopolitical might. Six years after their launch, the EU's negotiations with African, Caribbean and Pacific countries under the name of Economic Partnership Agreements (EPAs) were causing problems for the global trade power.

Although the EU applied political pressure to conclude agreements by the 31 December 2007, 43 out of 78 ACP countries did not sign a trade deal on that day. These economies figure among the world's poorest and most trade- and aid-dependent. Real life trade politics thus produced skewed results from the perspective of standard political economy accounts that understands trade policy formation as a function of states' economic and geopolitical interests as well as the two-level game logic in which trade talks are conceptually placed. My thesis addresses this unhappy state of theory through a study of the inclusion of civil society groups in the West African region's EPA negotiations.

Institutionally, West Africa negotiated as the Economic Community of West African States (ECOWAS). In line with ECOWAS' negotiating roadmap, so-called 'civil society' representatives were entitled to access the policy-making rooms and relevant, including unpublished documentation. They could also speak in internal meetings and at the negotiating table with the EU. I qualify the arrangement as participatory trade politics, which helped the region to resist Europe's political pressure.

* *Lectio praecursoria* held at the public examination of the doctoral dissertation at the University of Helsinki on 16 June 2012. Professor Magnus Ryner from Oxford Brooks University acted as opponent.

In my *lectio*, I first present my methodology and my research question. I also scrutinise the inability of standard political economy to conceptualise West African participatory trade politics. I then answer my research question by advancing analytical alternatives to trade policy formation that stress the social embeddedness of all political and, indeed, economic action. I conclude that my intervention redresses the bias against non-state, non-corporate social groups in debates on trade policy's possible democratisations.

In terms of method, I rely on empirical data that I gathered between 2009 and 2011 through personal interviews with West African and European EPA actors, official documents and media sources. Since West African participatory trade politics frustrates almost all assumptions of standard political economy approaches to trade policy formation, I make two terminological innovations.

In my thesis, I use the term 'civil society' as a label for the groups that interacted with the West African EPA process under its banner. I argue nonetheless that the term causes analytical and political problems, specifically in conjunction with the term 'representation'. Across the literature, civil society rather loosely denotes a social sphere that is constitutive of, mediates between and potentially holds in check the economy and the state. No single social group can ever embody in any meaningful way that which permeates everything. Conceptually, I therefore reject the term. Instead, I identify state and non-state actors in my thesis and differentiate among them according to their attitude towards current trade politics. I distinguish conformist and transformative actors or claims in trade politics, that either support or challenge the trade political status quo.

My second conceptual intervention concerns the trade political status quo. Since the 18th century, political economy has not moved beyond the protectionism *versus* free trade distinction, whereby protectionism denotes state intervention with trade flows that is allegedly absent under free trade policies. I contend that the dichotomy produces a mental image that obscures key power relations in global trade politics. The reason for this is simple and was in essence given by Karl Polanyi in *The Great Transformation* in 1944. Every economic activity requires a framework of norms and rules in order to be conducted successfully. I therefore argue that under current alleged 'free trade' or 'trade liberalisation' policies, regulation is shifted away from governing trade flows at the border, for example in the form of duties. Instead, global trade talks shape market access conditions through interference with other domestic policy areas. According to the Doha Ministerial Declaration, WTO members strive not only for market access in goods, but also in services, through intellectual property protection, facilitation of foreign direct investment, access to government procurement, and so forth.[1] The policies escape the comparative advantage logic first elaborated by David Ricardo. They also establish opportunities for monopolisation in the global economy for a narrow set of economic actors through what Polanyi

1. Ministerial Declaration, adopted at Doha, 14 November 2001, Doc. WT/MIN(01)/DEC/1 (20 November 2001).

would call 'centralised interventionism'. This makes the terms not only paradoxical, but analytically misleading. In my thesis, I understand the concepts 'free trade' and 'trade liberalisation' to have two functions in the world. Normatively, they create an image that shapes trade debates. Substantially, they are shorthand for a specific trade political outlook within a given historical, geographical and social context. I refer to this complex as the 'global trade agenda'.

Based on this terminology, I present West African participatory trade politics in the following way: in ECOWAS' negotiating team, a network of regional global justice NGOs, local NGO and movement platforms, and trade unions filled the civil society chair. This network called 'the Platform' held a transformative trade political stance. West African state actors, on the other hand, were favourably disposed towards the global trade agenda. Although West African public officials were initially sceptical about the inclusion of the Platform, they eventually accorded substantial participatory rights. Transformative groups were thus empowered to influence negotiations. In 2008, for example, the Platform commissioned a legal study to demonstrate that applicable WTO law did not demand an 80% market opening from ECOWAS, a legal interpretation that the EU had insisted on across all EPA regions. West Africa's 60% market access offer based on the alternative interpretation has stalled EU–ECOWAS talks since 2009, frustrating the EU's ambition to further the global trade agenda through EPAs.

West African participatory trade politics were not a smooth affair. Relations within the Platform, and among all West African actors as well as the ECOWAS and EU negotiating teams were, at times, confrontational. The question that my thesis thus asks is: why did ECOWAS include transformative actors that opposed the global trade agenda in participatory trade policy-making?

In search for an answer, I first investigate dominant political economy approaches to trade policy formation. I diagnose their inability to account for this transformation in West African trade politics. My inquiries into why standard theory is inapt provide insights that are relevant to the broader debate on trade and democracy, a point that I will return to in my conclusion.

My main criticism is that dominant approaches to trade policy formation rest on several dubious premises. As a result, they lack an analytical category for non-state, non-corporate actors. By way of example I now problematise two. First, wealth or welfare are defined as rising capital endowment and access to goods and services in the global economy. This defines away the possibility that a clean environment or decent labour conditions, for example, can be part of a society's wealth. Connected to this point is the second underlying assumption that the economic performance of the corporate sector is the appropriate proxy to represent the impact of trade policy on society as a whole. Rising capital endowment and access to goods and services for a specific social group are thus expected to indicate what the standard view somewhat cynically calls 'global welfare'.

I trace these premises to the evolution of trade theory within the discipline of political economy since the late 19th century. I show that at that time, marginalist scholars deliberately narrowed down the notions of welfare and of society with the pronounced and explicit intention to make the free trade argument appear theoretically flawless.

This conceptual and methodological choice provides the basis for today's standard view of trade policy-making as a rationalistic game played by unified actors whose interests mechanically arise from the structures of the global political economy. The choice implies that dominant theories ignore the most fundamental characteristic of the social world. Namely that it is a human creation, and that therefore our ideas about, perceptions of and interactions with the material world matter for its operation.

To reinsert this dimension into studies of trade policy formation, I apply Marisa von Bülow's relational approach that she develops in her examination of a transnational trade campaign in the Americas. In the second part of my thesis, I expand her framework to studying the interactions between West African trade political actors during the evolution and consolidation of participatory trade politics.

In West Africa, trade policy-making was initially exclusive, based on the widespread belief that critics of the global trade agenda cannot make positive contributions to trade policy formation. Over time, policy makers' appreciation of what types of social groups were legitimate actors in trade policy-making changed. My theoretical approach to tackle this transformation embraces four interconnected arguments. First, trade political actors are embedded in wider social and political configurations as well as in specific social relations with each other. Second, their ideas and interests are not external to this political environment, but arise from their interaction with and within it. Third, actors' understanding of the political environment, including awareness of existing and potential opportunities for transformation, varies. Fourth, in order to explain whether and how actors cooperate, we need to look at the social and political mechanisms emanating from their political environment by which they manage or fail to overcome differences and construct common purpose. All of these features provide resources for change in political practice.

Political economy accounts of trade policy are thus enriched by incorporating a focus on the way in which agents perceive their political environment, how they attempt to mould it and what the consequences of their actions are. Specific attention needs to be paid to the way in which trade actors manage or fail to create the opportunity for political change by framing the ideas and discourses that shape the perceptions of their political environment, including its structural features. In this sense, my break with standard political economy accounts of trade is not total. Considerations such as material interests or government's power aspirations feature prominently in my framework, because they are part and parcel of the political environment of trade negotiations.

Seen through this lens, my thesis draws a picture of West African participatory trade politics evolving as follows:

In West Africa, transformative actors had become convinced through previous trade political advocacy since the late 1990s that furthering the global trade agenda would hinder the region's efforts to escape its poor socio-economic condition. When they met resistance to their critical claims, they began to create the conditions for their participation in the policy-making process through three main tactics that evolved over time.

First, together with their political allies, they started to depict the EPA as a set of rules that needed to take the region's development needs into account, thus hijacking the process from the realm of trade technocracy and bringing it onto the contested terrain of development policy. As a consequence, general public protest against the EPA was more easily mounted. More importantly, perhaps, broader good governance norms and standards of behaviour, as well as rules anchored in related international and domestic legal orders also became frames of reference for negotiations. Second, realising that technical language is the currently privileged vehicle for trade political demands, the Platform activated its broader transnational networks to produce legal and economic expertise. This had the added benefit of countering imbalances in negotiating capacity between the ECOWAS Secretariat and the European Commission. Third, in efforts to create solidarity in the West African negotiating team, they helped to build and subsequently relied on a sense of unity among conformist and transformative trade political actors. To create this sense, they drew on ambiguous collective experiences with internationally-led trade policy reform in the post-colonial era and with West African-European trade during colonisation.

West African public officials changed their attitudes because transformative actors proved to be beneficial allies in trade negotiations. Added technical capacity and unexpected influence in the asymmetrical talks strengthened West African trade officials' existing belief in the legitimate nature of inclusive policy-making mechanisms.

While West African trade political actors struggled with certain aspects of participatory trade politics, such as the question of representation, they continued to engage in the participatory process based on these perceived benefits.

Power, then, did not boil down to the question of how states use material resources to get their way, as the grandfather quote however inelegantly suggested. Material, institutional and ideational forms of power and the various resources for resistance and transformation that their interplays offer are all key to the course of EU-ECOWAS trade talks. Overall, West African participatory trade politics demonstrates that economic policy-making remains a social process that, although far from being arbitrary, ultimately comprises the possibility of indeterminacy.

My final contention is that my thesis holds lessons for the debate on trade and democracy. My study contradicts the view that consultative arrangements with trade critics constitute the outer limits of democratising trade policy-making today and I draw several lessons from West Africa's concrete experiences. With reference to the theoretical debate, on the other hand, I deconstruct the argument that deviation from the global trade agenda leads to decreases in global welfare. Adam Smith defined political economy as a field of inquiry concerned with the nature, the creation and the distribution of wealth. My thesis reveals that we have dropped the questions of the nature and the distribution of wealth from accounts of trade policy-making and channel the last remaining ambition, studying the creation of wealth, through the concept of capital endowment and access to goods and services for the corporate sector. The view is one normative perspective on how the world should function among many others. Democratising exchanges between the competing perspectives in theory and practise remains not only a possible but, in my eyes, timely and urgent task.

Transformations in Trade Politics: West African Civil Society Participation in Economic Partnership Negotiations with the European Union by Silke Trommer. Doctoral Dissertation, University of Helsinki, 2012

I have read Ms Silke Trommer's thesis carefully and with great interest. Ms Trommer's investigation into trade policies and its limits to furthering social justice imparts significant theoretical and empirical light on questions regarding the relationship between trade and democracy. The dissertation is very good. It is lucidly written, meticulously researched, and persuasively argued. Moreover, the dissertation sets clearly defined objectives and makes original contributions primarily to the scholarly literature on trade theory and global governance, and, secondarily to the literature on development and globalization studies. Ms Trommer's thesis is unique in that it not only questions the underlying assumptions of trade studies and its limits to democratization processes, i.e., citizen participation, but also uses the case of European Union–West African trade relations to illustrate and develop her argument. My assessment is an unconditional recommendation to move forward with the public examination of *Transformations in Trade Politics*. In what follows, I elaborate on two key contributions of the dissertation. I then briefly mention two minor points that Ms Trommer might think about as she moves forward with the project.

Ms Trommer opens and centres her dissertation with an intriguing question: 'why did trade politics become participatory in West Africa?' Ms Trommer's attempt to answer this question entails a series of theoretical and empirical interventions into several core debates across the social sciences. The main focus of the discussion, however, centres rightfully on the economistic manner in which dominant theories of the political economy of trade and trade policy formation have failed to account for, and provide explanatory analyses about, the role played by political and social realms. Ms Trommer traces the limits of the dominant approaches to trade, which have continued to shape trade agreements and institutions, such as the World Trade Organization (WTO), to the fundamental assumptions rooted in neoclassical economics. Ms Trommer's subsequent engagement with these approaches, both theoretically and empirically, provides an important intervention into what have become common sense assumptions in trade policy and trade theory, particularly the belief that the sole objective of trade is the pursuit of wealth, the conflation of the impact of trade policy with the corporate sector, and the unquestioned supposition that trade liberalization is the only policy option to pursue to obtain growth. Unlike many studies that focus on regional trade agreements and the WTO, however, Ms Trommer's dissertation goes beyond a critical evaluation of the neoclassical premises of trade liberalization and their questionable effects on alleviating poverty in the global South in two ways. First, she provides a historically rich and empirically thorough account of the limits to neoclassical understandings of trade from the vantage point of both the European and Western African negotiators. Second, she moves us beyond the limits of comparative advantage, within which most critical analyses confine themselves, to shift our gaze to the political and social dimensions of trade. That is, Ms Trommer demonstrates that trade policy should not simply be regarded as an economic phenomenon, but one that is deeply influenced and thus constituted by the political and the social. From this starting point, Ms Trommer invites the reader to rethink the traditional (economistic and legalistic) analytical framework of trade policy formation, so as to make space available for social and political considerations, i.e., what Ms Trommer refers to as a 'political opportunity structure'. The latter theoretical frame, she convincingly contends, allows us to grasp dynamically 'why pre-existing conditions sparked political action and how such political action impacted on the very structure in which it operated'.

A second major contribution of Ms Trommer's thesis is its ability to complement and contribute to the debates on the role of public accountability in global governance. By drawing on the case of European Economic Partnership Agreements (EPA) and Western African countries, Ms Trommer explores the roles and impact of civil societies in democratizing trade policies that are said to be often formulated not only at supra-national spaces that are above and beyond the participation of people, but also involve highly technical language that is often believed to be beyond the comprehension of the ordinary citizen. Jan Aarte Scholte's work, which Ms Trommer cites in her thesis, represents one of the leading scholars in the politicization of transnational civil society. Scholte's work has sought to study and suggest ways to institutionalize the demands by civil society in trade policy in a meaningful, constructive, and well co-ordinated manner. Ms Trommer embraces Scholte's conceptualization of the democratizing effects of transnational civil society, but goes beyond his analysis by conducting a theoretical and empirical analysis of the roles played by various civil society organizations in Western African countries with regard to the EPA. Indeed, Ms Trommer, unlike many scholars writing on issues pertaining to global governance, asks and addresses questions of development from a perspective that is not only sensitive to the concerns and demands from the global South (Western Africa), but also incorporates their viewpoint into the analysis.

Furthermore, and in contrast to the existing literature on global governance, Ms Trommer not only explores the social and political terrain of the struggles relating to the EPA, but also the legal dimensions of contestation by concentrating on important questions such as who is granted legal rights to participation and why? Ms Trommer also queries, and answers, what is the meaning(s) of this participation with regard to the formulation (actual impact) on policy formation? Ms Trommer's analysis is unique in addressing these questions, as she reveals how existing trade agreements (e.g., the Cotonou Agreement) have been used by civil society organizations in Western African countries to legalize their rights to participation, which as led to the effective challenge of more powerful actor's (e.g., the EU) interpretation of principal trade agreements such as the GATT.

In addition, Ms Trommer's discussion is distinct from the existing debates because her research results reveal an important, although often overlooked, issue that has helped shaped Western African participatory trade politics, namely staff capacity. Given the central characteristic of the highly technical nature of trade policy, Ms Trommer insightfully reveals that '[s]taff capacity was crucial for dialogue, and, in West African EPA talks, it was a particularly powerful tool for gaining and maintaining access to public officials'. Ms Trommer's dissertation is also important to an informed understanding of the public accountability of global governance in that her research reveals that participatory trade politics are a highly dynamic, albeit conflict-ridden procedure, that must be understood as a continual learning process.

In sum, Ms Trommer's study has yielded interesting, well-substantiated and important results that further our understanding regarding the limits and possibilities of democratizing trade politics not only as it relates to the Afro-European trade relations, but also provides us with insightful premises and questions with which we can think through reforming the WTO to include, in a more meaningful manner, i.e., beyond rhetoric and tokenism, the voices of those most, and usually adversely, affected by trade policy formation (in the global North).

I would like to add a two minor points upon which I hope Ms Trommer will take into consideration. Before proceeding, however, I would like to stress these comments should *not* be construed as areas in need of revision in the dissertation; but instead, should be regarded as constructive criticisms aimed at strengthening the dissertation for future publication(s).

First, I think the study would have benefitted from moving and expanding on the historical framing of trade politics in the various Western African countries in consideration. It would have been helpful for readers to know more about the effects of, and reactions (political mobilizations) by NGOs to, past trade policies in these countries. Moreover, a deeper discussion regarding the political and material bases of relations of power of the NGOs involved in contesting official trade policy in the African countries in question would have been instructive in terms of providing a more comprehensive understanding the role of structures and agency in creating and contesting limits regarding trade policy formation.

Second, the thesis should have engaged with the debates surrounding the typology and theorizations of NGOs in the literature on global governance, anti-globalization, and development. The reasoning behind this suggestion is twofold. First, there is an implicit contribution made by the thesis regarding the role of NGOs that could be made more explicit and developed in the thesis. The discussion could serve to strengthen Ms Trommer's notion of the 'political opportunity structure', as well as add to the debates on NGOs with regard to global civil society as well as global governance, which is notoriously undertheorized and understudied. Second, a more succinct discussion of NGOs in the context of this particular case could also aid to define more rigorously what is understood by an NGO in the dissertation and its possible distinction from a civil society organization, which often seem to be conflated in the dissertation.

In closing, the dissertation has made clear and important contributions to several debates in International Relations/International Political Economy and various disciplines in the social sciences. It is my strongly held view that Ms Trommer should be permitted to defend, without any conditions, her dissertation in a public examination.

Susanne Soederberg
Professor and Canada Research Chair Department of
Global Development Studies and Department of Political Studies
Queen's University

Soft-law Cooperation in International Law: The Arctic Council's Efforts to Address Climate Change*

Md. Waliul Hasanat

Compared to other parts of the globe, the Arctic is a distinct region. It is particularly vulnerable to climate change, and changes which occur in the region happen rapidly and require immediate action. Arctic inhabitants include several groups of indigenous peoples who are not allowed to participate with states in any formal international organisation under classical international law. The region served militarily as a strategic arena during the Cold War for two world superpowers—the Soviet Union and the United States. The European Union has also emerged as a regional power by means of its two Arctic member states, Finland and Sweden. Even if Canada is not seen as a global superpower it clearly qualifies as an Arctic superpower, due to its strong geographical presence in the region and the fact that it greatly contributes to regional policy-making. Following suit with most superpowers, the United States has not agreed to most formal international organisations or treaties which generate legally binding obligations.

The doctoral dissertation I am about to defend has two main objectives. The first is to examine the concept of soft law in regard to international law, and to explain how it has come to influence Northern and Arctic forms of international cooperation. The second goal is to specifically evaluate the most prominent among Arctic soft law international cooperation institution—the Arctic Council. In particular I look at how the Council has conducted its climate policy. For instance, what kind of climate change related activities has it undertaken, and how the Council could make improvements so as to counter climate change related consequences in the Arctic more effectively.

Let me start with the first issue: the concept of soft law and how it applies to the Arctic. Soft law is a fairly new concept within international law, which emerged as an important means of conducting international cooperation. Incidentally, there are many differing views about what it is. Some perceive soft law or soft norms in international treaties to be morally or politically binding, while others simply deem soft law and norms as non-legally binding but nonetheless worthy of evaluation since they exercise compliance on nation states as well as others.

Soft law could be seen as flexible in the sense that amendments to the law can be effected without many national and international formalities or bureaucratic procedures that are usually encountered. It can respond quickly to new situations precisely because there are no strict formal procedures involved, and it can involve other actors more flexibly. Still, it seems fair to say that the mainstream of international law has had a hard time with soft law arrangements given that they do not squarely fit within the existing concepts of treaty and intergovernmental organisation.

* *Lectio praecursoria* held at the public examination of the doctoral dissertation at the University of Lapland on 4 September 2012. Professor Betsy Baker from Vermont Law School acted as opponent.

Since there are so many differing conceptions of soft law, one group of scholars in particular has engaged themselves in finding constructive solutions to discern how traditional international law could be used in a beneficial way when negotiating and working within these soft law forums and organisations. As an example, they have proposed an analogical use of treaty law to help solve problematic issues which might arise during the process of soft law cooperation.

In this study, soft law is perceived as a fact in international life which international law consequently needs to deal with. It is obvious that states (and other actors) are increasingly making use of soft law instruments and are doing so with intent. In the short-term, the best solution from a research viewpoint is to admit this reality. However, as argued in Global Administrative Law (GAL), a school of thought which has recently risen in status, there is a need to keep studying these new cooperation structures even if they do not clearly fit within the traditional confines of international law. They urge scholars to study these soft law forms not only from the viewpoint of how these processes unfold but also to assess how they perform on the basis of good governance criteria, such as transparency and accountability. Soft law instruments are used mostly by states as a testing ground for engaging in deeper and more ambitious cooperation, but in some cases they are capable of creating a strong governance system of their own. In the long run it will be interesting to see whether international law can evolve with the rapid changes taking place inside forms of international cooperation, and within an increasingly globalised society. This also applies to the phenomenon of soft law. If states continue resorting to these forms of cooperation, it may well be that international law will evolve and develop secondary rules for what we now deem as soft law instruments.

Sometimes soft law may create permanent international cooperation among states which I refer to as soft law cooperation in my dissertation. The dissertation analyses what the pros and cons are in relation to different types of international cooperation prevailing in the Arctic—i.e. Arctic cooperation, Barents cooperation and the Northern Forum. After undertaking my analysis, the research findings are applied to the Arctic context by examining inter-relationships between the three forms of soft law cooperation studied in the dissertation.

Soft law cooperation types include international governance—established without concluding any formal international treaty and allowing room for the regional actors to be involved in the process. The strong side of GAL is that it does not set out to criticise the status of different international cooperation forms. Instead it perceives them as authoritative and influential international forms of cooperation which need to be studied for the exact reason that they are powerful. Since they wield societal power, one should expect that these entities perform according to concepts of good governance criteria, such as transparency, public participation, accountability, etc.

Soft law cooperation usually exists in a complex variety of forms and therefore it is somewhat difficult to determine common characteristics among them. Soft law cannot create any legally binding obligations other than by generating voluntary responsibilities or political commitments. Thus decisions made by a soft law body remain recommendatory. All three soft-law forums that the dissertation focuses on try to advance wellbeing within the region and two of them involve northern indigenous peoples in their work. The Arctic Council particularly involves indigenous peoples, offering them a 'Permanent Participant' status—a status now demanded by indigenous peoples involved in Barents cooperation which is based on their right to self-determination. All three of these cooperation forms, which I will present to you now, relate to one another.

The Arctic Council (the present form of Arctic cooperation), is an international cooperative forum of eight Arctic states (Canada, Denmark, Finland, Iceland, Norway, Sweden, Russia, and the United States). It was established in 1996 with the adoption of the Ottawa Declaration, which was a direct outgrowth from the Arctic Environmental Protection Strategy (AEPS) of 1991 established by the same states. The Arctic Council was established with the intention of providing mechanisms for addressing common concerns and challenges faced by Arctic states and their inhabitants, such as environmental protection and sustainable development in the Arctic. This is a comparatively new approach to international cooperation and allows indigenous peoples to sit in the Council, side by side with state officials, to address present and future challenges faced in the Arctic, and to discuss their own active involvement in Arctic Council activities.

The Barents cooperation, established in 1993, includes two separate cooperative platforms: the Barents Euro-Arctic Council (BEAC) and the Barents Regional Council (BRC). The five Nordic states (Denmark, Finland, Iceland, Norway and Sweden) along with Russia and the then Commission of European Communities (now the European Union (EU)), established the BEAC in 1993 after signing the Kirkenes Declaration. The BEAC aims to promote sustainable economic and social development in the Barents region. Regional governments (e.g. provincial, county, and oblast governments) in the Barents region, together with the Saami Council, established the Barents Regional Council via a cooperation protocol, forging common interests in the same place, at the same time, and with the same objectives.

The Northern Forum (NF) is an international cooperation of sub-national governments (regional, sub-regional and municipal) established in 1991 which aims to improve the quality of lives in the north and to support sustainable development. The NF grants non-voting membership to business organisations (companies and associations, such as chambers of commerce) as an innovative mechanism for enabling cooperation between these groups and sub-national governments, with the purpose of involving all actors in the common development of the northern economy.

The three forms of cooperation examined in the dissertation include a number of actors with similar core objectives, which mostly focus on the wellbeing of the region with a particular emphasis on environmental protection and indigenous peoples living in the north. All of these forms of cooperation chosen from within the Arctic region were of a decidedly soft law nature, rather than formal international organisation in light of public international law. In recent years these three soft law cooperation forms have been moving towards stronger commitments by producing several international instruments despite their soft law character.

There is little evidence of inter-cooperation in daily operational activities. However, these initiatives have managed to build informal, indirect and conceptual connections while also establishing legally binding obligations to some extent. A more formalised association or partnership could allow for a stronger focus on relevant Arctic issues as well as an additional global orientation. This kind of coordination mechanism could provide Arctic governance with alternative ideas. It would promote a sharing of responsibilities during initiatives, as well as effect a reduction in the number of regional governance bodies through merger. This would allow for a more effective operational system and would provide better protection for the environment and its inhabitants.

Let me now address the second goal of this dissertation—which is to evaluate the Arctic Council's climate change policy—from both descriptive and normative viewpoints. In principle, as it is based on soft law cooperation, the Arctic Council can do little in the way of mitigating global climate change which requires CO_2 emission cuts from all parts of the world. However, since the Arctic is experiencing the most intense consequences from global climate change, there is evidence suggesting that a common need to take adaptive action in the region exists.

The Arctic Council's climate change work includes the establishment of the Arctic Climate Impact Assessment (ACIA), the ACIA Policy Document, the Arctic Council Focal Point, the Arctic Council Task Force on Short-lived Climate Forcers, the Climate Expert Group, numerous other climate change related projects, and the Arctic Council's involvement in the global climate change regime.

The Arctic Council performs best when it promotes scientific research, feeding its gathered information on potential threats to all national, sub-national and indigenous governing structures in the region, in order for these to respond adequately. The Arctic Council's presence as a science provider is evident in its increasingly relevant and abundant work on various aspects of climate change in the region which suggest adaptation and mitigation challenges, as well as options for action, in order to increase the overall adaptive capacity in the region.

Arctic cooperation started with the AEPS transformed into the Arctic Council, and since then the Arctic Council has never changed its legal status or financial mechanism. Its main shortcoming with respect to dealing with climate change related issues is its soft law character which is, however, gradually changing in a unique manner. A number of proposals recommend a formal legal instrument to handle the Arctic Council. Yet for many involved this does not seem to be a desirable direction, especially when considering that the region's states do not want to commit themselves to a legal instrument. The Arctic Council is a forum which requires the participation of local inhabitants so that the region may benefit well from its activities, policies or rules. Soft law can accommodate the special circumstances which relate to the Arctic region (e.g., Arctic issues, history and peoples) more effectively than any other regular international organisation.

It is clear that a hard law instrument is, in general, more authoritative and exercises stronger compliance pull on states. However, this should not be overstated. Very much depends on what the states' interests and concerns are with regard to the specific instrument in question. The Arctic Council's approaches seem to proceed with well-balanced strategy in this respect: the Council is a soft-law body, since it is established via a declaration, but it nonetheless uses both soft law and hard law instruments when confronting challenges to the Arctic.

The Arctic Council can handle climate change issues more effectively if it becomes stronger in general and develops expertise in climate change science which would be mainly relevant to the Arctic. A promising indication of strengthened cooperation is notable from the most recent development to have occurred in the Arctic Council; one which may even be considered to be a historically unique occurrence in international relations.

As well as the newly established process to establish a permanent secretariat to the Arctic Council in Tromsø, it is pertinent to ask whether the way forward is gradually becoming easier in regard to countering common challenges in the region. It is of crucial importance to emphasise the unique characteristics of this emerging practice as a soft law body which produces proactive instruments whilst also facilitating its member states as they create legally binding agreements on specific issues.

Yet it is not wise to say that there is no need for reform in the Arctic Council. There would clearly be the need to create a type of Arctic Regional Council, in order to include Arctic regional governments in the Arctic Council's work. Working groups should also be coordinated more effectively and their working boundaries should be clarified in such a way that Arctic Council projects could find a clear lead. The Senior Arctic Officials (nominated by each Arctic state to the Arctic Council) should not be changed too frequently. National governments should develop closer contacts with residents within the Arctic region and ensure their proper representation is ensured in national delegations. The proposed Arctic Regional Council could play an advocacy role in this regard, while further inclusion from regional representatives in national governments might be helpful when highlighting issues affecting the Arctic at a national level.

In terms of its climate mitigation role, the Arctic Council has become the main platform for assessing the pace and scale of climate change in the region, and thereby influencing global scientific processes such as Intergovernmental Panel on Climate Change assessments. In turn this has had an indirect impact on how decision-makers perceive climate change proceedings. Since decision-makers at various levels have to rely on established climate science to make climate change mitigation decisions, it can be argued that the Arctic Council plays a substantial role in the overall efforts to mitigate climate change. Yet the Council's climate science work does not only pertain to climate change mitigation but it also applies to efforts in developing climate change adaptation measures. As a main platform for assessing the consequences of climate change in the region, it simultaneously feeds information to various levels of Arctic governance. In respect to this, the Arctic Council needs to take into account how its activities are in line with cutting-edge knowledge on climate change in the region, and to take necessary measures to adapt to these circumstances. These roles would be enhanced by having a strong media centre, which could communicate the Arctic Council's main findings from its assessments more effectively and in a popularised manner.

Even though climate change is rapidly transforming the region, it does seem (at the time of writing) that the Arctic Council is moving in the right direction. This dissertation has presented proposals to make it even stronger. It has also analysed the three key international governance soft law forms functioning in the Arctic as a means of representing new ways of conducting international cooperation in a way that seems suited to Arctic issues. In this thesis it is proposed that these various soft law bodies operating in the region could synergise their activities in a way which might continue to keep up the pace of current Arctic Council progression. It is with scholarly attention to potential problems within the Arctic Council that we can help guide its progress, and to counter the challenges posed by climate change in the region.

Soft-law Cooperation in International Law: The Arctic Council's Efforts to Address Climate Change by Md. Waliul Hasanat. Doctoral Dissertation, University of Lapland, 2012

The Candidate for a doctoral degree in law, Md. Waliul Hasanat, defended his dissertation on 4 September 2012 at the Faculty of Law, University of Lapland. I provide this assessment of his dissertation in my capacity as Opponent and recommend that his thesis be accepted. This recommendation is based on the criteria indicated in Part I, below, and on the analyses and discussion in Part II.

Part I. Criteria for Recommendation

This recommendation applies the Faculty of Law's criteria for evaluation of doctoral dissertations. It can be said that the doctoral thesis demonstrates the following three points required by the Faculty's guidelines (at 14):

A. The candidate has the ability to apply scientific research methods independently. Each of the four published articles evidences an ability to apply scientific research methods, including structuring research questions, surveying relevant literature, describing objects studied and drawing conclusions from those studies. As specified in the Faculty guidelines (at 14), a conclusion accompanies the four publications and summarizes the findings they contain. The revised eighty page conclusion also shows the candidate's ability to summarize his earlier work and build upon it.

B. The candidate has a sound knowledge of his chosen field, which is international law generally and, more specifically, the law of international organizations, international environmental law, the Arctic Council, and climate change. He demonstrates familiarity with an adequate range of English language primary sources and secondary literature regarding the growth in international of law of non-binding 'soft law' and the contribution of international organizations to that growth. He is competent in using primary sources of international law to undergird his arguments. He also demonstrates an ease in incorporating insights from non-legal literature including political science and relevant scientific reports on climate change. The bulk of his analysis focuses on international organizational law, with attention to limited aspects of international environmental law (e.g. the climate change treaty regime) as necessary to support his discussion of the climate initiatives of the entities being studied.

C. The candidate has a profound knowledge of his own area of research, which is the role of soft law in efforts by various entities in the Arctic to address climate change. Chapter 2 shows a good understanding of the limits and promise of soft law, and contains some original recommendations about how to use soft law to address climate change in the Arctic (see details in Part II, below). Chapters 3–5 evidence a detailed familiarity with the internal structural workings of the entities studied (the Arctic Council, the Barents Euro-Arctic Regional Council and the Northern Forum). The dissertation focuses primarily on structural components of international institutional law for each of the entities studied, i.e. membership, functions of committees and working groups, funding and how the routine operations of each entity affect outcomes in different Arctic states and regions. Part of this primary focus is the nature of the cooperation between entities and the non-binding yet practical effect of the wide range of documents these entities produce—see, e.g., the discussion in Chapter 5 (at 9) of the 1994 Rovaniemi Code of Conduct of the Northern Forum, which encourages business and national and regional governments to introduce effective business policies that promote environmental safety, protections for investors' rights and rights of local populations. Because the documents produced by the entities studied do not have legally binding effects, the candidate spends more time on structural questions and less time analyzing substantive questions of international organizations law. However, he rightly observes that such documents evidence a solid cooperation between members of the entities studied and in turn 'support compliance with certain international legal instruments' (Chapter 4 at 307; see also Chapter 2 at 31).

Part II. Analyses and Discussion of the Dissertation

Mr Hasanat's dissertation provides a detailed study of three forms of soft-law cooperation in the Arctic—cooperation in the Arctic Council, cooperation in the Barents-Euro Region, and cooperation in the Northern Forum. The dissertation examines in detail how these three groups are structured to address climate change in the North, and explains why and how they are not subject to the law of treaties or the law of international organizations. Thus, the title of the dissertation is perhaps overly modest, as it refers only to 'The Arctic Council's Efforts to Address Climate Change'. In fact, the dissertation studies not only the Arctic Council. One of its six chapters is devoted to the Barents Region. This chapter details the structure of the state-based Barents Euro-Arctic Council (BEAC) which works with the county-based Barents Regional Council (BRC). Another chapter studies the Northern Forum, a gathering of sub-national governments. Thus, the dissertation places the climate change work of the Arctic Council in a much broader context of northern cooperation. The conclusion points in this direction by suggesting that the Arctic Council can serve as an 'umbrella for most forms of international cooperation in the Arctic', that its structure complements the county-based BRC's practical work on the regional level, and that both might be able to better coordinate with the Northern Forum's association of sub-national governments more effectively.

After an introductory chapter, the dissertation proceeds with a chapter on soft law. The major contribution of this chapter is to show how soft law can create permanent cooperation forums. The dissertation proposes a practical approach to evaluating these cooperation mechanisms, namely by asking: what practical results do they achieve? It shows how such permanent cooperation has developed from four different bodies that were created by soft law instruments, that is by instruments other than treaties, conventions or agreements that are intended to be binding under international law. The four bodies sketched in Chapter 2 are the Arctic Council, the BEAC, the Northern Forum, and the South Asian Association for Regional Cooperation. The chapter demonstrates how some scholars have overcome objections to considering soft law as a 'source' of international law by focusing on the non-legally binding obligations (that is, moral, political, reputational, see top of page 19) that arise from soft law instruments and result in practical cooperation. The chapter points out that these soft law forums advocate compliance with specific legal instruments and thus influence indirectly the effectiveness of binding rules of international law.

Chapter 3 focuses on the Arctic Council and emphasizes the collaboration between its members. This focus on the nuts and bolts of the Council's cooperative structure is the chapter's main contribution. The chapter offers an extensive description of Arctic Council structure and functions, with attention to its history and various working groups, and to the innovative mechanism of 'Permanent Participant' status for representatives of Arctic indigenous peoples. It also shows how the Arctic Council incorporated and, eventually, prioritized climate change in its work even though the topic was not explicitly part of its founding document, the Ottawa Declaration, or that of its predecessor, the Arctic Environmental Protection Strategy. The chapter also surveys literature regarding proposed reforms to the Arctic Council and weighs arguments for and against an Antarctic-style treaty, rejecting the need for a formal treaty to undergird the work of the Council. The freshest insight is that formalizing the Arctic Council cooperation could jeopardize the gains made by the unique status of the Permanent Participants.

The next chapter (Chapter 4) contributes a previously unavailable level of detail about the legal and structural underpinnings of two soft-law bodies: the BEAC and the BRC. Mr Hasanat demonstrates how the two groups cooperate to promote the well-being of the region and its people. He shows how the BEAC, as a state-based platform, and the BRC, as a regional platform, can influence one another precisely because they have independent legal structures. Mr Hasanat emphasizes the importance of non-legally binding cooperation in producing a regular practice, in this case for over two decades. His analysis of the permanent International Barents Secretariat is the most important contribution of this chapter, pointing to the fact that it possesses legal personality as 'evidence of a separate independent organ within the [BEAC] to carry out its particular functions'. He uses three characteristics for assessing the work of both the state-based BEAC and the county-based BRC. Those three characteristics are: the nature of their written products, the independence of their secretariats, and whether the body engages in self-evaluation, for example as when an 'inferior' secretariat evaluates a 'superior' council (see at 304–305). The approach offers a possible method for evaluating the legal status of other forms of cooperation in the North.

As Chapter 4 does for the Barents region forums, Chapter 5 contributes a previously unavailable level of detail about the legal and structural underpinnings of the Northern Forum. It highlights the innovation of allowing business organizations and subnational governments membership in the same forum. It details cooperation between the Northern Forum and international organizations and forums (see e.g. at 10, column 2). He uses this discussion in part to suggest the legal status of the Northern Forum. He reminds readers that the Northern Forum founding charter claims the status of both 'international organization' and 'nongovernmental organization', and that the Northern Forum is incorporated as a private non-profit corporation under municipal (Alaskan) law. Given these multiple characteristics of the Northern Forum, the chapter proposes a new typology for its legal status, calling it a 'hybrid soft-law body' to reflect the fact that it 'strictly follows self-made rules' but also is less formal and non-treaty based (at 11, column 2). The chapter also usefully shows how reference to interests of indigenous peoples in Northern Forum documents is more cosmetic than substantive.

Chapter 6 is the concluding chapter of the dissertation. It summarizes each of the previously published articles, and provides information on new developments since they were published, which was over a period of the four years from 2007 to 2011. Several of Mr Hasanat's conclusions are worth repeating here. All of the soft-law cooperative bodies studied in the dissertation were initiated in the early 1990s 'and came into operation following the end of the Cold War' (at 214). This raises an interesting question of whether the time and geopolitical context of their creation required a soft-law structure, and whether new circumstances today can allow that structure to become more firm. His basic conclusion is that states seem to prefer the flexibility that soft law provides. For each body studied he reaches slightly different conclusions as to their future: he concludes that, over time, the Arctic Council has had the most impact globally; that the Barents bodies have reached the very practical result of connecting regional cooperation with state cooperation; and that the Northern Forum is the weakest of the bodies because it lacks national government representation. With these conclusions he supports, whether intentionally or not, the continued importance of involving states—the classic actor in international law—for the success even of soft-law structures.

The preceding remarks indicate the nature of the subject dealt with in the thesis and its importance to the academic literature. I would also like to emphasize one more way in which the dissertation contributes to research. Mr Hasanat has put great effort into the sometimes thankless task of providing a new and important level of detail about the internal workings of organizations that are little known to outsiders. Very little attention has been paid, especially in the legal literature, to understanding how the Northern Forum, the Barents bodies and even the Arctic Council function. With his diligent work setting out the structure of these entities, Mr Hasanat has provided important raw materials for future researchers, who will be able to turn to his dissertation as a starting point for understanding these entities. But he has also highlighted questions about their legal character and their implications for responding to climate change, and suggested ways they might complement the climate change work of the Arctic Council.

Our exchange during the question and discussion phase of his defense covered a wide range of questions, focusing at first on his understanding of soft law, then on his innovative suggestion that '[i]f states continue resorting to these forms of co-operation, it may well be that the customary law of treaties evolves to develop secondary rules for what we now deem as soft-law instruments' (at 188). We also discussed his assertion that the cooperative forums he studied advocate compliance with specific legal instruments and thus influence indirectly the effectiveness of binding rules of international law. We discussed whether this supports or negates the argument that soft law is a source of international law; he could see arguments on both sides. We spent less time on the climate change activities of the Arctic Council and more time on discussions of soft law and possible directions in which the Arctic Council might develop.

In conclusion, Mr Hasanat has demonstrated an in-depth knowledge of his area of research, which is the role of soft law in efforts by various bodies in the Arctic to address climate change. As a formal matter, the dissertation consists in part of four previously published articles and in part of new material that meets the requirement of summarizing those articles and integrating new developments and observations. Here I note the calibre of the peer-reviewed journals that accepted these pieces for publication, including the esteemed *Polar Record* of the Scott Polar Institute at Cambridge University, the *Yearbook of International Environmental Law* and the *Yearbook of Polar Law*. Less well known to this audience is the journal in which the first of Mr Hasanat's articles appeared: the *Journal of the Asian-African Consultative Organization*. That international organization is over fifty years old, with forty-seven countries comprising almost all the major States from Asia and Africa. Its purposes include 'To serve as an advisory body to its Member States in the field of international law'.[1] Why do I take time to spell out this information in my final statement, which I was instructed should serve as an overall opinion of the thesis? Because the fact that the work of the Arctic Council, the Barents bodies and the Northern Forum has been elucidated in a journal from a decidedly non-northern part of the world is itself a service, by drawing the attention of its readers to the issues and challenges facing the Arctic.

Substantively, Mr Hasanat's dissertation shows a good grasp of the limits and promise of soft law, and contains some original recommendations about how to use soft law to address climate change in the Arctic. The dissertation also shows Mr Hasanat's detailed familiarity with the internal structural workings of the bodies he has studied: the Arctic Council, the Barents Euro-Arctic Regional Council and the Northern Forum. The work shows how each forum has contributed to the development of 'soft-law' cooperation, with non-legally binding but practical effects on its respective members. It demonstrates how the Arctic Council has used its soft-law structure of working groups to coordinate with other bodies, both hard and soft law. It illustrates how those efforts have produced studies of climate change's effect on the Arctic and raised awareness regionally and globally about those effects. Finally, the dissertation proposes how improved coordination between existing sub-structures of the Arctic Council and outreach to other constituencies can build on recent reforms to enhance the Arctic Council's ability to address climate change. The dissertation is well researched, the topic timely and the candidate's dedication to his work is clear.

I therefore propose to the faculty that the dissertation be accepted.

Betsy Baker
Associate Professor of Law
Vermont Law School

1. <www.aalco.int/scripts/view-posting.asp?recordid=1>.

Finnish State Practice

FINNISH STATE PRACTICE IN 2011–2012

Virpi Laukkanen*

1. Introduction

This article continues the series of reports on Finnish state practice published regularly in this Journal.[1] The article covers the years 2011–2012. The report covers only a few selected activities in the field of public international law taking place in Finland during this time period. Treaty practice is illustrated in the form of a list of multilateral and bilateral treaties entered into force in Finland (Annexes I and II) and objections to reservations made to treaties.

2. International Humanitarian Law

Finland's accession to the Ottawa Treaty banning anti-personnel mines was accepted by the Parliament in November 2011. The Treaty entered into force in Finland on 1 July 2012. The Ottawa Treaty, negotiated in 1997, prohibits the use, stockpiling, production and transfer of anti-personnel mines and defines their destruction. Finland has a plan for destroying the anti-personnel mines currently in possession of the defence forces. The mines will be destroyed in accordance with the Treaty within four years of the entry into force of the Treaty.

---

* The report has been written in the author's personal capacity and does not necessarily reflect the views of the Ministry for Foreign Affairs.

1. For Finnish practice in 2009–2010, see Virpi Laukkanen, XXI *Finnish Yearbook of International Law* (2010) 377–395. For Finnish state practice in 2007–2008, see Virpi Laukkanen, XVIV *Finnish Yearbook of International Law* (2008) 433–449 at 433. For Finnish practice in 2005–2006, see Juha Rainne, XVII *Finnish Yearbook of International Law* (2006) 149–169. For 2003–2004, see Juha Rainne, XV *Finnish Yearbook of International Law* (2004) 435–451. For 2001–2002, see Anna Sotaniemi, XIII *Finnish Yearbook of International Law* (2002) 371–379 and Anna Sotaniemi, XII *Finnish Yearbook of International Law* (2001) 461–467.

In 2011 and 2012 Finland participated actively in the negotiations on an international trade treaty on conventional arms. Finland was also one of the seven countries initiating the Arms Trade Treaty process. Finland together with Australia, Argentina, Costa Rica, Great Britain, Japan and Kenya were the co-authors of the 2006 United Nations General Assembly Resolution 61/89 marking the beginning of the long negotiations at the UN. The agreement was finally concluded in the spring 2013. During the negotiations Finland in particular called for strong language to be included on the agreement on respecting obligations related to human rights and international humanitarian law.

In November 2011 Finland joined the Montreux Document on Private Military and Security Companies. In the spring 2012, Ministry for Foreign Affairs established a national working group with the task to strengthen the national implementation of the document. The document reaffirms the obligation on States to ensure that private military and security companies operating in armed conflicts comply with international humanitarian and human rights law. The document also lists some 70 recommendations, derived from State practice. In accordance with the Document, states should also take concrete measures to ensure that the personnel of private military and security companies can be prosecuted when serious breaches of the law occur.

The Copenhagen Process was launched by the Danish Government in 2007 to address a range of practical and legal challenges to States and organizations involved in international military operations, in particular related to detention. As a result of these discussions, in October 2012, an outcome document containing a set of non-legally binding principles and guidelines on the handling of detainees in internal armed conflict and in peace operations was concluded. Finland was an active participant in these discussions and supported the conclusion of the outcome document.

3. International Tribunals

Fighting impunity for the most serious international crimes continues to be one of Finland's foreign policy priorities.

During 2011–2012, Finland has continued its' cooperation with the International Criminal Court (ICC) as well as other international criminal tribunals. The agreement between Finland and the ICC on the enforcement of sentences entered into force in April 2011.

Finland has continued to provide financial assistance to various projects related to the fight against impunity. Finland has also supported financially other international criminal law initiatives, such as the Justice Rapid Response

(JRR) facility, the intergovernmental stand-by facility of readily deployable criminal justice experts trained in international investigations. Finland is also a member of the Executive Board of the JRR.

In September 2012, Finland and Estonia organised a seminar in Tallinn with a focus on the status and rights of victims in pending ICC trials. The seminar marked the 10-year anniversary of the International Criminal Court. The event was opened by the Foreign Ministers of Finland and Estonia. Chair of the Board of Directors of the Trust Fund for Victims, ICC, Minister Elisabeth Rehn was the keynote speaker.

In October 2012, with a view to the strengthening the cooperation of States and international organizations with the ICC, an open debate on peace and justice took place at the United Nations Security Council on the initiative of a new State Party to the Rome Statute, Guatemala. This offered an opportunity to discuss challenges and opportunities arising in the context of the relationship between the ICC and the Security Council. Finland holds the view that strengthening the cooperation between these two organizations could greatly contribute to the effective functioning of the ICC, in particular where the Security Council has referred situations to the Court.

The newly elected Prosecutor of the International Criminal Court (ICC) Fatou Bensouda visited Helsinki in November 2012 at the invitation of Foreign Minister Erkki Tuomioja. During her visit, Prosecutor Bensouda was the main speaker in a seminar related to the decade-long history of the ICC, organised under the title "Peace and Justice: Reflections from the ICC Prosecutor" by the Ministry for Foreign Affairs and the Eric Castrén Institute of International Law and Human Rights (ECI).

4. The Sixth Committee of the United Nations General Assembly

Finland continued to actively participate in the deliberations of the Sixth Committee of the United Nations General Assembly on the items on its agenda. The Committee considered items such as the Criminal accountability of United Nations officials and experts on mission, Measures to eliminate international terrorism, Diplomatic protection and the Rule of law at the national and international levels.

The first high-level meeting of the General Assembly dedicated solely to the rule of law took place during the 67th UN General Assembly in September 2012. The meeting brought together governments and civil society to review progress made and challenges that exist at the national and international level to strengthen the rule of law. On the occasion of the High Level Meeting on the Rule of Law, the Governments of Finland and South Africa, along with UN Women, hosted also a high level event focusing on women's access to justice. Secretary-General of the United Nations, Mr Ban Ki-Moon, the President of Finland, Mr Sauli Niinistö and the President of South Africa, Mr Jacob Zuma were among speakers. Governments were invited to make concrete commitments to policy actions and highlight initiatives to advance women's access to justice. Finland for her part made several pledges in order to enhance women's access to justice at the international and national level.

5. International Cooperation to Combat Terrorism

5.1. Cooperation in the Framework of International Organizations

Finland condemns terrorism in all its forms and recognizes international terrorism as an important security threat. Finland also continues to hold the view that any measure against terrorism, whether international or national, must be compatible with human rights law, international humanitarian law and refugee law in order to be effective and legitimate.

The Executive Directorate of the UN Counter-Terrorism Committee (CTED) made an expert assessment visit to Finland in June 2012. The UN Counter-Terrorism Committee was established by Security Council Resolution 1373 (2001), which was adopted unanimously in the wake of the terrorist attacks of 11 September 2001. The Committee works to enhance the ability of UN Member States to prevent terrorist acts both within their borders and across regions. Country visits are a regular part of the Committee's work in order to assess the counter-terrorism situation in each individual country. The Ministry for Foreign Affairs acted as the coordinator of the visit to Finland.

In June 2012 the Government of Finland adopted the third Internal Security Programme (ISP) covering the years 2012–2015.[2] The Programme, "A Safer Tomorrow", was prepared through broad-based cooperation between public authorities, NGOs and business. The goal of the Programme is to continue the work started within the previous programmes and tackle new security challenges. New areas of focus in the third Internal Security Programme cover inter alia security of youth and schools, prevention of violent extremism and business security. The ISP also includes Finland's first national Action Plan to Prevent Violent Extremism.

2. Publications of the Ministry of Interior 26/2012 (Sisäasiainministeriön julkaisut 26/2012).

5.2. Sanctions Combating Terrorism

Finland, together with other like-minded countries, has continued to call for the strengthening of the due process rights of the individuals and entities listed by the UN Sanctions Committees. These countries have emphasized, among other things, the need to extend the powers of the Ombudsperson to review the listings of all UN Sanctions Committees and not only the listing decisions under the regime of Resolution 1267 (1999).

Ministry for Foreign Affairs set up a working group in February 2011 to prepare legislation that would enable the authorities to freeze terrorist funds in Finland. The working group was also given a task to review the responsibilities of national authorities in the implementation of UN and EU restrictive measures. The working group finalized its work on the freezing of terrorist funds in February 2012. After this it continued the consideration of the rest of its mandate.

As a result of the work of this group, Government proposal for an Act on the Freezing of Funds with a view to Combating Terrorism was submitted to the Parliament in June 2012.[3] The objective of the proposal for a new Act was to enable Finland to freeze, in an administrative procedure, funds and economic resources of 1) persons and entities suspected, prosecuted or convicted in Finland of involvement in terrorist crimes, 2) persons and entities designated by the Council of the European Union as being involved in terrorist acts but whose funds have not been frozen by a directly applicable EU regulation, 3) on the basis of a well-founded request by another country, persons and entities identified in that request as being involved in terrorism, and 4) entities owned or controlled by any of the above. Furthermore, the Act prohibits the making available, directly or indirectly, of funds and financial resources to designated persons or entities, and makes it a criminal offence to breach the asset freeze or to make funds or economic resources available to designated persons or entities.

6. International Financial Sanctions

As in the previous reports published, the notifications informing of the entry into force of the EU Sanctions regulations are listed below. Applicable penal provisions relating to violations of sanctions regulations are referred to in Section 2a of the Sanctions Act (659/1967).

3. Government proposal 61/2012.

In 2011, the Ministry for Foreign Affairs issued six notifications informing of the entry into force of the following EU Regulations: Council Regulation (EU) No 101/2011 of 4 February 2011 concerning restrictive measures directed against certain persons, entities and bodies in view of the situation in Tunisia,[4] Council Regulation (EU) No 204/2011 of 2 March 2011 concerning restrictive measures in view of the situation in Libya[5] and Council Regulation (EU) No 270/2011 of 21 March 2011 concerning restrictive measures directed against certain persons, entities and bodies in view of the situation in Egypt,[6] Council Regulation (EU) No 359/2011 of 12 April 2011 concerning restrictive measures directed against certain persons, entities and bodies in view of the situation in Iran,[7] Council Regulation (EU) No 442/2011 of 9 May 2011 concerning restrictive measures in view of the situation in Syria[8] and Council Regulation (EU) No 753/2011 of 1 August 2011 concerning restrictive measures directed against certain individuals, groups, undertakings and entities in view of the situation in Afghanistan.[9]

In 2012, the Ministry for Foreign Affairs issued three notifications informing of the entry into force of Council Regulation (EU) No 36/2012 of 18 January 2012 concerning restrictive measures in view of the situation in Syria and repealing Regulation (EU) No 442/2011,[10] Council Regulation (EU) No 267/2012 of 23 March 2012 concerning restrictive measures against Iran and repealing Regulation (EU) No 961/2010[11] and Council Regulation (EU) No 377/2012 of 3 May 2012 concerning restrictive measures directed against certain persons, entities and bodies threatening the peace, security or stability of the Republic of Guinea-Bissau.[12]

7. Treaty Relations

7.1. Treaties Brought into Force in Finland

The compilation of treaties, which entered into force in Finland in 2011 and 2012, is included in the Annexes to this report.

4. OJ 2011 No L 31, 5 February 2011, 1–12.
5. OJ 2011 No L 58, 3 March 2011, 1–13.
6. OJ 2011 No L 76, 22 March 2011, 4–12.
7. OJ 2011 No L 100, 14 April 2011, 1–11.
8. OJ 2011 No L 121, 10 May 2011, 1–10.
9. OJ 2011 No L 199, 2 August 2011, 1–22.
10. OJ 2012 No L 16, 19 January 2012, 1–32.
11. OJ 2012 L 88, 24 March 2012, 1–112.
12. OJ 2012 No L 119, 4 May 2012, 1–8.

7.2. Objections to Reservations

Finland monitors actively reservations made to international human rights conventions as well as other international treaties. The Government of Finland has a well-established practice in objecting to reservations deemed to be incompatible with the objective and purpose of a treaty.

On 3 March 2011 Finland objected to the reservation made by the Republic of Yemen upon the accession to the International Convention for the Suppression of the Financing of Terrorism (Article 2, subparagraph 1(b)):

> *"The Government of Finland has carefully examined the content of the reservation relating to subparagraph 1(b) of Article 2 of the International Convention for the Suppression of the Financing of Terrorism made by the Republic of Yemen upon accession.*
>
> *The reservation seeks to exclude from the scope of the Convention acts of terrorism defined in subparagraph 1(b) of Article 2. The Government of Finland considers the reservation to be in contradiction with the object and purpose of the Convention, namely the suppression of the financing of terrorist acts wherever and by whomever they may be carried out.*
>
> *The Government of Finland wishes to recall that, according to Article 19(c) of the Vienna Convention on the Law of Treaties and customary international law, a reservation contrary to the object and purpose of a treaty shall not be permitted. It is in the common interest of States that treaties to which they have chosen to become parties are respected as to their object and purpose and that States are prepared to undertake any legislative changes necessary to comply with their obligations under the treaties.*
>
> *The Government of Finland therefore objects to the reservation made by the Republic of Yemen in respect of subparagraph 1(b) of Article 2 of the Convention. This objection shall not preclude the entry into force of the Convention between the Republic of Yemen and Finland. The Convention will thus become operative between the two states without the Republic of Yemen benefiting from its reservation."*

On 28 June 2011 Finland objected to the reservation made by the Islamic Republic of Pakistan upon ratification of the International Covenant on Civil and Political Rights (Articles 3, 6, 7, 12, 13, 18, 19, 25, and 40):

> *"The Government of Finland welcomes the ratification of the International Covenant on Civil and Political Rights by the Islamic Republic of Pakistan. The Government of Finland has carefully examined the content of the reservations relating to Articles 3, 6, 7, 12, 13, 18, 19, 25 and 40 of the Covenant made by the Islamic Republic of Pakistan upon ratification.*
>
> *The Government of Finland notes that the Islamic Republic of Pakistan reserves the right to apply the provisions of Articles 3, 6, 7, 18 and 19 to the extent that they are not repugnant to the provisions of the Constitution of Pakistan and the Sharia laws, the provisions of Article 12 so as to be in conformity with the provisions of the Constitution*

of Pakistan, and the provisions of Article 25 to the extent that they are not repugnant to the provisions of the Constitution of Pakistan, and that, as regards the provisions of Article 13, the Islamic Republic of Pakistan reserves the right to apply its law relating to foreigners.

The Government of Finland notes that a reservation which consists of a general reference to national law without specifying its content does not clearly define to other Parties to the Covenant the extent to which the reserving State commits itself to the Covenant and creates serious doubts as to the commitment of the reserving State to fulfil its obligations under the Covenant. Such reservations are, furthermore, subject to the general principle of treaty interpretation according to which a party may not invoke the provisions of its domestic law as justification for a failure to perform its treaty obligations.

Furthermore, the Government of Finland notes that the Islamic Republic of Pakistan declares that it does not recognize the competence of the Human Rights Committee provided for in Article 40 of the Covenant. The reporting mechanism established under Article 40 is an essential feature of the system of human rights protection created by the Covenant and an integral undertaking of States Parties to the Covenant.

All of the above reservations seek to restrict essential obligations of the Islamic Republic of Pakistan under the Covenant and raise serious doubts as to the commitment of the Islamic Republic of Pakistan to the object and purpose of the Covenant. The Government of Finland wishes to recall that, according to Article 19(c) of the Vienna Convention on the Law of Treaties and customary international law, a reservation contrary to the object and purpose of a treaty shall not be permitted. It is in the common interest of States that treaties to which they have chosen to become parties are respected as to their object and purpose and that States are prepared to undertake any legislative changes necessary to comply with their obligations under the treaties.

The Government of Finland therefore objects to the reservations made by the Islamic Republic of Pakistan in respect of Articles 3, 6, 7, 12, 13, 18, 19, 25 and 40 of the Covenant. This objection shall not preclude the entry into force of the Covenant between the Islamic Republic of Pakistan and Finland.

The Covenant will thus become operative between the two states without the Islamic Republic of Pakistan benefiting from its reservations."

On 28 June 2011 Finland objected to the reservation made by the Islamic Republic of Pakistan upon ratification of the Convention against Torture and other Cruel, Inhuman or Degrading Treatment or Punishment (Articles 3, 4, 6, 12, 13, 16, 28 and 30):

"The Government of Finland welcomes the ratification of the Convention against Torture and other Cruel, Inhuman or Degrading Treatment or Punishment by the Islamic Republic of Pakistan. The Government of Finland has carefully examined the content of the reservations relating to Articles 3, 4, 6, 8, 12, 13, 16, 28 and 30 of the Convention made by the Islamic Republic of Pakistan upon ratification.

The Government of Finland notes that the Islamic Republic of Pakistan reserves the right to apply the provisions of Article 3 so as to be in conformity with the provisions of its laws relating to extradition and foreigners, and the provisions of Articles 4, 6, 12, 13 and 16 to the extent that they are not repugnant to the provisions of the Constitution of Pakistan and the Sharia laws.

The Government of Finland notes that a reservation which consists of a general reference to national law without specifying its content does not clearly define to other Parties to the Convention the extent to which the reserving State commits itself to the Convention and creates serious doubts as to the commitment of the reserving State to fulfil its obligations under the Convention. Such reservations are, furthermore, subject to the general principle of treaty interpretation according to which a party may not invoke the provisions of its domestic law as justification for a failure to perform its treaty obligations.

The reservations to Articles 3, 4, 6, 12, 13 and 16 seek to restrict essential obligations of the Islamic Republic of Pakistan under the Convention and raise serious doubts as to the commitment of the Islamic Republic of Pakistan to the object and purpose of the Convention. The Government of Finland wishes to recall that, according to Article 19(c) of the Vienna Convention on the Law of Treaties and customary international law, a reservation contrary to the object and purpose of a treaty shall not be permitted. It is in the common interest of States that treaties to which they have chosen to become parties are respected as to their object and purpose and that States are prepared to undertake any legislative changes necessary to comply with their obligations under the treaties.

The Government of Finland therefore objects to the reservations made by the Islamic Republic of Pakistan in respect of Articles 3, 4, 6, 12, 13 and 16 of the Convention. This objection shall not preclude the entry into force of the Convention between the Islamic Republic of Pakistan and Finland. The Convention will thus become operative between the two states without the Islamic Republic of Pakistan benefiting from its reservations."

ANNEX I: Treaties which Entered into Force in Finland in 2012[13]

Multilateral Treaties

Agreement between the Government of the Republic of Estonia, the Government of the Republic of Finland, the Government of the Federal Republic of Germany, the Government of the Republic of Iceland, the Government

13. The lists in the appendixes include the conventions and agreements published in the Finnish Treaty Series (FTS). Information on the agreements not published in the FTS is to be found in the FTS in the form of 'Notifications of the Ministry for Foreign Affairs'.

of the Republic of Latvia, the Government of the Republic of Lithuania, the Government of the Kingdom of Norway, the Government of the Republic of Poland, the Government of the Russian Federation and the Government of the Kingdom of Sweden on the Establishment of the Secretariat of the Northern Dimension Partnership in Public Health and Social Well-Being, NDPHS, 25 November 2011 (FTS 99/2012)

Agreement on the Establishment of the North European Functional Airspace Block between the Republic of Estonia, the Republic of Finland, the Republic of Latvia and the Kingdom of Norway, 4 June 2012 (FTS 93–94/2012)

Treaty establishing the European stability mechanism between the Kingdom of Belgium, the Federal Republic of Germany, the Republic of Estonia, Ireland, the Hellenic Republic, the Kingdom of Spain, the French Republic, the Republic of Cyprus, the Grand Duchy of Luxembourg, Malta, The Kingdom of the Netherlands, the Republic of Austria, the Portuguese Republic, the Republic of Slovenia, the Slovak Republic and the Republic of Finland, 2 February 2012 (FTS 74–75/2012)

Agreement between the Nordic Countries on extradition of criminals,[14] 15 December 2005 (FTS 71–72/2012)

Agreement between the Kingdom of Denmark, Republic of Finland, Republic of Iceland, Kingdom of Norway and Kingdom of Sweden on citizenship,[15] 13 September 2010 (FTS 68–69/2012)

Council of Europe Convention on Action against Trafficking in Human Beings, 16 May 2005 (FTS 43–44/2012)

European Convention on the Adoption of Children (Revised), 27 November 2008 (FTS 38–39/2012)

Joint Procurement Agreement to procure common auction platforms, 9 November 2012 (FTS 26–27/2012)

Joint Procurement Agreement to procure an auction monitor, 9 November 2012 (FTS 24–25/2012)

Agreement between the Governments in the Barents Euro-Arctic Region on Cooperation within the Field of Emergency Prevention, Preparedness and Response, 11 December 2008 (FTS 22–23/2012)

Convention on the prohibition of the use, stockpiling, production and transfer of anti-personnel mines and on their destruction, 18 September 1997 (FTS 12–13/2012)

14. Unofficial translation by the author.
15. Unofficial translation by the author.

Agreement between the Republic of Finland, the Kingdom of Norway and the Kingdom of Sweden on the Arctic Region Foundation of Vocational Training,[16] 23 November 2011 (FTS 9/2012)

Bilateral Treaties

Agreement between the Republic of Finland and Seychelles concerning information on tax matters, 30 March 2011 (FTS 84–85/2012)

Air Services Agreement between the Republic of Finland and Philippines, 13 August 2009 (FTS 66–67/2012)

Agreement between the Republic of Finland and the United States on enhancing cooperation in preventing and combating crime (PCSC), 17 March 2010 (FTS 62–63/2012)

Agreement between the Republic of Finland and Mauritius concerning information on tax matters, 1 December 2011 (FTS 59–60/2012)

Agreement between Republic of Finland and Bahrain concerning information on tax matters, 14 October 2011 (FTS 57–58/2012)

Agreement on promotion of cross-border cooperation between the Republic of Finland and the Russian Federation, 13 April 2012 (FTS 56/2012)

Agreement between the Republic of Finland and Grenada concerning information on tax matters, 19 May 2010 (FTS 54–55/2012)

Agreement between the Republic of Finland and Liechtenstein for the exchange of information relating to Tax Matters, 17 December 2010 (FTS 52–53/2012)

Agreement between the Republic of Finland and the Marshall Islands concerning information on tax matters, 28 September 2010 (FTS 50–51/2012)

Agreement and Protocol between the Republic of Finland and Turkey for the avoidance of double taxation with respect to taxes on income, 6 October 2009 (FTS 48–49/2012)

Agreement between the Republic of Finland and the Palestinian Authority on support to the development of land administration,[17] 13 June 2012 (FTS 42/2012)

Agreement between the Republic of Finland and Estonia on abolishing the requirement of legalisation for population register documents, 12 December 2011 (FTS 36–37/2012)

Agreement on mutual protection of classified information between the Government of the Republic of Finland and the Government of the State of Israel/through the Israeli Ministry of Defence, 5 May 2011 (FTS 34–35/2012)

16. Unofficial translation by the author

17. Unofficial translation by the author.

Agreement between the Department of Defense of the United States of America and the Ministry of Defence of Finland acting on behalf of the Government of the Republic of Finland for Research, Development, Testing and Evaluation Projects, 2 May 2011 (FTS 28–29/2012)

Agreement between the Republic of Finland and the Cook Islands concerning information on tax matters, 16 December 2009 (FTS 10–11/2012)

Agreement on the Leasing of the parts of the Saimaa Canal located in the territory of the Russian Federation, together with the associated land area to the Republic of Finland, and on the Canal traffic,[18] 27 May 2010 (FTS 7–8/2012)

Agreement between the Republic of Finland and Hong Kong concerning mutual legal assistance in criminal matters, 4 October 2007 (FTS 4–5/2012)

Agreements with International Organisations

Agreement between the Republic of Finland and the African Union Commission on support to the AU Mediation Support Capacity Project, 19 November 2012 (FTS 86/2012)

Memorandum of Understanding Contributing Resources to the United Nations Interim Force in Lebanon (UNIFIL), 31 May 2012 (FTS 64–65/2012)

ANNEX II: Treaties which Entered into Force in Finland in 2011[19]

Multilateral Treaties

International Tropical Timber Agreement, 27 January 2006 (FTS 120–121/2011)

Convention concerning the Construction and Operation of a Facility for Antiproton and Ion Research in Europe (FAIR), 30 September 2010 (FTS 108/2011)

Agreement on the participation of the Republic of Bulgaria and Republic of Romania in the European Economic Area, 25 July 2007 (FTS 106/2011)

Council of Europe Convention on the Protection of Children against sexual exploitation and sexual abuse, 26 October 2007 (FTS 87–88/2011)

18. Unofficial translation by the author.
19. The lists in the appendices include the conventions and agreements published in the Finnish Treaty Series (FTS). Information on the agreements not published in the FTS is to be found in the FTS in the form of 'Notifications of the Ministry for Foreign Affairs'.

Universal Postal Convention, 12 August 2008 (FTS 68–69/2011)

The Geneva Act of the Hague Agreement Concerning the International Registration of Industrial Designs and Common Regulations under the Act, 2 July 1999 (FTS 50–51/2011)

Statute of the International Renewable Energy Agency (IRENA), 26 January 2009 (FTS 25–26/2011)

Agreement among the Ministry of Defence of Finland acting on behalf of the Government of the Republic of Finland, the Minister of Defense of the French Republic, the Ministry of Defence of the Italian Republic, the Minister of National Defence of the Republic of Poland, the Ministry of Defense of the Kingdom of Spain, Försvarets Materielverk of the Kingdom of Sweden and the Department of Defense of the United States of America concerning Exchange of Secured Software-defined radio (SSDR) research and development information, 1 October 2010[20] (FTS 22–23/2011)

European Convention on the Exercise of Children's Rights, 25 January 1996 (FTS 12–13/2011)

Convention on the International Protection of Adults, 13 January 2000 (FTS 10–11/2011)

Convention on Jurisdiction, Applicable Law, Recognition, Enforcement and Cooperation in respect of Parental Responsibility and Measures for the Protection of Children, 19 October 1996 (FTS 8–9/2011)

Agreement on the Secretariat of the northern dimension partnership for transport and logistics, 8 June 2010 (FTS 6–7/2011)

Bilateral Treaties

Agreement between the Republic of Finland and Macao concerning the exchange of information on tax matters, 29 April 2011 (FTS 2–3/2012)

Agreement between the Republic of Finland and the United Kingdom/Montserrat concerning information on tax matters, 22 November 2010 (FTS 116–117/2011)

Agreement between the Republic of Finland and Saint Kitts and Nevis concerning Information on Tax Matters, 24 March 2010 (FTS 96–97/2011)

Agreement between the Republic of Finland and the Palestinian Authority on Finland's financial contribution to the Palestinian Authority through the "Mecanisme Palestino Europeen de Gestion et d'Aide socio-economique" (PEGASE), Programme "Vulnerable Palestinian Families", 31 May 2011 (FTS 77/2011)

20. Date of signature by the Republic of Finland.

Agreement between the Republic of Finland and the Palestinian Authority on Finland's financial contribution throught the "Mecanisme Palestino Europeen de Gestion et d'Aide socio economique" (PEGASE), Programme "Supporting Palestinian Public Administration and Services", 31 May 2011 (FTS 76/2011)

Agreement between the Republic of Finland and the Kingdom of the Netherlands in respect of Aruba for the exchange of information with respect to taxes, 10 September 2009 (FTS 64/2011)

Agreement between the Republic of Finland and the Kingdom of the Netherlands to promote economic relations in respect of Aruba, 10 September 2009 (FTS 65/2011)

Agreement in between the Republic of Finland and the Kingdom of the Netherlands in respect of the Netherlands Antilles for the Exchange of information with respect to taxes, 10 September 2009 (FTS 62/2011)

Agreement between the Republic of Finland and the Kingdom of the Netherlands to promote economic relations in respect of the Netherlands Antilles, 10 September 2009 (FTS 63/2011)

Agreement between the Republic of Finland and Antigua and Barbuda concerning information on tax matters, 19 May 2010 (FTS60–61/2011)

Agreement between the Republic of Finland and the United Kingdom/ the British Virgin Islands for the exchange of information relating to taxes, agreement for the avoidance of double taxation of individuals, agreement for the avoidance of double taxation with respect to enterprises operating ships or aircraft in international traffic and agreement on the access to mutual agreement procedures in connection with the adjustment of profits of associated enterprises, 20 November 2009 (FTS 58–59/2011)

Agreement between the Republic of Finland and Saint Lucia concerning information on tax matters, 19 May 2010 (FTS 55–56/2011)

Agreement between the Republic of Finland and Saint Vincent and the Grenadines concerning Information on Tax Matters, 24 March 2010 (FTS 53–54/2011)

Agreement between the Republic of Finland and the Kingdom of Sweden on cross border and firm boundary operations, 23 June 2010 (FTS 48–49/2011)

Agreement between the Republic of Finland and India on economic cooperation,[21] 26 March 2010 (FTS 47/2011)

21. Unofficial translation by the author.

Agreement between the Republic of Finland and the United Kingdom/ Turks and Caicos concerning information on tax matters, 14 December 2009 (FTS 43–44/2011)

Agreement between the Republic of Finland and the United Kingdom/ Anguilla concerning information on tax matters, 14 December 2009 (FTS 41–42/2011)

Agreement between the Republic of Finland and Kosovo on co-operation and mutual assistance in customs matters, 4 June 2010 (FTS 35–36/2011)

Agreement between the Republic of Finland and Indonesia concerning the co-operation in the energy and environment partnership 14 February 2011 (FTS 24/2011)

Agreement on the Republic of Finland's contribution to the Lake Victoria Basin partnership fund, 21 February 2011 (FTS 21/2011)

Agreement between the Republic of Finland and Vanuatu concerning information on tax matters, 13 October 2010 (FTS 19–20/2011)

Agreement between the Republic of Finland and the Palestinian Authority on Finland's support towards the funding of education development strategic plan 2008–2012, 1 February 2011 (FTS 17/2011)

Agreement between the Republic of Finland and Andorra concerning information on tax matters, 24 February 2010 (FTS 15–16/2011)

Agreement between the Republic of Finland and Nepal on the Promotion and Protection of Investments, 3 February 2009 (FTS 4–5/2011)

Agreement between the Republic of Finland and Belarus on cooperation and mutual assistance in customs matters, 18 December 2009 (FTS 2–3/2011)

Agreements with International Organisations

Agreement on the enforcement of sentences of the International Criminal Court, 1 June 2010 (FTS 37–38/2011)

Agreement between the Republic of Finland and Africa Institute for the environmentally sound management of hazardous and other wastes on the Co-operation in the Regional Basel Centre Support Programme, 5 January 2011 (FTS 14/2011)

Host Country Agreement between the Republic of Finland and the Nordic Investment Bank, 20 October 2010 (FTS 124–125/2010)